Assembly Language for the IBM-PC

Luis Salinas

Assembly Language for the IBM-PC

KIP R. IRVINE

Miami–Dade Community College—South

MACMILLAN PUBLISHING COMPANY • *New York*

COLLIER MACMILLAN PUBLISHERS • *London*

PRINTED IN THE UNITED STATES OF AMERICA

Macmillan Publishing Company
866 Third Avenue, New York, New York 10022
Collier Macmillan Canada, Inc.

Library of Congress Cataloging in Publication Data

Irvine, Kip R., (Date)
Assembly language for the IBM-PC / Kip R. Irvine.
p. cm.
ISBN 0-02-359840-9
1. IBM Personal Computer—Programming.
2. Assembler language (Computer program language)
I. Title. QA76.8.I2594I77 1989 005.265—dc19

88-28668
CIP

Printing: 2 3 4 5 6 7 8 Year: 9 0 1 2 3 4 5 6 7 8

To Jack and Candy Irvine

Preface

Few people who have taught assembly language on the IBM-PC will disagree when I say that finding a suitable textbook has been an ongoing trial. The available books were aimed at the trade book market and thus lacked the breadth and depth needed in a college text. The present book is designed to improve the situation.

Assembly Language for the IBM-PC directly addresses the needs of a college instructor by using a methodical, step-by-step approach. It begins with machine and operating system concepts. Then the assembler instruction set is gradually introduced, using short program examples. Finally, we see more complex applications that take advantage of advanced operating system functions, and learn how to link assembly language to high-level languages.

The book may be covered in one semester or two quarters at the sophomore or junior college level. It may also be used as a convenient self-study book, along with the sample programs disk available from the publisher.

I have chosen to emphasize two broad areas: (1) the IBM-PC *environment,* consisting of its hardware, firmware, and operating system; (2) *applications and methodology,* using assembly language as the primary tool. Structured programming concepts are emphasized throughout.

This book should help the student approach problems with the mindset of an assembly language programmer. Assembly programs are most effective when they directly manipulate system resources and data. If we acquire the ability to visualize solutions to programming problems at the systems level, we can be far more effective programmers. To accomplish this goal, I introduce numerous short program examples to show how instructions can be applied. Students remember how the instructions work *in context,* rather than by rote memorization.

In addition to the hundreds of short examples, *Assembly Language for the IBM-PC* contains over 75 ready-to-run programs, each newly written for this book, that demonstrate instructions or ideas as they are presented in the text. Reference materials such as guides to DOS interrupts and instruction mnemonics are available at the end of the book.

The reader should know how to program in at least one (preferably two) high-level computer languages. The intended audience includes students majoring in computer science, management information systems, computer information systems, and electrical engineering, as well as professional programmers. All programs have been tested using the Microsoft Macro Assembler, versions 5.0 and 5.1, and Borland's Turbo Assembler, version 1.0.

This book was field tested during the summer of 1988 at two different colleges. My own class at Miami–Dade tends to attract students with a wide range of backgrounds, from second-semester computer science majors to computer professionals conversant in numerous languages. Students find the book valuable for different reasons. Those with less programming experience appreciate the book's step-by-step pedagogical approach and easy readability. The computer professionals tend to skim through the early chapters and immediately study the sample programs. The book may be used as a resource book for understanding how programs in any language interact with DOS.

We have a great advantage when learning assembly language on a microcomputer, because we can communicate directly with DOS. System integrity or security are of no concern when only one user is involved. I constantly try to remove the mysteries shrouding high-level languages and DOS. Students acquire more confidence in their programming skills, and the principles learned here carry over to more advanced courses in operating systems and computer organization.

ORGANIZATION AND FORMAT

Presentation Sequence

Chapters 1–8 represent the basic foundation of IBM-PC assembly language, and are most effective if covered in order:

1. *Introduction to Assembly Language*. Basic concepts, machine language, numbering systems, elements of an assembly language program.
2. *Hardware and Software Architecture*. Hardware fundamentals and terminology, registers, system software, stack.
3. *Assembly Language Fundamentals*. Data definition, program structure, MOV, XCHG, INC, DEC, ADD, SUB, addressing modes.
4. *The Macro Assembler*. Assembling, linking, operators, expressions.
5. *Input–Output Services*. Interrupts, DOS function calls 01h–0Ch, video attributes and modes, INT 10h functions.
6. *Loops and Comparisons*. Direct and indirect addressing, LEA, JMP, LOOP, AND, OR, XOR, NOT, NEG, TEST, CMP, LOOPZ, LOOPNZ.
7. *Conditions and Procedures*. Conditional jumps, programming applications, procedures, PUSH, POP, CALL, RET, high-level logic structures.
8. *Arithmetic*. Shift and rotate instructions, multidigit arithmetic, multiplication and division, ASCII and packed decimal arithmetic.

Chapters 9 through 16 may be covered in any order, with one minor restriction: The CONSOLE.LIB library developed in Chapter 10 is used by nearly all programs in Chapters 11, 12, and 13. The instructor may, of course, supply the students with the library on disk if Chapter 11 is to be covered later.

9. *Numeric Conversions and Libraries*. Character translation (XLAT), binary–decimal conversion, separately assembled program modules.
10. *String Processing*. String storage methods, string primitive instructions, building a library of string routines.
11. *Disk Storage*. Disk storage fundamentals, directory, file allocation table, system-level file and directory access.
12. *File Processing*. Standard DOS file functions, text file applications, fixed-length record processing, random record retrieval and indexing, dynamic memory allocation, and bit-mapped field searching.
13. *Macros and Advanced MASM*. Defining macros, passing parameters, conditional assembly, using macros to call procedures, STRUC and RECORD directives, advanced operators.
14. *Advanced Topics*. IBM-PC system hardware, defining segments, COM and EXE differences.
15. *Numeric Processing*. Using pointers, flag manipulation, accessing I/O ports, defining real numbers, the Intel 8087 math coprocessor.
16. *High-Level Linking and Interrupts*. Linking to Turbo Pascal, QuickBASIC, and Turbo C; interrupt-handling routines.

FEATURES

Updated Version of Microsoft MASM. This book takes advantage of Microsoft's simplified segment directives (.CODE, .DATA, and .STACK) introduced with MASM 5.0. These directives simplify program development for the beginning assembly language student.

Complete Program Listings. The book contains over 75 assembled and tested programs. They are available on disk from Macmillan, along with selected solutions to programming exercises.

Programming Logic. Chapters 6 and 8 emphasize Boolean arithmetic for comparison and bit manipulation. This includes the AND, OR, XOR, NOT, TEST, shift, and rotate instructions. Chapter 12 shows how to code a bit-mapped search, with exclusive and nonexclusive matches and compound comparisons. Chapters 7 and 12 both show how to create and optimize high-level logic structures using assembly language, including WHILE, REPEAT, FOR-NEXT, and IF-ELSE.

Hardware and Operating System Concepts. Chapter 2 introduces basic hardware and DOS concepts, including registers, flags, stack, memory addressing, and memory mapping. Chapter 5 shows how assembly language interacts with DOS, using INT 10h and INT 21h. Chapter 12 introduces dynamic memory allocation, showing how application programs can allocate and release memory blocks.

Chapter 14 takes a closer look at the Intel microprocessor family, with an explanation of instruction timings, machine cycles, and differences between CPUs. Chapter 16 introduces interrupt handlers and memory-resident programs that replace DOS interrupt vectors.

Chapter Ending Materials. Each chapter contains valuable teaching materials to reinforce student learning. Such materials have been missing from nearly all trade books on IBM-PC assembly language.

The Points to Remember section summarizes each chapter and highlights important facts that must be remembered in subsequent chapters. The Review Questions ask both general and specific questions relating to chapter material. The Programming Exercises are based on information and skills presented during the chapter, set at varying levels of difficulty. The Answers to Review Questions answer all review questions posed in the chapter (except general discussion questions).

Special Programming Tips. Nearly every chapter has a box containing a special topic called a programming tip. This contains more advanced or specialized information related to the current chapter material. A programming tip in Chapter 11, for instance, discusses a well-known technique for recovering deleted files.

Two Chapters on Disk Storage and Files. Chapter 11 covers the details of disk storage and shows how to manipulate disk drives, directories, file attributes, and the file allocation table (FAT). This provides a valuable tool to systems programmers and application programmers alike, who must go beyond the standard file access methods available in high-level languages.

Chapter 12 concentrates on file applications, covering extended DOS functions, text files, fixed-length records, random access files, and indexed record retrieval.

Object Libraries. I emphasize a toolbox approach to programming, as do many professional programmers. A *toolbox* is a set of short input–output and arithmetic routines that are introduced as early as Chapter 5. Linking separately assembled modules is introduced in Chapter 9, and Chapter 10 shows how to use the Microsoft LIB utility to build a link-time library. Chapters 11 and 12 use and extend the library created in Chapter 10.

By the end of the book, the student should see that a toolbox of assembly routines can be a valuable resource to a programmer writing application programs on the IBM-PC. It allows one to go where conventional languages fear to tread.

Complete Chapter on Macros. Macros are an important topic in any assembly language course. They give the student a chance to learn about parameter passing and to see how high-level languages build on standard routines.

Chapter 13 is devoted to macros and advanced MASM operators and directives. This chapter might easily be covered immediately after Chapter 8. Special emphasis is given to showing how simple macros can streamline procedure calls.

Linkage to High-Level Languages. A topic of great interest today is the linking of assembly routines to high-level languages. In fact, this is the area where assembler is used most often.

Chapter 16 discusses the most common ways of passing arguments to subroutines, and of coordinating identifiers and segment declarations. It shows how to link to Microsoft QuickBASIC, Turbo Pascal, and Turbo C.

Other Instructional Aids. All program listings and libraries are available on disk from Macmillan. A comprehensive instructor's manual is also available (written by Bob Galivan), with topic outlines, solutions to programming exercises, lecture strategies, and transparency masters taken from selected figures in the text.

REFERENCE MATERIALS

One of the most important differences between a commercial trade book and a textbook lies in its special reference materials. I find that students have a difficult time reading the original manuals in most computer labs, so they depend on the following appendixes:

Appendix A: Binary and Hexadecimal Tutorial. Appendix A explains binary and hexadecimal numbers from the ground up. Special emphasis is placed on converting numbers from one format to another: binary–decimal, binary–hexadecimal, and decimal–hexadecimal.

Appendix B: DEBUG Tutorial. Appendix B contains a concise listing of DEBUG (debugging utility program) commands, as well as a hands-on tutorial showing examples of each DEBUG command. This appendix should be read before doing the exercises in Chapters 2 and 3. DEBUG is supplied with DOS, making it a vaulable tool for examining files and programs.

Appendix C: Descriptions of DOS and BIOS Interrupts. Appendix C contains a quick reference to all DOS and BIOS interrupts. The reader can quickly look up an interrupt, note its standard calling sequence, and add it to his or her program. More detailed information on individual interrupts is also available within the chapters themselves.

Appendix D: Complete Instruction Set Reference. Appendix D is a complete listing of the Intel 8086/8088 instruction set. A short explanation of each instruction tells which flags are affected, how the instruction works, and shows each of the standard syntax formats.

ASCII Codes and Keyboard Scan Codes. The back inside cover of the book contains tables showing the entire set of ASCII control characters and keyboard scan codes for extended keyboard keys. (I use these tables so often that I have considered tattooing them on my arm!) The front inside cover contains a chart of IBM-PC graphics characters.

ACKNOWLEDGMENTS

I want to express my warm thanks to the many people who contributed to this book's preparation. In particular: John Griffin, senior editor; Ron Harris, production editor.

Special thanks are due the following groups and individuals who contributed to the book:

Barry Brosch, Bruce DeSautel, and Richard White of the Computer Information Systems department at Miami–Dade Community College (South Campus) reviewed individual chapters and offered valuable suggestions.

Richard A. Beebe of Simpson College (Indianola, Iowa) field-tested the book in his class during the summer of 1988.

Bob Galivan wrote a marvelous instructor's manual, which really helps when planning lectures. Bob Galivan, Kenneth Stahl, and George Kamenz proofread the manuscript, catching many mistakes. Barbara Medina did an excellent job of keying in corrections to the manuscript.

Members of the Borland and Microsoft Compuserve forums generously donated information on MASM and DOS.

Microsoft Corporation and Borland International generously donated software.

I would also like to thank the many reviewers who offered suggestions for improvement: Richard A. Beebe, Simpson College; John V. Erhart, Northeast Missouri State University; Michael Walton, Miami–Dade Community College-North;

K. R. I.

Contents

1. Introduction to Assembly Language

7. Conditions and Procedures 173

8. Arithmetic 211

11. Disk Storage 351

12. File Processing 404

13. Macros and Advanced MASM 463

15. Numeric Processing 544

16. High-Level Linking and Interrupts 574

Appendixes

1

Introduction to Assembly Language

INTRODUCING ASSEMBLY LANGUAGE

Assembly language unlocks the secrets of your computer's hardware and software. It teaches you about the way the computer's hardware and operating system work together and how application programs communicate with the operating system.

To learn how a computer and its software really work, you need to view them at the machine level. This book is about assembly language programming on the IBM-PC, the PC/XT, and the PC/AT, as the title suggests. But the book is also about operating system concepts.

There is no single assembly language. Each computer or family of computers uses a different set of machine instructions and a different assembly language. Strictly speaking, IBM-PC assembly language consists only of the Intel 8086/8088 instruction set—with enhancements for the 80186, 80826, and 80386. The instructions for the Intel 8088 may be used without modification on all the processors previously listed.

An *assembler* is a program that converts source-code programs into machine language. Several excellent assemblers for the IBM-PC are available that run under the disk operating systems MS-DOS or PC-DOS. Two examples are the

Microsoft Macro Assembler, called MASM, and Borland's Turbo Assembler. The Microsoft assembler, on which this book is based, recognizes 50 or more *directives,* commands that control the way a program is assembled. Most programmers refer to IBM-PC assembly language as both the 8086/8088 instruction set and the complete set of Microsoft Macro Assembler directives. In this book we will do the same. The programs in this book will also work with Borland's Turbo Assembler.

Why Learn Assembly Language?

People learn assembly language for various reasons. The most obvious one may be to learn about the computer's architecture and operating system. You may want to learn more about the computer you work with and about the way computer languages generate machine code. Because of assembly language's close relationship to machine language, it is closely tied to the computer's hardware and software.

You may also want to learn assembly language for its *utility.* Certain types of programming are difficult or impossible to do in high-level languages. For example, direct communication with the computer's operating system may be necessary. A high-speed color graphics program may have to be written using a minimum of memory space. A special program may be needed to interface a printer to a computer. Perhaps you will need to write a telecommunications program for the IBM-PC. Clearly, the list of assembly language applications is endless.

Often there is a need to remove restrictions. High-level languages, out of necessity, impose rules about what is allowed in a program. For example, Pascal does not allow a character value to be assigned to an integer variable. This makes good sense *unless* there is a specific need to do just that. An experienced programmer will find a way around this restriction, but in doing so may end up writing code that is less portable to other computer systems and is difficult to read. Assembly language, in contrast, has very few restrictions or rules; nearly everything is left to the discretion of the programmer. The price for such freedom is the need to handle many details that would otherwise be taken care of by the programming language itself.

Assembly language's usefulness as a *learning tool* should not be underestimated. By having such intimate contact with the operating system, assembly language programmers come to know instinctively how the operating system works. Coupled with a knowledge of hardware and data storage, they gain a tremendous advantage when tackling unusual programming problems. They are able to look at a problem from a different viewpoint than the programmer who knows only high-level languages.

Assembly Language Applications

At first, the assembly language programs presented in this book will seem almost trivial. Those new to assembly language often cannot believe the amount of work required to perform relatively simple tasks. The language requires a great deal of attention to detail. Most programmers don't write large application programs in assembly language; instead they write short, specific routines.

Often we write subroutines in assembly language and call them from high-level language programs. You can take advantage of the strengths of high-level languages by using them to write applications. Then you can write assembly language subroutines to handle operations that are not available in the high-level language.

Suppose you are writing a business application program in COBOL for the IBM-PC. You then discover that you need to check the free space on the disk, create a subdirectory, write-protect a file, and create overlapping windows, all from within the program. Assuming that your COBOL compiler does not do all of this, you can then write assembly language subroutines to handle these tasks.

Let's use another example. You might be writing a word processor in C or Pascal but find that this language performs badly when updating the screen display. If you know how, you can write routines in assembly language to speed up critical parts of the application and allow the program to perform up to professional standards.

Large application programs written purely in assembly language, however, are somewhat beyond the scope of the person who has just finished this book. There are many people who write complete assembly language application programs for the IBM-PC. The few programmers I know in this group are familiar with several machine architectures and assemblers and have been programming professionally for at least several years. These fortunate individuals still had to start with a basic foundation, and this book is intended to help you acquire just that.

COMPUTER NUMBERING SYSTEMS

The explanation of computer numbering systems in this chapter is brief and is not meant to be a complete tutorial. For a much longer explanation of the process of converting numbers from one format to another, see Appendix A after reading this chapter.

There are four primary types of numbering systems used by programmers today: *binary, octal, decimal,* and *hexadecimal*. Of these, the octal system is rarely used on the IBM-PC. Each system has a *base,* or maximum number of values, that can be assigned to a single digit:

Base	Possible Digits
Binary	0 1
Octal	0 1 2 3 4 5 6 7
Decimal	0 1 2 3 4 5 6 7 8 9
Hexadecimal	0 1 2 3 4 5 6 7 8 9 A B C D E F

In the hexadecimal (base 16) numbering system, the letters *A* through *F* represent the decimal values 10 through 15. We will assume that all numbers are decimal unless stated otherwise.

Radix. When referring to binary, octal, and hexadecimal numbers, a single lowercase letter called a *radix* will be appended to the end of each number to identify its type. For example, hexadecimal 45 will be written as 45h, 76 octal will be 76o or 76q, and binary 11010011 will appear as 11010011b.

Binary Numbers

A computer stores both instructions and data as individual electronic charges. Representing these entities with numbers requires a system geared to the concepts of *on* and *off* or *true* and *false*. Binary is a base 2 numbering system in which each digit is either a 0 or a 1. The digit **1** indicates that the current is on, and the digit **0** indicates that the current is off:

1	0	1	0
on	off	on	off

or

1	0	1	0
true	false	true	false

At one time, computers actually had panels full of mechanical switches that were flipped by hand. Electromechanical relays were soon used instead, and later transistors were implemented. Eventually thousands of individual electronic switches and circuits were engraved on tiny microprocessor chips. Each binary digit (1 or 0) represents an on or off state in an electronic switch.

Computers store all instructions and data as sequences of binary digits, without any distinction between the two. For example, the first three letters of the alphabet would be stored in the IBM-PC as

010000010100001001000011 = "ABC"

At the same time, an instruction to add two numbers might be stored in memory as

0000010000000101

Bits and Bytes. Each digit in a binary number is called a *bit*. Eight of these make up a *byte,* which is the basic unit of storage on nearly all computers. Each location in the computer's memory holds exactly one byte, or 8 bits. On the IBM-PC and all compatible computers, a byte can hold a single instruction, a character, or a number. The next largest storage type is a *word,* which is 16 bits, or 2 bytes, long:

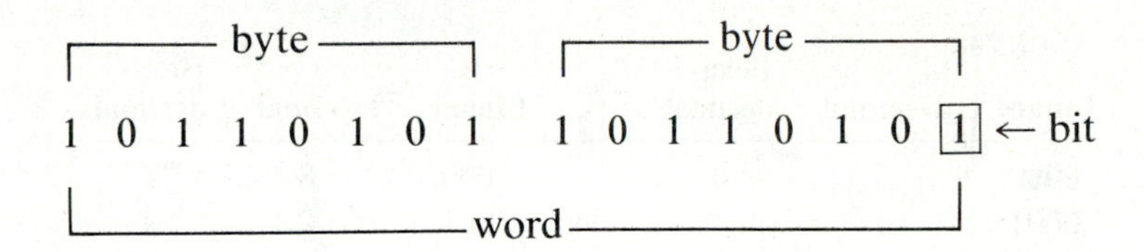

The IBM-PC is called a *16-bit* computer because its instructions can operate on 16-bit quantities.

Converting Binary to Decimal. There are many occasions when we need to find the decimal value of a binary number. Each bit position in a binary number is a power of 2, as the following illustration shows:

	2^7	2^6	2^5	2^4	2^3	2^2	2^1	2^0
value:	128	64	32	16	8	4	2	1

In order to find the decimal value, we add the value of each bit that equals 1 to the number's total value. Let's try this with the binary number 0 0 0 0 1 0 0 1:

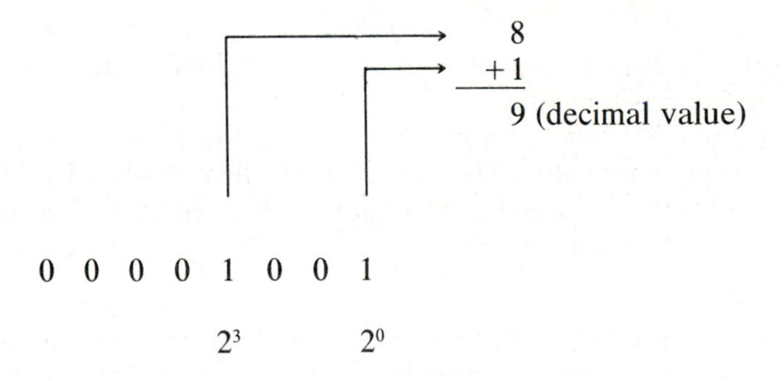

Hexadecimal Numbers

Large binary numbers are cumbersome to read, so *hexadecimal* numbers are usually used to represent computer memory or instructions. Each digit in a hexadecimal number represents 4 binary bits, and 2 hexadecimal digits represent a byte. In the following example, the binary number 000101100000011110010100 is represented by the hexadecimal number 160794:

1 6	0 7	9 4
00010110	00000111	10010100 = 160794h

A single hexadecimal digit may have a value from 0 to 15, so the letters *A* to *F* are used as well as the digits 0 to 9. The letter *A* = 10, *B* = 11, *C* = 12, *D* = 13, *E* = 14, and *F* = 15. The following table shows how each sequence of 4 binary bits translates into a decimal or hexadecimal value:

Binary	Decimal	Hexa-decimal	Binary	Decimal	Hexa-decimal
0000	0	0	1000	8	8
0001	1	1	1001	9	9
0010	2	2	1010	10	A
0011	3	3	1011	11	B
0100	4	4	1100	12	C
0101	5	5	1101	13	D
0110	6	6	1110	14	E
0111	7	7	1111	15	F

Hexadecimal Digit Positions. Each hexadecimal digit position represents a power of 16. This is helpful in calculating the value of a hexadecimal number:

	16^3	16^2	16^1	16^0
value:	4096	256	16	1

Numbers may be converted from hexadecimal to decimal by multiplying each digit by its position value.

Let's use 3BA4h as an example. First, the highest digit (3) is multiplied by 4096, its position value. The next digit (B) is multiplied by 256, the next digit (A) is multiplied by 16, and the last digit is multiplied by 1. The sum of these products is the decimal value 15,268:

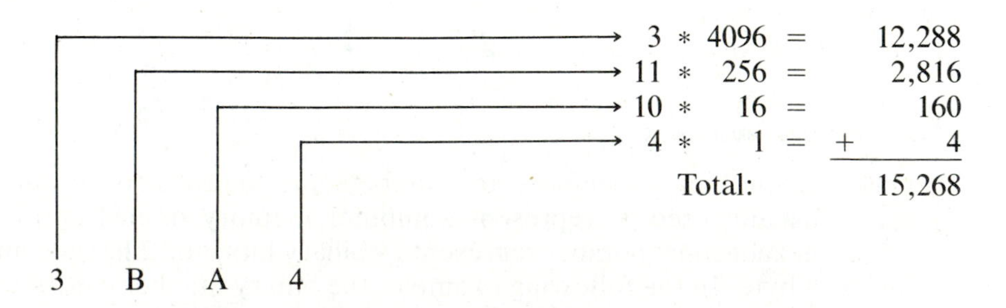

(When performing the multiplication, recall that the hexadecimal digit *B* = 11 and the digit *A* = 10.)

Signed Numbers

Binary numbers may be either *signed* or *unsigned*. Oddly, the central processing unit (CPU) performs arithmetic and comparison operations for both types equally well, without knowing which type it's operating on.

An *unsigned* byte uses all 8 bits for its numeric value. For example, 11111111 = 255. Therefore, 255 is the largest value that may be stored in an unsigned byte. The largest 16-bit value that may be stored in an unsigned word is 65,535.

A *signed* byte uses only 7 bits for its value; the highest bit is reserved for the sign. The number may be either positive or negative: If the sign bit equals 1, the number is negative; otherwise, the number is positive:

```
(sign bit)
    |
    1 0 0 0 1 0 1 0     (negative number)
    0 0 0 0 1 0 1 0     (positive number)
```

To calculate the *ones complement* of a number, reverse all of its bits. The ones complement of 11110000b, for example, is 00001111b.

Negative numbers are stored in a special format called a *twos complement*. In order to find out what the number's value really is, you have to calculate its twos complement.

To find the twos complement, calculate the ones complement and add 1. Let's use the negative number 11111010 as an example. Its ones complement is 00000101; if we add 1 to this, we end up with 6:

```
    1 1 1 1 1 0 1 0
    0 0 0 0 0 1 0 1   ←ones complement
+                 1   ←add 1
-------------------
    0 0 0 0 0 1 1 0   ←twos complement (6)
```

Now we append the negative sign to the decimal result and see that the original number (11111010) was equal to -6.

Maximum and Minimum Signed Values. The maximum signed byte value is +127 (01111111b, or 7Fh). The maximum signed word value is +32767 (0111111111111111b, or 7FFFh). The minimum signed byte and word values are -128 and -32768, respectively.

CHARACTER STORAGE

Computers can store only binary numbers, so how are characters such as "A" and "$" stored? A standard system used for translating characters into numbers is the *American Standard Code for Information Interchange* (*ASCII*). Another system, the *Extended Binary Code for Decimal Interchange* (*EBCDIC*), is used on IBM mini and mainframe computers. In each case, a unique numeric value is assigned to each character, including control characters used when printing or transmitting data between computers. ASCII codes are used on nearly all microcomputers, including the IBM-PC and IBM PS/2 series.

A table of ASCII codes is listed on the back inside cover of this book. Standard ASCII codes are actually only 7-bit codes, so the highest possible value is 7Fh. The eighth bit is optional and is used on the IBM-PC to extend the character set. Values 80h–FFh represent graphics symbols and Greek characters. Values 0–1Fh are control codes for printer, communications, and screen output.

All characters, including numbers and letters, are assigned unique ASCII codes. For example, the codes for the letters *ABC* and the numbers 123 follow:

	A	*B*	*C*	1	2	3
ASCII code	41h	42h	43h	31h	32h	33h

Binary Storage. Each letter or digit takes up 1 byte of storage. When we store numbers, however, we can be more efficient. The numeric value 123 can be stored in a single binary byte: 01111011b, or 7Bh. A byte in memory could be a single-byte numeric value or the ASCII representation of a character. The following sequence of memory bytes, for example, could be ASCII characters or four separate binary values:

30h	31h	32h	33h

Differences between instructions and data are purely artificial. High-level languages impose restrictions on the way variables and instructions may be manipulated, but assembly language does not. We might think of these restrictions as *boundaries* designed to help us avoid making fundamental errors. In assembly language there are few boundaries, but we are shouldered with the responsibility of taking care of many details.

ASSEMBLY LANGUAGE: AN INTRODUCTION

Assembly language is a specific set of instructions for a particular computer system. It provides a direct correspondence between symbolic statements and machine language. An *assembler* is a program that translates a program written in assembly language into machine language, which may in turn be executed by the computer. Each type of computer has a different assembly language, because the computer's design influences the instructions it can execute.

Machine Instructions

A *machine instruction* is a binary code that has special meaning for a computer's CPU—it tells the CPU to perform a task. The task might be to move a number from one location to another, compare two numbers, or add two numbers. Each machine instruction is precisely defined when the CPU is constructed, and it is specific to that type of CPU. The following list shows a few sample machine instructions for the IBM-PC:

```
0 0 0 0 0 1 0 0   Add a number to the AL register
1 0 0 0 0 0 0 1   Add a number to a variable
1 0 1 0 0 0 1 1   Move the AX register to another register
```

The *instruction set* is the entire body of machine instructions available for a single CPU, determined by its manufacturer. On IBM-PC and compatible computers, the CPU is one of the following, each made by Intel: iAPX 8088, iAPX 8086, iAPX 80286, or iAPX 80386. All of these CPUs have a common instruction set that will be used in this book. At the same time, the more advanced processors (80286 and 80386) have enhanced instructions that increase their flexibility.

A typical 2-byte IBM-PC machine instruction might be as follows: **B0 05**. The first byte is called the *operation code,* or *op code,* which identifies it as a MOV (move) instruction. The second byte (05) is called the *operand*. The complete instruction moves the number 5 to a register called AL. *Registers* are high-speed storage locations inside the CPU which are used by nearly every instruction. They are identified by two-letter names, such as AH, AL, AX, and so on. We refer to machine instructions using hexadecimal numbers, because they take up less space on the printed page.

Suppose we want to move the number 5 to a different register, the AH register. That machine instruction is **B4 05**. It has a different op code than our first example, but the operand is still the same.

Assembly Language Instructions

Although it is possible to program directly in machine language using numbers, assembly language makes the job easier. The assembly language instruction to move 5 to the AL register is

```
mov   al,5
```

Here it is understood that the first operand (AL) is the destination, and the number 5 is the source.

Assembly language is called a *low-level* language because it is close to machine language in structure and function. We can say that each assembly language instruction corresponds to one machine instruction. In contrast, *high-level* languages such as Pascal, BASIC, FORTRAN, and COBOL contain powerful statements that are translated into many machine instructions by the compiler.

Mnemonic. A *mnemonic* (pronounced ni-'män-ik) is a short alphabetic code that literally "assists the memory" in remembering a CPU instruction. It may be an *instruction* or a *directive*. An example of an instruction is MOV (move). An example of an assembler directive is DB (define byte), used to create memory variables.

Operand. An instruction may contain zero, one, or two operands. An operand may be a register, a memory variable, or an immediate value. For example:

```
10       (immediate value or constant)
count    (memory variable)
AX       (register)
```

The choice of operand is usually determined by the addressing mode. The *addressing mode* tells the assembler where to find the data in each operand: in a register, in memory, or as immediate data. Examples of instructions using operands are:

```
push  ax          ; one register
mov   ax,bx       ; two registers
add   count,cl    ; memory variable, register
mov   bx,1000h    ; register, immediate value
```

Comment. The beginning of a comment is marked by a semicolon (;) character. All other characters to the right of the semicolon are ignored by the assembler. You can even begin a line with a semicolon; in this case, the entire line will be treated as a comment. Assembly language statements should contain clear comments in order to help explain details about the program. Samples are as follows:

```
 ; This entire line is a comment
mov ax,bx   ; copy the BX register into AX
```

Programming Tip: Using a Debugger

In this chapter we begin looking at short assembly language programs and show the contents of registers and memory when they run. The best way to learn about these programs and about the way the computer works is to use a programmer's tool called a *debugger.* A debugger is a program that allows you to examine registers and memory and to step through a program one statement at a time to see what is going on. In assembly language, you will depend upon this ability to see what the CPU is doing. There are a number of debuggers to choose from: DEBUG is a simple, easy-to-use debugger supplied with DOS. The SYMDEB utility is supplied with Microsoft MASM 4.0, but not with version 5.0. It has all the DEBUG commands, with a number of useful enhancements. The CODEVIEW debugger was supplied by Microsoft beginning with MASM version 5.0 and is a full-featured source-level debugger. For a complete tutorial on using DEBUG, see Appendix B.

A Sample Program

Assembly language programs are made up primarily of instructions and operands. *Instructions* tell the CPU to carry out an action, while *variables* are memory locations where data are stored. In assembly language jargon, variables are also known as *memory operands*. *Immediate operands* are constant values, like 5 and 10. Let's write a short assembly language program that adds three numbers together and stores them in a variable called **sum**. The lines are numbered for your convenience.

```
1:   mov   ax,5       ; move 5 into the AX register
2:   add   ax,10h     ; add 10h to the AX register
3:   add   ax,20h     ; add 20h to the AX register
4:   mov   sum,ax     ; store AX in sum
5:   int   20         ; end the program
```

Each line in our example begins with an instruction mnemonic (MOV or ADD), followed by two operands. On the right side, any text following a semicolon is treated as a comment. There is no standard rule regarding the use of uppercase or lowercase letters.

The sample program may be understood with a little imagination. The MOV instruction tells the CPU to move, or copy data, from a *source* operand to a *destination* operand. Line 1 moves 5 into the AX register. Line 2 adds 10h to the AX register, making it equal to 15h. Line 3 adds 20h to AX, making it equal to 35h, and line 4 copies AX into the variable called **sum**. The last line halts the program.

We could have performed the addition using a single high-level language statement, but that's not the point. By writing the program in assembly language, we have communicated with the computer on its own level, and we can see exactly how the computer works.

Assemble and Test the Program. If you have DEBUG available, you can assemble and test our sample program. You will find a debugger to be the perfect tool for learning how assembler instructions work. It prompts for commands using the hyphen (-) character. The DEBUG commands to assemble and test the program are as follows:

```
DEBUG                 (load the DEBUG.COM program)
-A 100                (begin assembly at location 100)
  mov ax,5            (enter the rest of the program)
  add ax,10
  add ax,20
  mov [0120],ax       (SUM is at location 0120)
int 20                (end program)
-                     (press ENTER to end assembly)
-R                    (display registers)
-T                    (trace each instruction)
-T
-T
-G                    (execute the rest of the program)
-Q                    (quit DEBUG, and return to DOS)
```

The **A** (Assemble) command allows you to input a program and have it assembled into machine instructions. After typing the A command, you will be prompted for each assembler instruction.

The **T** (Trace) command executes a single instruction, displays the registers, and stops. The **R** (Register) command displays the registers. The **G** (Go) command executes all remaining instructions in the program, and the **Q** (Quit) command returns you to DOS.

As you assemble each line of the program, you will see a computer address appear at the left side of the screen. These addresses show the location of each instruction. For example:

```
-A  100
5511:0100  mov  ax,5
5511:0103  add  ax,10
.
.
```

After the last MOV instruction, press ENTER to return to DEBUG's command mode. If you would like to see the machine instructions that make up your program, type U for *Unassemble* (this is often called *disassembling* a program). A modified listing of the statements is as follows:

Machine Instruction			Assembly Instruction	
B8	05	00	MOV	AX,0005
05	10	00	ADD	AX,0010
05	20	00	ADD	AX,0020
A3	20	01	MOV	[0120],AX
CD	20		INT	20

DEBUG always displays numbers in hexadecimal. The number [0120] in brackets is DEBUG's way of referring to the contents of a memory location. The variable **sum** is located at address 0120h.

In each machine instruction shown here, the first byte is the op code and the next 2 bytes represent an immediate or memory operand. Of course, not all assembler instructions are 3 bytes long; their lengths vary between 1 and 6 bytes.

Note that 16-bit values are reversed when stored in memory. For example, the first instruction in the preceding table moves 0005h to AX, and the machine instruction reverses the 05h and the 00h. This reversal of bytes is characteristic of all processors in the Intel family and is performed for efficiency reasons. When 16-bit registers are loaded from memory back into registers, the bytes are re-reversed to their original form.

Our entire program could have been created by entering the following sequence of bytes into memory:

B8 05 00 05 10 00 05 20 00 A3 20 01 CD 20

The actual binary storage of the program would be

```
10111000 00000101 00000000 00000101 00010000 00000000
00000101 00100000 00000000 10100011 00100000 00000001
11001101 00100000
```

Believe it or not, early computers had to be programmed just this way, using mechanical switches to represent each binary bit. Most computer programs, fortunately, were very short.

In this book, we will not write programs using binary numbers, because it takes too long to look up the op code for each instruction. But it does illustrate a point: Computer programs are nothing more than meaningful sequences of numbers.

Trace the Program. Use DEBUG's **T** (Trace) command to execute each program statement. After each instruction is executed, DEBUG stops and displays the CPU registers and the next instruction. One advantage to using this procedure is that you can halt the program and return to DOS at any time. You can also change the contents of registers and variables before going on.

A trace of our sample program appears in Figure 1-1. As you look at it, carefully note the value of the AX register as it is changed by each instruction. You are now looking at what the program is doing directly at the machine level. This close contact with the CPU will be necessary throughout your study of assembly language.

Figure 1-1 Sample program trace, using DEBUG.

```
-R
AX=0000  BX=0000  CX=0000  DX=0000  SP=DF12  BP=0000  SI=0000  DI=0000
DS=1FDD  ES=1FDD  SS=1FDD  CS=1FDD  IP=0100   NV UP EI PL NZ NA PO NC
1FDD:0100  B80500        MOV  AX,0005

-T
AX=0005  BX=0000  CX=0000  DX=0000  SP=DF12  BP=0000  SI=0000  DI=0000
DS=1FDD  ES=1FDD  SS=1FDD  CS=1FDD  IP=0103  NV UP EI PL NZ NA PO NC
1FDD:0103  051000        ADD  AX,0010

-T
AX=0015  BX=0000  CX=0000  DX=0000  SP=DF12  BP=0000  SI=0000  DI=0000
DS=1FDD  ES=1FDD  SS=1FDD  CS=1FDD  IP=0106  NV UP EI PL NZ NA PO NC
1FDD:0106  052000        ADD  AX,0020

-T
AX=0035  BX=0000  CX=0000  DX=0000  SP=DF12  BP=0000  SI=0000  DI=0000
DS=1FDD  ES=1FDD  SS=1FDD  CS=1FDD  IP=0109  NV UP EI PL NZ NA PE NC
1FDD:0109  A32001        MOV  [0120],AX

-G
-D 120,121        (dump memory locations 120 through 121)
1FDD:0120  35 00  (bytes are reversed)
```

```
                              MASM CHARACTER SET

Letters: A-Z, a-z
Digits: 0-9

Special characters:

?                                        ,     (comma)
@                                        "     (double quotes)
_  (Underline symbol)                    &
$                                        %
:                                        !
.  (period)                              '     (apostrophe)
[ ]                                      ~     (tilde)
( )                                      |
< >                                      \
{ }                                      =
+                                        #
/                                        ^     (caret)
=                                        ;
                                         `     (accent char)
```

Figure 1-2 The Macro Assembler character set.

BASIC ELEMENTS OF ASSEMBLY LANGUAGE

In this section, we will elaborate on the basic building blocks of IBM-PC assembly language. Assembly language statements are made up of constants, literals, names, mnemonics, operands, and comments. Figure 1–2 shows the assembler's basic character set. These characters may be used to form numbers, names, statements, and comments.

Constant

A *constant* is a value that is either known or calculated at assembly time. A constant may be either a number or a string of characters. It cannot be changed at runtime. A *variable,* on the other hand, is a storage location that may be changed at runtime. The following are examples of constants:

```
'ABC'
2134
 5*6
(1+2)/3
```

Integer. An integer is made up of numeric digits with no decimal point, followed by an optional radix character (d = decimal, h = hexadecimal, o, q = octal, b

= binary). The radix character may be in uppercase or lowercase. If the radix is omitted, the number is assumed to be a decimal number. Examples:

Example	Radix
11110000b	Binary
200	Decimal (default)
300d	Decimal
4A6Bh	Hexadecimal
2047q	Octal
2047o	Octal

Real Number. A *real number* contains digits, a single decimal point, an optional exponent, and an optional leading sign. The syntax is

$$\left[\left\{\begin{matrix}+\\-\end{matrix}\right\}\right] \textit{digits.digits} \left[\mathrm{E}\left[\left\{\begin{matrix}+\\-\end{matrix}\right\}\right] \textit{digits}\right]$$

Examples

```
2.3
+200.576E+05
0.22222E-5
-6.0e3
```

Syntax Notation. In the preceding example and in all future syntax definitions, an optional element will be enclosed in brackets. Braces will identify a required selection. For example, if a leading sign is used in a real number, you must choose either a plus (+) or minus (-) sign. Required reserved words are in uppercase. Lowercase words in italics are predefined terms, such as *identifier, operand,* and *register.*

Character or String Constant. A single ASCII character or a string of characters may be enclosed in single or double quotation marks:

```
"a"
'B'
"STACK OVERFLOW"
'012#?%%A'
```

A *character constant* is 1 byte long. The length of a *string constant* is determined by its number of characters. The following constant is 5 bytes long:

```
'ABCDE'
```

An apostrophe may be enclosed in double quotation marks, or double quotation marks may be enclosed in single quotation marks. Single or double quotation marks may be embedded in their own string by repeating them immediately. All of the following are valid:

"That's not all..."
'The file "FIRST" was not found'
'That''s not all...'
"The file ""FIRST"" was not found"

Statement

An assembly language *statement* consists of a name, a mnemonic, operands, and a comment. Statements generally fall into two classes—instructions and directives. *Instructions* are executable statements, and *directives* are statements that provide information to assist the assembler in producing executable code. The general format of a statement is:

```
[name] [mnemonic] [operands] [;comment]
```

Statements are *free-form,* meaning that they may be written in any column with any number of spaces between each operand. Blank lines are permitted anywhere in a program. A statement must be written on a single line and may not extend past column 128.

A *directive,* or *pseudo-op,* is a statement that affects either the program listing or the way machine code is generated. For example, the DB directive tells MASM to create storage for a variable named **count** and initialize it to 50:

```
count db 50
```

An *instruction* is executed by the microprocessor at runtime. Instructions fall into general types: program control, data transfer, arithmetic, logical, and input-output. Instructions are always translated directly into machine code by the assembler. In fact, a feature of assembly language is that each assembler instruction translates directly into a single machine language instruction.

Name

A *name* identifies a label, variable, symbol, or reserved word. It may contain any of the following characters:

A–Z	a–z	0–9	?	_	@	$	.

Programmer-chosen names must adhere to the following restrictions:

- Only the first 31 characters are recognized.
- There is no distinction between upper- and lowercase letters.
- The first character may not be a digit.
- If it is used, the period (.) may be used only as the first character.
- A programmer-chosen name may not be the same as an assembler reserved word.

A name used before an assembler *directive* identifies a location or numeric value within the program. For example, the following memory variable has been given the name **count**:

```
count   db   50
```

If a name appears next to a program instruction, it is called a *label*. Labels serve as place markers whenever transfers of control are required within programs. In the following example, **start_program** is a label identifying a location in an assembly language program:

```
start_program:   mov ax,0
                 mov bx,0
```

A label can also appear on a blank line:

```
Label1: mov ax,0
```

Reserved Name. A reserved name, or *keyword,* has a special predefined meaning. Reserved names are *case insensitive*—they may contain uppercase letters, lowercase letters, or a combination of the two. Examples of reserved names in IBM-PC assembly language are MOV, PROC, TITLE, ADD, AX, and END. For example, the word MOV is an assembly language instruction mnemonic. It cannot be used as a label before an instruction, because it has a predefined meaning.

Another Program Example

We're going to write a program called ECHO, which inputs a character from the keyboard and echoes it on the screen. It demonstrates the way DOS handles input-output.

DOS has a set of *function calls* that provide a convenient set of input-output instructions for your programs. Each is activated by using the **INT 21h** instruction and by placing a function selector number in the AH register. First, to input a character from the keyboard, we use the following two instructions:

```
mov  ah,1   ; DOS function #1: keyboard input
int  21h    ; call DOS to do the work
```

The program will stop and wait for a key to be pressed; then the key's ASCII code will be placed in the AL register. Next, we will use DOS function 2 to display a character on the console. The ASCII code of the character must be in DL. We want to display the character currently in AL, so we move it to DL where DOS can display it:

```
mov  ah,2    ; DOS function #1: console output
mov  dl,al   ; display the character in AL
int  21h     ; call DOS
```

Complete Program. The complete program will now be listed, along with the DEBUG commands to be used when assembling and testing it. Remember not to use the **h** radix on numbers in DEBUG, because all numbers are assumed to be in hexadecimal anyway. Do not type the comments on the right side:

```
DEBUG
-A 100
mov ah,1
int 21          (input character will be in AL)
mov ah,2
mov dl,al       (move the character to DL)
int 21
int 20          (end the program)
                (press ENTER on the blank line)
-U              (unassemble the program)
-G              (Go-execute the program)
-Q              (Quit-return to DOS)
```

The Procedure Trace Command. To trace a program containing INT instructions, you have to use the P (Procedure trace) command instead of the T command. The T command would trace into DOS's input-output subroutines, and you would probably never get back to your own program. A sample trace of the program using DEBUG is shown in Figure 1–3.

POINTS TO REMEMBER

The first purpose of this chapter has been to explain what assembly language is, why it is used, and what types of programs assembly programmers write. Second, we have briefly covered the binary and hexadecimal numbering systems, because they are the foundation of data representation on the IBM-PC. When writing and debugging programs in assembly language, you must be able to *think* in binary and hexadecimal.

A tremendous amout of time and work goes into mastering IBM-PC assembly language. Many skills must be mastered before the process of programming in assembler seems natural. The IBM-PC appears deceptively simple, yet its as-

```
-R
AX=0000  BX=0000  CX=000C  DX=0000  SP=FFEE  BP=0000  SI=0000  DI=0000
DS=3D7D  ES=3D7D  SS=3D7D  CS=3D7D  IP=0100   NV UP EI PL NZ NA PO NC
3D7D:0100 B401          MOV     AH,01
-P

AX=0100  BX=0000  CX=000C  DX=0000  SP=FFEE  BP=0000  SI=0000  DI=0000
DS=3D7D  ES=3D7D  SS=3D7D  CS=3D7D  IP=0102   NV UP EI PL NZ NA PO NC
3D7D:0102 CD21          INT     21
-P

*
AX=012A  BX=0000  CX=000C  DX=0000  SP=FFEE  BP=0000  SI=0000  DI=0000
DS=3D7D  ES=3D7D  SS=3D7D  CS=3D7D  IP=0104   NV UP EI PL NZ NA PO NC
3D7D:0104 B402          MOV     AH,02
-P

AX=022A  BX=0000  CX=000C  DX=0000  SP=FFEE  BP=0000  SI=0000  DI=0000
DS=3D7D  ES=3D7D  SS=3D7D  CS=3D7D  IP=0106   NV UP EI PL NZ NA PO NC
3D7D:0106 88C2          MOV     DL,AL
-P

AX=022A  BX=0000  CX=000C  DX=002A  SP=FFEE  BP=0000  SI=0000  DI=0000
DS=3D7D  ES=3D7D  SS=3D7D  CS=3D7D  IP=0108   NV UP EI PL NZ NA PO NC
3D7D:0108 CD21          INT     21
-P

*
AX=022A  BX=0000  CX=000F  DX=002A  SP=FFEE  BP=0000  SI=0000  DI=0000
DS=3D7D  ES=3D7D  SS=3D7D  CS=3D7D  IP=010A   NV UP EI PL NZ NA PO NC
3D7D:010A CD20          INT     20
-P
```

Figure 1-3 Trace output of the ECHO program, using DEBUG.

sembly language is surprisingly complex. Within the next 10 years, you will probably learn three or four different assembly languages. You can take heart in knowing that many skills learned here will apply to other assemblers.

Debuggers. Use one of the debugging programs mentioned in this chapter (DEBUG, SYMDEB, or CODEVIEW), or another if one is available. There are also several excellent shareware debuggers available on electronic bulletin boards, including the nationwide Compuserve network. The reward for this effort is threefold: You will master specific skills in assembly language programming, you will gain a great deal of confidence in your ability to tackle systems-level programming on the IBM-PC, and you will gain insight into how high-level language compilers generate machine instructions.

We have introduced the following DEBUG commands:

A 100 — *Assemble* instructions into machine language, beginning at location 100.

G — *Go* (execute) from the current location to the end of the program.

P	*Procedure trace* a single instruction or DOS function call. This prevents you from having to trace instructions within DOS functions.
Q	*Quit* DEBUG and return to DOS.
R	*Register* display.
T	*Trace* a single instruction, and show the contents of the registers after it is executed.
U	*Unassemble*. Disassemble memory into assembly language instructions.

REVIEW QUESTIONS

1. Why should computer students learn assembly language?

2. Before reading this chapter, how did you think assembly language was used? Has your impression changed?

3. Can you recall a debugging problem that occurred when you were unable to proceed without help because you didn't know enough about the IBM-PC's operating system?

4. Think of at least two things that you cannot do in a high-level language that you would like to be able to do in assembly language.

5. Find a book, article, or other publication that uses octal notation.

6. Using a high-level language, show an example of converting data from character format to numeric format and vice versa.

7. Write the hexadecimal and binary representations of the characters 'XY', using the ASCII table at the end of this book.

8. Suppose your computer has 24-bit registers, and the highest bit of a signed number holds the sign. What would be the largest *positive* number, expressed in both binary and hexadecimal, that a register could hold?

9. How many bits does a word of storage contain on the IBM-PC?

10. What are the decimal values of the following signed numbers?
    a. 10000000b
    b. 01111111b

11. How does a low-level language differ from a high-level language?

12. Define the following terms in your own words:
    a. machine instruction
    b. instruction mnemonic
    c. operand
    d. register
    e. disassemble

13. In the following machine instruction, which byte probably contains the op code?

    05 0A 00

14. Which DEBUG command lets you do each of the following?
    a. Execute a single instruction, stop, and display all registers.
    b. Execute the remainder of a program.
    c. Begin assembling statements that will be converted to machine language.
    d. Return to DOS.

PROGRAMMING EXERCISES

DEBUG Exercises

For each of the following program excerpts, draw a diagram showing the movement of data as each instruction executes. Write down the final contents of the AX, BX, CX, and DX registers. Then assemble and trace the instructions using DEBUG, and verify your answers.

Exercise 1

```
mov   ah,7F
mov   ax,1234
mov   bh,al
mov   bl,ah
int   20
```

Exercise 2

Assuming that the numbers in this program excerpt are signed, explain what has happened to the signed result in the AL register. Use decimal values in your explanation.

```
mov   al,81
add   al,0FE
int   20
```

Exercise 3

(The following SUB instruction subtracts the second operand from the first.)

```
mov     al,FFFE
sub     al,2
mov     bl,8C
mov     bh,2D
add     bx,ax
int     20
```

Assuming that all values in the preceding program are signed, write down the signed decimal value in AX at the end of the program.

Exercise 4

(The NOT instruction reverses all bits in a number.)

```
mov     bl,FE
not     bl
add     bl,1
int     20
```

Exercise 5

(The INC instruction adds 1 to a number, and the DEC instruction subtracts 1.)

```
mov     ax,0
dec     ax
dec     ax
add     ax,2
inc     ax
int     20
```

ANSWERS TO REVIEW QUESTIONS

6. BASIC: N = ASC("B") : C$ = CHR$(66)
   Pascal: n := ord('Z'); ch := char(90);

7. a. 5859h b. 0101100001011001b

8. 011111111111111111111111b or 7FFFFFh

9. A word is 16 bits.

10. a. -128 b. +127

11. Each instruction in a low-level language matches one machine instruction; each instruction in a high-level language is translated into many machine instructions.

12. See the definitions in the chapter.

13. The first byte: 05

14. a. T (Trace) b. G (Go) c. A (Assemble) d. Q (Quit)

2

Hardware and Software Architecture

This chapter is a brief survey of the hardware and operating system of the IBM-PC. It is an important prelude to programming in its assembly language. Throughout this book, we deal with specific details of the IBM-PC and IBM-compatible computers. To do this effectively, we need to understand the computer's hardware configuration, the Intel iAPX 8088 processor, and the IBM operating system. Nearly everything said about the IBM-PC in this chapter applies to the IBM PC/XT and PC/AT computers as well.

Although this book is about the IBM-PC, the basic ideas in this chapter apply to many different microcomputers and operating systems. The Intel 8088 processor, for example, traces its roots to the earlier Intel 8080 and Z-80 microprocessors. The DOS operating system has many roots in the popular CP/M and Unix operating systems. Microcomputers and operating systems yet to come will, no doubt, draw on the rich legacy left by the IBM-PC and by DOS.

INSIDE THE SYSTEM UNIT

A diagram of the IBM-PC's system unit is shown in Figure 2–1. The system board lies flat inside the computer, containing the bulk of the microprocessors and memory.

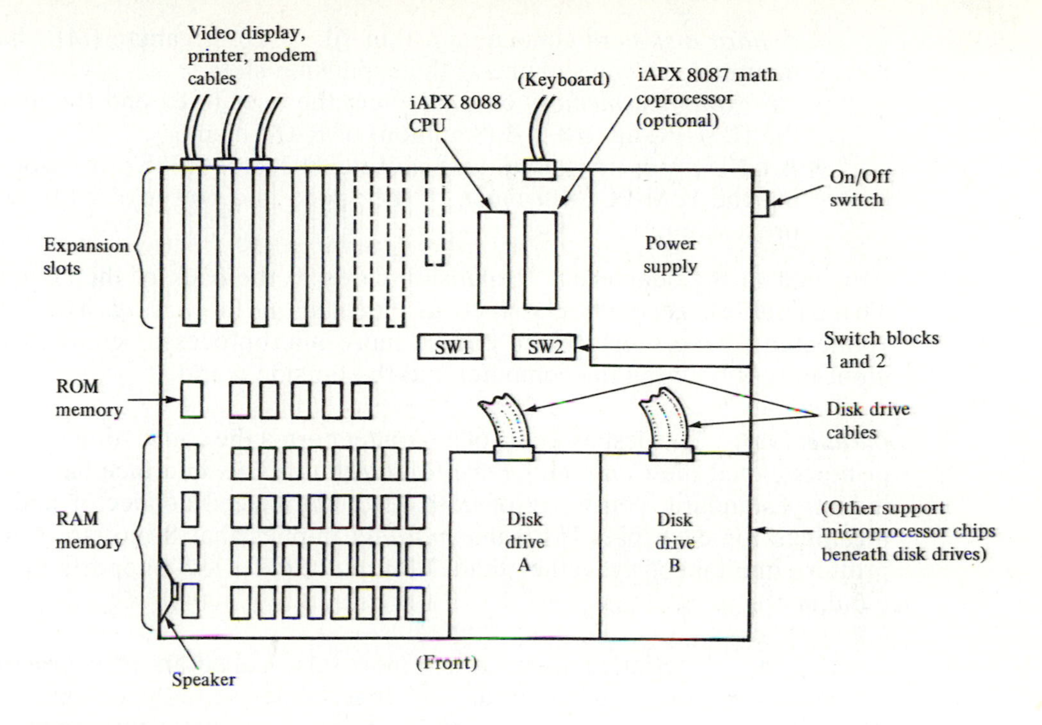

Figure 2-1 System unit, IBM-PC.

Expansion Slots. The IBM-PC has five expansion slots (eight on the XT and AT) holding expansion/adapter cards produced by IBM and other companies. The cards contain microprocessor chips and connectors for the video display, the disk drive controller, and the input-output ports. The following list is not meant to be all-inclusive, but it does illustrate some of the more popular expansion cards available today. At a minimum, a system includes the following adapter and controller cards:

- A *video display adapter* (monochrome, color, or enhanced color) with connectors for the video display and a parallel printer port.
- A *disk controller* for the floppy disk drives.

Most systems contain the following optional expansion cards:

- A *hard disk controller* to allow the addition of hard disk storage to the system.
- A *multipurpose expansion card* containing additional memory to bring the total random access memory (RAM) memory up to 640k, along with additional serial and parallel input-output ports.

Other popular options include the following:

- An *internal modem* allowing communications across telephone lines. Previously, it was necessary to connect a separate modem outside the computer to do this.

- A *hard disk card* containing a thin 10- or 20-megabyte (MB) hard disk mounted sideways in one of the expansion slots.
- An *expanded memory* card allowing the user to extend the memory of the IBM-PC up to 8 MB (8 million) of RAM memory.
- A *CPU processor board,* with an Intel 80286 or 80386 processor, providing the IBM-PC with much of the speed and power of more advanced processors.

Attached to the adapter and expansion cards at the back of the computer are various cables, generally classified as either *serial* or *parallel.* The cables are connected to *ports,* which are one or more microprocessor chips that permit input-output between the computer and the outside world.

Parallel Port. The best example of a parallel port is the connection used on most printers called the *Centronics Parallel Interface*. This interface has become an industry standard, consisting of both a standard-sized connector and specific meanings for each pin. The name *parallel* implies that 8 bits are sent to the printer simultaneously, rather than 1 bit at a time. DOS supports up to three parallel ports.

Serial Port. A serial communications port (also called an *asynchronous port*) connects a mouse, a modem, or any other serial device to the computer system. A serial port is used for asynchronous communications, where binary bits are sent one at a time rather than in parallel. The IBM-PC uses a standard *RS-232* serial interface. DOS supports up to two serial ports, called COM1 and COM2.

Central Processing Unit. Inside every microcomputer there is a microprocessor called the *central processing unit* (*CPU*). The CPU is the heart of the whole system. The IBM-PC uses the Intel iAPX 8088 processor and an optional Intel 8087 math coprocessor designed for high-speed floating-point math operations. The IBM-PC/AT uses the Intel 80286 processor, as do the newer IBM PS/2 models 50 and 60. The PS/2 model 80 uses the 80386 processor.

Switch Blocks. Below the 8088 and 8087 processors are two switch blocks called SW1 and SW2, used when configuring the computer's system to the available memory and devices. Each block contains eight manual switches that can be turned on or off by pressing on one end. The switches hold the following information:

Type of video display (monochrome or color)

Number of floppy disk drives

8087 math coprocessor

Hard disk installed (*yes* or *no*)

Amount of installed RAM memory

Memory. In the lower left corner of the system board are both read-only memory (ROM) and RAM memory. On many IBM-compatible computers, the ROM sockets are empty except one containing the ROM BIOS.

RAM memory is just below ROM, consisting of four banks of 9 chips each. Each chip represents 64 kilobits, so 8 of these make up 64K bytes of memory. The ninth chip in each bank is for parity checking, a way of catching errors when reading and writing memory. Four banks of 64K memory are equal to 256K of memory, which originally was the maximum memory that could be placed on the standard IBM-PC board. Many computers built more recently use memory chips with a greater capacity, usually 256 kilobits per chip. Most IBM-PCs today have an additional expansion board with another 384K of memory, to fill it up to the maximum 640K. Newer IBM-AT computers allow 1 MB of memory to be socketed on the system board.

THE CPU REGISTERS

Registers are special work areas inside the CPU designed to be accessed at high speed. The registers are 16 bits long, but you have the option of accessing the upper or lower halves of the four data registers:

Data registers	16-bit: AX, BX, CX, DX 8-bit: AH, AL, BH, BL, CH, CL, DH, DL
Segment registers	CS, DS, SS, ES
Index registers	SI, DI, BP
Special registers	IP, SP
Flags registers	Overflow, Direction, Interrupt, Trap, Sign, Zero, Auxiliary Carry, Parity, Carry

Data Registers. Four registers, named *data registers* or *general-purpose registers*, are used for arithmetic and data movement. Each register may be addressed as either a 16-bit or 8-bit value. For example, the AX register is a 16-bit register; its upper 8 bits are called AH, and its lower 8 bits are called AL. Bit positions are always numbered from right to left, starting with 0:

bits: 15 0

16-bit AX register	
AH register	AL register

bits: 7 . . . . 0 7 0

Instructions may address either 16-bit or 8-bit data registers from the following list:

AX		BX		CX		DX	
AH	AL	BH	BL	CH	CL	DH	DL

When a 16-bit register is modified, so is its corresponding 8-bit half register. Let's say, for example, that the AX register contains 0000h. If we move 126Fh to AX, AL will change to 6Fh.

Each general-purpose register has special attributes:

AX (*accumulator*). AX is called the accumulator register because it is favored by the CPU for arithmetic operations. Other operations are also slightly more efficient when performed using AX.

BX (*base*). Like the other general-purpose registers, the BX register can perform arithmetic and data movement, and it has special addressing abilities. It can hold a memory address that points to another variable. Three other registers with this ability are SI, DI, and BP.

CX (*counter*). The CX register acts as a counter for repeating or looping instructions. These instructions automatically repeat and decrement CX and quit when it equals 0.

DX (*data*). The DX register has a special role in multiply and divide operations. When multiplying, for example, DX holds the high 16 bits of the product.

Segment Registers

The CPU contains four *segment registers,* used as base locations for program instructions, data, and the stack. In fact, all references to memory on the IBM-PC involve a segment register used as a base location. The segment registers are:

CS (*code segment*). The CS register holds the base location of all executable instructions (code) in a program.

DS (*data segment*). The DS register is the default base location for memory variables. The CPU calculates the offsets of variables using the current value of DS.

SS (*stack segment*). The SS register contains the base location for the current program stack.

ES (*extra segment*). The ES register is an additional base location for memory variables.

Index Registers

Index registers contain the offsets of variables. The term *offset* refers to the distance of a variable, label, or instruction from its base segment. Index registers speed up processing of strings, arrays, and other data structures containing multiple elements. The index registers are:

SI (*source index*). This register takes its name from the 8088's string movement instructions, where the source string is pointed to by the SI register. SI usually contains an offset value from the DS register, but it can address any variable.

DI (*destination index*). The DI register acts as the destination for the 8088's string movement instructions. It usually contains an offset from the ES register, but it can address any variable.

BP (*base pointer*). The BP register contains an assumed offset from the SS register, as does the stack pointer. The BP register is often used by a subroutine to locate variables that were passed on the stack by a calling program.

Special Registers

The IP and SP registers are grouped together here, since they do not fit into any of the previous categories:

IP (*instruction pointer*). The IP register always contains the location of the next instruction to be executed. CS and IP registers combine to form the address of the next instruction about to be executed.

SP (*stack pointer*). The SP register contains the *offset*, or distance from the beginning of the stack segment to the top of the stack. The SS and SP registers combine to form the complete top-of-stack address.

Flags Register

The *flags* register is a special 16-bit register with individual bit positions assigned to show the status of the CPU or the results of arithmetic operations. Each relevant bit position is given a name; other positions are undefined:

Bit Position

15	14	13	12	11	10	9	8	7	6	5	4	3	2	1	0
x	x	x	x	O	D	I	T	S	Z	x	A	x	P	x	C

O = Overflow	S = Sign
D = Direction	Z = Zero
I = Interrupt	A = Auxiliary Carry
T = Trap	P = Parity
x = undefined	C = Carry

Fortunately, we do not have to memorize each flag position. Instead there are special 8088 instructions designed to test and manipulate the flags. A flag or bit is *set* when it equals 1; it is *clear* (or reset) when it equals 0. The CPU sets flags by turning on individual bits in the Flags register. There are two basic types of flags: *control flags* and *status flags*.

Control Flags. Individual bits may be set in the Flags register by the programmer to control the CPU's operation. These are the *Direction, Interrupt,* and *Trap* flags. Abbreviations used by DEBUG and CODEVIEW debugger programs are shown in parentheses.

The *Direction* flag controls the assumed direction used by string processing instructions. The flag values are 1 = Up (UP) and 0 = Down (DN). The programmer controls this flag, using the STD and CLD instructions.

The *Interrupt* flag makes it possible for external interrupts to occur. These interrupts are caused by hardware devices such as the keyboard, disk drives, and the system clock timer. The Interrupt flag is cleared by the programmer when an important operation is going on that must not be interrupted. The flag must then be set to allow the system to process interrupts normally again. The flag values are 1 = Enabled (EI) and 0 = Disabled (DI), and are controlled by the CLI and STI instructions.

The *Trap* flag determines whether the CPU should be halted after each instruction. Debugging programs use this flag to allow the user to execute one instruction at a time (called *tracing*). The flag values are 1 = Trap on and 0 = Trap off, and the flag may be set by the INT 3 instruction.

Status Flags. The status flag bits reflect the outcome of arithmetic and logical operations performed by the CPU. These are the *Overflow, Sign, Zero, Auxiliary Carry, Parity, and Carry* flags.

The *Carry* flag is set when the result of an arithmetic operation is too large to fit into the destination. For example, if the values 200 and 56 were added together and placed in an 8-bit destination, the result (256) would be too large and the Carry flag would be set. The flag values are 1 = Carry (CY) and 0 = No carry (NC).

The *Overflow* flag is set when the signed result of an arithmetic operation may be too large to fit into the destination area. The flag values are 1 = overflow (OV) and 0 = no overflow (NV).

The *Sign* flag is set when the result of an arithmetic or logical operation generates a negative result. Since a negative number always has a 1 in the highest bit position, the Sign flag is always a copy of the destination's sign bit. The flag values are Negative (NG) and Positive (PL).

The *Zero* flag is set when the result of an arithmetic or logical operation generates a result of zero. The flag is used primarily by jump and *loop* instructions, in order to allow branching to a new location in a program based on the comparison of two values. The flag values are Zero (ZR) and Not Zero (NZ).

The *Auxiliary Carry* flag is set when an operation causes a carry from bit 3 to bit 4 (or a borrow from bit 4 to bit 3) of an operand. It is rarely used by the programmer. The flag values are Aux Carry (AC) and No Aux Carry (NA).

The *Parity* flag reflects the number of bits in the result of an operation that are set. If there is an even number of bits, the Parity is even (displayed as PE). If there is an odd number of bits, the Parity is odd (displayed as PO). This flag is used by the operating system to verify memory integrity and by communications software to verify correct transmission of data.

SYSTEM SOFTWARE AND MEMORY

In this section, we will look at the IBM-PC's system software and memory organization. We will present only the fundamentals for now, and delve more deeply into specific DOS services in later chapters.

IBM-PC Memory Architecture

The IBM-PC can access 1 MB of memory using a standard 20-bit address. The memory is divided between RAM and ROM. A diagram of the IBM's memory is shown in Figure 2–2. RAM memory starts at location 00000h and extends to BFFFFh. ROM memory begins at location C0000h and extends to FFFFFh.

Interrupt Vectors. The lowest 1,024 bytes of memory (00000h to 003FFh) contain the *interrupt vector table*. These are addresses used by the CPU when processing hardware and software interrupts. When a device interrupts the system or when a program requests services from the operating system, the processor locates the appropriate location in the interrupt vector table. In this location, an address points to an operating system subroutine designed to handle the interrupt.

Figure 2-2 The IBM-PC/XT/AT memory map.

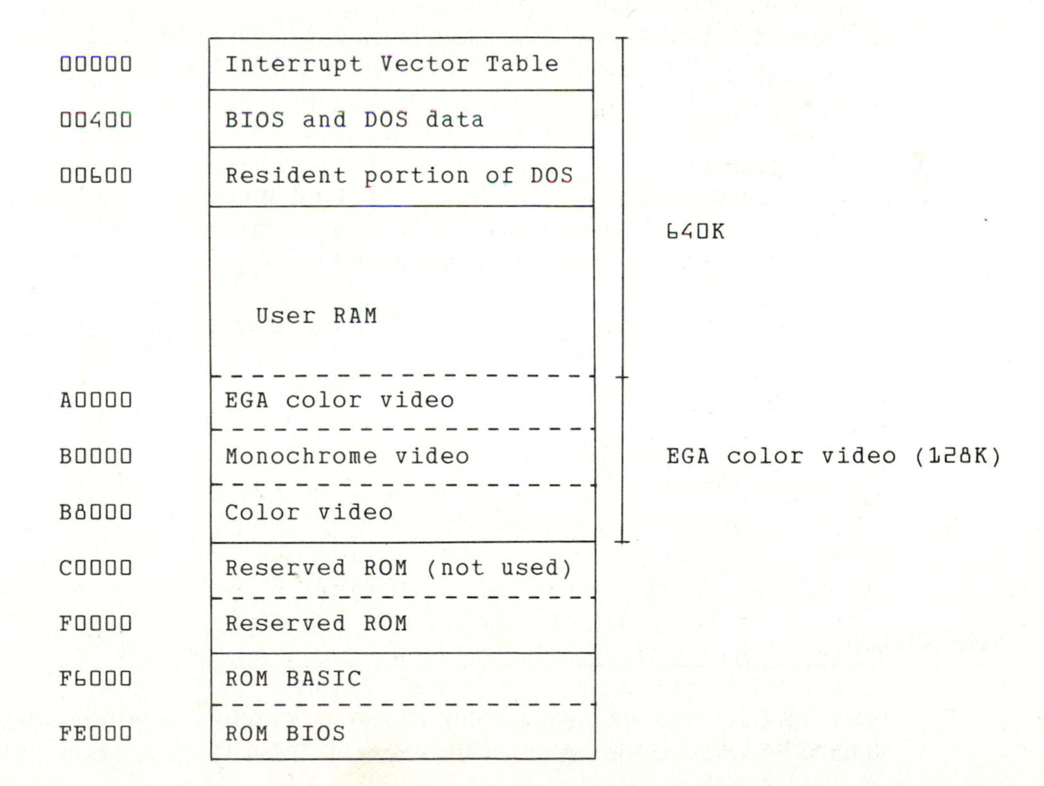

The DOS data area (00400h to 005FFh) contains variables used by DOS. For example:

- The keyboard buffer, where all keystrokes are stored until they can be processed.
- The keyboard status flag, showing which keys are currently being pressed.
- The locations of the printer ports.
- The locations of the serial ports.
- A description of the equipment available in the system: the amount of memory, number of disk drives, video monitor type, and so on.

User RAM. The resident portion of DOS is located at address 00600h, and free memory begins immediately above DOS. The size of DOS has increased steadily over the past several years, so its size will vary between 23K and 40K. The total amount of free RAM on the standard IBM-PC and PC/XT can be up to 640K, or address 9FFFFh. The IBM-PC/AT can address up to 1 MB of RAM.

Video Display Memory. The video display is *memory-mapped*. Rather than having to send each video character out through a port to the video display, the engineers at IBM decided that it would be more efficient to give each screen position a separate memory address. When DOS writes a character to the display, it calls a subroutine in the ROM BIOS, which in turn writes the character directly to a video memory address.

Video RAM memory (128K) extends from A0000h to BFFFFh, depending on the type of display used. The monochrome display uses only 4K of memory (B0000h to B7FFFh), the color graphics adapter (CGA) uses 16K of memory (B8000h to BBFFFh), and the enhanced graphics adapter (EGA) uses 128K. Many programs write characters directly to the video display buffer. A character written to the monochrome display area will not appear in the color display area because they are at different memory addresses. Programs that write directly to video memory must check the display type first.

ROM Area. Locations C0000h to FFFFFh are reserved by IBM for specialized ROM uses, including the hard disk controller and ROM BASIC. The latter is usually not included on IBM-compatible computers.

Finally, the ROM BIOS resides in locations F0000h to FFFFFh, the highest area of memory. The BIOS contains low-level subroutines used by DOS for input-output and other basic functions. Programs coded in ROM are often called *firmware*, because they are software stored in a hardware medium.

THE STACK

The *stack* is a special memory buffer used as a holding area for addresses and data. The stack resides in the stack segment. Each 16-bit location on the stack is pointed to by the SP register, called the *stack pointer.* The stack pointer holds the address of the last data element to be added to, or *pushed* on the stack. The last value added to a stack is also the first one to be removed, or *popped* from the stack, so we call it a *LIFO structure* ("Last In First Out").

Let's look at a program stack containing one value, 0006, on the left side of the following illustration. The stack pointer (notated by SP) points to the most recently added value:

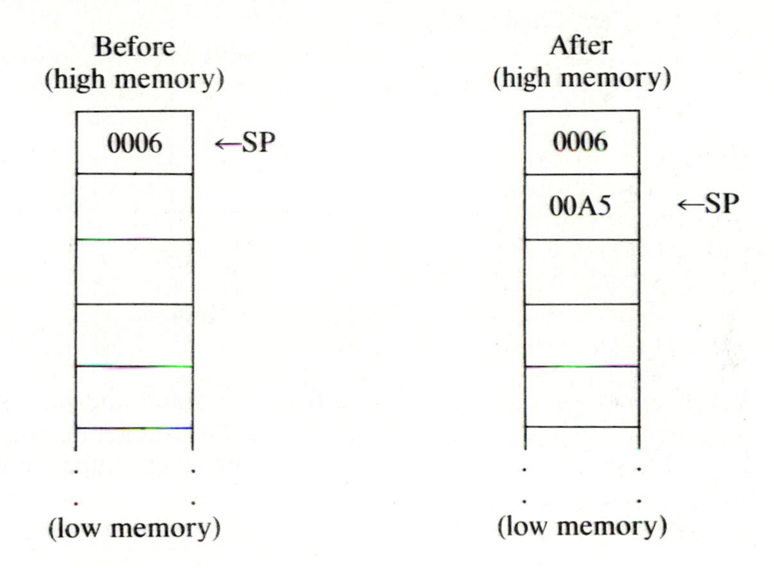

When we push a new value on the stack, as shown on the right side of this illustration, SP is decremented before the new value is pushed (SP always points to the last value pushed). We use the PUSH instruction to accomplish this, as shown by the following code:

```
mov    ax,00A5   ; move 00A5h to AX
push   ax        ; push AX on the stack
```

The PUSH instruction does not change the contents of AX; instead, it *copies* the contents of AX onto the stack.

As more values are pushed, the stack grows downward in memory. Let's assume that the BX and CX registers contain the values 0001 and 0002. The following instructions push them on the stack:

```
push   bx    ; push BX on the stack
push   cx    ; push CX on the stack
```

Now that 0001 and 0002 have been pushed on the stack, it appears as follows:

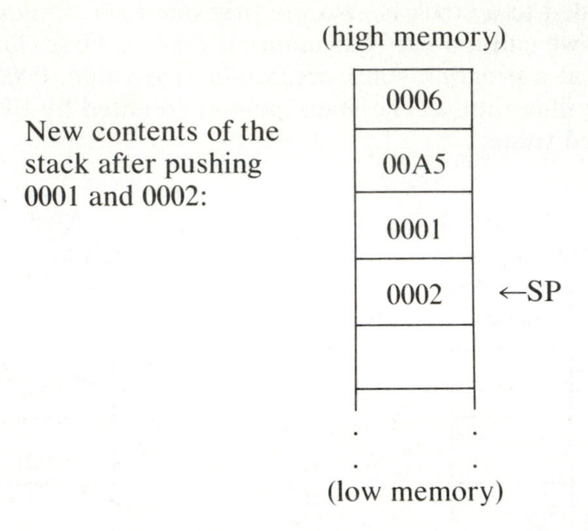

A pop operation removes a value from the stack and places it in a register or variable. After the value is popped from the stack, the stack pointer is incremented to point to the previous value on the stack. Suppose we want to execute the following instruction:

```
pop  ax   ; pop the top of stack into AX
```

We can see the stack before and after the instruction is executed in the following illustration:

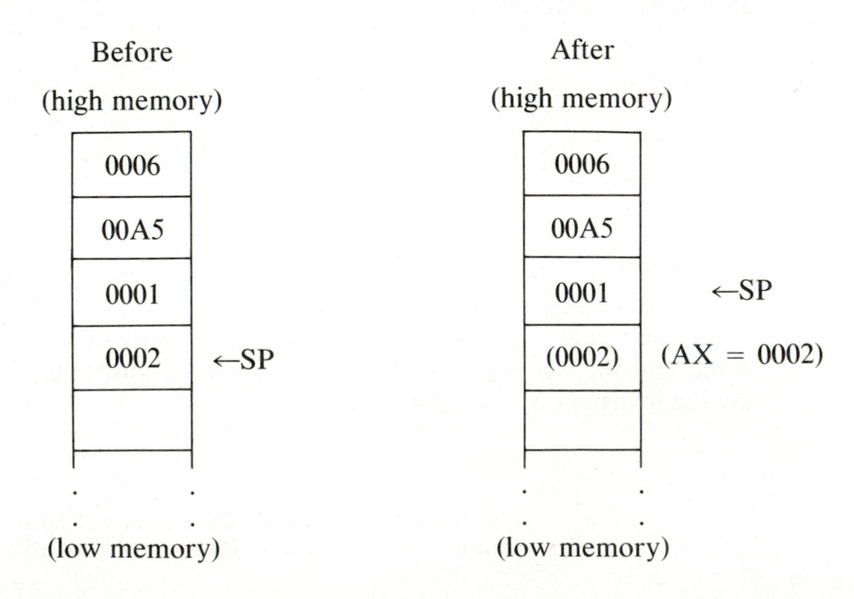

After the POP has taken place, AX contains the number that was at the top of the stack (0002). The stack pointer has moved up and is now pointing at 0001. The popped value (0002) is no longer available, and the area of the stack below the stack pointer is available for future use.

Programming Tip: What Happens to the Stack?

It is very easy to presume that data left on the stack below the stack pointer will remain there until we use the stack again. But that's not the case: We can only assume that data *above* the stack pointer remains intact.

The IBM-PC employs a system of hardware *interrupts,* which literally interrupt any program in progress when hardware devices signal the CPU. A device might be the keyboard, a disk drive, a serial communications port, or even the system timer, which ticks 18.2 times per second. An interrupt activates a subroutine in memory called an *interrupt handler,* which freely uses the stack for its own purposes. So, at any instant, data below the stack pointer can be erased without our knowing it. We will cover interrupt handling routines more thoroughly in Chapter 16.

There are three standard uses of stacks:

1. A stack makes an excellent *temporary save area* for registers if we need to preserve their values. We can then use the registers as a scratch area and restore them when finished.
2. When a subroutine is called, the program saves a *return address* on the stack, the location in the program to which the subroutine is to return.
3. High-level languages create an area on the stack inside subroutines called the *stack frame*. It is in this area that local variables are created while the subroutine is active. They are then discarded when the subroutine returns to the calling program.

ADDRESS CALCULATION

An *address* is a number that refers to an 8-bit memory location. Addresses are numbered consecutively starting at 0, going up to the highest location in memory. Addresses are expressed in one of two hexadecimal formats:

- A 32-bit *segment-offset* address, which combines a base location (segment) with an offset to represent an actual location. An example is 08F1:0100.
- A 20-bit *absolute* address, which refers to an exact memory location. An example is 09010.

Using 20 bits, the CPU can address up to 1,048,576 bytes of memory. But address registers are only 16 bits wide and can only hold a maximum value of 65,535. To solve this apparent dilemma, the CPU combines the segment and offset values to create an absolute address.

To illustrate, let us start with a hypothetical segment-offset address of 08F1:0100h. The CPU converts this to a 20- bit absolute address by adding the segment and offset together. The segment value is always understood to have 4 implied zero bits to the right. Therefore, a segment address of 08F1h really represents an absolute location of 08F10h:

0	8	F	1	(0)	←4 implied bits
0000	1000	1111	0001	0000	

The CPU then adds the offset to the segment, yielding the absolute address:

Segment value →	0	8	F	1	(0)
Add the offset →		0	1	0	0
Absolute address →	0	9	0	1	0

One might wonder why such a complicated method of addressing was created. Programmers using the earlier 8-bit microcomputers, for example, dealt only with 16-bit absolute addresses. There are at least two advantages to the segment-offset addressing method.

First, a program may be loaded into memory at any segment address without having to recalculate the addresses of variables within the program. Because other programs may have already been loaded into memory, it is impossible to know in advance the segment address a program will have.

Second, a program may access large data structures by setting the current segment address to a new block of memory.

Memory Addressing Using Registers. When referencing instructions and data, the CPU combines two registers. A base location, or *segment,* is placed in one register. An *offset* address is placed in another register and combined with the segment register to produce a complete address. For example, the combined code segment (CS) and instruction pointer (IP) registers point to the next instruction about to be executed. The combined SS and SP registers point to the stack. ES and DS may be combined with variables and registers:

```
DS + BX              ;BX is a base register
DS + SI              ;SI, DI are index registers
ES + DI
DS + variable_1
```

DOS Architecture

DOS is composed of a number of parts, all working together at different levels. Part of it is in ROM, called the BIOS, and the rest of it is supplied on disk. When the computer is booted, the following happens:

The CPU jumps to an initialization program in the ROM BIOS. The first thing this program does is to RAM memory, called a *power-on self-test.*

A program called the *bootstrap loader* loads the *boot record* from either drive A or drive C (if the computer has a hard disk). The boot record contains another program that executes as soon as it is loaded. The boot record program, in turn, loads two other DOS programs into memory if they are on the disk: IBMBIO.COM and IBMDOS.COM. Neither of these programs appears in the disk directory because their names are hidden. IBMBIO.COM comprises the software portion of the BIOS that complements the existing ROM BIOS routines, and IBMDOS.COM contains the resident portion of DOS.

The next program loaded into memory is the DOS *command processor* (COMMAND.COM), which consists of three parts. The *resident* part remains in memory all the time and provides all of the basic operating system services to application programs. The *initialization* part is used only temporarily when DOS is first loaded. The *transient* part is loaded into high RAM and interprets DOS commands typed at the keyboard.

When DOS has been loaded into memory, COMMAND.COM takes over; it prompts the user for the date and time, displays a prompt on the screen, and waits for a command. Finally, a number of utility programs supplied on the DOS disks provide the user with *external DOS commands*. Some examples are as follows:

DOS Program	Usage
FORMAT.COM	Format a new disk
CHKDSK.COM	Verify disk integrity
PRINT.COM	Print a text file
SORT.EXE	Sort a file

The AUTOEXEC.BAT File. DOS looks for a file called AUTOEXEC.BAT on the root directory of the boot disk. In general, any file with a .BAT extension is called a *batch* file, containing DOS commands to be executed in sequence as if they were typed from the keyboard. The AUTOEXEC.BAT file is special because it is automatically executed when the system is booted. Some commonly used commands are:

CLS — Clear the screen.
DATE — Simulate the prompt normally used by DOS when the system is booted, asking for today's date.
TIME — Simulate the prompt normally used by DOS when the system is booted, asking for the current time.

PATH Tell DOS where to search for executable programs and batch files when they cannot be found in the current directory.

PROMPT Allow the user to customize the DOS prompt. For example, PROMPT $P $G changes the prompt to display the current directory path, such as C:\ASM\PROGS > .

POINTS TO REMEMBER

There must be at least two expansion cards in an IBM-PC—the video controller and the disk controller. Expansion cards offer a variety of features not supplied on the original computer. Most common among these are the serial communications port and extra memory.

Registers. When an 8-bit register is modified, its corresponding 16-bit register is also modified. Moving a value to AH, for example, automatically affects the upper half of AX.

When you move data between registers, the register sizes must match. Suppose you want to copy the contents of the BL register into AL. The following instruction would be valid:

```
mov  al,bl
```

But you could not write the following, because AX is a 16-bit register:

```
mov  ax,bl
```

IBM-PC Memory. Application programs occupy memory just above DOS in the user RAM area. The total available memory on a standard IBM-PC is 640K, but some of this is already used up by DOS. It is possible to expand the available memory by adding a memory expansion board to the system.

Video Display. The video display is memory mapped, so characters may be moved directly to memory in order to be displayed quickly. You cannot do this, however, if your program is to be run in a multitasking or multiprocessing environment. Instead, video output must be routed through the ROM BIOS services.

Stack. A stack is a specialized buffer or array. We use it to save registers that must be altered, to store the return address when a subroutine is called, or to create local variables within subroutines. The PUSH instruction decrements the stack pointer (SP) and copies a value from a variable or register onto the stack. The POP instruction copies a value from the stack into a variable or register and then increments the stack pointer. Most programs shown in this book use a 256-byte stack.

Addressing. The IBM-PC uses a segment-offset method that addresses the entire range of memory. A 16-bit hexadecimal segment address is always assumed to have an extra implied zero in the lowest position. Thus, a segment of 1234h implies an address of 12340h. A 16-bit offset is added to a segment address in order to arrive at an absolute memory location. We always notate segment-offset addresses with a colon between the two numbers—1234:0200h, for example.

Additional DEBUG Commands. As always, the time to experiment with DEBUG and learn about the registers and stack is *now.* Write a few short programs using the ADD, SUB, MOV, INC, DEC, PUSH, and POP instructions, and find out how they work. The following DEBUG commands will prove useful. For more complete information, see the DEBUG tutorial in Appendix B. The AX register is used here for the purpose of illustration, but all other registers may be used.

Sample	Explanation
R	(Register) Display registers.
R AX	Modify a single register; DEBUG then prompts you for the new register contents.
D	(Dump) Dump 128 bytes of memory from the current location.
D 120	Dump 128 bytes from location DS:0120 (the DS register is considered the default base segment).
E 200 31	(Enter) Enter the value 31h at location DS:0200.
F 100,500 20	(Fill) Fill memory from DS:100 through DS:500 with the value 20h.

REVIEW QUESTIONS

1. Which two adapter and controller cards are required in every IBM-PC?

2. In addition to supplying extra serial and parallel ports, what might a multipurpose expansion card do?

3. Which peripheral device most often uses a parallel port?

4. Which peripheral devices most often use a serial port?

5. In addition to telling the system how much installed memory exists, what four other things do the switch blocks on the system board identify?

6. Why are there nine chips in each bank of RAM memory? What is the purpose of the ninth chip?

7. Name the four general-purpose data registers.

8. What is the name of the lower half of the CX register? How many bits can it hold?

9. Name the four segment registers.

10. When the upper half of a data register is changed, are the high 8 bits of the corresponding 16-bit register (AX) also changed?

11. What special purpose does the CX register serve?

12. Which register holds the high 16 bits of the product in a multiplication operation?

13. Which register acts as the base location for all executable instructions?

14. Which register acts as the base location for the stack?

15. Besides the stack pointer (SP), which other register points to variables passed on the stack by a calling program?

16. Name two index registers.

17. Which three flags are called *control flags*?

18. The *status flags* include the Auxiliary Carry, Parity, Carry, Overflow, and which two other flags?

19. Which flag is set when the result of an unsigned arithmetic operation is too large to fit into the destination?

20. Which flag is set when the result of an arithmetic or logical operation generates a negative result?

21. Which flag reflects the number of 1 bits in the result of an operation?

22. Assuming that your IBM-PC has 640K of RAM memory, what is the highest user RAM location in which you can store your programs?

23. What occupies the lowest 1,024 bytes of memory?

24. Name two examples of system data stored in the DOS and BIOS data areas.

25. If a character is written to the monochrome display buffer, will it also appear on the color display?

26. What is the name of the memory area containing low-level subroutines used by DOS for input-output?

27. What is the name of the base location of the stack?

28. Which register holds the offset of the last value pushed on the stack?

29. A PUSH operation adds a value to the stack, while a ______ operation removes a value from the stack.

30. When a value is pushed onto the stack, does the stack grow upward or downward in memory?

31. Why is the stack called a LIFO structure?

32. The two ways of describing an address on the IBM-PC are segment-offset and ____________.

33. True or false: Once a program has been assembled into machine language, it can be loaded into memory only at a predefined segment address coded within the program.

34. Which two registers combine to form the address of the next instruction that will be executed?

35. What does the IBMBIO.COM program do?

36. When is an AUTOEXEC.BAT file executed?

37. Convert the the following segment-offset addresses to absolute addresses:
    a. 0950:0100
    b. 08F1:0200

PROGRAMMING EXERCISES

Exercise 1 Expanded Memory

Find a book or technical journal article that relates to the LIM standard for expanded memory on the IBM-PC. After reading the article, write a short explanation of how DOS is able to access more than a megabyte of memory using only a 20-bit address. Suggested journals are *Microsoft Systems Journal, PC Tech Journal, and Dr. Dobbs Journal.*

Exercise 2 The Intel 80386 Processor

Find an article in a technical journal that describes the register set of the Intel 80386 processor chip, and give a short presentation to the class explaining how the 80386 registers differ from the registers on the 8086/8088.

Exercise 3 Asynchronous Communications

Find an article in a technical journal that explains why the ROM BIOS services for asynchronous communications are not adequate for most high-speed tasks. What solution to this problem is usually proposed?

Exercise 4 Memory Chips

Look inside the computer you are currently using and count the number of memory chips. Find out how much RAM is installed, and figure out how many kilobits each chip holds. Call a commercial distributor, and find out the memory access speed needed for a 10 MHz IBM-AT-compatible computer.

Exercise 5 Dumping Memory Variables

Use the E (Enter) command in DEBUG to initialize a variable at location 200 with the value 36h. Then assemble a short program that moves the byte at location 200 to the DL register. Finally, move the contents of DL to memory location 201. When you are finished, use the D (Dump) command to look at locations 200 and 201, and verify that both locations contain 36h.

Exercise 6 Moving Immediate Values to Registers

Using a debugger, find out by experimentation the registers to which you cannot move immediate values. Write down the names of these registers, and suggest a reason why the CPU does not allow immediate moves to them.

Exercise 7 Resetting the Instruction Pointer

The R (Register) command in DEBUG lets you modify registers and flags. For example, you can modify AX by typing

```
R AX
```

DEBUG will prompt you for the new value to give the register. Assemble the following program, and trace it to the last instruction. Use the R command to set the instruction pointer back to location 100, and trace the program again. The program is:

```
mov  ax,2000
mov  si,ax
mov  bx,si
mov  dx,bx
int  20
```

Exercise 8 Evaluating the Flags

Use DEBUG to assemble and trace the following program. Write down the contents of the Zero, Carry, and Sign flags after tracing each instruction. Write a short note next to each line explaining why any of the flags changed. The program is:

```
mov  al,FFFF
inc  al
sub  al,2
mov  dl,al
add  dx,2
int  20
```

Exercise 9 Video Buffer Display

Using DEBUG, inspect your computer's video buffer. For a monochrome adapter, the address is B000:0, and for color/EGA/VGA it is B800:0. Use the D (Dump) command and see if you can identify characters that had just appeared on the video display. (You may have to repeat the D command several times to see any meaningful text.) Notice that in the following sample every other byte contains the number 7. This is an attribute byte that is stored along with each screen byte.

```
B800:0260 20 07 20 07 20 07 20 07-20 07 20 07 20 07 20 07   . . . . . . . .
B800:0270 20 07 20 07 20 07 20 07-20 07 20 07 20 07 20 07   . . . . . . . .
B800:0280 20 07 56 07 6F 07 6C 07-75 07 6D 07 65 07 20 07   .V.o.l.u.m.e. .
B800:0290 69 07 6E 07 20 07 64 07-72 07 69 07 76 07 65 07  i.n. .d.r.i.v.e.
B800:02A0 20 07 43 07 20 07 68 07-61 07 73 07 20 07 6E 07   .C. .h.a.s. .n.
B800:02B0 6F 07 20 07 6C 07 61 07-62 07 65 07 6C 07 20 07  o. .l.a.b.e.l. .
B800:02C0 20 07 20 07 20 07 20 07-20 07 20 07 20 07 20 07   . . . . . . . .
B800:02D0 20 07 20 07 20 07 20 07-20 07 20 07 20 07 20 07   . . . . . . . .
B800:02E0 20 07 20 07 20 07 20 07-20 07 20 07 20 07 20 07   . . . . . . . .
B800:02F0 20 07 20 07 20 07 20 07-20 07 20 07 20 07 20 07   . . . . . . . .
B800:0300 20 07 20 07 20 07 20 07-20 07 20 07 20 07 20 07   . . . . . . . .
B800:0310 20 07 20 07 20 07 20 07-20 07 20 07 20 07 20 07   . . . . . . . .
B800:0320 20 07 44 07 69 07 72 07-65 07 63 07 74 07 6F 07   .D.i.r.e.c.t.o.
B800:0330 72 07 79 07 20 07 6F 07-66 07 20 07 20 07 43 07  r.y. .o.f. . .C.
B800:0340 3A 07 5C 07 41 07 53 07-4D 07 5C 07 43 07 48 07  :.\.A.S.M.\.C.H.
B800:0350 32 07 20 07 20 07 20 07-20 07 20 07 20 07 20 07  2. . . . . . . .
```

Exercise 10 **Filling the Video Buffer**

Use the F (Fill) command in DEBUG to fill the video buffer with 702A. Assuming a monochrome video display, the command is:

```
F B000:0,1000 2A,70
```

Provide a short explanation of why the video display looked as it did.

Exercise 11 **Stack Manipulation**

Assemble a short program using DEBUG that performs the following tasks in order:

a. Load the data registers with the following values:
AX=0001, BX=0002, CX=0003, DX=0004
b. Push each register on the stack, in the following order:
AX, BX, CX, DX.
c. Pop each register from the stack in the following order:
AX, BX, CX, DX.

After you have traced each instruction up through step (b), examine the stack using the D (Dump) command. Print a copy of the stack, using the keyboard Shift-PrtSc command. (Remember that the stack contents always begin from the current stack pointer position.)

Next, trace the program through step (c). After the last POP instruction, explain why the register values (AX, BX, CX, and DX) have changed. Use the Shift-PrtSc command to print out a dump of the registers.

ANSWERS TO REVIEW QUESTIONS

1. The video display adapter and the disk controller.
2. Increase RAM memory.
3. A printer.
4. A modem or a mouse.
5. The type of video display, the number of floppy disk drives, the presence of a math coprocessor, the presence of a hard disk.
6. Each chip represents 1 bit in 64K or 256K of memory. The ninth chip contains a parity check bit for each byte of memory.
7. AX, BX, CX, and DX.
8. The lower half of CX is CL; it holds 8 bits.

9. CS, DS, SS, and ES.

10. Yes.

11. It acts as a counter for repeating and looping instructions.

12. DX.

13. CS.

14. SS.

15. BP.

16. SI and DI.

17. The Direction, Interrupt, and Trap flags.

18. Sign and Zero.

19. Carry flag.

20. Sign flag.

21. Parity flag.

22. 9FFFFh, the last location before the video buffer.

23. Interrupt Vector Table.

24. Two of the following: keyboard buffer, keyboard status flag, addresses of the printer ports, addresses of the asynchronous adapter ports, and the equipment flag.

25. No, the monochrome and color displays use different memory areas.

26. The ROM BIOS.

27. Stack segment.

28. Stack pointer (SP).

29. POP.

30. Downward.

31. Because the last value pushed on the stack is the first value popped off—LIFO.

32. Absolute.

33. False. A program may be loaded into memory at any available segment address.

34. CS and IP.

35. It provides extensions to programs in the ROM BIOS.

36. When the system is booted or when the name AUTOEXEC is typed.

37. a. 09600h b. 09110h

3

Assembly Language Fundamentals

DATA DEFINITION DIRECTIVES

In assembly language, we define storage for variables using *data definition* directives. (The term *data declaration* is sometimes used to mean the same thing.) Data definition directives create storage at assembly time and can even initialize a variable to a starting value. The directives are summarized in the following table:

Directive	Description	Number of Bytes	Attribute
DB	Define byte	1	byte
DW	Define word	2	word
DD	Define doubleword	4	doubleword
DQ	Define quadword	8	quadword
DT	Define 10 bytes	10	tenbyte

As we see from this table, the variable being defined is given a particular *attribute*. The attribute refers to the basic unit of storage used when the variable was defined.

These directives also assign names to variables. For example, the following DB directive creates an 8-bit variable called **char**:

```
char  db 'A'
```

The assembler initializes the variable to a starting value, which in this example is 41h, the ASCII code for the letter *A*. The name of the variable is optional, but we normally supply it in order to be able to refer to the variable in an instruction.

Define Byte (DB)

The DB directive creates (allocates) storage for a byte or group of bytes, and optionally assigns starting values. The syntax is:

```
[name] DB initialvalue [,initialvalue] . . .
```

Initialvalue can be one or more 8-bit numeric values, a string constant, a constant expression, or a question mark (?). Commas separate the values when multiple bytes are defined:

```
list  db  10h,20h,41h,2
```

Let us assume that the variable **list** is stored at location 00h, as shown by the following illustration. Each number begins at the offset immediately following the previous one:

Offset:	00	01	02	03
Values:	10	20	41	02

This brings up a very important point: The name **list** identifies the *offset*, or location, of only the first byte in the list of numbers. The other bytes defined by **list** follow at the next few memory locations. Each constant may use a different radix when a list of items is defined:

```
list  db  10d,14h,41h,00000010b
```

Numeric, character, and string constants may be freely mixed:

```
db   10,'A',20h,'ABC'
```

Each storage byte for this data is shown here in hexadecimal:

Values:	0A	41	20	41	42	43

Memory contents may be left undefined by using the question mark (?) operator:

```
count   db   ?
```

A numeric expression can initialize a variable with a value that is calculated at assembly time:

```
count   db 10*20
```

The *DUP* operator repeats a single- or multiple-byte value. For example, 20 bytes containing all binary zeros would be coded as:

```
db   20  dup(0)
```

At the same time, an array containing 20 occurrences of the string 'stack' would be:

```
db   20  dup('stack')
```

This would allocate 100 bytes of storage: 'stack' is 5 bytes long and it occurs 20 times.

When a hexadecimal number begins with a letter (*A–F*), a leading zero is added to prevent the assembler from interpreting it as a label. Examples:

```
db A6h     ; incorrect
db 0A6h    ; correct
```

Define Word (DW)

The DW directive creates storage for a word or list of words and optionally gives them starting values. The syntax is:

```
[name] DW initialvalue [,initialvalue] ...
```

Initialvalue can be any 16-bit numeric value up to 0FFFFh (65535), a constant expression, or a question mark (?). If *initialvalue* is signed, the acceptable range is -32768 to +32767.

A character constant may be stored in the lower half of a word. The largest string constant that may be stored in a word is 2 characters long, such as: 'ab'.

Reversed Storage Format. The assembler reverses the bytes in a word value when storing it in memory; the lowest byte occurs at the lowest address. When the variable is moved to a 16-bit register, the CPU re-reverses the bytes. This is shown in the following illustration, where 2AB6h is stored in memory as B6 2A:

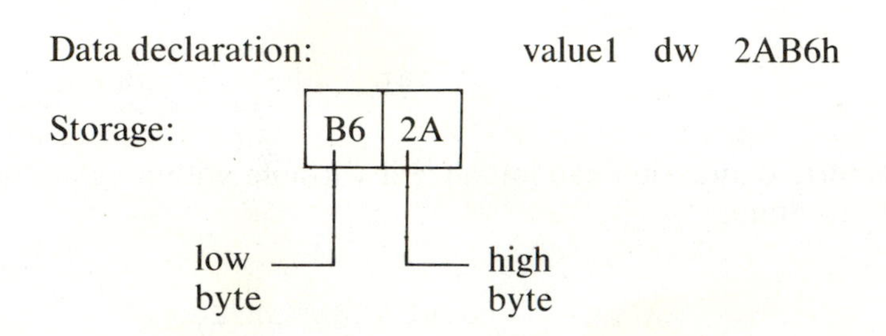

DUP operator. The DUP operator allocates multiple occurrences of a value. For example, the following DW directive creates a list of four 16-bit integers:

```
intarray   dw   4 dup(1234h)
```

As with all 16-bit values, each number is stored in reversed-byte format. Assuming that **intarray** starts at offset 00, we might picture the storage of bytes thus:

Offset:	00	01	02	03	04	05	06	07
Contents:	34	12	34	12	34	12	34	12

Additional examples using the DW directive are as follows:

```
dw   0,0,0                  ; define 3 words of storage
dw   0,65535                ; lowest and highest unsigned values
dw   -32768,+32767          ; lowest and highest signed values
dw   256*2                  ; constant expression = 512
dw   4000h                  ; hexadecimal value
dw   1111000011110000b      ; binary value
dw   1000h,4096,'AB',0      ; mixed data types
dw   ?                      ; single uninitialized word
dw   100 dup(?)             ; 100 uninitialized words
```

In the last two examples, the question mark (?) tells the assembler not to initialize the memory location to any value. Thus, the contents are undetermined at runtime.

Define Doubleword (DD)

The DD directive creates storage for a 32-bit doubleword variable, with the option of giving it a starting value. The syntax is:

```
[name] DD initialvalue [,initialvalue] . . .
```

Initialvalue can be a binary number up to 0FFFFFFFFh, a segment-offset address, a 4-byte encoded real number, or a decimal real number.

The bytes in a doubleword variable are stored in reverse order, so the least significant digits are stored at the lowest address. For instance, the value 12345678h would be stored in memory as

Offset:	00	01	02	03
	78	56	34	12

You can define a single doubleword location or a list of them. In the first example that follows, **far_pointer1** is uninitialized. In the second example, the assembler automatically initializes **far_pointer2** to the 32-bit segment-offset address of **subroutine1**. In the third example, **list32** marks the starting location of 20 doubleword memory locations:

```
far_pointer1   dd   ?
far_pointer2   dd   subroutine1
list32         dd   20 dup(0)
```

The LABEL Directive

The LABEL directive assigns a specific attribute (e.g., byte, word, doubleword) to a label. If LABEL is used in the code segment, the syntax is:

```
name LABEL distance
```

where *distance* may be either NEAR or FAR. This mainly affects the way a subroutine is called: from within the same segment (NEAR) or from another segment (FAR). We will delay a complete discussion of this until Chapter 7.

If LABEL is used with the name of a variable in the data segment, the syntax is:

```
name LABEL type
```

where *name* is a symbol assigned to the variable, and *type* may be BYTE, WORD, DWORD, QWORD, or TBYTE. This is where LABEL is the most useful, because it allows us to redefine a variable with a different name and/or attribute.

MASM's Type Checking. When a variable is created using DB, DW, DD, or any of the other data definition directives, MASM gives it a default attribute, or type (8-bit, 16-bit, etc.). This type is checked when you refer to the variable, and an error results if the types do not match. For instance, you might want to move the lowest byte of a 16-bit variable into an 8-bit register. The following MOV instruction would be flagged by MASM as an error, because it checks the type of each operand:

```
mov   al,count   ; error: operand sizes must match
.
.
count  dw  20h
```

Tips on Using DEBUG

DEBUG and other compatible debuggers have certain limitations when assembling programs:

- Labels cannot be used.
- All numbers must be coded in hexadecimal.
- References to the contents of a variable must be in the form [nnnn], where the number inside the brackets is the variable's offset.

Let's assume that the variable **count** is located at offset 0006h. The following statements are equivalent:

MASM Version	DEBUG Version
`mov    al,count`	`mov    al,[0006]`
`mov    dl,'A'`	`mov    dl,41`
`count  db 20h`	`count  db 20`

This type checking is usually a good idea because it helps us to avoid logic errors. If you need to disable it, you can use the LABEL directive to create a new name *at the same address*. The variable may now be accessed using either name:

```
mov    al,count_low        ; retrieve low byte of count
mov    cx,count            ; retrieve all of count
.
.
count_low label byte       ; byte attribute
count dw   20h             ; word attribute
```

PROGRAM STRUCTURE

In this section, we present an overview of the basic structure of an assembly language program. A program is divided into separate *segments*. Each segment contains instructions or data whose addresses are relative to a segment register (CS, DS, SS, or ES). Beginning with Version 5.0, MASM provides a simplified set of directives for declaring segments, called *simplified segment directives*. (We will deal here only with the simplified directives and will cover complete segment definitions in Chapter 14.)

Figure 3-1 shows the basic program structure to be used in most programs in this book. The optional TITLE directive defines a program title up to 128 characters long, which will be printed on the program listing. The DOSSEG directive

Figure 3-1 Structure of an assembly language program.

```
title  Sample Program Structure

dosseg                          ; set up segment order
.model small                    ; small memory model
.stack 100h                     ; set stack size

.code
main       proc
           mov  ax,bx           ; code (instructions)
           .
           .
main       endp

.data
count      db  10               ; data (variables)
           .
           .
end        main                 ; end of assembly
```

tells MASM to place the program segments in a standard order used by Microsoft high-level languages.

The MODEL Directive

The MODEL directive selects a standard memory model for your program. A *memory model* is a lot like a standard blueprint or configuration. It determines the way segments are linked together, as well as the maximum size of each segment.

The memory models are standard for Microsoft and Borland languages and are common to compilers written by many other companies. The models are defined by the number of bytes that may be used for code (instructions) and data (variables). When we limit code to 64K, for example, we indicate that all instructions must fit within a single 64K memory segment. The following table summarizes the differences between the types of models:

Model	Description
Tiny	Code and data together may not be greater than 64K
Small	Neither code nor data may be greater than 64K
Medium	Only the code may be greater than 64K
Compact	Only the data may be greater than 64K
Large	Both code and data may be greater than 64K
Huge	All available memory may be used for code and data

All of the program models except *tiny* result in the creation of .EXE programs. The *tiny* model creates a .COM program. Unfortunately, simplified segment directives may not be used with this model, and the CODEVIEW debugger does not work well with .COM programs. In this book, we will use the *small* memory model, as it is the smallest one that is fully supported by Microsoft. A complete discussion of .COM programs may be found in Chapter 14.

Program Segments

Three segment directives are normally used: .STACK, .CODE, and .DATA. They may be placed *in any order* within a program, since the DOSSEG directive determines their final order anyway. The .STACK directive sets aside stack space for use by the program. For most small programs, 256 bytes is a more than adequate amount of space. The .CODE directive identifies the start of code (instructions) in a program. Program execution always begins with the first instruction in this section. The .DATA directive identifies the start of the data segment, where variables are declared.

By using the DOSSEG, MODEL, .STACK, .CODE, and .DATA directives, we ensure that a program can be called as a subroutine from a Microsoft high-level language without any conflicts arising from segment definitions.

Procedures

A *procedure* is a group of related program instructions with a common function or purpose. A procedure is given a name that identifies its starting location. We use the PROC directive to identify a procedure. For example, the label **main_routine** defines the starting location of a procedure:

```
main_routine proc
```

Procedures are often called *routines* or *subroutines*. Every program has at least one procedure, and additional procedures may be added as a program expands.

The PROC directive shows where a procedure begins and the ENDP directive shows where it ends. If other procedures were to be added to the program in Figure 3-1, they would fall after the ENDP directive for **main** and before the .DATA directive:

```
.code
main    proc
        .
        .
main    endp

sub1    proc
        .
        .
sub1    endp

sub2    proc
        .
        .
sub2    endp
```

The END Directive. The END directive marks the last line in a source program to be assembled. Any lines of text placed after the END directive are ignored. In the main module of a program, the END directive is accompanied by a label that identifies the *entry point,* or start, of program execution. In Figure 3-1, the program entry point is **main**, the name of the only procedure.

MASM Versions 1.0 Through 4.0

Earlier versions of the Microsoft Assembler required you to declare the code, data, and stack segments yourself. Figure 3-2 shows the basic structure of such a program. First, it does not include the DOSSEG, .MODEL, .CODE, and .STACK directives. Instead, the segments' order is determined by their physical placement in the source program.

```
title  Sample Program Structure, MASM Version 4.0

code segment                 ; beginning of code segment

  assume cs:code,ds:data,ss:stack

  main proc                  ; main procedure

    mov  ax,data             ; (instructions here)
    mov  ds,ax
    .
    .

  main endp

code ends                    ; end of code segment

data segment                 ; beginning of data segment

  count  db  10              ; (variables here)
       .
       .
       .
data ends                    ; end of data segment

stack segment STACK          ; stack segment

  db 100h dup(0)

stack ends

end       main               ; end of assembly
```

Figure 3-2 *Structure of an assembly language program, MASM Versions 1.0 through 4.0.*

Some early versions of MASM placed the segments in alphabetical order, regardless of their order in the .ASM file. You can still choose alphabetical order by assembling with the /A option, but it's rarely necessary.

The segments can be given any names. In our example, we have chosen the names *code, data,* and *stack* only to make them easier to identify. Each segment begins and ends with the SEGMENT and ENDS directives. All variables, for example, are placed in the data segment:

```
data segment
  count  db  10   ; (variables here)
data ends
```

The SEGMENT directive for the stack segment in Figure 3-2 gives it a *combine type* of STACK. This tells MASM to initialize the SS register to the stack's base location and place the stack's size in SP (100h):

```
stack segment STACK
```

Finally, the ASSUME directive is needed in our sample program to identify the segment names used for the code, data, and stack. Because we can choose any segment names we want, MASM has no other way of knowing where variables and code are stored:

```
assume cs:code,ds:data,ss:stack
```

(The ss:stack designation is unnecessary, but it provides some documentation.)

You can use the complete segment directives shown in Figure 3-2 with MASM Version 5.0 with no problem. Chapter 14, in fact, includes a more complete discussion of segment directives, showing how they offer flexibility at the advanced programming level.

COM Format Programs

Often you will see assembly language programs written in COM format, intended to be assembled and linked into a file with an extension of .COM. They have a simpler structure, just a single segment, and load more quickly than .EXE pro-

Figure 3-3 *Structure of a COM format assembly language program, all versions of MASM.*

```
title  Sample Program Structure, COM format

code segment              ; beginning of the only segment

  assume cs:code,ds:code,ss:code

  org 100h                ; starting location counter

  main proc               ; main procedure
       .
       .                  ; (instructions here)
       .
  main endp

  count  db  10           ; (variables here)

code ends                 ; end of code segment

end  main                 ; end of assembly
```

grams. Programs assembled using DEBUG, for example, are in COM format. There has been a gradual shift away from using the COM format with the advent of the OS/2 operating system and other multitasking software, because a COM program does not share memory very well with other programs. Also, COM programs cannot use simplified segment directives or be debugged in source mode using Microsoft's CODEVIEW debugger. All these disadvantages aside, COM programs are easy to write and fine for small stand-alone applications.

Figure 3-3 (page 57) shows a COM program shell, which is identical for all versions of MASM. The only segment is called **code**, and the ASSUME directive has been adjusted accordingly. There is no stack segment because a stack area is automatically created at the end of the program segment. Variables may be located anywhere in the program segment, as long as you don't allow the CPU to accidentally process variables as instructions. I usually place variables right after the **main** procedure. A COM program must include the ORG 100h directive, which sets the instruction pointer (IP) to 100h when the program is loaded.

DATA TRANSFER INSTRUCTIONS

The MOV Instruction

The MOV instruction copies data from one operand to another using either 8-bit or 16-bit operands. MOV is called a *data transfer* instruction. The syntax is:

```
MOV   destination,source
```

Data is merely *copied* from the source to the destination, so the source operand is not changed. The *source* operand may be immediate data, a register, or a memory operand. The *destination* operand may be a register or a memory operand. The following types of data transfers are possible:

immediate data	to	register or memory
register	to	register
register	to	memory
memory	to	register

There are a few limitations on the types of operands:

- CS and IP may never be destination operands.
- Immediate data and segment registers may not be moved to segment registers.
- The source and destination operands must be the same size.
- If the source is immediate data, it must not exceed 255 (FFh) for an 8-bit destination or 65,535 (FFFFh) for a 16-bit destination.

MOV does not allow memory-to-memory transfers, so data must be transferred to a register first. For example, to copy **var1** into **var2**, one would have to write

```
mov   ax,var1
mov   var2,ax
```

Register Operands. A move involving only registers is the fastest type, taking only two clock cycles. (A *clock cycle* is the CPU's smallest unit of time measurement; it varies from 50 to 210 nanoseconds, depending on the type of CPU being used.) Registers should be used when an instruction must execute quickly.

Any register may be used as a source operand, and any registers except CS and IP may be destination operands. Some examples using register operands are as follows:

```
mov    ax,bx
mov    dl,al
mov    bx,cs
```

Immediate Operands. An immediate value (integer constant) may be moved to any register except a segment register or IP, and may be moved to any memory operand. A common error is to make the immediate value larger than the destination operand. Examples of valid immediate addressing are:

```
mov bl,01            ; move 8-bit value to BL
mov bx,01            ; move 16-bit value to BX
mov bx,1000h         ; move 16-bit value to BX
mov total,1000h      ; move 16-bit value to a variable
```

Direct Addressing. The name of a variable may be coded as one of the operands in a MOV instruction. This causes the contents of memory at the variable's address to be used. Let's say, for example, that an 8-bit variable named **count** contains the number 1. The following MOV statement copies the contents of **count** into AL:

```
mov   al,count
```

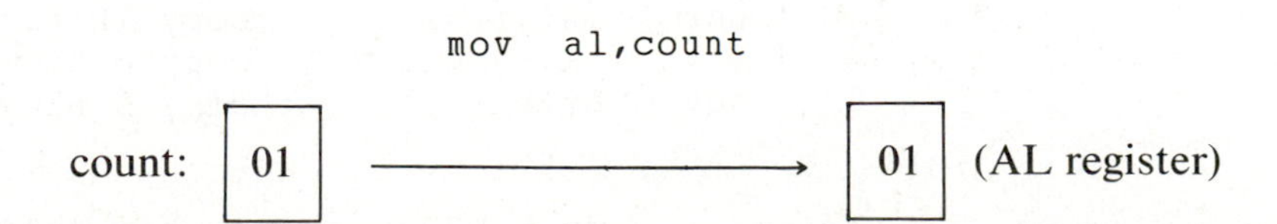

On the other hand, you might want to copy the BL register into the variable **count**:

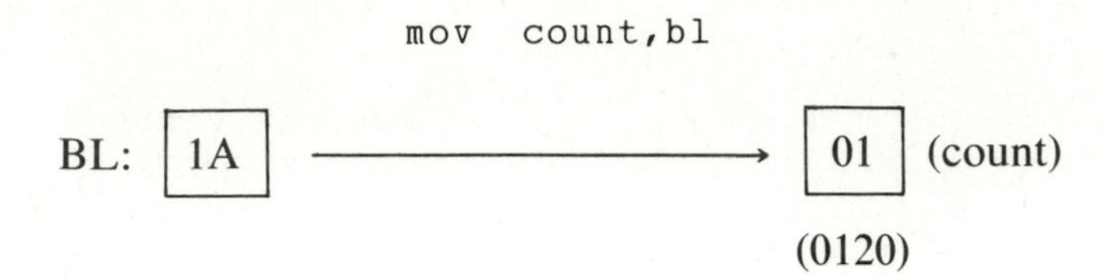

You can also add an offset to the name of a variable when using direct addressing. The name **array+1** refers to the location 1 byte beyond the offset of **array**. We call the notation **array** or **array+1** an *effective address,* or EA, because the operand's address is calculated by MASM, and this address is used to access memory at the given location. Assuming that **array** is a list of numbers, we might picture it as follows:

```
array  db 10h,20h,30h,40h,50h
```

array:	+0	+1	+2	+3	+4
	10h	20h	30h	40h	50h

Therefore, memory location **array+1** contains 20h. The following statements show different ways of accessing the array:

```
mov    al,array       ; contents = 10h
mov    dl,array+1     ; contents = 20h
mov    bh,array+4     ; contents = 50h
mov    array+2,0      ; third element = 0
```

As with register and immediate addressing, the *size attributes* (byte or word) of the two operands must match. For example, a variable named **int_1** created using the DW directive could only be paired with a 16-bit register. The variable **byte_1**, created by using DB, could only be paired with an 8-bit register. Both examples follow:

```
          mov    ax,int_1       ; copy 16 bits
          mov    int_1,si       ; copy 16 bits
          mov    al,byte_1      ; copy 8 bits
          mov    byte_1,dl      ; copy 8 bits
          .
          .
int_1        dw    1000h      ; 16-bit value
byte_1       db    10h        ; 8-bit value
```

PTR Operator. Occasionally you need to clarify an operand's type with the PTR operator. The name PTR incorrectly suggests the use of a pointer, but it really identifies the *attribute* of the memory operand. In the following example, WORD PTR identifies **count** as a word-sized variable, while BYTE PTR identifies **var2** as an 8-bit operand:

```
mov   word ptr count,10
mov   byte ptr var2,5
```

Illegal Moves. Certain combinations of operands are not valid with the MOV instruction:

1. Moves between two memory operands.
2. Moves of segment registers or immediate values to segment registers.
3. Moves to CS and IP.
4. Moves between registers of different sizes.
5. Moves between operands of different sizes unless the PTR operator overrides the default type of a memory operand.
6. Moves to immediate operands (this is probably obvious).

Samples of each illegal move are as follows:

```
        mov     word_1,word_2       ; memory to memory
        mov     ds,1000h            ; immediate to segment
        mov     ip,ax               ; IP destination
        mov     al,bx               ; mismatching register types
        mov     word_1,al           ; mismatching operand types
        mov     1000h,ax            ; immediate destination
        .
        .
word_1      dw    1000h
word_2      dw    0
```

Example. The following program moves immediate values to a register and then transfers values between registers. To get the maximum benefit from the example, assemble and trace it using DEBUG. The line numbers on the left side are not part of the program:

```
                               ;  AX   BX   CX   DX
1:    mov    ax,2B10           ; 2B10 0000 0000 0000
2:    mov    bx,ax             ; 2B10 2B10 0000 0000
3:    mov    dl,ah             ; 2B10 2B10 0000 002B
4:    mov    cl,bl             ; 2B10 2B10 0010 002B
5:    int    20                ; end program
```

(All numbers in the program listing are assumed to be in hexadecimal.) Line 1 moves 2B10h to AX, line 2 copies AX to BX, and line 3 copies AH to DL. AH is the *upper* half of AX, so 2Bh is copied to DL. Line 4 copies BL into CL. Line 5 halts the program and returns to DEBUG.

Sample Program: Move a List of Numbers

The following program may be assembled and run in DEBUG. The program moves three 16-bit integers from location 0120h to location 0130h:

```
mov  bx,[0120]
mov  [0130],bx
mov  cx,[0122]
mov  [0132],cx
mov  dx,[0124]
mov  [0134],dx
mov  ax,4C00
int  21
```

Use the A (Assemble) command to define the list of integers:

```
-A 120
DW 1000,2000,3000
```

The XCHG Instruction

The XCHG instruction exchanges the contents of two registers or of a register and a variable. The syntax is:

```
XCHG  op1,op2
```

The two operands may be registers or memory operands, as long as one operand is a register.

XCHG is the most efficient way to exchange two 8-bit or 16-bit operands, because you don't need a third register or variable to hold a temporary value. Particularly in sorting applications, this instruction provides a speed advantage.

One or both operands may be registers, or a register may be combined with a memory operand. Two memory operands may not be used togther. The following are all valid examples:

```
xchg  ax,bx      ; exchange BX with AX
xchg  ah,al      ; exchange upper, lower register halves
xchg  var1,bx    ; exchange memory operand with BX
```

Exchanging Memory Operands

The following statements load two variables from memory and exchange their contents:

```
1:  mov   al,value1    ; load value1 into AL
2:  xchg  al,value2    ; exchange AL with value2
3:  mov   value1,al    ; store AL in value1
     .
     .
  value1  db    0Ah    ; initialized variables
  value2  db    14h
```

(The line numbers are inserted for convenience and are not part of the program.)
On line 1, **value1** is copied to AL:

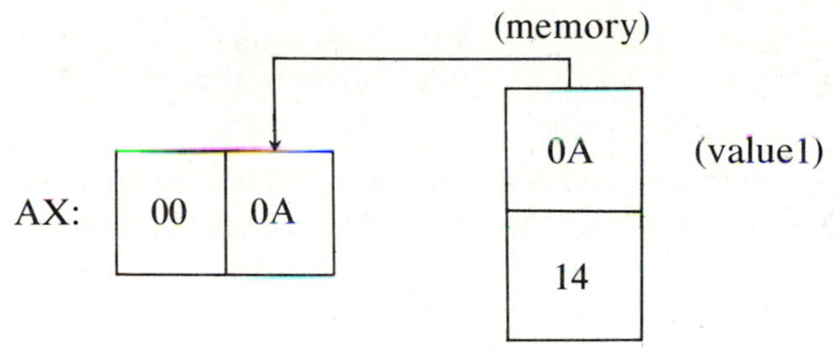

On line 2, AL is exchanged with **value2**:

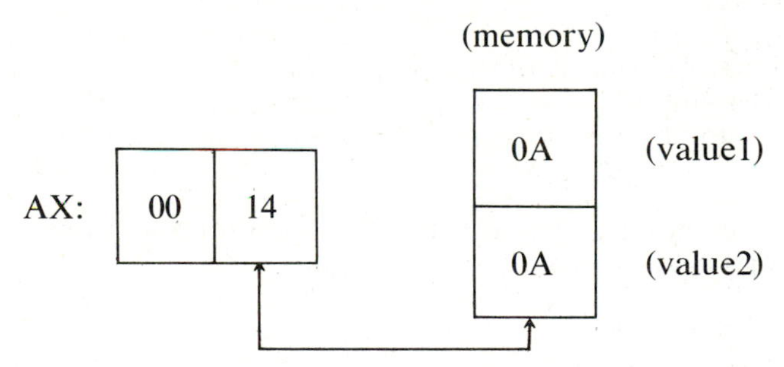

Line 3 moves AL to **value1**, completing the exchange of the two variables:

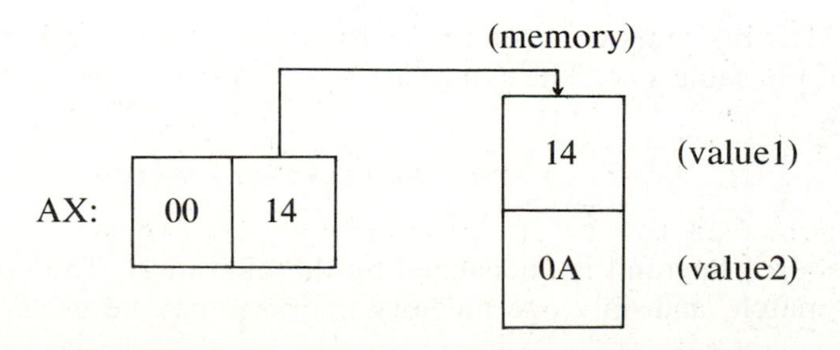

ARITHMETIC INSTRUCTIONS

Hardly any computer program could avoid performing arithmetic. The Intel instruction set has instructions for integer arithmetic, using 8-bit and 16-bit operands. Floating-point operations are handled by the 8087 Math Coprocessor.

In this section, we look at the most basic arithmetic instructions. The INC and DEC instructions add 1 to or subtract 1 from an operand; the ADD and SUB instructions perform 8-bit and 16-bit addition and subtraction.

The INC and DEC Instructions

The INC and DEC instructions add 1 to or subtract 1 from a single operand, respectively. Their syntax is:

```
INC  destination
DEC  destination
```

The destination operand may be an 8- or 16-bit register or memory variable. INC and DEC are faster than the ADD and SUB instructions, so they should be used where practical. All status flags are affected except the Carry flag. Examples are as follows:

```
inc al                  ; increment 8-bit register
dec bx                  ; decrement 16-bit register
inc membyte             ; increment memory operand
dec byte ptr membyte    ; increment 8-bit memory operand
dec memword             ; decrement 16-bit memory operand
inc word ptr memword    ; increment 16-bit memory operand
```

In these examples, the BYTE PTR operator identifies an 8-bit operand and WORD PTR identifies a 16-bit operand.

The ADD Instruction

The ADD instruction adds an 8- or 16-bit source operand to a destination operand of the same size. The syntax is:

```
ADD  destination,source
```

The source operand is unchanged by the operation. The sizes of the operands must match, and only one memory operand may be used. A segment register may not be the destination. All status flags are affected. Examples are as follows:

```
add al,1          ; add immediate value to 8-bit register
add cl,al         ; add 8-bit register to register
add bx,1000h      ; add immediate value to 16-bit register
add var1,ax       ; add 16-bit register to memory
add dx,var1       ; add 16-bit memory to register
add var1,10       ; add immediate value to memory
```

The SUB Instruction

The SUB instruction subtracts a source operand from a destination operand. The syntax for SUB is:

SUB *destination,source*

The sizes of the two operands must match, and only one may be a memory operand. A segment register may not be the destination operand. All status flags are affected. Examples are as follows:

```
sub al,1          ; subtract immediate value from 8-bit register
sub cl,al         ; subtract 8-bit register from register
sub bx,1000h      ; subtract immediate value from 16-bit register
sub var1,ax       ; subtract 16-bit register from memory
sub dx,var1       ; subtract 16-bit memory from register
sub var1,10       ; subtract immediate value from memory
```

Flags Affected by ADD and SUB

If the result of an addition operation is too large for the destination operand, the Carry flag is set. For example, the following result (300) is too large to fit into AL:

```
mov  al,250
add  al,50    ; Carry flag set
```

If the source is larger than the destination, a subtraction operation requires a borrow. This sets the Carry flag, as in the following example:

```
mov  al,5
sub  al,10    ; Carry flag set
```

If the result of an arithmetic operation is zero, the Zero flag is set. In the following examples, the ADD and SUB instructions set the Zero flag:

```
mov  bl,0
mov  al,0
add  al,bl    ; Zero flag set
mov  al,10
sub  al,10    ; Zero flag set
```

When an addition operation generates a result exactly 1 too large for the destination, it sets the Zero flag. The next example adds 1 to 255 in BL, causing BL to roll over to zero (much like an automobile speedometer when it reaches 100,000 miles):

```
mov  bl,255
add  bl,1       ; Zero flag set, and BL = 0h
```

The Overflow flag is set when an addition operation generates a signed number that is out of range. A signed 8-bit value is limited to the range -128 to +127, and a 16-bit value is limited to the range -32768 to +32767, because the highest bit is reserved for the sign. If we exceed this range, the Overflow flag is set and the result is invalid:

```
mov  cl,+126
add  cl,2       ; Overflow flag set, and CL = -128 (80h)
```

ADDRESSING MODES

Nearly every instruction involves one or two operands. The operands may be registers, immediate data (constants), or memory operands (variables). The way an instruction references its operands is called its *addressing mode,* which may be one of three basic types: *register, immediate,* or *memory.* Much of the CPU's power centers on its ability to handle a large variety of operand types, making it easy to access complex data structures.

Memory addressing may be further divided into types, shown by the following addressing mode table. In the table, a *displacement* is either a numeric value or the offset of a variable. The *effective address* of an operand refers to the distance of the data from the beginning of a segment. Each of the following examples refers to the *contents of memory* at the effective address:

ADDRESSING MODES

Mode	Example	Description
Direct	op1 bytelist	Effective address is displacement
Register indirect	[bx] [si] [di] [bp]	Effective address is the contents of a register
Based	list[bx] [bp+1]	Effective address is the sum of a base register and a displacement
Indexed	list[si] [list+di] [di+2]	Effective address is the sum of an index register and a displacement
Based indexed	[bx+si] [bx][di] [bp+di]	Effective address is the sum of a base and an index register
Based indexed with displacement	[bx+si+2]	Effective address is the sum of a base register, an index register, and a displacement

These examples are rudimentary and do not show the wide range of variations available. One might ask why so many addressing modes exist in the first place. Intel addressing modes, in fact, are some of the most complex available in any assembly language. This complexity results in greater convenience for the programmer, particularly when accessing tables of one, two, and three dimensions. You will see the register, immediate, direct, and register indirect modes used almost constantly; it's almost impossible to program without them. The remaining modes are less common, and one can easily work around them. But then, why not take advantage of the CPU's full power?

Types of Operands

Invariably, when referring to an addressing mode, we also refer to the type of operand used. The use of a register operand, for example, implies the register addressing mode.

Register Operand. A register operand may be one of the following 16-bit registers:

AX, BX, CX, DX, SI, DI, SP, BP, IP, CS, DS, ES, SS

Alternatively, it may be one of the following 8-bit registers:

AH, AL, BH, BL, CH, CL, DH, DL

In general, the register addressing mode is the most efficient because registers are part of the CPU and no memory access is required.

Immediate Operand. An immediate operand is a constant expression, such as a number, a character, or an arithmetic expression. (It is also possible to define a name as a constant; we will discuss this in Chapter 4.) MASM must be able to determine the value of an immediate operand at assembly time. Its value is inserted directly into the machine instruction. For example, the following instruction moves 5 to AL:

```
mov  al,5
```

The corresponding machine code generated by the assembler is

```
B0 05
```

where the first byte is the op code and the second is the immediate value 5.

Examples of immediate operands are shown here. The last one, (2+3)/5, is an expression that is evaluated at assembly time:

Example	Size (Bits)
10	8
'A'	8
'AB'	16
65535	16
(2+3)/5	8

Direct Operand. A direct operand refers to the contents of memory at an address implied by the name of a variable. Assuming that **count** was declared using a DB directive, the following examples are valid:

```
mov  count,cl    ; move CL to count
mov  al,count    ; move count to AL
```

Based and Indexed Operands. Based and indexed operands are essentially the same: The contents of a register are added to a displacement to generate an effective address. The register must be one of the following: SI, DI, BX, or BP. A *displacement* is either a number or a label whose offset is known at assembly time. The notation may take several equivalent forms:

Register added to an offset:

```
mov   dx,array[bx]
mov   dx,[di+array]
mov   dx,[array+si]
```

Register added to a constant:

```
mov   ax,[bp+2]
mov   dl,[di-2]    ; DI + (-2)
mov   dx,2[si]
```

If BX, SI, or DI is used, the effective address is usually an offset from the DS register. BP, on the other hand, usually contains an offset from the SS register. We will use BP only when calling assembly programs from high-level languages in Chapter 16.

Based Indexed Operand. The operand's effective address is formed by combining a base register with an index register. For example:

```
mov   al,[bp][si]
mov   dx,[bx+si]
add   cx,[di][bx]
```

Two base registers or two index registers cannot be combined, so the following would be incorrect:

```
mov dl,[bp+bx]   ; error: two base registers
mov ax,[si+di]   ; error: two index registers
```

Based Indexed with Displacement. The operand's effective address is formed by combining a base register, an index register, and a displacement. Examples are as follows:

```
mov   dx,array[bx][si]
mov   ax,[bx+si+array]
add   dl,[bx+si+3]
sub   cx,array[bp+si]
```

Two base registers or two index registers cannot be combined, so the following would be incorrect:

```
mov   ax,[bp+bx+2]
mov   dx,array[si+di]
```

Summing a List of Numbers

The following example shows how register indirect and based addressing modes may be used to access individual elements of an array. We add a list of numbers together and store the result in a variable called **sum**:

```
        mov   bx,offset list      ; get offset of list
        mov   ax,0
        mov   al,[bx]             ; get first number
        add   al,[bx+1]           ; add second number
        add   al,[bx+2]           ; add third number
        add   al,[bx+3]           ; add fourth number
        add   al,[bx+4]           ; add fifth number
        mov   sum,ax              ; store the sum
        .
        .
        .
list db   10h, 20h, 40h, 2h, 5h
sum  dw   0
```

When based addressing is used, an immediate value is added to a base register and the result is an effective address. We then take the contents of memory at the effective address and add it to AL:

```
add   al,[bx+1]
```

DEBUG version. A version of the foregoing program to be assembled in DEBUG is now shown. The references to **list** and **sum** have been replaced by hexadecimal addresses, and the **h** radix has been dropped from all numbers. When you trace the program using the T command, carefully observe the changing contents of AX (shown here in the diagram):

```
a 100                    (Changing values of AX)
mov  bx,0120
mov  ax,0
mov  al,[bx]                     0010
add  al,[bx+1]                   0030
add  al,[bx+2]                   0070
add  al,[bx+3]                   0072
add  al,[bx+4]                   0077
mov  [0125],ax
int  20

a    120
db   10,20,40,2,5
dw   0
```

POINTS TO REMEMBER

Programming in assembly language involves several skills: an understanding of the basic principles of computer architecture, specific knowledge of a computer's hardware and operating system, a knowledge of the CPU's instruction set, a knowledge of the available assembler directives, and the ability to apply all of the preceding skills when writing programs in assembly language.

Data Definition. Each of the data definition directives allocates memory storage in single units or groups of units. The primary types are as follows:

Directive	Storage Size (Bits)
DB (define byte)	8
DW (define word)	16
DD (define doubleword)	32
DQ (define quadword)	64
DT (define tenbyte)	80

The DUP operator makes it possible to define a list of values of the same storage type. The ? operator tells MASM not to initialize a variable to a starting value. When a 16-bit number is stored in memory, the bytes are stored in reverse order. Thus, the number 1234h would be stored as 34h,12h.

Program Structure. Programs are divided into separate areas according to their types of statements. These separate areas are called *segments.* Executable instructions belong in the code segment, and variables belong in the data segment. A third segment, the stack segment, is used as a temporary save area for registers and for return addresses when subroutines are called.

The simplified segment directives for creating segments are .CODE (code segment), .DATA (data segment), and .STACK (stack segment). One more directive, DOSSEG, orders the segments according to a standard method.

The MODEL directive selects a standard memory model, or configuration, for a program. This directive makes it easier to write assembly language subroutines that are compatible with high-level languages.

A *procedure* is a set of statements identified by a single name, having a unified function. The PROC directive identifies the start of a procedure, and the ENDP directive marks its end.

At the end of a program listing, the END directive identifies the location of the program entry point and marks the last line to be assembled.

Data Transfer and Arithmetic. The MOV instruction copies data from a source operand to a destination operand. The INC instruction adds 1 to an operand, and the DEC instruction subtracts 1 from an operand. The ADD instruction adds a source operand to a destination. The SUB instruction subtracts a source operand from a destination. The XCHG instruction exchanges two operands. The PTR operator either identifies or overrides the default size of a variable. Use it when you must access part of a variable or clarify the variable's size. The LABEL directive lets you redefine a variable or procedure, giving it another name and/or type. Labels in the code segment can be either NEAR or FAR, and labels in the data segment can be one of the following: BYTE, WORD, DWORD, QWORD, TBYTE.

Three types of operands are used: *Register* operands (e.g. AL, BX, or SI), *immediate* operands (e.g. 10, 35*4), and *memory* operands (variables).

REVIEW QUESTIONS

1. If any of the following MOV statements are illegal, explain why:
   a. mov ax,bx
   b. mov var_2,al
   c. mov ax,bl
   d. mov bh,4A6Fh
   e. mov dx,3
   f. mov var_1,bx
   g. mov al,var_3
   h. mov cs,0
   i. mov ip,ax
   j. mov word ptr var_3,10
   k. mov var_1,var_2
   l. mov ds,1000
   m. mov ds,es

```
var_1  dw  0
var_2  dw  6
var_3  db  5
```

2. Write a data definition for the following string:

   'MYFILE.DTA'

3. Write a data definition statement for a list of 8-bit memory operands containing the following values:

   3, 15h, 0F6h, 11010000b

4. Write a data declaration directive for a sequence of 500 words, each containing the value 1000h.

5. An *operand* may be a *memory variable*, a *register*, or __________ .

6. Which of the following registers may not be used as destination operands?

   AX, CL, IP, DX, CS, BH, SS, SP, BP

7. What will be the hexadecimal value of the destination operand after each of the following moves? (If any instruction is illegal, write the word ILLEGAL as the answer.)

Instruction	**Before**		**After**
a. mov ax,bx	AX=0023	BX=00A5	AX=
b. mov ah,3	AX=06AF		AX=
c. mov dl,count	DX=8F23	count=1A	DL=
d. mov bl,ax	BX=00A5	AX=4000	BL=
e. mov di,100h	DI=06E9		DI=
f. mov ds,cx	DS=0FB2	CX=0020	DS=
g. mov var1,bx	var1=0025	BX=A000	var1=
h. mov count,ax	count=25	AX=4000	count=
i. mov var1,var2	var1=0400	var2=0500	var1=

var1 and **var2** are 16-bit operands, and **count** is 8 bits long. All numbers are in hexadecimal format.

8. What will be the hexadecimal value of the destination operand after each of the following statements has executed? You may assume that **var1** is a word variable and that **count** and **var2** are byte variables. If any instruction is illegal, write the word ILLEGAL as the answer.

Instruction	Before		After
a. mov ah,bl	AX=0023	BX=00A5	AX=
b. add ah,3	AX=06AF		AX=
c. sub dl,count	DX=8F23	count=1A	DX=
d. inc bl	BX=FFFF		BX=
e. add di,100h	DI=06E9		DI=
f. dec cx	CX=0000		CX=
g. add var1,bx	var1=0025	BX=A000	var1=
h. xchg var2,al	var2=25	AL=41	var2=
i. sub var1,var2	var1=15A6	var2=B8	var1=
j. dec var2	var2=01		var2=

All numbers are in hexadecimal.

9. Write a data definition for the variable **arrayptr** that contains the offset address of the variable **intarray**.

10. What will AX equal after the following instructions have executed?

```
        mov     ax,array1
        inc     ax
        add     ah,1
        sub     ax,array1
        .
        .
array1   dw 10h,20h
array2   dw 30h,40h
```

11. As each of the following instructions is executed, fill in the hexadecimal value of the operand listed on the right-hand side:

```
        mov       ax,array1      ; a. AX=
        xchg      array2,ax      ; b. AX=
        dec       ax
        sub       array2,2       ; c. array2=
        mov       bx,array2
        add       ah,bl          ; d. AX=
        .
        .
array1   dw       20h,10h
array2   dw       30h,40h
```

PROGRAMMING EXERCISES

Exercise 1 Define a List of 8-Bit Numbers

Use DEBUG's Assemble command to create the following list of 8-bit hexadecimal numbers at offset 0120h:

1, 2, 30, 31, 32, 41, 42, 43

If a printer is available, toggle it on by pressing Ctrl-PrtSc. Then use the Dump command to display memory from locations 0120h through 0127h.

Exercise 2 Define a List of 16-Bit Numbers

Use DEBUG's Assemble command to create the following list of 16-bit hexadecimal numbers at offset 0120h:

1000, 2000, 7FFF, FFFF

If a printer is available, toggle it on by pressing Ctrl-PrtSc. Then use the Dump command to display memory from locations 0120h through 0127h. Draw a circle around each number, showing how the bytes are reversed.

Exercise 3 Fill a Buffer with a String

Use DEBUG's Assemble command to define the string 'STACK' at location 0100h. Use the DB directive and dump the result to the printer when you are finished.

Exercise 4 Arithmetic Program

Assemble the following program using DEBUG at location 100h. Before you run the program, write down what you think AX, BX, CX, and DX will contain at the end of the program.

Next, toggle the printer on with Ctrl-PrtSc and trace the program one instruction at a time. On the printout, circle the registers and flags that have changed after each instruction.

```
mov  ax,1234
mov  bx,ax
mov  cx,ax
add  ch,al
add  bl,ah
add  ax,FFFF
dec  bx
inc  ax
int  20
```

Exercise 5 **Arithmetic Sums**

Assemble a program using DEBUG with the following memory variables, beginning at location 0130h:

```
DB   10, 20, 30
DW   1000, 2000, 3000
```

Write the instructions to find the sum of the three byte variables and place it in the DL register. Find the sum of the three word variables and place it in the BX register. Trace the program and print out a dump of locations 0130h through 0138h.

Exercise 6 **Signed Numbers**

Assemble the following program at location 100h:

```
mov  ax,7FFF
inc  ax
mov  bx,8000
dec  bx
int  20
```

Before you run the program, write down what you think AX, BX, CX, and DX will contain at the end of the program. Trace the program one instruction at a time at the printer. On the printout, circle the registers and flags that have changed after each instruction. Assume that the numbers in AX and BX are signed and write an explanation of how and why the Carry and Overflow flags are affected.

Exercise 7 **Modify the SUM Program**

Modify the SUM program presented at the end of this chapter in the following ways:

1. Sum the following 16-bit numbers:

   1000, 2000, 7000, 03FF

2. Use the SI register as a base register instead of BX. Assemble the program using DEBUG. Trace each step of the program and print a dump of the four numbers and the sum.

ANSWERS TO REVIEW QUESTIONS

1. b. mismatching sizes
   c. mismatching sizes
   d. must be a 16-bit register
   h. cannot change CS
   i. cannot change IP

j. not illegal, but will overwrite next memory byte
k. memory-to-memory move
l. immediate value to segment register
m. segment register to segment register

2. filename db 'MYFILE.DTA'

3. db 3,15h,0F6h,11010000b

4. dw 500 dup(1000h)

5. an immediate operand

6. IP, CS

7. a. 00A5h
   b. 03AFh
   c. 8F1Ah
   d. illegal
   e. 0100h
   f. 0020h
   g. A000h
   h. illegal
   i. illegal

8. a. A523h
   b. 09AFh
   c. 8F09h
   d. FF00h
   e. 07E9h
   f. FFFFh
   g. A025h
   h. 41h
   i. illegal
   j. 00h

9. arrayptr dw intarray

10. AX=0101h

11. a. 0020h
    b. 0030h
    c. 001Eh
    d. 1E2Fh

4

The Macro Assembler

This chapter covers the entire process of assembling, linking, and executing assembly language programs. We will examine each of the files created at assembly time, as well as files created by the linker. Arithmetic and boolean operators will be introduced, along with the OFFSET and PTR operators that clarify the locations and sizes of memory variables. Last of all, we will present a debugging workshop, with examples of some common syntax errors found in assembly programs.

Two types of programs are typically written in assembly language: EXE and COM programs. Throughout most of the book, we will concentrate solely on EXE programs; they are more fully supported by the Macro Assembler and may be debugged using Microsoft CODEVIEW. To get the maximum benefit from this and later chapters, take time out from reading to assemble and run the sample programs. In programming, you learn by doing.

THE ASSEMBLY PROCESS

Figure 4-1 shows the process of assembling, linking, and executing an assembly program. (For the sake of simplicity, we will refer to all of these steps as the

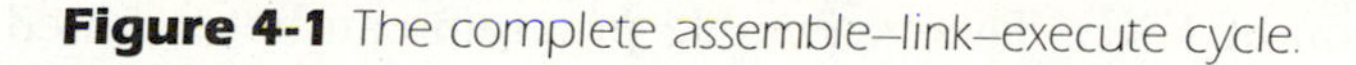

Figure 4-1 The complete assemble–link–execute cycle.

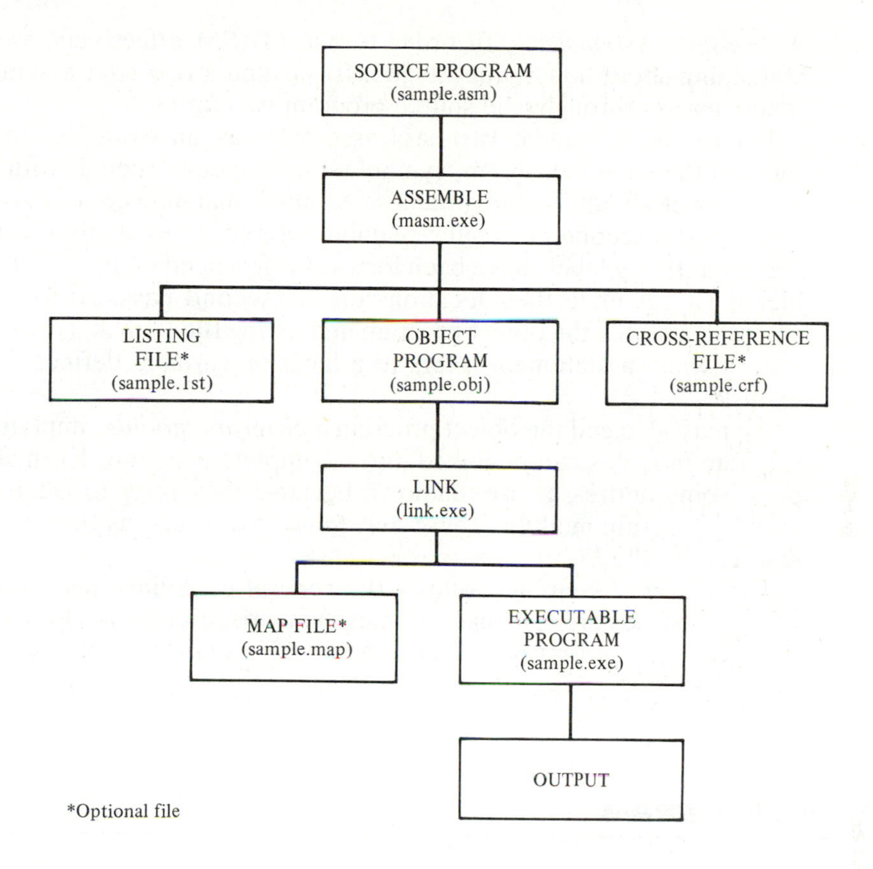

assembly process.) The steps are very similar to those used with high-level languages such as COBOL, FORTRAN, C, or Pascal. A *source program* is a collection of text characters making up a program that follows the rules of assembly language. It must be converted to machine language before it can be run.

Assembly Step. An *assembler* is a program designed to read an assembly language source program as input and generate an object program as output. The assembler may also create a *listing* file, which lists both the source statements and the machine code, and a *cross-reference* file with an alphabetized listing of all labels and identifiers in the program. An *object program* is a machine language interpretation of the original source program, lacking certain information needed by DOS before it may be executed.

Link Step. The *linker* supplied with the Macro Assembler reads an object program and generates an *executable* program. On the IBM-PC, an executable file has a file extension of EXE. The executable program can be executed just by typing its name.

A Two-Pass Assembler. In order to use MASM effectively, we should know something about how it does its job. It is called a *two-pass* assembler because it reads (passes through) the source program two times.

Let us use a typical two-pass assembler as an example. In the first pass through the source program, symbol tables are constructed, with the names and locations of all labels and variables. As much machine code is generated as possible. In the second pass, all remaining references to symbol locations must be resolved. If any labels have been forward-referenced on the first pass, the assembler must calculate their locations on the second pass. At the same time, the assembler writes the object program and listing file to disk. (A *forward reference* occurs when a statement refers to a label or variable defined later in the program.)

We may also call the object program a *program module,* implying that multiple program modules can be linked into a complete program. Even after the second pass, some addresses are unknown because they refer to labels outside of the current program module. These *unresolved externals,* as they are called, will be resolved by the *linker.*

The Macro Assembler follows the general guidelines just outlined. The two separate passes are transparent unless you specifically ask for a listing file to be generated on the first pass. The MASM *User's Guide* explains how to do this.

A SAMPLE PROGRAM

Let's write and assemble a program that exchanges the contents of two variables. First, the source program is created using a text editor (Figure 4-2). The format is free-form, so labels, comments, and instructions may be typed in any column position. All text typed to the right of a semicolon (;) is ignored. MASM is *case insensitive,* meaning that it doesn't recognize the difference between uppercase and lowercase letters.

Assembler Directives

A number of standard assembler directives used in the sample program are listed here:

.CODE	Mark the beginning of the code segment
.DATA	Mark the beginning of the data segment
DOSSEG	Use standard segment ordering
END	End of program assembly
ENDP	End of procedure

Figure 4-2 The SAMPLE.ASM program, written for MASM Version 5.0+.

```
page ,132

title  Exchange Two Variables                    (SAMPLE.ASM)

dosseg
.model small
.stack 100h

.code

main proc

     mov    ax,@data          ; initialize DS register
     mov    ds,ax
 swap:
     mov    al,value1         ; load the AL register
     xchg   value2,al         ; exchange AL and value2
     mov    value1,al         ; store AL back into value1
     mov    ax,4C00h          ; return to DOS
     int    21h

main endp

.data

value1   db     0Ah
value2   db     14h

end main
```

.MODEL	Determine the program memory model size
PAGE	Set a page format for the listing file
PROC	Begin procedure
.STACK	Set the size of the stack segment
TITLE	Title of listing file

Working from the first line to the last in Figure 4-2, we see the following directives:

PAGE. The PAGE directive is used either to begin a new page in the program listing or to select the number of lines per page and the length of each line. The default number of lines per page is 50.

The default line width is 80, which usually causes lines to wrap around when the file is printed. A value of 132 for the line width is preferable. Examples of settings for the page length and line width settings are as follows:

Example	Length	Width
PAGE	50	80
PAGE ,132	50	132
PAGE 40	40	80

The PAGE directive may be used anywhere in a listing. It forces the listing file to begin printing on a new page. In the program in Figure 4-2, the PAGE directive accepts the default page length and changes the line length to 132.

TITLE. The TITLE directive identifies the program listing title. Any text typed to the right of this directive is printed at the top of each page in the listing file.

DOSSEG. Microsoft high-level languages have a standard order for the code, data, and stack segments. The DOSSEG directive tells MASM to place the segments in the standard order. One can place the segments in any order in the source program without running into compatibility problems. (The segments are identified by the CODE, STACK, and DATA directives.)

.MODEL. The program in Figure 4-2 uses Microsoft's *small* memory model to determine the maximum size of the code and data. The small model is the most efficient model that may be debugged easily using CODEVIEW.

.STACK. The .STACK directive sets the size of the program stack, which may be any size up to 64K. A size of 100h is more than enough for most programs. The stack segment is addressed by the SS and SP registers.

.CODE. The .CODE directive identifies the part of the program that contains instructions (code). The *code segment,* as it is called, is addressed by the CS and IP registers.

PROC. The PROC directive creates a name and an address for the beginning of a procedure. A *procedure* is a group of instructions that is given a common name. We have called this procedure **main**, but any name up to 31 characters would be valid. Most assembly language programs have at least one procedure, the one that executes first.

ENDP. The ENDP directive marks the end of a procedure. Its name must match the name used by the PROC directive.

.DATA. All variables are defined in the area following the .DATA directive, called the data segment.

END. The END directive terminates assembly of the program, and any statements after it are ignored. The syntax is:

```
END [entrypoint]
```

Entrypoint tells the assembler and linker where the program will begin execution. In a program made up of separately compiled modules, only the first module has an *entrypoint* label after the END directive.

Program Instructions

The first two instructions in the program in Figure 4-2 initialize the DS register:

```
mov  ax,@data
mov  ds,ax
```

The name **@data** is a standard MASM identifier that stands for the location of the data segment. (The actual segment name varies, depending on which memory model is used.) By setting DS equal to the start of the data segment, we make it possible for MASM to locate variables correctly.

The next three instructions exchange the contents of **value1** and **value2**:

```
mov   al,value1
xchg  value2,al
mov   value1,al
```

Assembling and Linking

Before we assemble and link SAMPLE.ASM, the following programs must be in the current directory or DOS path:

MASM.EXE	Microsoft Macro Assembler
LINK.EXE	Linker
CREF.EXE	Cross-reference generator

Step 1. Assemble the Program. We will assume that the sample program has been created using a text editor and saved to disk as SAMPLE.ASM. To assemble it, we type

```
MASM/L/N/C SAMPLE;
```

in either uppercase or lowercase letters. MASM displays a copyright message and begins to read the source program. At the end of assembly, MASM displays statistics on the amount of available free space and the number of errors:

```
> MASM/L/N/C SAMPLE;

Microsoft (R) Macro Assembler Version 5.10
Copyright (C) Microsoft Corp 1981-1985, 1987. All rights reserved.

50592 + 271152 Bytes symbol space free

    0 Warning Errors
    0 Severe Errors
```

In this example, the program assembled successfully and no error messages were displayed. Otherwise, the source program would have to be edited and reassembled until all errors were corrected. There are a number of options available when assembling a program; these are listed in Figure 4-3. A few of the more useful ones are shown here with a source program named SAMPLE:

DOS Command Line	**Comment**
MASM SAMPLE;	Create only an object file named SAMPLE.OBJ.
MASM/L SAMPLE;	Create a listing file named SAMPLE.LST.
MASM/L/N SAMPLE;	Create a listing file but suppress the symbol tables that are usually printed at the end.
MASM/Z SAMPLE;	Create an object file and display source lines containing errors on the screen during assembly.
MASM/C SAMPLE;	Create a cross-reference file named SAMPLE.CRF that contains the line numbers of all names in the program.
MASM/ZI SAMPLE;	Place a list of symbols and line numbers in the object file for use by the CODEVIEW debugger.

Step 2. Link the Program. In the LINK step, the linker program (LINK.EXE) reads the object file as input (SAMPLE.OBJ), creates an executable file (SAMPLE.EXE), and optionally creates a map file (SAMPLE.MAP):

```
> LINK/M SAMPLE;

Microsoft (R) Overlay Linker Version 3.60
Copyright (C) Microsoft Corp 1983-1987. All rights reserved.
```

The map file lists the names of all segments in the program; this becomes important only when writing larger assembler programs or programs that link to

Figure 4-3 MASM Version 5.0 command line options.

Option	Action
/A	Writes segments in alphabetical order
/B*number*	Sets the buffer size
/C	Creates a cross-reference file
/D	Creates a pass 1 listing
/D*symbol*[= *value*]	Defines an assembler symbol
/E	Creates code for emulated floating-point instructions
/H	Lists command-line syntax and all assembler options
/I*path*	Sets the include-file search path
/L	Specifies an assembly-listing file
/ML	Makes names case sensitive
/MU	Converts names to uppercase letters
/MX	Makes public and external names case sensitive
/N	Suppresses tables in the listing file
/P	Checks for impure code
/T	Suppresses messages for successful assembly
/V	Displays extra statistics on the screen
/W{0|1|2}	Sets the error-display level
/Z	Displays erroneous source lines on the screen during assembly
/ZI	Creates a CODEVIEW-compatible object file

high-level languages. The LINK.EXE program supplied with the MASM disk must be used, rather than the linker supplied with DOS.

There is one important linker option, /CO. The command line to prepare an executable file for debugging with CODEVIEW is:

```
link/co sample;
```

The following files and programs were created during the assembly of SAMPLE.ASM:

Name	Comment	Command Used
SAMPLE.ASM	Source program	MASM
SAMPLE.OBJ	Object program	MASM
SAMPLE.LST	Listing file	MASM
SAMPLE.CRF	Cross-reference file	MASM
SAMPLE.EXE	Executable program	LINK
SAMPLE.MAP	Map file	LINK

Step 3. Run the Program. Once the SAMPLE program has been assembled and linked, it may be run by typing its name on the DOS command line. The program doesn't generate any output, so you will probably want to run the program using a debugger.

The SAMPLE.EXE program may be run repeatedly without having to assemble and link it. If we wish to modify the program, however, all changes must be made to the SAMPLE.ASM file. The program must then be assembled and linked again.

EXE Programs

Many assembly language programs are designed to be assembled as EXE programs. There are several reasons why EXE programs are preferred. First, CODEVIEW can display source statements only from EXE programs (not COM programs), making them better suited to debugging. Second, EXE-format assembler programs are more easily converted into subroutines for high-level languages.

The third reason has to do with memory management. To fully use a multitasking operating system, programs must be able to share computer memory and resources. An EXE program is easily able to do this.

Program Template. Figure 4-4 contains a program template to be used when creating new programs. Simplified segment directives are used, and one need only fill in the code and data sections when writing a new program.

Figure 4-4 EXE program template.

```
page ,132
title

dosseg
.model small
.stack 100h

.code
main proc
     mov   ax,@data        ; initialize the DS register
     mov   ds,ax


     mov   ax,4C00h        ; end program
     int   21h
main endp

.data     ;variables here

end main
```

Using a Batch File

Needless to say, it would be time-consuming to have to type all of the commands shown so far every time a program is assembled. Instead, a *batch* file may be used to perform both steps. A useful one is:

```
echo off
cls
masm/l/n %1;
if errorlevel 1 goto end
link %1;
:end
```

The ECHO OFF command tells DOS not to echo the commands to the screen while the batch file is executing. The messages generated directly by the assembler and linker still appear, however. The CLS command clears the screen. The MASM command invokes the Macro Assembler:

```
masm/l/n %1;
```

The batch file automatically halts after the MASM step if any assembly errors occurred by checking the error level returned by the Macro Assembler. An error level of 0 means that no errors occurred. An error level of 1 or more means that there were errors during assembly:

```
if errorlevel 1 goto end
```

The LINK command invokes the linker:

```
link %1;
```

Use a text editor to create this file, and call it CL.BAT (i.e., compile, link) or some other meaningful name. To run the batch file and assemble SAMPLE.ASM, type:

```
cl sample
```

Do not type a file extension—MASM assumes it is .ASM. The name SAMPLE is then substituted for each occurrence of %1 in the batch file, resulting in the following effective commands:

```
echo off
cls
masm/l/n sample;
if errorlevel 1 goto end
link sample;
:end
```

OTHER FILES CREATED DURING THE ASSEMBLY PROCESS

The Listing File

When MASM detects an error while assembling a program, a listing file can be useful. The listing file for the SAMPLE program (Figure 4-5) is called SAMPLE.LST. It contains a wealth of information about the program. Across the top line, the version of MASM used is shown. The program title (Exchange Two Variables) is printed at the top of each page.

The original source program statements are listed, with consecutive line numbers along the left margin. Just to the right are four-digit hexadecimal numbers representing the offset of each statement. An *offset* is the distance (in bytes) from the beginning of a segment to a statement's location.

To the right of each address is a hexadecimal representation of the machine language bytes generated by the instruction. In most cases, the hexadecimal bytes in the program listing are identical to those in the final EXE program. For example, the instruction to move **value1** to AL is on line 13 at address 0005h:

```
13 0005 A0 0000 R      mov al,value1
```

Figure 4-5 The SAMPLE.LST file.

```
Microsoft (R) Macro Assembler Version 5.10
Exchange Two Variables  (SAMPLE.ASM)                    Page   1-1

 1                          page ,132
 2                          title Exchange Two Variables         (SAMPLE.ASM)
 3
 4                          dosseg
 5                          .model small
 6 0100                     .stack 100h
 7
 8 0000                     .code
 9 0000                     main proc
10 0000  B8 ---- R               mov   ax,@data         ; initialize DS register
11 0003  8E D8                   mov   ds,ax
12 0005                     swap:
13 0005  A0 0000 R               mov   al,value1        ; load the AL register
14 0008  86 06 0001 R            xchg  al,value2        ; exchange AL with value2
15 000C  A2 0000 R               mov   value1,al        ; store new value of AL
16 000F  B8 4C00                 mov   ax,4C00h         ; return to DOS
17 0012  CD 21                   int   21h
18 0014                     main endp
19
20 0000                     .data
21 0000  0A                 value1   db    0Ah
22 0001  14                 value2   db    14h
23
24 0002                     end main
```

The instruction's op code is A0, and the address of **value1** is 0000. The letter *R* shown here indicates that **value1** is a *relocatable* operand, because its location is relative to the start of the data segment.

Other statements are given offset addresses but do not generate any machine code. The statement on line 9, for example, simply marks the beginning of the MAIN procedure.

The Cross-Reference File

A cross-reference listing can be helpful in tracking down the names of procedures, labels, and variables. A cross-reference file may be created during the assembly step, with an extension of CRF (i.e., SAMPLE.CRF). Then the CREF.EXE utility program is run, using SAMPLE.CRF as input, producing the sorted cross-reference listing (SAMPLE.REF). This file may be displayed or printed. The command to create a file called SAMPLE.REF is:

```
cref sample,;
```

The SAMPLE.REF file is shown in Figure 4-6.

Figure 4-6 The SAMPLE.REF file.

```
Microsoft Cross-Reference Version 5.10

  Symbol Cross-Reference    (# definition, + modification) Cref-1

CODE ...................    8

DATA ...................   20
DGROUP .................   10

MAIN ...................    9#   18    24

STACK ..................    6#    6
SWAP ...................   12#

VALUE1 .................   13    15+   21#
VALUE2 .................   14+   22#

_DATA ..................   20#
_TEXT ..................    8#

10 Symbols
```

The Map File

Created during the LINK step, a map file lists information about each of the program segments. In the following SAMPLE.MAP file, the starting and ending addresses and the length of each segment are shown:

```
Start    Stop     Length   Name       Class
00000H   00024H   00025H   _TEXT      CODE
00026H   00027H   00002H   _DATA      DATA
00030H   0012FH   00100H   STACK      STACK

Origin   Group
0002:0   DGROUP

Program entry point at 0000:0010
```

The columns labeled *Name* and *Class* identify each segment name and segment class. The linker automatically combines different segments of the same class into a single segment. This program was created using the .CODE, .DATA, and .STACK directives, so MASM has automatically initialized the name and class of each segment.

The segment attributes shown here are consistent with other Microsoft languages. This map file also shows the order of segments in memory, determined by the DOSSEG directive. When DOSSEG is used, 16 null bytes are automatically placed at the beginning of the code (_TEXT) segment. The *program entry point* in this example tells us that execution will begin at offset 0010h when the program is loaded.

After having looked at both the SAMPLE.LST file and the SAMPLE.MAP file, we can form a picture of the way the program is arranged in memory. The offsets from the beginning of the program are shown at the top; the contents of each part of the program are inside the boxes; the segment names are shown at the bottom:

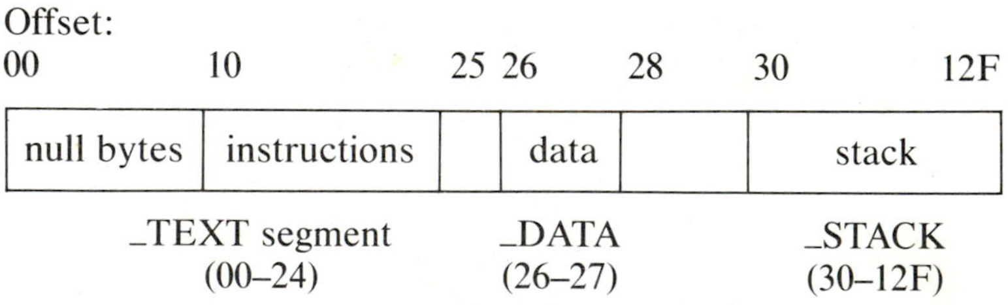

Offset:

00	10	25	26	28	30 … 12F
null bytes	instructions		data		stack

_TEXT segment (00–24) _DATA (26–27) _STACK (30–12F)

Alternate Versions of the SAMPLE.ASM Program

Figure 4-7 shows the SAMPLE.ASM program (originally in Figure 4-2) with complete segment directives. This may be assembled by MASM Versions 1.0 through 4.0.

Figure 4-7 The SAMPLE.ASM program, written for MASM versions 1.0 through 4.0.

```
page   ,132

title  Exchange Two Variables  (MASM Version 4.0)

code segment
     assume cs:code,ds:data,ss:stack

main proc

     mov   ax,data              ; initialize DS register
     mov   ds,ax

swap:
     mov   al, value1           ; load the AL register
     xchg  value2,al            ; exchange AL and value2
     mov   value1,al            ; store AL back into value1
     mov   ax,4C00h             ; return to DOS
     int   21h

main endp
code ends

data segment

value1   db    0Ah
value2   db    14h

data ends

stack segment STACK
   db 100h dup(0)
stack ends

end main
```

Figure 4-8 shows the same program written in COM format, which may be assembled by any version of MASM. The linker will display a warning message (*no stack segment*), which may be ignored. After SAMPLE.EXE has been created, you must run the EXE2BIN.EXE program (supplied with DOS) to convert the executable file to a COM file. Therefore, the following commands assemble, link, and convert SAMPLE.ASM to a COM file:

```
masm sample;
link sample;
exe2bin sample sample.com
```

Figure 4-8 The SAMPLE.ASM program, written in COM format.

```
page    ,132
title    Exchange Two Variables    (COM format)

code segment
     assume cs:code,ds:code,ss:code
     org 100h

main proc

 swap:
        mov   al, value1        ; load the AL register
        xchg  value2,al         ; exchange AL and value2
        mov   value1,al         ; store AL back into value1
        mov   ax,4C00h          ; return to DOS
        int   21h

main endp

value1   db    0Ah
value2   db    14h

code ends

end main
```

Programming Tip: The COMMENT Directive

As a matter of habit, assembly language programs should be carefully commented. In longer programs, one often provides comments at the beginning of each program module and procedure. Rather than writing a semicolon at the beginning of each line of comments, you may wish to begin a group of comment lines with the COMMENT directive. The syntax is:

```
COMMENT  delimiter
  text
delimiter    [text]
```

The *delimiter* may be any character not appearing within the text. Additional text on the same line as the last delimiter is also ignored by MASM. For example,

```
COMMENT @

    This program displays all 256 ASCII codes on the screen,
    using the LOOP instruction.

    Last update: 11/01/89
@
```

EQUATES

Equate directives allow constants and literals to be given symbolic names. A constant may be defined at the start of a program and, in some cases, redefined later on.

The Equal-Sign Directive

Known as a *redefinable equate,* the equal-sign directive creates an absolute symbol by assigning the value of a numeric expression to a name. The syntax is:

```
name = expression
```

In contrast to the DB and DW directives, the equal-sign directive allocates no storage. As the program is assembled, all occurrences of *name* are replaced by *expression.* The expression value may be from 0 to 65,535. Examples are as follows:

```
count      = 50          ; Assigns the value 50
prod       = 10 * 5      ; Evaluates an expression
maxint     = 7FFFh       ; Maximum signed value
maxUint    = 0FFFFh      ; Maximum unsigned value
string     = 'XY'        ; Up to two characters allowed
endvalue   = count + 1   ; May use a predefined symbol
```

A symbol defined with the equal-sign directive may be redefined as many times as desired. In the following program excerpt, **count** changes value several times. On the right side of the example, we see how MASM evaluates the constant:

Original	Assembled As
`count=5`	
`mov   al,count`	`mov   al,5`
`mov   dl,al`	`mov   dl,al`
`count=10`	
`mov   cx,count`	`mov   cx,10`
`mov   dx,count`	`mov   dx,10`
`count=2000`	
`mov   ax,count`	`mov   ax,2000`

The EQU Directive

The EQU directive assigns a symbolic name to a string or numeric constant. This increases the readability of a program and makes it possible to change constants in a single place at the beginning of a program.

There is one limitation imposed on EQU: A symbol defined with EQU may not be redefined later in the program. At the same time, EQU is very flexible:

- A name may be assigned to a string, allowing the name to be replaced by the string wherever it is found. For example, the **prompt1** string is defined here using the **continue** constant:

```
continue equ 'Do you wish to continue (Y/N)?'
.
.
.
prompt1 db continue
```

- An *alias*, which is a name representing another predefined symbol, may be created. For example:

Original	Assembled As
move equ mov	
address equ offset	
.	
.	
move bx,address value1	mov bx,offset value1
move al,20	mov al,20

Expressions involving integers evaluate to numeric values, but floating-point values evaluate to text strings. Also, beginning with MASM Version 5.0, string equates may be enclosed in angle brackets (< and >) to force their evaluation as string expressions. This eliminates ambiguity on the part of the assembler when assigning the correct type of value to a name:

Example			Type of Value
maxint	equ	32767	Numeric
maxuint	equ	0FFFFh	Numeric
count	equ	10 * 20	Numeric
float1	equ	<2.345>	String
msg1	equ	'Press [Enter] to Continue'	String
tl	equ	<top-line>	String
bpt	equ	<byte ptr>	String

OPERATORS AND EXPRESSIONS

An expression is a combination of operators and operands that is converted by the assembler into a single value. The size of the value must not be greater than the size of the destination operand, which is either 8 or 16 bits. MASM performs arithmetic and logical operations at assembly time, not at runtime. The result is calculated and placed in memory at the current program location. A list of the most frequently used operators follows.

Frequently Used Operators

Arithmetic Operators (+, −, *, /, MOD)
Addition, subtraction, multiplication, division, modulus arithmetic.

Boolean Operators (NOT, AND, OR, XOR)
Boolean operations.

Index Operator ([])
Adds the value between the square brackets to the operand outside. For example, the expression 4[2] is equal to 6.

OFFSET Operator
Returns the offset address of a variable or label.

SEG Operator
Returns the segment value of a variable, label, or any other symbol.

PTR Operator
Forces a variable or label to be given a specified type (i.e., BYTE, WORD, DWORD, QWORD, TBYTE, NEAR, or FAR).

Segment Override (CS:, DS:, ES:, SS:, segname:)
Forces the CPU to calculate the offset of a variable or label from the named segment.

Shift Operators (SHL, SHR)
Shifts an operand left or right *count* number of bits. The operand may be a single value or an expression.

SHORT Operator
Identifies a label as being within the range of -128 to +127 bytes from the current location. Used often with the JMP instruction.

Arithmetic Operators

Arithmetic operators may be used only with integers, with the exception of unary plus (+) and minus (−), which may also be used with real numbers. Examples of arithmetic expressions follow.

Example	Comment
`20 * 5`	Value is 100
`-4 + -2`	Value is -6
`count+2`	**Count** is a constant
`31 MOD 6`	Remainder is 1
`6/4`	Value is 1
`'2'-30h`	Value is 2

Each of the operators has a *precedence* level, meaning that it will be evaluated before another operator of lower precedence. The set of arithmetic operators in order of precedence is:

Operator	Description
()	Parentheses
+	Positive sign (unary)
–	Negative sign (unary)
*	Multiplication
/	Division
MOD	Modulus arithmetic
+	Addition
–	Subtraction

The order of operations is shown for each of the following examples:

Example	Order of Operations
3 + 2 * 5	Multiplication, addition
count / 5 MOD 3	Division, MOD
+4 * 3 – 1	Positive sign, multiplication, subtraction
(1000h – 30h) * 4	Subtraction, multiplication
–((count MOD 5) + 2) * 4	MOD, addition, negative sign, multiplication

Boolean Operators

The AND, OR, NOT, and XOR operators may be used in assembler expressions, which are evaluated at assembly time. Assuming that **status** and **count** have been declared using equates, the following expressions are valid:

```
status and 0Fh
(count or 10h) and 7Fh
not status
(count * 20) and 11001010b
```

OFFSET Operator

The OFFSET operator returns the distance of a label or variable from the beginning of its segment. The destination operand must be a 16-bit register, as in the following example:

```
mov   bx,offset count   ; BX points to count
```

We say that BX points to **count** because it contains the variable's address. When a register or variable holds an address, we call it a *pointer.* It may be easily manipulated to point to subsequent addresses.

SEG Operator

The SEG operator returns the segment value of a label or variable. We usually use it to place an address in a segment register. In the following example, the segment value must be transferred via AX because an immediate value may not be moved to a segment register:

```
mov  ax,seg array   ; set DS to segment of array
mov  ds,ax
```

PTR Operator

The PTR operator forces a variable or label to be used as if it were of a specified type. The syntax is:

```
type PTR
```

The various types of PTR operators follow. They are related to the characteristics of a memory variable or to the distance attribute of a label:

Operator	Description
Byte ptr	Byte operand
Word ptr	Word operand
Dword ptr	Doubleword (32-bit) operand
Qword ptr	Quadword (64-bit) operand
Tbyte ptr	Ten-byte (80-bit) operand
Near ptr	Within the current segment
Far ptr	Outside the current segment

PTR specifies the exact size of an operand, as in the following examples:

```
mov    ax,word ptr var1         ; Var1 is a word operand
mov    bl,byte ptr var2         ; Var2 is a byte operand
inc    dword ptr newaddress     ; Doubleword operand
call   far ptr clear_screen     ; Call a far subroutine
```

PTR can also override an operand's default type. Suppose the variable **wordval** contains 1026h, and we want to move its low byte into AL. Because word values are always stored in memory with the bytes in reverse order, the low byte is stored at the lowest address:

```
             mov    al,byte ptr wordval     ; al = 26h
81           .
82           .
83    wordval    dw   1026h                 ; stored as 26 10
84
```

Operands with Displacements

A particularly good use of the addition and subtraction operators (+, −) is to access a list of values. The addition operator adds to the *offset* of a label. For example, an instruction to move a byte at location **array** into BL is:

```
mov  bl,array
```

To access the byte following **array**, we add 1 to the label:

```
mov  bl,array+1
```

In the following series of instructions, the first byte of **array** is moved to AL, the second byte to BL, the third byte to CL, and the fourth byte to DL. The value of each register after the moves is shown on the right:

```
    mov  al,array      ; AL = 0Ah
    mov  bl,array+1    ; BL = 0Bh
    mov  cl,array+2    ; CL = 0Ch
    mov  dl,array+3    ; DL = 0Dh
    .
    .
array db 0Ah,0Bh,0Ch,0Dh
```

Although less typical, we may wish to subtract from a label's offset. In the following example, the label **endlist** is 1 byte beyond the last byte in **list**. To move the last byte in **list** to AL, we write:

```
        mov   al,endlist-1    ; move 5 to AL
        .
        .
list     db 1,2,3,4,5
endlist db 0
```

In a list of 16-bit values, you add 2 to the offset of any element to point to the next element. This is done here, using an array called **wvals**:

```
    mov    ax,wvals      ; AX = 1000h
    mov    bx,wvals+2    ; BX = 2000h
    mov    cx,wvals+4    ; CX = 3000h
    mov    dx,wvals+6    ; DX = 4000h
    .
    .
wvals dw 1000h,2000h,3000h,4000h
```

The addition or subtraction operator may be combined with the OFFSET operator to calculate the location of an item in a list. Assuming that the offset of **bytelist** is 0h in the following example, we will end up with the following values in AX and BX:

```
    mov   ax,offset bytelist      ; AX = 0000h
    mov   bx,offset bytelist+4    ; BX = 0004h
    .
    .
bytelist db '01234567890'
```

Programming Tip: Other MASM Operators

A number of other operators available in MASM are briefly described here. Consult the MASM manual for more complete information.

HIGH returns the high 8 bits of a constant expression.

LOW returns the low 8 bits of a constant expression.

LENGTH returns the number of byte, word, dword, qword, or tenbyte elements in a variable. This is meaningful only if the variable was initialized with the DUP operator.

MASK returns a bit mask for the bit positions in a field within a variable. A *bit mask* preserves just the important bits, setting all others equal to zero. The variable must be defined with the RECORD directive.

EQ, NE, LT, LE, GT, GE (relational operators) return a value of 0FFFFh when a relation is true or 0 when it is false.

SEG returns the segment value of an expression, whether it be a variable, a segment/group name, a label, or any other symbol.

SIZE returns the total number of bytes allocated for a variable. This is calculated as the LENGTH multiplied by the TYPE.

Structure Field-Name (.) identifies a field within a predefined structure by adding the offset of the field to the offset of the variable. The format is:

```
variable.field
```

THIS creates an operand of a specified type at the current program location. The type may be any of those used with the PTR operator or the LABEL directive.

TYPE returns a numeric value representing either the size of a variable or the type of a label. For example, the TYPE of a word variable is 2.

.TYPE returns a byte that defines the mode and scope of an expression. The result is bit mapped and used to show whether a label or variable is program related, data related, undefined, or external in scope.

WIDTH returns the number of bits of a given field within a variable. The variable must be defined using the RECORD directive.

DEBUGGING WORKSHOP

Most syntax errors result either from the incorrect use of assembler directives or from the use of invalid instruction operands. Several programs containing common errors are presented here. The general types of errors made at the beginning level are:

- Missing or misplaced .CODE, .DATA, and .STACK directives.
- Missing or misplaced PROC and ENDP directives.
- Missing END directive or a label missing after the END directive.
- Mismatching operand sizes.

When MASM displays an error message, it lists the name of the source program, the line number (from the listing file) in parentheses, the error number, and a description of the error. For example:

```
PROG1.ASM (7): warning A4031: Operand types must match
```

The name of the source file is PROG1.ASM, and the error occurred on line 7. The error number (A4031) refers you to a more complete explanation in the MASM manual. The message ("Operand types must match") says that a statement tried to mix operands of two different sizes. Although this is a warning message, the problem should be resolved before linking and running the program. Otherwise, MASM may generate incorrect object code.

In the sample error messages given in this chapter, we have omitted the file name, so the line number that caused the error is at the beginning of the error message.

Open Procedures. The error message "Open procedures" occurs when an ENDP directive is not found to mark the end of a procedure. The following program demonstrates this:

```
 1:   title Error Example
 2:   dosseg
 3:   .model small
 4:   .stack 100h
 5:   .code
 6:   main proc
 7:        mov ax,4C00h
 8:        int 21h
 9:                                   <- ENDP directive missing
10:   end main

Error message:  Open procedures: MAIN
```

Operand Sizes and Addressing Errors

Recent versions of MASM perform stronger type checking on memory operands than do earlier versions. By *type checking,* we mean ensuring that the sizes of both operands match. As a result, many older assembly language source programs must be modified to assemble correctly. Such errors are usually corrected by using the BYTE PTR or WORD PTR operators to identify the attributes of certain operands. This may seem to be an annoyance, but it often helps us avoid subtle logic errors.

Mismatching Operand Sizes. In the following program, the 8-bit size of **value1** does not match the 16-bit size of AX, and **value2** does not match the size of AH. This is probably the most common of all syntax errors, made by beginner and expert alike:

```
 1:   title Mismatching Operand Sizes
 2:   dosseg
 3:   .model small
 4:   .stack 100h
 5:   .code
 6:   main  proc
 7:         mov   ax,@data
 8:         mov   ds,ax
 9:         mov   ax,value1
10:         mov   ah,value2
11:         mov   ax,4C00h
12:         int   21h
13:   main  endp
14:
15:   .data
16:   value1  db    0Ah
17:   value2  dw    1000h
18:   end     main

 (9): warning A4031: Operand types must match
(10): warning A4031: Operand types must match
```

Figure 4-9 Program with numerous syntax errors.

```
 1:   title  Miscellaneous Errors
 2:   dosseg
 3:   .model small
 4:   .stack 100h
 5:   .code
 6:   main  proc
 7:         mov   ax,@data      ; initialize DS register
 8:         mov   ds,ax
 9:         mov   ax,bx * cx
10:         mov   bx,value1 * 2
11:         mov   byte ptr value3, al
12:         mov   cx,ax
13:         mov   cs,ds
14:         mov   ax,4C00h
15:         int   21h
16:   main  endp
17:   .data
18:   value1   db    0Ah
19:   value2   db    14h
20:   value3   dw    1000h
21:   end    main

         (9): error A2042: Constant expected
        (10): error A2042: Constant expected
        (13): error A2059: Illegal use of CS register
```

These errors may be corrected by adjusting the instruction operands to the correct sizes of the memory variables. We can rewrite lines 9 and 10 as follows:

```
mov  al,value1
mov  ax,value2
```

Miscellaneous Errors. In the program shown in Figure 4-9, a number of different mistakes were made. On line 9 the expression (bx * cx) is interpreted by MASM as an immediate operand. The values of BX and CX are known only at runtime, so MASM prints an error message. On line 10, the expression (value1 * 2) appears to be the product of two constants. When MASM encounters the declaration of **value1** (as a variable) later in the program, it declares the instruction illegal. The error message for line 13 reminds us that CS may not be used as a destination operand (nor may IP).

Programming Tip: Creating Your Own Segments

You can use the SEGMENT and ENDS directives to create additional segments. You might want to create a 64K buffer the size of an entire segment. Another use might be to isolate data inside each program module. Virtually any number of segments may appear in a single program.

To create a segment, begin with the SEGMENT directive. This is followed by instructions or data, which in turn are followed by the ENDS directive:

```
my_seg segment
   var1    db   10
   var2    dw   2000h
   .
   .
my_seg ends
```

Caution: You must set DS or ES to the desired segment location before trying to access a variable in the segment. The following program excerpt illustrates the use of two programmer-defined segments, along with the default data segment. The SEG operator may be used to obtain a variable's segment value, or the name of the segment itself may be used to obtain its location:

```
.code
mov   ax,seg value1    ; use the SEG operator
mov   ds,ax
mov   al,value1        ; result: AL = 1
mov   ax,seg2          ; use the segment's name
mov   ds,ax
mov   al,value2        ; result: AL = 2
mov   ax,@data         ; use predefined @DATA value
mov   ds,ax
mov   al,value3        ; result: AL = 3
.
.
seg1 segment
  value1  db   1
seg1 ends

seg2 segment
  value2  db   2
seg2 ends

.data
  value3  db   3
```

POINTS TO REMEMBER

A debugger should always be used when learning about data storage and assembly language instructions and when tracing executable programs.

The assembly process involves converting a source program to an executable program. Several other files are created at assembly time: a *listing* file containing a list of the program's source code, a *cross-reference* file containing the names of labels and other names, and a *map file* created by the linker identifying segment names in the program.

A *batch* file can make the assembly and link steps easier. A batch file is a short program containing commands that would otherwise have to be typed at the DOS command prompt.

REVIEW QUESTIONS

1. Why could a listing file not be assembled and linked?
2. Which three files could be created by MASM if the program PROJ1.ASM were assembled?
3. Name two files created during the LINK step.
4. What is the maximum length of an assembler statement?
5. If the program TEST.ASM has been designed as an EXE program, can the program TEST.OBJ be executed successfully?
6. What does the MODEL directive identify?
7. Name six different types of memory models.
8. After the cross-reference file (extension CRF) has been created, can it be printed?
9. What is the exact meaning of the following directive?

```
PAGE 55,132
```

10. During the first pass by the assembler, is any machine code generated for each instruction?
11. What happens when the length of an operand changes between the assembler's first and second passes?
12. In a program consisting of separately compiled modules, what is the assembler's name for a reference to a label outside the current module?
13. Which directive controls the segment order in a program?
14. If a variable name is coded in uppercase letters, must all references to the variable also be in uppercase?

15. If a program had two procedures, how could we be sure that one was executed before the other?

16. If the following statements were used in a batch file, would a program assemble and link properly?

```
masm %1,,,;
if errorlevel 0 goto end
link %1;
:end
```

17. Which distance attribute for PROC is the default?

18. Which directive marks the end of a procedure?

19. What is the significance of the label used with the END directive?

20. Would the following command (typed from DOS) generate an object file and a listing file?

```
masm test;
```

21. Which file(s) will be generated by the following LINK command?

```
link test;
```

22. When the listing file displays the *offset* of a statement, what does the offset indicate?

23. In the following excerpt from a program listing, what do the values B8 4C00 represent?

```
12 010E B8 4C00    mov   ax,4C00h
```

24. In the following program, do you think that the instruction at **label2** will be executed? Use a debugger to confirm the result.

```
title
dosseg
.model small
.stack 100h
.code
main proc
label1:
    mov   ax,20
    mov   ax,4C00h
    int   21h
label2:
    mov   ax,10
main endp
end main
```

25. Correct any erroneous lines in the following program, based on the error messages printed by MASM.

```
 1:   title Find The Errors
 2:   segdos
 3:   .model
 4:   .stack 100h
 5:
 6:   main proc
 7:         mov   bl,val1
 8:         mov   cx,val2
 9:         mov   ax,4C00h
10:         int   21h
11:   main endp
12:
13:   .data
14:   val1    db   10h
15:   val2    dw   1000h
16:   end  main
```

```
                      MASM Error Messages
------------------------------------------------------------------
(2):   error A2105: Expected: instruction or directive
(6):   error A2062: Missing or unreachable CS
(7):   error A2086: Data emitted with no segment
(8):   error A2086: Data emitted with no segment
(9):   error A2086: Data emitted with no segment
(10):  error A2086: Data emitted with no segment
```

26. The following program contains numerous errors. Write a correction next to each erroneous statement, and add any new lines you deem necessary.

```
 1:   title Find The Errors
 2:   dosseg
 3:   .model small
 4:   .stack 100h
 5:   .data
 6:         mov   ax,value1
 7:         mov   bx,value2
 8:         inc   bx,1
 9:         int   21h
10:         mov   4C00h,ax
11:   main   endp
12:
13:   value1   0Ah
14:   value2   1000h
15:   end main
```

```
                      MASM Error Messages
------------------------------------------------------------------
(6):   error A2009:   Symbol not defined: VALUE1
(7):   error A2009:   Symbol not defined: VALUE2
(8):   warning A4001: Extra characters on line
(10):  error A2056:   Immediate mode illegal
```

```
(11): error A2000:   Block nesting error
(13): error A2105:   Expected: instruction or directive
(14): error A2105:   Expected: instruction or directive
(15): error A2009:   Symbol not defined: MAIN
```

27. Assume that **array1** is located at offset address 0120. As each instruction is executed, fill in the value of the operand shown on the right side:

```
.code
  mov     ax,@data
  mov     ds,ax
  mov     ax,ptr1              ; a. AX =
  mov     bx,array1            ; b. BX =
  xchg    ax,bx                ; c. AX =
  sub     al,2                 ; d. AX =
  mov     ptr2,bx              ; e. ptr2 =
.data
  array1    dw   10h,20h
  ptr1      dw   array1
  ptr2      dw   0
```

28. Assume that **val1** is located at offset 0120h and that **ptr1** is located at offset 0122h. As each instruction is executed, fill in the value of the operand shown on the right-hand side.

```
.code
  mov     ax,@data
  mov     ds,ax
  mov     ax,0
  mov     al,byte ptr val1     ; a. AX =
  mov     bx,ptr1              ; b. BX =
  xchg    ax,bx                ; c. BX =
  sub     al,2                 ; d. AX =
  mov     ax,ptr2              ; e. AX =
.data
  val1     dw   3Ah
  ptr1     dw   val1
  ptr2     dw   ptr1
```

PROGRAMMING EXERCISES

Exercise 1 Define and Display 8-Bit Numbers

Write, assemble, and test a program to do the following:

Use the DB directive to define the following list of numbers with the label **array**:

31h, 32h, 33h, 34h

Write instructions to load each number into DL and display it on the console. (The following instructions display the byte in DL on the console:)

```
mov   ah,2
int   21h
```

Explain why the output on the screen is a series of single digits:

```
1234
```

Exercise 2 **Add a List of 16-Bit Numbers**

Write, assemble, and test a program to do the following: Use the DW directive to define the following list of 16-bit numbers:

```
1000h, 2000h, 1234h
```

Add each number to the AX register and move the sum to a variable called **sum**. Move the offset of the second number to BX, using the OFFSET operator. Move the third number into CX, using BX as a register indirect operand.

Exercise 3 **Using the = and EQU Directives**

Write, assemble, and test a program to do the following:

Define a variety of constants, using both the = and EQU directives. Include character strings, integers, and arithmetic expressions. Be sure to use the +, -, *, /, and MOD operators.

Move the constants to both 8-bit and 16-bit registers, trying to anticipate in advance which moves will generate syntax errors.

Exercise 4 **Using PTR and OFFSET**

Assemble the following program using MASM and trace the executable program using a debugger. Print a trace of the program. Before you run the program, write down what you think each register will contain after it is changed by an instruction. Assume that **first** is located at offset 0h:

```
            mov   al,byte ptr first + 1       ; AL =
            mov   bx,word ptr second + 2      ; BX =
            mov   dx,offset first + 2         ; DX =
            mov   ax,4C00h
            int   21h
            .
            .
first  dw 1234h
second dw 16386
third  db 10,20,30,40 ; (decimal values)
```

Exercise 5 **Arithmetic Sums**

Write, assemble, and trace a program that finds the sum of three byte variables and places it in memory at location **sums**. Find the sum of three word variables and place it in memory at location **sums+2**. Print out a dump of the variables.

Use the following variables:

```
byte_array  db  10h, 20h, 30h
word_array  dw  1000h, 2000h, 3000h
sums        dw  0, 0
```

Exercise 6 **Batch File for CODEVIEW**

Using the sample batch file presented in this chapter for compiling and linking, create your own for use with CODEVIEW. Test the file, and make sure that it works. You may want to have the batch file run CODEVIEW automatically.

ANSWERS TO REVIEW QUESTIONS

1. A listing file contains line numbers and a hexadecimal representation of the machine language program generated by the assembler. This would generate many syntax errors if it were used as input to the assembler.
2. PROJ1.LST, PROJ1.OBJ, and PROJ1.CRF.
3. An EXE file and a MAP file.
4. 128 characters.
5. No, it must be linked before it can be run.
6. The MODEL directive identifies the memory model to be used in assembling the program.
7. The models are tiny, small, medium, compact, large, and huge.
8. No, the CREF.EXE program must read the CRF file and generate a REF file, which may then be printed.
9. When the listing file is generated, the page length will be 55 lines, and the line length will be 132 characters.

10. Yes, the assembler generates as much machine code as possible, with the exception of offsets for variables that are forward referenced.

11. A phase error is generated, because all subsequent instructions and labels are shifted to new addresses.

12. A label outside the current module is an *unresolved external* whose address will not be known until the program is linked.

13. The DOSSEG directive.

14. No, MASM does not distinguish between uppercase and lowercase letters.

15. The procedure identified by the END directive would be executed first.

16. No, because the ERRORLEVEL 0 would return TRUE even when a program assembled successfully, causing the statement

```
GOTO END
```

to be executed. As a result, no program would ever be linked.

17. NEAR.

18. ENDP.

19. It refers to the location of the first executable instruction in the program, often known as the *entry point*.

20. Only an object file, TEST.OBJ.

21. Only an executable file, TEST.EXE.

22. The offset indicates the distance (in bytes) between the statement and the beginning of the segment in which the statement resides.

23. B8 is the op code for moving immediate data to the AX register, and 4C00 is the immediate data being moved.

24. The instruction at **label2** will not be executed because it is after the program terminate instructions (mov ax,4C00h; int 21h).

25. The errors are corrected in the following listing:

```
title Find The Errors
dosseg
.model small
.stack 100h
.code
```

```
main  proc
      mov  ax,@data
      mov  ds,ax
      mov  bl,val1
      mov  cx,val2
      mov  ax,4C00h
      int  21h
main  endp

.data
val1    db 10h
val2    dw 1000h
end main
```

26. The errors are corrected in the following listing:

```
title Find The Errors
dosseg
.model small
.stack 100h
.code
main  proc
      mov   ax,@data
      mov   ds,ax
      mov   al,value1
      mov   bx,value2
      inc   bx
      mov   ax,4C00h
      int   21h
main  endp
.data

value1   db 0Ah
value2   dw 1000h
end main
```

27. a. 0120
    b. 0010
    c. 0010
    d. 000E
    e. 0120

28. a. 003A
    b. 0120
    c. 003A
    d. 011E
    e. 0122

5

Input-Output Services

On the IBM-PC, requests for input-output take the form of calls to subroutines in the operating system. These subroutines, or *services,* are provided both by DOS and by the ROM BIOS. In this chapter we examine both levels of services. The DOS services work on all computers running under MS-DOS. The BIOS services work only on computers that have an IBM-compatible ROM BIOS.

INTERRUPTS

An *interrupt* occurs when any currently executing program is interrupted. Interrupts are generated for a variety of reasons, usually related to peripheral devices such as the keyboard, disk drive, or printer. The Intel CPU recognizes two types of interrupts. A *hardware interrupt* is generated when a peripheral device needs attention from the CPU. A *software interrupt* is a call to a subroutine located in the operating system, usually an input-output routine.

Keyboard. The keyboard provides a good example of a device that generates hardware interrupts. Pressing a key activates a hardware interrupt via the Intel 8259 Interrupt Controller chip. The CPU temporarily suspends the current program and executes a subroutine that stores the keyboard character. When finished, the original program resumes execution. If necessary, a program can briefly disable hardware interrupts so that it won't be interrupted.

Software Interrupt. Strictly speaking, a software interrupt is not an interrupt at all. It probably got its name because it mimics many of the actions of a hardware interrupt. A software interrupt provides a valuable tool for handling the details of everyday input-output. It would be far too time-consuming to take care of these details in each of our programs.

The INT (interrupt) instruction is used within application programs to request services from the operating system, usually for input-output. These services are actually small programs located both in the ROM BIOS and in the resident portion of DOS.

Suppose an application program needs to clear the screen. It issues an INT instruction to request this service from the operating system. The program could have accessed the video hardware directly, of course, but there are several difficulties involved. First, most high-level languages have no facilities for direct access to hardware, so some of the code would have to be written in assembly language. Second, hardware details vary greatly from one computer system to another, making it difficult to write a single program that controls all types of hardware correctly. Third, programs that directly control hardware can be time-consuming to debug.

Software interrupts are provided to make programming easier and to make the programs more portable from one computer system to another. In this chapter we will concentrate on the elementary interrupts for input-output, such as video, keyboard, and printer services.

The INT Instruction

The INT instruction calls an operating system subroutine, identified by a number in the range 0–FFh. Before the INT instruction is executed, AH usually contains a *function number* that identifies the desired subroutine. In addition, other values may be passed to the interrupt in registers. The syntax is:

```
INT number
```

We use the INT instruction for general console input-output, file and video manipulation, and many other services provided by the BIOS and DOS.

Interrupt Vector Table. The CPU processes an interrupt instruction using the *interrupt vector table,* a table of addresses in the lowest 1,024 bytes of memory. Each entry in this table is a 32-bit segment-offset address that points to an operating system subroutine. The actual addresses in this table vary from one machine to another.

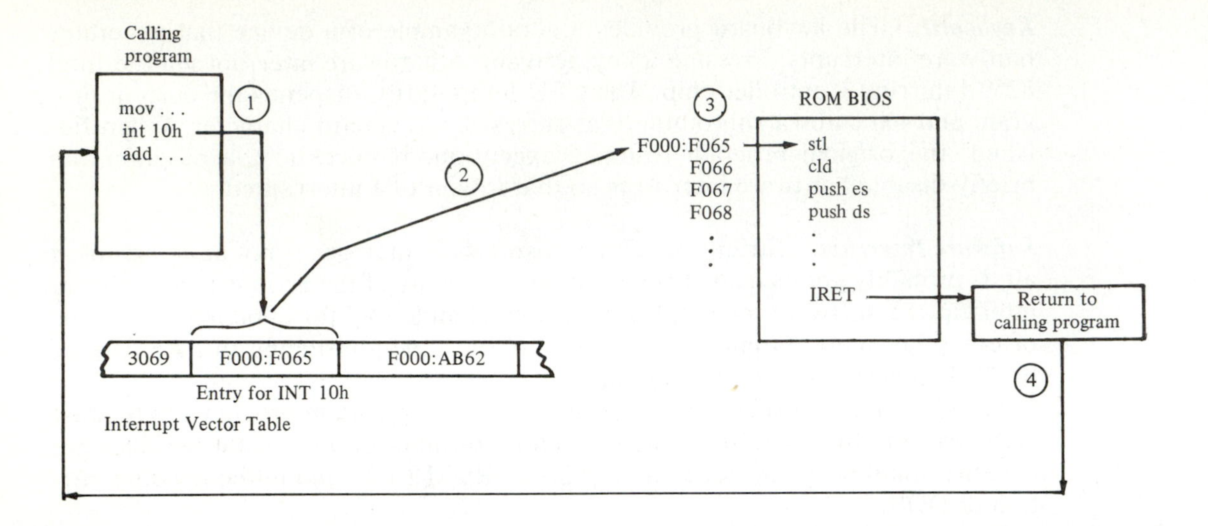

Figure 5-1 Interrupt vectoring in DOS.

Figure 5-1 illustrates the steps taken by the CPU when the INT instruction is invoked by a program:

1. The number following the INT mnemonic tells the CPU which entry to locate in the interrupt vector table. In the illustration, INT 10h requests a video service.
2. The CPU jumps to the address stored in the interrupt vector table (F000:F065).
3. The video service routine in the ROM BIOS at F000:F065 begins execution and finishes when the IRET instruction is reached.
4. IRET (interrupt return) causes the program to resume execution at the next instruction in the original calling program.

This seems to be an extraordinarily complex way of handling a subroutine call. It works well for us because the CPU does most of the work. We need only place one or more values in registers and invoke the INT instruction; DOS does the rest.

Common Software Interrupts. Software interrupts call subroutines either in the ROM BIOS or in the memory-resident part of DOS. The more often used interrupts are as follows:

- **INT 10h: Video Services**. Video display routines that control the cursor position, scroll the screen, and display video graphics.
- **INT 16h: Keyboard Services**. Routines that read the keyboard and check its status.
- **INT 17h: Printer Services**. Routines to initialize, print, and return the printer status.

- **INT 1Ah: Time of Day**. Routine that gets the number of clock ticks since the machine was turned on or sets the counter to a new value.
- **INT 1Ch: User Timer Interrupt**. An empty routine that is executed 18.2 times per second. It may be used by your own program.
- **INT 21h: DOS Services**. DOS service routines for input-output, file handling, memory management; also known as *DOS function calls*.

Device Names

Throughout this chapter, references will be made to the *standard input device* and the *standard output device*. The console is the standard device for both input and output, which may be thought of as the keyboard (input) and the video display (output). Either of these may be redirected to other devices or files. For example, a program named PROG1.EXE that writes to the standard output device may be redirected to write its output to the printer using the following DOS command line:

```
prog1 > prn
```

If PROG1 normally accepts standard input from the console, the input may be redirected from a disk file named INFILE with the following command line:

```
prog1 < infile
```

Both input and output may be redirected at the same time:

```
prog1 < infile > prn
```

A program user can choose actual devices to be used for input-output. Without this capability, programs would have to be substantially revised before their input-output could be changed. We will refer to the *console* as either the standard input or standard output device.

DOS uses the following as standard device names:

Device Name	Description
CON	Console (video display or keyboard)
LPT1 or PRN	First parallel printer
LPT2	Second parallel printer
LPT3	Third parallel printer
AUX or COM1*	First serial/parallel adapter port
COM2	Second serial/parallel adapter port
NUL	Nonexistent or dummy device

*Although AUX, COM1, and COM2 are listed as serial/parallel, they are almost always serial devices.

DOS FUNCTION CALLS

INT 21h is called a *DOS function call.* There are some 87 different functions supported by this interrupt, identified by a *function number* placed in the AH register. Functions 00h through 0Ch are listed in Figure 5-2.

Most DOS functions check to see if CTRL-BREAK has been pressed, the standard DOS command used to halt a program. If it is pressed while DOS is executing a service routine, DOS stops and returns to the calling program. In contrast, DOS functions 6 and 7 ignore CTRL-BREAK. In this chapter, we will say that CTRL-BREAK is *active* when it is recognized by DOS.

Figure 5-2 DOS function calls for console input–output.

Function Number	Description
0	*Terminate the current program.* INT 21h, function 4Ch is used instead.
1	*Console input with echo.* Wait for a character from the standard input device. The character is returned in AL and echoed. May be terminated using CTRL-BREAK.
2	*Character output.* Send the character in DL to the standard output device (console).
3	*Auxiliary input.* Wait for a character from the asynchronous port. The character is returned in AL (rarely used).
4	*Auxiliary output.* Send the character in DL to the asynchronous port (rarely used).
5	*Printer output.* Send the character in DL to the parallel printer port.
6	*Direct console input-output.* Either input an available character from the standard input device or send a character to standard output. Control characters are not filtered.
7	*Console input.* Wait for a character from the standard input device. The character is returned in AL, but not echoed. Control characters are not filtered.
8	*Console input without echo.* Wait for a character from the standard input device. The character is returned in AL, but not echoed. May be terminated using CTRL-BREAK.
9	*String output.* Send a string of characters to the standard output device. DX contains the offset address of the string.
0Ah	*Buffered input.* Wait for a string of characters from the standard input device. Characters are stored in a buffer pointed to by DX.
0Bh	*Get console input status.* Check to see if an input character is waiting. It returns AL = FFh if the character is ready, AL = 0 otherwise.
0Ch	*Clear input buffer, invoke input function.* Clears the console input (typeahead) buffer, and then executes the input function selected by the number in AL (only functions 1, 6, 7, 8, and 0Ah are allowed).

01h: Console Input with Echo

DOS function 1 waits for a character to be input from the console and stores the character in AL. CTRL-BREAK is active. The character is *echoed,* meaning that it is redisplayed on the console as soon as it is input. In the following example, a single character is input and placed in a variable named **char**:

```
mov  ah,1       ; console input function
int  21h        ; call DOS, key returned in AL
mov  char,al    ; save the character
```

Any character currently waiting in the keyboard typeahead buffer is automatically returned in AL. Otherwise DOS waits for a character to be input. The *typeahead* buffer is a 15-character circular buffer used by DOS to store keystrokes as they are pressed. This makes it possible for you to type faster than a program is able to act on the input: DOS will "remember" the keystrokes. If too many characters are backed up in the buffer, the computer beeps and extra keystrokes are ignored.

02h: Character Output

DOS function 2 sends a character to the console. CTRL-BREAK is active. You must place the character to be displayed in DL, as in the following example:

```
mov  ah,2      ; select DOS function 2
mov  dl,'*'    ; character to be displayed
int  21h       ; call DOS to do the job
```

AL may be modified by DOS during the call to INT 21h, so be sure to replace its contents after DOS finishes.

```
mov  byteval,al  ; save contents of AL
mov  ah,2
mov  dl,'*'      ; character to be displayed
int  21h         ; (DOS changes AL)
mov  al,byteval  ; restore original AL
```

05h: Printer Output

To print a character, place it in DL and call function 5. DOS waits until the printer is ready to accept the character. If necessary, you can terminate the wait by pressing CTRL-BREAK. The default output is to printer 1 (device name LPT1). You may also have to send a carriage-return character (0Dh) to force immediate printing. Many printers keep each character in an internal buffer until either the buffer is full or a carriage return is printed. The following program excerpt prints a dollar-sign ($) character:

```
mov  ah,5     ; select printer output
mov  dl,'$'   ; character to be printed
int  21h      ; call DOS
mov  dl,0Dh   ; print a carriage return
int  21h      ; call DOS
```

It is not necessary to reload AH with 5 before calling INT 21h the second time. This is true for INT 21h functions in general.

06h: Direct Console Input-Output

DOS function 6 either reads from or writes to the console. CTRL-BREAK is not active. In fact, any control characters may be read or written without being acted on, such as the carriage return, tab, and so on. The section entitled "ASCII Control Characters" later in this chapter provides many examples.

To request console input, DL must equal 0FFh. DOS does not wait for a character to be pressed, but will return a character in AL if one is waiting in the keyboard input buffer. If no character is available, the Zero flag is set.

To request console output, DL should equal the character to be displayed (other than 0FFh). Examples of both input and output are as follows:

Character input:

```
mov  ah,6        ; request DOS function 6
mov  dl,0FFh     ; look for input, don't wait
int  21h         ; if key pressed, AL=character,
                 ; otherwise the Zero flag is set
```

Character output:

```
mov  ah,6        ; request DOS function 6
mov  dl,'&'      ; character to be output
int  21h         ; call DOS
```

07h: Direct Console Input

Function 7 waits for a character from the console. The character is not echoed, and CTRL-BREAK is inactive. This input function is well suited to special keyboard characters such as function keys and cursor arrows:

```
mov  ah,7       ; console input function
int  21h        ; call DOS
mov  char,al    ; save the character
```

08h: Console Input Without Echo

Function 8 waits for a character from the console without echoing it, and CTRL-BREAK is active. The character is returned in AL. This input function is also appropriate for special keyboard characters:

```
mov  ah,7      ; console input function
int  21h       ; call DOS
mov  char,al   ; save the character
```

09h: String Output

Function 9 displays a character string on the console. The offset address of the string must be in DX, and the string must be terminated by the dollar-sign ($) character. Control characters such as tabs and carriage returns are recognized by DOS. In the following example, a string is displayed, followed by the carriage return (0Dh) and line feed (0Ah) characters:

```
        mov  ah,9                 ; string output function
        mov  dx,offset string     ; offset address of the string
        int  21h
        .
        .
string  db 'This is a byte string.',0Dh,0Ah,'$'
```

This DOS function has an obvious disadvantage, because a dollar-sign character cannot be displayed as part of a string. A curious thing happens when the dollar sign is omitted; DOS simply displays all subsequent characters in memory until the ASCII value for a dollar sign (24h) is found. Several hundred characters might be displayed before this happens.

0Ah: Buffered Console Input

Function 0Ah reads a character string of up to 255 characters from the console and stores it in a buffer. The backspace key may be used to erase characters and back up the cursor. You terminate the input by pressing ENTER. DOS filters out any extended keys, such as cursor arrows, PgDn, and so on, so they will not be stored in the buffer. CTRL-BREAK is active, and all characters are echoed on the console.

Before the function is called, DX must contain the offset of the keyboard parameter area. The format of this area is:

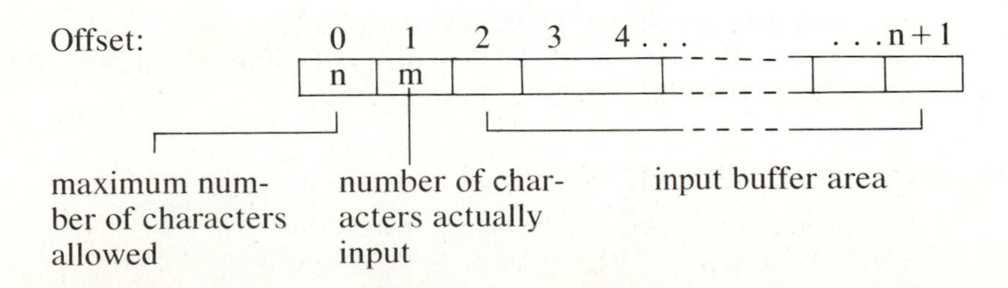

In the byte at offset 0, place a count of the maximum number of characters you wish to be input. If you choose a count of 5, for example, DOS will permit only 4 characters plus the Enter key to be input. After the interrupt is called, DOS places the number of keys *actually typed* in the byte at offset 1. This count doesn't include the Enter key. The characters themselves are placed by DOS in the buffer, beginning at offset 2.

In the following example, **max_keys** equals 32, **chars_input** is filled in by DOS, and **buffer** holds the input characters:

```
    mov ah,0Ah                 ; select console input
    mov dx,offset maxkeys      ; DX points to keyboard parameter area
    int 21h                    ; call DOS
    .
    .
max_keys db 32                 ; max characters allowed
chars_input db ?               ; characters actually input
buffer  db 32 dup(0)           ; holds the input
```

Let's assume that we have used these statements in a program, and then we input the following 21 characters from the console:

```
My name is Kip Irvine
```

A dump of the buffer after the characters are input shows that the byte at offset 0001 contains the number of characters actually input (15h), followed by the input characters. (The Enter key appears in the buffer as 0Dh, and the count [15h] does not include the extra key.)

```
 max_keys  chars_input
   ↓      ↙
  20 15
  4D 79 20 6E 61 6D 65 20 69 73 20   .My name is   ]  buffer
  4B 69 70 20 49 72 76 69 6E 65 0D   Kip Irvine.   ]
                                 ↑
                              Enter key
```

0Bh: Get Console Input Status

Function 0Bh checks the DOS keyboard buffer to see if a character is waiting in the typeahead buffer. If so, DOS returns 0FFh in AL; if not, DOS returns 00 in AL. CTRL-BREAK is active. For example:

```
mov  ah,0Bh   ; check keyboard status
int  21h      ; call DOS
```

(AL = FF if a character is available)
(AL = 00 if no character is available)

0Ch: Clear Input Buffer, Invoke Input Function

Function 0Ch clears the keyboard typeahead buffer and calls a console input function. The function to be called (1, 6, 7, or 8) is identified by a number in AL. The new input character will be returned in AL.

You may wish to prevent the user of a program from typing commands ahead of displayed prompts. If so, this DOS function is useful. In the following example, we clear the buffer and then call function 1 to input a character:

```
mov  ah,0Ch    ; clear buffer
mov  al,1      ; call function 1 after finished
int  21h       ; call DOS
mov  char,al   ; store the character
```

Extended Keyboard Keys

Many keys on the IBM-PC keyboard do not return a printable ASCII character value. Among these we include the programmable function keys, the cursor arrows, PgUp, PgDown, Home, End, and so on. If an extended key is pressed, 2 bytes are placed in the typeahead buffer. The first is equal to zero, and the second contains a numeric *keyboard scan code* for the key. To retrieve the scan code byte, your program must call a DOS console input function twice:

```
mov  ah,7   ; console input function, no echo
int  21h    ; call DOS, 0 returned in AL
int  21h    ; call DOS again, scan code returned in AL
```

In general, DOS functions 7 and 8 are best here because neither echoes the character on the screen. If function 1 were used, an ASCII character would be displayed that matches the scan code of the extended key. Since this would not be very helpful, function 1 is not used.

When we learn about conditional instructions in Chapter 8, we will be able to input the first character, test to see if it equals 0, and then input the scan code byte only if an extended key has been pressed. A short table of the extended key codes is given here, and a complete list appears on the inside back cover of the book.

Hexadecimal Scan Code	Key Name
47,4F	Home, End
77,75	Ctrl-Home, Ctrl-End
49,51	PgUp, PgDn

84,76	Ctrl-PgUp, Ctrl-PgDn
48,50	Cursor Up, Cursor Down
4B,4D	Cursor Left, Cursor Right
73,74	Ctrl-Cursor Left, Ctrl-Cursor Right
52,53	Ins, Del
3B–44	F1 to F10
85,86	F11, F12
54–5D	Shift-F1 to Shift-F10
5E–67	Ctrl-F1 to Ctrl-F10
68–71	Alt-F1 to Alt-F10
78–83	Alt 1, 2, 3, 4, 5, 6, 7, 8, 9, 0, –, =
10–19	Alt Q, W, E, R, T, Y, U, I, O, P
1E–26	Alt A, S, D, F, G, H, J, K, L
2C–32	Alt Z, X, C, V, B, N, M

ASCII Control Characters

The ASCII character set has a number of *control characters,* in the range 0–20 hex, which are acted on by DOS but not actually displayed. They are used for screen and printer control and for asynchronous communications. The more common ones used are as follows:

Hexadecimal	Decimal	Meaning
08	08	Backspace
09	09	Horizontal tab
0A	10	Line feed
0C	12	Form feed (printer only)
0D	13	Carriage return (Enter key)
1B	27	Escape

Characters 0Dh and 0Ah are the *carriage return* and *line feed* characters often found at the ends of lines in text files. When they are displayed on the screen, a carriage return moves the cursor to the left side of the screen, and a line feed moves the cursor down one line. Particularly when displaying more than one line on the screen, these characters must be present; otherwise, each new line overwrites the previous one. This would happen in the following example:

```
            mov   ah,9                      ; string output function
            mov   dx,offset message         ; offset of the string
            int   21h                       ; call DOS
            .
            .
message db   'This is line one',0Dh
        db   'This is line two','$'
```

To avoid this problem, the first line should end with both a carriage return and a line feed:

```
db  'This is line one',0Dh,0Ah
db  'This is line two',0Dh,0Ah,'$'
```

MANIPULATING THE VIDEO DISPLAY

The video display is controlled most effectively by using the INT 10h functions, located in the ROM BIOS. They are more efficient than INT 21h but are also less portable to other computers running under DOS. The functions shown here may not be redirected, as may the DOS functions; they apply only to the video display.

Aside from the basic services provided by DOS using INT 21h, certain operations are performed on the video display using INT 10h, including clearing the screen, locating the cursor, and setting the video mode. In this chapter we will concentrate on the basics.

The IBM-PC offers three basic video displays, named after the type of adapter card plugged into the IBM-PC expansion bus. The monochrome display adapter displays text in only one color, usually green. The color graphics adapter (CGA) displays both text and graphics, and the enhanced graphics adapter (EGA) displays high-resolution text and graphics. The Personal System/2 IBM microcomputers use an additional video adapter, called the Video Graphics Array (VGA), which is compatible with the standard display types already mentioned.

Video Attributes

Each position on the screen may hold a character, along with its own *attribute*. Examples of attributes are reverse video, blink, underline, and highlight. The standard DOS functions (INT 21h) allow you to display characters on the console without changing the current video attributes.

There is another way of using INT 21h which is less efficient but more portable. A video device driver called ANSI.SYS may be installed when the computer is booted, allowing screen cursor positioning and manipulation of video attributes, among other things. The ANSI.SYS driver is far too slow for most applications like word processing and spreadsheet manipulation.

The standard attributes for the monochrome display are:

Hex Value	Attribute
07	Normal
87	Blinking
0F	Bright (highlight)
70	Reverse (inverse)
01	Underline
09	Bright underline

Any of these attributes may be made to blink by setting the highest bit, bit 7. For example, normal blinking is 87h, bright blinking is 8Fh, reverse blinking is 0F0h, and so on. At the same time, bit 3 is the normal/bright bit, so an attribute may be made bright by setting bit 3 to 1.

The CGA and EGA adapters do not support the underline attribute, but they do allow the use of colors in text mode. The colors are divided into two categories. The foreground color is the color of text characters, and the background color is the color of the blocks behind the letters. It is possible, for example, to write a line of text in which every letter has a foreground and background color different from those of the previous letter. The background color is identified by bits 4, 5, and 6 of the attribute byte, and the foreground color is identified by bits 0, 1, and 2. Bit 3 is the high/low bit, which makes a color lighter when set, and bit 7 is the blink bit. Figure 5-3 shows how each color is controlled by attribute bits.

To see how this bit mapping works, let us create a few color attributes. To get gray letters on a blue background, we set the background bits to 001, set the foreground bits to 1000, and turn off the blink bit:

```
0 0 0 1 1 0 0 0
└───┘ └─────┘
 blue   gray
```

Figure 5-3 Mapping the color attribute bits.

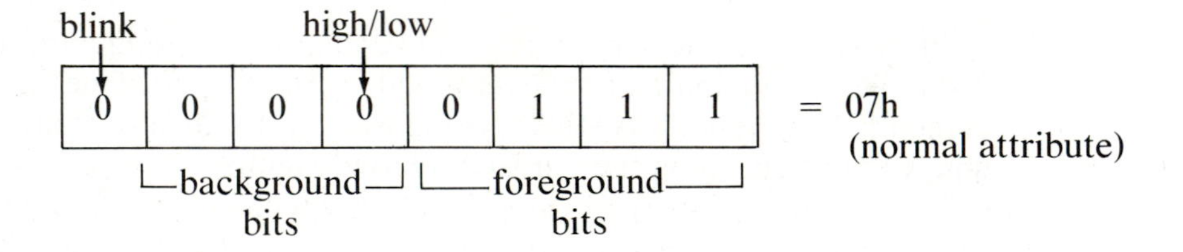

Foreground or Background		Foreground Only	
000	black	1000	gray
001	blue	1001	light blue
010	green	1010	light green
011	cyan	1011	light cyan
100	red	1100	light red
101	magenta	1101	light magenta
110	brown	1110	yellow
111	white	1111	bright white

To produce yellow letters on a brown background, we set the background to 110 and the foreground to 1110:

```
0 1 1 0 1 1 1 0
  └───┘ └─────┘
  brown  yellow
```

To produce blinking green letters on a magenta background, we use the following:

```
     1 1 0 1 0 0 1 0
     ↑ └───┘ └─────┘
blink  magenta  green
```

Video attributes may be controlled when writing individual characters or when scrolling the screen. The choice of colors and attributes is largely a matter of taste and can greatly influence the appearance of your software. In addition to the colors mentioned here, the EGA can switch to different color *palettes,* allowing a larger selection.

Video Modes

The color adapters (CGA, EGA, and VGA) can switch from video mode to another using INT 10h function calls. For example, the CGA is able to use text mode for word processing and then switch immediately to high-resolution graphics mode with 640 × 200 pixels in two colors. A *pixel* is a single dot on the screen that may be turned on and off. The more common video modes are as follows:

Mode	Description	
02h	80 × 25 black and white text	
03h	80 × 25 color text	
04h	320 × 400 4-color graphics	
06h	640 × 200 2-color graphics	
07h	80 × 25 black and white text ← monochrome adapter only	
0Dh	320 × 200 16-color graphics	
0Eh	640 × 200 16-color graphics	EGA and VGA only
0Fh	640 × 350 monochrome graphics	EGA and VGA only
10h	640 × 350 16-color graphics	EGA and VGA only

Application programs often use a call to INT 10h to find out what the current video mode is. For example, a program that displays high-resolution graphics

(640 × 200) must be sure that the program is currently running on a computer with a CGA, VGA, or EGA adapter.

Video Pages

All the color graphics adapters have the ability to store multiple video text screens, called *pages,* in memory. (The monochrome adapter may only display video page 0.) On the color adapters, one may write text to one page while another is being displayed, or flip back and forth between multiple video pages. The pages are numbered from 0 to 7, and the number of pages available depends on the current video mode.

Available Pages	Mode	Adapter
0	07h	Mono
0–7	00h, 01h	CGA
0–3	02h, 03h	CGA
0–7	02h, 03h	EGA
0–7	0Dh	EGA
0–3	0Eh	EGA
0–1	0Fh, 10h	EGA

A brief summary of the INT 10h functions discussed in this chapter appears in Figure 5-4. Several points should be made: Functions 09h and 0Ah do not advance the cursor to the next screen position; that must be done separately, using function 2 (set cursor position).

Figure 5-4 Summary of INT 10h functions.

Function Number (in AH)	Description
0	*Set Video Mode.* Set the video display to monochrome, text, graphics, or color mode.
1	*Set Cursor Lines.* Identify the starting and ending scan lines for the cursor.
2	*Set Cursor Position.* Position the cursor on the screen.
3	*Get Cursor Position.* Get the cursor's screen position and size.
4	*Read Light Pen.* Read the position and status of the light pen.
5	*Set Display Page.* Select the video page to be displayed.
6	*Scroll Window Up.* Scroll a window on the current video page upward, replacing scrolled lines with blanks.
7	*Scroll Window Down.* Scroll a window on the current video page downward, replacing scrolled lines with blanks.

Figure 5-4 *(cont.)*

8	*Read Character and Attribute*. Read the character and its attribute at the current cursor position.
9	*Write Character and Attribute*. Write a character and its attribute at the current cursor position.
0Ah	*Write Character*. Write a character only (no attribute) at the current cursor position.
0Bh	*Set Color Palette*. Select a group of available colors for the CGA adapter.
0Ch	*Write Dot*. Write a graphics pixel when in color graphics mode.
0Dh	*Read Dot*. Read the color of a single graphics pixel at a given location.
0Eh	*Write Character*. Write a character to the screen and advance the cursor.
0Fh	*Get Video Mode*. Get the current video mode, to find out if video is in text or graphics mode.

VIDEO FUNCTIONS

In this section, we take a look at the functions available under INT 10h. These functions control the video display by calling ROM BIOS routines. In general, INT 10h preserves only the BX, CX, DX, and segment registers. Any other registers that you wish to preserve should be pushed on the stack prior to the INT 10h instruction.

00h: Set Video Mode

To set the display to a particular video mode, move 0 to AH and place the video mode number in AL. The screen will be cleared automatically, unless the high bit in AL is set. The following example sets the mode to 80 X 25 color text:

```
mov   ah,0    ; set video mode
mov   al,3    ; choose mode 3
int   10h     ; call the ROM BIOS
```

To avoid clearing the screen, we could have set AL to 83h.

If there are two video adapters in the system, i.e. monochrome and color, the correct adapter will be selected. To find out what the current video mode is, see function 0Fh, *Get Video Mode*.

The following routine sets the video mode to high-resolution graphics, waits for a keystroke, and then sets the video mode to color text. It may be run using a CGA, EGA, or VGA video adapter.

```
mov  ah,0   ; set video mode
mov  al,6   ; 640 X 200 color graphics mode
int  10h
mov  ah,1   ; get a keystroke
int  21h
mov  ah,0   ; set video mode
mov  al,3   ; to color text
int  10h
```

01h: Set Cursor Lines

The cursor is displayed using starting and ending scan lines, which makes it possible for you to control its size. Application programs may do this in order to show the current status of an operation. For example, one text editor increases the cursor size when the NumLock key is toggled on; when it is pressed again, the cursor returns to its original size.

The monochrome display uses 12 lines for its cursor, while the CGA and EGA displays use only 8 lines. We can picture the cursor as a series of horizontal lines, numbered beginning at line 0. The default color cursor starts at line 6 and ends at line 7. The default monochrome cursor starts at line 0Bh and ends at line 0Ch. Both are pictured here graphically:

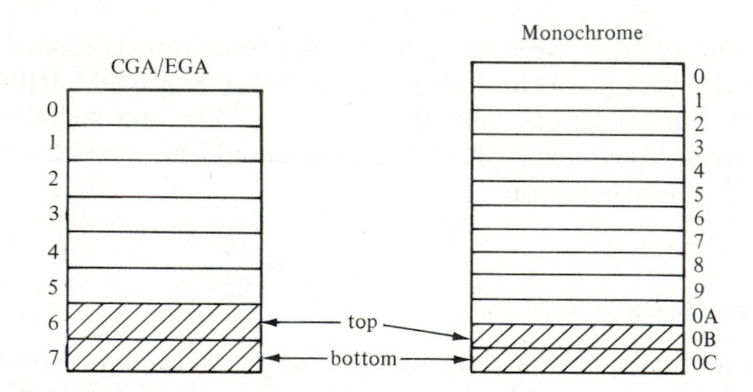

To call the set cursor lines function, set CH and CL to the top and bottom lines for the cursor and set AH to 1. The following instructions set the monochrome cursor to its maximum size, a solid block:

```
mov  ah,1     ; set cursor size
mov  ch,0     ; start line (top)
mov  cl,0Ch   ; end line (bottom)
```

It is a good idea to save the current cursor size in a variable before changing it and then to restore the cursor on exit. Software that ignores this common courtesy is annoying, to say the least. You can retrieve the cursor size using function 3, *Get Cursor Position*.

Many programs find it necessary to make the cursor invisible, which may be done in one of two ways. The starting scan line may be set to an illegal value by turning on bit 5 in CH. This works for most color and monochrome displays. The following instructions retrieve the current cursor lines and hide the cursor:

```
mov   ah,3              ; get current cursor
mov   bh,0              ; video page 0
int   10h               ; call BIOS
mov   savecursor,cx     ; save original cursor lines
mov   ah,1              ; set cursor lines
or    ch,00100000b      ; set bit 5, make cursor invisible
int   10h               ; call BIOS
```

Later, the same program can restore the cursor lines to their original values:

```
mov   ah,1              ; set cursor lines
mov   cx,savecursor     ; to original values
int   10h               ; call BIOS
```

Another approach is to set the cursor *position* off the end of the screen, using function 2, *Set Cursor Position*. The screen rows are numbered from 0 to 24, so you can set the cursor on any row number greater than 24 to make it invisible.

To protect yourself against those unscrupulous programs that destroy your cursor, run the following program from DOS whenever your cursor disappears. The program is written for the CGA and EGA, but you can move 0B0Ch to CX for the monochrome display:

```
mov   ah,1          ; set cursor lines
mov   cx,0607h      ; restore default CGA/EGA cursor
int   10h           ; call BIOS
mov   ax,4C00h      ; return to DOS
int   21h
```

02h: Set Cursor Position

Function 2 locates the cursor at a desired row and column. Set AH to 2, set DH to the desired cursor row, set DL to the column, and set BH to the current video page number (usually page 0). The following instructions position the cursor at row 10, column 20:

```
mov   ah,2      ; set cursor position
mov   dh,10     ; row 10
mov   dl,20     ; column 20
mov   bh,0      ; video page 0
int   10h       ; call BIOS
```

It is possible to set the cursor position on a video page not currently being displayed. Indirectly, this leads to a common error—forgetting to specify the current video page. Depending on the installed BIOS version, AL may be changed during the operation; it should be saved before and restored after calling INT 10h.

03h: Get Cursor Position

Function 3 returns the row and column positions of the cursor on a specified video page, as well as the starting and ending lines that determine the cursor's size. Set AH to 3 and BH to the current video page number. The values returned are:

Register	Value
CH	Starting scan line
CL	Ending scan line
DH	Row location
DL	Column location

The following routine retrieves and stores the cursor information:

```
mov   ah,3              ; get cursor position
mov   bh,0              ; video page 0
int   10h               ; call BIOS
mov   savecursor,cx     ; save the cursor lines
mov   current_row,dh    ; save the row
mov   current_col,dl    ; save the column
```

This function can be quite useful in programs where the user is moving the cursor around a menu. Depending on where the cursor is, you know which menu choice has been selected.

05h: Set Video Page

Function 5 is useful in text mode on the CGA and EGA adapters. Text written to one page is kept intact while another page is being displayed. To call this function, set AH to 5 and AL to the desired page number:

```
mov   ah,5     ; select display page
mov   al,1     ; page 1 selected
int   10h      ; call BIOS
```

Figure 5-5 lists PAGES.ASM, which displays text on video pages 0 and 1 and switches back and forth between the two. (This program will only work on a CGA, VGA, or EGA display.) After assembling the program, run it several times, and you will see the text from each of the previous runs still on the page 1 screen. This happens because most programs (and DOS) write only to page 0.

Figure 5-5 Example of switching video pages.

```
title   Video Pages Example                 (PAGES.ASM)

; This program switches back and forth between
; video pages 0 and 1 on the CGA or EGA display.

dosseg
.model small
.stack 100h

.code
main proc
        mov     ax,@data              ; initialize DS register
        mov     ds,ax
        mov     ah,9                  ; display a message
        mov     dx,offset page0
        int     21h
        mov     ah,1                  ; get a keystroke
        int     21h

to_page_1:
        mov     ah,5                  ; set video page
        mov     al,1                  ; to page 1
        int     10h
        mov     ah,9                  ; display a message
        mov     dx,offset page1
        int     21h
        mov     ah,1                  ; get a keystroke
        int     21h

to_page_0:
        mov     ah,5                  ; set video page
        mov     al,0                  ; to page 0
        int     10h
        mov     ax,4C00h              ; return to DOS
        int     21h
main endp

.data
page0    db    'This is video page zero.$'
page1    db    'This is video page one.$'
end main
```

06h, 07h: Scroll Window Up or Down

Functions 6 and 7 scroll a screen window. The term *scrolling a window* describes moving data on the video display up or down. As the display is scrolled up, for example, the bottom line is replaced by a blank line. A *window* is the area of the screen being scrolled. We define a window by using row and column coordinates for its upper left and lower right corners. Rows are numbered 0–24 from the top, and columns are numbered 0–79 from the left. Therefore, a window covering the entire screen would be from 0,0 to 24,79. Scrolling just one line or a few lines is as easy as scrolling the entire window. If all lines are scrolled, the window is cleared. Lines scrolled off the screen cannot be recovered. The input parameters for calling functions 6 and 7 are:

Register	Contents
AH	6 to scroll up or 7 to scroll down
AL	Number of lines (0 = all)
CH, CL	Row and column of the upper left window corner
DH, DL	Row and column of the lower right window corner
BH	Video attribute given to each blank line

The following statements clear the screen by scrolling it upward with a normal attribute:

```
mov   ah,6      ; scroll window up
mov   al,0      ; entire window
mov   ch,0      ; upper left row
mov   cl,0      ; upper left column
mov   dh,24     ; lower right row
mov   dl,79     ; lower right column
mov   bh,7      ; normal attribute for blank lines
int   10h       ; call BIOS
```

We can shorten the preceding statements somewhat by placing two input parameters in each 16-bit register. This works as long as the parameters are expressed in hexadecimal:

```
mov   ax,0600h    ; scroll entire window up
mov   cx,0000h    ; set upper left corner to 0,0
mov   dx,184Fh    ; set lower right corner to 24,79
mov   bh,7        ; normal attribute for blank lines
int   10h         ; call BIOS
```

The following routine scrolls a window from 10,20 to 15,60 downward two lines. The two scrolled lines are given a reverse video attribute:

```
mov   ax,0702h     ; scroll window down two lines
mov   cx,0A14h     ; upper left row, column (10,20)
mov   dx,0F3Ch     ; lower right row, column (15,60)
mov   bh,70h       ; reverse attribute for blank lines
int   10h          ; call BIOS
```

08h: Read Character and Attribute

Function 8 returns the character and its attribute at the current cursor position on the selected video page. Call this function by placing 8 in AH and the video page number in BH. INT 10h returns the character in AL and its attribute in AH. The following routine positions the cursor at row 5, column 1 and retrieves a character:

```
locate:
    mov   ah,2          ; set cursor position
    mov   bh,0          ; on video page 0
    mov   dx,0501h      ; at 5,1
    int   10h
getchar:
    mov   ah,8          ; read attribute/character
    mov   bh,0          ; on video page 0
    int   10h
    mov   char,al       ; save the character
    mov   attrib,ah     ; save the attribute
```

09h: Write Character and Attribute

Use function 9 to write one or more characters at the current cursor position. This function can display any ASCII character, including the special graphics characters for codes 1–31. None of these are interpreted as ASCII control codes, as they would be by INT 21h DOS services. The input parameters are:

AH	Function code 9
AL	Character to be written
BH	Video page
BL	Attribute
CX	Repetition factor

The *repetition factor* specifies how many times the character is to be repeated. (The character should not be repeated beyond the end of the current screen line.) After a character is written, you must call function 2 to move the cursor if more characters will be written.

The following statements write the graphics character identified by 0Ah on the screen 32 times, with a blinking attribute. You may recognize 0Ah as an ASCII *line feed* character, but it is interpreted here by INT 10h as a graphics character (white circle on a black background):

```
mov  ah,9      ; write character and attribute
mov  al,0Ah    ; ASCII character 0Ah
mov  bh,0      ; video page 0
mov  bl,87h    ; blinking attribute
mov  cx,32     ; display it 32 times
int  10h
```

0Ah: Write Character

Function 0Ah writes a character to the screen at the current cursor position without changing the current screen attribute. It is identical to function 9 in every way, except that the attribute is not specified. The following routine writes the letter *A* once at the current cursor position:

```
mov  ah,0Ah     ; write character only
mov  al,'A'     ; character 'A'
mov  bh,0       ; video page 0
mov  cx,1       ; display only once
int  10h
```

0Fh: Get Video Mode

Function 0Fh returns the number of video columns in AH, the current display mode in AL, and the active display page in BH.

A list of the more common video modes is given in the section of this chapter entitled "Video Modes." This function should be called before attempting to perform any color graphics functions or color-specific operations. The following statements get the current video mode and video page:

```
mov  ah,0Fh      ; get video mode
int  10h
mov  vmode,al    ; save the mode
mov  page,bh     ; save the page
```

POINTS TO REMEMBER

The most portable input-output services are offered by DOS, using INT 21h. The video services using INT 10h, on the other hand, are more efficient.

A *hardware interrupt* is activated when the CPU takes time to process a hardware device's request before resuming its normal operation. A *software interrupt* calls a subroutine in the operating system. The service routines provided by the operating system help to minimize differences between specific hardware used on various computers.

The *interrupt vector table* is used by the CPU to locate specific operating system subroutines; each address in the table points to a DOS or ROM BIOS subroutine.

DOS uses standard *device names* to identify the console, printer, asynchronous communications port, and so on. These names may be used to redirect program input and output.

DOS functions are accessed using the INT 21h instruction. These functions are used for standard input and output of both single characters and strings of characters. Standard ASCII codes may be input from the keyboard, as well as keyboard scan codes for special keys.

The video display is manipulated using the INT 10h instruction. INT 10h routines perform such critical tasks as setting the video mode, positioning the cursor, scrolling the screen, and writing characters.

The video mode must be set correctly in order to display color graphics, and one must be sure that the right type of video adapter is installed. Software authors must make their programs flexible enough to work with several types of video displays.

REVIEW QUESTIONS

1. What does an INT instruction do?
2. How is a software interrupt different from a hardware interrupt?
3. What are the largest and smallest possible interrupt numbers?
4. What are the numbers in the Interrupt Vector Table for?
5. What advantage do interrupt routines in the ROM BIOS have over those serviced by DOS?
6. Why would an application program not manipulate the IBM-PC's hardware directly?
7. Which interrupt (other than INT 21h) services the keyboard?
8. How are DOS function calls different from other interrupts?
9. When INT 21h displays a single character on the screen, which register holds the character to be displayed?
10. Why do the DOS functions use redirectable device names for input and output?

11. What is the DOS device name for the first asynchronous adapter port?
12. What is the DOS device name for a nonexistent device?
13. Which INT 21h service routines output a single character to the console?
14. Correct any errors in the following example:

```
        mov   al,9          ; string output function
        mov   dx,message
        int   21h
        .
        .
message db    'Hello, world!@'
```

15. The following example uses the DOS service routine for keyboard input. Which variable holds the number of keys actually typed, and which label points to the first keystroke?

```
          mov   dx,offset label1
          mov   ah,0Ah
          int   21h
          .
          .
label1    db    20
label2    db    0
label3    db    20 dup(' ')
```

16. Which two DOS service routines would be best when you wish to input special keyboard characters such as function keys and cursor arrows? Explain your choices.
17. If INT 21h function 9 is used to display a string, will ASCII control characters such as tabs and line feeds be interpreted correctly?
18. Application programs often clear the keyboard typeahead buffer before asking for more input. Which INT 21h service routine is best for this task?
19. What is a keyboard scan code?
20. Which ASCII control character returns the cursor to the left side of the screen?

21. Which interrupt clears the screen, and what value(s) should be placed in the AH register?

22. The three most popular video adapters for the IBM-PC are the monochrome, ______ , and ______ .

23. Name at least four video attributes that may be used with the monochrome adapter.

24. In the following table, fill in the binary value of each color video attribute (refer to Figure 5-3). The first is done for you:

	Blink	Background	Foreground	Bit Pattern
a.	Off	Brown	Yellow	01101110
b.	Off	White	Blue	
c.	Off	Blue	White	
d.	On	Cyan	Gray	
e.	Off	Black	Light magenta	
f.	On	Black	Bright white	

25. Which INT 10h function displays a character on the screen without changing any screen attributes?

26. Which INT 10h function sets the color adapter into medium-resolution graphics mode with four colors?

27. In the 640 × 200 graphics mode, what advantage does the EGA have over the CGA?

28. How many video pages does the monochrome adapter support?

29. What would happen if a program attempted to set the monochrome adapter into color graphics mode?

30. Complete the following statements to set the cursor size on the monochrome display to scan lines 6–12:

```
mov  ah,1    ; set cursor lines
mov  ch,
mov  cl,
int  10h
```

31. Complete the following statements to locate the cursor at row 5, column 10 on video page 0:

```
mov   ah,2
mov   dh,
mov   dl,
mov   bh,
int   10h
```

32. Complete the following statements to scroll the entire screen upward with a reverse video attribute:

```
mov   ah,
mov   al,
mov   ch,
mov   cl,
mov   dh,
mov   dl,
mov   bh,
int   10h
```

33. Assuming that a program named PROG1.EXE uses standard input-output, write a command to run the program and tell it to receive its input from a file called INPUT.TXT.

34. Using the same program from Question 33, write the command to tell the program to send its output to the printer.

PROGRAMMING EXERCISES

Exercise 1 Window Scroll Program

Write a short program to do the following:

- Scroll a window from row 5, column 10 to row 20, column 70, with a reverse video attribute.
- Locate the cursor at row 10, column 20.
- Display a line of text, such as:

```
THIS TEXT IS IN THE WINDOW
```

Exercise 2 Enhanced Window Scroll Program

Enhance the program written for Exercise 1 as follows:

1. After the line of text is displayed, wait for a key to be pressed.
2. Scroll a window from row 7, column 15 to row 18, column 68, with a normal attribute.
3. Write the character A with a blinking attribute in the middle of the window.
4. Wait for a keystroke, and then clear the entire screen with a normal attribute.

Exercise 3 Keyboard Echo Program

Write a program called ECHOC to input a single character from the console, and then write it on the console. Use DOS function 1 to input the character and function 2 to display it. After the program has been assembled, run it from DOS in the following ways:

a. ECHOC (from kybd to screen)
b. ECHOC < INFILE (from file to screen)
c. ECHOC > OUTFILE (from kybd to file)

For option b, you will need to create a text file with a single character in it. Your program will read the file as input.

Exercise 4 Compressed Type Setup

Write a program to set an Epson-compatible printer to compressed mode. This is useful if you want to print 132 columns on standard (8.5 x 11) size paper. The following hexadecimal number must be sent to the printer, using DOS function 5: 0Fh (change to compressed type). The number is placed in the DL register.

Next, run the program from DOS. Nothing will appear to happen until actual text is printed. Then print a line of output with the DOS COPY command:

```
copy con prn
This line is compressed
(press the F6 key)
```

(Pressing F6 sends an end-of-file character to DOS and ends the COPY command.) If ASCII code 15 does not compress the type on your printer, check its manual for the correct value.

Exercise 5 Uppercase Character Conversion

Write a program to convert any lowercase letter to uppercase. First, use DOS function 9 to display a prompt, such as:

```
Type a lowercase letter:
```

When the user types a lowercase letter, the program converts the character to uppercase and displays it. Since you do not want to echo the lowercase letter being input, use DOS function 8. Assume that only a valid lowercase letter will be entered.

Hint: If you look at the table of ASCII codes at the end of this book, note that uppercase ASCII codes are always 32 less than their lowercase counterparts. For example:

B = 66, b = 98

Type several extended keyboard keys, such as HOME, END, INS, DEL, or F1. When the program ends and returns to the DOS prompt, you will probably see an extra character appear. Offer an explanation of why this happens.

Exercise 6 Character String Printing

Write a program that writes the following line of text to the printer, with only the word *compressed* in compressed mode:

```
The word compressed is the only one that is small.
```

Use DOS function 9 to write the string. Run the program from DOS, redirecting its output to the printer. *Hint*: The Epson code to turn compressed mode on is 0Fh, while the code to turn it off is 12h. Write a carriage return and line feed at the end of the line to force the printer to empty its buffer.

Exercise 7 Line-Drawing Editor

Write a simple line-drawing program that reads the cursor arrow keys, moves the cursor in the desired direction, and draws a line on the screen. When turning a corner, be sure to use one of the corner characters. Here is an example of what the screen might look like after moving and drawing:

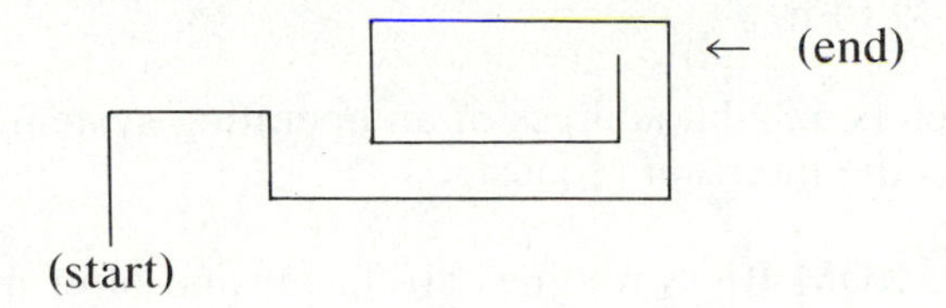

The following is a list of the ASCII characters to be used:

ASCII Code	Character
C0h	└
D9h	┘
C4h	─
B3h	│
DAh	┌
BFh	┐

The keyboard scan codes for the arrow keys are as follows:

Move left	4Bh
Move right	4Dh
Move up	48h
Move down	50h

Extra. Use the letters *D* and *E* to toggle back and forth between the *draw* mode and the *erase* mode. (Change the cursor size using INT 10h, function 01h, in order to show which mode is currently active.)

Display the + character when one line crosses another. You may want to use INT 10h, function 08h, to read a character from the screen at the current cursor position. Thus, you can check to see if you are crossing an existing line.

ANSWERS TO REVIEW QUESTIONS

1. An INT instruction calls a subroutine in the operating system to perform input-output.

2. A hardware interrupt is caused by a physical device that interrupts the CPU; a software interrupt is a call to a subroutine in the operating system.

3. 0 and FFh.

4. Each is a 32-bit address of an operating system subroutine designed to process the interrupt request.

5. The ROM BIOS routines are faster and offer more complete access to the computer's hardware.

6. Because of the variations among hardware on different IBM-compatible computers, the program might not run on all machines.

7. INT 16h provides BIOS-level access to the keyboard.

8. DOS function calls are called using INT 21h. They are tied to the resident part of DOS or MS-DOS, making them more portable to different IBM-compatible computers than other interrupts.

9. The DL register.

10. Redirection adds flexibility to programs running under DOS, because programs do not have to be modified in order to change their input-output.

11. COM1.

12. NUL.

13. Numbers 2 and 6.

14.
```
mov     ah,9
mov     dx,offset message
int     21h
message db 'Hello, world!$'
```

15. **Label2** holds the number of keys typed, and **label3** points to the first keystroke.

16. Functions 7 and 8, because neither echoes the character on the screen.

17. Yes, as discussed in the section entitled "ASCII Control Characters" in this chapter.

18. Service routine 0Ch clears the buffer and calls another input function.

19. A unique number identifying each key on the keyboard. It is particularly useful for identifying special keys, such as the cursor arrows, Ins, Del, and function keys.

20. The carriage return (0Dh).

21. INT 10h. Either 6 or 7 should be moved to AH in order to scroll a window on the screen.

22. CGA, EGA.

23. Choose four from the following: blinking, underline, reverse video, normal, bright.

24. a. 01101110
    b. 01110001
    c. 00010111
    d. 10111000
    e. 00001101
    f. 10001111

25. Function 0Ah.

26. Function 0, with AL = 4.

27. The EGA will display 16 colors, as opposed to only 2 colors on the CGA.

28. Only one—page 0.

29. The screen would go blank.

30.
```
mov  ah,1
mov  ch,6
mov  cl,12
int  10h
```

31.
```
mov  ah,2
mov  dh,5
mov  dl,10
mov  bh,0
int  10h
```

32.
```
mov  ah,6
mov  al,0
mov  ch,0
mov  cl,0
mov  dh,24
mov  dl,79
mov  bh,70h
int  10h
```

33. prog1 < input.txt.

34. prog > prn   (or prog1 > lpt1).

6

Loops and Comparisons

All the programs we have looked at so far lack one important characteristic: the ability to *loop,* or repeat a block of statements. This chapter introduces two instructions used for looping and transfer of control: JMP (jump) and LOOP. In the second half of the chapter, we will concentrate on boolean and comparison instructions. These give you the ability to manipulate individual bits and to test their values. They are introduced as preparation for the complete coverage of conditional jump instructions in Chapter 7.

In assembler, a *jump* is the same thing as a GO TO statement in a high-level language. A new address is moved to the IP (instruction pointer) register, which causes the CPU to begin executing instructions at the new location. JMP is called an *unconditional* transfer instruction because no test or condition is necessary; the jump always takes place.

The LOOP instruction is also a type of jump instruction that decrements and tests a counter. Therefore, LOOP is a *conditional transfer* instruction.

MORE ON ADDRESSING MODES

In Chapter 3 we looked briefly at all of the addressing modes, but at that time we had seen very few programs. Now it's time to take a closer look at the memory addressing modes. The MASM *Programmer's Guide* contains an excellent description of a direct memory operand:

> A direct memory operand is a symbol that represents the address (segment and offset) of an instruction or data. The offset address represented by a direct memory operand is calculated at assembly time. The address of each operand relative to the start of the program is calculated at link time. The actual (or effective) address is calculated at load time.*

This statement also tells us something about the assembly, link, and execution steps. The offset address of an operand is calculated during the assembly step and displayed in the listing file. The following instruction, for example, moves **count** to DL:

```
8A 16 0005 R    mov   dl,count
```

The R shown in the listing file identifies this as a *relocatable* operand, and 0005 is the operand's offset from the beginning of the data segment.

During the link step, segments are grouped together and placed in their correct order. The offsets of variables are recalculated as offsets from the start of a group of segments.

When a program is loaded into memory, DOS determines the absolute addresses of variables. The program's load address is always the lowest memory location that is currently not in use by another program.

A memory operand may be the name of a procedure, such as **main**, it may be the offset of a variable, as in

```
mov   bx,offset count
```

or it may refer to the contents of a variable:

```
mov   dl,count
```

There are several basic elements that can be combined to create a memory operand:

Base register	BX, BP
Index register	SI, DI
Displacement	The name of a label or variable, which represents an offset from the beginning of a segment
Direct operand	The contents of memory at a location identified by the operand's name
Indirect operand	An address stored in a register or variable that is used to locate another variable

*From the MASM 5.0 *Programmer's Guide*. Used by permission of Microsoft Corporation.

Much of the power of IBM-PC assembly language lies in its flexibility when addressing data. The Intel instruction set offers a wide variety of addressing modes that help to make programming easier. Chapter 3 introduced operands constructed from registers, immediate data, and memory variables. Let us add to what we know about direct and indirect addressing.

Direct Addressing Mode

The MASM documentation distinguishes between two types of operands used in direct addressing: direct-memory operands and relocatable operands. A *direct-memory* operand combines a segment value with an offset that represents an absolute memory address at runtime. A *relocatable* operand is any label or symbol identifying a 16-bit displacement from a segment register. The syntax for creating a direct-memory operand is:

```
segment:offset
```

Segment refers to either a segment register or a segment name. Its value is unknown at assembly time, because it depends on where DOS will eventually load the program. *Offset* may be an integer, symbol, label, or variable. Examples are:

```
mov   ax,ds:5        ; segment register and offset
mov   bx,cseg:2Ch    ; segment name and offset
mov   ax,es:count    ; segment register and variable
```

Relocatable operands are more common. Their location depends on the offset of a label from the beginning of a segment. Depending on which segment the label is located in, the following segment registers are used by default:

Type of Label	Default Segment Register
Program code (instructions)	CS
Variables (data)	DS

The ES register usually addresses variables, but it can contain the base location of any segment.

Indirect Addressing Mode

Indirect operands use registers to point to locations in memory. If a register is used in this way, we can change its value and access different memory locations at runtime. Two types of registers are used: *base* registers (BX, BP) and *index* registers (SI, DI). BP is assumed to contain an offset from the stack segment. SI, DI, and BX contain offsets from DS, the data segment register.

There are five indirect addressing modes, identified by the types of operands used:

Addressing Mode	Example
Register indirect	[bx]
Based	table[bx]
Indexed	table[si]
Based indexed	[bx+si]
Based indexed with displacement	[bx+si+2]

Register Indirect. Indirect operands are particularly powerful when processing lists or arrays, because a base or index register may be modified at runtime. In the following example, BX points to two different array elements:

```
     mov   bx,offset array   ; point to start of array
     mov   al,[bx]           ; get first element
     inc   bx                ; point to next
     mov   dl,[bx]           ; get second element
     .
     .
array  db  10h,20h,30h
```

The brackets around BX signify that we are referring to the *contents* of memory, using the address stored in BX.

In the following example, the three bytes in **array** are added together:

```
     mov   si,offset array   ; address of first byte
     mov   al,[si]           ; move the first byte to AL
     inc   si                ; point to next byte
     add   al,[si]           ; add second byte
     inc   si
     add   al,[si]           ; add third byte
     inc   si
     .
     .
array  db  10h,20h,30h
```

The LEA Instruction

The LEA (load effective address) instruction loads the offset of a variable into a register, as does the MOV . . . OFFSET instruction. The following instructions both place the same value in BX:

```
mov   bx,offset bytelist
lea   bx,bytelist
```

MOV . . . OFFSET is more efficient because the offset of **bytelist** is calculated by MASM at assembly time; the offset is assembled into a constant value. The LEA instruction, on the other hand, calculates the operand's offset at runtime, which slows the program down. LEA may be used effectively with more advanced addressing modes, such as the based mode, where the effective address is unknown until runtime. In the following example, the effective address is calculated by adding BX to the offset of **table**:

```
lea   dx,table[bx]
```

Notes on Using PTR

When indirect addressing is used, the PTR operator may be needed to identify a memory operand's size. For instance, if an immediate source operand is less than 256, MASM doesn't know whether the destination operand is a byte or word. In the following example, the first instruction generates a syntax error but the second does not:

```
mov   [bx],10h              ; incorrect
mov   byte ptr [bx],10h     ; correct
```

On the other hand, the following instruction assembles correctly because the source operand is greater than 255 and therefore must be 16 bits long:

```
mov   [bx],1000h
```

If one of the operands is a register, MASM deduces the size of an indirect operand from the register size:

```
mov   dl,[bx]     ; 8-bit move
mov   [bx],dx     ; 16-bit move
```

Another situation in which PTR is required is when the only operand is an indirect operand:

```
inc   word ptr [bx]
```

TRANSFER-OF-CONTROL INSTRUCTIONS

The CPU executes a program sequentially by loading the address of each instruction into IP. To repeat a block of statements, a transfer-of-control statement must be used. A *transfer of control,* or *branch,* is a way of altering the order in which statements are executed. All programming languages contain statements to do this. We divide such statements into two categories:

Unconditional Transfer. The program branches to a new location in all cases; a new value is loaded into the instruction pointer, causing execution to continue at the new address. The JMP instruction is a good example.

Conditional Transfer. The program branches if a certain condition is true. Intel provides a wide range of conditional transfer instructions that may be combined to make up conditional logic structures. The CPU interprets true/false conditions based on the contents of the CX and Flags registers.

The JMP Instruction

The JMP instruction tells the CPU to begin execution at another location. The location must be identified by a label, which is translated by MASM into an address. If the jump is to a label in the current segment, the label's offset is loaded into the IP register. If the label is in another segment, the segment's address is also loaded into CS. The syntax is

```
        [ { SHORT    } ]
JMP     [ { NEAR PTR } ]   destination
        [ { FAR PTR  } ]
```

where *destination* is a label or 32-bit segment-offset address.

The JMP instruction is amazingly flexible. It can jump to a label in the current procedure, from one procedure to another, from one segment to another, completely out of the current program, or to any place in RAM or ROM.* Structured programming discourages such jumps, but they are occasionally necessary in systems programming applications. Examples of various jumps are shown here:

```
jmp L1                ; NEAR:   dest. in current segment
jmp near ptr L1       ; NEAR:   dest. in current segment
jmp short nextval     ; SHORT:  dest. within -128 to +127
                                bytes
jmp far ptr error_rtn ; FAR:    dest. in another segment
```

*The Microsoft/IBM OS/2 operating system restricts a program's ability to jump outside the current memory partition. Also, the Intel 80386 processor offers hardware memory protection, further restricting such jumps.

The operator placed before the destination operand may be one of the following:

SHORT — Jump to a label in the range −128 to +127 bytes from the current location. An 8-bit signed value is added to IP.

NEAR PTR — Jump to a label anywhere in the current program segment. A 16-bit displacement is moved to IP.

FAR PTR — Jump to a label in another segment. The label's segment address is moved to CS, and its offset is moved to IP.

The SHORT operator is especially useful when coding a forward jump, because MASM doesn't know the destination's address until it assembles that part of the program. For example:

```
label1:  jmp short label2   ; use SHORT here
         .
         .
         .
label2:  jmp label1         ; automatically a SHORT jump
```

The NEAR PTR operator may be used to tell MASM that the destination label is in the same segment; usually this is assumed. If the jump is to a label outside the current segment, the FAR PTR operator may be required. Examples of each are shown here, using a label called **exit**:

```
jmp near ptr exit
jmp far  ptr exit
```

A looping program with only a JMP instruction causes a continuous loop, as the following statements show. Fortunately, the program calls INT 21h, so you can stop the program by pressing CTRL-BREAK:

```
start:  mov  ah,2
        mov  dl,'A'
        int  21h
        jmp  start
```

Programming Tip: Assembling a Short Jump

You may find it interesting to know something about the way MASM assembles JMP instructions. The following excerpt is from a listing file generated by MASM. At the beginning of each line is the hexadecimal address of each instruction, followed by the object code that was generated:

Address	Object Code		Source Code	
0100	B4 02	start:	mov ah,2	; start of loop
0102	B2 41		mov dl,'A'	; display "A"
0104	CD 21		int 21h	; call DOS
0106	EB F8		jmp start	; jump back to **start**
0108	...(etc.)			

Before assembling an instruction, MASM increments its own *location counter,* which tells it the offset of the next instruction. When assembling the instruction at 0106h, for example, MASM has already set the location counter to 0108h.

The jump at 0106h is automatically assembled as a short jump, because the distance from the location counter to the label **start** is less than 128 bytes. Two object code bytes are generated for the JMP at location 0106h: EBh and F8h. The first byte (EBh) is the op code for a short jump instruction. The second byte (F8h, or −8) is a *displacement* that tells the CPU how far to jump. MASM calculates this by subtracting the location counter (0108h) from the offset of the destination (0100h). The resulting displacement (F8h) is assembled as part of the instruction:

```
op code → EB F8 ← displacement
```

The LOOP Instruction

The LOOP instruction is the easiest way to repeat a block of statements a specific number of times. CX is automatically used as a counter and is decremented each time the loop repeats. Its syntax is:

```
LOOP destination
```

First, the LOOP instruction subtracts 1 from CX. Then, if CX is greater than zero, control transfers to *destination*. The destination operand must be a short label, in the range −128 to +127 bytes from the current location.

In the following example, the loop repeats five times:

```
         mov   cx,5    ; CX is the loop counter
start:
         .
         .
         loop  start   ; jump to START
```

If CX is equal to zero after having been decremented, no jump takes place and control passes to the following LOOP instruction. The flags are not affected when CX is decremented, even if it equals zero.

In the following example, the loop repeats five times, adding 1 to AX each time. When the loop ends, AX = 5 and CX = 0.

```
        mov   ax,0   ; set AX to 0
        mov   cx,5   ; loop count

top:    inc   ax     ; add 1 to AX
        loop top     ; repeat until CX = 0
```

Caution: If CX = 0 before the LOOP instruction is reached for the first time, CX becomes equal to FFFFh. The loop then repeats another 65,535 times!

Example: Repeat the Letter A. The following program excerpt prints the letter *A* on the screen 960 times, using the LOOP instruction. The count placed in CX represents 12 rows of the screen multiplied by 80 characters per row:

```
    mov    cx,12*80  ; set count to 960

next:
    mov    ah,2        ; function: display character
    mov    dl,'A'      ; display the letter A
    int    21h         ; call DOS
    loop   next        ; decrement CX and repeat
```

Indirect Addressing. The LOOP instruction is particularly powerful when used with an indirect operand. The following program excerpt copies 6 numbers from one array to another, using indirect addressing:

```
 1:          mov    si,offset array1   ; initialize SI and DI
 2:          mov    di,offset array2
 3:          mov    cx,6               ; initialize loop counter
 4:
 5:  move_byte:
 6:          mov    al,[si]            ; get a byte from array1
 7:          mov    [di],al            ; store it in array2
 8:          inc    si
 9:          inc    di
10:          loop   move_byte
11:          .
12:          .
13:  array1   db   10h,20h,30h,40h,50h,60h
14:  array2   db   6 dup(?)
```

On lines 1 and 2, the MOV instructions set SI and DI to the starting offsets of each array. Lines 6 and 7 copy a character from **array1** to **array2**. Lines 8 and 9 point both index registers to the next array position. The LOOP instruction on line 10 subtracts 1 from CX and jumps back to the label **move_byte**, as long as CX is greater than zero.

Example: Display a String. The following program excerpt displays each character in a string. Line 2 sets SI to the starting location of the string. Each character is moved to DL and displayed using INT 21h. We can let MASM calculate the length of the string by using the location counter operator ($). On line 13, the offset of **string** is subtracted from the location counter, which yields the string length:

```
 1:      mov    cx,len              ; counter value = length of string
 2:      mov    si,offset string    ; SI = the address of string
 3:
 4:  getchar:
 5:      mov    ah,2                ; display the character
 6:      mov    dl,[si]
 7:      int    21h
 8:      inc    si                  ; point to next character
 9:      loop   getchar             ; decrement CX, repeat until 0
10:      .
11:      .
12:  string  db   'This is a string.'
13:  len     dw   $ - string        ; calculate the string length
14:
```

Example: Sum an Integer Array. The following program excerpt accumulates the sum of an array in AX. Indirect addressing is used:

```
 1:      sum_an_array:
 2:         mov    ax,0                  ; zero the accumulator
 3:         mov    di,offset intarray    ; address of intarray
 4:         mov    cx,4                  ; number of integers
 5:      read_int:
 6:         add    ax,[di]               ; add integer to accumulator
 7:         add    di,2                  ; point to next integer
 8:         loop   read_int              ; repeat until CX = 0
 9:         .
10:         .
11:  intarray   dw 200h,100h,300h,600h
```

Line 3 sets DI to the offset of **intarray**. Line 4 sets up CX as a counter, so the LOOP instruction on line 8 will be repeated four times. The first time line 6 is executed, it adds 200h to AX. Line 7 adds 2 to DI, making it point to the next value in the array.

Example: Display ASCII Codes. A short program that displays ASCII codes 14–255 is shown in Figure 6-1. (Codes less than 14 are generally used as control characters.) Line 8 initializes CX to the number of characters to be displayed

```
 1:  title Display ASCII Codes 14-255   (ASCII.ASM)
 2:
 3:  dosseg
 4:  .model small
 5:  .stack 100h
 6:  .code
 7:  main proc
 8:       mov     cx,242     ; loop count = 242
 9:       mov     dl,14      ; starting ASCII code
10:       mov     ah,2       ; display char function
11:
12:  A1:  int     21h        ; call DOS
13:       inc     dl         ; next ASCII code
14:       loop    A1         ; display another character
15:
16:       mov   ax,4C00h     ; return to DOS
17:       int   21h
18:  main endp
19:  end main
```

Figure 6-1 A program to display ASCII codes 14–255.

because it is the loop counter. Line 9 places the starting ASCII code in DL, and line 12 displays the character using INT 21h. Line 13 increments the ASCII code in preparation for displaying the next character. The LOOP instruction on line 14 decrements CX and jumps to label A1 if CX is still greater than zero.

Example: Sum the Numbers 1–255. We can use the LOOP instruction to find the sum of the numbers 1–255 inclusive. The loop counter in CX varies from 255 down to 0, and each value is added to AX. The result is 7F80h (32,640):

```
        mov   ax,0     ; zero the accumulator
        mov   cx,255   ; loop counter

again:  add   ax,cx    ; top of loop: Add to the sum
        loop  again    ; repeat until CX = 0
```

Example: Delay Loop. If we want a program to pause before continuing to the next instruction, we can create a delay loop. The length of the delay varies inversely with the value in CX. The following sample routine beeps repeatedly, with a short delay between each beep:

```
start:  mov   ah,2      ; display character function
        mov   dl,7      ; ASCII char(7) sounds a beep
        int   21h       ; call DOS
        mov   cx,4096   ; set up delay value
delay:  loop  delay     ; loop 4096 times
        jmp   start     ; jump to start
```

There is a drawback to the method used here: The length of the delay depends on the speed of the computer. A more general approach would be to use the BIOS timer interrupt (INT 1Ch), which always ticks 18.2 times per second.

Changing the Loop Counter. One must be careful not to modify the register or variable being used as a loop counter. In the following example, CX is incremented within the loop. It never reaches zero, and the loop never ends:

```
        mov     ah,2      ; DOS function: display character
        mov     cx,10     ; loop counter
        mov     dl,'*'    ; character to be displayed

top:    int     21h       ; call DOS
        inc     cx        ; add 1 to CX (??)
        loop    top       ; loop until CX = 0
```

This principle, in fact, is universal among programming languages: Never modify a loop counter within its own loop.

Nested Loop. Occasionally you may want to code a nested loop, with one loop inside another. If so, CX must be saved before entering the inner loop and then restored after leaving the inner loop. The nested loop program in Figure 6-2 displays the letter *O* each time the outer loop repeats, and the letter *I* each time the inner loop repeats. The following output is generated by the program:

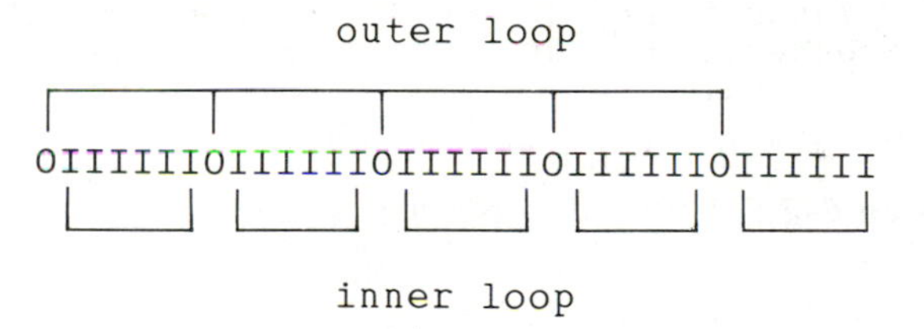

There are a few key points in the program worth mentioning. Line 13 sets CX to the outer loop count, which is 5. After entering the outer loop, two things happen: Line 18 stores CX back in the outer loop counter variable, and line 19 sets CX to the inner loop count. After the inner loop finishes, line 25 restores CX to the outer loop count so it can be tested by the LOOP instruction on line 26. An abbreviated diagram is shown here:

```
mov   cx,outer_count
outer:
      .
      .
      mov   outer_count,cx
      mov   cx,inner_count
      inner:
      .
      .
      loop  inner
      mov   cx,outer_count
loop outer
```

```
 1:  title  Nested Loop Example            (NLOOP.ASM)
 2:
 3:  ; This program prints the following pattern on the screen:
 4:  ;          OIIIIIIOIIIIIIOIIIIIIOIIIIIIOIIIIII
 5:
 6:  dosseg
 7:  .model small
 8:  .stack 100h
 9:  .code
10:  main proc
11:      mov   ax,@data          ; initialize DS register
12:      mov   ds,ax
13:      mov   cx,outer_count    ; outer loop count
14:  outer:
15:      mov   ah,2              ; display "O" for outer
16:      mov   dl,'O'
17:      int   21h
18:      mov   outer_count,cx    ; save outer count
19:      mov   cx,inner_count    ; inner loop count
20:  inner:
21:      mov   ah,2              ; display "I" for inner
22:      mov   dl,'I'
23:      int   21h
24:      loop  inner             ; repeat inner loop
25:      mov   cx,outer_count    ; restore CX
26:      loop  outer             ; repeat outer loop
27:      mov   ax,4C00h          ; return to DOS
28:      int   21h
29:  main endp
30:
31:  .data
32:  inner_count  dw   6   ; counters for inner and outer loops
33:  outer_count  dw   5
34:  end main
```

Figure 6-2 Example of a nested loop.

BOOLEAN AND COMPARISON INSTRUCTIONS

The CPU performs certain fundamental operations on binary numbers. *Boolean* operations are among the most important, as they make it possible to manipulate individual bits. Bit manipulation using boolean operators is an intrinsic part of assembly language, while it tends to be an extra feature not found in all high-level languages.

The Flags Register. Each of the instructions in this section affects the Flags register. The flags were discussed in Chapter 2, but we are now concerned primarily with the way the Zero, Carry, and Sign flags show the results of boolean and comparison instructions. Three important points to remember are:

- The *Zero* flag is set when the result of an operation is zero.
- The *Carry* flag is set when the result of an operation is too large for the destination operand or when a subtraction operation requires a borrow.

- The *Sign* flag is set when the high bit of the destination operand is set, indicating a negative result.

Boolean instructions are based on boolean algebra operations (invented by the mathematician George Boole). These operations allow modification of individual bits in binary numbers, as summarized in the following table:

Operation	Comment
AND	Result is 1 only when both input bits are 1
OR	Result is 1 when either input bit is 1
XOR	Result is 1 only when the input bits are different (called *exclusive-OR*)
NOT	Result is the reverse of the input bit (i.e., 1 becomes 0, and 0 becomes 1)

The AND Instruction

The AND instruction performs a boolean AND operation using two 8-bit or 16-bit operands and places the result in the destination operand. The syntax is:

```
AND destination,source
```

The operands must be the same size, and only one of them may be a memory operand. For each matching bit in the two operands, the following rule applies: If both bits equal 1, the result bit is 1; otherwise, it is 0. The following flags are affected: Overflow, Sign, Zero, Parity, Carry, and Auxiliary Carry. The following example shows the results of the boolean AND operation using two 4-bit numbers:

```
         0  0  1  1
         0  1  0  1
         ----------
Result:  0  0  0  1
```

Each bit position in the two operands is ANDed separately. For example:

```
mov al,00111011b
and al,00001111b   ; AL = 00001011b
```

More examples of the AND instruction follow:

```
and  ax,bx               ; 16-bit registers
and  bl,byteval          ; 8-bit register, memory
and  wordval,cx          ; 16-bit memory, register
and  al,30h              ; 8-bit register, immediate
and  val1,00111111b      ; 8-bit memory, immediate
and  byte ptr [bx],al    ; indirect operand, register
```

The AND instruction can force selected bits in an operand to zeros, while carefully preserving the states of others. The term *bit masking* describes this process, which is common when drawing video graphics and controlling hardware devices.

Example: Clearing High Bits. Suppose that we need to clear the high bit of each character in a file created by a word processing program. Some programs, WordStar, for example, use the high bit of characters to store text formatting information. Before such a file can be read by other programs, the high bit of each character must be cleared to zero.

The following program excerpt inputs a byte from a text file, clears the high bit, and writes the revised byte to standard output. Both the input and output may be redirected from the DOS command line, making it possible to read from one file and write to another. INT 21h function 6 is chosen because it prevents DOS from filtering out any characters and because it inputs the character without echoing it on the console:

```
mov    ah,6           ; console input function
mov    dl,0FFh        ; check for input character
int    21h            ; call DOS
and    al,01111111b   ; strip high bit
mov    dl,al          ; move char to DL
mov    ah,2           ; write char to standard output
int    21h
```

An input character, for example, might be the letter *A*. Instead of being 01000001b (41h), the high bit has been set by WordStar, and it equals 11000001b (C1h). The program ANDs the latter value with 01111111b (7Fh):

```
        11000001   (character A with high bit set)
(AND)   01111111   (strip high bit, using 7Fh)
        --------
        01000001   (result: 41h, the character A)
```

The OR Instruction

The OR instruction performs a boolean OR operation using the source and destination operands and places the result in the destination. Its syntax is:

```
OR destination,source
```

The operands may be 8 or 16 bits, as long as both are the same size. Only one of them may be a memory operand.

For each matching bit in the two operands, the following applies: If both bits are 0, the result bit is 0; otherwise, it is 1. The following flags are affected: Overflow, Sign, Zero, Parity, Auxiliary Carry, and Carry.

Examples of the OR instruction with different operands are:

```
or   ax,bx                ; 16-bit registers
or   bl,byteval           ; 8-bit register, memory
or   wordval,cx           ; 16-bit memory, register
or   al,30h               ; 8-bit register, immediate
or   val1,00111111b       ; 8-bit memory, immediate
or   byte ptr [bx],al     ; indirect operand, register
```

The following table shows the results of an OR operation using individual bits:

```
          0  0  1  1
          0  1  0  1
         -----------
Result:   0  1  1  1
```

For example, let us OR 3Bh with 0Fh:

```
mov  al,00111011b    ; 3Bh
or   al,00001111b    ; AL = 3Fh
```

The lower 4 bits of the result were set to 1's in this example, while the high 4 bits were preserved from the original value of AL.

This technique may be used to convert a single decimal digit to ASCII by forcing bits 4 and 5 on. If, for example, AL contains 5, we can convert it to the ASCII code for the digit 5: We OR the number with 30h, resulting in 35h, which would be displayed as '5':

binary value:	00000101	(05h)
boolean OR:	00110000	(30h)
Result:	00110101	(35h)

The assembly language instructions to do this are:

```
mov  dl,5     ; binary value
or   dl,30h   ; convert to ASCII
```

Checking the Sign or Value. You can use the OR instruction to find out if an operand is either negative or equal to zero. A number ORed with itself does not change, but the flags are affected:

```
or   al,al
```

If the Zero flag is set, then AL must be equal to 0; if the Sign flag is set, AL must be negative; if neither the Zero nor the Sign flag is set, AL must be greater than 0.

The XOR Instruction

The XOR (exclusive OR) instruction performs a boolean exclusive OR operation, using the source and destination operands, and places the result in the destination. The syntax is:

```
XOR destination,source
```

Only one operand may be a memory operand. For each matching bit in the two operands, the following applies: If both bits are the same (both 0 or both 1) the result is 0; otherwise, it is 1. The following flags are affected: Overflow, Sign, Zero, Parity, Auxiliary Carry, and Carry.

The following example shows the effect of XOR on individual bits. XOR produces a 1 only when the two input bits are different:

```
          0  0  1  1
          0  1  0  1
          ----------
Result:   0  1  1  0
```

The following instructions produce a result of 32h in AL:

```
mov   al,10110100b
xor   al,10000110b     ; AL = 00110010b, or 32h
```

More examples of XOR using different operands follow:

```
xor   ax,bx                ; 16-bit registers
xor   bl,byteval           ; 8-bit register, memory
xor   wordval,cx           ; 16-bit memory, register
xor   al,30h               ; 8-bit register, immediate
xor   val1,00111111b       ; 8-bit memory, immediate
xor   byte ptr [bx],al     ; indirect operand, register
```

Toggling Screen Bits. The XOR instruction may be used to generate high-speed color graphics. A pixel (dot) lights up on the screen when a single bit in video memory is set to 1. In order to achieve a blinking effect, a bit may be XORed repeatedly, toggling it on and off.

In the following example, the bits in the result are exactly the reverse of their original values. When the XOR is repeated, the number returns to its original value:

```
mov al,00111011b    ; AL = 00111011b
xor al,11111111b    ; AL = 11000100b
xor al,11111111b    ; AL = 00111011b
```

The NOT Instruction

The NOT instruction reverses all bits in an operand, changing ones to zeros and vice versa. The result is called the *ones complement*. The syntax is:

```
NOT destination
```

For example, the ones complement of F0h is 0Fh:

```
mov  al,11110000b    ; AL = 11110000b
not  al              ; AL = 00001111b
```

More examples follow:

```
not  al                ; 8-bit register
not  bx                ; 16-bit register
not  byte ptr [si]     ; indirect operand
not  word1             ; 16-bit memory
not  byteval           ; 8-bit memory
```

Twos Complement. The CPU stores negative numbers in twos complement form. You can create the twos complement of a number using the NOT and INC instructions:

```
mov al,1     ; AL = 00000001b (+1)
not al       ; AL = 11111110b
inc al       ; AL = 11111111b (-1)
```

The NEG Instruction

The NEG instruction converts a number from positive to negative, or vice versa. It does this by converting the number to its twos complement. The syntax is:

```
NEG destination
```

The instruction reverses all bits in the *destination* operand and adds 1 to the result. The following flags are affected: Overflow, Sign, Zero, Auxiliary Carry, Parity, and Carry. Examples of NEG are:

```
neg  al               ; 8-bit register
neg  bx               ; 16-bit register
neg  byte ptr [si]    ; indirect operand
neg  word1            ; 16-bit memory
neg  byteval          ; 8-bit memory
```

It's a good idea to check the size of a number being converted, or you might end up with incorrect results. For example, if we move −128 to AL and then NEG it, the result is still −128, with the Overflow flag set:

```
mov  al,-128    ; AL = 10000000b
neg  al         ; AL = 10000000b, OF = 1
```

On the other hand, if +127 is negated, the result is correct, and the Overflow flag is clear:

```
mov  al,+127    ; AL = 01111111b
neg  al         ; AL = 10000001b, OF = 0
```

The TEST Instruction

The TEST instruction performs an implied AND operation on the destination operand, using the source operand. The flags are affected, but neither operand is changed. The syntax is:

```
TEST destination,source
```

If any matching bit positions are set in both operands, the Zero flag is cleared. The following flags are affected: Overflow, Sign, Zero, Carry, Auxiliary Carry, and Parity.

The TEST instruction is particularly valuable when you want to know if individual bits in an operand are set. Examples are listed here:

```
test  ax,bx               ; 16-bit registers
test  bl,byteval          ; 8-bit register, memory
test  wordval,cx          ; 16-bit memory, register
test  al,30h              ; 8-bit register, immediate
test  val1,00111111b      ; 8-bit memory, immediate
test  byte ptr [bx],al    ; indirect operand, register
```

Example: Checking the Printer Status. INT 17h checks the status of the printer and returns a single byte in AL. If bit 5 is on, the printer is out of paper. The following TEST checks for this and clears the Zero flag if bit 5 is set:

```
mov   ah,2           ; function: read printer status
int   17h            ; call BIOS
test  al,00100000b   ; ZF = 0 if out of paper
```

The TEST instruction can check several bits at once, to see if any of them are set. Suppose we have read a byte from an I/O device, and we want to know if either bit 0 or bit 3 is set. From the following illustration, we can see that the Zero flag will be set only when both bits are clear:

Example 1: Bit 0 is set:

```
0 0 1 0 0 1 0 1  ← input value
0 0 0 0 1 0 0 1  ← test value
0 0 0 0 0 0 0 1  ← result: Zero flag clear
```

Example 2: Bits 0 and 3 are clear:

```
0 0 1 0 0 1 0 0  ← input value
0 0 0 0 1 0 0 1  ← test value
0 0 0 0 0 0 0 0  ← result: Zero flag set
```

The CMP Instruction

The CMP (compare) instruction offers a convenient way of comparing two 8-bit or 16-bit operands. The result is reflected in the state of the Flags register. The CMP instruction performs an implied subtraction of the source operand from the destination operand, but neither operand is actually changed. The syntax is:

```
CMP destination,source
```

Only one operand may be a memory operand. The destination operand can be neither an immediate operand nor the IP register. Neither operand may be a segment register. The following flags are affected: Overflow, Sign, Zero, Carry, Auxiliary Carry, and Parity.

Flag Conditions. Generally only three flags are important, as we will see when we use the CMP instruction in actual programs. The following table shows how the flags are affected by the CMP instruction:

Result of Comparison	Flag(s) Affected
Destination < source	Carry flag = 1
Destination = source	Zero flag = 1
Destination > source	Carry = 0, Zero = 0

The Intel instruction set contains *conditional jump* instructions that allow your programs to jump to a label based on specific flag settings (conditional jumps will be fully explored in Chapter 7).

CMP is a valuable instruction because it provides the basis for most conditional logic structures. The following examples show various operands used with CMP:

```
cmp  si,di               ; 16-bit registers
cmp  bl,1                ; 8-bit register, immediate
cmp  membyte,al          ; 8-bit memory, register
cmp  wordval,10          ; 16-bit memory, immediate
cmp  word ptr [si],cx    ; indirect operand, register
```

Examples. Let's look at three examples that show how the flags are set when numbers are compared. In Example 1, AL is less than 10, so the Carry flag is set. In Example 2, the Zero flag is set because both operands are equal. In Example 3, the destination (SI) is greater than the source, so both the Zero and Carry flags are clear.

Example 1:

```
mov  al,5
cmp  al,10     ; Carry flag = 1
```

Example 2:

```
mov  ax,1000
mov  cx,1000
cmp  cx,ax     ; Zero flag = 1
```

Example 3:

```
mov  si,105
cmp  si,0      ; Zero and Carry flags = 0
```

CONDITIONAL LOOPS

The LOOPZ (LOOPE) Instruction

The LOOPZ (LOOPE) instruction loops while CX > 0 and the Zero flag is set. The destination must be in the range of −128 to +127 bytes from the current location. The syntax is:

```
LOOPZ destination
LOOPE destination
```

First, CX is decremented. Then, if CX > 0 and the Zero flag is set, we jump to *destination*; otherwise, nothing happens, and control passes to the next instruction.

Example: Scan an Array. Let us scan through an array of 100 integers until a nonzero value is found. We can compare each integer to 0, setting the Zero flag whenever the values are the same. When a nonzero value is found, the LOOPZ instruction no longer jumps back to the top of the loop:

```
1:          mov     bx,offset intarray   ; point to the array
2:          sub     bx,2                 ; back up one word
3:          mov     cx,100               ; repeat 100 times
4:
5: next:    add     bx,2                 ; point to next entry
6:          cmp     word ptr [bx],0      ; compare array value to zero
7:          loopz   next                 ; loop while ZF = 1, CX > 0
            .
            .
  intarray   dw   100 dup(?)
```

Line 6 sets the Zero flag each time the current array element is equal to zero. Line 7 jumps to **next** if CX > 0 and ZF = 1. Of course, the entire array might contain only zeros. We would probably be wise to compare CX to zero right after the LOOPZ instruction to see if the entire array was processed.

Changing Flags. You must be careful not to change the flags between a CMP instruction and a subsequent conditional loop instruction. In the following example, the ADD instruction causes the loop to terminate too soon because it clears the Zero flag.

```
next:   cmp     [bx],ax   ; compare array value to zero
        add     bx,2      ; point to next entry
        loopz   next      ; error: Zero flag has changed
```

The LOOPNZ (LOOPNE) Instruction

The LOOPNZ (loop while not zero) instruction is the reverse of LOOPZ. The looping continues only if CX > 0 and the Zero flag is clear. The syntax is identical to that of LOOPZ. The following program excerpt scans each number in an 8-bit array until it reaches a positive value (a clear sign bit):

```
 1:      mov     si,offset array-1    ; point 1 byte before the array
 2:      mov     cx,array_len
 3:
 4:  next:
 5:      inc     si                   ; point to next value
 6:      test    byte ptr [si],80h    ; sign bit set?
 7:      loopnz  next                 ; yes: continue
 8:      .                            ; no: quit
 9:      .
10:  array       db  -3,-6,-1,-10,10,30,40,4
11:  array_len   equ $-array
```

The loop repeats until lines 6 and 7 detect a positive number. The INC instruction has been placed on line 5 in order to avoid incrementing SI before the LOOPNZ instruction. As we've seen before, the Zero flag must not be changed between the TEST and LOOPNZ instructions. Line 1 has to point SI 1 byte *before* the beginning of the array.

POINTS TO REMEMBER

When using direct addressing, be sure to distinguish between the *contents* of an operand and its *offset*. The offset is a 16-bit quantity, but the contents may be either 8 or 16 bits long. The following examples show the difference:

```
mov    al,count            ; contents
mov    bx,offset count     ; offset
```

Indirect addressing means using a register to point to a location in memory by placing a 16-bit offset address in the register. Either a base register (BX, BP) or an index register (SI, DI) may be used.

Arithmetic and comparison instructions set the flags in the following ways: The *Zero* flag is set when an operation produces a result of zero, the *Carry* flag is set when a carry or borrow is required, and the *Sign* flag is set when the result is negative.

Boolean instructions: Use AND when bits must be cleared, use OR when bits must be set, and use XOR when bits must be reversed.

The TEST instruction checks selected bits in a destination operand. The Zero flag is set when no matching bits are found. Use NOT to reverse all bits in an operand. Use NEG to reverse the sign of an operand by converting it to its twos complement.

The CMP instruction compares a destination operand to a source operand by performing an implied subtraction. The Zero and Carry flags are meaningful only if the operands are unsigned. If the operands are signed, the Sign, Zero, and Overflow flags are important.

The LOOP instruction may only be to a short label, which is within -128 to $+127$ bytes of the current location. The LOOP instruction decrements CX first. Then, if CX $>$ 0, control passes to the destination label. If CX $=$ 0, the jump is not taken and control passes to the next instruction. Be careful to initialize CX before beginning a loop; otherwise the loop will probably execute an undesired number of times.

The LOOPZ instruction loops while CX $>$ 0 and the Zero flag is set. The LOOPNZ instruction loops while CX $>$ 0 and the Zero flag is clear.

REVIEW QUESTIONS

1. Does the LOOP instruction terminate when the Zero flag is set?

2. Name an unconditional transfer-of-control instruction.

3. The three basic types of operands are *register, memory,* and ____________ .

4. Is the address of each operand relative to the start of the program calculated at assembly time or at link time?

5. In the following machine code from a listing file, what does the R tell us?

```
5B 0021 R    add   bx,val1
```

6. Which registers are called *base* registers?

7. Identify the types of operands (register, immediate, direct, or indirect) used in each of the following instructions:
   a. mov al,20
   b. add cx,wordval
   c. mov bx,offset count
   d. add dl,[bx]

8. Why is the PTR operator required in the following instruction?

```
add   word ptr [si],5
```

9. Would we need the PTR operator in each of the following instructions?

```
a.      mov   al,bval
b.      mov   dl,[bx]
c.      sub   [bx],2
d.      mov   cl,wval
e.      add   al,bval+1
        .
        .
   bval    db   10h,20h
   wval    dw   1000h
```

10. Mark and correct any syntax errors in the following listing:

```
        mov   al,blist
        add   al,wlist+1
        mov   bx,offset blist
        mov   dl,[bl]
        add   [bx],byte ptr 2
        mov   cx wlist
        mov   dx,cx
        inc   word ptr dx
        dec   ax
        inc   [cx]
        .
        .
blist   db 1,2,3,4,5
wlist   dw 6,7,8,9,0Ah
```

11. The following program fragment adds a list of 10 numbers together and places the result in **total**. If you see any syntax or logic errors, explain their causes and suggest corrections:

```
1:   begin:
2:           mov    cx,10
3:           mov    si,offset bytelist
4:
5:   nextbyte:
6:           add    dx,[si]
7:           inc    dx
8:           loop   begin
9:           mov    total,dx
10:
11:  .data
12:  bytelist     db   56,22,30,40,76,82,10,5,44,23
13:  total        dw   0
```

PROGRAMMING EXERCISES

Be sure to test each of the programs written here, using a debugger. You may want to print a copy of the trace output to keep as a reference.

Exercise 1 Copy an Array

Write a program that copies all numbers from one 16-bit array to another. Declare the arrays as follows:

```
array1  dw 1000h,2000h,3000h,4000h,5000h,6000h,7000h,8000h
array2  dw 8 dup(0)
```

Exercise 2 Copy an Array Backwards

Write a program that copies all numbers from **array1** to **array2**, reversing the numbers in the process. Make up your own data.

Exercise 3 Reverse an Array

Write a program that reverses the numbers in an 8-bit array. A sample array is shown here before and after being reversed:

10, 20, 30, 40, 50, 60, 70
70, 60, 50, 40, 30, 20, 10

Be sure to have MASM calculate the length of the array, using the location-counter operator ($).

Exercise 4 Reverse Doubleword Bytes

A 32-bit variable is stored in memory in reversed-byte format, with the least significant byte at the lowest address. Write a program that reverses the bytes of a 32-bit number, in place. Use the following variable:

```
double_word  dd  12345678h
```

Exercise 5 Fibonacci Series

Write a program that generates the first 15 numbers of the Fibonacci series, starting with 1: 1, 2, 3, 5, 8, 13 ... 987. Each number after 2 is the sum of the previous 2 numbers.

Exercise 6 Convert a Character to Lowercase

Write a program that inputs a string of up to 80 uppercase characters from the keyboard and displays them in lowercase. (An uppercase letter may be converted to lowercase by setting bit 5.)

Exercise 7 Convert a String to Uppercase

Write a program that inputs a string of up to 80 characters from the keyboard and displays them in uppercase. (A lowercase letter may be converted to uppercase by clearing bit 5.)

Exercise 8 Reverse Screen Bits

Write a program to read each position on the top line of the screen, using INT 10h. XOR the character with 0FFh, and then write the character back to the screen. Then wait for a keystroke, and restore the screen to its original state. *Extra:* Do the same for the entire screen.

Exercise 9 Test Individual Bits

Assume that a sequence of 10 bytes has been input from a communications port and placed in a buffer called **inbuff**. Write a program to check if bits 3 and 5 in each incoming byte are set. If they are, clear all bits except bits 0, 1, and 2, and add the resulting value to a variable called **total**. Create sample data to test the program.

ANSWERS TO REVIEW QUESTIONS

1. No, it terminates when CX equals 0.
2. JMP.
3. Immediate.
4. No, it is calculated at link time.
5. This instruction contains a relocatable operand.
6. BX and BP.
7. a. register, immediate
   b. register, direct
   c. register, direct
   d. register, indirect

8. Because the immediate operand's size is ambiguous—it could be either 8 or 16 bits. The destination operand, [si], also gives no indication of size.

9. a. PTR is not needed
   b. PTR is not needed
   c. sub byte ptr [bx],2
   d. mov cl,byte ptr wval
   e. PTR is not needed

10. The erroneous lines have been corrected:

```
.code
mov   al,blist
add   al,wlist+1          ; add ax,wlist+1
mov   bx,offset blist
mov   dl,[bl]             ; mov dl,[bx]
add   [bx],byte ptr 2     ; add byte ptr [bx],2
mov   cx wlist            ; mov cx,wlist
mov   dx,cx
inc   word ptr dx         ; inc dx
dec   ax
inc   [cx]                ; inc cx (CX may not be indirect)

.data
blist   db 1,2,3,4,5
wlist   dw 6,7,8,9,0Ah
```

11. Five errors were found. First, DX is not initialized to 0 at the beginning. The following instruction should be inserted within the first three lines:

```
mov   dx,0
```

Second, the instruction at line 6 would cause a mismatch of operand sizes and should be changed to:

```
add   dl,[si]
```

The alternative, adding [si] to DX, would not work because SI points to a list of byte values.

Third, line 7 should increment SI instead of DX:

```
inc   si
```

Fourth, line 8 should loop back to **nextbyte**, not **begin**:

```
loop   nextbyte
```

The fifth error is more subtle: Whenever the ADD instruction overflows DL, the Carry flag is set. To extend the sum into DH, we must insert the following instruction after the ADD:

```
adc   dh,0
```

The corrected program is:

```
.code
begin:
      mov   dx,0
      mov   cx,10
      mov   si,offset bytelist

nextbyte:
      add   dl,[si]
      adc   dh,0
      inc   si
      loop  nextbyte
      mov   total,dx

.data
bytelist  db  56,22,30,40,76,82,10,5,44,23
total     dw  0
```

7

Conditions and Procedures

CONDITIONAL JUMPS

There are no conditional logic structures in IBM-PC assembly language. But we can implement almost any structure using a combination of statements. A logic structure is simply a group of conditional statements working together. The WHILE structure, for instance, has an implied IF statement at its beginning that evaluates a condition:

Structured	**Unstructured**
DO WHILE (a < b)	L1: IF (a >= b) THEN
<statement–1>	jump to L2
<statement–2>	ENDIF
.	<statement–1>
.	<statement–2>
ENDDO	.
	jump to L1
	L2: (continue here)

We use angle brackets (<>) around the word *statement* in this chapter to identify a program statement.

Two steps are involved in executing an IF statement. First, an arithmetic or comparison instruction sets one or more flags based on its result. Second, a *conditional jump* instruction may cause the CPU to jump to a new address. The instructions used belong to one of two groups:

> Group 1: Comparison and arithmetic instructions, in which the CPU sets individual flags according to the result.
>
> Group 2: Conditional jump instructions, in which the CPU takes action based on the flags.

The instructions from the two groups work in tandem: An instruction from Group 1 is executed, affecting the flags. Then a conditional jump instruction from Group 2 executes, based on the value of one of the flags. In the following example, the JZ instruction jumps to **next** if AL = 0:

```
      cmp  al,0
      jz   next   ; jump if Zero flag is set
      .
      .
next:
```

Conditional Jump Instruction

A conditional jump instruction transfers control to a destination address when a flag condition is true. The syntax is:

```
Jcond destination
```

The destination address must be − 128 to + 127 bytes from the current location.* *Cond* refers to a flag condition, identifying the state of one or more flags. For example:

C	Carry flag set
NC	Carry flag not set (clear)
Z	Zero flag set
NZ	Zero flag not set (clear)

We have already seen that flags are set by arithmetic, comparison, and boolean instructions. Each conditional jump instruction checks one or more flags, returning a result of *true* or *false*. If the result is true, the jump is taken; otherwise, the program does nothing and continues to the next instruction. For ex-

*Since the CPU always increments IP before executing an instruction, the *current location* is actually the next address beyond the jump instruction.

ample, the following instruction says: If the Zero flag is set, jump to the address implied by the label **next_section**:

```
jz  next_section
```

Using CMP. Let's say we want to jump to location **equal** when AX and BX are the same. The CMP instruction compares AX to BX, and the JE instruction causes a jump if the Zero flag is set (i.e., the operands are equal):

```
1:          cmp  ax,bx      ; compare AX to BX
2:          je   equal
3:  not_equal:              ; continue here if AX ≠ BX
4:          .
5:          .
6:          jmp  quit
7:  equal:                  ; jump here if AX = BX
8:
9:  quit:                   ; always end up here
```

We can best understand this program by using different test values for AX and BX. Refer to the line numbers shown in the program during the following discussion:

Case 1: AX=5, BX=5. The CMP instruction (line 1) sets the Zero flag because AX and BX are equal. The JE instruction (line 2) jumps to the label **equal** on line 7. All statements from this point on are executed in sequence.

Case 2: AX=5, BX=6. CMP (line 1) clears the Zero flag because AX and BX are not equal. JE (line 2) has no effect, so the program falls through to line 3, executes all instructions through the JMP on line 6, and jumps to **quit**.

Table of Conditional Jump Instructions. A table of jumps based on unsigned comparisons is shown in Figure 7-1, and a table of jumps based on signed and miscellaneous comparisons is presented in Figure 7-2.

Figure 7-1 Jumps based on unsigned comparisons.

Jumps Based on Unsigned Comparisons

Mnemonic	Description	Flag Condition(s)
JZ JE	Jump if zero Jump if equal (if op1 = op2)	ZF = 1
JNZ JNE	Jump if not zero Jump if not equal (if op1 ≠ op2)	ZF = 0

Figure 7-1 *(Cont.)*

Mnemonic	Description	Flag Condition(s)
JA	Jump if above (if op1 > op2)	CF = 0 and ZF = 0
JNBE	Jump if not below or equal (if op1 not <= op2)	
JAE	Jump if above or equal (if op1 >= op2)	CF = 0
JNB	Jump if not below (if op1 not < op2)	
JNC	Jump if not carry	
JB	Jump if below (if op1 < op2)	CF = 1
JNAE	Jump if not above or equal (if op1 not >= op2)	
JC	Jump if carry	
JBE	Jump if below or equal (if op1 <= op2)	CF = 1 or ZF = 1
JNA	Jump if not above (if op1 not > op2)	

Figure 7-2 Jumps based on signed and miscellaneous comparisons.

Jumps Based on Signed Comparisons

Mnemonic	Description	Flag Condition(s)
JG	Jump if greater (if op1 > op2)	ZF = 0 and SF = OF
JNLE	Jump if not less than or equal (if op1 not <= op2)	
JGE	Jump if greater than or equal (if op1 >= op2)	SF = OF
JNL	Jump if not less (if op1 not < op2)	
JL	Jump if less (if op1 < op2)	SF ≠ OF
JNGE	Jump if not greater than or equal (if op1 not >= op2)	
JLE	Jump if less than or equal (if op1 <= op2)	ZF = 1 or SF ≠ OF
JNG	Jump if not greater (if op1 not > op2)	

Figure 7-2 *(Cont.)*

Miscellaneous Jumps

JCXZ	Jump if CX = 0	CX = 0
JS	Jump if sign	SF = 1
JNS	Jump if not sign	SF = 0
JO	Jump if overflow	OF = 1
JNO	Jump if not overflow	OF = 0
JP	Jump if parity even	PF = 1
JNP	Jump if no parity	PF = 0

APPLICATIONS USING CONDITIONAL JUMPS

In this section, we present a number of simple applications involving conditional jump instructions. To get the greatest benefit from these examples, assemble each one into a short program and trace it with a debugger.

Larger of Two Numbers. We might want to compare unsigned values in AX and BX and move the larger one to DX. Whenever a condition is true, the program jumps over instructions that follow:

```
            mov   dx,ax      ; assume AX is larger
            cmp   ax,bx      ; if AX is >= BX then
            jae   quit       ; jump to quit
            mov   dx,bx      ; else move BX to DX
quit:
```

Smallest of Three Numbers. The following instructions compare the unsigned values in AL, BL, and CL and move the smallest of these to a variable called **small**:

```
1:      mov  small,al     ; assume AL is the smallest
2:      cmp  small,bl     ; if small <= BL then
3:      jbe  L1           ; jump to L1
4:      mov  small,bl     ; else move BL to small
5:  L1: cmp  small,cl     ; if small <= CL then
6:      jbe  L2           ; jump to L2
7:      mov  small,cl     ; else move CL to small
8:  L2:
```

Let's test this program, using the following register values: AL = 10, BL = 18, and CL = 10. Line 1 moves 10 to **small**. Line 3 causes a jump to L1 because **small** < BL. The JBE on line 6 is taken because **small** = CL. When line 8 is reached, **small** = 10, the lowest of the three register values.

Keyboard Buffer Input

Let's look at a complete program (BUFIN.ASM, Figure 7-3) that inputs characters from the keyboard and stores them in a buffer. We want to read one character at a time until either ENTER is pressed or the buffer is full. For the sake of brevity, the program does not filter out ASCII control characters (e.g., tab, backspace, carriage return).

We use EQU to define two constant symbols: **enter** and **bufsize** (lines 12–13). **Bufsize** appears in three other places: line 20, where it is moved to the loop

Figure 7-3 The Buffer Input program.

```
 1:  title Buffer Input Program                  (BUFIN.ASM)
 2:
 3:  ;
 4:  ;  This program inputs characters from the keyboard
 5:  ;  and places them in a memory buffer.
 6:  ;
 7:
 8:  dosseg
 9:  .model small
10:  .stack 100h
11:
12:  enter      equ  0Dh      ; ASCII code for ENTER key
13:  bufsize    equ  30h      ; size of text buffer
14:
15:  .code
16:  main proc
17:      mov   ax,@data           ; initialize DS
18:      mov   ds,ax
19:      mov   si,offset buffer   ; SI points to the buffer
20:      mov   cx,bufsize         ; CX is the loop counter
21:
22:  A1: mov   ah,1               ; input a character with echo
23:      int   21h                ; call DOS
24:      cmp   al,enter           ; character = ENTER?
25:      je    A2                 ; yes: quit
26:      mov   [si],al            ; no: place character in buffer,
27:      inc   si                 ; point to next buffer position,
28:      loop  A1                 ; get another character
29:
30:  A2: sub   charstyped,cl      ; store number of characters typed
31:      mov   ax,4C00h           ; return to DOS
32:      int   21h
33:  main endp
34:
35:  .data
36:  charstyped db  bufsize          ; size of text buffer
37:  buffer     db  bufsize dup(0)   ; text is stored here
38:
39:  end main
```

counter, and lines 36–37, where it defines storage for the keyboard input buffer. We usually define constants with symbolic names to avoid hard-coding numbers within a program. It is much easier to locate a single constant definition at the beginning of a program than it is to track down all places where the constant is used.

Line 36 defines a buffer where we store the number of characters typed at the keyboard, and line 37 stores the characters themselves:

```
charstyped db   bufsize            ; number of characters input
buffer     db   bufsize dup(0)     ; text is stored here
```

This is also the format used by some high-level languages, Turbo Pascal for instance, to store a character string. The byte at the head of the string is a binary number called a *string descriptor,* which indicates how many characters in the string are currently in use. The remaining positions in the string contain undefined values:

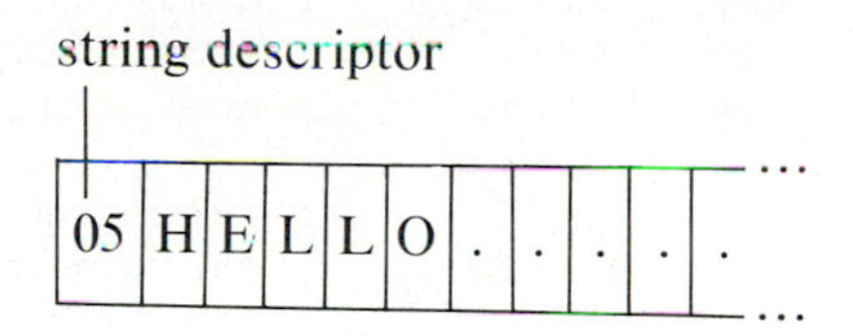

Line 19 (Figure 7-3) initializes SI to the beginning of the input buffer. Throughout the program, SI will be a pointer to the current buffer position as each character is typed. CX holds the buffer size and acts as a loop counter:

```
19:     mov   si,offset buffer
20:     mov   cx,bufsize
```

As each character is typed and stored in AL, we check for a certain value. If ENTER has been pressed, we jump to **A2**; otherwise, AL is placed in the buffer. Line 27 increments SI to make it point to the next buffer position. The LOOP instruction on line 28 jumps back and inputs another character as long as CX > 0.

When the loop ends, line 30 subtracts CL from **charstyped**, giving us the number of characters actually typed. This field was initialized to **bufsize** at assembly time. If 16 characters were typed, for example, CX would have been decremented to 20h:

30h − 20h = 10h

bufsize CL charstyped

```
 1:    title  Uppercase Display Program                (UPCASE.ASM)
 2:
 3:    ;
 4:    ;   This program converts each character input from
 5:    ;   the keyboard to uppercase. The program ends when
 6:    ;   ENTER is pressed.
 7:    ;
 8:
 9:    dosseg
10:    .model small
11:    .stack 100h
12:
13:    .code
14:    main proc
15:
16:    A1: mov   ah,8        ; input a character, no echo
17:        int   21h
18:        cmp   al,0Dh      ; ENTER pressed?
19:        je    A3          ; yes: quit
20:        cmp   al,'a'      ; character < 'a'?
21:        jb    A2          ; yes: display it
22:        cmp   al,'z'      ; character > 'z'?
23:        ja    A2          ; yes: display it
24:        sub   al,32       ; no: subtract 32 from ASCII code
25:
26:    A2: mov   ah,2        ; function: display character
27:        mov   dl,al       ; character is in DL
28:        int   21h         ; call DOS
29:        jmp   A1          ; get another character
30:
31:    A3: mov   ax,4C00h    ; return to DOS
32:        int   21h
33:
34:    main endp
35:    end main
```

Figure 7-4 The Uppercase Display program.

Uppercase Conversion

The UPCASE.ASM program (Figure 7-4) converts each character typed at the keyboard to uppercase. The program ends when ENTER is pressed. When you run the program, type a line of text containing a wide variety of letters and other characters. Only the lowercase letters will be modified.

The CMP, JB, and JA instructions are combined to create a conditional statement that checks to see if a character is lowercase. We can express the logic in pseudocode, using a single IF statement:

```
IF character < 'a' THEN
   display it
ELSE IF character > 'z' THEN
   display it
ELSE
   convert it to uppercase
ENDIF
```

This pseudocode translates into assembler as:

```
cmp  al,'a'     ; IF character < 'a' THEN
jb   display    ; display it
cmp  al,'z'     ; ELSE IF character > 'z' THEN
ja   display    ; display it
sub  al,32      ; ELSE convert it to uppercase
```

The ASCII codes for lowercase letters (*a–z*) are 97–122. Converting a character from lowercase to uppercase is as easy as subtracting 32 from its ASCII code. For example, the ASCII code for the letter *a* is 97, while the code for *A* is 65.

Text File Conversion

Many word processing programs set the highest bit of characters while formatting text files. These characters are difficult to read using DOS's TYPE command. We need to find a way to clear the high bit from each character. The CONVERT.ASM program (Figure 7-5) reads characters from standard input, screens out unwanted characters, and writes the resulting characters to standard output.

Figure 7-5 The File Conversion program.

```
 1:  title  File Conversion Program                    (CONVERT.ASM)
 2:
 3:  ;
 4:  ;  This program converts a text file to ASCII. It clears
 5:  ;  the high bit of each character and eliminates unwanted
 6:  ;  control characters.
 7:  ;
 8:
 9:  dosseg
10:  .model small
11:  .stack 100h
12:
13:  ; ------------- define ASCII codes -------------
14:  ctrlz      equ   1Ah     ; end-of-file marker
15:  cr         equ   0Dh     ; carriage return char
```

Figure 7-5 *(Cont.)*

```
16:   lf        equ   0Ah      ; linefeed character
17:   tab       equ   09h      ; tab character
18:   space     equ   20h      ; lowest printable code
19:
20:   .code
21:   main proc
22:
23:   A1: mov   ah,6            ; unfiltered console input
24:       mov   dl,0FFh         ; fetch waiting character
25:       int   21h             ; call DOS
26:       jz    A3              ; if zero, no characters waiting
27:
28:       ; Compare the character to several standard ASCII
29:       ; characters, and filter out unwanted values
30:
31:       cmp   al,ctrlz        ; end-of-file marker found?
32:       je    A3              ; yes: quit program
33:       and   al,01111111b    ; clear the high bit
34:       cmp   al,cr           ; carriage return?
35:       je    A2              ; yes: write it
36:       cmp   al,lf           ; line feed?
37:       je    A2              ; yes: write it
38:       cmp   al,tab          ; tab character?
39:       je    A2              ; yes: write it
40:       cmp   al,space        ; too low to be printable?
41:       jb    A1              ; yes: skip it
42:
43:       ; Use INT 21h, function 2 to display each character
44:
45:   A2: mov   dl,al           ; move character to DL
46:       mov   ah,2            ; function: display character
47:       int   21h             ; call DOS
48:       jmp   A1              ; get another character
49:
50:   A3: mov   ax,4C00h        ; return to DOS
51:       int   21h
52:   main endp
53:   end main
```

The program may be run from DOS using redirected input, with the results displayed on the screen:

```
convert < infile
```

The program can also read an input file and write the characters to another file, where FILE1 is the input file, and FILE2 is the output file:

```
convert < file1 > file2
```

The following operations are performed by the CONVERT program each time a character is input:

```
Input a character
If the character is an end-of-file marker,
  then quit
Clear high bit (AND with 01111111b)
If the character is a carriage return, line feed, or tab,
  then write it
If the ASCII code of the character is less than 20h,
  then skip it
Else
  write the character
```

Several constants are defined using EQU at the beginning of the program. In particular, the end of each line in a text file is marked by 2 bytes containing 0Dh (carriage return) and 0Ah (line feed); the end of a file is often marked with a byte containing 1Ah. The constant definitions appear in lines 14–18.

Lines 23–25 input a character using DOS function 6. This function does not filter out control characters, so we can read and manipulate each character ourselves.

Line 31 checks for the end-of-file marker (1Ah) character and jumps to the end of the program if it is found.

Line 33 clears the highest bit of the character in case it has been set.

Lines 34–39 check for selected control characters that we want to keep: carriage return, line feed, and tab.

If the ASCII code of the character is less than 20h (a space character), lines 40–41 skip over it without writing it to the output.

Largest and Smallest Array Values

The LGSMAL.ASM program (Figure 7-6) demonstrates a simple way to find the largest and smallest values in an array. The program could easily be modified to do the same for a character string.

The program uses the JGE (jump greater than or equal) instruction, because the array values are signed. The JAE (jump above or equal) instruction would not work correctly. For example, if we used JAE to compare −1 to 0, JAE would treat the numbers as unsigned and consider −1 (FFFFh) to be the larger number. JGE, on the other hand, would treat the numbers as signed and consider 0 to be greater than −1.

Line 16 sets DI to the offset of the array. Lines 17 and 18 initialize the variables **largest** and **smallest** to the first number in the array.

Lines 21–24 check the current array value to see if it is smaller than the variable **smallest**. If so, **smallest** is replaced. The same technique is used for the variable **largest** in lines 26–28. Line 30 points DI to the next array element, and the LOOP instruction on line 31 lets us continue scanning the rest of the array.

```
 1:  title  Largest and Smallest Signed Numbers (LGSMAL.ASM)
 2:
 3:  ;
 4:  ;   This program finds the largest and smallest
 5:  ;   signed numbers in an array of integers.
 6:  ;
 7:
 8:  dosseg
 9:  .model small
10:  .stack 100h
11:
12:  .code
13:  main      proc
14:      mov   ax,@data          ; initialize DS
15:      mov   ds,ax
16:      mov   di,offset array
17:      mov   ax,[di]
18:      mov   largest,ax        ; initialize largest
19:      mov   smallest,ax       ; initialize smallest
20:      mov   cx,6              ; loop counter
21:  A1: mov   ax,[di]           ; get array value
22:      cmp   ax,smallest       ; [DI] >= smallest?
23:      jge   A2                ; yes: skip
24:      mov   smallest,ax       ; no: move [DI] to smallest
25:
26:  A2: cmp   ax,largest        ; [DI] <= largest?
27:      jle   A3                ; yes: skip
28:      mov   largest,ax        ; no: move [DI] to largest
29:
30:  A3: add   di,2              ; point to next number
31:      loop  A1                ; repeat the loop until CX = 0
32:
33:      mov   ax,4C00h          ; return to DOS
34:      int   21h
35:  main endp
36:
37:  .data
38:  array     dw    -1,2000,-4000,32767,500,0
39:  largest   dw    ?
40:  smallest  dw    ?
41:
42:  end main
```

Figure 7-6 *Finding the largest and smallest signed numbers.*

Programming Tip: Choosing Variable Names

Variables should be clear and readable, although there is no set standard for choosing names. At the very least, you should make the naming style consistent within each program. The following names demonstrate various styles:

```
video_segment          cursor_position
buffer_size            search_string
input_file             integer_array
save_char              end_of_file_flag

bufsize      bytelist      fileprompt
intarray     stdmsgout     fptemp5w2

MAXLEN       COL           PROMPT
ERRCDE       OPNMSG        SAVE_CNT
```

In general, it is probably best to make the names all uppercase or all lowercase if you plan to link to a C language program. The C language recognizes differences in case; the names **Load_Buffer**, **LOAD_BUFFER**, and **load_buffer** would all be considered different.

PROCEDURES

With the introduction of procedures, we can now produce larger, better-constructed programs. If you write only short programs, readability is not a problem even when the programs contain a multitude of jumps and labels. As your programs become larger, however, you need to be able to break them up into separate procedures, or *subroutines*. The CPU uses the stack to keep track of the current program location so a program can find its way back from a procedure call. When a near procedure is called, the current value of IP is pushed on the stack. When the procedure returns, the value on the stack is popped back into IP. Before we embark on a more detailed discussion of the stack, let's review the way procedures are declared by the PROC directive.

PROC Directive

The PROC directive declares, or marks the beginning of, a procedure. The PROC directive has appeared in each of our sample programs so far, to identify the main procedure. From now on, we will use the PROC directive to declare all procedures in our programs. The following example shows a main procedure and a subroutine both declared in the code segment:

```
main proc
    .
    .
    .
main endp

subroutine proc
    .
    .
    .
subroutine endp
```

A procedure declaration should always be in the code segment. If necessary, one can alternate between code and data by prefacing each with the .CODE and .DATA directives, respectively. For example:

```
.code               ; begin code segment
main proc
    .
    .
    .
main endp
.data               ; begin data segment
value1  db  ?

.code               ; resume code segment
sub1 proc
    .
    .
    .
sub1 endp
```

The Stack

The stack, first introduced in Chapter 2, is simply a memory buffer or array to which we attach special meaning. Two registers address the stack: The SS (stack segment) register contains the base location of the stack; the SP (stack pointer) register contains the address of the top of the stack, where the last value was pushed.

A *push* operation places a new value on the stack and decrements the stack pointer by 2; thus the stack grows downward in memory as new values are pushed. A *pop* operation removes data from the stack by copying it into a register or memory operand, and increments the stack pointer by 2.

Each location on the stack is 2 bytes, so only 16-bit operands may be pushed or popped. In the course of a single program, the stack grows and shrinks constantly. Registers and operands are saved on the stack, and both subroutine calls and DOS use the stack. In general, a small program should reserve at least 256 bytes of stack space.

PUSH Instruction

The PUSH instruction subtracts 2 from SP and copies an operand onto the stack at the location pointed to by SP. The syntax is:

```
PUSH source
```

Source may be a 16-bit register or variable.

PUSH is useful for saving the contents of a register on the stack so that it may be restored later. As only a limited number of registers are available, their contents change often. We use the PUSH instruction to make sure we can retrieve old register values when we need them.

Figure 7-7 shows the stack before and after several values have been pushed on it. The PUSH instruction is efficient, so registers should be saved this way rather than by moving them to memory variables.

POP Instruction

The POP instruction copies the contents of the stack pointed to by SP into an operand and adds 2 to the stack pointer. The syntax is:

```
POP destination
```

Destination may be a 16-bit register (other than CS or IP), or a variable. POP can restore the contents of any 16-bit register or variable after it has been pushed.

Figure 7-7 Stack example 1

Stack example showing the stack after the values 1000h, 2000h, and 3000h have been pushed:

	Before		After	
SP→	0000		0000	
			1000	
			2000	
			3000	←SP

Saving and Restoring Registers. There are many occasions when a register must be reused. In the following example, DX and AX are assumed to have important values at the beginning that must be restored after the message is displayed:

```
    push    ax                   ; save AX
    push    dx                   ; save DX
    mov     ah,9                 ; function: display string
    mov     dx,offset message    ; DX points to the string
    int     21h                  ; call DOS
    pop     dx                   ; restore DX
    pop     ax                   ; restore AX
    .
    .
message  db  'This is a message.$'
```

Note the sequence of pushes and pops: The pops are always a mirror image of the pushes because the stack is a LIFO (last in, first out) structure. In other words, the last register to be pushed is the first register to be removed when the POP instruction occurs.

Subroutines. The most frequent uses of PUSH and POP are inside subroutines. When a program calls a subroutine, it has no way of knowing which registers the subroutine will use and cannot anticipate the ways in which the registers might be altered. It is the subroutine's responsibility to save and restore any registers it uses. We use the PUSH instruction at the beginning of the subroutine to save registers we plan to use. Before leaving the subroutine, we restore the same registers to their original values. PUSH and POP have little impact on the speed of a program if they are used with discretion.

CALL Instruction

The CALL instruction transfers control to a subroutine. Programmers trained in structured programming tend to divide their programs into short procedures. As much as possible, they try to write procedures that are tightly organized. The term *cohesive* applies to a procedure in which all statements are directed toward a single, specific task. Such a procedure is usually easier to debug than a long, noncohesive one. Cohesive procedures have another advantage: They can be reused many times, eliminating the need for duplicate code.

The syntax of the CALL instruction includes a version for calls to *near* procedures, which are in the current code segment, and *far* procedures, which are located in other segments:

```
CALL  near_procedure
CALL  far_procedure
```

When a *near procedure* is called, IP is incremented so that it points to the next instruction, and is then pushed on the stack. Then the offset of the called procedure is moved to IP.

When a *far procedure* is called, CS is pushed on the stack, followed by IP. Then the subroutine's segment address is moved to CS and its offset is moved to IP. A procedure may also be located in another program module. In this case, it is called an *external* procedure.

Examples of the CALL instruction are shown here:

```
call  writestr
call  near ptr sub1    ; procedure in the same segment
call  far ptr sub2     ; procedure in another segment
```

If the NEAR PTR or FAR PTR operators are not used in a CALL instruction, MASM usually assumes the procedure to be *near* (in the current segment). For this reason, a call to a *far* procedure should be labeled as such.

RET Instruction

The RET instruction is placed at the end of a procedure to return the CPU to the calling location. This is identical to the RETURN statement used in high-level languages. If the calling location is in the same segment, RET pops the stack into IP and increments SP. This causes the program to continue execution at the new address in IP. Figure 7-8, Example 1, shows a program excerpt that calls a *near* procedure.

When a procedure is called from a separate segment, MASM translates the RET instruction into the Intel RETF (return far) instruction. This pops the stack

Figure 7-8 Calling near and far procedures.

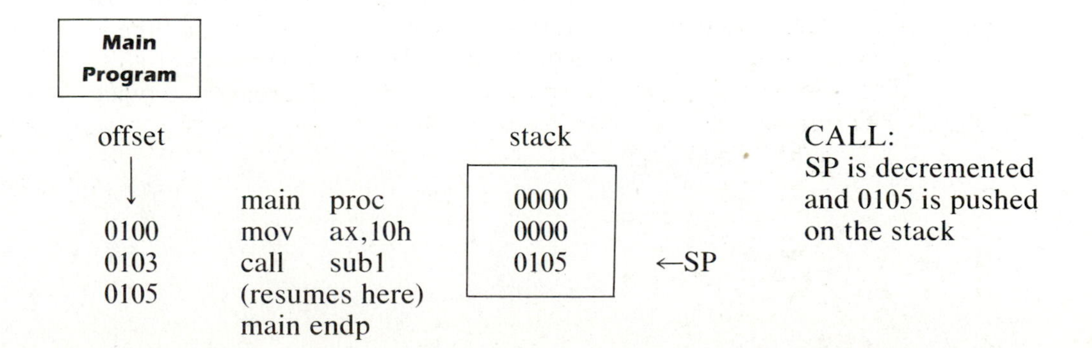

Figure 7-8 *(Cont.)*

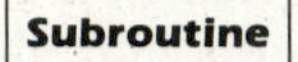

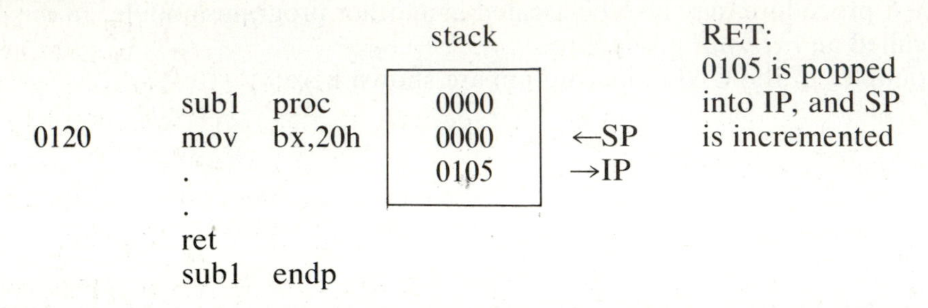

Example 2: Calling a FAR Procedure

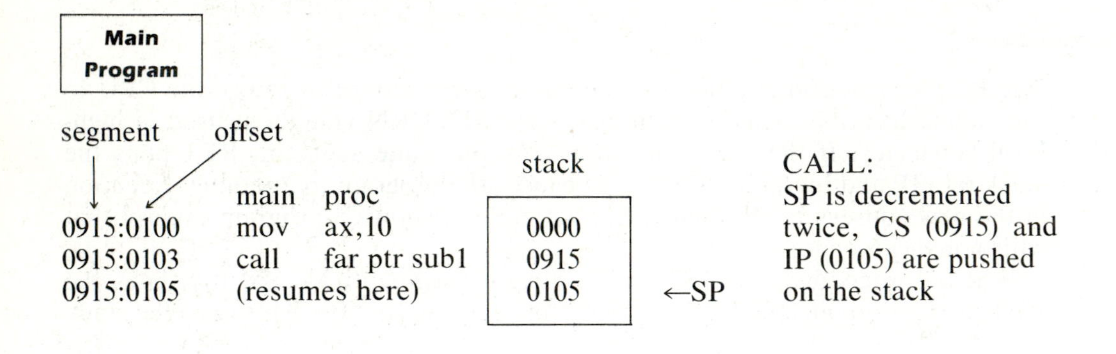

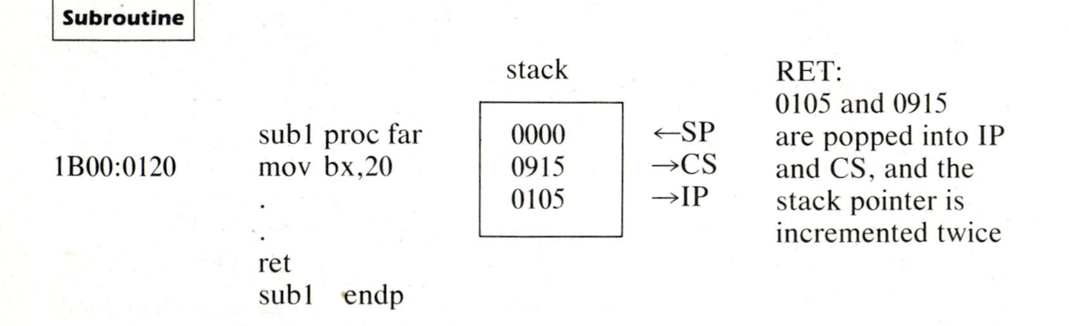

into IP, increments SP, pops the stack into CS, and increments SP. In Example 2 (Figure 7-8), the SUB1 procedure has a *far* attribute and is assumed to be in a different segment than the MAIN procedure.

Version 5.0 of MASM introduced the RETN and RETF instructions, which may be used to explicitly return from a near or far procedure, respectively. Using RETN, for example, one can call a label in the same segment that was not declared by the PROC and ENDP directives. At the same time, one must remember to use the appropriate return instruction (RETN or RETF). You will probably rely more on near and far procedure declarations than on RETN and RETF instructions.

Example Using CLRSCR and DISPLAY

The DISPLAY.ASM program (Figure 7-9) demonstrates a practical use for procedure calls in a short program. The two procedures are:

CLRSCR	Clear the screen, locate cursor at 1,1
DISPLAY	Display a string pointed to by DS:DX

Figure 7-9 The DISPLAY program.

```
 1:  title  CLRSCR and DISPLAY Procedures      (DISPLAY.ASM)
 2:
 3:  ;
 4:  ;   This program clears the screen and
 5:  ;   displays two strings using INT 21h.
 6:  ;
 7:
 8:  dosseg
 9:  .model small
10:  .stack 100h
11:
12:  .code
13:  main proc
14:      mov   ax,@data            ; initialize DS
15:      mov   ds,ax
16:      call  clrscr              ; clear the screen
17:      mov   dx,offset message1  ; display first string
18:      call  display
19:      mov   dx,offset message2  ; display second string
20:      call  display
21:      mov   ax,4C00h            ; return to DOS
22:      int   21h
23:  main endp
24:
25:  ; Clear the screen and move the cursor to row 0,
26:  ; column 0
27:
28:  clrscr proc
```

Figure 7-9 *(Cont.)*

```
29:         push  ax              ; save registers
30:         push  bx
31:         push  cx
32:         push  dx
33:         mov   ax,0600h        ; scroll entire window up
34:         mov   cx,0            ; upper left: 0, 0
35:         mov   dx,184Fh        ; lower right: 24,79
36:         mov   bh,7            ; use normal attribute
37:         int   10h             ; call BIOS
38:         mov   ah,2            ; set cursor position
39:         mov   dx,0            ; row 0, column 0
40:         mov   bh,0            ; video page 0
41:         int   10h             ; call BIOS
42:         pop   dx              ; restore registers
43:         pop   cx
44:         pop   bx
45:         pop   ax
46:         ret
47:     clrscr endp
48:
49:     ; Display a string that is pointed to by DX and terminated
50:     ; by the $ character
51:
52:     display proc
53:         push  ax
54:         mov   ah,9            ; function: display a string
55:         int   21h             ; call DOS
56:         pop   ax
57:         ret
58:     display endp
59:
60:     .data
61:     message1  db  'This is on line one, and ',0Dh,0Ah,'$'
62:     message2  db  'this message is on line two.',0Dh,0Ah,'$'
63:
64:     end   main
```

The CLRSCR procedure is taken directly from examples in Chapter 5 that dealt with video manipulation using INT 10h. Because of its length, it should not be coded more than once in a program. Instead, a single copy of the procedure is placed in the code segment and can be called as many times as desired. No values need be passed to CLRSCR.

The DISPLAY procedure assumes that DS contains the address of the data segment and that DX contains the offset of a string. In this way, the procedure is generic and may be used by nearly any program.

It is the calling program's responsibility to set DS and DX to their correct values before calling DISPLAY. To show how easily this procedure may be reused, we have called it twice in the sample program (lines 18 and 20). Each time we call DISPLAY, the offset of a different string is moved to DX.

Here is a general pattern for all our programs: The initial part of the program contains the main procedure, consisting mainly of CALL statements. In keeping with structured programming principles, all control will originate from and return to the main procedure.

The INCLUDE Directive. As program listings grow longer with the inclusion of separate procedures, one can place each procedure in an *include* file. This is a file containing text which is copied into the main ASM program as it is being assembled. Longer programs, in particular, are easier to edit if each include file is less than 100 lines long. The same include file may also be used by several programs. If an include file is modified, all programs using it must be assembled and linked again.

A file containing a procedure should be included after the main procedure and before the end of the code segment. The DISPLAY2 program uses two include files, shown in Figure 7-10.

Figure 7-10 The Display program, using the INCLUDE directive.

```
 1:  title  Display Program Using INCLUDE      (DISPLAY2.ASM)
 2:
 3:  dosseg
 4:  .model small
 5:  .stack 100h
 6:
 7:  .code
 8:  main proc
 9:      mov   ax,@data              ; initialize DS
10:      mov   ds,ax
11:      call  clrscr                ; clear the screen
12:      mov   dx,offset message1    ; display string
13:      call  display
14:      mov   dx,offset message2    ; display string
15:      call  display
16:      mov   ax,4C00h              ; return to DOS
17:      int   21h
18:  main endp
19:
20:  include   display.inc           ; other procedures
21:  include   clrscr.inc
22:
23:  .data
24:  message1  db  'This is on line one, and ',0Dh,0Ah,'$'
25:  message2  db  'this message is on line two.',0Dh,0Ah,'$'
26:
27:  end main
```

Programming Tip: Labels and Procedure Names

You may have noticed that some programs shown in this chapter use short label names, such as A1, A2, B3, and D4. Many programmers prefer to number their labels consecutively within each procedure, making them easy to locate.

One effective technique is to assign a different letter of the alphabet to each procedure. Thus, the first procedure will have labels beginning with the letter A (A1, A2, A3 . . .), the second procedure will use the letter B (B1, B2, B3 . . .), and so on. Using short label names also helps to differentiate them from the longer names used for procedures and variables.

Procedure names are easy to understand when they contain a verb and an object, at the very least. You can make liberal use of the underline character between words. You will probably find that comments next to procedure calls are unnecessary if the names are chosen carefully. Examples are:

```
load_directory        display_buffer
open_file             calculate_sum
read_sector           convert_to_binary
```

You may even wish to add an adjective to a procedure name, as in the following examples:

```
read_next_sector
display_all_lines
find_next_entry
```

HIGH-LEVEL LOGIC STRUCTURES

In IBM-PC assembly language there are no IF, ELSE, or WHILE statements. This is not a severe limitation, as several instructions can be combined to create any logical structure. In fact, you can optimize logic structures to make them execute much more efficiently than they would in a high-level language. The logic structures shown in this chapter are universal to all structured languages.

IF Statement

An IF statement comparing two values is often followed by a list of statements to be performed when the condition is true. In the following example, **op1** and **op2** might be immediate operands, registers, or memory operands:

```
IF (op1 = op2) THEN
  <statement1>
  <statement2>
ENDIF
```

A high-level language compiler would translate the preceding IF statement into a *compare* followed by one or more *conditional jump* instructions. The following is a sample of compiled code:

```
      cmp   op1, op2         ; IF op1 = op2 THEN
      je    next_label       ;   jump to next_label
                             ; ELSE
      jmp   end_if           ;   jump to end_if
next_label:                  ; ENDIF
      <statement1>           ; perform <statement1>
      <statement2>           ; perform <statement2>
end_if:
```

In assembly language, we can eliminate one of the jumps by reversing the comparison for *equal* to *not equal*:

```
      cmp   op1, op2         ; IF op1 ≠ op2 THEN
      jne   next_label       ;   jump to next_label
                             ; ELSE
        <statement1>         ;   <statement1>
        <statement2>         ;   <statement2>
  next_label:                ; ENDIF
```

Compound IF with the OR Operator. In many instances, assembly language is well suited to the evaluation of multiple conditions. Consider the following pseudocode, where any one of four conditions results in the execution of **statement1**:

```
IF  (AL > op1)
  OR  (AL >= op2)
  OR  (AL = op3)
  OR  (AL < op4) THEN
    <statement1>
ENDIF
```

This can be easily translated into assembly language if we remember that a false condition always falls through to the next statement. The following *linear nested-IF* structure chains through the series of conditions:

```
cmp   al,op1     ; IF AL > op1 THEN
jg    L1         ;   jump to L1
cmp   al,op2     ; ELSE IF AL >= op2 THEN
```

```
          jge  L1           ;   jump to L1
          cmp  al,op3       ; ELSE IF AL = op3 THEN
          je   L1           ;   jump to L1
          cmp  al,op4       ; ELSE IF AL < op4 THEN
          jl   L1           ;   jump to L1
          jmp  L2           ; ELSE jump to L2
      L1: <statement1>      ; ENDIF
      L2:
```

Compound IF with the AND Operator. The AND operator in high-level languages ties multiple conditions together. In the following pseudocode, all four conditions must be true in order for **statement1** to be executed:

```
IF  (AL > op1)
  AND  (AL >= op2)
  AND  (AL = op3)
  AND  (AL < op4) THEN
    <statement1>
ENDIF
```

The easiest way to translate this into assembly language is to reverse the conditions and jump to an exit label when any condition is true. The condition (AL > op1), for example, becomes NOT (AL > op1). If all of the conditional tests fail, control passes to **statement1**:

```
    cmp   al,op1        ; IF NOT (AL > op1) THEN
    jng   next_label    ;   jump to next_label
    cmp   al,op2        ; ELSE IF NOT (AL >= op2) THEN
    jnge  next_label    ;   jump to next_label
    cmp   al,op3        ; ELSE IF NOT (AL = op3) THEN
    jne   next_label    ;   jump to next_label
    cmp   al,op4        ; ELSE IF NOT (AL < op4) THEN
    jnl   next_label    ;   jump to next_label
                        ; ELSE
    <statement1>        ;   <statement1>  ; (no condition was true)
    .                   ; ENDIF
    .
next_label:             ; reached if any condition is true
```

WHILE Structure

The WHILE structure tests a condition first before performing a block of statements. As long as the test remains true, the statements are repeated:

```
DO WHILE (op1 < op2)
  <statement1>
  <statement2>
ENDDO
```

In assembly language, we would reverse the condition and jump to the label **enddo** when the condition becomes true:

```
do_while:
   cmp  op1,op2     ; IF NOT (op1 >= op2) THEN
   jnl  enddo       ;   jump to enddo
                    ; ELSE
   <statement1>     ;   <statement1>
   <statement2>     ;   <statement2>
   jmp do_while     ;   jump to do_while
enddo:
```

IF Statement Nested Inside a WHILE. High-level structured languages are particularly good at representing nested control structures. In the following example, an IF statement is nested inside a WHILE loop:

```
DO WHILE  (op1 < op2)
  <statement1>
  IF (op2 = op3) THEN
    <statement2>
    <statement3>
  ELSE
    <statement4>
  ENDIF
ENDDO
```

The assembly language version of the preceding structure is still practical, although harder to follow because of the number of labels involved. The following rendition of the WHILE loop follows the original pseudocode as closely as possible:

Assembly Code	**Pseudocode**
while:	
cmp op1,op2	DO WHILE (op < op2)
jnl L3	
<statement1>	<statement1>
cmp op2,op3	IF op2 = op3 THEN
jne L1	
<statement2>	<statement2>
<statement3>	<statement3>
jmp L2	
L1:	ELSE
<statement4>	<statement4>
L2: jmp while	ENDIF
L3:	ENDDO

Short label names (L1, L2, and L3) are used here to make the example read as clearly as possible; you may still find descriptive names more to your liking.

Be sure to apply the principle of *one entry and one exit* when designing a complex structure such as this. In our example, the label **while** is the entry point, and **L3** is the exit point.

REPEAT . . . UNTIL Structure

A REPEAT . . . UNTIL structure executes one or more statements within a block at least once and performs a test at the bottom of the loop. In the following example, two conditions are tested before the loop repeats:

```
REPEAT
  <statement1>
  <statement2>
  <statement3>
UNTIL (op1 = op2) OR (op1 > op3)
```

It might be interesting to look at the assembly code generated for this REPEAT loop by a high-level language compiler. In particular, the multiple condition generates a great deal of code. The result of the first test is pushed on the stack; after the second test, it is popped from the stack and ORed with the result of the second test:

```
 1:  repeat:
 2:         <statement1>
 3:         <statement2>
 4:         <statement3>
 5:
 6:  test1: mov  ax,0        ; assume result is false
 7:         cmp  op1,op2
 8:         jne  test2       ; IF op1 = op2 THEN
 9:         mov  ax,0FFh     ;   set result to true
10:                          ; ENDIF
11:  test2: push ax          ; save result of first test
12:         mov  ax,0        ; assume result is false
13:         cmp  op1,op3
14:         jng  test3       ; IF op1 > op3 THEN
15:         mov  ax,0FFh     ;   set result to true
16:                          ; ENDIF
17:  test3: pop  dx          ; retrieve first result
18:         or   dx,ax       ; OR with the second result
19:         jz   endup       ; exit if neither is true
20:         jmp  repeat      ; otherwise, jump to repeat
21:  endup:
```

The code generated by this compiler is not overly efficient, as it generates 13 instructions just for the REPEAT loop. It insists on evaluating both conditions even if the first returns *true* (some compilers can optimize their code generation and prevent this from happening).

If we code the same loop in assembly language, we can easily improve its performance. The best strategy is to fall through from one test to another if the first one fails. If the first test succeeds, we never reach the second test:

```
 1:   repeat:
 2:      <statement1>
 3:      <statement2>
 4:      <statement3>
 5:   test1:
 6:      cmp  op1,op2    ; IF op1 = op2 THEN
 7:      je   endup      ;   exit the loop
 8:   test2:             ; ELSE
 9:      cmp  op1,op3    ;   IF op1 NOT > op3 THEN
10:      jng   repeat    ;     repeat the loop
11:   endup:             ; ENDIF
```

Note that we have trimmed the original 13 instructions down to only 4. Line 6 performs the first comparison: If ZF = 1, line 7 exits the loop; otherwise, we fall through to line 9 and perform the second test. If the second test fails, control passes to line 11 and the loop ends.

This is precisely the type of optimization that must be incorporated into high-performance software. You can write an entire program in a high-level language, disassemble the code, and look for sluggish sections that need to be rewritten in assembly language. Many compilers, in fact, will automatically generate an assembly language source listing of your compiled program, making the whole job easier.

CASE Structure

The CASE structure allows a multiway branch by comparing a single value to a list of values. Using Pascal as an example, we can select a course of action based on the value of the variable **input**:

```
CASE input OF
 'A' : Process_A;
 'B' : Process_B;
 'C' : Process_C;
 'D' : Process_D
END;
```

In assembly language we might process each case with a separate comparison, followed by a jump to a label:

```
mov  al,input
cmp  al,'A'
je   Process_A
cmp  al,'B'
je   Process_B
cmp  al,'C'
je   Process_C
cmp  al,'D'
je   Process_D
```

If you would rather call a procedure when each individual case is selected, the CALL statement may be inserted, followed by a jump to the final label (**L4**) at the end of the case structure:

```
    mov   al,input          ; CASE al OF
    cmp   al,'A'            ; 'A':
    jne   L1
    call  Process_A         ;       call Process_A
    jmp   L4                ;       jump to L4
L1: cmp   al,'B'            ; 'B':
    jne   L2
    call  Process_B         ;       call Process_B
    jmp   L4                ;       jump to L4
L2: cmp   al,'C'            ; 'C':
    jne   L3
    call  Process_C         ;       call Process_C
    jmp   L4                ;       jump to L4
L3: cmp   al,'D'            ; 'D':
    jne   L4
    call  Process_D         ;       call Process_D
L4:                         ; END
```

Offset Table

A more efficient way to process a CASE structure is to create an *offset table* containing the offsets of labels or procedures. MASM can calculate a label's offset and place it in a variable.

An offset table is most effective when a large number of comparisons must be made. The following statements define a table containing the lookup values and addresses of procedures we want to call:

```
casetable db  'A'         ; lookup value
          dw  process_A   ; address of procedure
          db  'B'
          dw  process_B
          db  'C'
          dw  Process_C
          db  'D'
          dw  Process_D
```

Let's assume that PROCESS_A, PROCESS_B, PROCESS_C, and PROCESS_D are located at addresses 0120h, 0130h, 0140h, and 0150h, respectively. The table would be arranged in memory as follows:

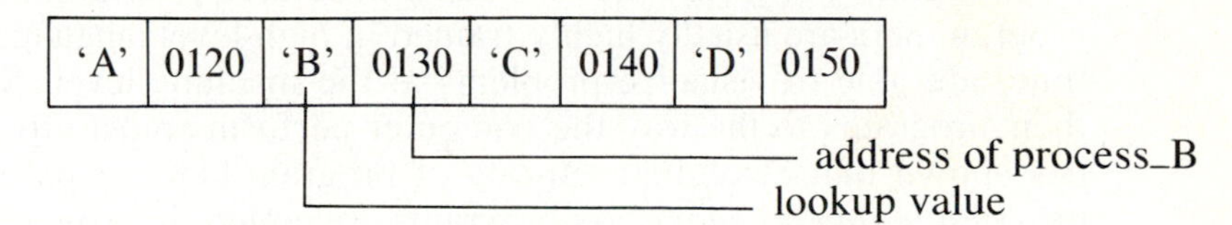

AL is compared to each entry in the table, using a loop. The first match found in the table causes a call to the procedure offset stored immediately after the lookup value:

```
        mov   al,input              ; value to be found
        mov   bx,offset casetable   ; point BX to the table
        mov   cx,4                  ; number of table entries

    L1: cmp   al,[bx]               ; match found?
        jne   L2                    ; no: continue
        call  word ptr [bx+1]       ; yes: call the procedure
        jmp   L3                    ; exit search
    L2: add   bx,3                  ; point BX to next entry
        loop  L1                    ; repeat until CX = 0
    L3:
```

This method involves some initial overhead, but it helps make the compiled program more efficient. A table can handle a large number of comparisons, and it may be more easily modified than a long series of compare, jump, and CALL instructions. Most importantly, an offset table may be modified at runtime, whereas a CASE statement is fixed at assembly time.

POINTS TO REMEMBER

A *near* procedure is located in the same segment as the point from which it is called. A *far* procedure is located in a different segment.

Whenever possible, structure your code carefully. Use procedure calls to simplify complex logic structures. Save and restore registers inside subroutines.

Take advantage of assembly language's natural strengths: its ability to initialize variables at assembly time, its automatic address calculations, and the control it provides over the design of logic structures. Assembly language allows one to make decisions that will optimize program speed and size.

Do not overdo optimization, however, if it makes your programs unintelligible. Any particularly tricky techniques you use should be carefully documented so that another programmer can understand exactly what you are doing.

Logic Structures. From our discussion on high-level logic structures, it is evident that any structure may be reproduced in assembly language. At the same time, it would be a mistake to force an assembly program into one of these standard formats simply to justify the result as a structured program. Successful assembly programmers are usually highly trained in high-level languages and, at the same time, are able to visualize problems at the machine level. Such persons adapt their programs to the way the computer performs most efficiently. Experience has shown that careful structuring of program logic helps to produce a better program *in any language*. As programs are coded, improvements may be added that take advantage of assembly language's natural strengths.

Many programmers view assembly language as being terminally unstructured. The constant use of jumps in assembly language may appear at first to be a throwback to past styles of unstructured "spaghetti" programming, but this may be misleading. If anything, an assembly language program must be highly structured in order to be successful. This is because assembly language imposes few restraints, making it necessary for you to impose your own in order to produce structured, bug-free, readable code. As you've probably guessed, a tremendous amount of self-discipline and attention to detail are required in assembly language programming.

REVIEW QUESTIONS

1. Explain the difference between the JMP and JZ instructions.

2. Which CPU flags are used in unsigned comparisons?

3. Which CPU flags are used in signed comparisons?

4. Which conditional jump is based on the contents of a general-purpose register?

5. What is the difference between the JA and JNBE instructions?

6. What is the difference between the JB and JL instructions?

7. Can a conditional jump instruction jump to a label anywhere in the same segment?

8. For a JB instruction to be executed, which flag must be set?

9. Assume that a CMP instruction has just compared two operands. For each of the conditional jump instructions shown here, the contents of four flags are shown. Indicate in the right column whether or not the jump would be taken. (You may want to refer to Figures 7-1 and 7-2.) The first exercise has been done for you:

	Instruction	Over-flow	Sign	Zero	Carry	Jump Taken?
a.	JNZ	0	0	1	0	No
b.	JA	1	0	1	0	
c.	JNB	1	0	1	0	
d.	JBE	0	0	1	0	
e.	JGE	1	1	0	0	
f.	JNLE	0	1	0	1	
g.	JNS	0	0	1	0	
h.	JNG	1	1	0	1	
i.	JE	1	0	1	0	
j.	JNAE	1	0	1	0	

10. After the following instructions are executed, what will be the values of AL and BL?

```
        mov   al,val1
        mov   bl,val2
        and   ax,0FB6h
        cmp   al,bl
        ja    label1
        mov   al,bl
        jmp   exit
label1:
        mov   bl,al
exit:

val1    db    6Bh
val2    db    3Fh
```

11. After the following instructions are executed, what will be the values of AL and BL?

```
        mov   al,val2
        mov   bl,val1
        or    bl,0Fh
        sub   al,bl
        jb    label1
        mov   al,1
        jmp   exit
label1:
        mov   bl,1
exit:

val1    db    6Bh
val2    db    3Fh
```

12. After the following instructions are executed, what will be the values of AL and BL?

```
          mov   al,val2
          mov   bl,val1
          xor   bl,0FFh
          test  al,3
          jz    label1
          mov   al,1
          jmp   exit
label1:
          mov   bl,1
exit:

val1  db  35h
val2  db  3Fh
```

13. After the following instructions are executed, what will be the values of CX, DX, and SI?

```
        mov   si,0
        mov   cx,val1
        mov   dx,val2
        and   cx,0FFh
        not   dx
        xchg  dx,val1
again:
        inc   si
        dec   dx
        loop  again

val1  dw  026Ah
val2  dw  3FD9h
```

14. After the following instructions are executed, what will be the values of CX, DX, SI, and **val2**? (Assume that **val1** is located at address 0006.)

```
          mov    si,offset val1
          mov    cx,[si]
          add    si,2
          mov    dx,[si]
          xchg   dx,val1
          and    dx,0FF00h
again:
          dec    word ptr [si]
          dec    dx
          cmp    dx,01FFh
          loopz  again

val1  dw  026Ah
val2  dw  3FD9h
```

PROGRAMMING EXERCISES

Exercise 1 Numeric Digit Test

Input a character from the keyboard into AL. Write a series of comparison and jump instructions to find out if AL contains a numeric digit. If it does, display it on the console using INT 21h; otherwise, jump to the label **exit**.

Exercise 2 Alphabetic Input

Write a short program to input only letters (*A–Z, a–z*) from the keyboard. Any other characters should be rejected without being echoed on the screen. Continue the input until ENTER is pressed.

Exercise 3 Decimal Number Input

Write a program to input a decimal number (up to 18 digits) from the keyboard. Any characters other than digits and a single decimal point should be rejected without being echoed on the screen. Quit when ENTER is pressed.

Exercise 4 Decimal Number Input with Leading Sign

Expand the program from Exercise 3 to include a single leading plus (+) or minus (−) sign. Store each character in a buffer, and redisplay the buffer at the end of the program.

Exercise 5 Reverse an Array

Write a program that reverses an array of 30 16-bit integers. The array should be reversed in place, without being copied to another array. Run the program using a debugger, and dump the array to the printer before and after it has been reversed.

Exercise 6 Display a String in Reverse

Write a program that inputs a string of up to 50 characters from the console and then displays the string in reverse order. Sample input:

```
This string was typed at the keyboard.
```

Output:

```
.draobyek eht ta depyt saw gnirts sihT
```

Exercise 7 Reverse the Words in a String

Write a program that inputs any sentence (up to 80 characters) from the console. Reverse the words in the sentence, but not the characters in each word. Sample input:

```
The quick brown fox jumped over the lazy dog's back.
```

Output:

```
back. dog's lazy the over jumped fox brown quick The
```

Exercise 8 Count the Words in a Text Line

Write a program that reads a line of text from standard input and counts the numbers of words and characters entered.

Exercise 9 Customer Account Program

Write a program with separate procedures to do the following:

- Clear the screen and display an input form with the following prompts:

```
              ACCOUNT INPUT SCREEN

NAME: ...............        ACCT NUM: .....
PREVIOUS BALANCE: ........
PAYMENTS: ........
CREDITS: ........
```

- Position the cursor on the first input field (NAME), and let the user type a name. When ENTER is pressed, move the cursor to the next field (ACCT NUM).
- As the user enters data, store each character in an input buffer for the field.
- When ENTER is pressed on the last field, end the input screen.

Exercise 10 Customer Account Program, Version 2

Add the following features to the program in Exercise 9:

- For the PREVIOUS BALANCE, PAYMENTS, and CREDITS fields, let the user type only numbers. The digits 0–9 may be typed in any position, but a plus or minus sign may be typed only in the first position. Only one decimal point may be typed. If any invalid characters are typed, reject them and sound a beep by writing ASCII character 7 to standard output.
- When the input screen ends, clear the screen and redisplay the contents of all fields to verify that all inputs worked correctly.

Exercise 11 Customer Account Program, Version 3

Add the following features to the program in Exercise 10:

- Numeric fields may contain a maximum of 8 digits.
- Display the field names in reverse video, using INT 10h.
- Allow the user to use the backspace key to edit field entries. Your pointer to the input buffer must back up one position so that the buffer will accurately reflect the contents of the field on the screen.
- The characters in the NAME field should be automatically converted to uppercase.

Exercise 12 Hard Returns to Soft Returns

Some word processing programs place a 2-character sequence (0Dh,0Ah) at the end of each line of text. Other programs (e.g. WordStar) use a different marker for these lines, called a *soft return* (8Dh,0Ah).

Write a program to convert all 0Dh characters to 8Dh, *except* when 0Dh is immediately preceded by 0Ah (this identifies the end of a paragraph). The following pseudocode may be of help:

```
prevchar := 0
input (ch)
DO WHILE NOT end of file
  IF (ch = 0Dh) and (prevchar ≠ 0Ah) THEN
     ch := 8Dh
  ENDIF
  write (ch)
  prevchar := ch
  input (ch)
ENDDO
```

Use INT 21h to input and output each character, and have DOS redirect the input and output. If the program is called SOFTRET.EXE, we can type

```
SOFTRET < infile > wsfile
```

which will copy **infile** to **wsfile** and perform the conversion.

Exercise 13 Student Registration Program

Assume that 10 records from a student registration file have been read and placed in a memory area called **buffer**. Each record has the following format:

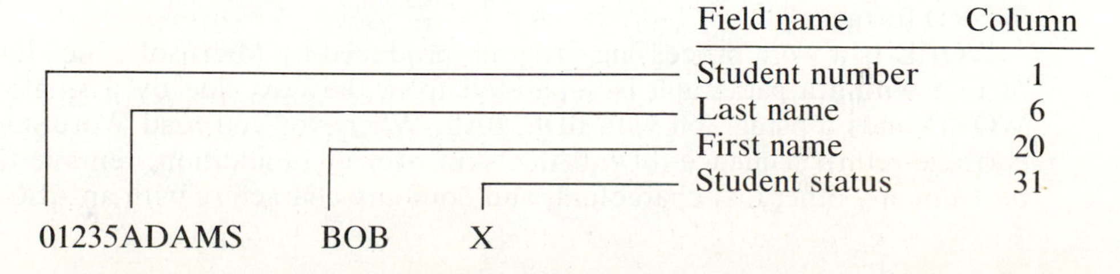

The Student status field is bit mapped, so that each bit corresponds to a different value:

Bit	Meaning
0	Degree seeking (1 = yes, 0 = no)
1	State resident (1 = yes, 0 = no)
2	Taken basic skills test (1 = yes, 0 = no)
3	Taken SAT test (1 = yes, 0 = no)
4	Probation (1 = yes, 0 = no)
5	Academic warning (1 = yes, 0 = no)
6	Dean's List (1 = yes, 0 = no)
7	Transfer student (1 = yes, 0 = no)

A great deal of information may be encoded in a single byte, as long as each field can be reduced to a value of 1 or 0. For each record, display the name, student number, and all status fields that are equal to "yes."

After displaying all records, use the TEST and CMP instructions to look for and display the names of any students who have taken the basic skills test, but not the SAT test.

Use the following data, or make up your own:

```
buffer  db '03343BROWN          BARRY      ',01101100b
        db '03566CARSON         CARMEN     ',11001010b
        db '16487CHONG          WAN FUN    ',11010011b
        db '32424FUKUNAGA       FRED       ',01001101b
        db '33648JEFFERSON      FRANKLIN   ',11000101b
        db '40001O'MALLEY       HENRY      ',00010110b
        db '40221PEARSON        MARY       ',11001001b
        db '45002PEREIRA        PETER      ',01001010b
        db '50000WRIGHT         WALTER     ',10101010b
        db '60200ZEDMORE        ZEKE       ',01001111b
```

Exercise 14 WordStar to WORD Format

Write a program that will convert a file produced by WordStar to Microsoft WORD format.

WORD is a word processing program produced by Microsoft, Inc. Each line of text within a paragraph is separated from the next line by a single space. WORD ends a paragraph with 0Dh, 0Ah. Whenever you read WordStar's soft carriage-return sequence (8Dh,0Ah), skip over it. In addition, remove the high bit from any other text characters, and omit any characters with an ASCII code of less than 32 (aside from 0Dh, 0Ah, and 09h). You may want to use the following pseudocode as a guide:

```
BEGIN
  REPEAT
    read ch
    IF (ch = 8Dh) THEN              ( soft return )
      read ch                       ( skip linefeed )
    ELSE
      and ch,7Fh                    ( clear high bit )
      IF (ch > 1Fh) OR
        (ch in [0Dh, 0Ah, 09h]) THEN
        write ch
      ENDIF
    ENDIF
  UNTIL (ch = 1Ah)                  ( end of file )
END
```

Use the DOS redirection symbols for input and output.

Exercise 15 **Bubble Sort Program**

Write a program that sorts a randomly ordered list of fifty 16-bit integers. The sort is to take place in memory. Use a debugger to dump the numbers to the printer before and after the sort.

ANSWERS TO REVIEW QUESTIONS

1. JMP is an unconditional jump instruction, because the jump is always taken. JZ is a conditional jump, because the jump is taken only if the Zero flag is set.

2. Zero and Carry.

3. Zero, Sign, and Overflow.

4. JCXZ.

5. Except for the mnemonic, they are the same.

6. JB is used for unsigned operands, and JL is used for signed operands.

7. No, it must use a *short* jump, within −128 to +127 bytes from the current location.

8. The Carry flag.

9. a. No
   b. No
   c. Yes
   d. Yes
   e. Yes
   f. No
   g. Yes
   h. No
   i. Yes
   j. Yes

10. AL = 3Fh, BL = 3Fh

11. AL = D0h, BL = 01h

12. AL = 01h, BL = CAh

13 CX = 0000h, DX = 0200h, SI = 006Ah

14. CX = 0268h, DX = 01FEh, SI = 0008h, val2 = 3FD7h

8

Arithmetic

Arithmetic in assembly language can be quite simple when only integers are involved, and quite complicated when floating-point arithmetic is attempted. In this chapter we will limit ourselves to integer arithemtic, showing the numerous enhancements available in IBM-PC assembly language.

Shift and rotate instructions are covered first, because they are strongly related to multiplication and division. Shifts and rotates are not generally available in high-level languages, so assembly language may be an absolute necessity in certain types of applications.

We will cover addition, subtraction, multiplication, and division instructions, all of which are designed to work on 8- or 16-bit operands.

Last of all, we will spend some time on arithmetic, using ASCII numbers (one digit per byte) and packed decimal (BCD) arithmetic. This chapter covers only the basic instructions and techniques in an effort to expose the reader to areas that may be of interest for later study.

SHL	Shift left
SHR	Shift right
SAL	Shift arithmetic left
SAR	Shift arithmetic right
ROL	Rotate left
ROR	Rotate right
RCL	Rotate carry left
RCR	Rotate carry right

(All instructions affect the Overflow and Carry flags)

Figure 8-1 Shift and rotate instructions.

SHIFT AND ROTATE INSTRUCTIONS

The shift and rotate instructions provide a way to move bits around in an operand. These instructions are listed in Figure 8-1. They are standard in assembly language but are rarely available in high-level languages.

SHL Instruction

The SHL (shift left) instruction shifts each bit in a destination operand to the left, filling the lowest bit with 0. The highest bit is moved to the Carry flag, and the bit that was in the Carry flag is lost:

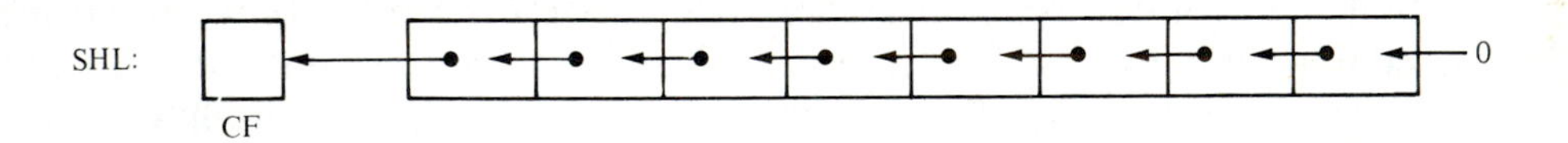

There are two formats for SHL. The first shifts a register or memory operand 1 bit to the left. The second uses a *shift count* in the CL register to determine how many times the destination operand is to be shifted:

```
SHL   dest,1
SHL   dest,CL
```

The CL register is not changed when SHL uses it as a shift counter. Examples using both register and memory operands are as follows:

```
shl  bl,1              ; shift BL 1 bit to the left
shl  wordval,1         ; 16-bit direct memory operand
shl  byte ptr[si],1    ; 8-bit indirect memory operand
mov  cl,4              ; place shift count in CL
shl  al,cl             ; shift AL left 4 bits
```

In the following example, BL is shifted once to the left. The highest bit is copied into the Carry flag, and the lowest bit position is filled with a 0:

```
mov  bl,8Fh       ; BL = 10001111b
shl  bl,1         ; BL = 00011110b, CF = 1
```

The following instructions will shift DX left 3 bits:

```
mov  dx,000Fh     ; DX = 0000000000001111b
mov  cl,3         ; shift count = 3
shl  dx,cl        ; DX = 0000000001111000b
```

In the following example, BL is shifted left four times; the low 4 bits are moved into the high four positions, and the low four bits are set to 0:

```
mov  bl,00001111b
mov  cl,4              ; shift left 4 times
shl  bl,cl             ; BL = 11110000b
```

Multiplication. One of the most powerful uses of the SHL instruction is for performing high-speed multiplication. The standard multiplication instructions are quite slow in comparison to SHL. The multiplication must always be a power of 2, and the number of times you shift is actually the exponent. For example, shifting left one position is the same as multiplying by 2^1; shifting two positions is the same as multiplying by 2^2, and so on. The following example shows the decimal value of DL after each shift:

```
mov  dl,1      ; DL = 1
shl  dl,1      ; DL = 2
shl  dl,1      ; DL = 4
shl  dl,1      ; DL = 8
shl  dl,1      ; DL = 16
shl  dl,1      ; DL = 32
(etc.)
```

Any number may be used as the starting value. If, for instance, we shift 21h left two times, the result is the same as multiplying it by 2^2 (4):

```
mov  ah,00100001b   ; AH = 21h
mov  cl,2
shl  ah,cl          ; AH = 84h
```

A word of caution: If you shift a signed value, the product must still be in a valid signed range.

SHR Instruction

The SHR (shift right) instruction shifts each bit to the right, replacing the highest bit with a 0. The lowest bit is copied into the Carry flag, and the bit that was in the Carry flag is lost.

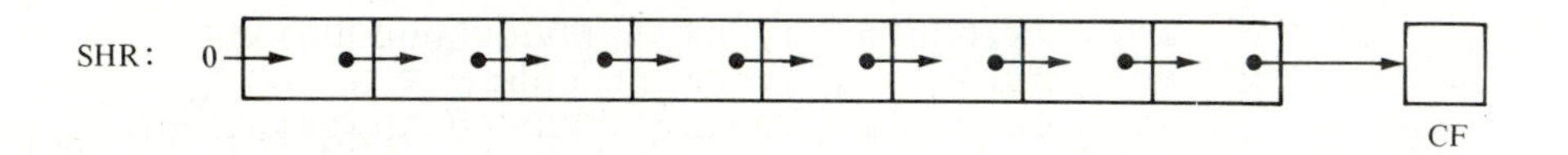

There are two formats for SHR. The first shifts a register or memory operand 1 bit to the right. The second uses the value in CL to repeat the shift.

```
SHR  dest,1
SHR  dest,CL
```

CL is unchanged. Examples using both register and memory operands are as follows:

```
shr  bl,1              ; shift BL 1 bit to the right
shr  wordval,1         ; 16-bit direct memory operand
shr  byte ptr[si],1    ; 8-bit indirect memory operand
mov  cl,4              ; place shift count in CL
shr  al,cl             ; shift AL right 4 bits
```

In the following example, a 0 is copied into the Carry flag and the highest bit position is filled with a 0:

```
mov  al,0D0h      ; AL = 11010000b
shr  al,1         ; AL = 01101000b, CF = 0
```

The SHR instruction may be used to divide a number by 2. For example, we can divide 32 by 2, yielding 16:

```
mov dl,32      ; 00100000b
shr dl,1       ; 00010000b    (DL = 16)
```

By coding several shifts in a row, we can divide an operand by a power of 2. In the following example, 64 is divided by 8 (2^3), so three divisions by 2 are used. The final result is 8:

```
mov   al,01000000b     ; AL = 64
shr   al,1             ; divide by 2, AL = 00100000b
shr   al,1             ; divide by 2, AL = 00010000b
shr   al,1             ; divide by 2, AL = 00001000b
```

If you plan to perform division by shifting signed numbers, it's best to use the SAR instruction, as it preserves the number's sign bit.

SAL and SAR Instructions

SAL (shift arithmetic left) and SAR (shift arithmetic right) are shift instructions specifically for signed numbers. SAL is identical to SHL and is included in the instruction set only for completeness. SAR shifts each bit to the right and makes a copy of the sign bit:

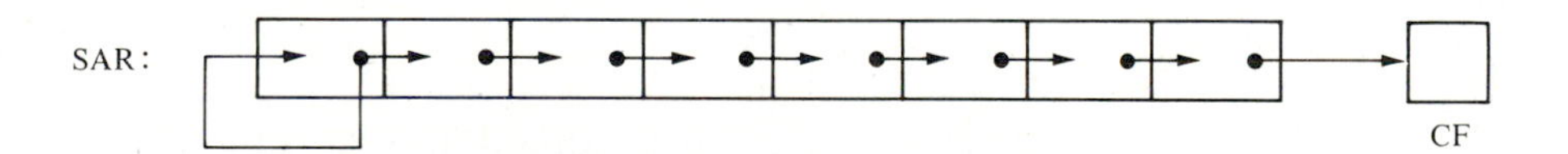

SAR copies the lowest bit of the destination operand into the Carry flag, shifts the operand right 1 bit position, and duplicates the original sign bit. You can also place a shift count in CL for multiple shifts. The syntax for SAR and SHR is identical to that of SHL and SHR:

```
SAR   dest,1
SHR   dest,CL
```

The following example shows how SAR duplicates the sign bit. AL is negative before and after it is shifted to the right:

```
mov   al,0F0h      ; AL = 11110000b (-16)
sar   al,1         ; AL = 11111000b (-8)   CF = 0
```

In the following example, −32768 is shifted right five times, which is the same as dividing it by 2^5 (32). The result is −1024:

```
mov   dx,8000h     ; DX = 1000000000000000b
mov   cl,5
sar   dx,cl        ; DX = 1111110000000000b
```

ROL Instruction

The ROL (rotate left) instruction moves each bit to the left. The highest bit is copied both into the Carry flag and into the lowest bit:

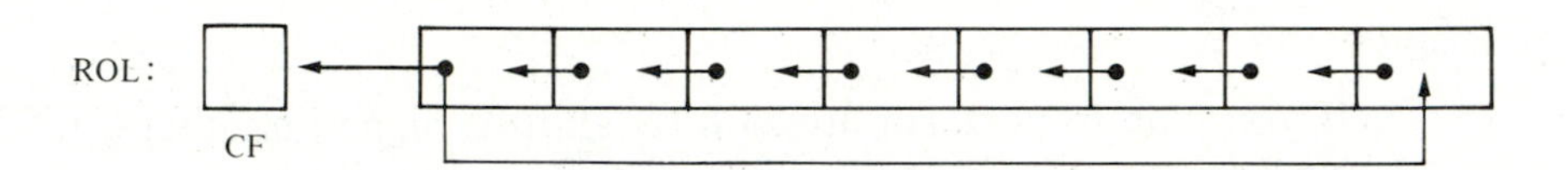

In general, rotate instructions are different from shift instructions because bits are never lost. A bit that is rotated off one end of a number appears again at the other end. The two formats are the same as for shift instructions:

```
ROL   dest,1
ROL   dest,CL
```

In the following example, the high bit is copied into both the Carry flag and into bit position 0:

```
mov   al,40h       ; AL = 01000000b
rol   al,1         ; AL = 10000000b, CF = 0
rol   al,1         ; AL = 00000001b, CF = 1
rol   al,1         ; AL = 00000010b, CF = 0
```

You can use ROL to exchange the high and low halves of an operand. The following examples demonstrate this for byte and word values:

```
byte_values:
     mov   cl,4           ; rotation count = 4
     mov   al,26h
     rol   al,cl          ; AL = 62h
     rol   byteval,cl     ; byteval = F0h
```

```
word_values:
        mov   cl,8           ; rotation count = 8
        mov   ax,0203h
        rol   ax,cl          ; AX = 0302h
        rol   wordval,cl     ; wordval = 3412h
        .
        .
byteval  db  0Fh
wordval  dw  1234h
```

ROR Instruction

The ROR (rotate right) instruction moves each bit to the right. The lowest bit is copied into the Carry flag and into the highest bit at the same time:

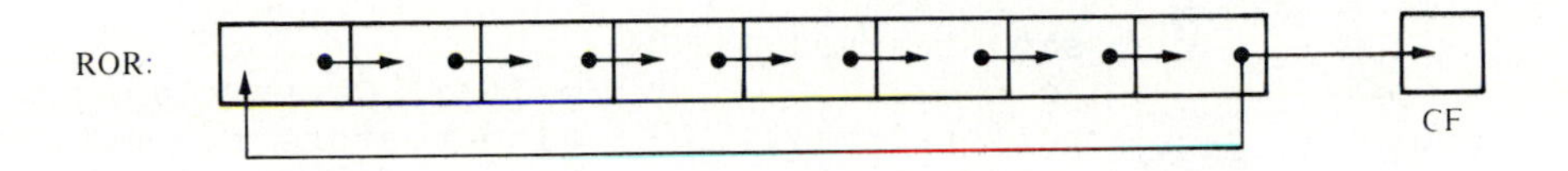

The two syntax formats are the same as for the ROL instruction:

```
ROR   dest,1
ROR   dest,CL
```

In the following example, the lowest bit is copied into the Carry flag and into the highest bit of the result:

```
mov al,01h        ; AL = 00000001b
ror al,1          ; AL = 10000000b, CF = 1
ror al,1          ; AL = 01000000b, CF = 0
```

RCL and RCR Instructions

The RCL (rotate carry left) instruction shifts each bit to the left and copies the highest bit into the Carry flag. The Carry flag is copied into the lowest bit of the result:

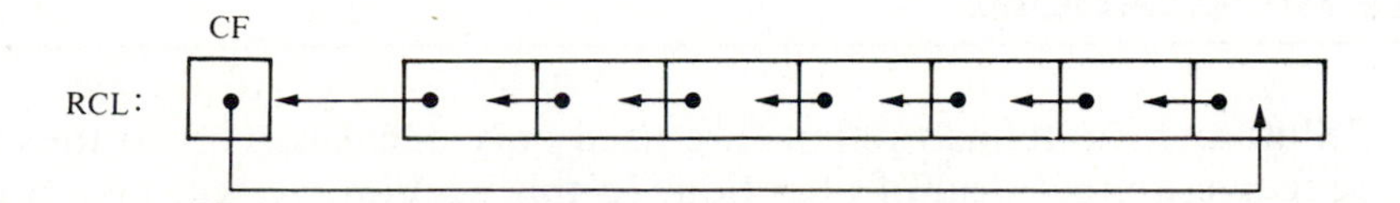

In the following example, the CLC instruction clears the Carry flag. The first RCL instruction moves the high bit of BL into the Carry flag and shifts all other bits to the left. The second RCL instruction moves the Carry flag into the lowest bit position and shifts all other bits to the left:

```
clc              ; CF = 0
mov   bl,88h     ; BL = 10001000b
rcl   bl,1       ; BL = 00010000b, CF = 1
rcl   bl,1       ; BL = 00100001b, CF = 0
```

Recover a Bit from the Carry Flag. RCL can recover a bit that has previously been shifted into the Carry flag. The following example checks the lowest bit of **testval** by shifting its lowest bit into the Carry flag. Then RCL restores the number to its original value:

```
        shr   testval,1
        jc    exit            ; exit if Carry flag set
        rcl   testval,1       ; else restore the number
        .
        .
testval   db   01101010b
```

RCR Instruction. The RCR (rotate carry right) instruction shifts each bit to the right and copies the lowest bit into the Carry flag. The Carry flag is copied into the highest bit of the result:

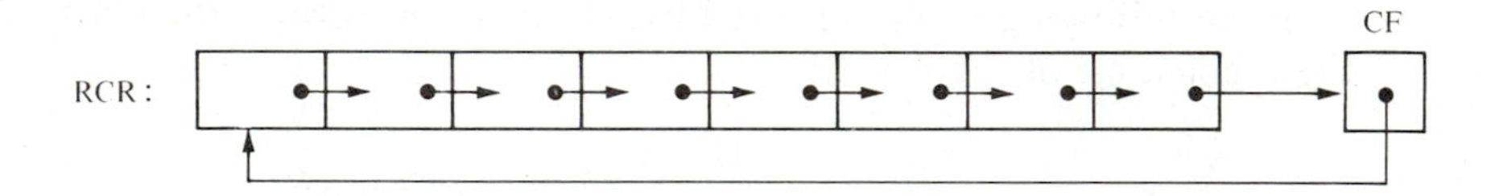

In the following example, STC sets the Carry flag before performing the rotation:

```
stc              ; CF = 1
mov   ah,10h     ; AH = 00010000b, CF = 1
rcr   ah,1       ; AH = 10001000b, CF = 0
```

SAMPLE APPLICATIONS

Shift and rotate instructions are used only occasionally, so they do not usually receive a great deal of attention. In this section we will take a look at several practical applications using shifts and rotates. The variety of possible examples is endless, of course.

Shifting Multiple Bytes

Suppose we wanted to shift all bits in a table to the right, as we might for a bit-mapped table containing a graphic image. Using three byte operands as an example, we can begin with the leftmost byte, shifting its low bit into the Carry flag. The results of a single shift to the right are as follows:

	byte1	**byte2**	**byte3**
Before:	00111011	01000110	11111111
After:	00011101	10100011	01111111

After being shifted, **byte1** equals 00011101b and CF = 1. Next, we use RCR to rotate **byte2** to the right while copying the contents of the Carry flag into the highest position of **byte2**. After the rotate, **byte2** equals 10100011b. Last, **byte3** is rotated to the right, resulting in the value 01111111b.

These three steps are repeated each time we shift all bits in the 3 bytes. The following instructions shift the bits in all 3 bytes to the right four times:

```
        mov   cx,4        ; repeat the shift four times
    again:
        shr   byte1,1     ; highest byte
        rcr   byte2,1     ; middle byte, include Carry flag
        rcr   byte3,1     ; low byte, include Carry flag
        loop  again

byte1  db   3Bh     ; after: 03h
byte2  db   46h     ; after: B4h
byte3  db   0FFh    ; after: 6Fh
```

Multiplication and Division

As we have already seen, SHL and SHR perform multiplication and division efficiently when at least one operand is a power of 2 (e.g., 2, 4, 8, 16, 32 . . .).

If neither operand is a power of 2, one may still be able to factor the number into two powers of 2. To multiply the number in BX by 36, for example, we take advantage of the distributive property of multiplication and add the products of 32 and 4 together:

$$\begin{aligned} BX * 36 &= BX * (32 + 4) \\ &= (BX * 32) + (BX * 4) \end{aligned}$$

The following example shows how a 16-bit variable called **intval** may be multiplied by 36. The result, 360, is the sum of two products, 320 and 40:

```
 1:          mov   bx,intval     ; get integer value
 2:          mov   cl,5          ; multiply by 32
 3:          shl   bx,cl         ; BX = 0140h (320d)
 4:          mov   product,bx    ; save first result
 5:          mov   bx,intval     ; get integer value again
 6:          shl   bx,1          ; multiply by 4
 7:          shl   bx,1          ; BX = 0028h (40d)
 8:          add   product,bx    ; add results together
 9:          .
10:          .
11:    intval    dw   0Ah      ; result = 0168h (360d)
12:    product   dw   ?
```

Programming Tip: Using a Repeat Count

A sequence of single shifts or rotates may execute more quickly when CL is used as a shift counter. For instance, Example 1 is faster than Example 2:

Example 1 (faster)

```
shr    ax,1
shr    ax,1
shr    ax,1
```

Example 2 (slower)

```
mov    cl,3
shr    ax,cl
```

When the number of shifts goes beyond four, however, the method used in Example 2 is more efficient. This is because it takes the CPU longer to fetch a shift or rotate instruction from memory than it does to execute it. After a few instructions, the arithmetic logic unit (ALU) finds itself waiting for the next instruction to be fetched, when it could be executing a repeated shift instruction instead.

You may want to read the article "Bit Rotation Speeds," by Michael Abrash, in the *PC Tech Journal,* May 1986, p. 47. He explains the way the CPU fetches and executes the shift and rotate instructions.

Sometimes the exact number of shifts is unknown at assembly time, so CL must be used as a counter for the shift. In the following example, the variable **countval** contains the number of desired shifts, but its value will be determined at runtime:

```
      mov  cl,countval     ; get number of shifts
      shr  bx,cl           ; perform the shift
      .
      .
countval  db  ?
```

Display a Number in ASCII Binary

A good way to apply the SHL instruction is to display a byte in ASCII binary format. We may take advantage of the fact that the highest bit is copied into the Carry flag each time the byte is shifted to the left.

The following BIN.ASM program displays each of the bits in the AL register. The output is the bit pattern of 6Ch: 01101100.

```
 1:   title Display ASCII Binary (BIN.ASM)
 2:
 3:   ;  This program displays a binary number as a string
 4:   ;  of digits.
 5:
 6:   dosseg
 7:   .model small
 8:   .stack 100h
 9:
10:   .code
11:   main     proc
12:            mov    al,6Ch         ; AL = 01101100b
13:            mov    cx,8           ; number of bits in AL
14:
15:      L1:   shl    al,1           ; shift AL left into Carry flag
16:            mov    dl,'0'         ; choose '0' as default digit
17:            jnc    L2             ; if no carry, then jump to L2
18:            mov    dl,'1'         ; else move '1' to DL
19:
20:      L2:   push   ax             ; save AX
21:            mov    ah,2           ; display DL
22:            int    21h
23:            pop    ax             ; restore AX
24:            loop   L1             ; shift another bit to left
25:
26:            mov    ax,4C00h       ; return to DOS
27:            int    21h
28:   main endp
29:   end  main
```

Lines 15–18 form the nucleus of the program, where each high bit is shifted into the Carry flag. If the Carry flag is set, we move the ASCII digit 1 to DL; otherwise, DL equals the digit 0.

Isolate a Bit String

Often a byte or word contains more than one field, so we extract short sequences of bits, called *bit strings*. For instance, DOS function 57h returns the date stamp of a file in DX. (The date stamp shows the date on which the file was last modified.) Bits 0–4 represent a day number between 1 and 31, bits 5–8 are the month number, and bits 9–15 hold the year number. For example, let us assume that a file was last modified on March 10, 1989. The file's date stamp would appear as follows in the DX register:

```
        DH              DL
0 0 0 1 0 0 1 0 0 1 1 0 1 0 1 0
```

Field:	Year	Month	Day
Bit numbers:	9–15	5–8	0–4

The year number is relative to 1980. In order to extract a single field, we shift its bits into the lowest part of DX, using the SHR instruction, and then AND the irrelevant bits with zeros.

To demonstrate, let's start with the day of the month. We make a copy of DL and mask off all bits not belonging to the field. AL now contains the value we want:

```
mov  al,dl          ; make a copy of DL
and  al,00011111b   ; clear bits 5-7
mov  day,al         ; save in day
```

To extract the month number, we move bits 5–8 into the low part of AL before clearing all other bits. AL is shifted right five positions, so the month number is in the lowest five positions:

```
mov  al,dl          ; make a copy of DL
mov  cl,5           ; shift count
shr  al,cl          ; shift right five positions
and  al,00001111b   ; clear bits 4-7
mov  month,al       ; save in month
```

The year number (bits 9–15) is completely within the DH register. We move this to AL and shift it right 1 bit:

```
mov  al,dh          ; make a copy of DH
shr  al,1           ; shift right one position
mov  ah,0           ; clear AH to zeros
add  ax,1980        ; year is relative to 1980
mov  year,ax        ; save in year
```

MULTIPLE ADDITION AND SUBTRACTION

ADC Instruction

The ADC (add with carry) instruction permits addition and subtraction of multibyte and multiword operands. Both the source operand and the Carry flag are added to the destination operand. The syntax is:

```
ADC dest,source
```

The source and destination operands may be 8-bit or 16-bit values.

The MULTIWORD_ADD procedure is demonstrated in Figure 8-2, which can add two multiword operands of any length and store the result. When calling it, we pass pointers to the input operands in SI and DI, a pointer to the result in BX, and a count of the number of words to be added in CX. Because we are passing only 16-bit pointers, all three operands must be in the segment pointed to by DS. The procedure assumes that each value is stored with its least significant word at the lowest address. Theoretically, MULTIWORD_ADD could add two 10,000-word numbers.

Figure 8-2 Example of multiword addition.

```
 1:  title  Multiword Addition Example           (MWADD.ASM)
 2:
 3:  ;
 4:  ;  Demonstrates a procedure that will add multiword
 5:  ;  operands together and store the sum in memory.
 6:  ;
 7:
 8:  dosseg
 9:  .model small
10:  .stack 100h
11:
12:  .code
13:  main proc
14:      mov   ax,@data              ; initialize DS
15:      mov   ds,ax
16:
17:  ;   Add two doubleword operands
18:
19:      mov   si,offset op1
20:      mov   di,offset op2
21:      mov   bx,offset result
22:      mov   cx,2                  ; add 2 words
23:      call  multiword_add
24:
25:      mov   ax,4C00h              ; return to DOS
```

Figure 8-2 *(Cont.)*

```
26:        int    21h
27:    main endp
28:
29:    .data
30:    op1         dd    0A2B2A406h
31:    op2         dd    080108700h
32:    result      dw    3 dup(0)     ; stored as 2B06h, 22C3h, 0001h
33:
34:    ;  Add any two multiword operands together. When the
35:    ;  procedure is called, SI and DI point to the two operands,
36:    ;  BX points to the destination operand, and CX contains the
37:    ;  number of words to be added.  No registers are changed.
38:
39:    .code
40:    multiword_add proc
41:        push   ax
42:        push   bx
43:        push   cx
44:        push   si
45:        push   di
46:        clc                        ; clear the Carry flag
47:
48:    L1: mov    ax,[si]            ; get the first operand
49:        adc    ax,[di]            ; add the second operand
50:        pushf                      ; save the Carry flag
51:        mov    [bx],ax            ; store the result
52:        add    si,2               ; advance all 3 pointers
53:        add    di,2
54:        add    bx,2
55:        popf                       ; restore the Carry flag
56:        loop   L1                 ; repeat for count passed in CX
57:
58:        adc    word ptr [bx],0    ; add any leftover carry
59:        pop    di
60:        pop    si
61:        pop    cx
62:        pop    bx
63:        pop    ax
64:        ret
65:    multiword_Add endp
66:
67:    end main
```

Let's look at a few details. Lines 19–22 load the appropriate pointer and counter registers before MULTIWORD_ADD is called. Lines 41–45 save all registers that we plan to change inside the procedure, so on return they may be restored. Line 46 clears the Carry flag, to prevent our accidentally adding it the first time through the loop, on line 49. Lines 48–51 add a single pair of words and store the result at the location pointed to by BX. We save the flags using the PUSHF (push flags) instruction, to preserve the Carry flag when returning to line 49 on the next pass through the loop. Lines 52–54 move the three pointers to the next set of values to be added, but they also modify the Carry flag. The POPF (pop flags) instruction on line 55 restores the Carry flag before looping back to label **L1**.

The following illustration shows the arithmetic performed by the program:

```
              A2  B2  A4  06   (op1)
         +    80  10  87  00   (op2)
---------------------------------
00   01   22  C3  2B  06   (result)
```

Programming Tip: The LABEL Directive

The LABEL directive lets you create a new label or variable starting at the same offset as another label. This is often used when a variable of one type (e.g., doubleword) must be accessed using a different-sized operand (e.g., word). For instance, accessing individual words in a 32-bit variable requires the use of WORD PTR.

```
mov    ax,word ptr dword_value
  .
  .
dword_value dd ?
```

The LABEL directive allows a 16-bit reference to any variable:

```
dword_value label word
            dd    0A2B2A406h
```

Now a reference to the operand may be made without using WORD PTR.

SBB Instruction

The SBB (subtract with borrow) instruction is useful for multibyte or multiword subtraction. The syntax is:

```
SBB dest,source
```

The destination and source operands may be 8- or 16-bit values. First, the source operand is subtracted from the destination; then the Carry flag is subtracted from the destination.

Quadword Example. In the following example, one quadword (8-byte) operand is subtracted from another:

```
 1:             mov cx,8            ; loop counter: 8 bytes
 2:             mov si,0            ; set index to 0
 3:             clc                 ; clear Carry flag
 4:      top:
 5:             mov   al,byte ptr op1[si]
 6:             sbb   al,byte ptr op2[si]
 7:             mov   byte ptr result[si],al
 8:             inc   si
 9:             loop  top
10:             .
11:             .
12:     op1  dq  20403004362047A1h
13:     op2  dq  055210304A2630B2h
14:   result dq  0   ; result = 1A EE 1F D3 EB FA 16 EF
```

Line 1 sets up a counter for a loop from lines 4–9. The SBB instruction on line 6 subtracts both the Carry flag and the contents of **op2** from AL.

The DQ directive stores the bytes in memory in reverse order, so we initialize SI to the lowest address of each operand. The subtraction may be summarized as follows:

op1		20	40	30	04	36	20	47	A1
op2	−	05	52	10	30	4A	26	30	B2
result		1A	EE	1F	D3	EB	FA	16	EF

In this example, **op1** is larger than **op2**, so the result is positive. If the result were negative, the Carry flag would also be set after the loop had finished, and the result would be stored in twos complement form.

On line 3, the CLC (clear carry) instruction clears the Carry flag. Be sure to do this before you execute an ADC or SBB instruction the first time; otherwise, a leftover value in the flag will affect the result. The STC (set carry) instruction sets the Carry flag to a 1.

SIGNED ARITHMETIC

When the CPU performs arithmetic, it treats the operands as unsigned binary numbers. If one intends the values to be *signed,* the flags must be carefully watched to make sure the result does not overflow the destination. Although the CPU performs arithmetic as if the operands are unsigned, signed values may still be computed correctly. This appears to be a contradiction, but it is not. Suppose, for example, that we add FFFFh to 3000h. The result is 2FFFh:

```
        mov   cx,3000h        ; starting value of CX
        add   cx,0FFFFh       ; add -1

    result:     CX = 2FFFh    Flags: NV PL NZ CY
```

The *unsigned* sum of 3000h and 0FFFFh is 12FFFh, which overflows CX. The highest digit is truncated, the Carry flag is set, and the result is incorrect. If the operands are signed, however, the statement is really adding -1 to 3000h. The result, 2FFFh, is correct. The Carry flag is irrelevant.

Signed Values Out of Range. The Overflow flag (notated OF) tells us something about the result of a signed addition or subtraction operation. If OF = 1, the signed result may be too large to fit into the destination operand or the result's sign bit may have changed. The CPU examines the sign bit of the result operand before and after the operation. If the bit has changed value, it sets the Overflow flag (OF = 1).

Let us compare two examples in which 1 is added to +127. In the first example, we store the result in AX, so OF = 0; in the second example, the result changes the sign bit of AL, so OF = 1:

Instruction	Before	After	Flags
1. add AX,1	AX = 007F (+127)	AX = 0080 (+128)	NV PL NC
2. add AL,1	AL = 7F (+127)	AL = 80 (−128)	OV NG NC

Figure 8-3 presents a more detailed description of these operations. In Example 1 the result in AX is correct (+128), and neither the Overflow flag nor the Sign flag is set. In Example 2 the result in AL is −128, although we added +1 to +127. The Overflow flag is set, showing that the sign bit was changed, and the result is invalid. The Sign flag is also set because the number in AL is negative.

MULTIPLICATION AND DIVISION

There are instructions to perform integer multiplication and division on 8-bit and 16-bit numbers. All operands are assumed to be binary, so if decimal or binary-coded decimal operands are involved, you must make all adjustments. Floating-point operations are handled either by a separate Intel math coprocessor or by

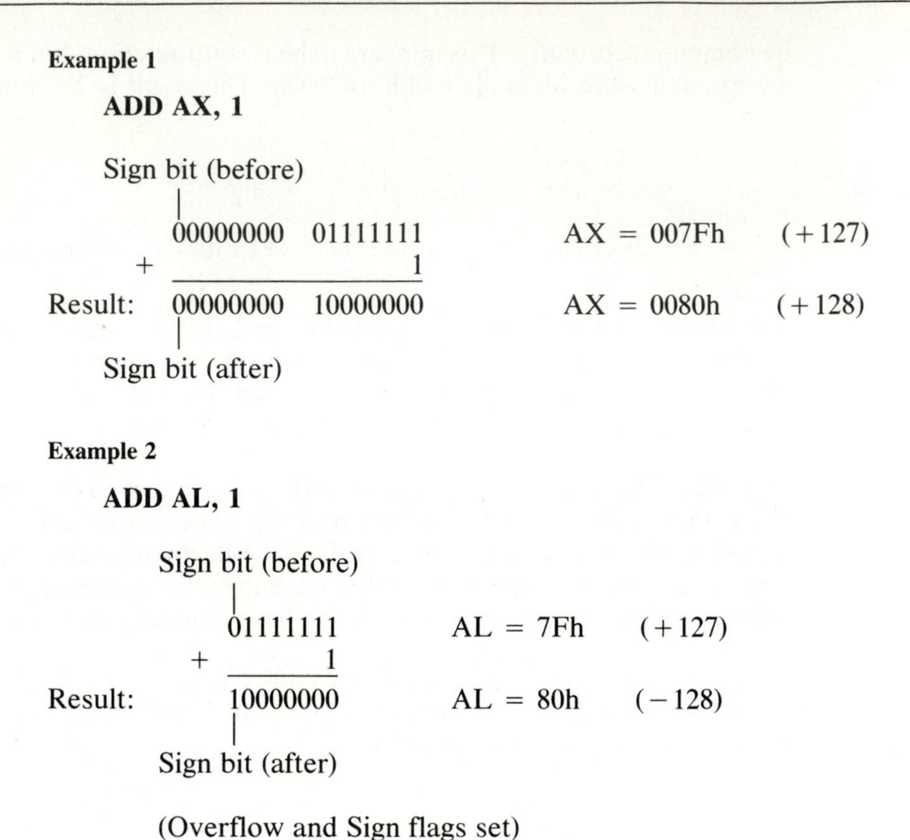

Figure 8-3 Examples of signed addition.

software emulation supplied in a language library. (See Chapter 15 for a discussion of the Intel 8087 math coprocessor.)

The MUL (multiply) and DIV (divide) instructions are for unsigned binary numbers. The IMUL (integer multiply) and IDIV (integer divide) instructions are for signed binary numbers.

MUL and IMUL Instructions

The MUL and IMUL instructions multiply an 8-bit or 16-bit operand by AL or AX. If an 8-bit source operand is supplied, it is automatically multiplied by AL, and the result is stored in AX. If a 16-bit source operand is supplied, it is multiplied by AX, and the result is stored in DX and AX (the high 16 bits are in DX). The syntax formats are:

```
MUL   source
IMUL  source
```

The source operand may be either a register or a memory operand, but it may not be immediate data. The destination (either AX or DX:AX) is implied and may not be changed.

Example 1. Multiply AL by 10h:

```
mov  al,5h
mov  bl,10h
mul  bl          ; AX = 0050h
```

Example 2. Multiply AX by 10h:

```
      mov     ax,val1
      mul     val2        ; DX = 0002h, AX = 0000h
      .
      .
val1  dw   2000h
val2  dw   0010h
```

Example 3. Multiply *integer1* by *byte1* and store the product in a 32-bit variable named *result:*

```
          mov   ax,integer1             ; get word operand
          mov   bh,0
          mov   bl,byte1                ; get byte operand
          mul   bx                      ; DX:AX = 0002:4680h
          mov   word ptr result,ax      ; low word of result
          mov   word ptr result+2,dx    ; high word of result
          .
          .
   byte1    db   20h
integer1    dw   1234h
  result    dd   ?
```

IMUL Instruction. The IMUL (integer multiply) instruction multiplies signed binary values. It sign-extends the result through the highest bit of AX or DX:AX, depending on the size of the source operand. A result of −10h, for example, would be extended into AH if an 8-bit operation had taken place or into DX for a 16-bit operation:

RESULT = −10h	
8-bit operation:	AX = FFF0h
16-bit operation:	DX = FFFFh, AX = FFF0h

Interpreting the Flags. If the product fits completely within the lower half of the destination (AL or AX), the Carry and Overflow flags are cleared. In the following example, the result of the 8-bit IMUL operation is −1, so AX equals 1111111111111111b. The Carry and Overflow flags are clear:

```
mov    al,1
mov    bl,-1
imul   bl          ; AX = 1111111111111111b
                   ; CF = 0, OF = 0
```

16-Bit Multiplication Example. The following instructions multiply 10 by −48 and store the product in a variable named **result**. The 32-bit result is FFFFFE20h:

```
        mov    ax,10d
        mov    cx,-48d
        imul   cx              ; DX:AX = FFFF:FE20h (-480d)
        mov    result,ax
        mov    result+2,dx
        .
        .
result  dw     0,0
```

DIV and IDIV Instructions

The DIV and IDIV instructions perform both 8- and 16-bit division, signed and unsigned. A single operand is supplied (register or memory operand), which is assumed to be the divisor. The syntax formats for DIV and IDIV are:

```
DIV   source
IDIV  source
```

If the divisor is 8 bits long, AX is the dividend, AL the quotient, and AH the remainder. If the divisor is 16 bits, DX:AX is the dividend, AX the quotient, and DX the remainder:

Dividend /	Divisor =	Quotient	Remainder
AX	Operand	AL	AH
DX:AX	Operand	AX	DX

Example 1. 8-bit division (83h / 2 = 40h, remainder 3):

```
mov    ax,0083h    ; dividend
mov    bl,2        ; divisor
div    bl          ; AL = 40h, AH = 03h
```

Example 2. 16-bit division (8003h / 100h = 80h, remainder 3). DX contains the high part of the dividend, so we must clear it before dividing. After the division, the quotient is in AX and the remainder is in DX:

```
mov   dx,0        ; clear dividend, high
mov   ax,8003h    ; dividend, low
mov   cx,100h     ; divisor
div   cx          ; AX = 0080h, DX = 0003h
```

Example 3. 16-bit division using a memory operand as the divisor:

```
    mov   dx,0            ; clear dividend, high
    mov   ax,dividend
    div   divisor         ; AX = 0080h, DX = 0003h
    .
    .
dividend  dw  8003h
divisor   dw  100h
```

IDIV Instruction. When performing signed division, the CPU preserves the sign only if the dividend has been properly prepared. For example, if we want to divide −48 by 5, we might be tempted to write

```
mov    ah,0
mov    al,-48
mov    bl,5          ; AX = 00D0h
idiv   bl
```

But the result would be wrong. To see why, look at AX before the division takes place. The sign bit in AL has not been extended into AH, so the number is really equal to +208:

```
   AH        AL
00000000  11010000    (00D0h or +208d)
```

To correct this error, insert the CBW (convert byte to word) instruction, which sign extends AL into AH:

```
mov    al,-48        ; AL = D0h
cbw                  ; AX = FFD0h
mov    bl,5
idiv   bl            ; AL = -9, AH =-3
```

For 32-bit dividends, the CWD (convert word to doubleword) instruction sign extends AX into DX:

```
mov    ax,-5000     ; AX = EC78h
cwd                 ; DX:AX = FFFFEC78h
mov    bx,256
idiv   bx           ; AX = FFEDh, (-19) quotient
                    ; DX = FF78h, (-136) remainder
```

Divide Overflow

When a division operation generates too large a result, a *divide overflow* condition results, which calls system interrupt 0. On many machines this hangs the computer system, requiring a cold start. An attempt to divide by 0 will also produce a divide overflow. High-level languages have built-in protection against this, of course, but the CPU itself does not perform any error checking before dividing.

One solution is to always break up a 32-bit dividend into two separate 16-bit operands. For example, if we divide 08010020h by 10h, we will generate a divide overflow, because the quotient (801002h) does not fit into AX. The division may be performed in two steps, as shown here:

```
1:          mov   ax,dividend+2       ; dividend, high
2:          cwd                       ; sign extend
3:          mov   cx,divisor
4:          div   cx                  ; AX = quotient (high)
5:                                    ; DX = remainder (high)
6:          mov   bx,ax               ; save quotient, high
7:          mov   ax,dividend         ; dividend, low
8:          div   cx                  ; AX = quotient (low)
9:          mov   remainder,dx        ; save remainder (low)
10:         .                         ; BX:AX = 0080:1002h
11:         .
12:   dividend    label word
13:               dd     08010020h
14:   divisor     dw     10h
15:   remainder   dw     ?            ; result = 0000h
```

First, we divide the most significant word of the dividend. Lines 1 and 2 load the dividend into AX and sign-extend it into DX. Line 4 divides the high part of the dividend (0801h) by 10h. The quotient is 0080h and the remainder is 0001h:

0000:0801h	/	10h	=	0080h,	remainder 1
(DX:AX)		(CX)		(AX)	(DX)

Line 6 saves the high quotient in BX. The remainder (DX) will become the most significant part of the new dividend. When line 7 loads AX with the low half of the dividend, DX:AX equals 0001:0020h. When this is divided by 10h, the quotient (AX) equals 1002h and the remainder (DX) is zero:

```
0001:0020h  /   10h  =  1002h,   remainder 0000h
 (DX:AX)       (CX)     (AX)          (DX)
```

Therefore, the 32-bit quotient in BX:AX equals 0080:1002h.

ASCII ARITHMETIC

The arithmetic shown so far has dealt only with binary values. The CPU calculates in binary, but we often need to perform arithmetic on numbers that have been input from the console or a file. Such numbers may be called *ASCII digit strings*.

Suppose we want to input two numbers from the console and add them together. No doubt, you have written such a program in a high-level language. The following is a sample console session:

```
Enter first number:    3402
Enter second number:   1256
The sum is:            4658
```

As each digit is input, we would store its ASCII code in a memory byte. After the first number was input, the number would be stored as follows:

33	34	30	32	(hexadecimal storage)
3	4	0	2	(ASCII digits)

In order to calculate the sum, we have two alternatives: We can convert each ASCII digit string to a 16-bit binary value, which in turn can be used in the calculation; or we can add the ASCII digits themselves. The first option will be demonstrated in Chapter 9. The second will be shown in this chapter, where we use standard instructions to perform the arithmetic and adjust the result.

Four adjustment instructions are available: the AAA (ASCII adjust after addition), AAS (ASCII adjust after subtraction), AAM (ASCII adjust after multiplication), and AAD (ASCII adjust before division).

For addition and subtraction, the operands may be in either ASCII format or in *unpacked BCD* format. The high 4 bits of an unpacked BCD number are always zeros, whereas the high 4 bits of an ASCII number equal 0011b. The following example shows how 3,402 would be stored using both formats:

ASCII format:	33	34	30	32
Unpacked BCD:	03	04	00	02

(all values are in hexadecimal)

For multiplication and division, however, the unpacked BCD format must be used. Therefore, the high 4 bits of each byte must be cleared first.

In general, ASCII arithmetic is slow because it must be performed digit by digit. But it offers an advantage, the ability to process large numbers. For example, the number

234,567,800,026,365,383,456

may be represented accurately in ASCII format.

AAA Instruction

The AAA (ASCII adjust after addition) instruction adjusts the binary result of an ADD or ADC instruction. It makes the result in AL consistent with ASCII digit representation, using the following steps:

- If bits 0–3 of AL contain a value greater than 9, or if the Auxiliary Carry flag is set, the CPU adds 6 to AL and adds 1 to AH. The Auxiliary Carry and Carry flags are both set.
- In all cases, bits 4–7 of AL are set to zero.

Sample Addition. Let's add the ASCII digits 2 and 6 (32h and 36h). The binary result is 68h. We can clear the high 4 bits of this sum, ending up with 08h. This is converted back to ASCII by ORing it with 30h:

```
mov   al,32h    ; '2'
add   al,36h    ; + '6' = 68h
and   al,0Fh    ; clear high 4 bits (AL = 08h)
or    al,30h    ; convert to ASCII  (AL = 38h)
```

However, this solution will not always work. If the ASCII digits 8 and 2 are added, the result is 6Ah. When we convert this to ASCII, the result is 3Ah, clearly not the result we intended:

```
mov   al,38h
add   al,32h    ; AL = 6Ah
and   al,0Fh    ; AL = 0Ah
or    al,30h    ; AL = 3Ah, which is incorrect
```

Clearly, this is a case where the AAA instruction is needed so we can adjust the result of the addition to compensate for the ASCII digit representation.

AAA Example. The following example shows how to add the ASCII digits 8 and 2 correctly, using the AAA instruction. Remember to clear AH to zero before performing the addition:

```
mov  ah,0
mov  al,'8'       ; AX = 0038h
add  al,'2'       ; AX = 006Ah
aaa               ; AX = 0100h             (ASCII adjust result)
or   ax,3030h     ; AX = 3130h = '10'      (convert to ASCII)
```

The last instruction converts both AH and AL to ASCII digits.

Longer Digit Strings. Any two ASCII digit strings can be added together using a loop. The ASCADD.ASM program (Figure 8-4) adds together two eight-digit ASCII digit strings, both equal to 09999999. The result, 19999998, is also stored as a string. We could instruct this program to process longer digit strings by simply changing the loop counter value.

Figure 8-4 Example of ASCII decimal addition.

```
 1:   title  ASCII Decimal Addition          (ASCADD.ASM)
 2:
 3:   ;
 4:   ;  Demonstration of ASCII addition, using two
 5:   ;  8-digit strings.  The AAA instruction adjusts
 6:   ;  the result after each addition.
 7:   ;
 8:   dosseg
 9:   .model small
10:   .stack 100h
11:
12:       numdigits  equ  8      ; number of digits
13:
14:   .code
15:   main proc
16:       mov   ax,@data         ; initialize DS
17:       mov   ds,ax
18:       mov   cx,numdigits     ; set loop counter
19:       mov   si,numdigits-1   ; point SI to first digit
```

Figure 8-4 *(Cont.)*

```
20:        mov    ax,0                 ; initialize AX
21:
22:    nextdigit:
23:        mov    al,val1[si]          ; get digit from val1
24:        add    al,ah                ; add previous carry
25:        mov    ah,0
26:        add    al,val2[si]          ; add digit from val2
27:        aaa                         ; AX = adjusted result
28:        or     al,30h               ; convert digit to ASCII
29:        mov    result[si],al        ; store digit in result
30:        dec    si                   ; back up the index
31:        loop   nextdigit
32:
33:        mov    ax,4C00h             ; return to DOS
34:        int    21h
35:    main endp
36:
37:    .data
38:
39:    val1      db   '09999999'             ; input operand
40:    val2      db   '09999999'             ; input operand
41:    result    db   numdigits dup(0)       ; result = '19999998'
42:
43:    end main
```

A single index register (SI) points to the current position in each digit string, as well as the result string. The loop portion of the program reads each digit from **val1**, adds it to the corresponding digit in **val2**, and uses the AAA instruction to adjust the result.

Let's look at specific lines. Line 19 sets SI to the offset of the least significant (lowest) digit in each of the strings, which is 7. This is done because we need to start with the lowest digits and work our way up to the highest digits in order to preserve the Carry flag correctly.

Lines 22–31 are the core of the program. A digit is read from **val1**, and any carry that resulted from a previous addition is added to AL. The AAA instruction places a carry value in AH after adjusting the result of an addition. The following listing of lines 22–31 shows the hexadecimal values in AX during the first pass through the loop:

```
                                              AX
22:    nextdigit:
23:        mov    al,val1[si]                0039
24:        add    al,ah                        .
25:        mov    ah,0                         .
26:        add    al,val2[si]                0072
27:        aaa                               0108
28:        or     al,30h                     0138
29:        mov    result[si],al                .
30:        dec    si                           .
31:        loop   nextdigit
```

AAS Instruction

The AAS (ASCII adjust after subtraction) instruction adjusts the binary result of a SUB or SBB instruction. It makes the result in AL consistent with ASCII digit representation, using the following steps:

- If bits 0–3 contain a value greater than 9, or if the Auxiliary Carry flag is set, 6 is subtracted from AL and 1 is subtracted from AH. The Auxiliary Carry and Carry flags are both set.
- In all cases, bits 4–7 of AL are set to zero, and the Carry flag is set to the same value as the Auxiliary Carry flag.

Adjustment is necessary only when the subtraction generates a negative result.

Example. Let's subtract ASCII 9 from 8. After the SUB instruction, AX equals 00FFh (−1). The AAS instruction converts AX to FF09h, the tens complement of −1:

```
        mov   ah,0
        mov   al,val1    ; AX = 0038h
        sub   al,val2    ; AX = 00FFh
        aas              ; AX = FF09h
        or    al,30h     ; AX = FF39h
        .
        .
val1    db '8'
val2    db '9'
```

At first, this makes no sense at all. But consider what happens when we perform multidigit subtraction by hand. When the lowest digits of each number in the following example are subtracted, the result is 9 and a borrow is required:

```
Step:      (1)        (2)        (3)

          1 2 8      1 2 8      1 2 8
        - 0 0 9    - 0 0 9    - 0 0 9
        -------    -------    -------
              9        1 9      1 1 9
```

This is exactly the operation performed by the AAS instruction. The binary result (00FFh) is adjusted to FF09h, and the Carry flag is set. The 09 is converted to ASCII and stored in the lowest digit of the result:

ASCII:			9
Hexadecimal:			39

As the next two digits (2 − 0) are subtracted, we use the SBB instruction to subtract the Carry flag from 2. The result is converted to ASCII and placed in the result. The same is done for the highest digit, and the result is stored as follows:

ASCII:	1	1	9
Hexadecimal:	31	31	39

AAM Instruction

The AAM (ASCII adjust after multiplication) instruction adjusts the binary result of a MUL instruction. The multiplication must have been performed on *unpacked* BCD numbers.

Multiplication may not be performed on ASCII numbers until the high 4 bits of each number are cleared. If, for instance, we want to multiply the ASCII digits 6 and 2, we must convert them to 06h and 02h. The following operations are performed by AAM:

- AL is divided by 10; the quotient is stored in AH and the remainder in AL.
- The Sign flag is set to the high bit of AL, and the Zero flag reflects the contents of AL.

For example, (6 * 2) = 0Ch. After AAM, AX = 0102h.

Example. Multiply 5 by 6, and adjust the result in AX. After adjusting the result, AX = 0300h, which is the unpacked BCD representation of 30:

```
         mov   bl,val1    ; first operand
         mov   al,val2    ; second operand
         mul   bl         ; AX = 001Eh
         aam              ; AX = 0300h
         .
         .
val1     db    05h
val2     db    06h
```

AAD Instruction

The AAD (ASCII adjust before division) instruction adjusts the unpacked BCD dividend in AX *before* a division operation. Three steps are involved:

- AH is multiplied by 10 and added to AL.
- AH is set to zero.
- The Zero flag reflects the contents of AL, and the Sign flag is set to the high bit of AL.

Let's divide ASCII 37 by 5. First, the AAD instruction converts 0307h to 0025h. Then the DIV instruction yields a quotient of 07h in AL and a remainder of 02h in AH:

```
        mov  ax,0307h      ; dividend
        aad                ; AX = 0025h
        mov  bl,5          ; divisor
        div  bl            ; AX = 0207h
        mov  quotient,al
        mov  remainder,ah
        .
        .
quotient  db  ?
remainder db  ?
```

PACKED DECIMAL ARITHMETIC

Packed decimal numbers (packed BCD) contain 2 decimal digits per byte. Each decimal digit is represented by 4 bits, as in the BCD storage of 2,405:

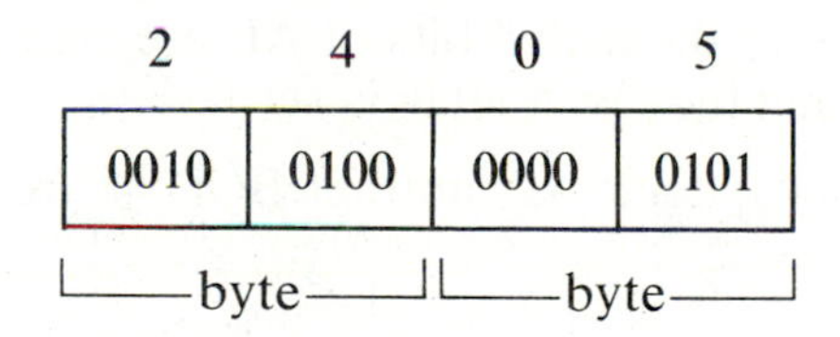

Packed BCD format has at least three strengths:

- The numbers may have almost any number of significant digits. This makes possible calculations with a great deal of accuracy.
- Conversion of packed BCD numbers to ASCII (and vice versa) is relatively fast.
- An implied decimal point may be used by keeping track of its position in a separate variable.

Two instructions, DAA (decimal adjust after addition) and DAS (decimal adjust after subtraction), adjust the result of an addition or subtraction operation on packed BCD numbers. Unfortunately, no such instructions exist for multiplication and division. In those cases, the number must be unpacked, multiplied or divided, and then packed again.

DAA Instruction

The DAA (decimal adjust after addition) instruction converts the binary result of an ADD or ADC instruction in AL to packed BCD format. The following steps are taken:

- If the Auxiliary Carry flag is set or the low 4 bits of AL are greater than 9, 6 is added to AL and the Auxiliary Carry flag is set.
- If the Carry flag is set or the high 4 bits of AL are greater than 9, 60h is added to AL and the Carry Flag is set.

For example, the following instructions add packed BCD 35 and 48. The lower digit of 7Dh is greater than 9, so it is adjusted. The upper digit, which is 8 after the first adjustment, is not adjusted:

```
mov   al,35h
add   al,48h      ; AL = 7Dh
daa               ; AL = 83h (adjusted result)
```

DAS Instruction

The DAS (decimal adjust after subtraction) instruction converts the binary result of a SUB or SBB instruction in AL to packed BCD format. The steps are similar to those of DAA:

- If the Auxiliary Carry flag is set or the low 4 bits of AL are greater than 9, 6 is subtracted from AL and the Auxiliary Carry flag is set.
- If the Carry flag is set or the high 4 bits of AL are greater than 9, 60h is subtracted from AL and the Carry Flag is set.

For example, the following statements subtract BCD 48 from 85 and adjust the result:

```
mov   bl,48h
mov   al,85h
sub   al,bl      ; AL = 3Dh
das              ; AL = 37h (adjusted result)
```

BCD Addition Example

The BCDADD.ASM program (Figure 8-5) adds two 10-byte packed BCD numbers. The DT storage directive was specifically designed for packed BCD numbers. MASM stores the bytes in reverse order, with an extra byte reserved for the sign in the most significant byte. A maximum of 18 significant digits may be encoded, as demonstrated by **val1** (lines 36–37). Assuming no decimal point, this represents about 98 quadrillion.

At the beginning of the program, we set up a loop counter in CX to process 9 bytes (18 digits). The lowest digit is stored at the lowest address, so we set SI to zero; thus, we plan to index from the start of **val1**, **val2**, and **result**. Line 19 clears

```
 1:  title  Packed Decimal Addition              (BCDADD.ASM)
 2:
 3:  ;
 4:  ;  Demonstrates BCD addition, using two packed
 5:  ;  decimal numbers.  The DAA instruction adjusts
 6:  ;  the result after each addition.  Each number
 7:  ;  is 9 bytes (18 digits) long.
 8:  ;
 9:  dosseg
10:  .model small
11:  .stack 100h
12:
13:  .code
14:  main proc
15:       mov    ax,@data          ; initialize DS
16:       mov    ds,ax
17:       mov    cx,9              ; process 9 bytes
18:       mov    si,0              ; start at lowest digit
19:       clc                      ; clear Carry flag
20:
21:  nextdigit:
22:       mov    al,val1[si]       ; get digit from val1
23:       adc    al,val2[si]       ; add digit from val2 + carry
24:       daa                      ; AL contains adjusted result
25:       mov    result[si],al     ; store the digit
26:       inc    si                ; point to next byte
27:       loop   nextdigit
28:
29:       mov    result[si],0      ; store positive sign
30:       mov    ax,4C00h          ; return to DOS
31:       int    21h
32:  main endp
33:
34:  .data
35:
36:  val1     label byte
37:           dt     098765438746498376    ; 18 digits, stored
38:  val2     label byte                   ; in reverse order
39:           dt     000876543232728405
40:  result   label byte
41:           dt     ?
42:  end main
```

Figure 8-5 *Example of packed decimal addition.*

the Carry flag because the ADC (add carry) instruction on line 23 must not include any carry value the first time it executes.

A handy way of addressing the two operands is to add the same index value to the offset of each operand. As we increment SI on line 26, it points to the corresponding positions in **val1**, **val2**, and **result**.

The signs of both numbers are assumed here to be positive. If either value were negative, however, its sign byte would contain 80h and it would have to be subtracted from the other operand.

POINTS TO REMEMBER

Shift and Rotate Instructions. A shift or rotate operation may be coded using single or multiple instructions. A multiple shift or rotate uses CL as a counter.

The SHL and SHR instructions shift bits left and right, respectively. Each bit shifted out of the number goes into the Carry flag, and each bit shifted into the number is a zero. The SAR instruction replicates the highest bit of the number to avoid changing the number's sign.

The ROL and ROR instructions rotate an operand right or left. As a bit disappears from one end of the number, it appears at the other end. Thus, bits may be rotated without being lost. RCL and RCR rotate each bit off the end of a number into the Carry flag, while the bit in the Carry flag is moved to the other end of the number.

Two applications involving shifting were shown: displaying a number in binary ASCII format (e.g., 10110101 . . .) and isolating bit strings from the date stamp of a file.

Multibyte Addition and Subtraction. The ADC (add with carry) and SBB (subtract with borrow) instructions make it possible to include the value of the Carry flag in an addition or subtraction operation. The CLC and STC instructions clear and set the Carry flag, respectively. In particular, CLC should be used before entering a loop in which either ADC or SBB will be used.

Signed Arithmetic. When performing signed arithmetic, take special care to check the Overflow flag. It is set when the sign bit of a result operand has changed. This means that the operand's magnitude is too large and the sign bit has been overwritten. The Carry flag is meaningful only when performing unsigned arithmetic.

Multiplication and Division. The MUL and DIV instructions work on either 8-bit or 16-bit unsigned integers. The IMUL and IDIV instructions are used with signed integers.

Special care must be taken to clear AH before performing 8-bit unsigned division, and to clear DX when performing 16-bit unsigned division. When performing signed division, use CBW or CWD to sign-extend the dividend into AH or DX, respectively.

A division operation should avoid a *divide overflow* condition, in which the quotient is too large to fit into the destination operand. If necessary, 32-bit division may be performed to allow for a larger result.

ASCII and Packed Decimal Arithmetic. When ASCII digits are added, the AAA (ASCII adjust after addition) instruction converts the binary result to ASCII format. AAS performs the same operation after subtraction, and AAM is used after multiplication. AAD (ASCII adjust before division) modifies AX before division takes place. All of these instructions are valid only for 8-bit operations.

Two instructions adjust the result of packed decimal operations: The DAA (decimal adjust after addition) and DAS (decimal adjust after subtraction) instructions adjust the contents of AL after 8-bit addition or subtraction, respectively.

REVIEW QUESTIONS

1. a. Discuss possible ways that decimal addition might be performed using the following two ASCII decimal numbers:

   2.1234
   300.5

   b. Devise a generalized algorithm for decimal point scaling that would make it possible to add any two ASCII decimal numbers (up to 18 digits of precision).

2. Name at least two popular high-level languages that contain shift instructions.

3. Do you know of any high-level language that contains rotate instructions?

4. Which two instructions move each bit in an operand to the left and copy the highest bit into both the Carry flag and the lowest bit position?

5. Which instruction moves each bit to the right, copies the low bit into the Carry flag, and copies the Carry flag into the high bit position?

6. Which instruction moves each bit to the right and makes the highest 2 bits exactly the same?

7. Which instruction moves each bit to the left, copies the Carry flag into the low bit position, and copies the highest bit into the Carry flag?

8. Which set of instructions will execute more quickly?

Example 1

```
mov  cl,2
shl  al,cl
```

Example 2

```
shl  al,1
shl  al,1
```

9. What happens to the original contents of the Carry flag when the SHR instruction is executed?

10. To multiply a number by 16, how many times must it be shifted to the left?

11. Write two instructions to divide BX by 4 using shift instructions.

12. Write a short program to multiply AL by 12 using SHR instructions.

13. What will be the contents of AL after each of the following instructions is executed? (Assume that AL = EAh, CL = 2, and the Carry flag is clear before each instruction is executed.)

Instruction	Contents of AL
a. shl al,1	
b. shl al,cl	
c. shr al,1	
d. sar al,1	
e. rol al,1	
f. rol al,cl	
g. ror al,1	
h. rcl al,1	
i. rcr al,1	
j. rcr al,cl	

14. Write two instructions that will exchange the high and low halves of the DL register.

15. Write an instruction that shifts the highest bit in the DL register into the lowest bit position of DH.

16. What will be the contents of DX after the following instructions are executed?

```
mov  dx,5
stc
mov  ax,10h
adc  dx,ax
```

17. The following program is supposed to subtract **val1** from **val2**. How many logic errors can you find?

```
mov cx,8          ; loop counter: 8 bytes
mov si,val1       ; set index to start
mov di,val2
clc               ; clear Carry flag
```

```
top:
          mov   al,byte ptr [si]    ; get first number
          sbb   al,byte ptr [di]    ; subtract second
          mov   byte ptr [si],al    ; store the result
          dec   si
          dec   di
          loop  top
          .
          .
 val1   dq   20403004362047A1h
 val2   dq   055210304A2630B2h
result  dq   0
```

18. What will be the contents of AX after the following operation?

```
mov   ax,22h
mov   cl,2
mul   cl
```

19. What will be the contents of AX and DX after the following operation?

```
mov   dx,0
mov   ax,222h
mov   cx,100h
mul   cx
```

20. What will be the contents of AX after the following operation?

```
mov   al,63h
mov   bl,10h
div   bl
```

21. What will be the contents of AX and DX after the following operation?

```
mov   ax,1234h
mov   dx,0
mov   bx,10h
div   bx
```

22. What will be the contents of AX and DX after the following operation?

```
mov   ax,4000h
mov   dx,500h
mov   bx,10h
div   bx
```

23. Write the instructions to multiply −5 by 3 and store the result in the 16-bit variable **val1**.

24. Write the instructions to divide −276 by 10 and store the result in the 16-bit variable **val1**.

25. Write the instructions to divide 20000000h by 10h and store the result in **result_hi** and **result_lo**. *Hint:* 32-bit division must be used to avoid a divide overflow condition.

PROGRAMMING EXERCISES

Exercise 1 Backwards Binary Display

Write a program that will display the binary bits in any 8-bit variable *backwards*. For example, the number 84h would be displayed as 00100001.

Exercise 2 Packed Decimal Coversion

Write a program to convert a packed BCD number to individual ASCII digits. Display the number on the screen. Use the following test value:

```
packedval dt 273645193846571425
```

Exercise 3 Room Schedule

Assume that you have read a record from a room scheduling file. One field, called **roomstatus**, is bit mapped, so each bit or group of bits is actually a subfield:

Bit Position	Usage
0–1	Type of room (0, 1, 2, 3)
2–7	Number of seats (0–63)
8–12	Department ID (0–31)
13	Overhead projector (0, 1)
14	Blackboard (0, 1)
15	P.A. system (0, 1)

Using the following data definitions, write a program that extracts each bit string from **roomstatus** and places it in its corresponding 8-bit variable:

```
roomstatus   dw   0110011101011101b
roomtype     db   ?
numseats     db   ?
deptID       db   ?
projector    db   ?
blackboard   db   ?
PAsystem     db   ?
```

Exercise 4 Multibyte Addition Program

Write a program that adds the following two binary numbers together:

```
val1   dq   0000263BA4502109h
val2   dq   000000206B1F2C44h
```

Store the sum in memory. Dump the contents of all variables to the printer before and after the addition.

Exercise 5 Add 10-Digit Numbers

Write a program to do the following:

a. Input two 10-digit ASCII decimal numbers and store them in memory.
b. Add the two numbers together and display the result.
c. Prompt the user to find out if he or she wants to add another pair of numbers.

The screen display should resemble the following:

```
                 ASCII Addition Program

First Number        → 0142536475
Second Number       → 0023466722

Result              → 0166003197


Action:   Q)uit     R)esume
```

Exercise 6 Multidigit BCD Multiplication

Write a program that multiplies two unpacked BCD numbers together and stores the result in a variable named **product**. Run the program using a debugger, and dump the contents of **product** before and after the multiplication takes place. The variables may be declared as follows:

```
factor1  dd 01020304h
factor2  dd 00000105h
product  db 8 dup(0)
```

In order to reserve enough space for the product, its size should be the sum of the digit positions of the two factors (4 + 2 = 6).

You may want to use the same approach as in traditional longhand multiplication. After each multiply operation, AH contains the carry value, that is, the value to be added to the next product.

```
           01 02 03 04      (1,234)
      *          01 05      (   15)
        --------------
        00 06 01 07 00      (product1)
   + 00 01 02 03 04 00      (product2)
   -------------------
     00 01 08 05 01 00      (18,510)
```

Using the lowest 2 digits of each number as an example, 4 * 5 = 20. AX will equal 0200h. The 2 in AH is added to the next product (3 * 5 = 15), giving us 17. The 7 becomes part of **product1**, and the 1 in AH is added to the next multiply operation.

Exercise 7 ASCII Multiplication Program

Write a procedure that multiplies two ASCII numbers together and displays the result. Test the procedure by calling it from a main program and passing the addresses of the numbers in SI and DI. Input the numbers from the console.

Exercise 8 ASCII Division Program

Write a procedure to divide one 6-byte ASCII number by another and display the result. Test the procedure by calling it from a main program. Continue entering each pair of numbers from the console and performing the division until the user presses ENTER on a blank line to quit.

Exercise 9 Average Value Calculation

Calculate and display the average of a list of ASCII digit strings. Be sure to place the decimal point in the correct position when displaying the result. Use the following numbers, hard coded in the data segment of your program:

```
ntable  db  '00012.30'
        db  '00140.00'
        db  '01000.20'
        db  '00050.50'
        db  '00230.10'
        db  '01400.00'
        db  '00300.00'
        db  '00050.10'
```

Extra: Write a routine to input the numbers from the console and store them in **ntable**. Limit the number of digits that may be typed on either side of the decimal point. Also, insert a comma in the computed average and suppress any leading zeros.

Exercise 10 The DIV32 Procedure

Write a general procedure that performs 32-bit division. Pass the dividend's offset in SI, and pass the divisor in CX. The dividend should be stored in reversed-byte order. For example, the value 12345678h would be stored in memory as follows:

78	56	34	12

Dump the contents of all relevant registers and variables just before and after the procedure is called.

ANSWERS TO REVIEW QUESTIONS

1. (Discussion question).
2. The C language and Turbo Pascal.
3. I don't know of any.
4. ROL.
5. RCR.
6. SAR.
7. RCL.

8. Example 2 is slightly faster.

9. The original contents are overwritten by bit 0.

10. Four.

11. Multiply BX by 4:

```
shr bx,1
shr bx,1
```

12. Multiply AL by 12:

```
push ax       ; save original value
shl  al,1     ; AL * 2
shl  al,1     ; AL * 4
shl  al,1     ; AL * 8
mov  dl,al    ; save first result
pop  ax       ; retrieve original value
shl  al,1     ; AL * 2
shl  al,1     ; AL * 4
add  al,dl    ; add results
```

Another possible solution:

```
mov   dl,al
shl   dl,1       ; DL * 8
shl   dl,1
shl   dl,1
shl   al,1       ; AL * 4
shl   al,1
add   dl,al      ; DL = DL + AL
```

13. a. D4h
    b. A8h
    c. 75h
    d. F5h
    e. D5h
    f. ABh
    g. 75h
    h. D4h
    i. 75h
    j. 3Ah

14. mov cl,4
    ror dl,cl ; (or: rol dl,cl)

15. shl dx,1

16. DX = 0016h

17. The following instruction, as coded in the program, will not store the result. Instead, it will place each arithmetic result back in **val1**:

```
mov  byte ptr [si],al
```

    Also, the SI and DI registers should be incremented rather than decremented because they have been set to the starting addresses of the two operands.

18. AX = 0044h

19. DX = 0002h, AX = 2200h

20. AX = 0306h

21. AX = 0123h, DX = 0004h

22. This will create a divide overflow because the quotient (500400h) is too big to fit into AX.

23.
```
mov   al,-5
mov   bl,3
imul  bl
mov   val1,ax
```

24.
```
mov   ax,-276
mov   bl,10
idiv  bl
mov   val1,ax
```

25. The following program performs 32-bit division:

```
mov  ax,dividend+2   ; dividend, high
cwd
mov  cx,divisor
div  cx
mov  result_hi,ax    ; save result
mov  ax,dividend     ; dividend, low
div  cx
mov  result_lo,ax
mov  remainder,dx

dividend     label word
             dd    20000000h
divisor      dw    10h
result_hi    dw    ?
result_lo    dw    ?
```

9

Numeric Conversions and Libraries

In this chapter we will discuss ways to translate numbers from one format to another, using assembly language. Numeric conversions are not automatic in the Intel instruction set; they must be handled completely by our software. This chapter also introduces external subroutines, showing how to link a program to separately compiled object files.

Numeric Formats. We will refer to several standard numeric formats throughout this chapter. *Binary* format refers to the encoded binary value of a number. One byte holds a value from 0 to 255, 2 bytes hold a value up to 65,535, and so on. In *unpacked BCD* format, each byte holds the binary value of a single digit. In *packed BCD* format, each half of a byte stores the binary value of a single decimal digit. There are several types of ASCII formats, in which each numeric digit is stored in a separate byte. A number in *ASCII decimal* format holds the ASCII code of each decimal digit. The *ASCII binary* format holds the ASCII code of each binary digit. The *ASCII hexadecimal* and *ASCII octal* formats are the same for hexadecimal and octal digits, respectively. The following examples demonstrate seven ways of representing the number 32:

```
db 20h              ; binary
db 03h,02h          ; unpacked BCD
db 32h              ; packed BCD
db '32'             ; ASCII decimal (30h, 32h)
db '00100000'       ; ASCII binary
db '20'             ; ASCII hexadecimal
db '40'             ; ASCII octal
```

This chapter focuses on two types of conversions:

Binary to ASCII Decimal. When the CPU performs arithmetic using binary numbers, the numbers must be translated to decimal ASCII format before they can be displayed or printed.

ASCII Decimal to Binary. If a program inputs a number from the console as a string of ASCII digits, we usually translate it to binary before using it in calculations.

Assembly programmers write all of the conversion routines themselves and eventually store them in a library. A *library* is simply a collection of related procedures that may be linked to a main program.

CHARACTER TRANSLATION USING XLAT

One task that assembly language programs handle best is character translation. There are many computer applications for this. The rapidly expanding field of data encryption is one, where data files must be securely stored and transmitted between computers while their contents are kept secret. Another application is data communications, where keyboard and screen codes must be translated in order to emulate various terminals. Often we need to translate characters from one encoding system to another—from ASCII to EBCDIC, for example. A critical factor in each of these applications is speed, which just happens to be a feature of assembly language.

The XLAT Instruction

The XLAT instruction adds the contents of AL to BX and uses the resulting offset to point to an entry in an 8-bit *translate table*. This table contains values that are substituted for the original value in AL. The byte in the table entry pointed to by BX + AL is moved to AL. The syntax is

```
XLAT  [tablename]
```

Tablename is optional because the table is assumed to be pointed to by BX. Therefore, be sure to load BX with the offset of the translate table before invoking XLAT. The flags are not affected by this instruction.

The table may have a maximum of 256 entries, the same range of values possible in the 8-bit AL register.

Example. Let's store the characters representing all 16 hexadecimal digits in **table**:

```
table  db  '0123456789ABCDEF'
```

The table contains the ASCII code of each hexadecimal digit:

Offset:	00	01	02	03	04	05	06	07	08	09	0A	0B	0C	0D	0E	0F
Contents:	30	31	32	33	34	35	36	37	38	39	41	42	43	44	45	46

(all values are in hexadecimal)

If we place 0Ah in AL with the thought of converting it to ASCII, we need to set BX to the table offset and invoke XLAT. This instruction will do the following:

- Add BX and AL, generating an effective address that points to the eleventh entry in the table.
- Move the contents of this table entry to AL.

In other words, XLAT sets AL to 41h because this value is located at table offset 0Ah. 41h is the ASCII code for the letter *A*. The following instructions accomplish this:

```
mov   al,0Ah              ; index value
mov   bx,offset table     ; offset of the table
xlat                      ; AL = 41h, or 'A'
```

Without the XLAT instruction, we could accomplish the table lookup as follows:

```
mov   al,0Ah              ; index value
mov   bx,offset table     ; offset of the table
push  bx                  ; save the offset
add   bl,al               ; add to offset
mov   al,[bx]             ; retrieve the entry
pop   bx                  ; restore BX
```

Character Filtering

One of the best uses of XLAT is to filter out unwanted characters from a stream of text. Suppose we want to input a string of characters from the keyboard but echo only those with ASCII values from 32 to 127. We can set up a translate table, place a zero in each table position corresponding to an invalid character, and place 0FFh in each valid position:

```
validchars db 32 dup(0)    ; invalid chars: 0-31
           db 96 dup(0FFh) ; valid chars: 32-127
           db 128 dup(0)   ; invalid chars: 128-255
```

The XLAT.ASM program (Figure 9-1) contains statements that input a character and use it to look up a value in the **validchars** table. If XLAT returns a value of zero in AL, we skip the character and jump back to the top of the loop. (When AL is ORed with itself, the Zero flag is set if AL equals 0.) If the character is valid, 0FFh is returned in AL, and we use INT 21 to display the character in DL (lines 26–28).

Figure 9-1 The XLAT program.

```
 1:   title  Character Filtering Example                    (XLAT.ASM)
 2:
 3:   ;
 4:   ;  This program filters input from the console
 5:   ;  by screening out all ASCII codes less than
 6:   ;  32 or greater than 127.
 7:   ;
 8:   dosseg
 9:   .model small
10:   .stack 100h
11:
12:   .code
13:   main proc
14:       mov   ax,@data
15:       mov   ds,ax
16:       mov   bx,offset validchars   ; BX points to the table
17:       mov   cx,20                  ; set loop to 20 characters
18:
19:   getchar:
20:       mov   ah,8                   ; input character, no echo
21:       int   21h                    ; call DOS
22:       mov   dl,al                  ; save copy in DL
23:       xlat  validchars             ; look up char in AL
24:       or    al,al                  ; is the character invalid?
25:       jz    getchar                ; yes: get another
26:       mov   ah,2                   ; no: write DL to output
27:       int   21h                    ; call DOS
28:       loop  getchar
```

Figure 9-1 *(Cont.)*

```
29:
30:        mov    ax,4C00h                  ; return to DOS
31:        int    21h
32:     main endp
33:
34:     .data
35:     validchars  db 32 dup(0)     ; invalid chars: 0-31
36:                 db 96 dup(0FFh) ; valid chars:   32-127
37:                 db 128 dup(0)   ; invalid chars: 128-255
38:
39:     end main
```

Character Encoding

The XLAT instruction provides a simple way to encode data so it cannot be read by unauthorized persons. When messages are transferred across telephone lines, for instance, encoding can be a way of preventing others from reading them. Imagine a table in which all the possible digits and letters have been rearranged. A program could read each character from standard input, use XLAT to look it up in a table, and write its encoded value to standard output. A sample table is as follows:

```
codetable db 48 dup(0)                       ; no translation
          db '4590821367'                    ; 0-9
          db 7 dup (0)                       ; no translation
          db 'GVHZUSOBMIKPJCADLFTYEQNWXR'    ; A-Z
          db 6 dup (0)                       ; no translation
          db 'gvhzusobmikpjcadlftyeqnwxr'    ; a-z
          db 133 dup(0)                      ; no translation
```

Certain ranges in the table are set to zeros; characters in these ranges are not translated. The $ character (ASCII 36), for example, is not translated because position 36 in the table contains 0.

Sample Program. The character encoding program (ENCODE.ASM, Figure 9-2) encodes each character read from an input file. When running the program, one can redirect standard input from a file, using the < symbol. For example:

```
encode < infile
```

The program output will appear on the screen. One can also redirect the output to a file:

```
encode < infile > outfile
```

Figure 9-2 The ENCODE program.

```
 1:  title  Character Encoding Program                    (ENCODE.ASM)
 2:
 3:  ;
 4:  ;   This program reads an input file and encodes
 5:  ;   the output.
 6:  ;
 7:  dosseg
 8:  .model small
 9:  .stack 100h
10:
11:  .code
12:  main proc
13:      mov   ax,@data           ; initialize DS
14:      mov   ds,ax
15:      mov   bx,offset codetable    ; point to lookup table
16:  getchar:
17:      mov   ah,6               ; console input, no wait
18:      mov   dl,0FFh            ; specify input request
19:      int   21h                ; call DOS
20:      jz    quit               ; quit if no input is waiting
21:      mov   dl,al              ; save character in DL
22:      xlat  codetable          ; translate the character
23:      cmp   al,0               ; translatable?
24:      je    putchar            ; no: write it as is
25:      mov   dl,al              ; yes: move new character to DL
26:
27:  putchar:
28:      mov   ah,2               ; write DL to output
29:      int   21h                ; call DOS
30:      jmp   getchar            ; get another character
31:
32:  quit:
33:      mov   ax,4C00h           ; return to DOS
34:      int   21h
35:  main endp
36:
37:  .data
38:  codetable db   48 dup(0)       ; no translation
39:            db  '4590821367'     ; ASCII codes 48-57
40:            db   7 dup (0)       ; no translation
41:            db  'GVHZUSOBMIKPJCADLFTYEQNWXR'
42:            db   6 dup (0)       ; no translation
43:            db  'gvhzusobmikpjcadlftyeqnwxr'
44:            db   133 dup(0)      ; no translation
45:
46:  end main
```

The following example shows a line from an input file that has been encoded:

```
This is a SECRET Message    (read from input file)
Ybmt mt g TUHFUY Juttgou    (encoded output)
```

The program may not use the keyboard as the standard input device because it would quit looking for input as soon as the keyboard buffer is empty. (One would have to type fast enough to keep the keyboard buffer full.)

Program Overview. Line 15 moves the offset of the lookup table into BX, as required by the XLAT instruction. Within the main loop of the program, we use DOS function 6 to check for an input character (lines 16–20). When using function 6, place 0FFh in DL to request console input. If no character is waiting, DOS sets the Zero flag and the program quits.

As soon as a character is read, we look it up in the translate table, using XLAT (line 22). If a value other than 0 is found in the lookup table, line 25 moves it to DL.

Lines 28 and 29 write the character to standard output using DOS function 2, and line 30 jumps back to input a new character.

We should not have any delusions about the security level demonstrated here; the code can be broken. At the same time, a novice might be discouraged from trying. One might also use this translate table as a basis for further manipulation of the character values.

BINARY TO DECIMAL CONVERSION

To display or print a binary value, one converts it to a string of ASCII digits. Simply moving a binary value to DL and writing it to the console does not yield the desired result. For example, we might move the number 65 to DL and display it as follows:

```
mov   ah,2      ; console output function
mov   dl,65     ; character to be displayed
int   21h       ; call DOS
```

But these statements would cause the letter *A* to be displayed on the console, since 65 is the ASCII code for *A*. To display the actual digits in the number 65, we would write two characters to the console:

```
mov   ah,2      ; console output function
mov   dl,'6'    ; digit to be displayed
int   21h       ; call DOS
mov   dl,'5'    ; next digit to be displayed
int   21h       ; call DOS
```

Therefore, a binary number must be converted to individual ASCII digits before it can be displayed correctly.

The WRINT Procedure

Figure 9-3 contains a general-purpose procedure called WRINT that displays an unsigned binary value on the console. The number to be displayed is placed in AX before WRINT is called.

This procedure uses a standard algorithm to convert an internal binary number to ASCII decimal. We divide the number repeatedly by 10 until the quotient is equal to 0. The remainder from each division step becomes a digit in the ASCII digit string. For example, the number 4096 is converted as follows:

Dividend	/	10	=	Quotient	Remainder
4096	/	10	=	409	6
409	/	10	=	40	9
40	/	10	=	4	0
4	/	10	=	0	4

Result: 4 0 9 6

As each digit is calculated we put it in a buffer, which is later written to standard output. A pseudocode listing of WRINT follows:

```
REPEAT
  Divide AX by 10
  Convert remainder (DL) to ASCII
  Place DL in the buffer
UNTIL AX = 0

REPEAT
  Move digit from buffer to DL
  Display the digit
  Point to next digit in buffer
UNTIL all digits displayed
```

Description of WRINT. We place the binary number to be converted in AX before calling WRINT. In Figure 9-3, lines 14 and 15 initialize the digit counter (CX) to zero and point DI 1 byte beyond the end of the buffer (the digits will be inserted at the end of the buffer, working backward).

Next is the actual conversion. The number in AX is divided by 10. Each time DIV is executed (line 21), a remainder is left in DX. This remainder is converted to an ASCII digit (line 22), which is placed in the output buffer. Converting the remainder in DL to ASCII is accomplished by ORing it with 00110000b (30h). The value 2, for example, would become 32h, the ASCII code for the digit 2.

Figure 9-3 The WRINT procedure.

```
 1:  ;
 2:  ;  WRINT displays a 16-bit unsigned binary number
 3:  ;  in ASCII decimal format.  AX contains the
 4:  ;  binary value when the procedure is called.
 5:  ;
 6:
 7:  .code
 8:  wrint proc
 9:      push  ax              ; save registers
10:      push  bx
11:      push  cx
12:      push  dx
13:      push  di
14:      mov   cx,0                ; set digit counter to zero
15:      mov   di,offset buffer_A + 6  ; point past end of buffer
16:
17:      ; Divide AX, convert remainder to ASCII.
18:
19:      mov   bx,10           ; divisor = 10
20:  A1: mov   dx,0            ; clear dividend to 0
21:      div   bx              ; divide AX by 10
22:      or    dl,30h          ; convert remainder to ASCII
23:      dec   di              ; reverse through the buffer
24:      mov   [di],dl         ; store ASCII digit
25:      inc   cx              ; increment count
26:      or    ax,ax           ; quotient = 0?
27:      jnz   A1              ; no: divide again
28:
29:      ; Display the buffer, using CX as a counter.
30:
31:  A2: mov   ah,2            ; function: display character
32:      mov   dl,[di]         ; get digit from buffer
33:      int   21h             ; call DOS
34:      inc   di              ; point to next digit
35:      loop  A2
36:
37:      pop   di              ; restore registers
38:      pop   dx
39:      pop   cx
40:      pop   bx
41:      pop   ax
42:      ret
43:  wrint endp
44:
45:  .data
46:  buffer_A  db  6 dup(' ')
```

Lines 26 and 27 check the quotient in AX and repeat the loop only if AX is greater than 0. Lines 31–35 display all digits stored in the buffer.

Choosing Label Names. Beginning with the WRINT procedure, we are using a new format for code labels that makes it easier to manage larger programs. The labels within each procedure start with the same letter (*A, B, C,* etc.) and are numbered sequentially. In large programs with many procedures, each procedure's labels will begin with a different letter.

The WRITESINT Procedure

The WRITESINT procedure (Figure 9-4) displays a signed number in ASCII decimal format. The algorithm used is nearly the same as that in the WRINT procedure, with two important differences. First, if AX is negative at the beginning of the procedure, we set a flag to *true*. Second, we add a leading negative sign (–) to the final ASCII digit string if the original number was negative.

Line 18 checks the number's sign by ORing AX with itself. If the Sign flag is set, we assume AX is negative, set **neg_flag** to *true,* and reverse the sign of AX.

After the ASCII digits have been stored in the buffer, we check **neg_flag**. If it equals 1, we insert a negative (–) sign at the beginning of the number.

Figure 9-4 The WRITESINT procedure.

```
 1:  ;
 2:  ;     WRITESINT displays a signed binary integer in
 3:  ;     ASCII decimal format.  The number to be displayed
 4:  ;     is in AX when the procedure is called.
 5:  ;
 6:
 7:      true  equ   1                    ; define boolean constants
 8:      false equ   0
 9:
10:  .code
11:  writesint proc
12:      push  ax                         ; save registers
13:      push  bx
14:      push  cx
15:      push  dx
16:      push  di
17:      mov   neg_flag,false             ; assume neg_flag is false
18:      or    ax,ax                      ; is AX positive?
19:      jns   B1                         ; yes: jump to B1
20:      neg   ax                         ; no: make it positive
21:      mov   neg_flag,true              ; set neg_flag to true
22:
23:  B1: mov   cx,0                       ; digit count = 0
24:      mov   di,offset buffer_B+6       ; point past end of buffer
25:      mov   bx,10                      ; will divide by 10
26:
```

Figure 9-4 *(Cont.)*

```
27:   B2: mov   dx,0                      ; set dividend to 0
28:       div   bx                        ; divide AX by 10
29:       or    dl,30h                    ; convert remainder to ASCII
30:       dec   di                        ; reverse through the buffer
31:       mov   [di],dl                   ; store ASCII digit
32:       inc   cx                        ; increment digit count
33:       or    ax,ax                     ; quotient > 0?
34:       jnz   B2                        ; yes: divide again
35:
36:       ; Check for a sign.
37:
38:       cmp   neg_flag,false            ; was the number positive?
39:       jz    B3                        ; yes: display it
40:       dec   di                        ; no: backup up in buffer
41:       mov   byte ptr [di],'-'         ; store negative sign
42:       inc   cx                        ; increment counter
43:
44:       ; Display the digits in the buffer.
45:
46:   B3: mov   ah,2                      ; function: display character
47:       mov   dl,[di]                   ; get digit from buffer
48:       int   21h                       ; call DOS
49:       inc   di                        ; point to next digit
50:       loop  B3
51:
52:       pop   di                        ; restore registers
53:       pop   dx
54:       pop   cx
55:       pop   bx
56:       pop   ax
57:       ret
58:   writesint endp
59:
60:   .data
61:   buffer_B   db  6 dup(' ')           ; buffer holding digits
62:   neg_flag   db  ?
```

Testing WRINT and WRITESINT. Let's look at a short program (TEST1.ASM, Figure 9-5) that tests the WRINT and WRITESINT procedures. The program loops through two lists of 16-bit integers, first unsigned, then signed.

The first loop (lines 18–23) loads five unsigned numbers into AX, one at a time, and calls the WRINT procedure. Five numbers are displayed in ASCII decimal format:

```
0 65535 32768 2 4096
```

```
 1:  title  ASCII Display Program                    (TEST1.ASM)
 2:
 3:  ;
 4:  ;   This program tests the WRINT and WRITESINT
 5:  ;   procedures.
 6:  ;
 7:  dosseg
 8:  .model small
 9:  .stack 100h
10:
11:  .code
12:  main proc
13:      mov   ax,@data              ; initialize DS
14:      mov   ds,ax
15:      mov   si,0                  ; index = 0
16:      mov   cx,5                  ; loop count
17:
18:  main1:
19:      mov   ax,unsigned [si]      ; get an unsigned number
20:      call  wrint                 ; display it
21:      call  space                 ; write a space
22:      add   si,2                  ; point to next number
23:      loop  main1                 ; repeat five times
24:
25:      call  space                 ; write an extra space
26:      mov   si,0                  ; index = 0
27:      mov   cx,5                  ; loop count
28:
29:  main2:
30:      mov   ax,signed [si]        ; get a signed number
31:      call  writesint             ; display it
32:      call  space                 ; write a space
33:      add   si,2                  ; point to next number
34:      loop  main2                 ; repeat five times
35:
36:      mov   ax,4C00h              ; return to DOS
37:      int   21h
38:  main endp
39:
40:  include  WRINT.INC              ; the WRINT procedure
41:  include  WRSINT.INC             ; the WRITESINT procedure
42:
43:  .code
44:  space proc                      ; write a space character
45:      mov   ah,2
46:      mov   dl,32
47:      int   21h
48:      ret
49:  space endp
50:
51:  .data
52:  unsigned dw  0, 65535, 32768, 2, 4096
53:  signed   dw  1024, -4096,-1, 32767, -32768
54:
55:  end main
```

Figure 9-5 *Test of the WRINT and WRITESINT procedures.*

The second loop (lines 29–34) reads five signed numbers and calls WRITESINT. The output from this loop is:

```
1024 -4096 -1 32767 -32768
```

Converting to Another Radix

The WRINT procedure (Figure 9-3) displays binary numbers in ASCII decimal notation, but it cannot display them in hexadecimal, binary, or octal. We need a more flexible procedure that will convert to any radix between 2 and 16. The new procedure will be called WRITEINT. We can pass a radix value (2–16) in BX to the procedure, and we will assume that all values are unsigned. Sample procedure calls to display AX in various ASCII formats are as follows:

SAMPLE CALLS TO WRITEINT

ASCII decimal format

```
mov   bx,10           ; decimal radix
mov   ax,wordvalue    ; value to be displayed
call  writeint
```

ASCII hexadecimal format

```
mov   bx,16           ; hexadecimal radix
mov   ax,wordvalue    ; value to be displayed
call  writeint
```

ASCII binary format

```
mov   bx,2            ; binary radix
mov   ax,wordvalue    ; value to be displayed
call  writeint
```

Clearly, this procedure is more useful than WRINT. To convert a binary number to ASCII hexadecimal, for instance, we repeatedly divide the number by 16; the remainder becomes a digit in the result. The number 4,096 is used as an example here:

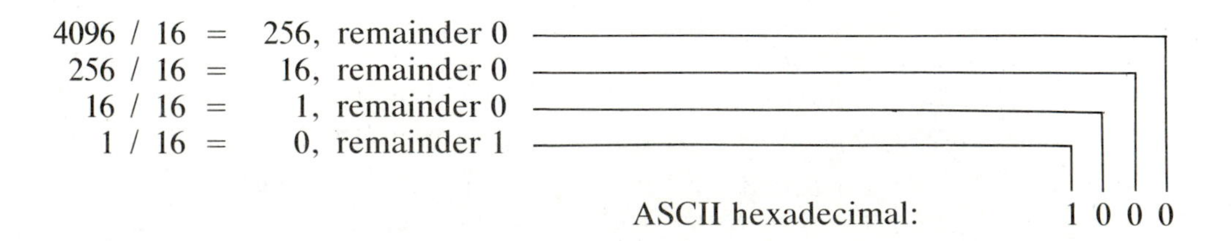

The same approach will work for any radix if we change the divisor to the desired radix.

The WRITEINT Procedure

The TEST2.ASM program (Figure 9-6a) demonstrates the WRITEINT procedure, and Figure 9-6b shows the program output. When using FFFFh as the value to be converted, for example, the output is:

```
1111111111111111     (binary)
177777               (octal)
65535                (decimal)
FFFF                 (hexadecimal)
```

Let's look at a few specific lines in Figure 9-6a. The radix to be used when converting the number is passed in BX by the calling program. Lines 65–70 ensure that BX is in the range 2–16; otherwise, BX is set to 10, the default radix.

The main loop begins at line 76, where we clear the high part of the dividend and divide AX by the radix. Each time we execute line 77, AX contains the remaining value of the binary number that has not yet been converted.

In this program, we use a translate table and the XLAT instruction (line 84) to look up the digit in AL. In earlier programs, we converted a digit to ASCII decimal by ORing it with 30h; here the translate table accommodates any radix up to 16. Lines 95–99 loop through the buffer and display each digit.

Figure 9-6a *ASCII Conversion, using WRITEINT.*

```
 1:  title  Binary to ASCII Conversion Program     (TEST2.ASM)
 2:
 3:  ;
 4:  ;  This program demonstrates the WRITEINT procedure,
 5:  ;  which displays a 16-bit integer in binary,
 6:  ;  octal, decimal, or hexadecimal ASCII.
 7:  ;
 8:  dosseg
 9:  .model small
10:  .stack 100h
11:
12:      binary   equ   2         ; radix definitions
13:      octal    equ   8
14:      decimal  equ  10
15:      hex      equ  16
16:
17:  .code
18:  main proc
19:      mov   ax,@data           ; initialize DS
20:      mov   ds,ax
21:      mov   cx,5               ; loop count
22:      mov   si,offset intlist  ; list of integers
23:
```

Figure 9-6a *(Cont.)*

```
24:  nextvalue:
25:       mov   ax,[si]                 ; get word value
26:       mov   bx,binary               ; binary radix
27:       call  writeint                ; display integer
28:       call  writecrlf               ; output carriage return
29:
30:       mov   bx,octal                ; octal radix
31:       call  writeint
32:       call  writecrlf
33:
34:       mov   bx,decimal              ; decimal radix
35:       call  writeint
36:       call  writecrlf
37:
38:       mov   bx,hex                  ; hexadecimal radix
39:       call  writeint
40:       call  writecrlf
41:       call  writecrlf               ; write a blank line
42:       add   si,2                    ; point to next integer
43:       loop  nextvalue               ; repeat five times
44:
45:       mov   ax,4C00h                ; return to DOS
46:       int   21h
47:  main endp
48:
49:  ;
50:  ;  WRITEINT converts a 16-bit unsigned binary number
51:  ;  to ASCII and writes it to standard output.  The
52:  ;  procedure must be called with a binary value in AX
53:  ;  and a radix value (2-16) in BX.
54:  ;
55:
56:  writeint proc
57:        push  ax                     ; save registers
58:        push  bx
59:        push  cx
60:        push  dx
61:        push  di
62:
63:        ; The radix passed in BX must be from 2 to 16
64:
65:        cmp   bx,2                   ; if radix < 2
66:        jb    L1                     ;   set it to 10
67:        cmp   bx,16                  ; if radix > 16
68:        ja    L1                     ;   set it to 10
69:        jmp   L2                     ; else jump to L2
70:  L1:   mov   bx,10                  ; default radix = 10
71:  L2:   mov   cx,0                   ; digit count = 0
72:        mov   di,offset buffer+16 ; point past end of buffer
73:
74:        ; Begin converting AX to ASCII
75:
```

Figure 9-6a *(Cont.)*

```
 76:   L3:  mov   dx,0                   ; clear dividend to 0
 77:        div   bx                     ; divide AX by the radix
 78:
 79:        ; Translate the digit in AL to ASCII, store in buffer
 80:
 81:        xchg  ax,dx                  ; exchange quotient, remainder
 82:        push  bx
 83:        mov   bx,offset table        ; point to translate table
 84:        xlat                         ; look up ASCII digit
 85:        pop   bx
 86:        dec   di                     ; back up in buffer
 87:        mov   [di],al                ; move digit into buffer
 88:        xchg  ax,dx                  ; swap quotient back into AX
 89:        inc   cx                     ; increment digit count
 90:        or    ax,ax                  ; quotient = 0?
 91:        jnz   L3                     ; no: divide again
 92:
 93:        ; Display the buffer, using CX as a counter
 94:
 95:   L4:  mov   ah,2                   ; function: display character
 96:        mov   dl,[di]                ; character to be displayed
 97:        mov   21h                    ; call DOS
 98:        inc   di                     ; point to next character
 99:        loop  L4
100:
101:        pop   di                     ; restore saved registers
102:        pop   dx
103:        pop   cx
104:        pop   bx
105:        pop   ax
106:        ret
107:   writeint     endp
108:
109:   writecrlf   proc      ; write a CR/LF
110:        push ax
111:        push dx
112:        mov  dx,offset creturn
113:        mov  ah,9
114:        int  21h
115:        pop  dx
116:        pop  ax
117:        ret
118:   writecrlf   endp
119:
120:   .data
121:   buffer    db  16 dup (' ')             ; buffer to hold chars
122:   table     db  '0123456789ABCDEF'       ; translate table
123:   intlist   dw  1,11010001b,4096,65535,9000h
124:   creturn   db  0Dh,0Ah,'$'
125:
126:   end main
```

```
1                ← binary
1                ← octal
1                ← decimal
1                ← hexadecimal

11010001         ← binary
321              ← octal
209              ← decimal
D1               ← hexadecimal
                 (etc.)

1000000000000
10000
4096
1000

1111111111111111
177777
65535
FFFF

1001000000000000
110000
36864
9000
```

Figure 9-6b Output from the TEST2.ASM program.

DECIMAL TO BINARY CONVERSION

When a string of ASCII decimal digits is input from either the keyboard or a file, the string is usually converted to binary. This helps us to take advantage of the CPU's greater speed when processing binary numbers. Arithmetic may be performed using ASCII digit strings, as we saw in Chapter 8, but this forces us to perform calculations 1 digit at a time. To convert a number from ASCII decimal to binary, we multiply it successively by 10. This is the reverse of the process used when converting binary numbers to ASCII.

Let's use the ASCII string "4096" as an example. AX is initialized to zero. As we read each ASCII digit, we multiply AX by 10, and the digit's binary value is added to AX. After all digits have been read, AX contains the binary value of the number 4096:

AX Before			New Digit		AX After	
0	* 10	+	4	=	4	
4	* 10	+	0	=	40	
40	* 10	+	9	=	409	
409	* 10	+	6	=	4096	← final value

The READINT Procedure

The TEST3.ASM program (Figure 9-7) demonstrates the READINT procedure. It inputs an ASCII decimal number from the console, converts it to binary, and stores the converted value in AX. Leading spaces are skipped, and the procedure checks for a leading sign (+ or −). The end of the number is found when the first nondigit character is found.

Lines 45–47 call DOS function 0Ah to input a string of digits. Lines 48–50 get DOS's count of the number of digits typed and move it to CX. Lines 51–54 check the number of digits entered; if none were typed, we set AX to zero and exit.

Lines 56–61 skip over leading spaces at the beginning of the number, using CX as a loop counter. We exit if the number contains all spaces, which would happen only if CX were decremented all the way to zero.

Lines 63–68 check for a leading negative (−) or positive (+) sign. **Sign** is set to −1 if a negative sign is found. If either no sign or a positive sign is found, **sign** is set to 1. Lines 77–81 make sure that DL contains a valid ASCII digit, and line 82 converts it to binary by clearing its high 4 bits.

Line 84 multiplies the binary value of the number so far by 10; to this we add DL. These instructions detect overflow by checking the Carry flag after the MUL and ADD instructions (lines 86 and 88). You may recall that a 16-bit multiply operation sets the Carry flag when its result is larger than 16 bits. If the result is larger than 16 bits, we display the following message on the screen and exit, because the value returned by READINT is no longer valid (lines 94–97):

```
<integer overflow>
```

An Interesting Bug. Often we learn more by the mistakes made while writing programs than we do when they work the first time. See if you can catch an error I made while developing the first version of READINT. I wrote the following code to multiply the number in AX by 10 and add the value of the most recent digit:

```
and  dx,000Fh     ; convert digit to binary
mul  bl           ; AX = AL * 10
add  ax,dx        ; add new digit to AX
```

```
 1:   title  ASCII to Binary Conversion Program       (TEST3.ASM)
 2:
 3:   ;
 4:   ;   Demonstration of the READINT procedure: Converts
 5:   ;   an ASCII digit string to a 16-bit binary value.
 6:   ;   No output will appear, so the program should be
 7:   ;   tested using a debugger.
 8:   ;
 9:   dosseg
10:   .model small
11:   .stack 100h
12:
13:   .code
14:   main proc
15:           mov   ax,@data           ; initialize DS
16:           mov   ds,ax
17:           mov   cx,2               ; loop count = 2
18:   nextvalue:
19:           mov   ah,9               ; display a prompt
20:           mov   dx,offset prompt
21:           int   21h
22:           call  readint            ; input a number
23:           mov   ah,9               ; display a CR/LF
24:           mov   dx,offset crlf
25:           int   21h
26:           loop  nextvalue          ; repeat 2 times
27:
28:           mov   ax,4C00h           ; return to DOS
29:           int   21h
30:   main endp
31:
32:   ;
33:   ;   READINT inputs an ASCII decimal number from the
34:   ;   console, including digits 0-9 and an optional leading
35:   ;   sign. Leading spaces are skipped. It returns the 16-bit
36:   ;   binary value of the number in AX. No other registers
37:   ;   are changed.
38:   ;
39:
40:   readint proc
41:       push  bx
42:       push  cx
43:       push  dx
44:       push  si
45:       mov   dx,offset inputarea   ; input the string
46:       mov   ah,0Ah
47:       int   21h
48:       mov   si,offset inputarea+2
49:       mov   cx,0                 ; scan for leading spaces
50:       mov   cl,inputarea+1       ; get number of chars entered
51:       or    cx,cx                ; any chars entered?
```

Figure 9-7 *ASCII to Binary Conversion, using READINT.*

Figure 9-7 *(Cont.)*

```
 52:        jnz    L1                    ; yes: continue
 53:        mov    ax,0                  ; no: set value to 0
 54:        jmp    L7                    ; exit procedure
 55:
 56:    L1: mov    al,[si]               ; get a character from buffer
 57:        cmp    al,' '                ; space character found?
 58:        jnz    L2                    ; no: check for a sign
 59:        inc    si                    ; yes: point to next char
 60:        loop   L1
 61:        jmp    L7                    ; quit if all spaces
 62:
 63:    L2: mov    sign,1                ; assume number is positive
 64:        cmp    al,'-'                ; minus sign found?
 65:        jnz    L3                    ; no: look for plus sign
 66:        mov    sign,-1               ; yes: sign is negative
 67:        inc    si                    ; point to next char
 68:        jmp    L4
 69:
 70:    L3: cmp    al,'+'                ; plus sign found?
 71:        jnz    L4                    ; no: must be a digit
 72:        inc    si                    ; yes: skip over the sign
 73:
 74:    L4: mov    ax,0                  ; clear accumulator
 75:        mov    bx,10                 ; BX is the multiplier
 76:
 77:    L5: mov    dl,[si]               ; get character from buffer
 78:        cmp    dl,'0'                ; character < '0'?
 79:        jl     L7                    ; yes: resolve sign and exit
 80:        cmp    dl,'9'                ; character > '9'?
 81:        jg     L7                    ; yes: resolve sign and exit
 82:        and    dx,000Fh              ; no: convert to binary
 83:        push   dx                    ; save the digit
 84:        mul    bx                    ; DX:AX = AX * BX
 85:        pop    dx                    ; restore the digit
 86:        jc     L6                    ; quit if result too large
 87:        add    ax,dx                 ; add new digit to AX
 88:        jc     L6                    ; quit if result too large
 89:        inc    si                    ; point to next digit
 90:        jmp    L5                    ; get another digit
 91:
 92:        ; Overflow must have occurred
 93:
 94:    L6: mov    dx,offset overflow_msg
 95:        mov    ah,9
 96:        int    21h
 97:        mov    ax,0                  ; set result to zero
 98:
 99:    L7: mul    sign                  ; AX = AX * sign
100:        pop    si
101:        pop    dx
102:        pop    cx
```

Figure 9-7 *(Cont.)*

```
103:        pop    bx
104:        ret
105:    readint endp
106:
107:    .data
108:    sign            dw   ?
109:    inputarea       db   10,0,10 dup(' ')   ; up to 9 digits
110:    overflow_msg    db   ' <integer overflow> $'
111:    prompt          db   'Enter a number: $'
112:    crlf            db   0Dh,0Ah,'$'
113:
114:    end main
```

Before these instructions are reached, BX always contains 10. Let's say that AX = 0020h and DL = 2. AL is multiplied by BL, so AX = 0140h. DL is added to AX, yielding AX = 0142h. The routine seems to work correctly.

But let's try another example, with AX = 0200h and DL = 02. AL * BL yields AX = 0. DL is added to this, so AX = 0002h. The solution, as we now see it, is that we must multiply using BX, not BL. This means the result will be stored in both DX and AX:

```
DX:AX = AX * BX
```

Of course, as soon as we do this, we destroy the digit that was being held in DL, so we have a new bug:

```
and   dx,000Fh       ; convert digit to binary
mul   bx             ; DX:AX = AX * 10
add   ax,dx          ; add new digit to AX
```

This is also a hard bug to catch unless you know that a 16-bit multiply always replaces the contents of DX, no matter how small the product is. So we must push DX on the stack before the multiplication and restore it afterward:

```
and    dx,000Fh      ; convert digit to binary
push   dx            ; save the digit
mul    bx            ; DX:AX = AX * 10
pop    dx            ; restore the digit
add    ax,dx         ; add new digit to AX
```

The only difference between this code and the complete procedure is the use of the two JC instructions to check for integer overflow. In retrospect, the error seems all too obvious, because the number in AX must always be multiplied by 10. If only such answers would seem obvious from the start!

SEPARATELY ASSEMBLED MODULES

Many programs use the input-output facilities available from DOS to perform the simplest keyboard and screen operations. In addition, programs need to have ways of converting numbers from one format to another. These features are generally available in high-level languages. In assembly language, however, you have to write your own long and detailed routines. We need a way of making these routines callable from any program. We can accomplish this by using a *toolbox,* or *library,* that is available to any program.

One approach has already been shown; the INCLUDE directive can copy a procedure's source code directly into a program while it is being assembled. This method has one drawback, however: A source program may become very large when several INCLUDE files are used. This tends to slow down the assembly process.

We are much better off writing programs in separate modules. Each module is assembled and converted to an OBJ file. This, in fact, is the real reason for having a linker. Otherwise, all programs would simply be assembled and converted to an EXE or COM format in a single step. The linker (LINK.EXE) collects one or more OBJ files and combines them into a single EXE program. This process is much faster than assembly, so large programs may be quickly constructed from many small modules.

An important structured programming principle here is *modularity.* When programs are assembled separately, we must define interfaces between the modules. These *interfaces* are the method by which data are passed back and forth. When two program modules have no interaction with each other except through their interfaces, it is easier to solve incompatibility problems that arise. There is also less chance that modifying a variable within one module will accidentally modify a variable with the same name in another module.

Of course, these are restrictions that we have come to respect in modern high-level languages. To a large extent, restrictions in assembly language are an illusion. We make our own rules as we construct programs, and we are wholly responsible for their outcomes. In the next section, we will create a collection of useful routines and show how to link them to an application program.

The EXTRN Directive

When MASM finds a reference to a name that is not in the current source file, it cannot calculate the name's effective address. We use the EXTRN directive to identify names that exist outside of the current source file. This tells MASM that the name's address will be filled in by the linker. The basic format of the EXTRN directive is

```
EXTRN  name:type
```

Name is the name of the procedure or label, and *type* is a size or distance attribute associated with the name. A list of allowable types follows:

Type	Explanation
ABS	A name defined with EQU or =
PROC	Default type for a procedure
NEAR	Name is in the same segment
FAR	Name is in a different segment
BYTE	Size is 8 bits
WORD	Size is 16 bits
DWORD	Size is 32 bits
FWORD	Size is 48 bits
QWORD	Size is 64 bits
TBYTE	Size is 10 bytes

Simplified Segment Directives. If your program uses simplified segment directives (e.g., .CODE, .DATA, .STACK, .MODEL), the EXTRN directive should use the PROC type for all procedure names. For a program declared with a small memory model (.MODEL SMALL), the PROC type will default to *near,* meaning that the procedure is located in the same segment. If the model type is medium, large, or huge, the PROC type will default to *far.* We will assume that simplified segment directives are being used for each of the examples here.

Examples. The following directive refers to an external procedure named WRITEINT:

```
extrn writeint:proc
```

In a small model program, the procedure being called could also be declared as near:

```
extrn writeint:near
```

In a medium, large, or huge model program, the procedure could be declared as far:

```
extrn writeint:far
```

The following EXTRN refers to the absolute symbols **true** and **false,** assumed to have been created using an equate operator:

```
extrn true:abs,false:abs
```

Notice that multiple names may be declared using a single EXTRN directive.

The following refers to three 8-bit variables named **bufsize**, **keystyped,** and **keybuf**:

```
extrn bufsize:byte, keystyped:byte, keybuf:byte
```

The PUBLIC Directive

The PUBLIC directive is required when a program module contains names that will be accessed by other modules. A procedure, symbol, or variable literally becomes public to any other part of the program. The general format is:

```
PUBLIC name
```

Multiple names may be declared together:

```
PUBLIC name1, name2, name3 . . .
```

A PUBLIC directive may be placed anywhere in a program module. If a PUBLIC declaration is made for an absolute symbol, it may only represent a 1- or 2-byte integer. In the following program, **count** may be declared public, but **message** may not:

```
dosseg
.model small
public  count, writestr

count   equ   25
message equ   'File not found'

.code
writestr proc   ; a public procedure
.
.
writestr endp
```

This example also declares WRITESTR public, so it may be accessed by other program modules.

Calling DISPLAY from Another Module

In this section, we will look at a program called EXTRN1.ASM that calls the DISPLAY procedure from another ASM module. Both modules are shown in Figure 9-8. The main module is EXTRN1.ASM. It declares the DISPLAY procedure external on line 12. After initializing DS to the data segment, it moves the offset of **message** to DX and calls DISPLAY.

```
EXTRN1.ASM:
 1:   title  Display a String                    (EXTRN1.ASM)
 2:
 3:   ;
 4:   ;  This program calls the DISPLAY procedure,
 5:   ;  located in the EXTRN1A.ASM module.
 6:   ;
 7:   dosseg
 8:   .model small
 9:   .stack 100h
10:
11:   .code
12:   extrn  display:proc
13:
14:   main proc
15:       mov   ax,@data            ; initialize DS
16:       mov   ds,ax
17:       mov   dx,offset message   ; point to message
18:       call  display
19:       mov   ax,4C00h            ; return to DOS
20:       int   21h
21:   main endp
22:
23:   .data
24:   message  db  'This message is displayed by the '
25:            db  'DISPLAY procedure.',0Dh,0Ah,'$'
26:
27:   end main
```

```
EXTRN1A.ASM:
 1:   title  The DISPLAY Procedure      (EXTRN1A.ASM)
 2:
 3:   ;
 4:   ;  This module is linked to EXTRN1.ASM.
 5:   ;
 6:   dosseg
 7:   .model small
 8:   .code
 9:   public  display
10:
11:   ; Display a string pointed to by DX
12:
13:   display proc
14:       push  ax         ; save AX
15:       mov   ah,9       ; function: display a string
16:       int   21h        ; call DOS
17:       pop   ax         ; restore AX
18:       ret
19:   display endp
20:
21:   end
```

Figure 9-8 External procedure call example.

The second module (EXTRN1A.ASM) contains the DISPLAY procedure, which displays any string pointed to by DX. It declares DISPLAY public, making it accessible to other programs (line 9).

This module also contains the DOSSEG, .MODEL, and CODE directives in order to maintain compatibility with the main module. One very important point: A label should be supplied only with the END directive of the main module. The label defines the *startaddress*, the address where a program begins execution. As one might assume, a program can have only one starting address.

Each module must be assembled separately and the two object files linked together. EXTRN1.ASM is the main program, so it appears first on the linker command line. The three commands used to assemble, link, and produce EXTRN1.EXE are shown here:

```
masm extrn1;
masm extrn1a;
link extrn1 extrn1a;
```

Using CODEVIEW. If you want to debug the EXTRN1.EXE program using CODEVIEW, you will have a pleasant surprise: The debugger automatically loads the source file of the second module when DISPLAY is called. The following commands assemble and link the programs and then run CODEVIEW:

```
masm/zi extrn1;
masm/zi extrn1a;
link/co extrn1 extrn1a;
cv extrn1
```

(Depending on your hardware setup, you may have to supply additional command line options when running CODEVIEW.)

CREATING EXTERNAL SUBROUTINES

Once you've written a standard input-output routine, you will probably want to use it in other programs. The next logical step is to create a library, or collection of these routines that can be linked to any program. We will use the name *procedure* for any group of statements delimited by the PROC and ENDP directives. A *subroutine* is a specific type of procedure; it is called by a main program to carry out a function. Each subroutine will be assembled into a separate .OBJ file. The subroutines presented in this section are described in the following list:

Procedure	Description
CLRSCR	Clear the screen and locate the cursor at the upper left corner
DISPLAY	Display a $-terminated string on the console
GETVMODE	Get the current video mode

LOCATE	Locate the cursor at a specified position
READINT	Read an ASCII decimal string from the console, and convert it to a signed binary value in AX
READKEY	Wait for a keystroke and place it in AL
READSTR	Read a string from the console
SCROLLWIN	Scroll all lines in a screen window
SETVPAGE	Set the current video page
WRITECRLF	Write a carriage return/line feed to the console
WRITEINT	Write an unsigned 16-bit binary integer to the console
WRITESINT	Write a signed 16-bit binary integer to the console

As we've said before, the interface is the manner in which values are passed by a calling program to a subroutine. The values passed by a calling program are called *arguments.** *Parameters,* on the other hand, are the same values after they have been received by the subroutine.

The interface between procedures is usually a trade-off between simplicity and flexibility. We want to write as few instructions as possible so the program will execute quickly, and we want the procedures to be useful in a variety of situations.

A subroutine should be as general as possible so it may be called by different programs. For example, the LOCATE procedure shown in the foregoing list expects the row and column values to be passed from the calling program. To code specific values within LOCATE would be a mistake because the subroutine would work only for a specific row and column.

Other decisions may not be quite as clear. The SCROLLWIN procedure, for instance, scrolls a window defined by the upper left and lower right corner positions passed by a calling program. What attribute should be used for the scrolled lines, and how many lines should be scrolled? If these are coded as constants within the subroutine, we lose flexibility; if they must be passed by the calling program, the procedure call becomes more cumbersome. Six values would have to be passed to the procedure:

Upper left corner row, column (two values)

Lower right corner row, column (two values)

Attribute for scrolled lines

Number of lines to scroll

And yet, if we omit any of these values, we may find ourselves creating separate SCROLLWIN procedures for different situations. There is no clear solution to this problem. It depends on the situation and on whether or not the subroutines need to be completely flexible.

*The distinction made here between arguments and parameters is not universal among reference materials provided with language compilers. Some refer to both the values passed to a subroutine and the values used within the subroutine as *parameters*. Either term is acceptable, as long as it is clear from the context which one is being used.

Passing Arguments. There are two basic ways to pass arguments to a subroutine. First, they may be passed in registers as 16-bit data or addresses. This method is simpler and faster but is limited by the number of available registers.

The second method involves pushing arguments on the stack before a subroutine is called. This is the method used by high-level languages. Using this method, even large amounts of data can be passed with a small loss of execution speed. A subroutine using this method may be called by either an assembler program or a high-level language program.

Of course, the whole issue of passing arguments could be avoided by simply declaring global variables and placing values in these variables before calling subroutines. But this approach involves an element of danger: You may accidentally alter global variables from any location in the program. Such errors are difficult to correct. Also, subroutines using global variables are inflexible, as they must always refer to the same variable names.

Individual Subroutine Descriptions

Let's take a detailed look at each subroutine. We will pass arguments in registers because this method is the most efficient and easiest to use. In each of the following descriptions, assume that no registers are modified by the subroutine unless they are specified as return values. When offsets of memory operands are passed, assume that DS points to their base segment.

CLRSCR. Clear the screen and locate the cursor at row 0, column 0. No values are passed or returned. Sample call:

```
call  clrscr
```

DISPLAY. Write an ASCII string that is terminated by the $ character (24h) to standard output. When calling the procedure, pass the string's offset in DX. No values are returned. Sample call:

```
mov   dx,offset message
call  display
```

GETVMODE. Get the current video mode using INT 10h, and store it in the global variable **videomode**. Get the current video page, and store it in **videopage**. This procedure should be called before using any of the color video modes. No values are passed or returned. Sample call:

```
call  getvmode   ; initializes videomode
```

LOCATE. Locate the cursor at a given row and column on the screen. When calling LOCATE, place the desired screen row in DH and the column in DL. No values are returned. Sample call:

```
mov   dh,row
mov   dl,col
call  locate
```

READINT. Read a signed ASCII decimal string from the console, and convert it to binary. The string may contain leading spaces and a sign (+ or −). The procedure checks the size of the number as it is being input. If overflow occurs, READINT sets the Carry flag and displays the following message:

```
<integer overflow>
```

No arguments are passed, and the binary value is returned in AX. Sample call:

```
call  readint          ; input a number
jc    out_range        ; if out of range then abort
mov   inputvalue,ax    ; size ok: save the number
```

READKEY. Wait for a keystroke (no echo), and place it in AL. If a normal key has been pressed, the Carry flag is clear and AL contains the ASCII code. If an extended key has been pressed, the Carry flag is set and the keyboard scan code is returned in AL. No arguments are passed. Sample call:

```
     call  readkey          ; wait for a key
     jc    extended_code    ; extended key pressed?
     mov   key,al           ; no: normal ASCII character
     .
     .
  extended_code:            ; yes: extended key
```

READSTR. Read an ASCII string from the keyboard. Place the address of the input area in DX when calling READSTR. The input area follows the format of INT 21h, function 0Ah:

Offset	Value
0	Buffer size (set by the calling program)
1	Keys typed (returned by DOS)
2	Input buffer area

Sample call:

```
            mov       dx,offset inbuffer_area
            call      readstr
            .
            .
    inbuffer_area  10h,0,10h dup(0)
```

SCROLLWIN. Scroll all lines in a window. No range checking is performed on the passed parameters. Pass the row and column values of the upper left corner in CH and CL, and pass the row and column values of the lower right corner in DH and DL. In addition, the following 8-bit global variables will be used by SCROLLWIN:

Variable	Description	Default Value
winattribute	Attribute of scrolled lines (monochrome display)	07h (normal)
winforeground	Color/attribute, foreground, scrolled lines (CGA, EGA)	07h (white)
winbackground	Color/attribute, background, scrolled lines (CGA, EGA)	00h (black)

These attributes remain in effect until they are changed by the calling program. When in monochrome mode, only **winattribute** should be used. When in color text mode, both **winforeground** and **winbackground** may be used. The following is a sample call using the default attribute values:

```
mov   cx,050Ah      ; ul corner: row 5, col 10
mov   dx,0A30h      ; lr corner: row 10, col 48
call  scrollwin
```

The following is a sample call with a monochrome reverse video attribute:

```
mov   winattribute,reverse
mov   cx,050Ah      ; ul corner: row 5, col 10
mov   dx,0A30h      ; lr corner: row 10, col 48
call  scrollwin
```

The following is a sample call with color attributes:

```
mov   winforeground,yellow
mov   winbackground,blue
mov   cx,050Ah     ; ul corner: row 5, col 10
mov   dx,0A30h     ; lr corner: row 10, col 48
call  scrollwin
```

SETVPAGE. Set the video page, using the page number passed in DL. This subroutine is valid for the CGA, EGA, and VGA displays. The default video page is 0. No values are returned. Sample call:

```
mov   dl,1        ; select video page 1
call  setvpage
```

WRITECRLF. Write a carriage return, line feed sequence (0Dh,0Ah) to standard output. No values are passed or returned. Sample call:

```
call   writecrlf
```

WRITEINT. Write an unsigned 16-bit binary integer to the console in one of the following ASCII formats: binary, octal, decimal, or hexadecimal. Pass the number to be written in AX and place a radix value (2–16) in BX, to be used when writing the number. No values are returned. Sample call:

```
   mov   ax,intvalue  ; get the number
   mov   bx,16        ; choose hexadecimal format
   call  writeint
   .
   .
intvalue dw  ?
```

WRITESINT. Write a signed 16-bit binary integer to the console in ASCII decimal format. Pass the number in AX when calling the subroutine. Sample call:

```
   mov   ax,signedvalue
   call  writesint
   .
   .
signedvalue dw  ?
```

Build the Modules. The first step is to create a module containing all global variables and constants (Figure 9-9). We must then assemble this and create LVARS.OBJ. The latter may be linked to any program that calls the library pro-

Constant	Value	
true	01h	← general-purpose constants
false	00h	
cr	0Dh	
lf	0Ah	
eof	1Ah	
monomode	07h	
colortextmode	03h	
uparrow	48h	← scan codes of extended keys on the keyboard
dnarrow	50h	
lftarrow	4Bh	
rtarrow	4Dh	
homekey	47h	
endkey	4Fh	
pgupkey	49h	
pgdnkey	51h	
inskey	52h	
delkey	53h	
attr_normal	07h	← monochrome video attributes
attr_reverse	70h	
attr_underline	01h	
attr_bright	0Fh	
blue	01h	← color video attributes
green	02h	
cyan	03h	
red	04h	
magenta	05h	
brown	06h	
white	07h	
gray	08h	
lblue	09h	
lgreen	0Ah	
lcyan	0Bh	
lred	0Ch	
lmagenta	0Dh	
yellow	0Eh	
brightwhite	0Fh	

Variable	Type	Description
videomode	Byte	Current video mode
videopage	Byte	Current video page
winforeground	Byte	Attribute for foreground characters when in color text mode
winbackground	Byte	Attribute for background when in color text mode
winattribute	Byte	Attribute for scrolled windows when in monochrome mode

Figure 9-9 Constants and variables in LVARS.ASM.

cedures. Using a program called MAIN, the following LINK command would do the job:

```
link main lvars;
```

Three of the procedures, WRITESINT, WRITEINT, and READINT, were shown earlier in this chapter. The remaining procedures are listed in Figure 9-10. Each procedure must be placed in a separate .ASM file and assembled into an .OBJ file. The procedures and their respective filenames are as follows:

Procedure	**Filename**
[1]	LVARS.ASM
CLRSCR	LCLRSCR.ASM
DISPLAY	LDISPLAY.ASM
GETVMODE	LGETVMOD.ASM
LOCATE	LLOCATE.ASM
READINT	LREADINT.ASM
READKEY	LREADKEY.ASM
READSTR	LREADSTR.ASM
SCROLL	LSCROLL.ASM
SETVPAGE	LSETVPAG.ASM
WRITEINT	LWRINT.ASM
WRITECRLF	LWRITECR.ASM
WRITESINT	LWRSINT.ASM

[1]All global constants and variables

Note that each filename has the letter *L* at the beginning to identify it as a library file. This is not a requirement, but it is an easy way to identify the source of a file.

When you want to call a subroutine from this list, its object file must be linked to the main program. Suppose that a program named MAIN calls CLRSCR and LOCATE. The main program would be linked to LVARS.OBJ, LCLRSCR.OBJ, and LLOCATE.OBJ, using the following command:

```
link main lvars lclrscr llocate;
```

Figure 9-10 Object library routines.

```
Individual Object Library Routines

;  (LCLRSCR.ASM)
;
;  CLRSCR clears the entire screen and locates the
;  cursor at row 0, column 0.
;
dosseg
.model small
public clrscr
extrn videopage:byte

.code
clrscr proc
     push    ax
     push    bx
     push    cx
     push    dx
     push    si
     push    di
     mov     ax,0600h     ; scroll entire screen up
     mov     cx,0         ; upper left corner (0,0)
     mov     dx,184Fh     ; lower right corner (24,79)
     mov     bh,7         ; normal attribute
     int     10h          ; call BIOS
     mov     ah,2         ; locate cursor at 0,0
     mov     bh,videopage
     mov     dx,0
     int     10h
     pop     di
     pop     si
     pop     dx
     pop     cx
     pop     bx
     pop     ax
     ret
clrscr endp
end

; (LDISPLAY.ASM)
;
;  DISPLAY writes a $-terminated string to standard
;  output.  Call it with the string's address in DX.
;
dosseg
.model small
public display
```

Figure 9-10 *(Cont.)*

```
.code
display proc
     push    ax
     mov     ah,9        ; DOS function: display a string
     int     21h
     pop     ax
     ret
display endp
end

; (LGETVMOD.ASM)
;
; LGETVMOD gets the current video mode and video page,
; using INT 10h.  Call this procedure before attempting
; to write to the color display.
;
dosseg
.model small
public getvmode
extrn videomode:byte, videopage:byte

.code
getvmode proc
     push  ax
     push  bx
     push  si
     push  di
     mov   ah,0Fh              ; get video mode
     int   10h                 ; call the BIOS
     mov   videomode,al        ; save the mode
     mov   videopage,bh        ; save the page
     pop   di
     pop   si
     pop   bx
     pop   ax
     ret
getvmode  endp
end

; (LLOCATE.ASM)
;
; LOCATE positions the cursor at row, column on the
; current video page.  Call it with the row in DH
; and the column in DL.
;
dosseg
.model small
public locate
extrn videopage:byte

.code
```

Figure 9-10 *(Cont.)*

```
locate proc
    push    ax
    push    bx
    push    dx
    push    si
    push    di
    mov     ah,2
    mov     bh,videopage    ; global variable
    int     10h
    pop     di
    pop     si
    pop     dx
    pop     bx
    pop     ax
    ret
locate endp
end

;  (LREADKEY.ASM)
;
; READKEY waits for a keystroke and places it in AL.
; If a normal key has been pressed, CF = 0 and AL contains
; the ASCII code.  If an extended key has been pressed,
; CF = 1 and the scan code is returned in AL.
;
dosseg
.model small
public readkey

.code
readkey proc
     mov    ah,7          ; read keyboard, no echo
     int    21h
     or     al,al         ; extended code?
     jz     L2            ; yes: get second byte
     clc                  ; no: normal ASCII character
     jmp    L3            ; exit
L2:  int    21h           ; second byte is extended code
     stc                  ; extended key
L3:  ret
readkey endp
end

;  (LREADSTR.ASM)
;
; READSTR gets an input string from the keyboard.
; Pass the address of the input area in DX.  The
; input buffer follows the format of DOS function 0Ah.
;
dosseg
.model small
```

Figure 9-10 *(Cont.)*

```
public readstr

.code
readstr proc
     push   ax
     push   dx
     mov    ah,0Ah           ; console input function
     int    21h              ; call DOS
     pop    dx
     pop    ax
     ret
readstr endp
end

;  (LSCROLL.ASM)
;
; SCROLLWIN scrolls all lines in a window.  No range
; checking is performed on the passed arguments.
; Set the following registers and variables before
; calling SCROLLWIN:
;
;   CH              Row of upper left corner
;   CL              Column of upper left corner
;   DH              Row of lower right corner
;   DL              Column of lower right corner
;
; Optionally, you may modify the following global
; variables before calling SCROLLWIN:
;
;   winattribute    Attribute of scrolled lines
;   winforeground   Color of foreground text
;   winbackground   Color of background text
;
dosseg
.model small
public scrollwin
extrn videomode:byte, colortextmode:abs
extrn winforeground:byte, winbackground:byte
extrn winattribute:byte

.code
scrollwin proc
     push   ax
     push   bx
     push   cx
     push   dx
     push   si
     push   di

     ; Set up the attribute byte.
```

Figure 9-10 *(Cont.)*

```
        cmp     videomode,colortextmode   ; are we in color?
        jne     L1                        ; no, jump to monochrome
        mov     bh,winforeground          ; yes: set window colors
        mov     al,winbackground
        shl     al,1                      ; shift into bits 4-7
        shl     al,1                      ; of the attribute byte
        shl     al,1
        shl     al,1
        or      bh,al                     ; add to BH to form attribute
        jmp     L2

L1:     mov     bh,winattribute           ; monochrome attribute
L2:     mov     ax,0600h        ; function: scroll window up
        int     10h             ; call BIOS
        pop     di
        pop     si
        pop     dx
        pop     cx
        pop     bx
        pop     ax
        ret
scrollwin endp
end

; (LSETVPAG.ASM)
;
;  SETVPAGE sets the video page to the value in
;  DL.  It has no effect on a monochrome display.
;
dosseg
.model small
public setvpage
extrn getvmode:proc
extrn videomode:byte, monomode:abs

.code
setvpage proc
    push  ax
    push  dx
    push  si
    push  di
    call  getvmode              ; if monochrome display
    cmp   videomode,monomode    ; then quit
    je    L1
    mov   ah,5                  ; select display page
    mov   al,dl                 ; page number is in DL
    int   10h                   ; call the BIOS
L1: pop   di
    pop   si
    pop   dx
```

Figure 9-10 *(Cont.)*

```
    pop    ax
    ret
setvpage endp
end

;  (LWRITECR.ASM)
;
;  WRITECR writes a carriage return and a line
;  feed sequence (0Dh,0Ah) to standard output.
;
dosseg
.model small
public writecrlf

.code
writecrlf proc
     push  ax
     push  dx
     mov   ah,2       ; function: write character
     mov   dl,0Dh     ; carriage return
     int   21h
     mov   dl,0Ah     ; line feed
     int   21h
     pop   dx
     pop   ax
     ret
writecrlf endp
end
```

TWO TEST PROGRAMS

To test the new procedures presented here, we will write two short programs. Each will be assembled into an object file and linked to individual subroutines. The link step is surprisingly fast because the individual subroutines have already been assembled.

TEST4.ASM.

The test program in Figure 9-11 clears a window in the middle of the screen, writes a message, inputs an integer, and redisplays the number in hexadecimal. Sample output from the program is as follows, with the bold text typed by the user:

```
Test of object library routines (TEST4.EXE).

Enter a signed or unsigned integer: 45424
In hexadecimal, the number is B170
```

```
 1:   title   Object Library Test                        (TEST4.ASM)
 2:
 3:   ;
 4:   ;  This program tests individual object library
 5:   ;  procedures. It displays a window, reads a 16-bit
 6:   ;  number from the keyboard, and echoes it back in
 7:   ;  hexadecimal.  It works on both color and
 8:   ;  monochrome displays.
 9:   ;
10:   dosseg
11:   .model small
12:   .stack 100h
13:
14:             ; External declarations
15:
16:   extrn colortextmode:abs, yellow:abs, blue:abs
17:   extrn attr_reverse:abs, winforeground:byte
18:   extrn winbackground:byte, winattribute:byte
19:   extrn videopage:byte, videomode:byte
20:   extrn clrscr:proc, display:proc, getvmode:proc
21:   extrn locate:proc, readint:proc, scrollwin:proc
22:   extrn writecrlf:proc, writeint:proc
23:
24:             ; Constant definitions
25:
26:   upperleft  equ  070Ah   ; UL window corner =   7, 10
27:   loweright  equ  0D46h   ; LR window corner =  13, 70
28:   titlepos   equ  0A12h   ; program title position = 10, 18
29:
30:   .code
31:   main proc
32:        mov   ax,@data              ; initialize DS
33:        mov   ds,ax
34:        call  getvmode              ; get videomode
35:        call  clrscr                ; clear the screen
36:
37:        ; Set the window color
38:
39:   L1:  cmp   videomode,colortextmode ; color display?
40:        jne   L2                      ; no: must be monochrome
41:        mov   winforeground,yellow    ; yes: set text color
42:        mov   winbackground,blue      ; set window color
43:        jmp   L3
44:   L2:  mov   winattribute,attr_reverse ; set reverse video
45:
46:        ; Display the window
47:
48:   L3:  mov   cx,upperleft          ; set window corners
49:        mov   dx,loweright
50:        call  scrollwin             ; scroll the window
51:        mov   dx,titlepos           ; locate the cursor
52:        call  locate
```

Figure 9-11 Object library test (TEST4.ASM).

Figure 9-11 *(Cont.)*

```
53:          mov   dx,offset progtitle ; display the title
54:          call  display
55:
56:          ; Prompt for an ASCII decimal number
57:
58:          mov   dx,1200h            ; locate at 18,0
59:          call  locate
60:          mov   dx,offset prompt1   ; display first prompt
61:          call  display
62:          call  readint             ; read number into AX
63:          mov   intvalue,ax         ; save the input number
64:          call  writecrlf           ; write a CR/LF
65:
66:          ; Display the number in hexadecimal format
67:
68:          mov   dx,offset prompt2   ; display second prompt
69:          call  display
70:          mov   ax,intvalue         ; get the input number
71:          mov   bx,16               ; choose hexadecimal radix
72:          call  writeint            ; display the number
73:
74:          mov   ax,4C00h            ; end program
75:          int   21h
76:     main endp
77:
78:     .data
79:
80:     progtitle db  'Test of object libary routines (TEST4.EXE).$'
81:     prompt1   db  'Enter a signed or unsigned integer: $'
82:     prompt2   db  'In hexadecimal, the number is $'
83:     intvalue  dw  ?
84:
85:     end main
```

A sample batch file for assembling and linking is listed here. The object file names must be typed on the same line, before you press ENTER:

```
masm test4;
link test4 lvars lgetvmod lclrscr lscroll llocate ldisplay lreadint lwritecr lwrint;
```

The TEST4 program contains three constants that define the position of each window corner, as well as the position where the program title is to be displayed:

```
upperleft   equ   070Ah
loweright   equ   0D46h
titlepos    equ   0A12h
```

Line 34 calls GETVMODE to find out whether the video display is in monochrome or color mode. GETVMODE initializes the global variable **videomode**.

Line 39 determines whether the video mode is set to color text mode. If it is, the window color is set to blue with yellow letters. If the display is in monochrome mode, line 44 sets the window attribute to reverse video.

Line 50 calls SCROLLWIN, which uses the the global variables **winforeground**, **winbackground**, and **winattribute**. The window corner positions must be passed in CH, CL, DH, and DL. On lines 48 and 49, we double up each register pair by using 16-bit values.

After displaying the program title, lines 60 and 61 prompt for a number. READINT is called (line 62) to read the ASCII number and convert it to internal binary. Line 72 uses the WRITEINT procedure to display the number in hexadecimal.

TEST5.ASM

The TEST5.ASM program in Figure 9–12 performs addition, using two signed numbers input from the keyboard. The result is displayed in signed decimal. The MAIN procedure begins by clearing the screen, displaying a greeting message, and prompting for the first number (lines 21–23). Sample screen output for the program is as follows:

```
Test of object library routines (TEST5.EXE).

Enter two integers, and the sum will be calculated.


First number: -4096
+ second number: 20
is equal to: -4076
```

Figure 9-12 Object library test (TEST5.ASM).

```
 1:    title  Object Library Test                              (TEST5.ASM)
 2:
 3:    ;
 4:    ;   This program tests individual object library
 5:    ;   routines.  Two numbers are input from the console,
 6:    ;   they are added together, and the result is displayed.
 7:    ;
 8:    dosseg
 9:    .model small
10:    .stack 100h
11:    extrn clrscr:proc, display:proc, readint:proc
12:    extrn writecrlf:proc, writesint:proc, readkey:proc
13:    extrn cr:abs, lf:abs
14:
15:    .code
```

Figure 9-12 *(Cont.)*

```
16:   main proc
17:         mov   ax,@data             ; initialize DS
18:         mov   ds,ax
19:
20:   first_number:
21:         call  clrscr               ; clear the screen
22:         mov   dx,offset greeting   ; display a greeting
23:         call  display
24:         call  readint              ; read first number
25:         call  writecrlf
26:         cmp   ax,0                 ; 0 or [ENTER] pressed?
27:         je    quit                 ; yes: quit
28:         mov   integer1,ax          ; no: store the number
29:         mov   dx,offset prompt2    ; prompt for second number
30:         call  display
31:         call  readint              ; read second number
32:         call  writecrlf
33:         add   ax,integer1          ; add the numbers together
34:         mov   dx,offset equals     ; display an equal sign
35:         call  display
36:         call  writesint            ; display the result
37:         call  readkey              ; wait for a keystroke,
38:         jmp   first_number         ; then repeat
39:
40:   quit:
41:         mov   ax,4C00h             ; end program
42:         int   21h
43:   main endp
44:
45:   .data
46:   greeting db  'Test of object library routines (TESTS.EXE).'
47:            db   cr,lf,cr,lf
48:            db  'Enter two integers, and the sum will be '
49:            db  'calculated. ',cr,lf,cr,lf,cr,lf
50:            db  'First number: $'
51:   prompt2  db  '+ second number: $'
52:   equals   db  'is equal to: $'
53:   integer1 dw   ?
54:
55:   end main
```

The READINT procedure call (line 24) inputs a number from the keyboard, and WRITECRLF moves the cursor to the next line. If READINT returns 0 in AX, we assume the operator has either just pressed ENTER or has input a value of zero. If either is true, we jump to the label **quit**.

Lines 29–31 prompt for the second number and call READINT again. We add the new number to the first, stored in **integer1**. The WRITESINT procedure (line 36) displays the sum in signed ASCII decimal format.

READKEY (line 37) waits for a keystroke before repeating the loop again. The same steps repeat until the user presses ENTER to quit.

The test programs presented here demonstrate several useful routines. Just as one takes input-output statements for granted in high-level languages, the same will be true for us as our library expands.

POINTS TO REMEMBER

This chapter had two goals. The first was to show how to create a group of useful numeric conversion routines. The second was to show how to create a library of input-output routines that may be used by any assembly program. We will use these routines throughout the rest of the book.

To display or print a 16-bit binary number, we must convert it to an ASCII digit string. By contrast, a number that is input from the keyboard must be converted from ASCII digits to binary.

The XLAT instruction offers a convenient way of translating 8-bit numeric or character values. Before XLAT is invoked, BX points to a translation table and AL contains an index value. After XLAT executes, AL contains a lookup value from the table.

When converting a number from binary to ASCII decimal, repeatedly divide the number by 10 and save each remainder. Each remainder becomes an ASCII digit.

To convert an ASCII decimal string to binary, multiply each digit by 10 and add the value of the next digit.

To write a negative signed integer to the console, reverse its sign and perform the conversion to ASCII as if the number were unsigned. Then append a negative sign to the beginning of the number.

Construct large programs using separately assembled modules, in order to ease program development and maintenance. Common routines used by many programs may be placed in an object library. Also, sections of a large program that have already been tested need not be constantly reassembled.

Assembling and Linking. When any change is made to a subroutine, remember to reassemble it. If any of your programs use this subroutine, they should be relinked to the subroutine.

More About the Microsoft Linker

As we know, the linker converts one or more object files to a single executable file. It is a powerful tool when used correctly. It carries out the following steps:

1. Reads the input object files.
2. Searches any specified libraries in order to resolve external references.

3. Assigns addresses to segments and public symbols.
4. Reads code and data in the segments.
5. Reads relocation references in the object files.
6. Fixes up references to segment addresses by program instructions.
7. Creates an executable file containing an image of the program and a program header. The header supplies relocation information used by DOS when the program is loaded and run.

Linker Options. The Microsoft LINK.EXE program has a number of powerful options, described in the *CodeView and Utilities Manual*. Each of these options may be typed after the word LINK on the command line, as in the following:

```
link/he     ( Display linker options )
```

A partial list of options is as follows:

LINKER OPTIONS

/HE	Display available linker options.
/PAU	Pause before generating an .EXE file to allow switching of disks.
/I	Display information during the linking process.
/E	Pack the .EXE file and remove repeated bytes.
/M	Create a .MAP file with a list of public symbols.
/LI	Create a .MAP file and include source line numbers.
/NOI	Do not ignore case for names (when linking to C).
/ST	Set the stack size, using the format /ST:*number,* where *number* may be from 1 to 65,535.
/CP	Set the maximum allocation space when the program is loaded into memory.
/SE	Set the maximum number of segments (default = 128).
/DO	Use standard Microsoft segment ordering (same as the .DOSSEG directive).
/DS	Load data in the high end of the data segment.
/HI	Load the .EXE file as high in memory as possible.
/CO	Prepare for debugging with CODEVIEW.
/Q	Produce a "quick library," suitable for use with Microsoft QuickBASIC or QuickC.

REVIEW QUESTIONS

1. What is the difference between an ASCII decimal number and a binary number?

2. If we stored the ASCII decimal number 4096 in 4 bytes of memory, what would be the hexadecimal contents of each byte?

3. Which register is used by XLAT to hold the address of a translate table?

4. (Y/N) Can the XLAT instruction work with a table containing 16-bit values?

5. If the name of a table is coded as an operand, will XLAT use its address rather than the one in BX?

6. Which flags are affected by the XLAT instruction?

7. What will AL contain after the following instructions have executed?

```
          mov   bx,offset chars
          mov   al,6
          xlat
          .
          .
   chars  db    'ABCDEFGHIJ'
```

8. What will be the hexadecimal value of AL after the following instructions have been executed? (Assume that **ptr1** is located at address 0106h.)

```
          mov   bx,ptr2
          mov   al,byte ptr ptr3+1
          xlat
          .
          .
   table  db    '1234567890'
   ptr1   dw    ptr2
   ptr2   dw    table
   ptr3   dw    ptr1
```

9. Design a table that could be used by XLAT to translate lowercase letters into uppercase.

10. Demonstrate the algorithm used in this chapter for conversion from binary to ASCII decimal, using the number 302h.

11. Demonstrate the algorithm used in this chapter for conversion from ASCII decimal to binary, using the value '8196'.

12. Show how the ASCII hexadecimal number '3F62' could be converted to binary.

13. So far, we have been able to convert only 16-bit binary numbers into ASCII decimal. If we wanted to convert the 32-bit number 00011000h to ASCII, for example, we would have to modify our approach. Can you think of a way of separating the number into two halves and converting each half?

14. The following program excerpt is designed to take each character from **inputlist**, check it against **validchars**, and print the character unless the XLAT instruction returns 0 in AL. Correct any syntax or logic errors that you find:

```
          mov    bx,validchars
          mov    di,offset inputlist
      getchar:
          mov    al,[si]
          xlat   validchars
          or     al,al
          jz     getchar
          int    21h
          loop   getchar
          .
          .
      inputlist    db 5,26,45,96,88,128
      validchars   db 32 dup(0)       ; invalid chars: 0-31
                   db 96 dup(0FFh)   ; valid chars: 32-127
                   db 128 dup(0)      ; invalid chars: 128-255
```

15. The following excerpt is adapted from the WRINT procedure that was introduced earlier in this chapter. To test your understanding of the procedure, add explanatory comments to lines 1, 4, 6, 8, 10, and 11:

```
1         mov   cx,0             ; ________________
2         mov   di,offset buffer+6
3         mov   bx,10
4    L1:  mov   dx,0             ; ________________
5         div   bx
6         or    dl,30h           ; ________________
7         dec   di
8         mov   [di],dl          ; ________________
9         inc   cx
10        or    ax,ax            ; ________________
11        jnz   L1               ; ________________
          .
          .
     buffer   db   6 dup(' ')
```

16. In the sample program in Question 15, if AX contained 0600h at the beginning, what would be the value of DX each time after executing line 5?
    a.   b.   c.   d.

PROGRAMMING EXERCISES

Exercise 1 Display the System Date

Write a procedure that will write the system date to standard output in either of the following formats:

Format 1: 8/20/89
Format 2: 20-Aug-1989

Use DOS function 2Ah to obtain the current date from the operating system. DOS places the year in CX, the month in DH, the day of the month in DL, and the day of the week in AL. When the procedure is called, pass it a value of 1 or 2 in AL to choose the display format. Test the procedure by calling it from a main program.

Exercise 2 Set the System Date

Write a program that uses a date input from the keyboard to set the system date. Test your procedure by calling it from an existing program.

DOS function 2Bh (set system date) requires the year number to be in CX, the month number to be in DH, and the day number in DL. For example:

```
mov   ah,2Bh        ; set system date
mov   cx,1989       ; year = 1989
mov   dh,10         ; month = October
mov   dl,18         ; day = 18
int   21h
```

After running the program, use the DOS DATE command to verify that the program worked.

Exercise 3 Character Encoding Program

Modify the ENCODE.ASM program presented in Figure 9-2 so that all text may be entered from the keyboard. When ENTER is pressed at the end of each line, redisplay the line in its encoded format. Then prompt for a new input line. Continue in this manner until the ESC key is pressed. At that point, display the last encoded line and a count of the number of lines that were typed, and return to DOS.

Exercise 4 Character Decoding Program

Run the ENCODE.ASM program shown in Figure 9-2. Write a new program, which decodes the file produced by ENCODE.ASM and displays the decoded text.

Exercise 5 Advanced Character Encoding

As mentioned in the discussion of the ENCODE.ASM program (Figure 9-2), the code used by the program could easily be broken. Improve the algorithm by using part of the current system date to control the number of bits each byte in the table is rotated. For a guide to getting the system date from DOS, see the explanation of DOS function 2Ah in Exercise 1.

Suppose that the month and day for July 1st returned by DOS in DX is 0701h

(1,793). We can divide DX by 10 and retain the remainder, which is 3. After each byte is looked up in the translate table, the result can then be rotated 3 bits to the left. After encoding a string and copying it to a new file, append the binary value in DX to the file.

Exercise 6 Advanced Character Decoding

Write a program that will decode the output file created by the program in Exercise 5.

Exercise 7 Window Application Program

Write a program to do the following:

1. Find out whether a color or monochrome display is being used, and store the result in the variable **videomode**.
2. Clear the screen, and divide it into four windows. If a color display is being used, make each window a different color.
3. Position the cursor in the first window, and prompt the user for a line of text using lowercase letters.
4. Display the text from window 1 in window 2 in all uppercase letters.
5. In window 3, have the user input an unsigned integer. Redisplay the integer in window 4 in binary, octal, decimal, and hexadecimal. Label each as it is displayed—for example:

Binary	→ 10010101
Octal	→ 225
Decimal	→ 149
Hexadecimal	→ 95

Link your program to the various subroutines presented in this chapter that will help you complete the program.

Exercise 8 The BIN8TOHEX Procedure

Write a general procedure named BIN8TOHEX that converts an 8-bit binary number in AL to two ASCII hexadecimal digits. Include an option to print a trailing radix indicator (h) after the number. When calling the procedure, let SI point to a 3-byte buffer where the digits will be stored. Test the procedure by calling it from a program and passing it at least ten different values.

Exercise 9 Modified BIN8TOHEX Procedure

Modify the BIN8TOHEX procedure created in Exercise 8, so it will convert a binary value to ASCII digits: either binary, octal, decimal, or hexadecimal. Test the procedure by calling it from a program and passing it at least ten different values. Display the final digit string, using the WRITESTRING procedure from this chapter.

Exercise 10 The BINTOASC Procedure

Write a procedure that converts an unsigned 16-bit binary number to an ASCII decimal string terminated by a binary zero byte (called an *ASCIIZ string*). Assemble the procedure into its own OBJ file, and test it by calling it from an external program. Pass the number to be converted in AX, and a pointer to the ASCII digit buffer in SI. Pass at least five different numbers to the procedure, and display each number on the console.

Exercise 11 Display Formatted Numbers

Using the WRITESINT procedure as a guide, write a new procedure that displays a signed ASCII decimal number in a fixed-length format. In addition to passing the binary value in AX, let CX equal the desired format size. As the number is written to standared output, insert leading spaces to right-justify the number. For example, the number 4096, with a length of 9 in CX, would be displayed with five leading spaces:

```
"     4096"
```

Assemble the procedure as an independent object module. Test it by calling it from an external main program. Write two vertically aligned columns of numbers to standard output:

```
  200      3
  -26  -5120
-3321  32767
```

Exercise 12 Display a 32-Bit Number

Write a procedure that displays an unsigned 32-bit binary number in ASCII decimal. Call this procedure from a program and pass it a variety of test values.

Let's say that DX and AX contain the 32-bit number 00011000h. The number would be displayed as 69632.

Method 1. One approach is to begin by dividing the number by 10,000:

69,632 / 10,000 = 6, remainder 9,632

First, convert the remainder to ASCII; then convert the quotient. When we place the quotient in front of the remainder, we get the ASCII decimal value:

"6" + "9632" = "69632"

Be careful, however, to insert the correct number of leading zeros in the remainder to make it 4 digits long. In the following example, the remainder must be stored with three leading zeros:

500,001 / 10,000 = 50, remainder 1
ASCII decimal value: "50" + "0001"

Method 2. A simpler approach is to use 32-bit division. For example, the number 12,345,678 can be repeatedly divided by 10. Each remainder becomes a digit in the resulting ASCII string. This is identical to the algorithm used by the WRINT procedure shown in Figure 9-3:

Dividend	/ 10	=	Quotient	Remainder
12,345,678			1,234,567	8
1,234,567			123,456	7
123,456			12,345	6
(etc.)				

The only difficulty is to write a 32-bit division procedure. You may wish to refer to the 32-bit division example in Chapter 8.

Exercise 13 Hexadecimal Memory Dump

Write a program that dumps a 128-byte block of memory in ASCII hexadecimal, similar to the format used by DEBUG. Of course, you may use the routines presented in this chapter and add a routine of your own to handle conversion from 8-bit binary to hexadecimal.

Display a heading showing the current segment value, and display the offset address of the first byte in each row along the left side. Display 16 bytes in each row. Sample:

```
                Memory Contents at Segment 38FF

0100   30 68 2C 20 66 75 6E 63 74 69 6F 6E 20 30 31 68
0110   2C 20 69 6E 20 6F 72 64 65 72 20 74 6F 20 0D 0A
0120   73 68 6F 77 20 77 68 69 63 68 20 6D 6F 64 65 20
0130   69 73 20 63 75 72 72 65 6E 74 6C 79 20 61 63 74
0140   69 76 65 2E 29 20 20 0D 0A 20 20 20 20 45 78 74
0150   72 61 20 23 32 3A 20 44 69 73 70 6C 61 79 20 74
0160   68 65 20 C5 20 63 68 61 72 61 63 74 65 72 20 77
0170   68 65 6E 20 6F 6E 65 20 6C 69 6E 65 20 63 72 6F
```

Exercise 14 Enhanced Hexadecimal Memory Dump

Enhance the program written for Exercise 13 as follows:

- Prompt the operator for the starting segment and offset values to be dumped.
- After each block is displayed, wait for a keystroke, clear the screen, and display the next block of memory. Quit when ESC is pressed.

Exercise 15 Hexadecimal File Dump

Read a file from standard input and dump the file in hexadecimal. Use the format shown in Exercise 13 as a reference (do not display the segment value). Dump each 128-byte block, clear the screen, wait for a keystroke, and continue dumping the file until you reach its end. *Extra*: Display an ASCII dump of each line on the right-hand side of the hexadecimal dump. Sample:

```
0100   30 68 2C 20 66 75 6E 63 74 69 6F 6E 20 30 31 68   0h, function 01h
0110   2C 20 69 6E 20 6F 72 64 65 72 20 74 6F 20 0D 0A   , in order to ..
0120   73 68 6F 77 20 77 68 69 63 68 20 6D 6F 64 65 20   show which mode
0130   69 73 20 63 75 72 72 65 6E 74 6C 79 20 61 63 74   is currently act
0140   69 76 65 2E 29 20 20 0D 0A 20 20 20 20 45 78 74   ive.)  ..    Ext
0150   72 61 20 23 32 3A 20 44 69 73 70 6C 61 79 20 74   ra #2: Display t
0160   68 65 20 C5 20 63 68 61 72 61 63 74 65 72 20 77   he E character w
0170   68 65 6E 20 6F 6E 65 20 6C 69 6E 65 20 63 72 6F   hen one line cro
```

Exercise 16 Register Snapshot Program

Write a procedure that prints a "snapshot" of selected CPU registers and flags on the printer. This is a simplified version of the utility often referred to as a SNAP on mainframe computers. Many large computer systems do not have an interactive source-level debugger like CODEVIEW, so the next best option is to print periodic snapshots of memory and registers. Design the output so it is easy to read and contains only essential information. A sample register display follows:

```
08FF:0100
 AX=0000 BX=0000 CX=0000 DX=0000 SI=0000 DI=0000 DS=38FF ES=38FF SS=38FF
 Sign=1  Zero=0  Carry=0 Oflow=0 Dir=0
```

Test your SNAP procedure by calling it several times from a program.

Exercise 17 Fibonacci Numbers

The well-known Fibonacci number series, discovered by Leonardo of Pisa around the year 1202, has been valued for centuries for its universal qualities by artists, mathematicians, and composers. Each number in the series after the number 1 is the sum of the two previous numbers:

1, 1, 2, 3, 5, 8, 13, 21, 34, 55 . . .

Write a program that generates and displays the first 24 numbers in the Fibonacci series, beginning with 1 and ending with 46,368.

Extra: For any number greater than 999, insert a comma in the correct position when it is displayed.

Exercise 18 4 by 4 Matrix Program

Write a program that reads 16 numbers (range, 0–200) from standard input and displays them on the screen as a 4 by 4 matrix. Right-justify the numbers and leave a blank line between rows. Example:

```
  0    50     2   200

 66    21    54    20

  1     3     4     6

100   150   120    99
```

Perform the following operations:

a. Compute and display the sum of row 1.
b. Compute and display the sum of column 2.
c. Count and display the number of values > 100.
d. Wait for a key to be pressed, interchange rows 1 and 2, and redisplay the matrix.

ANSWERS TO REVIEW QUESTIONS

1. Each digit of an ASCII decimal number is stored in a separate byte as its ASCII equivalent. A binary number is stored using encoded binary bits.

2. The contents of the four bytes would be 34h, 30h, 39h, 36h.

3. BX.

4. No, only 8-bit values.

5. No, BX must still be set to the table offset.

6. No flags are affected.

7. The ASCII code for the letter G (47h).

8. **Ptr3** = 0106h, with the bytes stored in reverse order. Thus before the XLAT, AL = 01h, and after the XLAT, AL = 32h.

9. Translate table for lowercase to uppercase:

```
UpTable  db 97 dup(0)   ; no translation
         db 'ABCDEFGHIJKLMNOPQRSTUVWXYZ'
         db 133 dup(0) ; no translation
```

10. The algorithm involves dividing the number successively by 10:

302h / 10 = 4Dh, remainder 0
4Dh / 10 = 7, remainder 7
7 / 10 = 0, remainder 7

ASCII decimal value: 7 7 0

11. Converting an ASCII decimal number to binary involves multiplying the total by 10 and adding the value of the most recent digit. This is shown here for the ASCII digits 8, 1, 9, and 6:

Old Total	*	10	+	Digit	=	New Total
0	*	10	+	8	=	8
8	*	10	+	1	=	81
81	*	10	+	9	=	819
819	*	10	+	6	=	8,196

12. Using similar logic to that of Question 11, we multiply the total value by 16 and add each new digit:

Old Total	*	16	+	Digit	=	New Total
0	*	16	+	3	=	3
3	*	16	+	F	=	63
63	*	16	+	6	=	1,014
1,014	*	16	+	2	=	16,226

13. One way is to first divide the number by 10,000. Convert the remainder to ASCII, and then convert the quotient to ASCII. Print the digits for the quotient before the digits for the remainder. The number 00011000h, for example, is divided as follows:

$$\frac{00011000\text{h}}{10000} = 6, \text{ remainder } 9632$$

We can print the quotient digit (6), then print the remainder digits (9632), and end up with the number 69632.

14. This is the correct version:

```
        mov  bx,offset validchars
        mov  si,offset inputlist
        mov  cx,6            ; set loop counter
getchar:
        mov  al,[si]
        mov  dl,al           ; save character
        xlat validchars
        or   al,al
        jz   getchar
        mov  ah,2            ; function: display character
        int  21h             ; display contents of DL
        loop getchar
        .
        .
inputlist   db 5,26,45,96,88,128
validchars  db 32 dup(0)      ; invalid chars: 0-31
            db 96 dup(0FFh)   ; valid chars:   32-127
            db 128 dup(0)     ; invalid chars: 128-255
```

15. Comment lines are added here:

```
1        mov  cx,0           ; initialize digit counter
2        mov  di,offset buffer+6
3        mov  bx,10
4   L1:  mov  dx,0           ; DX holds the converted value
5        div  bx
6        or   dl,30h         ; convert digit to ASCII
7        dec  di
8        mov  [di],dl        ; place digit in buffer
9        inc  cx
10       or   ax,ax          ; quotient = 0?
11       jnz  L1             ; no: continue conversion
         .
         .
    buffer  db  6 dup(' ')
```

16. a. 6 b. 3 c. 5 d. 1

10

String Processing

This chapter concentrates on specific instructions designed for string processing and shows how to create a library of useful string procedures. Let us broaden the usual definition of strings here to include arrays of 8-bit or 16-bit integers. A table, in fact, may be seen as a string if it includes only one element per row.

String processing is ideally suited to assembly language because it consists of small tasks that are repeated many times. Word processing and database management programs, for example, must carry out string operations without a noticeable loss of speed. Language compilers also require a great deal of string manipulation. In most cases, programmers optimize critical string handling routines by writing them in assembly language.

First, we will look at the way strings are stored. This is more complicated than it sounds because high-level languages use different string storage formats. An assembly language program must be able to adapt to all of them.

Next, we will examine the *string primitive* instructions in the Intel instruction set. These powerful, efficient instructions simplify string handling.

Last, we will develop a library containing general-purpose string routines (procedures) and write an application program that tests them. The Microsoft LIB utility program will be demonstrated as we collect our string-handling routines into a single library file that may be linked to other programs.

STRING STORAGE METHODS

Nearly all programming languages allow processing of character strings. They differ greatly, however, in the way they store and manipulate strings. We will define a *character string* as an array, or list of characters. Three basic formats are used most often:

1. A fixed-length buffer holds the characters, and unused positions at the end are filled with spaces. This method is used by COBOL, for instance:

S	T	R	I	N	G		O	N	E											

   This string would be declared in assembly language as

```
db 'STRING ONE          '
```

2. A *length descriptor* may be stored at the beginning of a string. In Turbo Pascal, for example, this format allows a string to vary in length from 0 to the number of bytes reserved by the string's declaration. Unused positions in the string have undetermined values, shown here by the period (.) character:

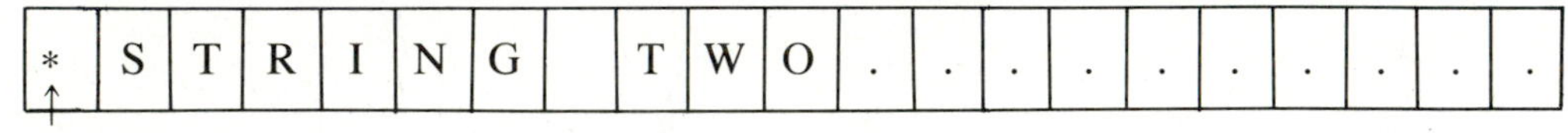

   This string would be declared in assembly language as

```
db 0Ah,'STRING TWO',10 dup(?)
```

3. An *ASCIIZ string* is a string of characters terminated by a binary 0 byte. The active length of the string may vary from 0 to the number of bytes reserved by the string's declaration. Unused positions have an undetermined value, shown here by the period (.) character. This format is used by the C language, for instance:

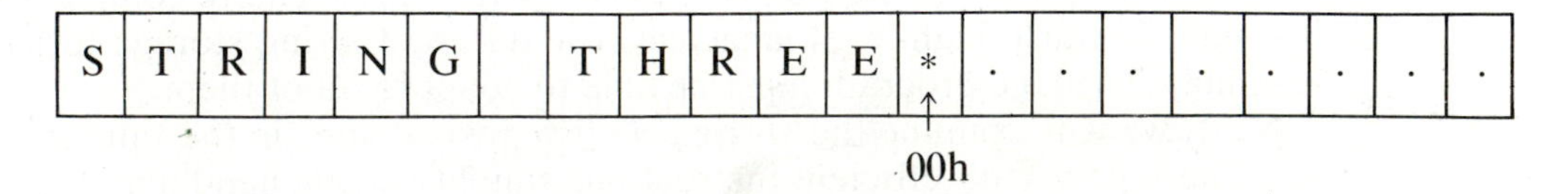

   This would be declared in assembly language as

```
db 'STRING THREE',0,8 dup(?)
```

Because of the variety of string formats, transferring strings between languages is somewhat awkward. It is also difficult to write assembly language routines that work with different high-level languages.

It may even be necessary to have separate string-handling procedures for each high-level language. As an alternative, we can write routines to convert strings from one format to another.

STRING PRIMITIVE INSTRUCTIONS

There are five specialized string-handling instructions, called *string primitives,* that operate on strings of 8-bit or 16-bit values. Each instruction involves at least one memory operand:

MOVS	Move a byte or word in memory to another memory location.
CMPS	Compare a byte or word in memory to another memory location.
SCAS	Compare a byte in AL or a word in AX to a memory location.
STOS	Store (copy) a byte in AL or a word in AX in a memory location.
LODS	Load (copy) a byte or word in memory into AL or AX.

String primitives can be automatically repeated, making them especially useful. They can also deal with two memory operands, a feature missing in other instructions.

As we've said earlier, we will let the term *string* identify any sequence of 8-bit or 16-bit values stored in memory. The assembler instructions themselves make no distinction between the two. A string, for example, might contain ASCII characters, 16-bit signed integers, or 8-bit binary values.

Figure 10-1 contains a brief summary of the string primitive instructions. The

Figure 10-1 Summary of string primitive instructions.

String Primitive Instructions

Instruction	Description	Implied Operands
MOVS	Move (copy) a byte or word in memory to another memory location.	MOVS [DI],[SI]
CMPS	Compare a byte or word in memory to another memory location.	CMPS [SI],[DI]
SCAS	Compare a byte in AL or a word in AX to a memory location.	SCAS [DI],AL SCAS [DI],AX
STOS	Store (copy) a byte in AL or a word in AX to a memory location.	STOS [DI],AL STOS [DI],AX
LODS	Load (copy) a byte or word in memory into AL or AX.	LODS AL,[SI] LODS AX,[SI]

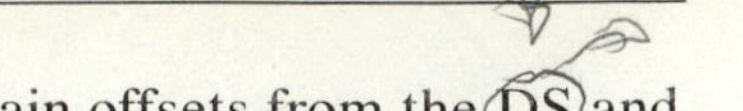

instructions require us to use DI and SI, which contain offsets from the DS and ES, respectively.

Further, a *source* operand is a location addressed by DS:SI, and a *destination* operand is addressed by ES:DI. The ES register must be initialized to the starting location of the data segment before we can use a string instruction with a destination operand. ES may be initialized at the same time as DS:

```
mov  ax,@data     ; get address of data segment
mov  ds,ax        ; initialize DS
mov  es,ax        ; initialize ES
```

Each string primitive instruction has three possible formats. The *general* format may be used with either byte or word operands. The formats ending with *B* (MOVSB, CMPSB, . . .) imply the use of 8-bit operands, and those ending with *W* imply 16-bit operands:

INSTRUCTION FORMATS

General	Specific Size	Description
MOVS	MOVSB	Move string byte
	MOVSW	Move string word
CMPS	CMPSB	Compare string byte
	CMPSW	Compare string word
SCAS	SCASB	Scan string byte
	SCASW	Scan string word
STOS	STOSB	Store string byte
	STOSW	Store string word
LODS	LODSB	Load string byte
	LODSW	Load string word

The *general* format does not specify an operand size (e.g., MOVS or SCAS), so the operands must be coded explicitly:

```
MOVS   dest,source    ; move source to destination
CMPS   dest,source    ; compare source to destination
SCAS   dest           ; scan destination string
STOS   dest           ; store accumulator into destination
LODS   source         ; load accumulator from source
```

If a specific operand size is specified, the operands need not be supplied with the instruction. In any case, SI and DI *must be set to the offsets of the operands*. In Example 1, the MOVSB instruction is used only after SI and DI are initialized.

In Example 2, operands are coded with the instruction, but SI and DI must still be initialized:

Example 1: Implied operands

```
mov    si,offset source     ; point SI to source
mov    di,offset dest       ; point DI to destination
movsb                       ; move from source to destination
```

Example 2: Explicit operands

```
mov    si,offset source     ; point SI to source
mov    di,offset dest       ; point DI to destination
movs   es:dest,source       ; move from source to destination
```

Most programmers prefer using implied operands, as in Example 1, because they are simpler. In Example 2, a segment override (ES:) lets MASM know that **dest** represents an offset from ES. This segment override is required if you use simplified segment directives (.CODE, .DATA, and .STACK).

Repeat Prefix. A string primitive instruction processes only a single byte or word at a time, but it may be preceded by a *repeat prefix*. This causes the instruction to be repeated, making it possible to process an entire with only one instruction. The following repeat prefixes are used:

REP	Repeat while CX > 0
REPZ, REPE	Repeat while the Zero flag is set and CX > 0
REPNZ, REPNE	Repeat while the Zero flag is clear and CX > 0

When using a repeat prefix, move a counter value to CX prior to the instruction. In the following example, the value in CX will make the MOVSB repeat 10 times:

```
mov  si,offset string1  ; SI points to source
mov  di,offset string2  ; DI points to destination
mov  cx,10              ; set counter to 10
rep  movsb              ; move 10 bytes
```

The repeat prefix is assembled into a single byte of machine code that precedes the string instruction. An assembly of the preceding example is as follows:

```
BE 0000 R    mov  si,offset string1
BF 000A R    mov  di,offset string2
B9 000A      mov  cx,10
F3/ A4       rep  movsb
```

You may recall that the letter *R* next to the addresses for **string1** and **string2** identifies these as relocatable operands, because the location of the data segment is unknown until runtime. The REP prefix generates the machine instruction F3, and MOVSB consists of just a single byte: A4.

String primitive instructions use the Direction flag to determine whether SI and DI will be incremented or decremented after a string instruction:

Value of the Direction Flag	Effect on SI and DI	Address Sequence
0 (up)	Incremented	Low-high
1 (down)	Decremented	High-low

The Direction flag may only be changed using the CLD and STD instructions:

```
CLD    ; clear Direction flag, set it to up
STD    ; set Direction flag, set it to down
```

MOVS (Move String)

The MOVS instruction moves (copies) data from a *source* location pointed to by DS:SI to a *destination* location pointed to by ES:DI. The syntax is:

```
MOVS   dest,source
MOVSB
MOVSW
```

ES:DI holds the address of the destination operand. MOVS requires both operands to be supplied. IF MOVSB is used, byte operands are assumed, and if MOVSW is used, word operands are assumed. The Direction flag determines the incrementing or decrementing of SI and DI. MOVSB increments or decrements SI and DI by 1; if MOVSW is used, the increment/decrement value is 2. The MOVS instruction uses the operands' attributes to determine the increment/decrement value.

Copy a List of Bytes. In the following example, 10 bytes are copied from **source** to **dest**. After we copy the bytes, both fields contain the same string, and SI and DI point 1 byte beyond the end of each string:

```
cld                      ; direction = up
mov  cx,10               ; set counter to 10
mov  si,offset source    ; DS:SI points to source
mov  di,offset dest      ; ES:DI points to destination
```

```
        rep  movsb         ; byte operands specified
        .
        .
source db  'ABCDEFGHIJ'
dest   db  10 dup(?)
```

In this example, the REP prefix causes MOVSB to repeat until CX is decremented to 0. Unlike the LOOP instruction, the REP prefix first tests to see if CX = 0 *before* executing the MOVSB instruction. If it does, the instruction is ignored and control passes to the next line in the program. If CX > 0, it is decremented and the instruction repeats. In the following example, the MOVSB instruction is not executed because CX = 0 and a REP prefix is used:

```
mov   cx,0
rep   movsb
```

Copy a List of Words. In the next example, MOVSW copies a list of 16-bit integers from **word_list** to **word_dest**:

```
      cld                        ; direction = up
      mov   si,offset word_list  ; DS:SI points to source
      mov   di,offset word_dest  ; ES:DI points to destination
      mov   cx,4                 ; set repeat count to 4
      rep   movsw                ; carry out the move
      .
      .
word_list   dw   1000h,2000h,3000h,4000h
word_dest   dw   4 dup(0)
```

Save the Video Screen to a Buffer. Many programs use pop-up windows to enhance a program with attractive menus. Before a window is displayed, the data underneath the window must be saved. Later, when the window is removed, the previous contents of the screen are restored. To illustrate this process, we will use an assembly routine that copies the entire screen to a buffer. The buffer may be defined as an array of 2000 words:

```
buffer  dw  2000 dup(?)
```

ES:DI will point to each position in the buffer, so we must initialize ES to the start of the data segment and set DS to the start of the video buffer segment

(0B000h for monochrome and 0B800h for CGA, EGA, and VGA). The instructions to copy the monochrome screen contents to the buffer are:

```
cld                        ; direction = up
mov  ax,0B000h             ; monochrome screen address
mov  ds,ax                 ; set DS to screen address
mov  cx,2000               ; number of positions on screen
mov  si,0                  ; SI points to the screen area
mov  di,offset buffer ; DI points to the buffer
rep  movsw                 ; copy from DS:SI to ES:DI
```

(To modify this routine for color, substitute 0B800h for 0B000h.) You may notice that we move 2,000 words, not bytes. There are 25 rows and 80 columns on the screen, which total 2,000 characters. Each character position on the screen consists of 2 bytes; one holds a displayable character, and the other holds a binary number defining the character's attribute. (Video attributes were discussed in Chapter 5.)

The SCREEN.ASM program shown in Figure 10-2 provides a more complete demonstration. It saves the screen to a buffer, prints a message, and then restores the screen.

Figure 10-2 Saving and restoring the screen.

```
 1:   title  Screen Snapshot Program                          (SCREEN.ASM)
 2:
 3:   ;
 4:   ;   This program takes a snapshot of the screen and saves
 5:   ;   it in a buffer.  It then displays a message, waits for
 6:   ;   a keystroke, and restores the original screen.  It
 7:   ;   calls the CLRSCR procedure from CONSOLE.OBJ.
 8:   ;
 9:   dosseg
10:   .model small
11:   .stack 100h
12:   extrn clrscr:proc
13:
14:   videoseg  equ  0B800h        ; use 0B800h for color
15:
16:   .code
17:   main  proc
18:       mov     ax,@data         ; initialize DS and ES
19:       mov     ds,ax
20:       mov     es,ax
21:
22:   save_screen:
23:       cld                      ; clear direction flag
24:       push    ds               ; save DS
25:       mov     ax,videoseg      ; screen segment
26:       mov     ds,ax            ; point to screen buffer
```

Figure 10-2 *(Cont.)*

```
27:        mov     cx,2000           ; number of positions on screen
28:        mov     si,0              ; SI points to screen area
29:        lea     di,buffer         ; DI points to hold_buffer
30:        rep     movsw             ; copy the screen to buffer
31:
32:   display_message:
33:        call    clrscr            ; clear the screen
34:        pop     ds                ; restore DS
35:        lea     dx,msg            ; display a message
36:        mov     ah,9
37:        int     21h
38:        mov     ah,8              ; wait for a keystroke
39:        int     21h
40:
41:   restore_screen:
42:        mov     di,0              ; DI points to start of screen area
43:        mov     ax,videoseg       ; ES points to screen segment
44:        mov     es,ax             ; ES:DI points to screen buffer
45:        lea     si,buffer         ; DS:SI points to hold_buffer
46:        mov     cx,2000           ; word count
47:        rep     movsw             ; restore screen
48:        mov     ax,4C00h          ; return to DOS
49:        int     21h
50:   main  endp
51:
52:   .data
53:   buffer  dw  2000 dup(?)
54:   msg     db  'The previous contents of the screen have been'
55:           db  0Dh,0Ah,'saved, so the screen will be restored when'
56:           db  0Dh,0Ah,'you press any key...$'
57:   end main
```

CMPS (Compare Strings)

The CMPS instruction compares the source operand, pointed to by DS:SI, to the destination operand, pointed to by ES:DI. The syntax is:

```
CMPS  dest,source
CMPSB
CMPSW
```

(The comparison is in the reverse order of the CMP instruction.) If we use CMPS, both operands must be supplied. If we use CMPSB, byte operands are assumed, and if CMPSW is used, word operands are assumed. The direction flag determines the incrementing or decrementing of SI and DI. The following repeat prefixes may be used:

REPNE, REPNZ	Repeat while source ≠ destination
REP, REPE, REPZ	Repeat while source = destination

If the source string is less than the destination, the Carry flag is set; if the strings are equal, the Zero flag is set; if the source is greater than the destination, the Zero and Carry flags are cleared. We can summarize the conditional jumps following CMPS as follows:

	Appropriate Jump	
Condition	**Unsigned**	**Signed**
source < dest	JB	JL
source <= dest	JBE	JLE
source ≠ dest	JNE (JNZ)	JNE (JNZ)
source = dest	JE (JZ)	JE (JZ)
source >= dest	JAE	JGE
source > dest	JA	JG

Implied Order of Operands. Be careful when following the CMPS instruction with a conditional jump. The order of operands is not the same as it is for CMP, which compares the destination operand to the source operand. In the following example, CMP implies subtraction of the source from the destination. CMPS, however, implies subtraction of the destination from the source:

```
mov   ax,10
cmp   ax,5               ; implies (AX - 5)
cmps  es:dest,source ; implies (source - dest)
```

In the next example, the conditional jump to **source_smaller** is taken because the seventh character in **source** is smaller than the corresponding character in **dest**:

```
      cld                     ; direction = up
      mov  si,offset source ; point to source
      mov  di,offset dest   ; point to destination
      mov  cx,8             ; length of strings
      repe cmpsb            ; compare source to destination
      jb   source_smaller   ; jump if source < destination
      .
      .
source_smaller:
      .
      .
source   db  'MARTIN  '
dest     db  'MARTINEZ'
```

We might picture the two strings as follows before and after the comparison:

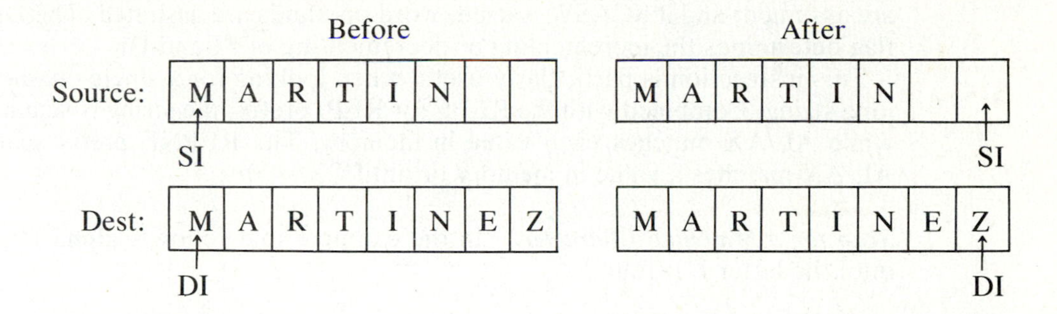

We start by setting SI and DI to the offsets of the two strings. Both registers are incremented until a difference between the strings in position 7 is found. After the CMPSB finishes, SI and DI are left pointing 1 byte beyond the characters that were different.

Comparing Signed Integers. The CMPSW instruction can compare two lists of signed integers. In the following example, each number in **array1** is compared to **array2**. **Array1** is found to be smaller, because its third number is −4, while the corresponding number in **array2** is 3:

```
    cld                        ; direction = up
    mov  si,offset array1      ; source
    mov  di,offset array2      ; destination
    mov  cx,4                  ; counter
    repe cmpsw                 ; compare source to dest
    jl   array1_smaller        ; jump if array1 < array2
    .
    .
array1_smaller:
    .
    .
array1  dw  -1,2,-4,20
array2  dw  -1,2,3,20
```

SCAS (Scan String)

The SCAS instruction compares a value in AL or AX to a byte or word in memory addressed by ES:DI. The syntax is:

```
SCAS  dest
SCASB
SCASW
```

ES:DI holds the address of the destination operand. If SCAS is used, the name of the destination operand must be supplied. If SCASB is used, byte operands are assumed, and if SCASW is used, word operands are assumed. The Direction flag determines the incrementing or decrementing of SI and DI.

This instruction is particularly useful when looking for a single character in a long string. Combined with the REPE (or REP) prefix, the string is scanned only while AL/AX matches each value in memory. The REPNE prefix scans until AL/AX matches a value in memory or until CX = 0.

Scan for a Matching Character. In the example that follows, **alpha** is scanned until the letter *F* is found:

```
    cld                      ; direction = up
    mov   di,offset alpha    ; ES:DI points to the string
    mov   al,'F'             ; search for the letter 'F'
    mov   cx,8               ; set the search count
    repne scasb              ; repeat while not equal
    jnz   exit               ; quit if letter is not found
    dec   di                 ; found: back up DI one character
    .
    .
alpha  db  'ABCDEFGH',0
```

We are assuming here that ES points to the segment where **alpha** is stored. When the letter *F* is found, DI points 1 byte beyond the matching character and must be decremented so that it points to the *F*:

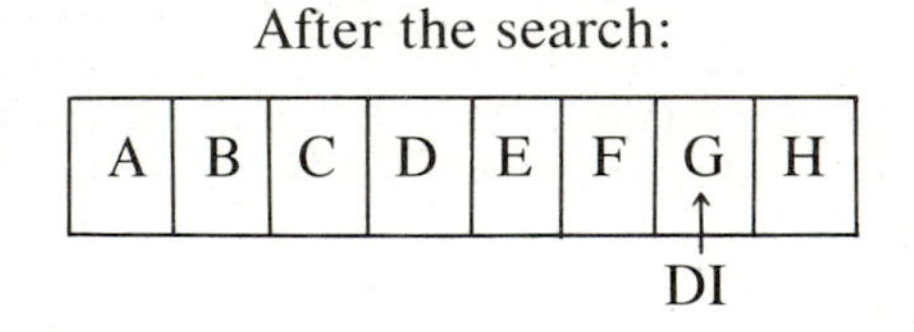

Using a Jump Instruction. When a CMPSB ends, you don't know if it stopped because CX = 0, or because a matching character was found in the string. In fact, the two may even happen at the same time.

In the case of REPNZ, use a JNZ instruction to jump when the character was not found. You might think of it this way: If the Zero flag is clear, the character was not found. If the Zero flag is set, the character was found:

```
          repnz cmpsb
          jnz   not_found
     or
          repnz cmpsb
          jz    found
```

Don't make the mistake of using the JCXZ instruction to find out whether the character was found. The problem is, the character might have been found in the last position scanned, but CX would still equal zero after the last comparison. The following would be incorrect:

```
repnz  scasb
jcxz   not_found
```

Remove Trailing Blanks. The SCASB instruction can be used to remove all trailing blanks from an ASCIIZ string. In the following example, DI points to the last byte in the string, CX equals the string length, AL = 20h (space character), and DF = 1. We use the REPE prefix in order to repeat the loop while AL matches each character in memory:

```
         std                         ; direction = down
         mov    di,offset dest       ; get string offset
         add    di,destlen-1         ; point to last byte
         mov    cx,destlen           ; set up counter
         mov    al,20h               ; look for spaces
         repe   scasb                ; scan the string
         jnz    exit                 ; quit if none found
         mov    byte ptr [di+2],0 ; insert new terminator byte
exit:
         .
         .
dest     db    'DESTINATION STRING      ',0
destlen equ    $-dest
```

After finding the first nonblank character, we insert a zero terminator just after it; this sets the string to its correct length. The instruction

```
mov  byte ptr [di+2],0
```

is correct; SCASB leaves DI pointing at the character just before the first nonblank character. To refer to the position following the character, we add 2 to DI.

STOS (Store in String)

The STOS instruction stores the contents of AL or AX in memory at ES:DI. The syntax is:

```
STOS  dest
STOSB
STOSW
```

ES:DI holds the address of the destination operand. STOS requires the name of the destination operand to be supplied. STOSB assumes that byte operands are being used, and STOSW assumes that word operands are used. The Direction flag determines the incrementing or decrementing of SI and DI.

You can use STOS to initialize a block of memory to a single value. The following example initializes each byte in **string1** to 0FFh (all binary 1's).

```
    cld                          ; direction = up
    mov  al,0FFh                 ; value to be stored
    mov  di,offset string1       ; ES:DI points to destination
    mov  cx,100                  ; character count
    rep  stosb                   ; fill with contents of AL
    .
    .
string1   db  100 dup(?)
```

LODS (Load String)

The LODS instruction loads a byte or word from memory at DS:SI into AL or AX. The syntax is:

```
LODS  dest
LODSB
LODSW
```

DS:SI holds the address of the source operand. LODS requires the name of the source operand to be supplied. LODSB assumes that byte operands are used, and LODSW assumes that word operands are used. The direction flag determines whether SI and DI will be incremented or decremented.

Repeat prefixes are rarely used with LODS because each new value loaded into AL or AX destroys its previous contents. As a single instruction, however, LODSB substitutes for the following two instructions:

```
mov  al,[si]    ; move byte at DS:SI to AL
inc  si         ; point to next byte
```

The next example scans through **buffer**, clears the high bit from each character, and stores it in **output**:

```
    cld                          ; direction = up
    mov   si,offset buffer       ; source buffer
    mov   di,offset output       ; destination buffer
    mov   cx,10                  ; buffer length

L1: lodsb                        ; copy DS:[SI] into AL
    and   al,7Fh                 ; clear high bit
```

```
        stosb                         ; store AL at ES:[DI]
        loop  L1
        .
        .
    buffer  db 0C8h,0FBh,0F5h,0CAh,41h,42h,43h,64h,87h,8Ch
    output  db 10 dup(?)
```

This example generates the following values in the output string. Each byte is the same as in the original, except that its highest bit has been cleared:

48 7B 75 4A 41 42 43 64 07 0C

A LIBRARY OF STRING ROUTINES

In this section, we will develop a library of string routines that may be called from other programs. Tasks performed by these routines are probably familiar to you from your experience with high-level languages. Some languages contain built-in string instructions, while others are supplemented by a separate library of string-handling routines. We will borrow a few ideas from these libraries and invent some new routines. These will be collected into a library that may be linked to assembly language programs.

String routines written in assembly language can mirror those available in high-level languages and, at the same time, can be more compact and efficient. We will use the ASCIIZ string format here, and pass and return pointers to strings in SI and DI. This makes the individual routines easier to write, and provides a smooth transition when a main program calls several routines one after another. The following string routines are presented:

READSTRING	Read an ASCIIZ string from the console
STRCHR	Scan a string for a character
STRCOMP	Compare two strings
STRCOPY	Copy a source string to a destination string
STRDEL	Delete characters from a string
STREXCH	Exchange two strings
STRLEN	Find the length of a string
STRSTR	Find a string within a string
WRITESTRING	Write a string to the console
ZTOPAS	Convert an ASCIIZ string to Turbo Pascal format

The READSTRING Procedure

The READSTRING procedure reads an ASCIIZ string from the console. When calling the procedure, let DS:DX point to an input buffer area and place a count in CX specifying the maximum number of characters to be input. Make the input buffer 2 positions larger than needed. When a string is input from the keyboard, DOS inserts the CR/LF (0Dh,0Ah) characters at the end of the buffer. Sample call:

```
mov    cx,20
mov    dx,offset input_buffer
call   readstring
```

READSTRING adds 2 to the count passed in CX, because DOS automatically shortens the count to allow for the CR and LF characters it tags onto the string. DOS function 3Fh (read from a file or device) is used. The device handle for the keyboard (0) is placed in BX, and DX points to the input buffer. After the string is input, DOS returns the number of characters typed in AX, and READSTRING inserts a binary 0 at the end of the string:

```
readstring proc          ; DS:DX points to string
    push  bx             ; CX = maximum string size
    push  cx
    push  dx
    add   cx,2           ; add 2 to count for CR=LF
    mov   ah,3Fh         ; function: read from device
    mov   bx,0           ; device = keyboard
    int   21h
    mov   bx,dx          ; get offset of string
    sub   ax,2           ; subtract CR/LF from length
    add   bx,ax          ; add number of characters entered
    mov   byte ptr[bx],0   ; insert binary 0
    pop   dx
    pop   cx
    pop   bx
    ret                  ; AX = size of input string
readstring endp
```

The STRCHR Procedure

The STRCHR procedure searches the string pointed to by ES:DI for the character in AL. If the character is found, DI contains its offset and the Carry flag is cleared; otherwise, the Carry flag is set, and DI is restored to its original value:

```
1:   strchr  proc
2:       push  ax
3:       push  cx
4:       push  di          ; save pointer to string
5:       push  ax          ; save the character
6:       call  strlen      ; get string length
7:       mov   cx,ax
8:       pop   ax          ; retrieve the character
9:       cld               ; set direction to up
```

```
10:        repne scasb      ; character found?
11:        jnz   L1         ; not: set Carry flag and quit
12:        dec   di         ; yes: save position in DI
13:        clc              ; clear the Carry flag and exit
14:        pop   ax         ; throw away old DI on stack
15:        jmp   L2
16:
17:    L1: stc              ; character not found: set Carry flag
18:        pop   di         ; restore old value of DI
19:
20:    L2: pop   cx         ; restore saved registers
21:        pop   ax
22:        ret
23:    strchr  endp
```

Let's look at a few important lines in this procedure. The SCASB instruction requires the character you are looking for to be in AL. We push this on the stack (line 5) before calling STRLEN, because this routine returns the string's length in AX. The string length then becomes a repeat count for the SCASB instruction (line 10).

Probably most interesting is the way STRCHR handles the return value in DI. If the character we are searching for is not found, line 18 pops DI off the stack and restores it. If the character *is* found, we resort to a little trickery in order to avoid restoring DI to its old value. Line 14 removes the old value of DI from the stack by popping it into AX, and line 15 jumps over the POP on line 18. This is a classic case of direct stack manipulation. Such code must be debugged carefully to prevent corrupting the stack and halting the program. When you test such a routine, examine the stack pointer at the beginning and end of the procedure, and pass the routine a variety of test values.

The method used in STRCHR to return information to the calling program was chosen for a reason. The return values should be usable by the calling program with a minimum of effort. Certain ways of passing and returning information work well—passing values in registers and flags, for example. The flags can directly affect conditional jump instructions. In the following sample call to STRCHR, the JC instruction uses the Carry flag to branch when the character is not found:

```
mov   di,offset inbuff  ; point to string
mov   al,'*'            ; look for '*'
call  strchr            ; was the character found?
jc    not_found         ; no: jump to not_found
```

The STRCOMP Procedure

The STRCOMP procedure compares a source string at DS:SI to a destination string at ES:DI and sets the flags accordingly. If the source string is less than the destination, the Carry flag is set. If the strings are equal, the Zero flag is set. If the source is greater than the destination, the Zero and Carry flags are both cleared. If, for example, we wished to know if **string1** was less than **string2**, we would call STRCOMP:

```
        mov    si,offset string1    ; source is string1
        mov    di,offset string2    ; destination is string2
        call   strcomp              ; compare, set the flags
        jb     string1_less         ; jump if string1 is less
        .
        .
    string1_less:
```

Within the STRCOMP procedure, we call STRLEN to find the length of the source string, which will be used as a counter. We clear the Direction flag to *up* and compare the two strings:

```
strcomp   proc
    push  ax
    push  cx
    push  si
    push  di
    call  strlen     ; get length of destination
    mov   cx,ax      ; store in CX
    cld              ; clear direction to up
    rep   cmpsb      ; compare and set the flags
    pop   di
    pop   si
    pop   cx
    pop   ax
    ret
strcomp   endp
```

The STRCOPY Procedure

The STRCOPY procedure copies a source string at DS:SI to a destination string at ES:DI. The following diagram shows what happens when a string is copied:

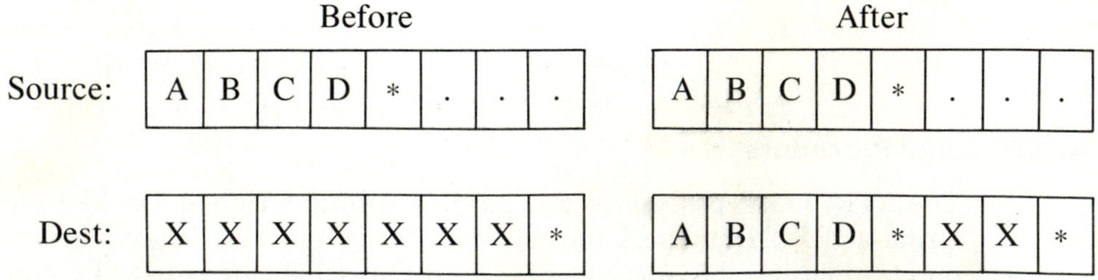

	Before								After							
Source:	A	B	C	D	*	.	.	.	A	B	C	D	*	.	.	.
Dest:	X	X	X	X	X	X	X	*	A	B	C	D	*	X	X	*

* = zero terminator byte.

A listing of STRCOPY follows. Line 8 calls STRLEN to get the length of the source string. This value is incremented, allowing the zero terminator byte to be copied. Line 7 copies SI to DI before calling STRLEN, because the latter requires DI to point to a string. Once we know the length of the source string, MOVSB copies the string (line 13).

```
 1:   strcopy   proc
 2:       push  ax
 3:       push  cx
 4:       push  si
 5:       push  di
 6:       push  di          ; save destination pointer
 7:       mov   di,si       ; get length of source string
 8:       call  strlen      ; returns length in AX
 9:       pop   di          ; restore destination pointer
10:       inc   ax          ; add 1 for zero terminator
11:       mov   cx,ax       ; set CX to length
12:       cld               ; clear direction to up
13:       rep   movsb       ; copy the string
14:       pop   di
15:       pop   si
16:       pop   cx
17:       pop   ax
18:       ret
19:   strcopy endp
```

Length of Destination String. STRCOPY requires the destination string to be long enough to accommodate all copied characters. It stops only when it reaches the end of the source string, but has no way of knowing how long the destination string is. Locating the destination string's zero terminator byte would not help, because the string might have more space allocated to it than its current length. One solution might be to have a *length constant* for each string that indicates how many bytes are allocated to it. The destination length would then be checked before beginning a copy operation.

The STRDEL Procedure

The STRDEL procedure deletes a specified number of characters from any position in a string. When calling STRDEL, point ES:DI to the first character to be deleted and set CX to the number of characters to be deleted.

To delete characters from a string, STRDEL copies characters forward so they overwrite previous characters. CX indicates the number of characters to delete, so we add CX to DI to get the source position. This is the position from which the first character will be copied.

To find out how many characters we want to copy, we take the length of the string (in AX), subtract the number of characters to be deleted (CX), and add 1.

This value is stored in CX. STRDEL is listed here:

```
strdel    proc     ; ES:DI points to first character
    push  ax       ; to be deleted.
    push  cx       ; CX = number of chars to delete
    push  si
    push  di
    call  strlen   ; how many chars available?
    cmp   ax,cx    ; more than CX?
    ja    L1       ; yes: CX stays the same
    mov   cx,ax    ; no: CX = number avail chars

L1: mov   si,di    ; find position to copy from:
    add   si,cx    ; SI = DI + CX
    sub   ax,cx    ; calc number bytes to move:
    inc   ax       ; CX = (AX - CX) + 1
    mov   cx,ax
    cld            ; set direction to up
    rep   movsb    ; copy the bytes
    pop   di
    pop   si
    pop   cx
    pop   ax
    ret
strdel  endp
```

Example. Suppose we wish to delete the string "XXXX" from the string "ABCXXXXDEF". The following illustration shows the string before and after the deletion:

Before:

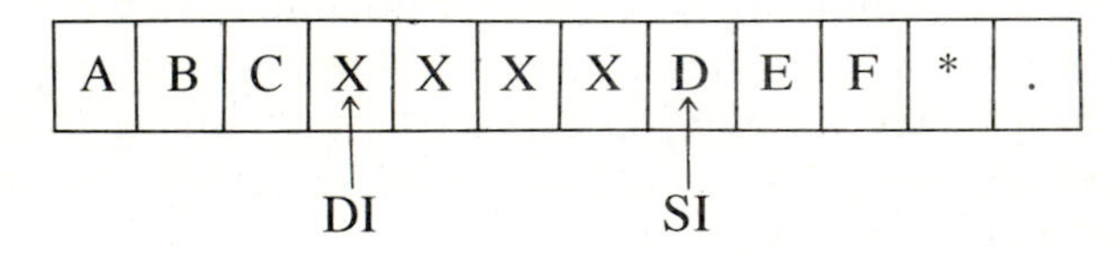

Four characters are copied from SI to DI, including the zero terminator byte.

After:

A	B	C	D	E	F	*	.	.	.	.	.

* = zero terminator byte.

The STREXCH Procedure

The STREXCH procedure exchanges the contents of two ASCIIZ strings. The calling program passes the addresses of the strings in DS:SI and ES:DI. A word of caution: Be sure there is enough storage for each string to hold the necessary characters. The following diagram shows the effect of a call to STREXCH:

Before

Source:	A	B	C	D	*	.	.	.
Dest:	V	W	X	Y	Z	*	.	.

After

Source:	V	W	X	Y	Z	*	.	.
Dest:	A	B	C	D	*	.	.	.

* = zero terminator byte.

The algorithm used in STREXCH boils down to a simple check for the ends of the strings:

```
DO WHILE (source ≠ 0) and (dest ≠ 0)
  Exchange source, dest
ENDDO
```

The STREXCH procedure is as follows:

```
strexch  proc
    push   ax
    push   si
    push   di

L1: cmp    byte ptr [si],0   ; term byte in source?
    jne    L2                ; no: continue
    cmp    byte ptr [di],0   ; term byte in destination?
    jne    L2                ; no: continue
    jmp    L3                ; yes: finished

L2: mov    al,[di]           ; get destination byte
    xchg   al,[si]           ; exchange with source
    mov    [di],al
    inc    si                ; move to next position
    inc    di
    jmp    L1                ; get next two characters

L3: pop    di
    pop    si
    pop    ax
    ret
strexch  endp
```

The STRLEN Procedure

The STRLEN procedure scans an ASCIIZ string pointed to by ES:DI for a zero terminator byte and returns the length of the string in AX. It uses SCASB to find the zero terminator. From this location we subtract the address of the string, yielding the string length. Let's suppose a string begins at location 0004h and its zero terminator is found at 0009h. The length is 5 bytes:

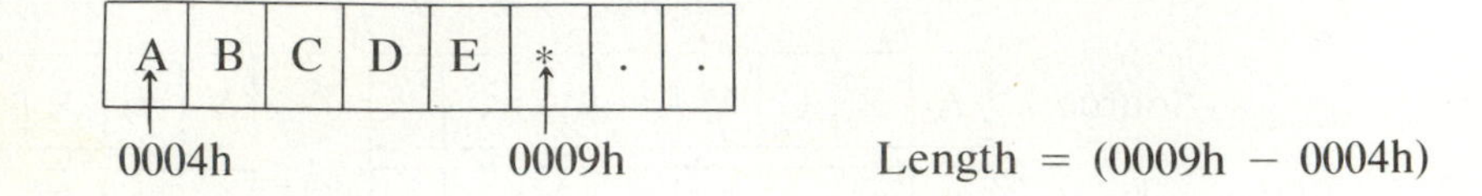

A listing of STRLEN appears here:

```
strlen      proc          ; ES:DI points to the string
    push    cx
    push    di            ; save pointer to string
    mov     cx,0FFFFh     ; set CX to maximum word value
    mov     al,0          ; scan for zero terminator
    cld                   ; direction = up
    repnz   scasb         ; compare AL to ES:[DI]
    dec     di            ; back up one position
    mov     ax,di         ; get ending pointer
    pop     di            ; retrieve starting pointer
    sub     ax,di         ; subtract start from end
    pop     cx
    ret                   ; AX = string length
strlen endp
```

The STRSTR Procedure

The STRSTR procedure finds the first occurrence of a *source* string inside a *destination* string. When you call STRSTR, point DS:SI to the source string and place its length in DX. Point ES:DI to the destination string and place its length in BX. If the source string is found, STRSTR clears the Carry flag and points ES:DI to the target position in the destination string. If the source string is not found, STRSTR sets the Carry flag and DI's value is undetermined.

The algorithm used here is simple and straightforward, based on three steps:

1. Scan the destination for a character that matches the first character in the source string.
2. Compare the remainder of the source string to the subsequent bytes in the destination string. If a match is found, clear the Carry flag and exit, with ES:DI pointing to the position where the matching string was found.
3. If a match was not found in step 2, move DI one more position beyond the position matched in step 1. Return to step 1 and look for another match.

The calling program passes a pointer to the source string in DS:SI, and DX contains its length. ES:DI points to the destination string, and BX contains its length. The pseudocode is as follows:

```
DO WHILE source length <= destination length:
  Scan destination for the first source character
  IF character not found THEN
    Set the Carry flag and exit
  ELSE
    IF source = destination THEN
      DI = DI - 1
      Clear the Carry flag and exit
    ENDIF
  ENDIF
ENDDO
```

A complete listing of the STRSTR procedure is given in Figure 10-3. In particular, note that we have tried to keep the routine as efficient as possible by using registers to hold the lengths of the source and destination strings. At line 12, BX holds the number of characters in the destination string yet to be scanned. Line 13 exits if the destination is shorter than the source. Line 16 takes the leading character of the source string and searches for a match in the destination.

If the character is not found, lines 18 and 19 set the Carry flag and exit. Otherwise, CX holds the new count of remaining characters in the destination. Line 27 again checks to see if enough characters remain in the destination. Line 29 calls COMPARE to match the remaining characters in the source string against the destination string. COMPARE sets the Zero flag if both strings are equal.

If COMPARE tells us that both strings are equal, we need only back up DI one position so it points to the matching string and exit (lines 36 and 37). If COMPARE finds no match, we return to line 12 and continue searching. This basic process continues until either a match is found or there are too few remaining characters in the destination string.

Figure 10-3 The STRSTR procedure.

```
 1:  strstr      proc
 2:      push    ax
 3:      push    bx
 4:      push    cx
 5:      push    dx
 6:      push    si
 7:      cld                    ; direction = up
 8:
 9:      ; Scan the destination for the first
10:      ; character in the source string.
11:
12:  L1: cmp     bx,dx          ; destination shorter than source?
13:      jb      L4             ; yes: exit with CF = 1
14:      mov     cx,bx          ; get destination length
15:      mov     al,[si]        ; get first byte of source
16:      repne   scasb          ; was the character found?
```

Figure 10-3 *(Cont.)*

```
17:         jz      L2          ; yes: continue matching
18:         stc                 ; no: set the Carry flag
19:         jmp     L4          ; quit searching
20:
21:         ; Try to match the rest of the source string.
22:
23:     L2: mov     bx,cx       ; save new destination length
24:         mov     cx,dx       ; get the source length
25:         dec     cx          ; and subtract 1 from it
26:         jz      L3          ; exit if source is now empty
27:         cmp     bx,cx       ; destination shorter than source?
28:         jb      L4          ; yes: exit with CF = 1
29:         call    compare     ; source = destination?
30:         jz      L3          ; yes: get ready to exit
31:         inc     di          ; no: move to next character
32:         jmp     L1          ; continue to scan destination
33:
34:         ; A matching string was found.
35:
36:     L3: dec     di          ; back up the destination pointer
37:         clc                 ; clear the Carry flag
38:
39:     L4: pop     si          ; restore registers and exit
40:         pop     dx
41:         pop     cx
42:         pop     bx
43:         pop     ax
44:         ret
45:     strstr  endp
46:
47:     compare proc           ; called by STRSTR only
48:         push    si
49:         push    di
50:         inc     si         ; point to second character of source
51:         repe    cmpsb      ; compare remaining characters
52:         pop     di
53:         pop     si
54:         ret
55:     compare endp
56:     end
```

The WRITESTRING Procedure

When calling the WRITESTRING procedure, we pass it the address of an ASCIIZ string in DS:DX. WRITESTRING is more flexible than the DISPLAY procedure introduced in Chapter 9, because the string may be up to 65,535 characters long and the $ character is not required as a string terminator.

DOS Function 40h. DOS function 40h writes to a file or device. It is more efficient than DOS function 2, which only displays individual characters. The address of the string must be in DS:DX, CX must contain the number of bytes to write, and BX must contain a file handle (in this case, 0001h for the console). The complete procedure is as follows:

```
writestring proc
    push    ax
    push    cx
    push    di
    mov     di,dx
    call    strlen     ; return length of string in AX
    mov     cx,ax      ; CX = number of bytes to write
    mov     ah,40h     ; write to file or device
    mov     bx,1       ; choose console output
    int     21h        ; call DOS
    pop     di
    pop     cx
    pop     ax
    ret
writestring  endp
```

The ZTOPAS Procedure

The ZTOPAS procedure converts an ASCIIZ string to Turbo Pascal format, in which a single byte at the beginning of the string indicates its length. The following illustration shows how the string "PASCAL" looks before and after conversion:

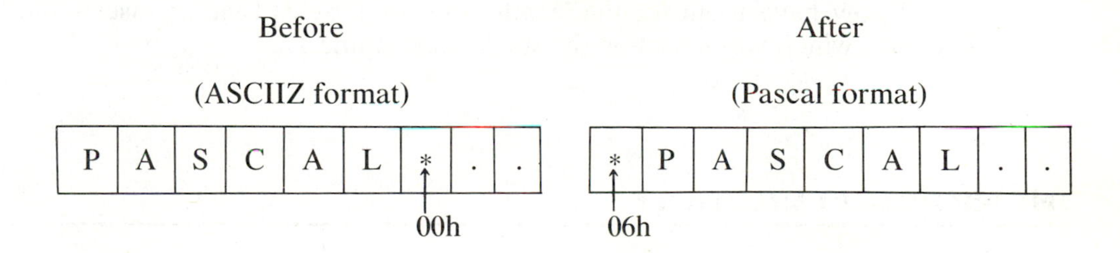

Basically we need to do three things: calculate the string length, shift all bytes backward one position, and place a byte in the first position showing the string's length. If the string is more than 255 characters long, we set the Carry flag and exit without converting the string. A complete listing is shown here:

```
1:    ztopas      proc        ; convert ASCIIZ string to
2:        push    ax          ; Turbo Pascal format.
3:        push    bx
4:        push    cx
5:        push    di          ; ES:DI points to the string
```

```
 6:        mov    bx,di          ; save start location
 7:        call   strlen         ; get the string length
 8:        cmp    ax,255         ; is the length > 255?
 9:        jna    L1             ; no: continue
10:        stc                   ; yes: set Carry flag and exit
11:        jmp    L3
12:    L1: mov    cx,ax          ; set loop count to string length
13:        inc    cx             ; add 1 for the terminator byte
14:        add    di,ax          ; point to first byte to be moved
15:        push   ax             ; save the string length
16:    L2: mov    al,[di]        ; get string[n]
17:        mov    [di+1],al      ; move to string[n+1]
18:        dec    di             ; back up one position
19:        loop   L2             ; repeat until CX = 0
20:        pop    ax             ; retrieve the string length
21:        mov    [bx],al        ; insert at head of string
22:        clc                   ; clear Carry flag
23:    L3: pop    di             ; restore registers and exit
24:        pop    cx
25:        pop    bx
26:        pop    ax
27:        ret
28:    ztopas endp
```

Lines 6–11 check the string's length and exit if it is greater than 255. As in many of our other string routines, the STRLEN procedure proves useful.

Lines 12–15 are housekeeping chores needed before the main loop begins. We initialize the loop counter in CX and point DI to the last string byte in the string.

Lines 16–18 shift a byte backward from the position pointed to by DI. When we finally reach the beginning of the string, we have shifted all bytes backward and now have room for the length descriptor byte. Line 21 inserts the length count, which was saved on the stack back at line 15.

THE MICROSOFT LIB UTILITY

Now that we have a group of useful string manipulation routines, we must assemble them and place them in a library for use by other programs. In the previous chapter, we linked each subroutine to a calling program. This time, however, we will create a *library* file (CONSOLE.LIB) containing a separate object module for each procedure. Each calling program is linked to the library, and *only the called procedures* actually become part of the final .EXE program. With this selective linking ability, libraries are invaluable when building larger programs.

Step 1: Assemble the Procedures. A separate .ASM module must be built for each procedure (or copied from the sample program disk available from the publisher). Each module is assembled into an object file. The following names are used on the sample disk:

readstr.asm	strcomp.asm	strcopy.asm
strdel.asm	strlen.asm	strstr.asm
writestr.asm	ztopas.asm	strchr.asm
strexch.asm		

Figure 10-4 lists the STRCOMP.ASM module. When building the .ASM modules, note the following: Many of the routines call STRLEN; therefore, each must contain an EXTRN directive for it. Each routine also must contain the DOSSEG, .MODEL, .CODE, PUBLIC, and END directives, but not the .STACK directive. The TITLE directive is optional. No label should be supplied with the END directive.

Figure 10-4 The STRCOMP.ASM module, ready for inclusion in CONSOLE.LIB.

```
 1:  title              STRCOMP Library Module
 2:
 3:  dosseg
 4:  .model small
 5:  .code
 6:  ;
 7:  ;                  STRCOMP  procedure
 8:  ;  Compares two ASCIIZ strings and sets the flags
 9:  ;  accordingly.  DS:SI points to the source string,
10:  ;  and ES:DI points to the destination string.
11:  ;
12:
13:      extrn  strlen:proc ; will be calling STRLEN
14:      public strcomp     ; make available to other modules
15:
16:  strcomp    proc
17:      push   ax
18:      push   cx
19:      push   si
20:      push   di
21:      call   strlen      ; get length of destination
22:      mov    cx,ax       ; store in CX
23:      cld                ; clear direction to up
24:      rep    cmpsb       ; compare and set the flags
25:      pop    di
26:      pop    si
27:      pop    cx
28:      pop    ax
29:      ret
30:  strcomp    endp
31:  end
```

Step 2: Create the CONSOLE Library. Once the modules have been assembled into .OBJ files, they are ready to be added to the library. Use the LIB utility supplied with MASM to create the CONSOLE library. With LIB.EXE in the current directory or on the system path, type the following command to create the library:

```
lib console;
```

Now add each object module to it, as is done here for STRCOMP. We assume here that STRCOMP.OBJ is in the current directory:

```
lib console +strcomp;
```

Multiple modules may be added at one time:

```
lib console +strchr + readstr + strcopy;
```

You will also want to include all the object files created in Chapter 9. Sample commands to create the entire library are shown here:

```
lib console;
lib console +readstr +strcomp +strcopy +strdel;
lib console +strlen +strstr +writestr +ztopas;
lib console +strchr +strexch;
lib console +lvars +lclrscr +ldisplay +lgetvmod +llocate +lreadint;
lib console +lreadkey +lreadstr +lscroll +lsetvpag +lwrint;
lib console +lwritecr +lwrsint;
```

Library Listing. You can display a cross-reference listing of the library that lists all symbols, variables, and procedures. A sample listing of CONSOLE.LIB appears in Figure 10-5, created by the following command:

```
lib console,con
```

Each name in the library appears next to the name of its object file name. LIB follows this with another listing that displays the size of each module (not shown).

Calling Routines. Any program can call routines in the library by including the library name on the LINK command line. Let's say that MAIN.OBJ calls routines in CONSOLE.LIB. The LINK command should be:

```
link main,,,console;
```

Label Name	File Name	Procedure Name	File Name
ATTR_BRIGHT	lvars	ATTR_NORMAL	lvars
ATTR_REVERSE	lvars	ATTR_UNDERLINE	lvars
BLUE	lvars	BRIGHTWHITE	lvars
BROWN	lvars	CLRSCR	lclrscr
COLORTEXTMODE	lvars	CR	lvars
CYAN	lvars	DELKEY	lvars
DISPLAY	ldisplay	DNARROW	lvars
ENDKEY	lvars	EOF	lvars
FALSE	lvars	GETVMODE	lgetvmod
GRAY	lvars	GREEN	lvars
HOMEKEY	lvars	INSKEY	lvars
LBLUE	lvars	LCYAN	lvars
LF	lvars	LFTARROW	lvars
LGREEN	lvars	LMAGENTA	lvars
LOCATE	llocate	LRED	lvars
MAGENTA	lvars	MONOMODE	lvars
PGDNKEY	lvars	PGUPKEY	lvars
READINT	lreadint	READKEY	lreadkey
READSTR	lreadstr	READSTRING	readstr
RED	lvars	RTARROW	lvars
SCROLLWIN	lscroll	SETVPAGE	lsetvpag
STRCHR	strchr	STRCOMP	strcomp
STRCOPY	strcopy	STRDEL	strdel
STREXCH	strexch	STRLEN	strlen
STRSTR	strstr	TRUE	lvars
UPARROW	lvars	VIDEOMODE	lvars
VIDEOPAGE	lvars	WHITE	lvars
WINATTRIBUTE	lvars	WINBACKGROUND	lvars
WINFOREGROUND	lvars	WRITECRLF	lwritecr
WRITEINT	lwrint	WRITESINT	lwrsint
WRITESTRING	writestr	YELLOW	lvars
ZTOPAS	ztopas		

Figure 10-5 Partial listing of CONSOLE.LIB after all procedures have been added.

Other LIB Options

The basic command line format of LIB.EXE is:

```
LIB oldlibrary [/PAGESIZE:number] [commands][,[listfile][,[newlibrary]]][;]
```

A brief explanation of the options is now given.

oldlibrary Specify the name of an existing library or a new one you wish to create.

PAGESIZE Set or change the page size for aligning modules in the library. The default is 16 bytes and rarely needs to be changed.

commands These are command symbols for adding, deleting, replacing, or moving library modules.

listfile This is the name of a cross-reference listing file with information about all symbols and modules in the library.

newlibrary Specify the name of a new library to be created, containing any changes required by the *commands* field. If this field is blank, LIB still creates a backup copy of the library (same filename, extension .BAK).

The commands used for adding, replacing, and deleting modules are:

Command Symbol	Meaning
+	Add a module to the library. For example, we can add the module NEW to the CONSOLE library using the following command: `LIB CONSOLE +NEW;`
–	Delete a module from the library. We would delete the module NEW using the following command: `LIB CONSOLE -NEW;`
–+	Replace a module in the library. We would replace the module STRSTR with STRSTR.OBJ using the following command: `LIB CONSOLE -+STRSTR;`
*	Copy a module from the library to an object file by the same name. This may also be thought of as *extracting* a module. To extract the module NEW from a library and copy it to NEW.OBJ, we would write: `LIB CONSOLE *NEW;`
–*	Move a module from the library to an object file. This is identical to copying, except that the module is also deleted from the library.

APPLICATION: STRING DEMONSTRATION PROGRAM

Let's write a program that provides a simple test of our new library routines. The String Demonstration program (STRDEMO.ASM, Figure 10-6) calls eight different procedures in CONSOLE.LIB. *Important point:* Both DS and ES must be initialized to the address of the data segment at the start of the program.

An EXTRN directive must be included in the calling program for each procedure called from the CONSOLE library. This program contains EXTRN directives for eight procedures.

The rest of STRDEMO is clearly documented, so a long explanation of it is unnecessary. Only one of the procedures generates screen output, so be sure to trace the program using a debugger. Figure 10-7 shows a trace of STRDEMO.EXE, using CODEVIEW. Compare this figure to the listing of the String Demonstration program in Figure 10-6.

```
 1:  title  String Demonstration Program              (STRDEMO.ASM)
 2:
 3:  ;
 4:  ; This program demonstrates the string procedures
 5:  ; in CONSOLE.LIB.
 6:  ;
 7:  dosseg
 8:  .model small
 9:  .stack 100h
10:  extrn strchr:proc, strcopy:proc, strdel:proc, strcomp:proc
11:  extrn strstr:proc, writestring:proc, strexch:proc, ztopas:proc
12:
13:  .code
14:  main  proc
15:      mov   ax,@data           ; initialize DS, ES
16:      mov   ds,ax
17:      mov   es,ax
18:
19:      mov   dx,offset str1     ; display str1 and str3
20:      call  writestring
21:      mov   dx,offset str3
22:      call  writestring
23:
24:      mov   si,offset str1     ; copy str1 to str2
25:      mov   di,offset str2
26:      call  strcopy
27:
28:      mov   al,'R'             ; search for 'R' in str2
29:      mov   di,offset str2
30:      call  strchr             ; (ES:DI points to position)
31:
32:      mov   cx,5               ; delete 5 characters from str2
33:      call  strdel
34:
35:      mov   si,offset str1     ; compare str1 to str2
36:      mov   di,offset str2
37:      call  strcomp            ; str1 > str2, so CF = 0, ZF = 0
38:
39:      mov   si,offset searchstr ; search for 'ONE' in str1
40:      mov   di,offset str1
41:      mov   dx,3               ; length of source
42:      mov   bx,40              ; length of destination
43:      call  strstr             ; ES:DI points to position found
44:
45:      mov   si,offset str1     ; exchange str1 and str3
46:      mov   di,offset str3
47:      call  strexch
48:
49:      mov   di,offset str1     ; convert str1 to Pascal format
50:      call  ztopas
51:      mov   ax,4C00h           ; return to DOS
52:      int   21h
```

Figure 10-6 The String Demonstration program (STRDEMO.ASM).

Figure 10-6 *(Cont.)*

```
53:   main  endp
54:
55:   .data
56:   str1         db  'THIS IS STRING ONE.',21 dup(0)
57:   str2         db   40 dup(0)
58:   str3         db  'THIS IS STRING THREE.',19 dup(0)
59:   searchstr    db  'ONE',0
60:
61:   end main
```

Figure 10-7 Trace of STRDEMO.EXE, using CODEVIEW.

```
AX=0000  BX=0000  CX=0534  DX=0000  SP=0100  BP=0000  SI=0000  DI=0000
DS=30B7  ES=30B7  SS=30E6  CS=30C7  IP=0010   NV UP EI PL NZ NA PO NC
30C7:0010 B8DD30        MOV       AX,@DATA

AX=6175  BX=0000  CX=0000  DX=0000  SP=0100  BP=0000  SI=0000  DI=0000
DS=614F  ES=614F  SS=617E  CS=615F  IP=0013  NV UP DI PL NZ NA PO NC
615F:0013 8ED8          MOV       DS,AX

AX=6175  BX=0000  CX=0000  DX=000A  SP=0100  BP=0000  SI=0000  DI=0000
DS=6175  ES=6175  SS=617E  CS=615F  IP=001A  NV UP DI PL NZ NA PO NC
615F:001A E8E100        CALL      WRITESTRING (00FE)

AX=6175  BX=0000  CX=0000  DX=000A  SP=0100  BP=0000  SI=0000  DI=0000
DS=6175  ES=6175  SS=617E  CS=615F  IP=001D  NV UP DI PL NZ NA PO NC
615F:001D BA5A00        MOV       DX,005A

AX=6175  BX=0001  CX=0000  DX=005A  SP=0100  BP=0000  SI=0000  DI=0000
DS=6175  ES=6175  SS=617E  CS=615F  IP=0020  NV UP EI NG NZ AC PE NC
615F:0020 E8DB00        CALL      WRITESTRING (00FE)

AX=6175  BX=0001  CX=0000  DX=005A  SP=0100  BP=0000  SI=0000  DI=0000
DS=6175  ES=6175  SS=617E  CS=615F  IP=0023  NV UP EI NG NZ AC PE NC
615F:0023 BE0A00        MOV       SI,STR1 (000A)

AX=6175  BX=0001  CX=0000  DX=005A  SP=0100  BP=0000  SI=000A  DI=0000
DS=6175  ES=6175  SS=617E  CS=615F  IP=0026  NV UP EI NG NZ AC PE NC
615F:0026 BF3200        MOV       DI,STR2 (0032)

AX=6175  BX=0001  CX=0000  DX=005A  SP=0100  BP=0000  SI=000A  DI=0032
DS=6175  ES=6175  SS=617E  CS=615F  IP=0029  NV UP EI NG NZ AC PE NC
615F:0029 E84C00        CALL      STRCOPY (0078)

AX=6175  BX=0001  CX=0000  DX=005A  SP=0100  BP=0000  SI=000A  DI=0032
DS=6175  ES=6175  SS=617E  CS=615F  IP=002C  NV UP EI PL NZ NA PE NC
615F:002C B052          MOV       AL,52

AX=6152  BX=0001  CX=0000  DX=005A  SP=0100  BP=0000  SI=000A  DI=0032
DS=6175  ES=6175  SS=617E  CS=615F  IP=002E  NV UP EI PL NZ NA PE NC
615F:002E BF3200        MOV       DI,STR2 (0032)

AX=6152  BX=0001  CX=0000  DX=005A  SP=0100  BP=0000  SI=000A  DI=0032
DS=6175  ES=6175  SS=617E  CS=615F  IP=0031  NV UP EI PL NZ NA PE NC
615F:0031 E80A01        CALL      STRCHR (013E)
```

Figure 10-7 *(Cont.)*

```
AX=6152  BX=0001  CX=0000  DX=005A  SP=0100  BP=0000  SI=000A  DI=003C
DS=6175  ES=6175  SS=617E  CS=615F  IP=0034  NV UP EI PL NZ NA PE NC
615F:0034 B90500        MOV     CX,0005

AX=6152  BX=0001  CX=0005  DX=005A  SP=0100  BP=0000  SI=000A  DI=003C
DS=6175  ES=6175  SS=617E  CS=615F  IP=0037  NV UP EI PL NZ NA PE NC
615F:0037 E88800        CALL    STRDEL (00C2)

AX=6152  BX=0001  CX=0005  DX=005A  SP=0100  BP=0000  SI=000A  DI=003C
DS=6175  ES=6175  SS=617E  CS=615F  IP=003A  NV UP EI PL NZ NA PE NC
615F:003A BE0A00        MOV     SI,STR1 (000A)

AX=6152  BX=0001  CX=0005  DX=005A  SP=0100  BP=0000  SI=000A  DI=003C
DS=6175  ES=6175  SS=617E  CS=615F  IP=003D  NV UP EI PL NZ NA PE NC
615F:003D BF3200        MOV     DI,STR2 (0032)

AX=6152  BX=0001  CX=0005  DX=005A  SP=0100  BP=0000  SI=000A  DI=0032
DS=6175  ES=6175  SS=617E  CS=615F  IP=0040  NV UP EI PL NZ NA PE NC
615F:0040 E82300        CALL    STRCOMP (0066)

AX=6152  BX=0001  CX=0005  DX=005A  SP=0100  BP=0000  SI=000A  DI=0032
DS=6175  ES=6175  SS=617E  CS=615F  IP=0043  NV UP EI PL NZ AC PE NC
615F:0043 BE8200        MOV     SI,SEARCHSTR (0082)

AX=6152  BX=0001  CX=0005  DX=005A  SP=0100  BP=0000  SI=0082  DI=0032
DS=6175  ES=6175  SS=617E  CS=615F  IP=0046  NV UP EI PL NZ AC PE NC
615F:0046 BF0A00        MOV     DI,STR1 (000A)

AX=6152  BX=0001  CX=0005  DX=005A  SP=0100  BP=0000  SI=0082  DI=000A
DS=6175  ES=6175  SS=617E  CS=615F  IP=0049  NV UP EI PL NZ AC PE NC
615F:0049 BA0300        MOV     DX,0003

AX=6152  BX=0001  CX=0005  DX=0003  SP=0100  BP=0000  SI=0082  DI=000A
DS=6175  ES=6175  SS=617E  CS=615F  IP=004C  NV UP EI PL NZ AC PE NC
615F:004C BB2800        MOV     BX,0028

AX=6152  BX=0028  CX=0005  DX=0003  SP=0100  BP=0000  SI=0082  DI=000A
DS=6175  ES=6175  SS=617E  CS=615F  IP=004F  NV UP EI PL NZ AC PE NC
615F:004F E83C00        CALL    STRSTR (008E)

AX=6152  BX=0028  CX=0005  DX=0003  SP=0100  BP=0000  SI=0082  DI=0019
DS=6175  ES=6175  SS=617E  CS=615F  IP=0052  NV UP EI PL NZ NA PO NC
615F:0052 BE0A00        MOV     SI,STR1 (000A)

AX=6152  BX=0028  CX=0005  DX=0003  SP=0100  BP=0000  SI=000A  DI=0019
DS=6175  ES=6175  SS=617E  CS=615F  IP=0055  NV UP EI PL NZ NA PO NC
615F:0055 BF5A00        MOV     DI,STR3 (005A)

AX=6152  BX=0028  CX=0005  DX=0003  SP=0100  BP=0000  SI=000A  DI=005A
DS=6175  ES=6175  SS=617E  CS=615F  IP=0058  NV UP EI PL NZ NA PO NC
615F:0058 E88500        CALL    STREXCH (00E0)

AX=6152  BX=0028  CX=0005  DX=0003  SP=0100  BP=0000  SI=000A  DI=005A
DS=6175  ES=6175  SS=617E  CS=615F  IP=005B  NV UP EI PL ZR NA PE NC
615F:005B BF0A00        MOV     DI,STR1 (000A)

AX=6152  BX=0028  CX=0005  DX=0003  SP=0100  BP=0000  SI=000A  DI=000A
DS=6175  ES=6175  SS=617E  CS=615F  IP=005E  NV UP EI PL ZR NA PE NC
615F:005E E8B300        CALL    ZTOPAS (0114)
```

Figure 10-7 *(Cont.)*

```
AX=6152  BX=0028  CX=0005  DX=0003  SP=0100  BP=0000  SI=000A  DI=000A
DS=6175  ES=6175  SS=617E  CS=615F  IP=0061  NV UP EI PL NZ NA PE NC
615F:0061 B8004C         MOV      AX,4C00

AX=4C00  BX=0028  CX=0005  DX=0003  SP=0100  BP=0000  SI=000A  DI=000A
DS=6175  ES=6175  SS=617E  CS=615F  IP=0064  NV UP EI PL NZ NA PE NC
615F:0064 CD21           INT      21
```

POINTS TO REMEMBER

String Storage Formats. This chapter introduced three standard string storage formats:

- A fixed-length string with unused positions filled by spaces
- A variable-length string with a length descriptor byte at the beginning
- A variable-length area consisting of the string characters followed by a zero terminator byte

There are many examples of these formats among high-level languages. COBOL uses the first type of format, Turbo Pascal uses the second, and the C language uses the third. In this chapter, we have concentrated on the last of these formats, often called the *ASCIIZ format*.

String Primitives. The five string primitive instructions are:

MOVS	Move bytes or words from one location to another
CMPS	Compare two strings
SCAS	Scan a string, looking for a byte or word
STOS	Store a byte or word into memory
LODS	Load a byte or word from memory

When used with *byte* operands, they are coded as MOVSB, CMPSB, SCASB, STOSB, and LODSB. When used with *word* operands, they are coded as MOVSW, CMPSW, SCASW, STOSW, and LODSW. Each instruction uses one or more of the following index registers:

Register(s) Used	Instruction
SI, DI	MOVS, CMPS
DI	SCAS, STOS
SI	LODS

The DS:SI register combination always points to the *source* string, and the ES:DI register always points to the *destination* string. Even if the names of the operands are explicitly coded in a string primitive instruction, you must still place the operands' offsets in SI and DI.

Each string primitive can use a *repeat prefix* that causes the instruction to repeat based on a counter in CX. The repetition ends when CX equals 0 or when the Zero flag changes.

REP	Repeat while CX is greater than zero
REPZ, REPE	Repeat while the Zero flag is set and CX is greater than zero
REPNZ,REPNE	Repeat while the Zero flag is clear and CX is greater than zero

The Direction flag determines whether a string primitive instruction will increment or decrement the SI and DI registers. The CLD instruction clears the Direction flag, causing SI and DI to be incremented. The STD instruction sets the flag, causing SI and DI to be decremented.

There is an important difference in the way the CMP and CMPS instructions compare operands. The CMP instruction compares the *destination* to the *source*:

```
CMP  destination, source
```

The CMPS instruction, however, compares the *source* to the *destination*. Therefore, the two instructions have the opposite effect on the flags. Remember that CMPS subtracts the destination from the source.

The Microsoft LIB Utility. LIB.EXE is ideal for creating a library of object modules that will be linked to your main programs. Of course, it is still possible to link separate .OBJ files to your programs or even to combine several routines into a single program module. But the LIB utility links only those routines called by your main program and excludes all others. Because of their convenience, object libraries are used by most high-level languages.

REVIEW QUESTIONS

1. Aside from the three string storage formats introduced in this chapter, can you think of another one used by a high-level language?

2. Name at least three string operations performed by a text editor that might be easily implemented in assembly language.

3. COBOL treats a string as a fixed-length alphabetic or alphanumeric field. What happens when a longer string is copied to a shorter string?

4. What happens to a Turbo Pascal string when the length descriptor byte is set to zero?

5. The STRCOPY routine discussed in this chapter doesn't check to see if the destination string area is large enough to hold the source string. Code specific changes to STRCOPY to prevent it from exceeding the storage area for the destination string.

6. In the following excerpt, a list of 16-bit integers is copied from **sourcew** to **destw**. Which repeat prefix should be used: REP, REPZ, or REPNZ?

```
cld
mov    cx,count
mov    si,offset sourcew
mov    di,offset destw
movsw
```

7. Assemble and trace the following two examples, using a debugger. How many bytes are loaded into AL by each?

Example 1:

```
mov    cx,0
mov    si,offset source
lodsb
```

Example 2:

```
mov   cx,0
mov   si,offset source
rep   lodsb
```

8. What will be the value of DI at the end of the following excerpt? (Assume that **dest** begins at location 0006h.)

```
       cld
       mov     al,'A'
       mov     di,offset dest
       mov     cx,9
       repnz   scasb
       .
       .
dest  db   'XXXXAXXXX'
```

9. In the following example, we want to compare two integer arrays. At the point where the two arrays differ, we want to move the lowest array element into AX. Identify and correct all logic errors:

```
cld
lea    si,list01
lea    di,list02
mov    cx,4
repe   cmpsw
```

```
            jl     L1
            dec    si
            mov    ax,[si]      ; move list01 to AX
            jmp    L2
    L1:     sub    di,2
            mov    ax,[di]      ; move list02 to AX
    L2:     ret
            .
            .
  list01   DW   -1,2,-4,20
  list02   DW   -1,2,3,20
```

10. The following example scans a string backwards, looking for the @ character. Identify and correct all logical errors:

```
lookforit:
      std                        ; direction = down
      mov    dl,'@'              ; DL = byte to be found
      mov    di,bigstring

      repz   scasb
      dec    di                  ; adjust DI when found
      .
      .
bigstring   db   'JOISD6H37DN398CX@98DF876743'
biglen      dw   $-bigstring
```

PROGRAMMING EXERCISES

Exercise 1 The STRSET Procedure

Write and test a procedure called STRSET that sets all characters in an ASCIIZ (zero-terminated) string to a single value. The length of the string is not to be changed. When you call the procedure, let ES:DI point to the string and let AL contain the value to be placed in the string.

Exercise 2 Fill a String

Write the necessary statements to fill a string with 500 occurrences of the following string:

'***/'

Write additional statements that remove all slash (/) characters from the string. There should be no gaps in the string.

Exercise 3 **Enhanced STRCHR Procedure**

The STRCHR procedure introduced earlier in this chapter searches an ASCIIZ string for the character in AL. Add the following improvement: In addition to returning a pointer to the first offset where the character was found, let CX equal the number of matches that were found.

Exercise 4 **The STRRCHR Procedure**

Write and test a procedure called STRRCHR that scans backward from the position in a string pointed to by ES:DI for the character in AL. Use the same return values as for the STRCHR procedure in Exercise 3.

Exercise 5 **Enhanced WRITESINT Procedure**

As written, the WRITESINT procedure from Chapter 9 prints a 16-bit integer with an optional leading sign. Modify the procedure so that you can pass DX as a pointer to a format string. Allow the following characters to be used in your format strings:

- 9 Print a digit
- B Print a space
- – Print a minus sign only if the number is negative
- + Print a plus sign if the number is positive or a minus sign if it is negative
- $ Print a dollar sign
- , Print a comma

Suppose the value passed in AX is 1000h (4096). The following table shows how the number would be printed depending on the format string pointed to by DX:

Format String	Displayed Result
9999	4096
+9999	+4096
99999	04096
99,999	04,096
$9,999	$4,096
$B9,999	$ 4,096

Exercise 6 **The TRANSFORM Procedure**

IBM COBOL has a verb called TRANSFORM that translates one set of characters to another. Write your own version of TRANSFORM in assembly language. For each character in **string2**, if it is found in **string1**, change the character to the corresponding character in **string3**. When you call TRANSFORM, point DS:BX to **string1**, point DS:SI to **string2**, and point ES:DI to **string3**.

Let's use the following three strings as examples. Each letter *A* in **string1** is changed to *Z* because the *Z* in **string3** matches the *A* in **string2**. Each letter *E* in **string1** is changed to *X* because *E* and *X* match in **string2** and **string3**. The letters *S* and *T* are also transformed:

```
string1  'THIS IS A SECRET MESSAGE'
string2  'AEST'
string3  'ZXBW'
```

(new contents of **string1**: 'WHIB IB Z BXCRXW MXBBZGX')

Exercise 7 The PASTOZ Procedure

Write and test a procedure called PASTOZ that converts a Turbo Pascal format string to an ASCIIZ string. Pass a pointer to the string in ES:DI. Suppose we wish to convert the string 'FRED' to ASCIIZ format. The following diagram shows the string before and after the conversion:

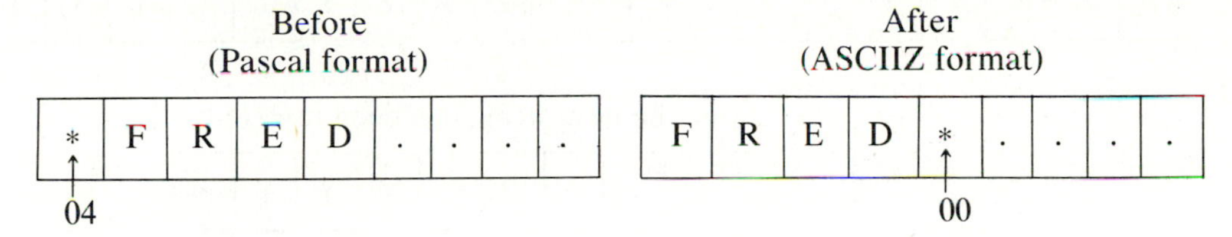

Exercise 8 The STRCAT Procedure

Write and test a procedure called STRCAT that concatenates two ASCIIZ strings (i.e., adds the *source* string to the end of the *destination* string). When you call STRCAT, point DS:SI to the source string and point ES:DI to the destination string.

Exercise 9 The STRPACK Procedure

Write and test a procedure named STRPACK that removes all leading, trailing, and duplicate blanks from an ASCIIZ string. A sample string is shown here before and after packing:

```
 THIS   IS  A   STRING    *
```

```
THIS IS A STRING*
```

* = zero terminator byte

Exercise 10 The STRINS Procedure

Write and test a procedure called STRINS that inserts one ASCIIZ string inside another. Pass a pointer to the string to be inserted in DS:SI, and let ES:DI point to the position in the destination string where the characters will be inserted. Two steps are involved:

1. Use the MOVSB instruction to copy all characters in the destination string from the insert position backward. This will make space for the new string.
2. Insert the source string into the destination string.

Let's say we want to insert the string 'ABC' in the string 'ZZZYYY' at position 4. The following illustration shows the destination string before and after the space has been created and then after the new string has been inserted:

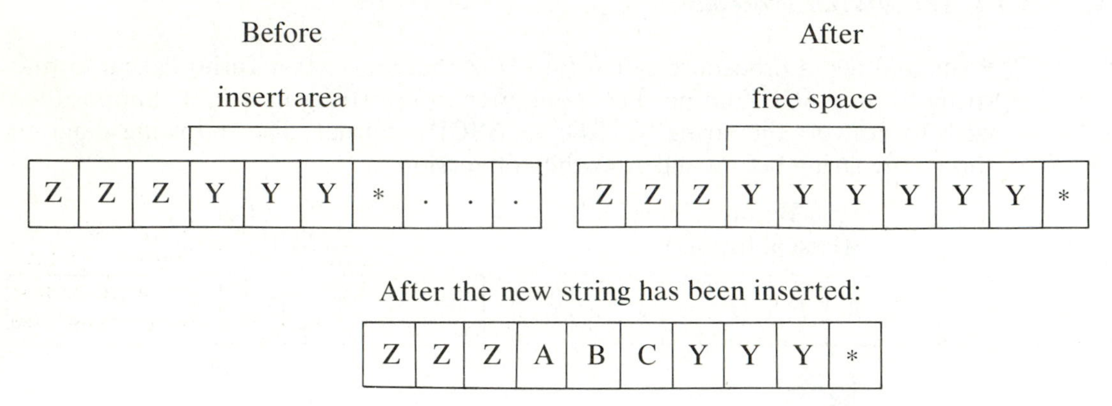

Exercise 11 Clear the Screen Using STOSW

Write and test a procedure to clear the screen using the STOSW instruction (rather than INT 10h). This method is fast because it accesses video memory directly rather than going through the ROM BIOS. Note the following:

The monochrome video segment begins at address B000h, whereas the CGA and EGA segments begin at B800h.

To clear the screen with a normal attribute, move the value 0720h to each of the 2,000 16-bit locations: 0000, 0002, 0004, 0006, and so on. The bytes are reversed in memory, so a dump of screen memory would appear as a sequence of characters alternating with attribute bytes:

Address:	0000	0001	0002	0003	0004	0005
Contents:	20	07	20	07	20	07
	char	attr	char	attr	char	attr

Exercise 12 Parse the Command Line

Write and test a program called PARSECOM that will locate and copy a string that was typed on the DOS command line. When a program is run from DOS, any characters typed on the command line are saved in memory at location PSP:0081h (offset 81h from the beginning of the program segment prefix). DOS also places a count of the number of characters typed at location PSP:0080h.

Look for the string following the first slash (/) character up to the next space or slash character. If a string is found, copy it to an ASCIIZ string called **param1**. For example, a program called TEST could be run from DOS with the following command line:

```
test /zi
```

The procedure would copy the string "zi" to **param1**.

Exercise 13 Parse Multiple Fields from the Command Line

Modify the PARSECOM program in Exercise 12 to copy up to four strings from the command line into separate ASCIIZ strings. The strings should be called **param1**, **param2**, **param3**, and **param4**. In addition, set the variable **paramcount** to the number of parameters found. In the following example, the command line has been parsed into three individual strings.

Sample command line: TEST /zi/abc FILE1

param1 = /zi
param2 = /abc
param3 = FILE1
paramcount = 3

Exercise 14 Line Editor Program

Some older computer systems have only a line-oriented text editor available for student use. Write a program that simulates just a few commands of a line editor. It should hold only one line of text and interpret the following commands:

I Input a line
D Delete a line
R Replace one string with another
Q Quit

Only a single line of text will be stored by this editor. In each of the following sample screens, the line of text is displayed after the 1> prompt, and commands are entered after the ?> prompt. The following is a sample console session. The user types *I* for input, followed by a line of text:

```
            << LINE EDITOR PROGRAM >>
1>
?> I This is the string input by the user.
```

The string is displayed, and the user decides to replace "string" with "sentence":

```
            << LINE EDITOR PROGRAM >>

1> This is the string input by the user.
?> R /string/sentence/
```

The text is redisplayed with the change, and the user enters *D* to delete the line:

```
            << LINE EDITOR PROGRAM >>

1> This is the sentence input by the user.
?> D
```

The line of text has been deleted, and the user enters *Q* to quit:

```
            << LINE EDITOR PROGRAM >>

1>
?> Q
```

The program returns to DOS.

Exercise 15 Obtain the Current DOS Path

Write a procedure that copies the DOS COMSPEC to a string variable pointed to by DS:DX. The COMSPEC is the part of the DOS environment string that tells where COMMAND.COM is located.

DOS keeps a pointer to the DOS environment block at location PSP:002Ch, which you move to a segment register (the environment block begins at offset zero from this segment). The COMSPEC is the first ASCIIZ string in the environment block. Sample:

COMSPEC = C:\COMMAND.COM<0>

The environment block is terminated by two consecutive zero bytes.

ANSWERS TO REVIEW QUESTIONS

1. Some versions of BASIC use a 4-byte string descriptor, where 2 bytes contain the offset of the string and 2 additional bytes contain a count of the

string's length. This makes it possible for strings to grow and shrink in size, because the actual string characters are kept in a separate buffer area.

2. Choose three from the following list: insert, delete, search for a string within a string, uppercase/lowercase conversion, concatenate strings, remove leading and trailing spaces.

3. Extra characters at the end are truncated.

4. The characters in the string are not changed at all, but Pascal will assume the string is empty when it reads the string's length descriptor.

5. One way might be to include a 16-bit integer at the beginning of the string that specifies the amount of memory allocated for the string. Procedures like STRCOPY could check their loop counters against this header value to avoid copying too many bytes.

6. REP should be used because the Zero flag is not important when using MOVS.

7. In Example 1, a single byte will be loaded into AL. In Example 2, no bytes will be loaded, because the REP prefix causes LODSB to be ignored when CX is equal to 0. Actually, the REP prefix is rarely used with LODSB, because the previous contents of AL are overwritten each time the instruction repeats.

8. DI will equal 000Bh, the location immediately following the letter *A*.

9. Both errors in this excerpt are subtle. On line 6, the JL instruction should be JG, because CMPSW compares the source operand to the destination operand. Thus, if the word at DS:SI (list01) is greater than the word at ES:DI (list02), we wish to jump to label L1 and move the word in list02 to AX. On line 7, the DEC instruction should be changed to

   ```
   sub si,2
   ```

   because we are dealing with 16-bit values, and CMPSW leaves SI pointing *two* bytes beyond the correct position in the list.

10. This program has a number of errors:
    Line 3: The character to be found must be placed in AL, not DL.
    Line 4: DI must be set to the offset of the last character in the string. The current instruction would also generate a syntax error, because we are attempting to move an 8-bit value into a 16-bit register.
    Line 5: CX has not been set to the length of the string, so we have no way of knowing how many times the SCASB will repeat.
    Line 6: The REPZ prefix is incorrect, because it will cause SCASB to repeat only while the character in AL is the same as each character in **bigstring**. REPNZ should be used instead.

Line 7: We must *increment* DI, because the backward search will leave DI pointing one position ahead of where the @ character was found.

The corrected program follows:

```
lookforit:
    std                           ; direction = down
    mov    al,'@'                 ; AL = byte to be found
    mov    di,offset biglen-1     ; point to end of string
    mov    cx,biglen              ; loop counter
    repnz  scasb
    inc    di                     ; adjust DI when found
    .
    .
bigstring  db   'JOISD6H37DN398CX@98DF876743'
biglen     dw   $-bigstring
```

11

Disk Storage

Assembly language rises above all other languages in its ability to tackle the details of disk storage. We can view disk storage on two levels: the hardware/BIOS level and the software/DOS level. The first level deals with the way data are physically and logically stored on disks. The second level is governed by the powerful DOS file facilities that help to make application programs easier to write.

We can bypass DOS completely when accessing data. Not that this is always a good idea; operating systems were specifically created to help programmers avoid picky low-level programming. When working at this level, we run the risk of having to adapt programs to individual machines. At the same time, low-level file access can be justified as a learning experience that prepares us for situations in which conventional software solutions will not work. For instance, we may need to store and retrieve data stored in an unconventional format or recover lost data.

The first half of this chapter concentrates on the storage of data on disks and on ways to access disk data directly. The second half covers the high-level DOS functions used for drive and directory manipulation.

DISK STORAGE FUNDAMENTALS

Let's start with the physical characteristics of disks. All disks function essentially the same way—they turn in circles, they allow direct access to data, they have a directory with the names of files, and they usually contain a table that maps out the physical and logical storage of files.

Physical and Logical Characteristics

At the hardware level are tracks, cylinders, and sectors, all of which describe the physical layout of a disk. At the software level are clusters and files, which DOS uses to locate data.

The surface of a disk is divided into invisible circular *tracks,* on which data are stored magnetically. Tracks are permanently marked on a disk when it is manufactured. A disk's *density* refers to its number of tracks per inch. The standard terminology when referring to floppy disks is as follows: *Single-density* disks have 20 tracks per side, *double-density* disks have 40, and *quad-density* disks have 80. On a fixed disk, a *cylinder* refers to the same track on multiple-disk platters. It represents all the tracks that are available on multiple-disk surfaces from a single position of the read/write heads.

A *sector* is a 512-byte segment of a track. Within each track, the sectors are numbered. In addition, each sector on a disk is assigned a separate *logical sector number.* In this chapter we will use only logical sector numbers.

A *cluster* is a logical group of adjacent sectors. It is also the smallest amount of disk space that may be allocated to a file. Therefore, a file containing only 1 byte still occupies a full cluster. The number of bytes per cluster varies among different types of disks. DOS keeps track of each file by storing its starting cluster number in the disk directory and all remaining cluster numbers in a separate table on the disk called the *file allocation table* (known as the *FAT*).

Primary Disk Areas. A standard 5.25-inch, 360K floppy disk is divided into the following areas:

Sector	Contents
0	Boot record
1–4	FAT
5–11	Directory
12–719	Data area

The *boot record* in sector 0 contains a short program with information about the disk storage format and the name of the computer system. It checks to see if the system files IBMBIO.COM and IBMDOS.COM are the first two entries in the root directory; if they are, it loads them into memory.

The FAT is a table containing linked lists of cluster numbers. Each list tells DOS which clusters are allocated to a particular file. The *disk directory* is a list of all files stored on the disk. Each directory entry contains information about a file, including its name, size, attribute, and starting cluster number. The *data area* of the disk is where files are stored.

Types of Disks

360K Floppy Disk. A standard 5.25-inch floppy disk is usually double-sided and double-density. It has two disk sides (side 0 and side 1), 40 tracks on either side, and stores 360K of data (tracks are physically marked on the disk by the manufacturer and cannot be altered by a program).

Each track is divided into 9 sectors of 512 bytes each (early versions of DOS supported only 8 sectors per track). Each sector is given a number (1–9), which may be used to identify its location. Thus, if we wish to refer to a specific physical sector, we must identify its side number, track number, and sector number:

Side 0, Track 1, Sector 4

Calculating the number of sectors on a disk is easy: Multiply the total number of tracks (80) by 9 sectors per track, yielding 720 sectors.

1.2-MB Floppy Disk. The PC/AT is equipped with a 5.25-inch floppy disk drive capable of storing 1.2 megabytes of data on special high-capacity diskettes. A *megabyte* (*MB*) is roughly 1 million bytes. These are often called *quad-density diskettes,* with 80 tracks per side and 15 sectors per track.

Micro-Floppy Disk. Many IBM and IBM-compatible computers are equipped with 3.5-inch disks capable of storing either 720K or 1.5 MB of data. The IBM PS/2 models 25 and 30 use the 720K format, while models 50, 60, and 80 use the 1.5-MB format.

Fixed Disk. A fixed disk, also called a *hard* disk, is usually made up of several platters. A typical 30-MB disk has three platters with six sides, for example. Each side has its own read/write head. The heads all move together, so at any given time they point to the same track on each side. The number of tracks on each side is far greater than than for a floppy disk because of the high quality of the recording surface.

Most fixed disks on IBM-PC systems store 10–32 MB of data. The original IBM-PC/AT, for example, was designed to work with disk sizes of up to 32 MB. With the introduction of DOS 4.0, the disk may be any size.

Disk Formats

Various disk formats are compared in the following table:

Disk Type	Sides	Tracks Per Side	Sectors Per Track	Total Sectors	Cluster Size	Total Bytes
360K	2	40	9	720	1,024	368,640
720K	2	80	9	1,440	512	737,280
1.2 MB	2	80	15	2,400	512	1,228,800
1.5 MB	2	80	18	2,880	512	1,474,560
32 MB	6	614	17	62,610	2,048	32,056,832*

*If you multiply together the number of sides, the tracks per side, the sectors per track, and 512, the result is larger: (6 * 614 * 17 * 512) = 32,065,536. The first head/cylinder contains the *partition table/master boot record,* which accounts for the missing 8,704 bytes.

Note that the disk sizes are often rounded off for convenience; a 360K floppy disk, for instance, actually stores 368,640 bytes of data. By multiplying the cluster size by the number of clusters, you arrive at a number smaller than the total disk size. The difference reflects the sectors taken up by the disk's directory, boot record, and FAT.

When trying to locate the FAT and disk directory, we must take into account the differences between disks:

Disk Type	Maximum Files, Root Directory	FAT Sectors	Directory Sectors	First Data Sector
360K	112	1–4	5–11	12
720K	112	1–6	7–13	14
1.2 MB	224	1–14	15–28	29
1.5 MB	224	1–18	19–32	33
30 MB	512	1–122	123–154	155

Disk Directory

Every disk has a *root directory,* which is the primary list of files on the disk. The root directory may also contain the names of other directories, called subdirectories. A *subdirectory* may be thought of as a directory whose name appears in some other directory—the latter is known as the *parent directory*. Each subdirectory may contain filenames and additional directory names. The result is a treelike structure with the root directory at the top, branching out to other directories at lower levels. For example:

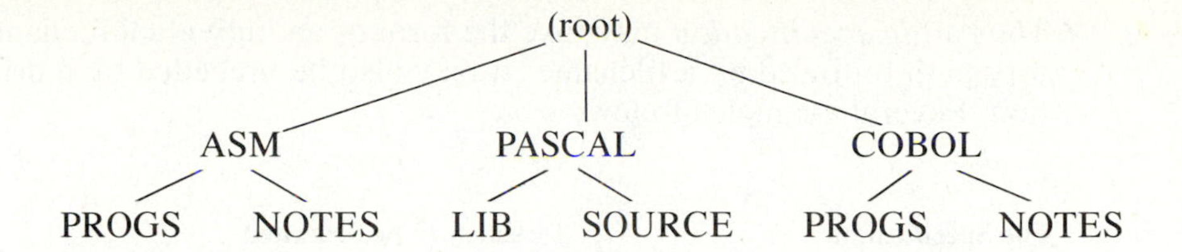

Each directory name and each file within a directory is qualified by the names of the directories above it, called the *path*. For example, the path for the file PROG1.ASM in the PROGS directory below ASM is:

C:\ASM\PROGS\PROG1.ASM

A copy of the file PROG1.ASM could be stored in another directory, and it would have a different path:

C:\ASM\NOTES\PROG1.ASM

Generally, the drive letter may be omitted from the path when an input-output operation is carried out on the current disk drive.

A complete list of the directory names in our sample directory tree follows:

C:\
\ASM
\ASM\PROGS
\ASM\NOTES
\PASCAL
\PASCAL\LIB
\PASCAL\SOURCE
\COBOL
\COBOL\PROGS
\COBOL\NOTES

The COBOL and ASM directories each have a subdirectiory called PROGS. This would seem to cause confusion, but it doesn't because DOS always looks at the complete path of a directory. The paths of the two PROGS directories are:

\ASM\PROGS
\COBOL\PROGS

We refer to the parent of the current directory by using the double-period (..) symbol. If, for example, we are currently in the \ASM\PROGS directory, we could view FILE1.DOC in the \ASM directory by using the following command:

```
TYPE ..\FILE1.DOC
```

Thus a *file specification* may take the form of an individual filename or a directory path followed by a filename. It may also be preceded by a drive specification. Several examples follow:

File Specification	Directory to be Searched
FILE1.DOC	Current directory
..\FILE1.DOC	Parent directory
\FILE1.DOC	Root directory
\ASM\PROGS\FILE1.DOC	\ASM\PROGS directory
C:\COB\NOTES\FILE1.DOC	\COB\NOTES directory on drive C
B:\FILE1.DOC	Root directory on drive B

Directory Format

On a 360K floppy disk, the root directory is stored in sectors 5–11. Each directory entry is 32 bytes long and contains the following fields:

Hexadecimal Offset	Field Name	Format
00–07	Filename	ASCII
08–0A	Extension	ASCII
0B	Attribute	8-bit binary
0C–15	Reserved by DOS	
16–17	Time stamp	16-bit binary
18–19	Date stamp	16-bit binary
1A–1B	Starting cluster number	16-bit binary
1C–1F	File size	32-bit binary

Filename. The filename field holds the name of a file, a subdirectory, or the disk volume label. The first byte may indicate the file's status. Any nonstatus character in the first byte is the first character of an actual filename. The possible status values are:

00h	The entry has never been used.
05h	The first character of the filename is actually the E5h character (rare).
E5h	The entry contains a filename, but the file has been erased.
2Eh	The entry is for a directory name. If the second byte is also 2Eh (..), the cluster field contains the cluster number of this directory's parent directory.

Extension. The extension field contains spaces if the entry is a volume name, a directory name, or a filename without an extension.

Attribute. The attribute field identifies the type of file. The field is bit-mapped and contains a combination of the following values:

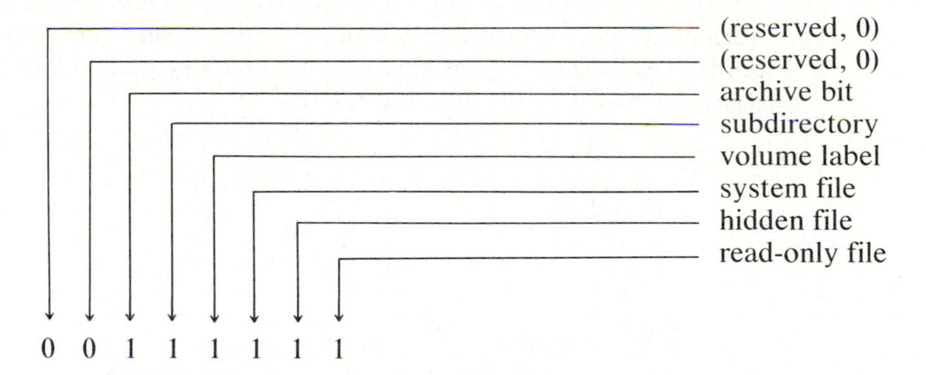

The two *reserved* bits should always be 0. The *archive* bit is set whenever a file has been modified. The *subdirectory* bit is set if the entry contains the name of a subdirectory. The *volume label* identifies the entry as the name of a disk volume, created if the disk was formatted using the /V option. The *system file* bit indicates that the file is part of the operating system. The *hidden file* bit makes the file hidden; it can't be found by normal DOS searches, and its name doesn't appear in the directory. The *read-only* bit prevents the file from being deleted or modified in any way.

Time Stamp. The time stamp field indicates the time when the file was created or last changed, expressed as a bit-mapped value:

1 1 1 1 1 1 1 1 1 1 1 1 1 1 1 1
hours minutes seconds

The hours may be 0–23, the minutes 0–59, and the seconds are stored in 2-second increments (e.g., a value of 10100b would actually indicate 40 seconds).

Date Stamp. The date stamp field indicates the date when the file was created or last changed, expressed as a bit-mapped value:

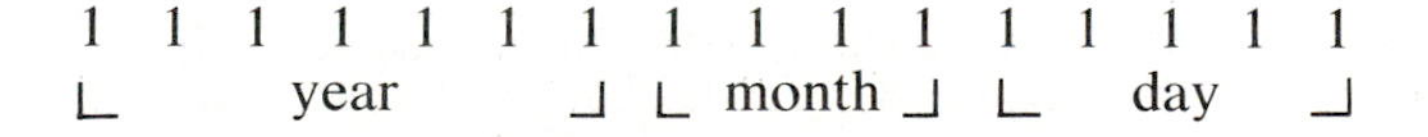

The years may be 0–119 (e.g., 1980–2099), the months may be 1–12, and the days may be 1–31.

Starting Cluster Number. The starting cluster number field refers to the number of the first cluster allocated to the file, as well as its starting entry in the FAT.

File Size. The file size field is a 32-bit number that shows the file size in bytes.

Sample Disk Directory

Let's look at an example of a 360K floppy disk containing several different types of files. The root directory entry displayed by DOS appears as follows. It was formatted as a data disk with the /V option, and the volume name is VOLUMENAME (not very original). A subdirectory named DIR1 has also been created, identified by the notation <DIR>:

```
 Volume in drive B is VOLUMENAME             ← volume name
 Directory of  B:\                           ← root directory

FILE1     ASM       1120  12-06-87    8:53p
FILE2     DOC        778  12-05-87    4:24p
DIR1         <DIR>        12-17-87    1:01p  ← subdirectory name
FILE4     DOC        269  12-05-87    4:45p
        4 File(s)     356352 bytes free
```

FILE5.DOC is hidden, and FILE6.DOC was deleted.

Now let's look at a dump of the directory, shown in Figure 11-1. This was viewed on the sample disk using DEBUG, with the following commands:

```
-L 100 1 5 6        (load sectors 5 and 6)
-D 100 1F7          (dump memory)
```

These commands tell DEBUG to load sectors 5 through 6 from disk drive 1 (B:) into memory at location DS:0100 and then dump memory from 0100h-01F7h. The numbers will vary, depending on the disk type.

Let's examine a single file entry (FILE1.ASM) more closely. This file has a normal attribute (20h), its starting cluster number is 2, and its size is 460h (1,120) bytes:

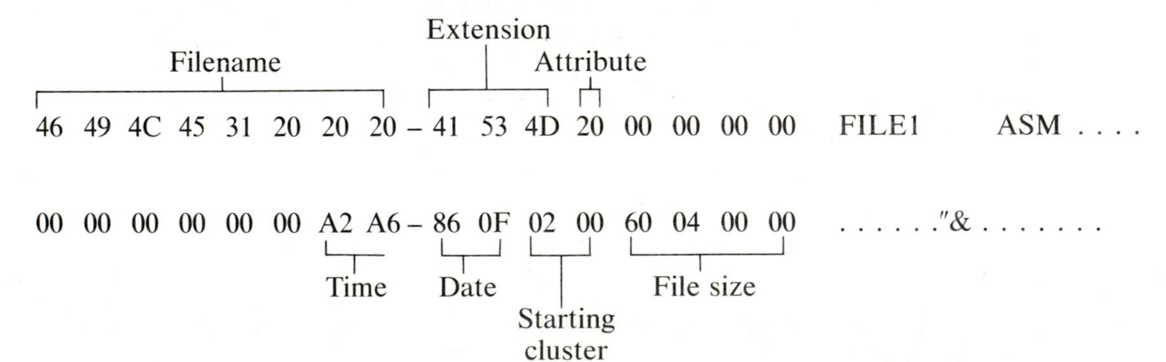

Of course, most of this information is already displayed by the DIR command in DOS. There are times, however, when we have to perform a few tricks using the directory—when recovering deleted files or lost clusters, for example. In order

```
56 4F 4C 55 4D 45 4E 41-4D 45 20 28 00 00 00 00 VOLUMENAME (....   ← volume name
00 00 00 00 00 00 00 68-91 0F 00 00 00 00 00 00 .......h........     (attribute = 28h)
46 49 4C 45 31 20 20 20-41 53 4D 20 00 00 00 00 FILE1   ASM ....   ← normal file
00 00 00 00 00 00 A2 A6-86 0F 02 00 60 04 00 00 ......"&....'...
46 49 4C 45 32 20 20 20-44 4F 43 20 00 00 00 00 FILE2   DOC ....
00 00 00 00 00 00 02 83-85 0F 04 00 0A 03 00 00 ................
44 49 52 31 20 20 20 20-20 20 20 10 00 00 00 00 DIR1        .....   ← subdirectory
00 00 00 00 00 00 37 68-91 0F 05 00 00 00 00 00 ......7h........     (attribute = 10h)
46 49 4C 45 34 20 20 20-44 4F 43 20 00 00 00 00 FILE4   DOC ....
00 00 00 00 00 00 AE 85-85 0F 06 00 0D 01 00 00 ................
46 49 4C 45 35 20 20 20-44 4F 43 22 00 00 00 00 FILES   DOC"....   ← hidden file
00 00 00 00 00 00 AE 85-85 0F 07 00 0D 01 00 00 ................     (attribute = 22h)
E5 49 4C 45 36 20 20 20-44 4F 43 20 00 00 00 00 eILE6   DOC ....   ← deleted file
00 00 00 00 00 00 AE 85-85 0F 08 00 0D 01 00 00 ................
00 00 00 00 00 00 00 00-00 00 00 00 00 00 00 00 ................
00 00 00 00 00 00 00 00-00 00 00 00 00 00 00 00 ................
```

Figure 11-1 Sample dump of a disk directory.

to fully understand disk storage, we will explore the area least understood by programmers—the FAT.

File Allocation Table (FAT)

The FAT is a map of all clusters on the disk, showing their ownership by specific files. Each entry corresponds to a cluster number, and each cluster is tied to one or more sectors. In other words, the 10th FAT entry identifies the 10th cluster on the disk, the 11th entry identifies the 11th cluster, and so on. On a disk that holds 10 MB or less, each FAT entry is 12 bits long; on larger disks, each entry is 16 bits long.

The first two entries identify the size and format of the disk. We can determine if each FAT entry is 12 or 16 bits by looking at the *media descriptor byte* at the beginning of the FAT. The table in Figure 11-2 shows how to interpret it. The

Figure 11-2 The media descriptor byte at offset 0 in the FAT.

Value	Type of Disk	FAT Entry Size (Bits)
FF	Dual sided, 8 sectors per track	12
FE	Single sided, 8 sectors per track	12
FD	Dual sided, 9 sectors per track (most common)	12
FC	Single sided, 9 sectors per track	12
F9	Dual sided, 15 sectors per track (high-density disk, PC/AT)	12
F8	Fixed disk	12 (<= 10 MB) 16 (> 10 MB)

only values commonly found are FD, F9, and F8. The remaining bytes in the first two FAT entries contain FFh.

Now let's look at the FAT table in sector 1 for our sample 360-K diskette. A value of FFF identifies the last cluster allocated to a file, a value of 000 shows that a cluster is unused and available, and a value of FF7 (not shown here) identifies a bad cluster. We can see that clusters 2 through 7 are currently in use:

FAT TABLE

Disk type (FD)

```
┌────────┐  ┌──2-3──┐  ┌──4-5──┐  ┌──6-7──┐
FD  FF  FF  03  F0  FF  FF  FF  FF  FF  FF  FF  00 00 00 00
00  00  00  00  00  00  00  00  00  00  00  00  00 00 00 00
00  00  00  00  00  00  00  00  00  00  00  00  00 00 00 00
00  00  00  00  00  00  00  00  00  00  00  00  00 00 00 00
(etc.)
```

The IBM *DOS Technical Reference* manual suggests the following procedure for finding each next cluster in a 12-bit FAT:

1. Multiply the cluster number by 1.5, and retain the whole number part. This is the *offset* into the FAT table. Thus, (2 * 1.5) = 3.0, so we find offset 3 in the table.
2. Move the word at this new offset into a register. The 2 bytes will be reversed. In our example, that would yield F003h.
3. If the previous cluster number was even, keep the lowest 12 bits; otherwise, keep the highest 12 bits. Our previous cluster number was 2, so we keep the lowest 12 bits (003), which tell us that cluster 3 is allocated to the file.
4. Repeating the process, INT (0003 * 1.5) = 4. After loading the word at offset 4, we get FFF0h. Our previous cluster number (3) was odd, so we keep the high 12 bits: FFFh.
5. When the resulting cluster number is FFFh, we know we have reached the last cluster in the file.

After performing these calculations, we know that FILE1.ASM occupies clusters 2 and 3. The next problem is to find the sectors that match each cluster:

1. Subtract 2 from the cluster number, and multiply the result by the number of sectors per cluster. A 360K disk has two sectors per cluster, so we multiply by 2.
2. Add the starting sector number of the data area. On a 360K disk, this is sector 12.

Let's do these calculations for FILE1.ASM: It begins with cluster number 2, which begins at sector 12:

$$\text{Sector} = ((2 - 2) * 2) + 12 = 12$$

Programming Tip: When a File Is Deleted, What Do You Do?

You may remember that FILE6.DOC appears as a deleted file in the sample disk directory shown in Figure 11-1. We know this because the first byte of the name contains the value E5h. The first cluster assigned to the file (cluster 8) still contains data from the file, although the file has been deleted. If another file should come along looking for an available cluster in which to park itself, cluster 8 would be taken first.

When a file is deleted, DOS modifies the FAT by setting all clusters allocated to the file to zeros. This means a file cannot be recovered simply by changing the first character of its filename; its cluster chain in the FAT must be carefully rebuilt. Only files occupying 1 cluster can be recovered simply by changing their first directory byte.

The best way to recover a deleted file is to use a disk utility program—the Norton Utilities, PC-Tools, or the Mace Utilities, to name a few. An excellent way is to write a utility of your own. Writing such a program provides a superior test of one's assembly language and DOS skills.

The basic steps in rebuilding a cluster chain are straightforward. From the file size value stored in the directory, you know how many clusters are needed to complete the file. Hunt through the FAT, looking for any clusters not already allocated to other files that appear to contain data. Each of these clusters should be added to the linked list for the file being recovered. Of course, the process is not perfect. There could be clusters that do not belong to the file in question; these would have to be discarded.

Reading and Writing Disk Sectors

There are two ways one can read individual disk sectors. INT 13h is at the lowest level, where you have to specify the track, sector, and the disk side. One rarely uses this interrupt, because the input information is so detailed.

INT 25h (DOS disk read) is much easier to use, because we need only provide the drive number and the logical sector number. The disk drives are numbered starting at 0: A = 0, B = 1, C = 2, and so on. INT 25h has an unusual characteristic: It doesn't pop the Flags register off the stack when it returns, so you have to do it yourself. All registers except segment registers are destroyed when the interrupt is called. The following sample routine reads sector 12 from drive B into **buffer**:

```
read_sector:
        mov    al,1                 ; select drive B
        mov    cx,1                 ; read 1 sector
        mov    dx,12                ; sector number 12
        mov    bx,offset buffer
        int    25h
```

```
        pop    ax                    ; pop flags off stack
        jc     error_routine         ; CF = 1 if error occurred
        .
        .
    buffer db  512 dup(0)
```

If DOS is unable to read the requested sector, it sets the Carry flag and places an 8-bit error code in AH. The most common errors are 0Fh (invalid drive designation), 15h (drive not ready), and 17h (data error).

You can write a sector to disk using INT 26h. The same registers are passed to DOS as for INT 25h, specifying the drive number, buffer, number of sectors, and so forth. As in the case of INT 25h, you must pop the flags off the stack after calling the interrupt, and the Carry flag is set when an error occurs.

APPLICATION: SECTOR DISPLAY PROGRAM

Let's put what we've learned about sectors to good use by writing a program that displays individual disk sectors in ASCII format. The Sector Display program (SECTOR.ASM, Figure 11-3) begins reading sector 12 (the first data sector) and continues reading and displaying sectors until ESC is pressed. The current sector number is displayed at the top of the screen. The program must be linked to CONSOLE.LIB because it calls the CLRSCR, DISPLAY, READKEY, and WRITEINT procedures. The pseudocode is listed here:

```
sector_number = 12
DO WHILE (keystroke ≠ ESC)
  Display heading
  Read sector
  IF DOS error, THEN exit
  Display sector
  Wait for a keystroke
  Increment sector_number
ENDDO
```

MAIN Procedure. At the core of the program is the routine that reads each sector from the disk. Lines 21–23 display a program heading. Lines 24–28 read a single sector from the disk, using **sector_number**. The sector data are placed in a buffer (line 55). Lines 36 and 37 display the sector by calling the DISPLAY procedure, and lines 38–42 wait for a keystroke and repeat the loop unless ESC is pressed.

```
 1:  title  Sector Display Program                 (SECTOR.ASM)
 2:
 3:  ;
 4:  ;   This program reads and displays disk sectors,
 5:  ;   starting at sector 12.  It uses the following
 6:  ;   routines from CONSOLE.LIB: CLRSCR, DISPLAY,
 7:  ;   READKEY, WRITEINT.
 8:  ;
 9:  dosseg
10:  .model small
11:  .stack 100h
12:  extrn clrscr:proc, display:proc, readkey:proc
13:  extrn writeint:proc, cr:abs, lf:abs
14:
15:  .code
16:  main  proc
17:       mov   ax,@data           ; initialize DS
18:       mov   ds,ax
19:       mov   sector_number,12 ; start with data sector
20:
21:  A1: call   clrscr             ; clear the screen
22:       mov   dx,offset heading ; display screen heading
23:       call  display
24:       mov   al,1               ; choose drive B
25:       mov   cx,1               ; read 1 sector
26:       mov   bx,offset buffer ; point to input buffer
27:       mov   dx,sector_number
28:       int   25h                ; read disk sector
29:       pop   ax                 ; pop flags off stack
30:       jc    A2                 ; quit if error in reading
31:       mov   ax,sector_number ; display the sector number
32:       mov   bx,10              ; choose decimal radix
33:       call  writeint           ;
34:       mov   dx,offset line     ; display horizontal line
35:       call  display
36:       mov   dx,offset buffer ; display sector contents
37:       call  display
38:       call  readkey            ; wait for a keystroke
39:       cmp   al,1Bh             ; ESC pressed?
40:       je    A3                 ; yes: quit
41:       inc   sector_number
42:       jmp   A1                 ; read another sector
43:
44:  A2: mov    dx,offset error_message ; "DOS error ..."
45:       call  display
46:
47:  A3: mov    ax,4C00h           ; return to DOS
48:       int   21h
49:  main endp
```

Figure 11-3 The Sector Display program.

Figure 11-3 *(Cont.)*

```
50:
51:    .data
52:
53:    line           db    cr,lf,79 dup(0C4h),cr,lf,'$'
54:    sector_number dw    ?
55:    buffer         db    512 dup(0),'$'
56:
57:    heading db     'Sector Display Program                   (SECTOR.EXE)'
58:            db    cr,lf,cr,lf,'Reading sector: $'
59:
60:    error_message db    cr,lf,'DOS error occurred while trying '
61:                  db   'to read the sector.',cr,lf
62:                  db   'Returning to DOS.$'
63:
64:    end main
```

If DOS encounters an error while trying to read a sector, the program jumps to line 44, where an error message is displayed. For example:

```
Sector Display Program                  (SECTOR.EXE)

Reading sector:
DOS error occurred while trying to read the sector.
Returning to DOS.
```

APPLICATION: CLUSTER DISPLAY PROGRAM

Using what we have learned about FATs and directories, it should be possible to write a program that displays a list of clusters allocated to each disk file. A program such as this is actually easier to write in assembly language than in a high-level language, because the details of the disk directory are readily accessible.

We will make a few assumptions to simplify the task. The disk will be a 360K floppy disk located in drive B. As a programming exercise at the end of the chapter, you will be asked to write a routine that returns the starting sector number of the disk directory for *any* disk. A listing of the Cluster Display program (CLUSTER.ASM) is given in Figure 11-4.

Lines 122 and 123 contain data definitions for buffers to hold the directory and the FAT. The FAT must be declared with a word attribute, so entries may be loaded into a 16-bit register:

```
fattable dw   FATsize * 256 dup(0)   ; file allocation table
dirbuf   db   dirsize * 512 dup(0)   ; input buffer
```

```
 1:   title  Cluster Display Program               (CLUSTER.ASM)
 2:
 3:   ;
 4:   ;   This program reads a disk directory, decodes the File
 5:   ;   Allocation Table, and displays the list of clusters
 6:   ;   allocated to each file.  Uses the following routines
 7:   ;   from CONSOLE.LIB: CLRSCR, DISPLAY, WRITEINT.
 8:   ;
 9:
10:   ; Modify the following equates to analyze other disks:
11:
12:       drive         equ  1     ; A = 0, B = 1, C = 2, etc.
13:       FATsize       equ  4     ; number of sectors for FAT
14:       dirsize       equ  7     ; number of directory sectors
15:
16:   dosseg
17:   .model small
18:   .stack 100h
19:   extrn clrscr:proc, display:proc, writeint:proc
20:   extrn cr:abs, lf:abs
21:
22:   .code
23:   main proc
24:       mov   ax,@data              ; initialize DS, ES
25:       mov   ds,ax
26:       mov   es,ax
27:       call  clrscr
28:       mov   dx,offset heading    ; display program heading
29:       call  display
30:       call  load_FAT_and_directory
31:       jc    A3                    ; quit if we failed
32:       mov   si,offset dirbuf     ; point to the directory
33:
34:   A1: cmp   byte ptr [si],0      ; entry never used?
35:       je    A3                    ; yes: must be the end
36:       cmp   byte ptr [si],0E5h   ; entry deleted?
37:       je    A2                    ; yes: skip to next entry
38:       cmp   byte ptr [si],2Eh    ; parent directory?
39:       je    A2                    ; yes: skip to next entry
40:       test  byte ptr [si+11],18h  ; vol or directory name?
41:       jnz   A2                     ; yes: skip to next entry
42:       call  display_file_clusters ; must be a valid entry
43:
44:   A2: add   si,32                 ; point to next entry
45:       jmp   A1
46:
47:   A3: mov   ax,4C00h              ; return to DOS
48:       int   21h
49:   main endp
50:
51:   load_FAT_and_directory proc
52:       mov   al,drive              ; select drive number
```

Figure 11-4 The Cluster Display program.

Figure 11-4 *(Cont.)*

```
 53:        mov   cx,FATsize+dirsize  ; number of sectors
 54:        mov   dx,1                ; start at sector 1
 55:        mov   bx,offset fattable
 56:        int   25h                 ; read sectors
 57:        pop   ax                  ; pop old flags off stack
 58:        ret
 59:    load_FAT_and_directory endp
 60:
 61:    display_file_clusters proc   ; SI points to directory entry
 62:        push  ax
 63:        call  display_filename   ; display the filename
 64:        mov   ax,[si+1Ah]        ; get first cluster
 65:    C1: cmp   ax,0FFFh           ; last cluster?
 66:        je    C2                 ; yes: quit
 67:        mov   bx,10              ; choose decimal radix
 68:        call  writeint           ; display the number
 69:        call  write_space        ; display a space
 70:        call  next_FAT_entry     ; returns next cluster number in AX
 71:        jmp   C1                 ; find next cluster
 72:    C2: mov   ah,9               ; write a carriage return
 73:        mov   dx,offset crlf     ; go to next line on console
 74:        int   21h
 75:        pop   ax
 76:        ret
 77:    display_file_clusters endp
 78:
 79:    write_space proc
 80:        push  ax
 81:        mov   ah,2         ; function: display character
 82:        mov   dl,20h       ; 20h = space
 83:        int   21h
 84:        pop   ax
 85:        ret
 86:    write_space endp
 87:
 88:    ;   Find next cluster in the FAT, return number in AX
 89:
 90:    next_FAT_entry proc           ; cluster number is in AX
 91:        push   bx                 ; save registers
 92:        push   cx
 93:        mov    bx,ax              ; copy the number
 94:        shr    bx,1               ; divide by 2
 95:        add    bx,ax              ; new cluster offset
 96:        mov    dx,fattable[bx]    ; DX = new cluster value
 97:        shr    ax,1               ; old cluster even?
 98:        jc     E1                 ; no: keep high 12 bits
 99:        and    dx,0FFFh           ; yes: keep low 12 bits
100:        jmp    E2
101:    E1: mov    cl,4               ; shift 4 bits to the right
102:        shr    dx,cl
103:    E2: mov    ax,dx              ; return new cluster number
```

Figure 11-4 *(Cont.)*

```
104:        pop     cx                        ; restore registers
105:        pop     bx
106:        ret
107:    next_FAT_entry endp
108:
109:    display_filename proc
110:        mov     byte ptr [si+11],'$'    ; SI points to filename
111:        mov     dx,si
112:        mov     ah,9                    ; function: display a string
113:        int     21h
114:        mov     ah,2                    ; display a space
115:        mov     dl,20h
116:        int     21h
117:        ret
118:    display_filename endp
119:
120:    .data
121:
122:    fattable dw FATsize * 256 dup(0) ; file allocation table
123:    dirbuf   db dirsize * 512 dup(0) ; input buffer
124:    crlf     db cr,lf,'$'             ; carriage return
125:
126:    heading  label byte
127:    db  'Cluster Display Program                (CLUSTER.EXE)'
128:    db   cr,lf,cr,lf,'The following clusters are allocated '
129:    db  'to each file on drive B:',cr,lf,cr,lf,'$'
130:
131:    end main
```

MAIN Procedure. The MAIN procedure (lines 23–49) displays a greeting, loads the directory and FAT into memory, and loops through each directory entry. The most important task here is to check the first character of each directory entry to see if it refers to a filename. If it does, we check the file's attribute byte at offset 0Bh to make sure the entry is not a volume label or directory name. Lines 34–40 screen out directory entries with attributes of 00h, E5h, 2Eh, and 18h.

Regarding the attribute byte: Bit 3 is set if the entry is a volume name, and bit 4 is set if it is a directory name. The TEST instruction (line 40) sets the Zero flag only if both bits are clear.

Load the FAT and the Directory. The LOAD_FAT_AND_DIRECTORY procedure (lines 51–59) loads the disk directory and the FAT into **fattable**. A single read of 11 sectors does the job, because the FAT and directory are stored in contiguous sectors.

Display File Clusters. The DISPLAY_FILE_CLUSTERS procedure (lines 61–77) displays all cluster numbers allocated to a single file. The disk directory has already been read into **dirbuf**, and we assume that SI points to the current directory entry. Line 63 displays the filename, and line 64 retrieves the starting cluster number at offset 1Ah from the beginning of the current directory entry. Lines 65–71 display all clusters allocated to the file.

Find the Next FAT Entry. The NEXT_FAT_ENTRY procedure (lines 90–107) takes the current cluster number passed in AX, calculates the *next* cluster number, and returns it in AX. To calculate the offset of the next FAT entry, lines 94 and 95 divide the current cluster number by 2 and add the result to the original number (this multiplies the integer portion of the original cluster number by 1.5).

Line 97 checks to see if the previous cluster number was even by shifting its lowest bit into the Carry flag. If it was, we retain the low 12 bits of DX; otherwise, we keep the high 12 bits. The new cluster number is returned in AX.

To run the program using a 720K micro-floppy disk in drive B, one would just modify the **fatsize** equate:

```
fatsize   equ  6
```

Program Output. The following output appeared on the screen when the program was run with the sample 360K disk shown earlier in this chapter:

```
Cluster Display Program          (CLUSTERS.EXE)

The following clusters are allocated
to each file on drive B:

FILE1   ASM 2 3
FILE2   DOC 4
FILE4   DOC 6
FILE5   DOC 7
```

SYSTEM-LEVEL FILE FUNCTIONS

In programming applications, we occasionally need to manipulate directories and files at the DOS level. If possible, we try to avoid loading and executing a second copy of the command processor (COMMAND.COM), because it uses up valuable memory and time. Calling DOS functions directly via INT 21h, however, is far more efficient.

INT 21h provides many functions that create and change directories, change file attributes, find matching files, and so forth. These functions tend to be less available in high-level languages and are usually specific extensions to the language, at that. In the list of the more common DOS functions shown in Figure 11-5, we assume that the function number is placed in AH when the function is called. Other registers contain additional values passed to DOS.

AH Register*	Description
0Eh	Set default disk drive
19h	Get default disk drive
36h	Get disk free space
39h	Create subdirectory
3Ah	Remove subdirectory
3Bh	Set current directory
41h	Delete file
43h	Get/set file attribute
47h	Get current directory path
4Eh	Find first matching file
4Fh	Find next matching file
56h	Rename file
57h	Get/set file date and time
59h	Get extended error information

*The function number is placed in AH

Figure 11-5 Selected list of system-level INT 21h disk functions.

DOS Error Codes

When a DOS function is called, a hardware or software error may occur. For example, the disk may be full, a file may not be found, the disk drive door might have been left open, and so forth. If this happens, DOS sets the Carry flag and places a 16-bit *error code* in AX. A list of the DOS error codes 01h-1Fh and their corresponding descriptions is shown in Figure 11-6. Only a few of these errors are relevant to each DOS function. Additional codes, not shown here, have been introduced to cover networks. You can place a table of DOS error messages in your own library so that when an error occurs, the number returned by DOS may be used to locate and display an appropriate message.

Beginning with DOS 3.0, function call 59h provides additional information about DOS errors. INT 59h provides three values: an error class, an error action, and a locus. Each is described here:

- The *error class* indicates the type of error that has occurred (i.e., hardware, software, temporary situation).
- The *error action* indicates what recommended action the program should take. You may wish to retry the action, delay and then retry, ask the user to reenter input, abort, and so on.
- The *locus* helps to locate the area of the computer system involved in the failure, such as a block device (usually the disk), a network, a serial device, or memory.

Hexadecimal Code	Error Description
01	Invalid function number
02	File not found
03	Path not found
04	Too many open files (no handles left)
05	Access denied
06	Invalid handle
07	Memory control blocks destroyed
08	Insufficient memory
09	Invalid memory block address
0A	Invalid environment
0B	Invalid format
0C	Invalid access code
0D	Invalid data
0E	Reserved
0F	Invalid drive was specified
10	Attempt to remove the current directory
11	Not same device
12	No more files
13	Diskette write protected*
14	Unknown unit
15	Drive not ready
16	Unknown command
17	Data error (CRC)
18	Bad request structure length
19	Seek error
1A	Unknown media type
1B	Sector not found
1C	Printer out of paper
1D	Write fault
1E	Read fault
1F	General failure

*Errors 13h–1Fh duplicate errors 0–0Ch from the critical error handler, INT 24h.

Figure 11-6 DOS extended error codes 01h–1Fh.

Displaying DOS Error Messages

Several examples of DOS function calls will be given in this chapter. Each will include a JC (jump carry) instruction that jumps to a label called **display_error**. At this label, we will assume that the DOS_ERROR procedure displays an error message based on the error code returned by DOS. For example, we might be trying to get the current directory path for drive D. If drive D is an invalid drive specification, DOS will set the Carry flag and return 0Fh in AX:

```
      mov    ah,47h               ; get current directory
      mov    dl,4                 ; for drive D
      mov    si,offset pathname ; point to a buffer
      int    21h
      jc     display_error        ; Carry flag set? Display message
      .
      .
  display_error:
      call   DOS_error            ; display the message
```

The DOS_ERROR procedure uses the error code in AX to look up an appropriate message in a table and writes it to the console, using device handle 2. This is the handle for the standard error output device (console) that cannot be redirected. An advantage to using it is that we can still redirect other program output to the printer or a file without affecting DOS error messages.

DOS Error Message Handler

The DOSERR.ASM module in Figure 11-7 should be assembled and added to the CONSOLE library in order to make it accessible to all future programs. The table of error messages used by the procedure consists of a series of fixed-length strings.

The DOS_ERROR procedure writes the string "DOS error:" to the console. Lines 25–28 check to see if AX = 0 or if AX is greater than the number of entries in the error message table. In the latter case, we jump to label L1 and display the message "unknown error."

If a valid error code is found, lines 29–33 calculate the position of its message in the **errmsg** table. We subtract 1 from the error code and multiply it by the length of each table entry. This may be expressed as

DX → start of table
AX = (AX − 1) * msglen
table position = DX + AX

Constants. Line 66 calculates a constant called **msglen** by subtracting the offset of **errmsg** from the current location counter. This constant helps us to index into a specific table position, using a DOS error number.

The **num_entries** constant (line 98) is calculated as the offset of the next byte beyond the table minus the offset of the beginning of the table, divided by the length of each message.

```
 1:  title  DOS Error Message Routine              (DOSERR.ASM)
 2:
 3:  ;
 4:  ;   DOS_ERROR writes an error message to DOS handle
 5:  ;   2, the error output device. This cannot be
 6:  ;   redirected.  When calling DOS_ERROR, the error
 7:  ;   code should be in AX.
 8:  ;
 9:
10:  dosseg
11:  .model small
12:  extrn writeint:proc
13:  public DOS_error
14:
15:  .code
16:  DOS_error proc
17:      push ax
18:      push bx
19:      push cx
20:      push dx
21:      pushf                    ; save all flags on entry
22:      mov   dx,offset message ; "DOS error: "
23:      mov   cx,11
24:      call  errout
25:      cmp   ax,0               ; error code = 0?
26:      je    L1                 ; unknown error
27:      cmp   ax,num_entries ; out of range?
28:      ja    L1                 ; unknown error
29:      dec   ax                 ; calculate position in table:
30:      mov   bx,msglen          ; (errorcode - 1) * msglen
31:      mul   bl
32:      mov   dx,offset errmsg
33:      add   dx,ax              ; point to message
34:      mov   cx,msglen          ; length of each entry
35:      call  errout             ; display error message
36:      jmp   L2
37:
38:   L1: mov   dx,offset unknown ; display "Unknown error"
39:      mov   cx,13
40:      call  errout
41:
42:   L2: mov   dx,offset crlf ; display a CR/LF
43:      mov   cx,2
44:      call  errout
45:      popf                     ; restore all flags
46:      pop   dx
47:      pop   cx
48:      pop   bx
49:      pop   ax
50:      ret
51:   DOS_error endp
```

Figure 11-7 The DOS Error Message routine.

Figure 11-7 *(Cont.)*

```
 52:
 53:   errout proc              ; write string to error device
 54:       push  ax
 55:       mov   ah,40h         ; function: write to file/device
 56:       mov   bx,2           ; use error output handle
 57:       int   21h
 58:       pop   ax
 59:       ret
 60:   errout endp
 61:
 62:   .data
 63:
 64:   errmsg  label byte
 65:       db  'Invalid function number           '
 66:   msglen equ $-errmsg
 67:       db  'File not found                    '
 68:       db  'Path not found                    '
 69:       db  'Too many open files               '
 70:       db  'Access denied                     '
 71:       db  'Invalid handle                    '
 72:       db  'Memory control blocks destroyed   '
 73:       db  'Insufficient memory               '
 74:       db  'Invalid memory block address      '
 75:       db  'Invalid environment               '
 76:       db  'Invalid format                    '
 77:       db  'Invalid access code               '
 78:       db  'Invalid data                      '
 79:       db  'Reserved                          '
 80:       db  'Invalid drive was specified       '
 81:       db  'Attempt to remove current dir     '
 82:       db  'Not same device                   '
 83:       db  'No more files                     '
 84:       db  'Diskette write protected          '
 85:       db  'Unknown unit                      '
 86:       db  'Drive not ready                   '
 87:       db  'Unknown command                   '
 88:       db  'Data error (CRC)                  '
 89:       db  'Bad request structure length      '
 90:       db  'Seek error                        '
 91:       db  'Unknown media type                '
 92:       db  'Sector not found                  '
 93:       db  'Printer out of paper              '
 94:       db  'Write fault                       '
 95:       db  'Read fault                        '
 96:       db  'General failure                   '
 97:
 98:   num_entries  equ  ($ - errmsg) / msglen
 99:
100:   message db  'DOS error: '
101:   unknown db  'Unknown error'
102:   crlf    db   0Dh,0Ah
103:   end
```

File Specifications

Many DOS functions require you to pass a pointer (usually in DX) to a *file specification*. This is always an ASCIIZ string containing part or all of the following: a drive, path, filename, and extension, followed by a binary zero terminator byte. Only the filename is required. All of the following are valid examples:

```
db  'B:FILE1.ASM',0
db  'C:\FILE1.DOC',0
db  'C:\PROGS\PROG2.ASM',0
db  '*.TXT',0
db  'PROG2.*',0
```

The second example refers to a file in the *root* directory of drive C. The third example refers to a file in a subdirectory on drive C named PROGS. Some of the DOS functions used in this chapter allow the use of wildcard characters (* and ?). DOS expands wildcard characters to match all available filenames in the specified directory. For example:

*.TXT	Files with extensions of .TXT
FILE?.DOC	FILE1.DOC, FILE2.DOC, FILEX.DOC, etc.

READING THE DOS COMMAND TAIL

In the programs that follow, we will often pass information to programs on the command line. Suppose we needed to pass the name FILE1.DOC to a program named ATTR.EXE. The DOS command line would be:

```
attr file1.doc
```

When a program is executed, any text typed after the program name is automatically stored in the *DOS command tail* area, part of the Program Segment Prefix (PSP) just ahead of the program. It is stored at PSP:80h, its maximum size is 128 bytes, and the first byte contains a count of the number of characters entered. Using our example of the ATTR.EXE program, the hexadecimal contents of the command tail are as follows:

Offset:	80	81	82	83	84	85	86	87	88	89	8A	8B
Contents:	0A	20	46	49	4C	45	31	2E	44	4F	43	0D
			F	I	L	E	1	.	D	O	C	

You can see this using a debugger if you load the program and pass it a command line. When running CODEVIEW, for example, you can pass information on the same line as the program being debugged. The first of the following commands loads CODEVIEW and ATTR.EXE and passes them the name FILE1.DOC. The second dumps memory at offset 80 from the DS register, which always points to the PSP when a program is loaded:

```
cv attr file1.doc
d 80
```

There is one exception to the rule that DOS stores all characters after the command or program name: It doesn't keep the file and device names used when redirecting input-output. For example, DOS does not save any text in the command tail when the following command is typed, because both INFILE and PRN are used for redirection:

```
prog1 < infile > prn
```

Finding the PSP. When DOS loads an EXE program, DS and ES point to the PSP. We normally reset those registers to the data segment at the beginning of the program. But once we do this, we lose the segment address of the PSP. First, we need to make a copy of the DOS command tail and store it in an ASCIIZ string for later use. We can call a procedure named GET_COMMAND_TAIL after we have saved the PSP segment in BX. The instructions used to initialize the segment registers and copy the command tail to an area in the program called **buffer** are shown here. This will serve as a standard startup routine for many of our programs:

```
mov     bx,ds              ; get copy of PSP segment
mov     ax,@data           ; initialize DS, ES
mov     ds,ax
mov     es,ax
mov     dx,offset buffer   ; point to buffer
call    get_command_tail   ; get copy of command tail
```

The GET_COMMAND_TAIL procedure follows. When calling it, place the PSP segment address in BX and point DS:DX to the buffer where the command tail will be copied. The input buffer should be initialized to binary zeros.

```
1:  get_command_tail proc  ; DS:DX points to input buffer
2:       push ax           ; BX = PSP segment
3:       push cx
4:       push si
5:       push di
```

```
 6:      push es
 7:      mov  es,bx           ; BX = PSP segment
 8:      mov  si,dx           ; DX points to buffer
 9:      mov  di,81h          ; point to command tail
10:      mov  cx,0            ; clear CX
11:      mov  cl,es:[di-1]    ; CX = length of tail
12:      cmp  cx,0            ; length = 0?
13:      je   L2              ; if so, quit
14:      mov  al,20h          ; compare using a space
15:      repz scasb           ; find first nonspace
16:      jz   L2              ; quit if all spaces
17:      dec  di              ; back up one position
18:      inc  cx              ; adjust count in CX
19:  L1: mov  al,es:[di]      ; copy rest of tail to filename
20:      mov  [si],al
21:      inc  si
22:      inc  di
23:      loop L1
24:      clc             ; clear Carry - command tail found
25:      jmp  L3
26:
27:  L2: stc             ; set Carry - command tail not found
28:  L3: pop  es         ; restore registers
29:      pop  di
30:      pop  si
31:      pop  cx
32:      pop  ax
33:      ret
34:  get_command_tail endp
```

The procedure skips over leading spaces and sets the Carry flag if the command tail is empty. This makes it easy for the calling program to execute a JC (jump carry) instruction if nothing was typed on the command line. Future programs in this book will use the GET_COMMAND_TAIL procedure, so it should be added to your copy of the CONSOLE library.

DRIVE AND DIRECTORY MANIPULATION

The functions used to manipulate the default drive and directory are based on commands that can be input from the DOS prompt. But imagine being able to change directories or to create a subdirectory without leaving your program. The DOS file functions presented in this section include those to get and set the default drive, get the disk free space, get or set the current directory, and create or remove a subdirectory.

Set Default Disk Drive (0Eh)

To set the default, or logged, disk drive, call function 0Eh and pass it a number in DL corresponding to a disk drive (0 = A, 1 = B, 2 = C, etc.). If the number in DL is too large, DOS ignores the request but does *not* set the Carry flag. The following instructions set the default drive to A:

```
mov   ah,0Eh          ; set default drive
mov   dl,0            ; select drive A
int   21h
mov   number_of_drives,al
```

The number of logical disk drives is returned by DOS in AL. This count includes all types of block devices, including RAM disks and logically partitioned fixed disks.

Get Default Disk Drive (19h)

To find out which drive is currently the default drive, call function 19h. DOS returns the number of the logged drive in AL (0 = A, 1 = B, etc.). For example:

```
mov   ah,19h              ; get default drive
int   21h
mov   current_drive,al
```

Get Disk Free Space (36h)

To find out how much free space is available on a particular disk, call this function and pass it the disk drive number in DL. The following is returned by DOS:

AX = sectors per cluster
BX = number of available clusters
CX = bytes per sector
DX = clusters per drive

Drive 0 is the current default drive, 1 = A, 2 = B, and so on. If the drive number passed in DL is invalid, DOS returns FFFFh in AX and the other registers are undefined. DOS functions 1Bh (allocation table information for the default drive) and 1Ch (allocation table information for a specific device) return the same basic information. But functions 1Bh and 1Ch do not return the amount of free space, and function 1Bh applies only to the default drive.

Sample Routine. The following routine was used to get the amount of free space and total disk capacity on a 32-MB fixed disk:

```
        mov   ah,36h   ; get disk space
        mov   dl,3     ; select drive C
        int   21h

; Return values: AX = sectors per cluster  BX = available clusters
;                CX = bytes per sector     DX = clusters per drive
```

```
; (Calculate disk free space)
push  dx       ; clusters per drive
mul   cx       ; AX = AX * CX = bytes per cluster
push  ax       ; AX = cluster size (bytes)
mul   bx       ; DX:AX = available bytes

; (Get total disk capacity)
pop   ax       ; cluster size
pop   dx       ; clusters per drive
mul   dx       ; DX:AX = total disk capacity
```

After function 36h was called, the result registers contained the following:

Register	Contents	Usage	
AX	0004	Sectors per cluster	
BX	144B	Available clusters	(5,195)
CX	0200	Bytes per sector	(512)
DX	3CFE	Clusters per disk	(15,614)

After calculating the disk free space, DX:AX = 00A25800h (10,639,360 bytes). After calculating the total disk capacity, DX:AX = 01E7F000h (31,977,472 bytes).

Get Current Directory Path (47h)

To get the current directory path, call function 47h, pass it a drive code in DL (0 = default, 1 = A, 2 = B, etc.), and point DS:SI to a 64-byte buffer. In this buffer, DOS places an ASCIIZ string with the full pathname from the root directory to the current directory (the drive letter and leading backslash are omitted). If the Carry flag is set by DOS, the only error return code is 0Fh (invalid drive specification).

In the following example, DOS returns the current directory path on the default drive. Assuming that the current directory is C:\ASM\PROGS, the ASCIIZ string returned by DOS is **ASM\PROGS**:

```
    mov  ah,47h      ; get current directory path
    mov  dl,0        ; default drive
    mov  si,offset pathname ; point to the scratch buffer
    int  21h
    jc   display_error
    .
    .
pathname db 64 dup(0)   ; path stored here by DOS
```

Set Current Directory (3Bh)

Function 3Bh lets you set the current directory by supplying DOS with a pointer in DS:DX to an ASCIIZ string with the desired drive and path. Let's say we wish to move to the directory C:\ASM\PROGS. We would write:

```
            mov   ah,3Bh       ; set current directory
            mov   dx,offset pathname
            int   21h
            jc    display_error
            .
            .
pathname    db    'C:\ASM\PROGS',0
```

Create Subdirectory (39h)

To create a new subdirectory, call function 39h with DS:DX pointing to an ASCIIZ string containing a path specification. The following example shows how to create a new subdirectory called ASM off the root directory of the default drive:

```
            mov   ah,39h       ; create subdirectory
            mov   dx,offset pathname
            int   21h
            jc    display_error
            .
            .
pathname    db    '\ASM',0
```

If the Carry flag is set by DOS, the possible error return codes are 3 and 5. Error 3 (path not found) means that part of the pathname does not exist. Suppose we have asked DOS to create the directory ASM\PROG\NEW, but the path ASM\PROG does not exist. This would generate error 3.

Error 5 (access denied) indicates that the proposed subdirectory already exists, or the first directory in the path is the root directory and it is already full. For example, \COB specifies the root directory as the parent directory.

Remove Subdirectory (3Ah)

To remove an existing subdirectory, pass DOS a pointer to the desired drive and path in DS:DX. If the drive name is left out, the default drive is assumed. The following example removes the \ASM directory from drive C:

```
            mov   ah,3Ah
            mov   dx,offset pathname
            int   21h
            jc    display_error
            .
            .
pathname    db    'C:\ASM',0
```

The Carry flag is set if the function fails, and the possible error codes are 3 (path not found), 5 (access denied: the directory contains files), and 16 (attempt to remove current directory).

FILE MANIPULATION

The next set of DOS file manipulation routines allows powerful control of files, often beyond that allowed at the DOS command prompt. For example, we can hide or unhide a file, change a normal file to read-only, or change the time and date stamp on a file. We can also search for all files matching a file specifier with a wildcard character such as *.ASM.

Get/Set File Attribute (43h)

Function 43h may be used to either retrieve or change the attribute of a file. We set a flag in AL to decide which action to perform. The following input registers are used:

AH	43h
AL	0= get attribute, 1 = set attribute
CX	New attribute (if AL = 1)
DS:DX	Points to an ASCIIZ string with a file specification

The Carry flag is set if the function fails, and the error return codes are 1 (function code invalid), 2 (file not found), 3 (path not found), and 5 (access denied).

You may want to refer to the discussion of file attributes earlier in this chapter. Sample values are shown in the following table. In addition, the archive bit (5) may be set.

	Archive Bit	
File Attribute	**On**	**Off**
Normal file	20h	00h
Read-only	21h	01h
Hidden file	22h	02h
Hidden, read-only	23h	03h
System file	24h	04h
Hidden, system, read-only	27h	07h

If AL = 0 (get attribute function), DOS returns the file attribute in CX. In addition to those shown in the preceding table, the attribute may also indicate a volume label (08h) or a subdirectory (10h). The following instructions set a file's attributes to hidden and read-only:

```
        mov   ah,43h
        mov   al,1         ; set file attribute
        mov   cx,3         ; hidden, read-only
        mov   dx,offset filename
        int   21h
        jc    display_error
        .
        .
filename  db  'TEST.DOC',0
```

One reason this DOS function is important is that it allows you to hide a file so it won't appear when the DIR, DEL, and COPY commands are used. You can also give a file a read-only attribute to prevent it from being changed. In fact, the only way to delete or update a read-only file using DOS is to first change its attribute to normal.

Delete File (41h)

To delete a file, set DS:DX to the address of an ASCIIZ string containing a file specification. The specification may contain a drive and path name, but wildcard characters are not allowed. For example, the following four statements delete SAMPLE.OBJ from drive B:

```
        mov   ah,41h
        mov   dx,offset filespec
        int   21h
        jc    display_error
        .
        .
filespec  db  'B:SAMPLE.OBJ',0
```

If DOS fails and the Carry flag is set, the possible error codes are 2 (file not found), 3 (path not found), and 5 (access denied because the file has a read-only attribute). To delete a file that has a read-only attribute, you must first call function 43h (change file mode) to change its attribute.

Rename File (56h)

Function 56h renames a file if you pass a pointer to the current name in DS:DX and a pointer to the new name in ES:DI. Both names must be ASCIIZ strings, without any wildcard characters. This function may also be used to move a file from one directory to another, because you can specify a different path for each filename. Moving a file is different from copying it; the file no longer exists in its original place.

If DOS sets the Carry flag, the possible error codes are 2 (file not found), 3 (path not found), 5 (access denied), and 11h (not same device). Error 11h occurs when you refer to filenames on different disk drives.

The following routine renames PROG1.ASM to PROG2.ASM:

```
          mov   ah,56h
          mov   dx,offset oldname
          mov   di,offset newname
          int   21h
          jc    display_error
          .
          .
oldname   db    'PROG1.ASM',0
newname   db    'PROG2.ASM',0
```

The following routine moves PROG1.ASM from the current directory to the \ASM\PROGS directory:

```
          mov   ah,56h
          mov   dx,offset oldname
          mov   di,offset newname
          int   21h
          jc    display_error
          .
          .
oldname   db    'PROG1.ASM',0
newname   db    '\ASM\PROGS\PROG1.ASM',0
```

Get/Set File Date and Time (57h)

Function 57h may be used to read or modify the date and time stamps of a file. Both are automatically updated when a file is modified, but there may be occasions when you wish to set them to some other value.

In order to call function 57h, the file must already be open. If you wish to read the file's date and time, set AL to 0 and set BX to the file handle. To set the date and time, set AL to 1, set BX to the file handle, CX to the time, and DX to the date. The time and date values are bit-mapped exactly as they are in the directory:

```
Time:  1 1 1 1 1 1 1 1 1 1 1 1 1 1 1 1
       └ hours  ┘ └ minutes    ┘ └ seconds ┘

Date:  1 1 1 1 1 1 1 1 1 1 1 1 1 1 1 1
       └   year      ┘ └ month ┘ └  day    ┘
```

The seconds are stored in increments of 2. A time of 10:02:02, for example, would be mapped as

0101000001000001

The year value is assumed to be added to 1980, so the date April 16, 1989 (890416) would be stored as

0001001010010000

If you simply want to get a file's date and time, function call 4Eh (find first matching file) is easier to use because it does not require the file to be open.

Find First Matching File (4Eh)

To search for a file in a particular directory, call function 4Eh. Pass a pointer to an ASCIIZ file specification in DS:DX and set CX to the attribute of the files you wish to find.

The file specification may include wildcard characters (* and ?), making this function particularly well suited to searches for multiple files. For example, to look for all files with an extension of ASM in the C:\ASM\PROGS directory, we would use the following:

```
        mov   ah,4Eh                ; find first matching file
        mov   cx,0                  ; find normal files only
        mov   dx,offset filespec
        int   21h
        jc    display_error
        .
        .
filespec   db   'C:\ASM\PROGS\*.ASM',0
```

If a matching file is found, DOS creates a 43-byte file description in memory at the current *disk transfer address* (often called the DTA). The location defaults to offset 80h from the PSP, but we usually reset it to a location within the data segment, using DOS function call 1Ah (set disk transfer address). The following is a description of the DTA when DOS finds a matching file:

Offset	File Information
0–20	Reserved by DOS
21	Attribute
22–23	Time stamp
24–25	Date stamp
26–29	Size (doubleword)
30–42	Filename (ASCIIZ string)

This function provides a convenient way to get the time and date stamp of a file without having to open it.

If the search fails, the Carry flag is set and AX equals either 2 (invalid path) or 18 (no more files). The latter means that no matching files were found.

Find Next Matching File (4Fh)

Once function 4Eh has found the first matching file, all subsequent matches may be found using function 4Fh (find next matching file). This presumes that a file specification with a wildcard character is being used, such as PROG?.EXE or *.ASM.

Function 4Fh uses the same disk transfer address as function 4Eh, and updates it with information about each new file that is found. When function 4Fh finally fails to find another matching file, the Carry flag is set. For a list of the file information in the DTA, see the explanation of function 4Eh (find first matching file). To call function 4Fh, you need only place the function number in AH:

```
mov   ah,4Fh    ; find next matching file
int   21h
jc    no_more_files
```

Set Disk Transfer Address (1Ah)

The *disk transfer address* is an area set aside by DOS for the transfer of file data to memory. It is used primarily by the pre-DOS 2.0 file functions, where file control blocks were used to access disk files. Its primary use with DOS 2.0 and above is by the find first matching file (4Eh) and find next matching file (4Fh) functions.

One uses function 1Ah to set the DTA to a location in the data segment. Otherwise, the DTA defaults to offset 80h from the start of the PSP. There are at least two advantages to resetting the DTA:

When an EXE program is loaded, both DS and ES point to the PSP. But we usually reset DS and ES to point to the data segment, thereby losing the original PSP segment address. If we allow function 4Eh to transfer data into the PSP, it then becomes harder for our program to access the data.

Second, the default DTA is the same location as the DOS command tail. Thus, the original command tail would be overwritten the first time DOS performed a disk transfer.

To set the DTA to a buffer called **my_DTA**, we might write the following:

```
mov   ah,1Ah               ; set DTA
mov   dx,offset my_DTA     ; to buffer in data segment
int   21h
```

APPLICATION: CHANGE FILE ATTRIBUTES

The File Attribute program (ATTR.ASM) shown in Figure 11-8 allows an operator to change the *hidden* and *read-only* attributes of a file. It represents a small

```
 1:   title  File Attribute Program                         (ATTR.ASM)
 2:
 3:   ;
 4:   ;  This program lets you change the read-only and
 5:   ;  hidden attributes of a file.  Command format:
 6:   ;  ATTR [d:][path]filename[.ext].  It uses the following
 7:   ;  routines from CONSOLE.LIB: CLRSCR, DISPLAY,
 8:   ;  DOS_ERROR, GET_COMMAND_TAIL, WRITESTRING.
 9:   ;
10:   dosseg
11:   .model small
12:   .stack 100h
13:   extrn clrscr:proc, display:proc, DOS_error:proc
14:   extrn get_command_tail:proc, writestring:proc
15:   extrn cr:abs,lf:abs
16:
17:   .code
18:   main  proc
19:       mov   bx,ds                 ; get copy of PSP segment
20:       mov   ax,@data              ; initialize DS, ES
21:       mov   ds,ax
22:       mov   es,ax
23:       mov   dx,offset filename    ; point to filename
24:       call  get_command_tail      ; get copy of command tail
25:       jc    A1                    ; quit if no filename
26:       call  get_attribute         ; get current file attribute
27:       jc    A2                    ; quit if file not found
28:       call  clrscr
29:       mov   dx,offset heading     ; display program heading
30:       call  display
31:       mov   dx,offset filename    ; display the filename
32:       call  writestring           ; (write ASCIIZ string)
33:       mov   dx,offset prompt2     ; prompt for new attribute
34:       call  display
35:       call  choose_attribute      ; input a keystroke and evaluate
36:       call  set_attribute         ; set file to new attribute
37:       jmp   A2                    ; exit program
38:
39:   A1: mov   dx,offset syntax_msg  ; no filename entered
40:       call  display
41:
42:   A2: mov   ax,4C00h              ; return to DOS
43:       int   21h
44:   main  endp
45:
46:   get_attribute proc ; get the file's current attribute
47:       mov   ax,4300h              ; get file attribute
48:       mov   dx,offset filename
49:       int   21h
50:       jnc   B1                    ; if DOS error occurred,
51:       call  DOS_error             ; display message
52:   B1: mov   attribute,CX
```

Figure 11-8 The File Attribute program.

Figure 11-8 *(Cont.)*

```
 53:        ret
 54:    get_attribute endp
 55:
 56:    choose_attribute proc   ; input and evaluate the attribute
 57:        mov   ah,7          ; input character, no echo
 58:        int   21h
 59:        and   al,11011111b         ; convert to uppercase
 60:    D1: cmp   al,'H'               ; hide?
 61:        jne   D2
 62:        or    attribute,00000010b ; set bit 1
 63:        jmp   D5
 64:    D2: cmp   al,'U'               ; unhide?
 65:        jne   D3
 66:        and   attribute,11111101b ; clear bit 1
 67:        jmp   D5
 68:    D3: cmp   al,'R'               ; read-only?
 69:        jne   D4
 70:        or    attribute,00000001b ; set bit 0
 71:        jmp   D5
 72:    D4: cmp   al,'W'               ; write-enable?
 73:        jne   D5
 74:        and   attribute,11111110b ; clear bit 0
 75:    D5: ret
 76:    choose_attribute endp
 77:
 78:    set_attribute proc
 79:        mov   ax,4301h             ; set file attribute
 80:        mov   cx,attribute
 81:        mov   dx,offset filename
 82:        int   21h
 83:        jnc   E1                   ; if DOS error occurred,
 84:        call  DOS_error            ; display error message
 85:    E1: ret
 86:    set_attribute endp
 87:
 88:    .data
 89:
 90:    attribute     dw   0
 91:    filename      db   42 dup(0)
 92:
 93:    heading  db  'File Attribute Program              (ATTR.EXE)'
 94:             db   cr,lf,cr,lf
 95:             db  'About to change the attribute of: $'
 96:
 97:    prompt2  db   cr,lf,cr,lf
 98:             db  '(H)ide, (U)nhide, (R)ead-only, (W)rite-enable :$'
 99:
100:    syntax_msg   db   'The correct syntax is:  '
101:                 db   'ATTR [d:][path]filename[.ext]',cr,lf,'$'
102:    end main
```

extension of the DOS ATTRIB command, which only modifies a file's read-only attribute. When you run the program, you need to enter the name of a file specification on the command line. For example:

```
attr file1.doc
attr tempfil
attr b:prog2.exe
```

One practical application is this: You may want to remove the DOS system files from a diskette so all of its space may be used for data. Run the ATTR program, remove the hidden and read-only attributes, and use the DEL command to delete them.

If no filename is entered, a message is displayed showing the correct syntax for running the program. The square brackets identify items that are optional:

```
ATTR [d:][path]filename[.ext]
```

The program will locate any file, even if it has a hidden attribute. The name of the file is displayed along with a prompt, asking for the new attribute. This is demonstrated here, using the file SAMPLE.DOC:

```
File Attribute Program                    (ATTR.EXE)
About to change the attribute of: SAMPLE.DOC
(H)ide, (U)nhide, (R)ead-only, (W)rite-enable :_
```

The *write-enable* (W) choice clears the read-only attribute bit so you can delete or modify the file. Note that a hidden file cannot be deleted using the DOS DEL command, because it is excluded from normal directory searches. You would have to use the *unhide* (U) option before deleting such a file.

The File Attribute program is designed so that unrelated attributes remain in effect. For example, if the file SAMPLE.DOC is set to archive and read-only, we can hide it without changing any of its other attributes. Conversely, if a file is currently a hidden file, we can set its attribute to write-enable and still leave it hidden. A by-product of this feature is a small limitation: The program cannot hide a subdirectory. This is because DOS will not allow an attribute to be both a directory name and hidden (00010010b). This problem can be corrected simply by checking to see if the file specifier is a directory name; if it is, force its attribute to 02h.

The Command Tail

At the beginning of the program (lines 19–24), we save the segment address of the PSP in BX so it may be passed to GET_COMMAND_TAIL a few lines later. This procedure copies the filename entered on the command line to the variable named **filename**. We also get the file's current attribute and quit if the file is not found (lines 26 and 27).

Lines 28–32 clear the screen and display the program heading. We prompt the operator for a new file attribute and call the CHOOSE_ATTRIBUTE and SET_ATTRIBUTES procedures (lines 33–36).

CHOOSE_ATTRIBUTE (lines 56–76) awaits a keystroke with the desired attribute and compares it with one of the known attribute codes (H, U, R, W). This is really a CASE statement (lines 60–74). In each case, one of the attribute bits is either set or cleared, corresponding to the bit mapping used in the file's attribute byte in the disk directory. This value is stored in the variable **attribute** and subsequently used by SET_ATTRIBUTE.

SET_ATTRIBUTE (lines 78–86) calls DOS function 43h, using the variable **attribute**, to modify the file. This returns to the main procedure, which returns to DOS (see lines 37 and 42).

APPLICATION: DISPLAY FILENAMES AND DATES

Using what we have learned about finding matching files and the date stamp of a file, we will write a program that looks for a file or group of files and displays each name, along with its date. This should provide some insight on how the DOS DIR command works. We would also like to be able to enter a file specification on the command line that includes optional wildcard characters.

The Date Stamp program (DAT.ASM) in Figure 11-9 does the following:

- It retrieves the filename typed on the DOS command line. If no name is found, a message is displayed showing the program syntax.
- It finds the first matching file. If none is found, an appropriate message is displayed before returning to DOS.
- It decodes the date stamp and stores the day, month, and year in variables.
- It displays the filename and date.
- It finds the next matching file.

The last 3 steps are repeated until no more files are found.

The MAIN Procedure. The MAIN procedure calls routines to retrieve the command tail and find the first matching file (lines 19–29). From that point on, it is essentially a loop that decodes and displays the date and looks for a new matching file (line 32–37).

The FIND_FIRST_MATCH Procedure. FIND_FIRST_MATCH (lines 49–60) calls DOS function 1Ah to set the disk transfer address, where file information will be stored when matching files are found. We call function 4Eh to find the first matching file and return to MAIN. The Carry flag is set by DOS if no matching files were found.

```
 1:   title  Date Stamp Program                              (DAT.ASM)
 2:
 3:   ;
 4:   ;   This program displays the name and date stamp for
 5:   ;   each file matching a file specification entered
 6:   ;   on the DOS command line.  It uses the following
 7:   ;   routines from CONSOLE.LIB: DISPLAY, DOS_ERROR,
 8:   ;   GET_COMMAND_TAIL, STRLEN, WRITEINT, and WRITESTRING.
 9:   ;
10:   dosseg
11:   .model small
12:   .stack 100h
13:
14:   extrn display:proc, DOS_error:proc, get_command_tail:proc
15:   extrn strlen:proc, writeint:proc, writestring:proc
16:   extrn cr:abs, lf:abs
17:
18:   .code
19:   main proc
20:       mov   bx,ds
21:       mov   ax,@data                ; initialize DS, ES
22:       mov   ds,ax
23:       mov   es,ax
24:       mov   dx,offset filespec      ; get filespec from
25:       call  get_command_tail        ; the command line
26:       jc    A2                      ; quit if none supplied
27:       mov   dx,offset heading       ; display program heading
28:       call  display
29:       call  find_first_match
30:       jc    A3                      ; quit if no files found
31:
32:   A1: call  decode_the_date
33:       call  display_filename_and_date
34:       mov   ah,4Fh                  ; find next matching file
35:       int   21h
36:       jnc   A1                      ; continue searching
37:       jmp   A3                      ; until no more matches
38:
39:   A2: mov   dx,offset syntax_msg ; display command syntax
40:       call  display
41:
42:   A3: mov   ax,4C00h                ; return to DOS
43:       int   21h
44:   main endp
45
46:       ; Find the first file that matches the file
47:       ; specification entered on the command line.
48:
49:   find_first_match proc
50:       mov   ah,1Ah                  ; set disk transfer address
```

Figure 11-9 Displaying filenames and dates: The DAT.ASM program.

Figure 11-9 *(Cont.)*

```
51:        mov   dx,offset DTA
52:        int   21h
53:        mov   ah,4Eh                    ; find first matching file
54:        mov   cx,0                      ; normal attributes only
55:        lea   dx,filespec               ; DX points to the name
56:        int   21h
57:        jnc   B1                        ; if DOS error occurred,
58:        call  DOS_error                 ; display a message
59:    B1: ret
60:    find_first_match endp
61:
62:        ; Translate the encoded bit format of a file's
63:        ; date stamp.
64:
65:    decode_the_date proc
66:        mov   bx,offset file_date
67:        mov   dx,[bx]                   ; get the day
68:        mov   ax,dx
69:        and   ax,001Fh                  ; clear bits 5-15
70:        mov   day,ax
71:        mov   ax,dx                     ; get the month
72:        mov   cl,5
73:        shr   ax,cl                     ; shift right 5 bits
74:        and   ax,000Fh                  ; clear bits 4-15
75:        mov   month,ax
76:        mov   ax,dx                     ; get the year
77:        mov   cl,9
78:        shr   ax,cl                     ; shift right 9 bits
79:        add   ax,80                     ; year is relative to 1980
80:        mov   year,ax
81:        ret
82:    decode_the_date endp
83:
84:        ; Write both the filename and its date stamp to
85:        ; the console.
86:
87:    display_filename_and_date proc
88:        mov   dx,offset file_name
89:        call  writestring               ; display the file name
90:        call  fill_with_spaces
91:        mov   bx,10                     ; choose decimal radix
92:        mov   ax,month                  ; display the month
93:        call  writeint
94:        call  write_dash                ; display a "-"
95:        mov   ax,day                    ; display the day
96:        call  writeint
97:        call  write_dash                ; display a "-"
98:        mov   ax,year                   ; display the year
99:        call  writeint
```

Figure 11-9 *(Cont.)*

```
100:        mov   dx,offset crlf          ; display CR/LF
101:        call  display
102:        ret
103:    display_filename_and_date endp
104:
105:
106:        ; Pad the right side of the filename with spaces.
107:
108:    fill_with_spaces proc
109:        mov   cx,15                   ; max file size plus 3 spaces
110:        mov   di,offset file_name     ; get length
111:        call  strlen                  ; AX = length of filename
112:        sub   cx,ax
113:        mov   ah,2                    ; display character
114:        mov   dl,20h                  ; space
115:    E1: int   21h                     ; write spaces
116:        loop  E1                      ; until CX = 0
117:        ret
118:    fill_with_spaces endp
119:
120:    write_dash proc          ; write a dash
121:         mov  ah,2
122:         mov  dl,'-'
123:         int  21h
124:         ret
125:    write_dash endp
126:
127:    .data
128:
129:    month        dw   ?                ; temporary storage for
130:    day          dw   ?                ; month, day, year
131:    year         dw   ?
132:
133:    filespec     db   40 dup(0)        ; DOS command line
134:    heading      db  'Date Stamp Program               (DAT.EXE)'
135:                 db   cr,lf,cr,lf,'$'
136:    syntax_msg   db  'The correct syntax is:  '
137:                 db  'DAT [d:][path]filename[.ext]',cr,lf,'$'
138:    crlf         db   cr,lf,'$'
139:
140:    ;------ (the following fields must be in order) ------
141:
142:    DTA       db 22 dup(?)     ; header info - not used
143:    file_time dw ?             ; time stamp of file
144:    file_date dw ?             ; date stamp of file
145:    file_size dd ?             ; size of file: not used
146:    file_name db 13 dup(0)     ; name of file found by DOS
147:
148:    end main
```

The DECODE_THE_DATE Procedure. DECODE_THE_DATE (lines 65–82) is the most complex procedure here, because each field (day, month, year) must be masked and shifted to the right. As each value is isolated, it is stored in a variable.

The day of the week occupies bits 0–4, so we clear bits 5–15 and move the result to **day** (lines 67–70).

The month number is stored in bits 5–8, so AX is shifted 5 bits to the right. We clear all other bits and store the result in **month** (lines 71–75).

The year number is stored in bits 9–15, so we shift AX 9 bits to the right. We add 80 because the date is always relative to 1980 (lines 76–80).

The DISPLAY_FILENAME_AND_DATE procedure (lines 87–103) calls WRITESTRING to display the filename and WRITEINT to display the month, day, and year values.

POINTS TO REMEMBER

Disk storage may be viewed on two levels: the hardware/BIOS level and the software/DOS level. In assembly language we can program on both levels, either by directly accessing physical areas of the disk or by calling DOS functions. Programs written at the hardware/BIOS level run faster and can manipulate the hardware. Such programs, however, may not be portable from one computer system to another. Programs written at the DOS level are portable to any system running under DOS or MS-DOS and still have more flexibility and speed than those written in most high-level languages.

Tracks are concentric circles that store data on disks. On a fixed disk with multiple platters, a cylinder is a combination of all tracks accessible from one position of the read/write heads. A typical fixed disk might have three platters with six heads. Tracks are divided into sectors, each of which holds 512 bytes.

There are several common disk storage formats used on IBM-compatible computers. A 5.25-inch disk holds either 360K or 1.2 MB of data, a 3.5-inch disk holds either 720K or 1.5 MB, and fixed disks hold 10 to 100 MB. Files are organized into logical units called clusters, each of which is made up of one or more sectors. Clusters vary in size from one disk format to another.

All IBM-PC disks have a boot record in their first sector. This contains disk format information, and loads some of the DOS system files into memory. Following the boot record is the file allocation table (FAT), which keeps track of all clusters assigned to each file. Following the FAT is the root directory, in which each entry contains a file, volume, or subdirectory name, the file's attribute, its length, its starting cluster number, its date stamp, and its time stamp. The root directory may also contain references to other subdirectories on the disk.

Individual disk sectors may be read using INT 25h and written using INT 26h. When calling these interrupts, you must tell DOS which drive to read, the starting sector number, the number of sectors, and the location of the input buffer.

The Sector Display program (SECTOR.ASM, Figure 11-3) demonstrates how to read and display individual disk sectors. The Cluster Display program (CLUSTER.ASM, Figure 11-4) reads the disk directory and file allocation table directly into memory and displays a list of the clusters allocated to each file. This program has a routine showing how to decode a FAT with 12-bit entries.

DOS Error Codes. When a DOS function manipulates files or directories, an error may occur. DOS signals the error by setting the Carry flag and placing an error code in AX. A list of codes 1–31 was shown in Figure 11-6.

Drive and Directory Manipulation. The most common functions used to manipulate disk drive assignments and directories are the following:

Set default disk drive	0Eh
Get default disk drive	19h
Get disk free space	36h
Get current directory path	47h
Set current directory	3Bh
Create subdirectory	39h
Remove subdirectory	3Ah

File Manipulation. The most common functions for manipulating files (other than opening, closing, reading, and writing) are the following:

Get/set file attribute	43h
Delete a file	41h
Rename file	56h
Get/set file date and time	57h
Find first matching file	4Eh
Find next matching file	4Fh
Set disk transfer address	1Ah

Applications. The File Attribute program (ATTR.ASM, Figure 11-8) was introduced, which reads a filename from the command line and allows the operator to change selected attributes of the file. The Date Stamp program (DAT.ASM, Figure 11-9) reads a file specification on the command line and uses DOS functions 4Eh and 4Fh (find first and find next) to display the name and date stamp of all matching files.

REVIEW QUESTIONS

1. Using a Pascal, BASIC, or C compiler manual, check to see how many of the following system-level DOS functions are available:

Create directory	Get/set file attribute
Remove directory	Find first matching file
Change logged directory	Get/set file date and time

2. For each of the following terms, write a single-sentence definition:
   a track
   b. sector
   c. cluster
   d. cylinder
   e. FAT
   f. subdirectory
   g. command tail
   h. date stamp
   i. attribute byte
   j. boot record
   k. parent directory
   l. file specification
   m. directory path
   n. media descriptor byte

3. For each of the following DOS error codes returned when INT 21h is called, write a single-sentence explanation of what probably caused the error.

	Error Number	Function Being Called
a.	03h	56h (Rename file)
b.	05h	41h (Delete file)
c.	06h	57h (Set date/time)
d.	10h	3Ah (Remove directory)
e.	11h	56h (Rename file)
f.	12h	4Eh (Find first matching file)

4. If a two-sided disk has 40 tracks per side and each track contains eight 512-byte sectors, what is the total disk capacity?

5. Which sector is the first data sector on a 1.2-MB floppy disk?

6. Within each entry in a disk directory, what is the offset of the file size?

7. If a file is only 2 bytes long, how much space will it take up on a 360-K disk?

8. Which area of a disk includes information about its cluster size, number of tracks per side, and number of sectors per track?

9. What does the notation (..) in the name field of a directory entry identify?

10. If a directory entry has an attribute of 10h, what kind of entry is it?

11. What date is indicated by the following file date stamp?

    0000011011100011

12. Calculate the starting sector number for the following file: It begins in cluster 2, the disk has 4 sectors per cluster, and the disk data area begins at sector 155.

13. What does it mean when the first byte of a filename in a directory entry contains E5h?

14. If an entry in a directory has an attribute of 10h, will its name be displayed by the DIR command?

15. If a file containing 5 clusters has been deleted, how much of the file *may* be recovered by removing the marker from the first character of its name?

16. In the following dump of a directory entry, what is the file size and starting cluster number?

```
46 49 4C 45 31 20 20 20-41 53 4D 20 00 00 00 00  FILE1   ASM ....
00 00 00 00 00 00 A2 A6-86 OF 04 00 20 00 00 00  ......"&....'...
```

17. How many bits long is each entry in the file allocation table of a 30-MB fixed disk?

18. Why is recovery of a deleted file much harder when the file is *fragmented,* that is, stored in noncontiguous clusters? Is the problem increased if the free clusters on the disk were once used by other files?

19. Assuming that **buffer** is a 512-byte memory buffer, what is wrong with the following subroutine that reads a single sector from drive B?

```
read_sector proc
    mov   al,1                 ; drive B
    mov   cx,1                 ; read 1 sector
    mov   dx,12                ; sector number 12
    mov   bx,offset buffer ; point to buffer
    int   25h                  ; read the sector
    ret
read_sector endp
```

20. Is there any way to tell INT 25h to read a sector from the current default drive? If so, how?

21. In the Cluster Display program (Figure 11-4), the following instruction is executed after SI is set to the offset of each directory entry. What is its purpose?

```
test  byte ptr [si+11],18h
```

22. Assume that you are decoding the file allocation table of a 360K floppy disk. AX contains the previous cluster number, and DX contains the current offset

into the FAT. Write a series of assembly language statements that will calculate the new cluster number and place it in AX.

23. At what location is the DOS command tail?

PROGRAMMING EXERCISES

Note: Many of the programs suggested here will alter your disk or directory. Be sure to make a backup copy of any disk affected by these programs, or create a temporary scratch disk to be used while testing them. *Under no circumstances should you run the programs on a fixed disk until you have tested them carefully!*

Exercise 1 Get Default Disk Drive

Write a routine to determine which is the current (default) disk drive. Then read sector 12 from the disk.

Exercise 2 Set Default Disk Drive

Write a routine to prompt the operator for a disk drive letter (*A, B, C,* or *D*), and then set the default drive to the value that was input.

Exercise 3 Disk Free Space

Write a routine that gets the amount of disk free space and prints it out (in bytes).

Exercise 4 Create a Hidden Directory

Write a routine that creates a hidden directory named TEMP. Use the DIR command to verify its hidden status. Try copying files to the new directory.

Exercise 5 Decode a 16-Bit FAT Entry

Write a routine that decodes a 16-bit file allocation table. Replace the NEXT_FAT ENTRY procedure in the CLUSTER.ASM program with your routine. Make other necessary adjustments to the program, and run the program on a fixed disk. *Caution:* To avoid losing any data on your fixed disk, double-check the LOAD_FAT_AND_DIRECTORY procedure to make sure you are *reading* sectors, not writing to them.

Exercise 6 **Search for Subdirectories**

Write a routine that searches for all entries in a directory with an attribute of 08h (subdirectory name). Display the names.

Exercise 7 **Display a Subdirectory**

Write a routine that finds the first subdirectory entry in the root directory, moves to the subdirectory, and displays a list of all of its files.

Exercise 8 **Hide Multiple Files**

Write a program called HIDE.EXE that hides all files matching a file specification on the command line. Allow wildcard characters, such as HIDE *.* or HIDE *.ASM. Write a second program that unhides all specified files.

Exercise 9 **Purge Multiple Files**

Write a program named PURGE.EXE that takes a file specification from the command line, displays the name of each matching file, and asks if the file is to be deleted. Each time the operator enters Y next to a filename, delete the file. This will turn out to be a handy utility program, allowing you to clean up a disk directory quickly.

Exercise 10 **Search for Files by Date**

Write a program that searches for all files in the current directory that have a date stamp less than the current system date and displays their names. To obtain the system date, call INT 21h function 2Ah. The year is returned in CX, the month in DH, and the day in DL. For example, October 12, 1990, would be returned as:

CX=07C6h, DH=0Ah, DL=0Ch

Exercise 11 **Modified Cluster Display Program**

Modify the Cluster Display program shown in Figure 11-4 so it displays the *sector numbers* allocated to each file, rather than the clusters. The following algorithm may be used to convert a cluster number to a sector number.

- Subtract 2 from the cluster number and multiply the result by 2 (two sectors per cluster).
- Add the starting sector number of the data area (12). The values shown in parentheses apply to a standard 360K floppy disk. Remember that a cluster consists of two adjacent sectors on a 360K disk.

Exercise 12 **Check Disk Free Space**

Write a program called CHKSPACE that will display the following information on the screen (with labels) for the default drive: (The numbers shown are only a sample.)

```
Default drive          :B
Sectors per cluster    :2
Clusters per disk      :360
Available clusters     :100
Available sectors      :720
```

Use DOS function call 36h. The program must produce the correct values for any standard disk type.

Exercise 13 **Modified CHKSPACE Program**

Modify the CHKSPACE program written for Exercise 12 so that it displays the following information about the default drive:

```
Default drive          :B
Sectors per cluster    :2
Total disk space       :368640
Available bytes        :102400
```

You will need to implement a 32-bit binary to ASCII conversion routine for this exercise. Refer to the discussion of this procedure in Chapter 9.

Exercise 14 **Enhanced File Attribute Program**

Modify the File Attribute program in Figure 11-8 as follows:

- Display the attributes of the file entered on the command line. For example:

```
File Attribute Program                          (ATTR.EXE)

FILE1.DOC has the following attributes:
Archive  Read-only

(H)ide, (U)nhide, (R)ead-only, (W)rite-enable, (Q)uit:_
```

- When the operator changes one of the attributes, redisplay the file's new attributes without scrolling the screen. Allow the user to continue modifying the file attributes until Q is entered to quit.

Exercise 15 Enhanced Sector Display Program

Earlier in this chapter, the Sector Display program (Figure 11-3) was presented as a way of reading and displaying individual disk sectors. As a programming exercise, enhance the program in the following ways:

a. The operator should be able to select the disk drive, using either an uppercase or a lowercase letter. If no letter is supplied, it should default to A. A varying number of spaces may occur after the program name on the DOS command line. Examples:

```
SECTOR A
SECTOR   B
SECTOR b
SECTOR     b
SECTOR C
SECTOR                    ( defaults to drive A )
```

b. Prompt the user for the starting and ending sector numbers. Example:

```
Starting sector: 12
Ending sector  : 25
```

c. Improve the message at the top of the screen when each sector is displayed by displaying the sector number and drive letter:

```
Reading sector 12 on drive B
-----------------------------
(sector data appears here)
-----------------------------
```

Exercise 16 Enhanced Sector Display Program, Version 2

Using the program from Exercise 15 as a starting point, add the following enhancement: As a sector is displayed, let the operator press F2 to display the same sector in hexadecimal, with 16 bytes on each line. The offset of the first byte in each line should be displayed at the beginning of the line:

```
0000  17 31 16 25 25 42 5B 75 27 9A 49 09 20 0D 06 55
0010  27 3A 46 55 25 32 4B 55 27 3A 49 59 29 3D 46 55
(etc)
```

Exercise 17 Simple DOS Shell Program

A *DOS shell* is a program that lets an operator run DOS commands from a menu and select filenames by pointing the cursor. The effect is to make DOS commands more convenient. We will focus on the DIR, DEL, and REN commands here, but you are free to add additional commands.

- Display the contents of the current disk directory on the screen, and load all filenames into a table of ASCIIZ strings.
- Use the cursor arrow keys to move a highlighted bar from one filename to another. Whenever a filename is highlighted, it is considered the current filename.
- Interpret the following single-keystroke commands:

D	Delete the current filename
R	Rename the current filename

For the delete operation, prompt the user with "Delete this file (Y/N)?" before deleting the file. For the rename operation, prompt the user for the new filename. Do not allow the new name to contain a different drive letter than the current drive. After a delete or rename operation, update your table of filenames and redisplay the screen.

Exercise 18 Simple DOS Shell Program, Version 2

Use the DOS shell program written in Exercise 17 as a starting point. Add the following features: Display the size of each file in bytes, along with its date. If all filenames will not fit on the screen, use the cursor arrow keys to scroll up and down through the names. (This will require pointers to be kept in the table of filenames in order to identify the first and last filenames currently being displayed.)

Display the attributes of each file, using the following codes:

A	Archive	R	Read-only
D	Directory name	S	System
H	Hidden	V	Volume label

For example, if FILE1.DOC had the archive, hidden, and system attribute bits set, it would be displayed as

```
FILE1.DOC  5/20/89   A H S
```

Allow the following additional command:

A	Change the current file's attribute

You can then prompt for the attribute, set the file's attribute, and update the directory listing on the screen.

ANSWERS TO REVIEW QUESTIONS

1. Probably the greatest number of system-level functions are available in either C or Turbo Pascal. In addition, libraries are available for other languages that greatly extend their capability.

2. Definitions:
   a. *track*: Circular pattern on disk used to store data.
   b. *sector*: A 512-byte segment of a track.
   c. *cluster*: Smallest logical unit of storage used by DOS to store a file; equal to 1, 2, or 4 sectors.
   d. *cylinder*: All tracks available on multiple disk surfaces from a single position of the read/write heads.
   e. *FAT*: The file allocation table, where DOS assigns individual clusters to files.
   f. *subdirectory*: A directory whose name belongs to a parent directory.
   g. *command tail*: The area of memory used by DOS to store all characters typed on the command line after the command or program name.
   h. *date stamp*: The date of the creation or last modification of a disk file, stored in its directory entry.
   i. *attribute byte*: A byte in each directory entry that identifies the type of entry (e.g., volume name, normal file).
   j. *boot record*: The first sector on a disk, containing information about the disk type, as well as a short program that loads the operating system.
   k. *parent directory*: A directory that holds the name of one or more subdirectories.
   l. *file specification*: A combination of the following information used to locate a file or group of files: drive letter, pathname, filename, extension.
   m. *directory path*: A list of all directory names leading up to and including a particular directory.
   n. *media descriptor byte*: A single byte at offset 0 in the FAT that identifies the type of disk.

3. a. Path not found: One is trying to rename a file, but the path contains an invalid directory name.
   b. Access denied: The file is either a directory name, a volume label, or a file that has a read-only attribute.
   c. Invalid handle: The file may not have been opened yet, or a nonexistent file handle may have been placed in BX.
   d. Attempt to remove the current directory: DOS will not let you remove the current directory. Instead, you must move to a different directory (function 3Bh) before calling function 3Ah.
   e. Not same device: You have tried to rename a file across disk drives, which DOS does not allow. Both filenames must refer to the same drive.
   f. No more files: No files in the specified directory could be found to match the file specification pointed to by DS:DX.

4. If we multiply 40 * 2 * 8 * 512, the result is 327,680 bytes.

5. Sector 29. See the table in the subsection entitled "Disk Formats" in the "Disk Storage Fundamentals" section at the beginning of this chapter.

6. The doubleword at offset 1Ch contains the file size.

7. The file would use up 1 cluster of disk space, because a cluster is the smallest allocation size.

8. The boot record in sector 0.

9. The notation (..) identifies the parent directory entry.

10. An attribute of 10h identifies a subdirectory entry.

11. Year: 0000011 = 3   Month: 0111 = 7   Day: 00011 = 3.
    Answer: July 3, 1983.

12. Subtract 2 from the cluster number, multiply by the number of sectors per cluster, and add the starting sector number of the data area: ((2 − 2) * 4) + 155 = sector 155.

13. The file has been deleted.

14. Yes. It is a subdirectory name, and it will be displayed.

15. At most, one cluster, using the starting cluster number in the directory entry.

16. The file size is 00000020h, or 32 bytes. The starting cluster number is 4.

17. Sixteen bits.

18. Rebuilding the linked list in the FAT table requires jumping around from entry to entry, rather than dealing with contiguous entries. If the free clusters were once used by other files, the problem is more difficult, because they contain data that *may or may not* be part of the file we are attempting to reconstruct.

19. The RET instruction will not return to the calling program, because we neglected to pop the flags off the stack (left there by DOS). Insert the following instruction just before the RET:

```
pop  ax   ; discard old flags from stack
```

20. Yes. Call function 19h to get the default drive, and then call INT 25, using the drive number.

21. This checks to see if either bit 3 or bit 4 is set in the attribute byte. These bits identify a subdirectory name or volume label, neither of which is displayed by the program.

22. The following solution is taken from the CLUSTERS.ASM program:

```
        shr  ax,1         ; old cluster even?
        jc   E1           ; no: keep high 12 bits
        and  dx,0FFFh     ; yes: keep low 12 bits
        jmp  E2
    E1: mov  cl,4         ; shift high 12 bits right
        shr  dx,cl
    E2: mov  ax,dx        ; return new cluster number
```

23. The DOS command tail is located at offset 80h from the beginning of the program segment prefix area of the current program.

12

File Processing

Having developed a good understanding of disk file organization, let's now examine the multitude of DOS function calls relating to files. DOS uses the technique, borrowed from the UNIX operating system, of using *handles* to access files and devices. In many cases, DOS sees no distinction between files and devices such as keyboards and video monitors. A handle is a 16-bit number used by DOS to identify an open file or device. There are five standard device handles recognized by DOS. Each of these supports redirection at the DOS command prompt except the error output device:

0 Keyboard (standard input)
1 Console (standard output)
2 Error output
3 Auxiliary device (asynchronous)
4 Printer

These handles are predefined and do not have to be opened before being used. For example, one can write to the console using handle 1, without any advance preparation.

Basic File Functions. Let's start by looking at a list of the most commonly used file functions, defined by a *function number* placed in AH. All of the following functions are available in high-level languages:

BASIC FILE FUNCTIONS

3Ch	Create file Create a new file or set the length of an existing file to 0 bytes in preparation for writing new data to the file.
3Dh	Open file Open an existing file for input, output, or input-output.
3Eh	Close file handle
3Fh	Read from file or device Read a predetermined number of bytes from a file into an input buffer.
40h	Write to file or device Write a predetermined number of bytes from memory to a file.
42h	Move file pointer Position the DOS file pointer before reading or writing to a file.

STANDARD DOS FILE FUNCTIONS

Create File (3Ch)

To create a new file or to truncate an existing file to 0 bytes, function 3Ch should be used. The file is automatically opened for both reading and writing. DS:DX must point to an ASCIIZ string with the name of the file, and CX should contain one or more of the following attribute values:

00h	Normal file
01h	Read-only file
02h	Hidden file
04h	System file (rarely used)

A sample routine that creates a file with a normal attribute is shown here. The file is created on the default drive in the current directory:

```
create_file:
    mov  ah,3Ch              ; function: create file
    mov  dx,offset newfile ; ASCIIZ string with file name
```

```
        mov   cx,0                ; normal attribute
        int   21h                 ; call DOS
        jc    display_error       ; error? display a message
        mov   newfilehandle,ax    ; no error: save the handle
        .
        .
    newfile         db   'NEWFILE.DOC',0
    newfilehandle   dw   ?
```

If the file was opened successfully, DOS returns a 16-bit file handle in AX. The number is usually 5 if this is the first file being opened, but it will vary when other files are already open.

Protecting Existing Files. One disadvantage of using function 3Ch (create file) is that one can inadvertently destroy an existing file with the same name. There are a couple of solutions to this problem. One can attempt to open the file for input, using function 3Dh (open file). If DOS sets the Carry flag and returns error 2 (file not found), you can safely use the create file function.

Another solution is to use DOS function 5Bh (create new file), introduced with DOS 3.0. It aborts and returns error 50h if the file already exists. For example:

```
        mov   ah,5Bh                  ; create new file
        mov   cx,0                    ; normal attribute
        mov   dx,offset filename
        int   21h
        jc    error_routine
        .
        .
    filename  db  'FILE1.DOC',0
```

Error Codes. If DOS sets the Carry flag, the error number it returns should be 3, 4, or 5. Error 3 (path not found) means the file specifier pointed to by DX probably contains a nonexistent directory name. For example, you may have specified

```
    filename  db  'C:\ASMS\FILE1.ASM',0
```

when in fact the subdirectory name is ASM, not ASMS.

Error 4 (too many open files) occurs when you have exceeded the maximum number of open files set by DOS. It limits the number of open files to 8 by default or to a larger number as specified in the CONFIG.SYS file (DOS looks at this file only when the system is booted). The following statement in CONFIG.SYS sets the maximum number of open files to 20, the largest number possible:

```
files=20
```

Bear in mind that five files are always open, based on the standard DOS device handles 0–4. An application program can therefore open as many as 15 additional files.

Error 5 (access denied) indicates that you may be trying to create a file that already exists and has a read-only attribute. You may be trying to create a file with the same name as a subdirectory. You may also be trying to add a new entry to a root directory that is already full.

Although it is not documented, error 2 (file not found) can be generated by leaving a carriage return at the end of a file specifier. Be sure you use a valid filename when calling functions to create or open files. The following is an invalid filename because of the trailing carriage return (0Dh) character:

N	E	W	F	I	L	.	A	S	M	0D	00

Open File (3Dh)

Function 3Dh lets you open an existing file in one of three modes: input, output, or input-output. AL contains the file mode to be used, and DS:DX points to a filename. Normal and hidden files may be opened. If the open is successful, DOS returns a valid file handle in AX.

```
    mov  ah,3Dh               ; function: open file
    mov  al,0                 ; choose the input mode
    mov  dx,offset filename
    int  21h                  ; call DOS
    jc   display_error        ; error? display a message
    mov  infilehandle,ax      ; no error: save the handle
    .
    .
infile        db  'B:\FILE1.DOC',0
infilehandle  dw  ?
```

File Mode. The file mode value placed in AL may have one of three values:

AL	Mode
0	Input (read only)
1	Output (write only)
2	Input-output

To open a file in output mode for sequential writing, function 3Ch (create file) is probably best. On the other hand, to read and write data to a file, function 3Dh (open file) is best. Specifically, random-access file updating requires function 3Dh.

Error Codes. If the Carry flag is set, AX contains one of the following error codes: Error 1 (invalid function number) means you are trying to share a file without having loaded the DOS file-sharing software. Error 2 (file not found) indicates that DOS was not able to find the requested file. Error 3 (path not found) means you specified an incorrect directory name in the filename's path. Error 4 (too many open files) indicates that too many files are currently open. Error 5 (access denied) means the file may be set to read-only, or it may be a subdirectory or volume name.

Close File Handle (3Eh)

To close a file, call function 3Eh and place the file's handle in BX. This function flushes DOS's internal file buffer by writing any remaining data to disk and makes the file handle available to other files. If the file has been written to, it is saved with a new file size, time stamp, and date stamp. The following instructions close the file identified by **infilehandle**:

```
          mov ah,3Eh            ; close file handle
          mov bx,infilehandle
          int 21h
          jc  display_error
          .
          .
infile         db  'B:\FILE1.DOC',0
infilehandle   dw  ?
```

The only possible error code is 6 (invalid handle), which means the file handle in BX does not refer to an open file.

Read from File or Device (3Fh)

Function 3Fh transfers bytes from a file into a memory buffer. When the interrupt is called, BX contains a valid file handle, CX contains the number of bytes to read, and DS:DX points to the input buffer. It is your responsibility to make the input buffer large enough to hold the data.

If the Carry flag is set, the error code will be either 5 or 6. Error 5 (access denied) probably means the file was open in the output mode, and error 6 (invalid handle) indicates that the file handle passed in BX does not refer to an open file.

End of File. If the Carry flag is clear after the operation, AX contains the number of bytes read. This information can be useful in detecting the end of a file. If the end is reached, AX will contain either 0 or a value smaller than the number of bytes originally requested (in CX). Suppose we have asked DOS to read 512 bytes in the following example, but AX returns with a value of only 256. Clearly, the end of the input file has been reached:

```
mov   ah,3Fh              ; read from file or device
mov   bx,infilehandle     ; BX = file handle
mov   cx,512              ; number of bytes to read
mov   dx,offset infilebuffer
int   21h
jc    display_error       ; display message if Carry set
cmp   ax,cx               ; fewer bytes read?
jb    eof_reached         ; yes: quit reading
```

When the input buffer size is the same as the logical record length and we have reached the end of the file, AX returns with a value of zero. (This will also happen if the input buffer is a multiple of the record size.) Assume that we are reading a sequential file with fixed-length, 80-byte records in this next example. The final attempt at reading will return a value of zero in AX:

```
mov   ah,3Fh              ; read from file or device
mov   bx,infilehandle
mov   cx,80               ; read 80 bytes
mov   dx,offset infilebuffer
int   21h
jc    display_error       ; display message if Carry set
cmp   ax,0                ; EOF reached?
je    eof_reached         ; yes: quit reading
```

Reading from the Keyboard. Function 3Fh may be used to read input characters from the keyboard, and it terminates when ENTER is pressed. Set BX to 1 (the keyboard handle), set CX to the maximum number of characters to be typed, and point DX to the input buffer:

```
mov   ah,3Fh              ; read from file or device
mov   bx,0                ; device = keyboard
mov   cx,127              ; request 127 bytes maximum
mov   dx,offset kbuff
int   21h
```

The backspace and left arrow keys may be used to edit the input, just as for DOS function 0Ah. When ENTER is pressed, DOS adds both a carriage return (0Dh) and a line feed (0Ah) to the input buffer and adds 2 to the character count in AX. The character count placed in CX should include the CR/LF characters that DOS appends to the string. DOS allows up to 127 characters to be typed, but only the number of characters specified in CX will be stored in the input buffer.

Write to File or Device (40h)

DOS function 40h is convenient for writing to either a device or a file. Place a valid file handle in BX, place the number of bytes to write in CX, and point

DS:DX to the buffer where the data are stored. DOS automatically updates the file pointer after writing to the file, so the next call to function 40h will write beyond the current position.

If the Carry flag is set, AX contains error code 5 or 6. Error 5 (access denied) means either the file was opened in the input mode or the file has a read-only attribute. Error 6 (invalid handle) means the file handle in BX does not refer to a currently open file.

If the Carry flag is clear but AX contains a number that is less than the number of bytes requested to be written, some type of input-output error occurred; for example, the disk may be full. In the following example, we write the contents of **buffer** to the file identified by **handle**:

```
write_to_file:
    mov  ah,40h              ; write to file/device
    mov  bx,handle           ; file handle returned by OPEN
    mov  cx,100h             ; number of bytes to write
    mov  dx,offset buffer    ; DX points to the buffer
    int  21h                 ; call DOS
    jc   display_error       ; error? display message.
    cmp  ax,100h             ; all bytes written?
    jne  close_file          ; no: disk is full
    .
    .
buffer  db   100h dup(?)     ; output buffer
handle  dw   ?               ; file handle
```

APPLICATION: CREATE A TEXT FILE

The next two application programs shown in this chapter deal with text files. A *text file* contains a sequence of ASCII characters delimited by an end-of-line marker at the end of each record. The marker varies from one computer system to another, but DOS recognizes the 0Dh (carriage return) and 0Ah (line feed) characters. Word processors all use some variation of these characters to delimit the end of each line; for example, some use only the 0Dh character.

Another standard character is the end-of-file character, 1Ah. Some text editors use this character to mark the end of a file. The DOS TYPE command, for instance, halts when 1Ah is found in a text file.

Finally, the tab character (09h) is used by many text editors to make the cursor skip to column numbers that are multiples of 8.

Text File Creation Program

Let's write a simple program to do the following:

1. Read the name of the file to be created from the command line. If no file is found, display an error message and exit.

2. Clear the screen, and display the name of the text file being created. Create the file, and open it for output.
3. Begin prompting the user for each line of text. As it is typed, each line of text is stored in the output file. Continue until ENTER is pressed on a blank line.
4. Close the file.

A complete program listing of MAKEFIL.ASM is shown in Figure 12-1. It relies on standard DOS functions to do most of the work. Note that we have

Figure 12-1 The Text File Creation program (MAKEFIL.ASM).

```
 1:  title  Text File Creation Program              (MAKEFIL.ASM)
 2:
 3:  ;
 4:  ;   This program creates a text file.  It prompts for
 5:  ;   each line of text and writes it to the file.  It
 6:  ;   uses the following procedures and constants from
 7:  ;   CONSOLE.LIB: CLRSCR, GET_COMMAND_TAIL, DISPLAY,
 8:  ;   DOS_ERROR, WRITESTRING, CR, LF.
 9:  ;
10:
11:  dosseg
12:  .model small
13:  .stack 100h
14:  extrn  clrscr:proc, display:proc, DOS_error:proc
15:  extrn  get_command_tail:proc, writestring:proc
16:  extrn  cr:abs, lf:abs
17:
18:  .code
19:  main  proc
20:      mov   bx,ds               ; get copy of PSP location
21:      mov   ax,@data            ; initialize DS, ES
22:      mov   ds,ax
23:      mov   es,ax
24:      mov   dx,offset newfile   ; get filename from
25:      call  get_command_tail    ; the command line
26:      jc    A3                  ; quit if none entered
27:      call  display_heading     ; display program heading
28:      mov   dx,offset newfile   ; create the new file
29:      call  create_file
30:      jc    A4                  ; quit if Carry set
31:
32:  A1: call  get_text_line       ; get a line of text
33:      cmp   buflen,2            ; only ENTER pressed?
34:      je    A2                  ; yes: quit
35:      call  write_buffer        ; no: write the buffer
36:      jmp   A1                  ; continue reading lines
37:
38:  A2: mov   bx,filehandle       ; close the file
39:      mov   ah,3Eh
40:      int   21h
```

Figure 12-1 *(Cont.)*

```
41:       jmp   A4
42:
43:   A3: mov   dx,offset syntax_msg ; no file was specified
44:       call  display
45:   A4: mov   ax,4C00h            ; return to DOS
46:       int   21h
47:   main  endp
48:
49:
50:   display_heading proc          ; display program heading
51:       call  clrscr              ; clear the screen
52:       mov   dx,offset greeting  ; display program logo
53:       call  display
54:       mov   dx,offset newfile   ; display name of file
55:       call  writestring         ; (ASCIIZ string)
56:       mov   dx,offset crlf2     ; write 2 CR/LF
57:       call  display
58:       ret
59:   display_heading endp
60:
61:
62:   create_file proc              ; DX points to filename
63:       mov   ah,3Ch              ; function: create file
64:       mov   cx,0                ; normal file attribute
65:       int   21h
66:       jnc   C1                  ; if DOS error,
67:       call  DOS_error           ; display error message
68:   C1: mov   filehandle,ax
69:       ret
70:   create_file endp
71:
72:
73:   get_text_line proc            ; input a line of text
74:       mov   ah,2                ; display prompt character
75:       mov   dl,'>'
76:       int   21h
77:       mov   ah,3Fh              ; read from file/device
78:       mov   bx,0                ; choose keyboard
79:       mov   cx,80               ; max characters to read
80:       mov   dx,offset buffer    ; point to input buffer
81:       int   21h
82:       mov   buflen,ax           ; number of bytes in buffer
83:       ret
84:   get_text_line endp
85:
86:
87:   write_buffer proc             ; write to output file
88:       clc                       ; assume no error
89:       mov   ah,40h              ; write to file/device
90:       mov   bx,filehandle
91:       mov   cx,buflen           ; number of bytes to write
```

Figure 12-1 *(Cont.)*

```
 92:         mov   dx,offset buffer      ; DX points to the buffer
 93:         int   21h
 94:         jnc   E1                    ; if DOS error,
 95:         call  DOS_error             ; display a message
 96:         jmp   E2
 97:     E1: cmp   ax,buflen             ; all bytes written?
 98:         je    E2                    ; yes: exit
 99:         mov   dx,offset diskfullmsg
100:         call  display               ; no: display "Disk full"
101:         stc                         ; set Carry flag
102:     E2: ret
103:     write_buffer endp
104:
105:     .data
106:
107:     buffer        db   82 dup(0)   ; output buffer area
108:     buflen        dw   0           ; current buffer size
109:     filehandle    dw   ?
110:     newfile       db   40 dup(0)  ; output file specifier
111:
112:     greeting      db  'Text File Creation Program'
113:                   db  '         (MAKEFIL.EXE)'
114:                   db   cr,lf,cr,lf,'Creating: $'
115:
116:     diskfullmsg   db   cr,lf,'Disk full.  '
117:                   db   'Closing the file.',cr,lf,'$'
118:
119:     DOSerrmsg     db   cr,lf,'DOS error occurred: $'
120:
121:     syntax_msg    db  'The correct syntax is: '
122:                   db  'MAKEFIL [d:][path]filename[.ext]$'
123:
124:     crlf2         db   cr,lf,cr,lf,'$'
125:
126:     end main
```

linked the program to CONSOLE.LIB, so we can call CLRSCR, DISPLAY, GET_COMMAND_TAIL, DOS_ERROR, and WRITESTRING. Sample output from the program is shown here:

```
Text File Creation Program         (MAKEFIL.EXE)
Creating: C:\ASM\FILE1.DOC
>This is the first line.
>This is line two.
>This is the third line.
>This is line four, in FILE1.DOC.
>This is the fifth line.
>
```

MAIN Procedure. In MAIN, we save the segment address of the PSP in BX so it will be available to GET_COMMAND_TAIL. The DOS command tail is copied into **newfile**, the file that will be created (lines 24–25).

CREATE_FILE Procedure. When CREATE_FILE is called from line 29, it attempts to create a new file (or truncate an old one), using the name in **newfile** (lines 62–70). If it fails for any reason, DOS sets the Carry flag, and it remains set when the procedure returns. Thus, a JC instruction on line 30 exits to DOS if the file was not created successfully.

Assuming that the file was created, the main program loop (lines 32–36) is where the operator enters a line of text, using GET_TEXT_LINE. If the line is not empty, line 35 calls WRITE_BUFFER to write the text to the output file. Line 33 checks for a value of 2 in **buflen**, which would tell us that only ENTER had been pressed.

The DISPLAY_HEADING procedure (lines 50–59) clears the screen and displays both the program name and the filename being created.

The CREATE_FILE procedure (lines 62–70) looks for an existing file with the name stored in **newfile**. If it exists, the procedure truncates it to 0 bytes; otherwise, it creates a new file. The file is opened for input–output, and the Carry flag is set if a DOS error occurs.

The GET_TEXT_LINE procedure (lines 73–84) reads a line of up to 80 characters from the keyboard and stores the number of characters entered in **buflen**.

The WRITE_BUFFER procedure (lines 87–103) writes the contents of **buffer** to the output file. The only likely DOS error that could happen here would occur if the disk were full.

If DOS sets the Carry flag after any file input-output operation, we call the DOS_ERROR procedure in the CONSOLE library to display an appropriate message. For instance, DOS error 3 generates the following message:

```
DOS error: access denied
```

Variables. The variables in this program include input buffers for the filename and the text lines written to the file, called **newfile** (line 110) and **buffer** (line 107), respectively. **Filehandle** contains the 16-bit file handle returned by DOS when the file is opened. It is used when writing to and closing the file. **Buflen** tells us how many characters were just typed by the operator in the most recent line of text.

Creating a Hidden, Read-Only File

In order to have the File Creation program create a hidden, read-only file, one could just modify the CREATE_FILE procedure. Bits 0 and 1 in CX would be set:

```
create_file proc
   mov  ah,3Ch              ; function: create file
   mov  dx,offset newfile
```

```
    mov  cx,3                ; hidden, read-only attribute
    int  21h
    .
    .
    ret
create_file endp
```

This is a good technique for storing important data, such as a password file or a control file, to protect them from being accidentally modified or erased.

A hidden, read-only file does not show up in the directory and it cannot be deleted from the DOS command line. It may, however, be opened for input by a program that knows it exists. The only way the file can be modified is by changing its attribute first.

APPLICATION: LIST A TEXT FILE

No discussion of file handling would be complete without an example that shows how to read individual lines of text from a sequential file. In this section, we will write a program that reads blocks of 512 bytes into a buffer and displays text lines one at a time.

High-level languages perform record buffering automatically, so when we read a line of text from a file, the input stops at the first end-of-line character. This is not as easy to accomplish as it sounds. The following steps are involved:

- Read a fixed-length block of data into an input buffer, and keep a pointer to the last character that was read.
- Copy bytes from the input buffer to a text line until the end-of-line marker is reached.
- When the next request is made for a line of input text, copy any remaining characters from the input buffer to the text line. If the end of the input buffer is reached before the end-of-line marker is found, the buffer must be refilled from the input file, and more bytes must be transferred to the text line.

In our program, we will use the following registers and variables:

Register or Variable	Usage
inbuf	A 512-byte input buffer
text_line	Buffer where a single line of text is stored before being displayed
SI	Pointer to the current position in the input buffer
DI	Pointer to the current position in the text line
inbufend	Pointer to the last valid character read into the input buffer
text_count	Number of characters moved to the text line

The Buffering Process. To see how record buffering works, let's look at the starting pointer values after the first block of data has been read from the input file. In the following discussion, we will assume that the input buffer is 128 bytes long and the text line is 80 bytes long. The dots in the input buffer represent end-of-line characters (0Dh,0Ah):

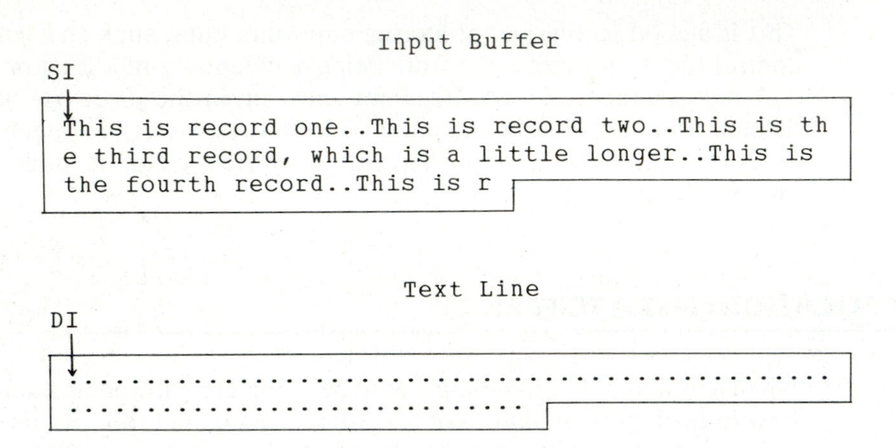

Next, the program copies the first text record to the text line, leaving both pointers after the 0Dh,0Ah bytes found at the end of the record. Most high-level languages strip off these bytes, but I have chosen to copy them. This will make it easier to display the records later:

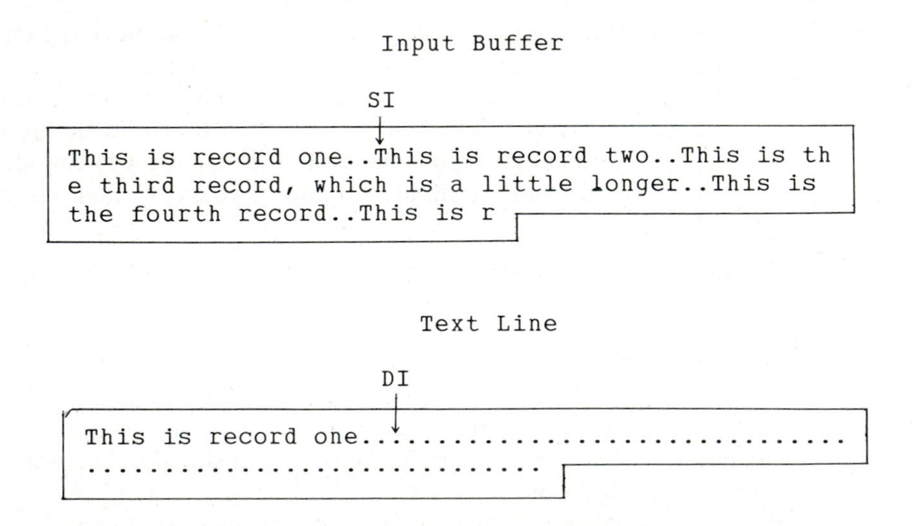

Each time a request for another record is made by the program, we reset DI to the beginning of the text line and copy another record from the input buffer. The same steps continue until the end of the input buffer is reached:

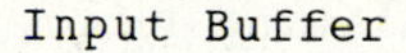

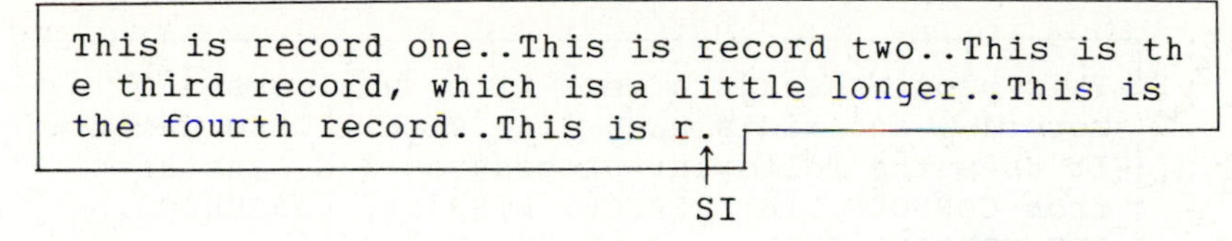

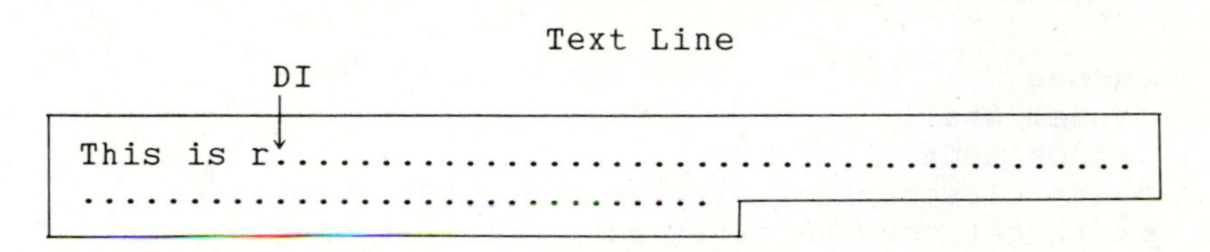

When the end of the input buffer is reached, we stop copying records, save the current position in the text line, and refill the input buffer. This time, perhaps, the end of the input file is reached, so the input buffer is not full. **Inbufend** points to the last valid character in the input buffer:

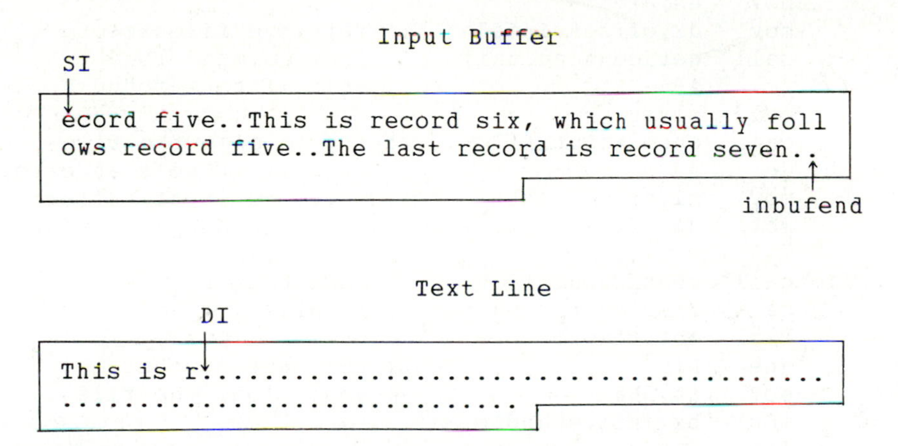

The remainder of record five is copied to the text line. The same process repeats until SI becomes equal to **inbufend**. The next attempted read returns 0 in AX because the end of the input file has been reached.

The File Listing Program

The File Listing program (LISTFIL.ASM) in Figure 12-2 carries out all the actions we have just described. It calls the CLRSCR, DISPLAY, DOS_ERROR, GET_COMMAND_TAIL, and WRITEINT procedures from the CONSOLE library. When running the program, type the name of the file you wish to list on the command line. For example, to list a file called PERFECT.PAS, type

```
listfil perfect.pas
```

```
 1:  title  Text File Listing Program                    (LISTFIL.ASM)
 2:
 3:  ;
 4:  ;   This program reads a text file, deblocks the
 5:  ;   records, and lists each line with a line number.
 6:  ;   It uses the following procedures and constants
 7:  ;   from CONSOLE.LIB: CLRSCR, DISPLAY, DOS_ERROR,
 8:  ;   GET_COMMAND_TAIL, and WRITEINT.
 9:  ;
10:
11:  dosseg
12:  .model small
13:  .stack 100h
14:  extrn clrscr:proc, display:proc, DOS_error:proc
15:  extrn get_command_tail:proc, writeint:proc
16:
17:  .code
18:  main proc
19:      mov   bx,ds                ; get copy of PSP segment
20:      mov   ax,@data             ; initialize DS, ES
21:      mov   ds,ax
22:      mov   es,ax
23:      mov   dx,offset infile     ; retrieve filename
24:      call  get_command_tail     ; from command line
25:      jc    A2                   ; quit if none found
26:      call  clrscr
27:      call  open_input_file      ; try to open the file
28:      jc    A3                   ; quit if there's an error
29:      mov   si,offset inbuf      ; point to input buffer
30:      mov   di,offset text_line  ; point to output buffer
31:
32:  A1: call  read_input_line      ; read text from file
33:      call  display_the_buffer   ; display a line
34:      cmp   eof_flag,1           ; end of file?
35:      jne   A1                   ; no: read another
36:      mov   ah,3Eh               ; yes: close the file
37:      mov   bx,infilehandle
38:      int   21h
39:      jmp   A3                   ; exit program
40:
41:  A2: mov   dx,offset syntax_msg  ; no filename entered
42:      call  display
43:  A3: mov   ax,4C00h             ; return to DOS
44:      int   21h
45:  main endp
46:
47:
48:  ;   Read a line of text from the input buffer.  If
49:  ;   the buffer is empty, read another block of data.
50:
51:  read_input_line proc           ; SI -> input buffer
```

Figure 12-2 The Text File Listing program (LISTFIL.ASM).

Figure 12-2 *(Cont.)*

```
 52:                                        ; DI -> output buffer
 53:    B1: cmp   si,bufend                 ; beyond end of inbuf?
 54:        ja    B2                        ; yes: read next record
 55:        movsb                           ; no: copy to output buffer
 56:        inc   text_count                ; add 1 to output count
 57:        cmp   byte ptr [si-1],0Ah       ; end of line?
 58:        je    B4                        ; yes: exit procedure
 59:        jmp   B1                        ; no: copy more characters
 60:
 61:    B2: mov   ah,3Fh                    ; read the file
 62:        mov   bx,infilehandle
 63:        mov   cx,512                    ; read 512 characters
 64:        mov   dx,offset inbuf           ; point to input buffer
 65:        int   21h
 66:        jnc   B3                        ; if DOS error,
 67:        call  DOS_error                 ;   print error message
 68:        jmp   B4                        ;   and exit
 69:
 70:    B3: mov   bufend,offset inbuf-1
 71:        add   bufend,ax                 ; points to last character
 72:        mov   si,offset inbuf           ; reset input pointer
 73:        cmp   ax,0                      ; end of file reached?
 74:        jne   B1                        ; no: continue
 75:        mov   eof_flag,1                ; yes: set EOF
 76:    B4: ret
 77:    read_input_line endp
 78:
 79:
 80:    display_the_buffer proc
 81:        inc   word ptr linenum          ; increment line number
 82:        mov   ax,linenum                ; display the line number
 83:        mov   bx,10                     ; choose decimal radix
 84:        call  writeint                  ; print the line number
 85:        mov   dx,offset colon           ; display ": "
 86:        mov   ah,9
 87:        int   21h
 88:        mov   ah,40h                    ; display the output buffer
 89:        mov   bx,1                      ; handle = console
 90:        mov   cx,text_count             ; number of bytes to write
 91:        mov   dx,offset text_line       ; DX points to the buffer
 92:        int   21h
 93:        mov   di,offset text_line       ; reset the output pointer
 94:        mov   text_count,0              ; reset text_line counter
 95:        ret
 96:    display_the_buffer endp
 97:
 98:
 99:    open_input_file proc
100:        mov   ah,3Dh                    ; function: open file
101:        mov   al,0                      ; choose the input mode
102:        mov   dx,offset infile
103:        int   21h                       ; call DOS
```

Figure 12-2 *(Cont.)*

```
104:        jnc    D1                    ; if DOS error,
105:        call   DOS_error             ;   display error message
106:    D1: mov    infilehandle,ax       ; no error: save the handle
107:        ret
108:    open_input_file endp
109:
110:    .data
111:
112:    infile        db   40 dup(0)        ; holds the filename
113:    inbuf         db   512 dup(0)       ; input buffer area
114:    text_line     db   128 dup(0)       ; output buffer area
115:    text_count    dw   0                ; bytes in text_line
116:    linenum       dw   0                ; current line number
117:    bufend        dw   offset inbuf-1   ; ptr to end of inbuf
118:    infilehandle  dw   ?                ; file handle
119:    eof_flag      dw   0                ; end of file flag
120:    colon         db   ':  $'
121:
122:    syntax_msg    db   'The correct syntax is: '
123:                  db   'LISTFIL [d:][path]filename[.ext]$'
124:
125:    end main
```

The output from this program may also be redirected to either disk or printer, making it useful as a file listing utility. The file PERFECT.PAS could be listed on the printer, using the following command:

```
listfil perfect.pas > prn
```

Sample output from the program when it was used to list a Pascal program is shown here:

```
1:   Program PerfectNumbers;
2:
3:    VAR
4:     n,
5:     limit        :Integer;
6:
7:      Function  SumFactors(n :Integer)  :Integer;
8:    {---------------------------------------------}
9:      VAR
10:       sum,i     :Integer;
11:      BEGIN
12:        sum := 1;
13:        FOR i := 2 to (n div 2) DO
14:          IF (n mod i) = 0 THEN
15:            sum := sum + i;
. . .
```

Let's look at a few of the more important parts of the program. Lines 19–30 retrieve the input filename from the command line, clear the screen, and open the input file.

The main program loop reads a line of text from the input buffer and writes it to the console (lines 32–35).

The READ_INPUT_LINE procedure (lines 51–77) is the most complicated; it handles the deblocking, or buffering, of records. By *deblocking,* we mean the breaking down of a buffer with multiple records into individual records. Languages such as Pascal, BASIC, and COBOL do this automatically.

SI always points to the current position in the input buffer, and DI points to the current position in the text line. The algorithm used to deblock the records is

```
REPEAT
   DO WHILE (SI <= bufend)
      [DI] = [SI]
      increment SI, DI, text_count
      IF [SI-1] = 0Ah, exit procedure
   ENDDO
   read the input file         ; AX = number of bytes read
   bufend = (inbuf - 1) + AX
   SI = offset inbuff
UNTIL (AX = 0)                 ; end of file
eof_flag = 1
```

The DISPLAY_THE_BUFFER procedure (lines 80–96) displays a line number followed by the contents of the output buffer, called **text_line**. It uses **text_count** to determine the number of bytes to be written and calls DOS function 40h (write to file or device).

FIXED-LENGTH RECORD PROCESSING

A file with fixed-length records has no delimiter at the end of each record, but it may be read more efficiently than a text file. To read a record sequentially, we need only tell DOS the file's handle and the record length. To speed up the input, a block, or group of records, may be read at one time. If the record length is 32 bytes, for example, the buffer should be a multiple of the record size (64, 128, 512, 1024, 2048, etc.). A 2,048-byte buffer, for instance, would require the disk to be accessed only once for every 64 records.

Fields. Fields within a record are located by knowing their exact lengths. Let's use part of a student information record as an example. The student number is 7 bytes long, the last name is 15 bytes, the first name is 8 bytes, and the scholarship amount is a 16-bit binary number. Each field must be a specific length so the program can locate other fields in the record:

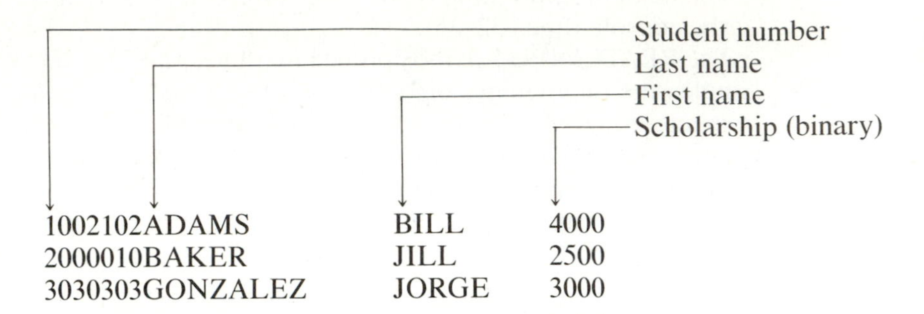

This illustrates another advantage to reading fixed-length records. Binary numbers cannot be stored in text files, because they conflict with standard ASCII control codes (carriage return, line feed, tab, end-of-file, etc.).

Random Retrieval. A file with fixed-length records may be read randomly by calculating the offset, or position, of any record in the file. Suppose we want to read the fifth record from a file containing 32-byte records. Assuming that the records are numbered starting at 1, the record offset is calculated by subtracting 1 from the record number and multiplying it by the record length:

$$\text{offset (80h)} = (5 - 1) * 20\text{h}$$

APPLICATION: DISPLAY A STUDENT INFORMATION FILE

In this section, we will write a program that reads and displays each fixed-length record from a student information file. For now, we will access the file sequentially, but eventually we plan to retrieve individual records from anywhere in the file.

The Student Information File

The Student Information file contains data on college students that might be used for general record keeping or course registration. It is much shorter than actual student records, of course, but it contains essential information such as the student number, last name, scholarship amount, and credits earned. The record layout is shown here. The fields are stored in ASCII format to make them easier to display, but they could just as easily be stored as binary numbers. Each record is 35 bytes long:

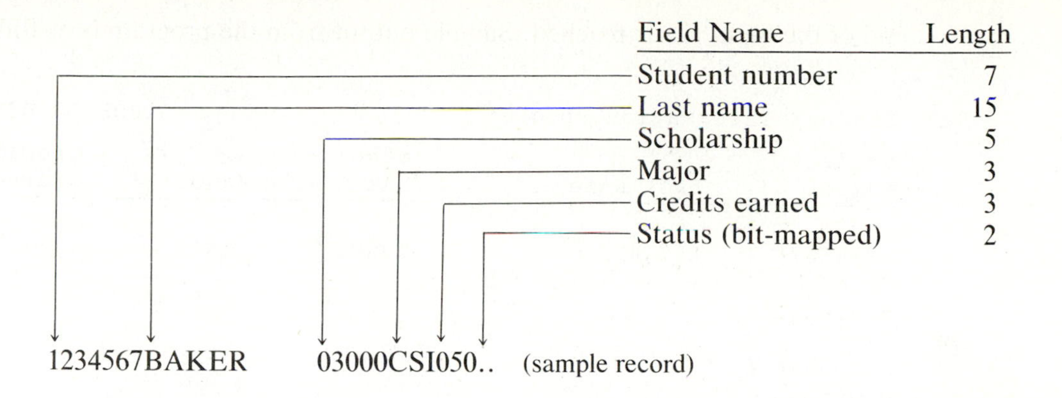

The STATUS Field. We will take advantage of one of assembly language's strengths: its ability to decode individual bits. The **status** field is bit-mapped, making it as compact as possible. Unless otherwise indicated, a bit value of 1 means "yes" and a value of 0 means "no." The following is a sample field value with each of the bits identified, showing that the student is a male disabled Hispanic nonresident on the Dean's List:

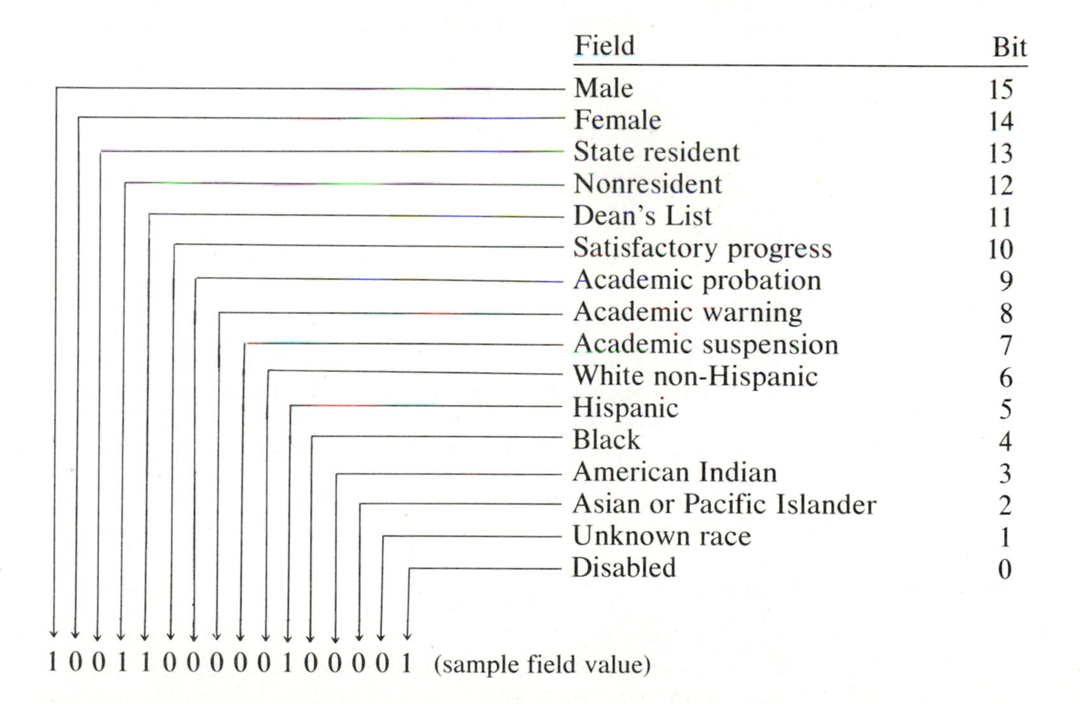

The Student Information Program

The complete Student Information program (STUDENTS.ASM) is shown in Figure 12–3. It reads the Student Information file and displays records until the end of the input file is reached. Sample output from the program is as follows:

```
Student Information Program                              (STUDENTS.EXE)
Student                               Schol                   Credits
Number       Last Name                 Amt       Major         Earned
------------------------------------------------------------------------

6234567      ALVAREZ                  03000       CSI           050
Male
Nonresident
Deans list
Hispanic
Disabled

2000000      GONZALEZ                 02500       MTH           036
Female
State resident
Satisfactory progress
Hispanic

1000000      MOORE                    13000       ENG           100
Male
State resident
Deans list
Black
.
.
(etc.)
```

Figure 12-3 The Student Information program (STUDENTS.ASM).

```
 1:   title  Student Information Program        (STUDENTS.ASM)
 2:
 3:   ;
 4:   ;   This program reads a Student Information file
 5:   ;   containing fixed-length records and displays
 6:   ;   them on the screen. It illustrates the use of a
 7:   ;   bit-mapped field. It uses the following routines
 8:   ;   from CONSOLE.LIB: CLRSCR, DISPLAY, and DOS_ERROR.
 9:   ;
10:
11:   dosseg
12:   .model small
13:   .stack 100h
14:   extrn clrscr:proc, display:proc, DOS_error:proc
15:   extrn cr:abs, lf:abs
16:
17:   .code
18:   main  proc
19:       call  setup               ; open input file
20:       jc    A3                  ; quit if not found
21:       mov   filehandle,ax       ; else save handle
```

Figure 12-3 *(Cont.)*

```
22:         mov    dx,offset heading    ; display program heading
23:         call   display
24:
25:     A1: call   read_record          ; read an input record
26:         jc     A2                   ; quit if end of file
27:         call   display_record
28:         jmp    A1                   ; continue until EOF
29:
30:     A2: mov    ah,3Eh               ; close the file
31:         mov    bx,filehandle
32:         int    21h
33:     A3: mov    ax,4C00h             ; return to DOS
34:         int    21h
35:     main  endp
36:
37:
38:     ;   Initialize variables, open Student file for input
39:
40:     setup proc
41:         mov    ax,@data             ; initialize DS, ES
42:         mov    ds,ax
43:         mov    es,ax
44:         cld                         ; set Direction flag to up
45:         call   clrscr
46:         mov    ah,3Dh               ; open the input file
47:         mov    al,0                 ; AL = input mode
48:         mov    dx,offset filename
49:         int    21h
50:         jnc    B1                   ; if DOS error occurred,
51:         call   DOS_error            ;   display a message
52:     B1: ret
53:     setup endp
54:
55:
56:     ;   Display a single record from the Student file
57:
58:     display_record proc
59:         mov     si,offset stu_num        ; student number
60:         mov     di,offset dl_stu_num
61:         mov     cx,7                     ; field length
62:         rep     movsb
63:         mov     si,offset last_name      ; last name
64:         mov     di,offset dl_last_name
65:         mov     cx,15
66:         rep     movsb
67:         mov     si,offset scholarship    ; scholarship
68:         mov     di,offset dl_scholarship
69:         mov     cx,5
70:         rep     movsb
71:         mov     si,offset major          ; major
72:         mov     di,offset dl_major
73:         mov     cx,3
74:         rep     movsb
```

Figure 12-3 *(Cont.)*

```
 75:        mov    si,offset credits          ; credits
 76:        mov    di,offset dl_credits
 77:        mov    cx,3
 78:        rep    movsb
 79:        mov    dx,offset detail_line      ; write detail line
 80:        call   display
 81:        call   display_status_field
 82:        ret
 83:    display_record endp
 84:
 85:
 86:    ;   Display the individual bits in the student status
 87:    ;   field by rotating each bit into the Carry flag.
 88:
 89:    display_status_field proc
 90:        mov    dx,offset status_table
 91:        mov    cx,table_size
 92:    D1: rol    status,1            ; rotate high bit into CF
 93:        jnc    D2                  ; exit if not set
 94:        mov    ah,40h              ; write to device
 95:        mov    bx,1                ; console output
 96:        push   cx                  ; save loop counter
 97:        mov    cx,entry_size       ; length of table entry
 98:        int    21h                 ; display the entry
 99:        pop    cx                  ; restore loop counter
100:    D2: add    dx,entry_size       ; point to next entry
101:        loop   D1                  ; repeat for 16 bits
102:        ret
103:    display_status_field endp
104:
105:
106:    read_record proc
107:        mov    ah,3Fh          ; read file/device
108:        mov    bx,filehandle
109:        mov    cx,student_record_size
110:        mov    dx,offset student_record
111:        int    21h
112:        jnc    E1              ; if DOS error occurred,
113:        call   DOS_error       ;   then display message
114:        jmp    E2
115:    E1: cmp    ax,cx           ; all bytes read?
116:        je     E2              ; yes: continue
117:        stc                    ; no: end of file
118:    E2: ret
119:    read_record endp
120:
121:    .data
122:
123:    entry_size    equ  25
124:
125:    filename    db  'STUDENTS.DTA',0
126:    filehandle  dw  ?
127:
```

Figure 12-3 *(Cont.)*

```
128:   student_record label byte              ; input record
129:     stu_num      db  7 dup(?)
130:     last_name    db  15 dup(?)
131:     scholarship db  5 dup(?)
132:     major        db  3 dup(?)
133:     credits      db  3 dup(?)
134:     status       dw  ?
135:   student_record_size equ  ($ - student_record)
136:
137:   detail_line label byte                  ; output record
138:                     db  cr,lf
139:     dl_stu_num      db  7 dup(?)
140:                     db  3 dup(' ')
141:     dl_last_name    db  15 dup(?)
142:                     db  3 dup(' ')
143:     dl_scholarship  db  5 dup(?)
144:                     db  5 dup(' ')
145:     dl_major        db  3 dup(?)
146:                     db  6 dup(' ')
147:     dl_credits      db  3 dup(?)
148:                     db  3 dup(' ')
149:                     db  cr,lf,'$'
150:
151:   status_table label byte   ; each entry is 25 bytes
152:       db  'Male                     ',cr,lf
153:       db  'Female                   ',cr,lf
154:       db  'State resident           ',cr,lf
155:       db  'Nonresident              ',cr,lf
156:       db  'Deans list               ',cr,lf
157:       db  'Satisfactory progress    ',cr,lf
158:       db  'Academic probation       ',cr,lf
159:       db  'Academic warning         ',cr,lf
160:       db  'Academic suspension      ',cr,lf
161:       db  'White Non-Hispanic       ',cr,lf
162:       db  'Hispanic                 ',cr,lf
163:       db  'Black                    ',cr,lf
164:       db  'American Indian          ',cr,lf
165:       db  'Asian/Pacific Islander ',cr,lf
166:       db  'Unknown race             ',cr,lf
167:       db  'Disabled                 ',cr,lf
168:
169:   table_size equ ($ - status_table) / entry_size
170:
171:   heading label byte
172:   db  'Student Information Program                     (STUDENTS.EXE)'
173:   db   cr,lf,cr,lf
174:   db  'Student                        Schol                       Credits'
175:   db   cr,lf
176:   db  'Number          Last Name      Amt       Major         Earned '
177:   db   cr,lf,51 dup('-'),cr,lf,'$'
178:
179:   end main
```

The SETUP procedure (lines 40–53) opens the input file and stores its handle in **filehandle**. The MAIN procedure has a repeating loop (lines 25–28) in which each input record is read and displayed.

The READ_RECORD procedure (lines 106–119) uses DOS function 3Fh to read from the input file. If the count returned by DOS in AX is smaller than CX, we know the end of the file has been reached, so we set the Carry flag (line 117) and exit. We don't have to worry about clearing the Carry flag, because the JNC on line 112 assures us that the flag is clear. In fact, the STC is unnecessary because the previous CMP instruction sets the Carry flag when AX is less than CX. (This rather subtle point might be missed by the casual reader, so the STC instruction makes the logic clearer.)

Displaying ASCII Fields. To display the record in report format, I have made up a record description called **detail_line** (lines 137–149), with a separate label for each field. The record includes filler fields containing spaces to be printed between fields. The DISPLAY_RECORD procedure (lines 58–83) moves each field from the input record to **detail_line** and writes the detail line.

Displaying the Status. Because the status field is bit mapped, we need to devise a convenient way of displaying the individual bit values. By using a bit pattern, we can avoid a complicated set of comparison and jump instructions. The first step is to create a table of field descriptions, called **status_table** (lines 151–167). The **table_size** constant is initialized by MASM. The notation

```
($ - status_table)
```

calculates the number of bytes between the current location and the beginning of the table. When this is divided by **entry_size**, the result is the number of entries in the table: 16.

The DISPLAY_STATUS_FIELD procedure (lines 89–103) inspects each bit of the status field. We rotate the status field leftward into the Carry flag. When the rotated bit sets the Carry flag (line 92), we print the current table entry. The table pointer is moved to the next table entry, and the loop is repeated 16 times, once for each bit.

INDEXING THE STUDENT INFORMATION FILE

The Student Information program that we have just looked at requires records to be read sequentially. This makes it difficult to locate individual records. To find student number 2000000, for example, we would have to read the first record, compare its student number to 2000000, read the next record, and so on. For a large file application, this would be too slow.

A much better way would be to create an index for the file, which would be stored in a separate file (see Figure 12-4). There are many ways to create an

Student Number	Status	Record Pointer
1000000	A810	0002
2000000	6420	0001
2222222	A440	0006
3230000	5808	0005
3333333	A840	0007
4000000	A240	0003
4444444	A840	0008
5000000	5404	0004
5200000	A404	0009
6000000	A205	000A
6234567	9821	0000
7000000	6410	000B
7777777	9402	000D
8000000	9140	000E
8888888	A810	000F
9000000	9410	000C

Figure 12-4 The STUDENTS.NDX file, listed in hexadecimal and ASCII.

index, but the one we will use is a simple sequential table. It consists of the student number and status fields from each student record, along with a 16-bit record number showing where each student is located.

Each index entry shown in Figure 12-4 is only 11 bytes long, which makes it easy to keep a large number of entries in memory. The index is sorted in ascending order by student number, making a binary search on this field possible. The status field is placed in the index so one can search for records based on any combination of values (e.g., female, state resident, Dean's List).

The Student Index Program

A listing of the Student Index program is shown in Figure 12-5. It may be broken down into the following major steps:

```
Open the student file
DO WHILE not end of file
   Read a student record
   Move the student number and status fields
      to the index
   Store the record number in the index
ENDDO
Close the student file
Sort the index in ascending order
Write the index to the index file
```

Figure 12-5 The Student Index program (INDEX.ASM).

```
 1:  title  Student Index Program                    (INDEX.ASM)
 2:
 3:  ;
 4:  ;   This program builds a sorted index from the
 5:  ;   Student Information file and writes the index to
 6:  ;   a file named STUDENTS.NDX.  It uses the following
 7:  ;   routines from CONSOLE: CLRSCR, DISPLAY, WRITEINT.
 8:  ;
 9:
10:  dosseg
11:  .model small
12:  .stack 100h
13:
14:  .code
15:  extrn clrscr:proc, display:proc, writeint:proc
16:  extrn cr:abs, lf:abs
17:
18:  main  proc
19:      call  setup                  ; open input file, etc.
20:      jc    A3                     ; quit if file not found
21:
22:  A1: call  read_record            ; read an input record
23:      jc    A2                     ; if end of file, close
24:      call  add_to_index           ; add entry to index
25:      jnc   A1                     ; continue if no error
26:
27:  A2: mov   ah,3Eh                 ; close the file
28:      mov   bx,filehandle
29:      int   21h
30:      call  sort_index             ; sort by student number
31:      call  write_index            ; write it to a file
32:      jmp   A4                     ; exit program
33:
34:  A3: mov   dx,offset not_found_msg  ; "file not found"
35:      call  display
36:  A4: mov   ax,4C00h               ; return to DOS
37:      int   21h
38:  main  endp
39:
40:
41:  ;   Initialize variables, open Student file for input.
42:
43:  setup proc
44:      mov   ax,@data               ; initialize DS, ES
45:      mov   ds,ax
46:      mov   es,ax
47:      cld                          ; direction flag = up
48:      call  clrscr
49:      mov   ax,3D00h               ; open Student file
50:      mov   dx,offset filename
51:      int   21h
52:      jc    B1                     ; quit if not found
```

Figure 12-5 *(Cont.)*

```
 53:        mov   filehandle,ax         ; else save handle
 54:        mov   dx,offset heading
 55:        call  display
 56:        mov   di,offset index       ; point to the index
 57:    B1: ret
 58:    setup endp
 59:
 60:
 61:    ;   Read a record from the Student file.
 62:
 63:    read_record proc
 64:        mov   ah,3Fh          ; read file/device
 65:        mov   bx,filehandle
 66:        mov   cx,student_record_len
 67:        mov   dx,offset student_record
 68:        int   21h
 69:        jc    C1              ; error: exit
 70:        cmp   ax,cx           ; all bytes read?
 71:        je    C1              ; yes: continue
 72:        stc                   ; no: end of file
 73:    C1: ret
 74:    read_record endp
 75:
 76:
 77:    ;  Add a new entry to the Index table.
 78:
 79:    add_to_index proc
 80:        mov   si,offset stu_num
 81:        mov   cx,key_len
 82:        rep   movsb               ; copy the student number
 83:        mov   ax,status           ; copy the status word
 84:        stosw
 85:        mov   ax,record_pointer  ; insert record pointer
 86:        stosw
 87:        inc   record_pointer
 88:        inc   num_entries
 89:        cmp   num_entries,max_entries    ; exceeded table?
 90:        ja    D1                         ; yes: error
 91:        clc                              ; no: clear Carry
 92:        jmp   D2
 93:    D1: mov   dx,offset table_size_msg  ; error message
 94:        call  display
 95:        stc                       ; set Carry to indicate error
 96:    D2: ret
 97:    add_to_index endp
 98:
 99:
100:    ;   Sort the index in ascending order by student number.
101:
102:    sort_index proc
103:        mov   ax,num_entries    ; number of index entries
104:        mov   iloop,ax          ; inner loop counter
```

Figure 12-5 *(Cont.)*

```
105:        dec    ax
106:        mov    oloop,ax            ; outer loop counter
107:
108:    E1: dec    word ptr iloop      ; adjust inner loop counter
109:        mov    cx,iloop            ; inner loop counter
110:        mov    exchflag,0          ; exchflag = false
111:        mov    si,offset index     ; SI -> first entry
112:        mov    di,offset index + indexrec_len
113:
114:    E2: call   compare             ; compare two entries
115:        jbe    E3                  ; source <= dest?
116:        call   exchange            ; exchange dest, source
117:        mov    exchflag,1          ; set exchflag to true
118:
119:    E3: add    si,indexrec_len     ; point to next two table rows
120:        add    di,indexrec_len
121:        loop   E2                  ; repeat inner loop if CX > 0
122:        dec    word ptr oloop      ; outer loop count = 0?
123:        jz     E4                  ; yes: quit
124:        cmp    exchflag,1          ; any exchanges done?
125:        je     E1                  ; yes: repeat outer loop
126:    E4: ret
127:    sort_index endp
128:
129:
130:    ;   Compare two entries in the index.
131:
132:    compare proc           ; compare source string (SI)
133:        push  si           ; to destination string (DI)
134:        push  di
135:        push  cx           ; preserve loop counter
136:        mov   cx,key_len   ; length of student number
137:        rep   cmpsb        ; repeat until ZF = 0
138:        pop   cx           ; restore registers
139:        pop   di
140:        pop   si
141:        ret
142:    compare endp
143:
144:
145:    ;   Exchange two index entries
146:
147:    exchange proc
148:        push  si           ; pointed to by SI and DI
149:        push  di
150:        push  cx           ; preserve loop counter
151:        mov   cx,indexrec_len
152:
153:    G1: mov   al,[di]      ; get char from destination
154:        xchg  al,[si]      ; exchange with source
155:        stosb              ; store source character
156:        inc   si           ; point to next character
```

Figure 12-5 *(Cont.)*

```
157:        loop   G1          ; repeat until CX = 0
158:
159:        pop    cx          ; restore registers
160:        pop    di
161:        pop    si
162:        ret
163:    exchange endp
164:
165:
166:    ;   Store the index in the STUDENTS.NDX file.
167:
168:    write_index proc
169:        mov    ah,3Ch              ; create file
170:        mov    cx,0                ; normal attribute
171:        mov    dx,offset indexfilename
172:        int    21h
173:        mov    bx,ax               ; save handle
174:        mov    ax,num_entries      ; number of index entries
175:        mov    cx,indexrec_len     ; multiplied by record length
176:        mul    cx                  ;
177:        mov    cx,ax               ; CX = number of bytes
178:        mov    ah,40h              ; write to file/device
179:        mov    dx,offset index     ; write the index
180:        int    21h
181:        mov    ah,3Eh              ; close the file
182:        int    21h                 ; handle is in BX
183:        mov    ax,num_entries      ; display num records written
184:        mov    bx,10               ; decimal radix
185:        call   writeint
186:        mov    dx,offset count_msg
187:        call   display
188:        ret
189:    write_index endp
190:
191:    ; --------------------- constants --------------------
192:    max_entries     equ   50      ; maximum index entries
193:    key_len         equ    7      ; length of student number
194:    indexrec_len    equ   11      ; length of index record
195:
196:    ; --------------------- variables --------------------
197:    .data
198:
199:    filename        db    'STUDENTS.DTA',0
200:    indexfilename   db    'STUDENTS.NDX',0
201:    filehandle      dw    ?      ; handle for data file
202:    record_pointer  dw    0      ; data record number
203:    num_entries     dw    0      ; number of index entries
204:    oloop           dw    0      ; outer loop counter
205:    iloop           dw    0      ; inner loop counter
206:    exchflag        db    0      ; indicates exchange made
207:
208:
```

Figure 12-5 *(Cont.)*

```
209:   student_record label byte  ; input record description
210:     stu_num        db    7 dup(?)
211:     last_name      db   15 dup(?)
212:     scholarship    db    5 dup(?)
213:     major          db    3 dup(?)
214:     credits        db    3 dup(?)
215:     status         dw    ?
216:   student_record_len equ  ($ - student_record)
217:
218:   index label byte           ; index stored here
219:   rept max_entries           ; create space for the index
220:       db  7 dup(?)           ; student number
221:       dw  ?                  ; status
222:       dw  ?                  ; record pointer
223:   endm
224:
225:   heading label byte
226:    db  'Student Index program                  (INDEX.EXE)'
227:    db   cr,lf
228:    db  'Reading STUDENTS.DTA, and creating STUDENTS.NDX.'
229:    db   cr,lf,cr,lf,'$'
230:
231:   not_found_msg  db  'STUDENTS.DTA not found.$'
232:   table_size_msg db  'Warning: maximum number '
233:                  db  'of index entries exceeded.',cr,lf,'$'
234:   count_msg      db  ' records were indexed.$'
235:
236:   end main
```

Constant Definitions. Lines 192–194 define constants that make the program easier to read and modify. **Max_entries** is the most important, because it determines the amount of memory allocated for the index. **Key_len** and **indexrec_len** are used throughout the program—when a new entry is added to the index, when the index is sorted, and when it is written to the new file. For example, the WRITE_INDEX procedure uses **indexrec_len** when calculating the number of bytes to write to the index file (line 175).

The REPT Directive

The Student Index program uses the REPT directive to allocate space for the index. Its syntax is:

```
REPT expression
 (statement)
 .
 .
ENDM
```

Expression must evaluate to a 16-bit quantity at assembly time. Any data or instructions may be coded between REPT and ENDM (end macro), which mark the beginning and end of the block. A number, expression, or predefined constant may be used after REPT. For example:

```
rept 5
rept (count * 10)
rept max_entries
```

We can define variables for one index table entry and then use REPT to generate all the other entries. This technique is used in the Student Index program (lines 219–223).

When referring to the index, one can set a base or index register to any given index entry. Offsets can then be added in order to access each of the fields:

```
mov  si,index
.
.
mov  ax,[si+7]     ; status field
mov  bx,[si+9]     ; record pointer
```

The indexed notation used here is not the easiest to read. A simple enhancement would be to predefine each field offset, using EQU:

```
ix_status          equ  [si+7] ; predefined offsets
ix_record_pointer equ  [si+9]
.
.
mov  si,index                ; point to the index
.
.
mov  ax,ix_status            ; status field
mov  bx,ix_record_pointer ; record pointer
```

Although it would be convenient, it is not possible to use labels within a REPT block, because this would result in a duplicate definition of the labels.

MAIN Procedure. Let us refer to the Student Index program again (Figure 12-5). The MAIN procedure calls SETUP (lines 43–58) to open the input file and display a heading. The main program loop begins at line 22, where READ_RECORD gets the next record from the input file and ADD_TO_INDEX adds a new entry to the index. Line 30 calls SORT_INDEX to sort the index in ascending order, and the next line calls WRITE_INDEX to store the index in an output file.

The READ_RECORD procedure (lines 63–74) reads a single student record from the input file and stores it in the buffer called **student_record**.

ADD_TO_INDEX Procedure. After a record is read from the input file, ADD_TO_INDEX (lines 79–97) moves the student number and status fields from the input record to the index. It also stores **record_pointer**, the current record number.

DI is set to the first index entry in the SETUP procedure (line 56). Each time ADD_TO_INDEX is called, DI points to the next index entry and is incremented by the MOVSB and STOSW instructions (lines 82, 84, and 86).

The variable **num_entries** contains a count of the number of entries added to the table. Line 89 compares this to **max_entries**, to avoid overflowing the index table.

SORT_INDEX Procedure. When all index entries have been loaded from the input file, SORT_INDEX (lines 102–127) sorts the index in ascending order by student number. A standard *bubble sort* algorithm is used. The sort is optimized in two ways: It quits when a single pass through the list yields no exchanges, and the number of comparisons in the inner loop is decreased by 1 after each pass. The following registers, variables, and procedures are used:

Register, Variable, or Procedure	**Usage**
num_entries	Number of entries in the index
oloop	Outer loop counter, which controls the number of passes through the index
iloop	Inner loop counter, which controls the number of comparisons within a single pass
exchflag	Set to 1 when two entries have been exchanged
index	The starting location of the index
SI	Points to the current index entry
DI	Points to index entry + 1
CX	Uses the value of the inner loop counter
COMPARE	Procedure that compares two student numbers
EXCHANGE	Procedure that exchanges two index entries

In the pseudocode version of SORT_INDEX shown here, a right arrow (−>) is used to show an operand that points to another, e.g., SI −> first entry.

```
iloop = num_entries
oloop = num_entries - 1
REPEAT
  Decrement iloop
  exchflag = 0
  SI -> first entry
  DI -> second entry
  DO WHILE iloop > 0
    Compare entry to entry + 1
    IF entry > entry + 1 THEN
      Exchange (entry, entry + 1)
      exchflag = 1
    ENDIF
    Point SI, DI to next two entries
  ENDDO
  Decrement oloop
UNTIL (exchflag = 0) OR (oloop = 0)
```

The COMPARE procedure is called by SORT_INDEX to compare the table entries pointed to by SI and DI. A single CMPSB does the job efficiently and sets the flags to show the result. The EXCHANGE procedure exchanges two table entries when the first entry is greater than the second.

WRITE_INDEX Procedure. After the index has been sorted, MAIN calls WRITE_INDEX (lines 168–189) to store the index in a file. We use two values to calculate the number of bytes to be written: **Num_entries** represents the number of entries in the index, and **indexrec_len** represents the length of each index record.

DYNAMIC MEMORY ALLOCATION

A weakness of the Student Index program is that we have to estimate the size of the index before compiling the program. This same problem exists for all programs containing tables and arrays. One solution would be to place a label at the end of the program listing without actually reserving any memory for the index. Thus the index would use any available memory above the program:

```
.data
(other variables first)
.
.
index label byte    ; index starts here at the
end main            ; end of the program
```

The problem with this approach is that under multitasking software, a program has to release any memory it is not actually using. This allows other programs to share the computer's remaining memory. In such an environment, our student index would not be able to grow in size without interfering with other programs. To make matters worse, programs written under DOS do not automatically release unused memory. COM programs allocate all of available memory, and EXE programs allocate a variable amount of memory, depending on the parameters specified in the EXE file header.

The real answer lies in the DOS *allocate memory* function, whereby memory may be allocated dynamically (at runtime). As space is needed for a buffer or array, one can request additional memory from DOS. Mastery of this technique is beyond the scope of this book, but the three basic DOS functions for memory management will be discussed here.

Modify Memory Blocks (4Ah)

When a program is loaded, it can call DOS function 4Ah to release all memory it does not need for its code, data, and stack. In order to find out how much memory is needed by a program, you can look at the statistics printed by MASM at the end of the listing file (extension .LST). The Student Index program, for instance, requires 540h bytes, the sum of the lengths of its three segments. The following table is printed by MASM in the STUDENTS.LST file:

```
Segments and Groups:

                N a m e          Length

_DATA    . . . . . . . . . . . .   0313    (data segment)
 STACK   . . . . . . . . . . . .   0100    (stack segment)
_TEXT    . . . . . . . . . . . .   012D    (code segment)
(total)                            0540
```

DOS allocates memory in 16-byte blocks called *paragraphs*. To find out how many paragraphs are needed, add another 16 blocks for the PSP, and divide the result by 16; drop the lowest digit of 550h (round upward if necessary):

550h = 55h paragraphs

Let's modify the SETUP procedure in the Student Index program to show how it works. When calling function 4Ah, we pass the PSP segment location in ES and the number of requested paragraphs in BX:

```
setup proc
      mov   ah,4Ah     ; modify memory blocks
      mov   bx,55h     ; keep 550h bytes
      int   21h
      mov   ax,@data ; initialize DS, ES
      mov   ds,ax
      mov   es,ax
      .
      .
```

Allocate Memory (48h)

When additional memory is needed for a large buffer, for instance, use DOS function 48h (allocate memory). BX should contain the number of requested paragraphs. If CF = 0, DOS returns the initial segment of the allocated block in AX. If CF = 1, there probably was not enough memory available, and BX contains the size of the largest available block (in paragraphs). The following example requests a 16K block of memory:

```
mov   ah,48h              ; allocate memory
mov   bx,400h             ; request 400h paragraphs
int   21h                 ; (16,384 bytes)
jc    not_enough_memory
mov   buffer_seg,ax       ; segment address of new block
```

A problem one might face in the Student Index program is in deciding how much memory to allocate for the index. One solution is to use DOS function 4Eh (find first matching file) to get the size of the index file. This value can then be divided by 16 to give us the number of paragraphs we need to allocate. After the memory is allocated, the index can be loaded into memory.

Release Allocated Memory (49h)

If your program has allocated a block of memory with function 48h, you can release the block when it is no longer needed. Call function 49h with the block's starting segment in ES:

```
mov   ah,49h           ; release allocated memory
mov   es,buffer_seg    ; segment of allocated block
int   21h
```

DOS sets the Carry flag if a program tries to release a memory block that either does not belong to it or was not previously allocated by function 48h. With any of the three memory allocation functions (48h, 49h, 4Ah), DOS fails if its own memory control blocks have been destroyed. This happens only when a program has accidentally corrupted a part of memory reserved by DOS.

RANDOM FILE ACCESS

Random file processing is surprisingly simple in assembly language. Only one new function needs to be added to what we already know—the *move file pointer* function (42h), which makes it possible to locate any record in a file. Each high-level language tends to have a specific syntax for random file processing. DOS, on the other hand, makes very little distinction between sequential and random files.

Random access is possible only when the records in a file have a *fixed length*. This is because the record length is used to calculate each record's offset from the beginning of the file. A text file (by definition) has *variable-length* records, each delimited by a carriage-return line feed sequence (0Dh,0Ah). There is no practical way to locate a record randomly in a text file, because the record's offset is not a function of its length.

In the following illustration, File 1 has fixed-length records, so we calculate the beginning of any record by multiplying the record number minus 1 by 20. File 2 stores the same data in a sequential file created by a BASIC program. There are comma delimiters between fields and a CR/LF (0Dh,0Ah) at the end of each record. The position of any one record may not be calculated, because each record has a different length. Record 2 begins at offset 15, record 3 at offset 34, and so on:

File 1: 20-Byte, Fixed-Length Records

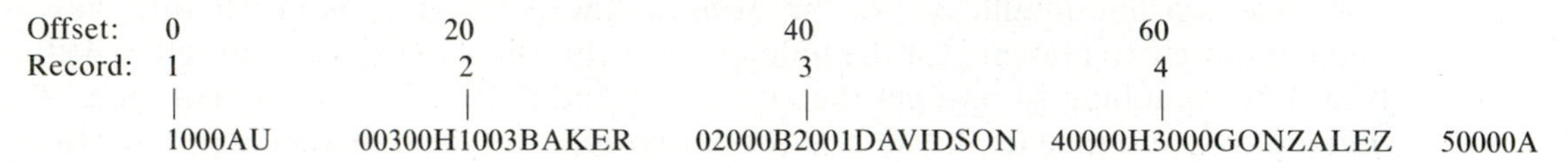

File 2: Text File, Variable-Length Records

```
Offset:  0             15                 34                     57
Record:  1              2                  3                      4
         |              |                  |                      |
         1000,AU,300,H..1003,BAKER,2000,B..2001,DAVIDSON,40000,H..3000,GONZALEZ,50000,A..
```

(.. = 0Dh,0Ah sequence)

Move File Pointer (42h)

DOS function 42h moves the file pointer to a new location (the file must be open). The input registers are:

AH	42h
AL	Method code (type of offset)
BX	File handle
CX	Offset, high
DX	Offset, low

The *offset* may be relative to the beginning of the file, the end of the file, or the current file position. When the function is called, AL contains a *method code* that identifies how the pointer will be set, and CX:DX contains a 32-bit offset:

AL	Contents of CX:DX
0	Offset from the beginning of the file
1	Offset from the current location
2	Offset from the end of the file

Result Values. If the Carry flag is set after the function is called, DOS returns either error 1 (invalid function number) or error 6 (invalid handle). If the operation is successful, the Carry flag is cleared and DX:AX returns the new location of the file pointer relative to the start of the file (regardless of which method code was used).

Example: Locate a Record. Suppose we are processing a random file with 80-byte records, and we want to find a specific record. The LSEEK procedure shown here moves the DOS file pointer to the position implied by the record number passed in AX. Assuming that records are numbered beginning at 0, we multiply the record number by the record length to find its offset in the file:

```
lseek proc              ; AX contains a record number
    mov   bx,80         ; CX:DX = (AX * 80)
    mul   bx
    mov   cx,dx         ; upper half of offset
    mov   dx,ax         ; lower half of offset
    mov   ah,42h
    mov   al,0          ; method: offset from beginning
    mov   bx,handle
    int   21h           ; locate the file pointer
    ret
lseek endp
```

For example, record 9 would be located at offset 720, and record 0 would be located at offset 0:

$$\text{Offset} = 9 * 80 = 720$$
$$\text{Offset} = 0 * 80 = 0$$

To read a record, we simply place the desired record number in AX, call LSEEK, and then call READ_RECORD:

```
mov    ax,record_number
call   lseek
call   read_record
```

The READ_RECORD procedure uses function 3Fh to read 80 bytes from the file:

```
read_record proc
    mov   ah,3Fh
    mov   bx,handle
    mov   cx,80
    mov   dx,offset buffer
    int   21h
    ret
read_record endp
```

Example: Append to a File. Function 42h is also used to append to a file. The file may be either a text file with variable-length records or a file with fixed-length records. The trick is to use method code 2, to position the file pointer at the end of the file before writing any new records. The following routine does this:

```
mov  ah,42h       ; position file pointer
mov  al,2         ; relative to end of file
mov  bx,handle
mov  cx,0         ; offset, high
mov  dx,0         ; offset, low
int  21h
```

Using a Negative Offset. If the method code in AL is either 1 or 2, the offset value may be either positive or negative, presenting some interesting possibilities. For example, one can "back up" the file pointer from the current position, using method 1, and reread a record. This also works for a text file with variable-length records:

```
mov  ah,42h          ; function: move pointer
mov  al,1            ; method: relative to current position
mov  bx,handle
mov  cx,0
mov  dx,-10          ; back up 10 bytes
int  21h
jc   error_routine ; exit if there is an error
mov  ah,3Fh          ; function: read file
mov  cx,10           ; read 10 bytes
mov  dx,offset inbuf  ; input buffer
int  21h
```

APPLICATION: INDEXED RECORD RETRIEVAL

We have discussed how to read the Student file sequentially and how to create an index for the file. A further step would be to access records randomly. This is actually quite easy, as it means placing the offset of a record in AX and calling DOS function 42h (move file pointer). Once the file pointer is positioned correctly, the record may be read by function 3Fh (read from file or device).

But we want to go one step further and retrieve records using student numbers. The student number field is called the *record key* because it is the field that was used when the index was created and sorted.

Retrieving a Record. In order to show how the Student file could be used for indexed record retrieval, let's list the major steps involved. In the following list, steps 3–5 repeat until the operator decides to quit:

1. Open the Student file for input.

2. Open the Index file for input, read it into the index table, and close the file.
3. Prompt for a student number, and input it from the console. If the operator presses ENTER without typing a student number, close the Student file and return to DOS.
4. Search the index using the student number that was input. If a matching entry is found, extract the record number from the index that points to the correct record in the Student file.
5. Set the DOS file pointer to the beginning location of the requested record. Then read and display the record.

Student Retrieval Program

The Student Retrieval program (RETRIEVE.ASM) in Figure 12–6 carries out each of the steps needed to perform indexed retrieval of records. It doesn't do any maintenance, such as adding or deleting records, but these features could be added to the program.

MAIN Procedure. The MAIN procedure calls SETUP, LOAD_INDEX, GET_STUDENT_ID, SEARCH_INDEX, and DISPLAY_RECORD. Each of these corresponds to one of the major steps already outlined for the program. All but the last of these are followed by JC instructions, forcing the program to quit when CF = 1.

GET_STUDENT_ID Procedure. GET_STUDENT_ID (lines 95–106) clears the screen, displays a prompt, and inputs a 7-digit student number from the operator. A sample is shown here:

```
Student Retrieval Program.          (RETRIEVE.EXE)

Enter the student number you wish to find:4444444_
```

If the operator presses ENTER without entering a student number, this is taken as a signal to end the program. The Carry flag is set, which tells MAIN to exit to DOS.

SEARCH_INDEX Procedure. Once a student number has been entered, SEARCH_INDEX (lines 112–129) checks it against each entry in the index. A sequential lookup is used here. COMPARE is called from here, with SI pointing to the student number entered by the operator and DI pointing to the current entry in the index. Upon returning from COMPARE, the flags are set according to the comparison. If the string pointed to by SI is less than that pointed to by DI, the Carry flag is set. If the strings are equal, the Zero flag is set.

Each index entry contains three fields: the student number, the status, and the record number. When a matching entry in the table is found, its record number is copied from the index entry to **record_pointer**. The latter is used by the

```
 1:  title  Student Retrieval Program               (RETRIEVE.ASM)
 2:
 3:  ;
 4:  ;   This program retrieves and displays records from
 5:  ;   the Student Information file, using an index
 6:  ;   based on the student number field.  It uses the
 7:  ;   following routines from CONSOLE.LIB: CLRSCR,
 8:  ;   DISPLAY, READSTRING, WRITESTRING.
 9:  ;
10:
11:  dosseg
12:  .model small
13:  .stack 100h
14:  extrn clrscr:proc, display:proc, readstring:proc
15:  extrn writestring:proc, cr:abs, lf:abs
16:
17:  .code
18:  main  proc
19:      call  setup                  ; open input file, etc.
20:      jc    A3                     ; quit if file not found
21:      call  load_index             ; load the index file
22:      jc    A2                     ; quit if error occurred
23:
24:  A1: call  get_student_id         ; read an input record
25:      jc    A2                     ; quit if ENTER pressed
26:      call  search_index           ; find index entry
27:      jc    A1                     ; prompt again if not found
28:      call  display_record         ; display the record
29:      jmp   A1                     ; prompt for another
30:
31:  A2: mov   ah,3Eh                 ; close the Student file
32:      mov   bx,filehandle
33:      int   21h
34:
35:  A3: mov   ax,4C00h               ; return to DOS
36:      int   21h
37:  main  endp
38:
39:
40:  ;   Initialize segment registers, open Student file
41:
42:  setup proc
43:      mov   ax,@data       ; initialize DS, ES
44:      mov   ds,ax
45:      mov   es,ax
46:      cld                  ; direction flag = up
47:      mov   ax,3D00h       ; open input Student file
48:      mov   dx,offset studentfilename
49:      int   21h            ; returns handle in AX
50:      mov   filehandle,ax  ; save handle
51:      jnc   B1             ; exit if no error
```

Figure 12-6 The Student Retrieval program (RETRIEVE.ASM).

Figure 12-6 *(Cont.)*

```
 52:        mov    dx,offset no_studentfile
 53:        call   display
 54:        stc                          ; Carry indicates an error
 55:    B1: ret
 56:    setup endp
 57:
 58:
 59:    ;   Load the Index file into memory
 60:
 61:    load_index proc
 62:        mov    ax,3D00h          ; open input index file
 63:        mov    dx,offset indexfilename
 64:        int    21h
 65:        jc     C1                ; quit if not found
 66:        mov    bx,ax             ; save file handle
 67:        mov    ax,3F00h          ; read the index file
 68:        mov    cx,index_size     ; CX = number of bytes
 69:        mov    dx,offset index
 70:        int    21h               ; AX = number of bytes read
 71:        cmp    ax,index_size     ; entire table full?
 72:        je     C2                ; yes: index possibly too large
 73:        mov    cx,indexrec_len
 74:        div    cl                ; bytes read / record len
 75:        mov    num_entries,ax    ; number of entries in table
 76:        mov    ah,3Eh            ; close the index file
 77:        int    21h
 78:        jmp    C3                ; return to MAIN
 79:
 80:    C1: mov    dx,offset no_indexfile ; file not found
 81:        call   display                ; display message
 82:        stc                           ; make sure Carry is set
 83:        jmp    C3                     ; return to MAIN
 84:
 85:    C2: mov    dx,offset table_size_msg
 86:        call   display           ; display warning message
 87:        stc                      ; set Carry flag
 88:    C3: ret
 89:    load_index endp
 90:
 91:
 92:    ;   Display a prompt and input a student number
 93:    ;   to be used when searching for a record
 94:
 95:    get_student_id proc
 96:        call   clrscr                ; clear the screen
 97:        mov    dx,offset heading     ; display a prompt
 98:        call   display
 99:        mov    cx,7                  ; read 7-digit student_ID
100:        mov    dx,offset student_ID
101:        call   readstring
102:        cmp    ax,0                  ; ENTER pressed?
```

Figure 12-6 *(Cont.)*

```
103:        jne   D1                     ; no: continue
104:        stc                          ; yes: set Carry flag
105:    D1: ret
106:    get_student_id endp
107:
108:
109:    ;   Search the index for a matching student_ID,
110:    ;   and place the result in record_pointer
111:
112:    search_index proc
113:        mov   si,offset student_ID
114:        mov   di,offset index
115:        mov   cx,num_entries     ; number of index entries
116:
117:    E1: call  compare            ; compare student_ID
118:        jne   E2                 ; skip if no match
119:        mov   ax,[di+9]          ; get pointer from index
120:        mov   record_pointer,ax  ; save it in a variable
121:        clc                      ; clear Carry to show success
122:        jmp   E3                 ; exit procedure
123:
124:    E2: add   di,indexrec_len    ; point to next entry
125:        loop  E1                 ; repeat for all entries
126:        stc                      ; search must have failed
127:
128:    E3: ret
129:    search_index endp
130:
131:
132:    ;   Compare two index entries
133:
134:    compare proc           ; compare source string (SI)
135:        push  si           ; to destination string (DI)
136:        push  di
137:        push  cx           ; preserve loop counter
138:        mov   cx,key_len   ; length of student number
139:        rep   cmpsb        ; repeat until ZF = 0
140:        pop   cx           ; restore registers
141:        pop   di
142:        pop   si
143:        ret
144:    compare endp
145:
146:
147:    ;   Display the record from the student
148:    ;   file pointed to by record_pointer
149:
150:    display_record proc
151:        call  lseek        ; set the file pointer
152:        jc    G1           ; exit if DOS failed
153:        mov   ah,3Fh       ; read from the file
```

Figure 12-6 *(Cont.)*

```
154:        mov    cx,student_record_len
155:        mov    dx,offset student_record
156:        int    21h
157:        mov    student_record+33,0  ; set zero terminator
158:        call   writestring    ; display the record
159:        mov    ah,1                ; wait for a keystroke
160:        int    21h
161:    G1: ret
162:    display_record endp
163:
164:
165:    ;   Move the file pointer to the desired record
166:
167:    lseek proc
168:        mov    ax,record_pointer
169:        mov    bx,student_record_len  ; CX:DX = AX * 35
170:        mul    bx
171:        mov    cx,dx       ; upper half of offset
172:        mov    dx,ax       ; lower half of offset
173:        mov    ah,42h      ; move file pointer
174:        mov    al,0        ; method: offset from beginning
175:        mov    bx,filehandle
176:        int    21h
177:        ret
178:    lseek endp
179:
180:    ; --------------- Constant definitions ----------------
181:
182:    max_entries  equ   50          ; max number index entries
183:    key_len              equ    7   ; length of student number
184:    indexrec_len         equ   11   ; length of index record
185:    student_record_len equ   35   ; length of student record
186:    index_size           equ  max_entries * indexrec_len
187:
188:    ; -------------------- Variables -----------------------
189:    .data
190:
191:    filehandle     dw    ?          ; handle for data file
192:    record_pointer dw    0          ; data record number
193:    num_entries    dw    0          ; number of index entries
194:    student_record db   35 dup(?)  ; input record
195:    student_ID     db    7 dup(0)  ; used for searching index
196:
197:    index label byte                ; index stored here
198:    rept max_entries                ; create space for the index
199:       db  7 dup(?)                 ; student number
200:       dw  ?                        ; status
201:       dw  ?                        ; record pointer
202:    endm
203:
204:    studentfilename  db   'STUDENTS.DTA',0
```

Figure 12-6 *(Cont.)*

```
205:   indexfilename    db    'STUDENTS.NDX',0
206:
207:   heading label byte
208:     db  'Student Retrieval Program                (RETRIEVE.EXE)'
209:     db  cr,lf,cr,lf,cr,lf
210:     db  'Enter the student number you wish to find: $'
211:
212:   no_studentfile  db  'STUDENTS.DTA not found.$'
213:   no_indexfile    db  'STUDENTS.NDX not found.$'
214:   table_size_msg  db  'Warning: maximum number '
215:                   db  'of index entries exceeded.',cr,lf,'$'
216:
217:   end main
```

LSEEK procedure to position the file pointer. Suppose we are looking for student number 2222222. The point at which we find a matching index entry is illustrated here:

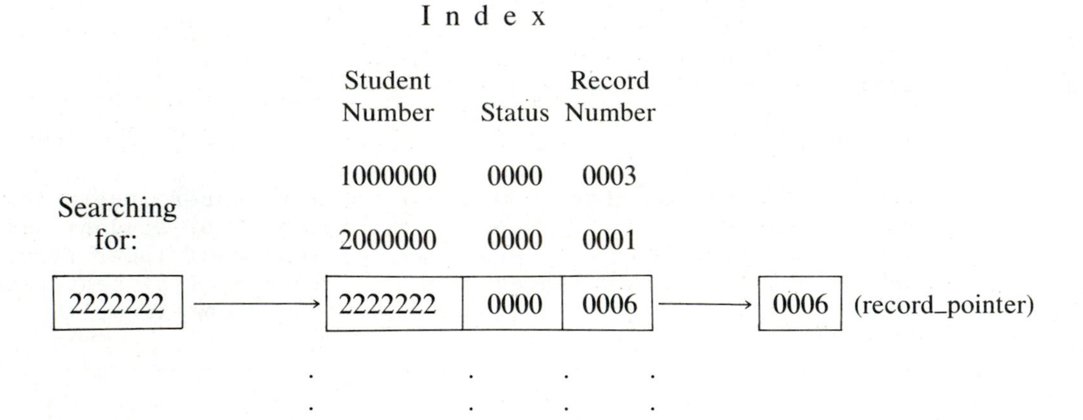

DISPLAY_RECORD Procedure. Once a correct record pointer has been obtained from the index, DISPLAY_RECORD (lines 150–162) locates, reads, and displays the student record. It calls LSEEK to set the file pointer and then reads the record into a buffer called **student_record**. In this program, we are not displaying the status field, so a zero terminator byte is placed in the record immediately after the credits field. For a complete list of the field names, see the Student Information program in Figure 12-3. After displaying the record, we wait for a keystroke and return to MAIN.

LSEEK Procedure. LSEEK (lines 167–178) moves the DOS file pointer to the file offset determined by **record_pointer**. The record pointer values start at 0 for the first record, so a record's offset is calculated by multiplying its record pointer by the record length. When passing the record offset to DOS, remember to place the high word in CX and the low word in DX, as we do in this program.

SEARCHING A BIT-MAPPED FIELD

As written, the Student Retrieval program retrieves records only by student number. You may recall, however, that we placed in the index a copy of the status field from each student record. This field is bit-mapped, making it possible to store a great deal of information in a single field. At the same time, there is another advantage to this format—efficient searches for combinations of values are possible.

Exclusive Matches (AND)

An exclusive match would involve searching for multiple characteristics in the status field, all of which must be matched in order for the record to be selected. For instance, we might want to find a student who satisfies the following criteria:

IF female AND Hispanic AND state resident
AND satisfactory progress

If these attributes were stored in separate fields, we would have to write a complex series of comparisons and jumps. Using a single bit-mapped field, however, only a single comparison is necessary.

First, we define constants with bits matching the attributes we are looking for, and from these a search pattern is constructed. We let the assembler generate the search pattern by ORing it with each of the constants:

```
female       equ 4000h    ; predefined bit patterns
resident     equ 2000h
satisfactory equ 0400h
Hispanic     equ 0020h

pattern equ female or resident or satisfactory or Hispanic
```

If the search pattern is known only at runtime, it can still be constructed using OR instructions:

```
mov  pattern,female
or   pattern,resident
or   pattern,satisfactory
or   pattern,Hispanic
.
.
pattern  dw  0
```

When searching for a record that matches a particular bit pattern, we don't want to look at any of the other bits. First, we AND the field with the search pattern, which clears any irrelevant bits. Then when the field is compared to the pattern, all bits must match in order for the Zero flag to be set:

```
mov  ax,ix_status   ; get status field from index
and  ax,pattern     ; clear any irrelevant bits
cmp  ax,pattern     ; does the field match?
jz   match_found    ; yes: successful search
```

Nonexclusive Matches (OR)

When looking for a record that matches only one of several criteria, one uses the TEST instruction. To find students who are *either* female *or* state residents *or* are on the Dean's List, set bits 11, 13, and 14 in the search pattern:

```
female          equ 4000h
state_resident  equ 2000h
deans_list      equ 0800h
pattern  equ female or state_resident or deans_list
.
.
test  ix_status,pattern   ; any bits match?
jnz   match_found         ; yes: successful search
```

Combinations of AND and OR

The most difficult situation to handle is one in which a comparison uses both AND and OR. Suppose we wanted to find all records matching the following:

male AND (Black OR Hispanic)

A single matching bit pattern for this does not immediately come to mind, because we don't know whether to use the TEST or CMP instruction. But if we can rephrase the search so as to eliminate all nonmatching records from the search, the solution is clearer. Essentially, we are looking for students who do not have any of the following characteristics: female, white non-Hispanic, American Indian, Asian, or unknown race. This may be expressed as

NOT (female OR white non-Hispanic OR American Indian OR Asian OR unknown)

We then take the preceding values and construct a bit pattern. A record matching any one of the bits in the following word would fail the search:

0 1 0 0 0 0 0 0 0 0 1 0 0 1 1 1 0

Assuming AX contains this value, the TEST instruction should be followed by a conditional jump:

```
test  ix_status,ax   ; compare status field
jnz   no_match       ; fail if any bits match
```

Input Routine

One problem remains—that of finding a way to input the search pattern. A possible way is to display a menu of all the status fields, and let the operator use the space bar and cursor arrow keys to toggle each field between *yes, no,* and *d/c* (don't care). The following is a sample input screen:

```
     SELECT FIELDS TO BE USED IN SEARCH:

  1  Male                          yes
     Female                        no

  2  State resident                d/c
     Nonresident                   d/c

  3  Dean's List                   d/c
     Satisfactory progress         d/c
     Academic probation            d/c
     Academic warning              d/c
     Academic suspension           d/c

  4  White non-Hispanic            no
     Hispanic                      yes
     Black                         yes
     American Indian               no
     Asian or Pacific Islander     no
     Unknown race                  no

  5  Disabled                      d/c
```

Setting any byte to *d/c* causes all other bytes in the group to be set to the same value. If the input values are stored in a table, we can step through it and set bits in the search pattern for entries that contain *no*. We will assume that 1 = *yes,* 0 = *no,* and 2 = *d/c*. Thus, the sample input screen just shown implies the following table contents:

01	00	02	02	02	02	02	02	02	00	01	01	00	00	00	02

(00 = no, 01 = yes, 02 = don't care)

The following routine steps through each byte in **scrtable** and constructs a bit pattern:

```
        mov   pattern,0    ; search pattern
        mov   bx,offset scrtable ; table screen entries
        mov   cx,16        ; process 16 entries

    L1: mov   al,[bx]      ; get a table entry
        cmp   al,0         ; set to no?
        jne   L2           ; no: continue
        or    pattern,1    ; yes: set the lowest bit
    L2: rol   pattern,1    ; rotate pattern to the left
        inc   bx           ; point to next table entry
        loop  L1           ; continue until CX = 0

        ror   pattern,1    ; readjust bit positions
        .
        .
  scrtable  db  16 dup(?)
  pattern   dw  ?
```

This routine stores the final sequence of bits in **pattern**. Each time a value of 0 is found, we set the lowest bit of **pattern** and shift the bit one position to the left. ROR is used because the shifting within the loop goes one position too far; the ROR adjusts the bits back to their original positions.

For each value of *no,* we set the corresponding bit; for each value of *yes* or *d/c,* we will clear the corresponding bit. Using the values from the sample input screen, we would expect the bit pattern to be the following:

0 1 0 0 0 0 0 0 0 1 0 0 1 1 1 0

Now when we conduct a search using this bit pattern, we reject any record that matches one of these bits. This brings us back to the TEST instruction presented earlier:

```
mov   ax,pattern     ; get search pattern
test  ix_status,ax   ; compare status field
jnz   no_match       ; fail if any bits match
```

POINTS TO REMEMBER

A handle is a 16-bit number used by DOS to refer to a standard device or an open file. The handle must be used when calling certain DOS functions—in particular, functions 3Fh (read from file or device) and 40h (write to file or device). The standard device handles used most often are 0 (keyboard), 1 (console), 2 (error output), and 4 (printer). An advantage to using handles is that input and output may be redirected to other files or devices at runtime, making programs more flexible.

All DOS functions require a function number to be placed in AH before calling INT 21h. Other data registers may be used to pass values. By convention, CX usually contains a count or size value, DX usually contains an offset address pointing to either a filename or a buffer, and BX usually contains a file handle.

The basic file functions presented in this chapter are 3Ch (create file), 3Dh (open file), 3Eh (close file handle), 3Fh (read from file or device), 40h (write to file or device), and 42h (move file read/write pointer).

When you want to create a new file or open a sequential file for output, use function 3Ch. Any existing file with the same name will be truncated to 0 bytes.

To open an existing file for input, use function 3Dh (AL = 0 for input mode) and function 3Fh to read from the file.

To append to an existing sequential file, use function 3Dh to open the file (AL = 1 for output mode), function 42h to point to the end of the file, and function 40h to write to the file.

To open a file for random reading and writing, use function 3Dh (AL = 2 for input-output mode), function 42h to position the file pointer, and functions 3Fh (read) and 40h (write).

DOS Error Codes. When DOS tries to carry out a requested operation and fails, it sets the Carry flag and returns a 16-bit error code that helps explain the cause of the error. With the introduction of DOS 3.0, there are 83 possible error codes.

End of File. When using function 3Fh to read from a file, check AX after the operation to find out if all requested bytes were read. A smaller value in AX indicates that the end of the file has been reached. If you continue reading from the file, AX just returns 0, showing that no more bytes are available.

Function 3Fh may also be used to read from the keyboard. When using this function for keyboard input, remember that any extra input characters (beyond the number requested in CX) are discarded by DOS.

Text Files. A text file is a stream of ASCII characters whose records are delimited by the values 0Dh and 0Ah. Other nonprintable characters are TAB (09h) and EOF (1Ah, end-of-file). The Text File Creation program (Figure 12-1) presented in this chapter showed how to create a text file, using input from the console. The Text File Listing program (Figure 12-2) showed how to read a text file, buffer the records, and display each line of text.

Fixed-Length Record Processing. When all records have the same length, individual records may be read randomly. The offset of any record is a function of its length and record number. Fixed-length records can also hold binary values, helping to save storage space and processing time. (Text files cannot hold binary values because the bytes might be confused with ASCII control characters.)

In this chapter, we looked at three programs relating to files with fixed-length records. The Student Information program (Figure 12-3) displayed the contents of the Student file, including one field that was bit-mapped. The Student Index program (Figure 12-5) showed how to create and sort an index for the Student file. The Student Retrieval program (Figure 12-6) loaded the index created by the Student Index program and allowed record retrieval by student number.

Bit-Mapped Fields. The Student Information file used in this chapter contained a bit-mapped field called status. A bit-mapped field is an efficient way to store boolean (true/false) information, and it may be easily searched for multiple criteria using AND, CMP, and TEST instructions. The Student Information program (Figure 12-3) used a lookup table to display the values of individual bits in the status field. Routines were also shown that took input from the keyboard and constructed a bit pattern used for searching the status field.

REVIEW QUESTIONS

1. If a file currently does not exist, what will happen if function 3Dh opens the file in the output mode?

2. If a file is created using function 3Ch, can it be both written to and read from before it is closed? What if it was created with a read-only attribute?

3. If you want to create a new file but do not want to accidentally erase an existing file with the same name, what steps should your program take?

4. What do the following instructions imply?

```
          mov   ah,3Dh
          mov   al,2
          mov   dx,offset filename
          int   21h
          .
          .
filename  db    'FIRST.RND',0
```

5. When a file is closed, do you need to point DX to its filename?

6. What do you think the effect of the following instructions would be?

```
mov   ah,3Eh
mov   bx,0
int   21h
```

7. When function 3Eh (read from file or device) is called, what does it mean when the Carry flag is set and DOS sets AX to 6?

8. When function 3Eh is called (with CX = 80h), what does it mean when DOS clears the Carry flag and returns a value of 20h in AX?

9. When function 3Eh is used to read from the keyboard and CX is set to 0Ah, what will be the contents of the input buffer when the following string is input?

```
1234567890
```

10. When function 40h writes a string to the console, must the string be terminated by a zero byte?

11. When using function 40h to write to an output file, does DOS automatically update the file pointer?

12. If you have just read a record from a random file and you want to rewrite it back to the same position in the file, what steps must you take?

13. Is it possible to move the DOS file pointer within a text file?

14. Write the necessary instructions to locate the file pointer 20 bytes beyond the end of the file identified by **filehandle**.

15. What is the offset of the 20th record in a file that contains 50-byte fixed-length records?

16. What is the purpose of buffering input records?

17. Assuming that bits 0–4 hold a department number and bits 5–7 hold a store number within the following bit-mapped field, what are the values shown here?

11000101	store =	department =
00101001	store =	department =
01010101	store =	department =

18. The following WRITE_BUFFER procedure is supposed to write the contents of **buffer** to the file identified by **filehandle**. The variable **buflen** contains the current length of the buffer. If the disk is full, the procedure should print an appropriate message. What is wrong with the procedure's logic?

```
write_buffer proc
    mov   ah,40h
    mov   bx,filehandle
    mov   cx,buflen
    mov   dx,offset buffer
    int   21h
    jnc   L1
    mov   dx,offset message
    call  display
L1: ret
```

```
write_buffer endp
    .
    .
.data
filehandle   dw   ?
buflen       dw   ?
buffer       db   80 dup(?)
message      db   'Disk is full.$'
```

19. The GET_COMMAND_TAIL procedure copies the DOS command line from PSP:80h to the buffer pointed to by DX. What is wrong with the way the following instructions call GET_COMMAND_TAIL?

```
main  proc
      mov   ax,@data
      mov   ds,ax
      mov   es,ax
      mov   bx,ds
      mov   dx,offset buffer
      call  get_command_tail
      .
      .
.data
buffer  db  128 dup(0)
```

PROGRAMMING EXERCISES

Exercise 1 The Student Information Program

Construct a bit pattern in AX that could be used to search the status field from the Student Information file. See the explanation of this file earlier in the chapter, along with the Student Information program (Figure 12-3). Your pattern should be used to find all female American Indian students who are on the Dean's List. Code the necessary instructions to place the test pattern in AX, and jump to the label **no_match** if the comparison fails.

Exercise 2 The Text File Listing Program

Identify at least three major improvements you could make to the Text File Listing program (Figure 12-2). Create a pseudocode or flowchart listing showing where in the program the changes should be made.

Exercise 3 **The Text File Creation Program**

Modify the Text File Creation program introduced in Figure 12-1 as follows: After the file has been closed, reopen it for input and display all records. Display a line number at the beginning of each record. For example:

```
1: This is line one.
2: This is the second line.
3: This is line 3.
4: This is the fourth line in the file.
```

Exercise 4 **Text Matching Program**

Write a program called SEARCH.EXE that opens a text file for input and lets you search for a string within the file. If the string is found, display all lines of text on which it appeared, with a line number at the beginning of each line. For example:

```
> SEARCH FILE1.DOC
Text to find? line

 2: This is line 2.
10: On line 10, we have even more text.
11: This is a single text line that is even longer.
(no more matches)
```

Create a 60K input buffer to hold the input file, and fill the buffer twice, if necessary. The search should be *case insensitive,* so all case differences will be ignored.

Exercise 5 **Enhanced Text Matching Program**

Improve the Text Matching program created for Exercise 4 as follows: Let the operator use wildcard characters in the file specification. Load and search each matching file. For example, assume the files FILE1.DOC, FILE1.ASM, and FILE1.TXT are in the current directory. The FIND program would search all three files, with the following command:

```
> find file1.*
```

Exercise 6 **File Listing Program**

Write a program that reads a text file into a buffer and displays the first 24 lines of text. Write the text directly to video memory for the best performance. You will need to use routines from CONSOLE.LIB to check for the current video adapter so the program will work properly on a color or monochrome display.

Provide the following keyboard command functions:

Key	Function
PgUp	Scroll up 24 lines
PgDn	Scroll down 24 lines
UpArrow	Scroll up 1 line
DnArrow	Scroll down 1 line
Esc	Exit to DOS

Of course, if the beginning of the buffer is currently being displayed, don't scroll up. And if you are at the end of the buffer, don't scroll down.

Exercise 7 Random File Creation Program

Write a program that creates a random file containing student academic information, using data entered from the console. Each record is 27 bytes long, and there should be at least 20 records. The record format is shown here:

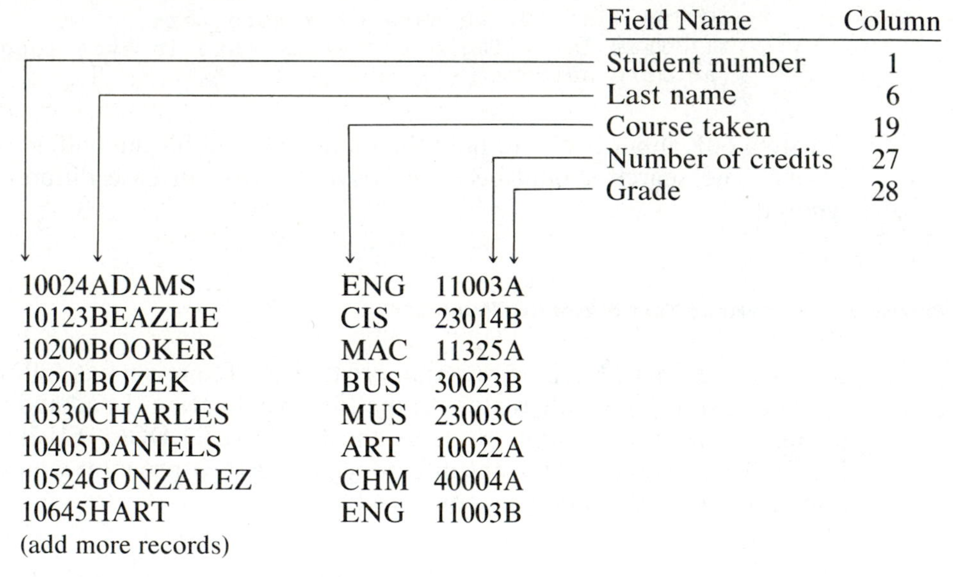

Prompt the operator for each record, and copy the record to the random file.

Exercise 8 Student File Maintenance Program

Using the file created in Exercise 7, write a random file update program. Display a menu offering the operator the following options:

STUDENT FILE MAINTENANCE

S Show a single record
A Add a new record
C Change (edit) a record
D Delete a record
E Exit program

The operator will select records by their number. Each time one of the menu functions is carried out, return to the menu. Run the program several times to make sure that records were added, deleted, and changed correctly.

Exercise 9 Enhanced Sector Display Program

Using the Sector Display program from Exercises 14 and 15 in Chapter 11 as a starting point, add the following enhancement: As a sector is displayed, let the operator press [F3] to write the sector to an output file. Prompt for the filename, and if it already exists, append the current sector to the end of the file. This helps to make the program a useful tool for recovering lost sectors on a disk, as the sectors can be reconverted into files.

Exercise 10 Enhanced Date Display Program

Modify the Date Display Program introduced in Chapter 11 so it displays all matching files in ascending order by date. You will need to load all matching filenames and dates into a table and then sort and display the table. If the operator types /N after the program name, sort the table in ascending order by filename. The following command, for example, would display all files with an extension of .ASM, sorted in ascending order by filename:

```
DAT/N *.ASM
```

The /N should be case insensitive, so /n will work as well.

Exercise 11 Student Index Program

Modify the Student Index program presented in Figure 12-5 by replacing the bubble sort with either a *quicksort* or *shell sort*.

Exercise 12 Student Retrieval Program, Version 1

Enhance the Student Retrieval program presented in Figure 12-6 in the following ways:

1. Display the fields in the student record with spaces between the fields, and display the bit-mapped status field.
2. Read the name of the student file from the DOS command line.

Exercise 13 **Student Retrieval Program, Version 2**

Enhance the Student Retrieval program presented in Figure 12-6 in the following ways:

1. Use the allocate memory function to create space for the index after calling a DOS function to get the size of the index file.
2. Offer the option of searching for records, using the status field.
3. Replace the sequential lookup in SEARCH_INDEX with a binary search.

ANSWERS TO REVIEW QUESTIONS

1. DOS will set the Carry flag and return error 2 (file not found).

2. Yes, it is automatically opened for reading and writing. If it is created with a read-only attribute, you can still write to the file. This means that the attribute has no effect until the file is closed.

3. One possibility is to try to open the file, using function 3Dh; if DOS can't find the file, you can safely call function 3Ch to create a new file with the same name. The other way to do it is to call function 5Bh (create new file), which will set the Carry flag and return AX = 50h if the file already exists.

4. The file named FIRST.RND is presumed to exist and is being opened for both input and output.

5. No. The file is identified by its handle, which must be placed in BX before calling function 3Eh (close file).

6. This would close the standard input device and cause DOS to ignore all keyboard input. The system would have to be cold started, so you would never do this intentionally.

7. Error message 6 (invalid file handle) probably means that we were trying to read from a file that had not been opened. Alternatively, we may not have placed the correct file handle in BX before calling the function.

8. When reading from a file, AX always contains the number of characters just read. If the Carry flag is clear, there is no DOS error, but it would mean that we have reached the end of the file.

9. The buffer will contain digits 1–8, plus the carriage return and line feed characters inserted by DOS. The last two input digits (9 and 0) will be ignored. The hexadecimal contents of the buffer will be:

31	32	33	34	35	36	37	38	0D	0A

10. When function 40h writes to the console (or a file), CX contains the number of bytes to be written. Thus, no zero terminator byte is necessary.

11. Yes, DOS automatically moves the file pointer forward to the position just after the last byte written.

12. Before rewriting the same record back to the file, you would have to move the pointer backward by an amount equal to the number of bytes in the record. When calling function 42h (move file pointer), you could set AL to 1, telling it that the contents of CX:DX will be a relative offset from the current location. Assuming that the length of the record just read is 80 bytes, you would place the value −80 in DX:

```
mov     ah,42h      ; move file pointer
mov     al,1        ; CX:DX is offset from current location
mov     bx,handle   ; file handle
mov     cx,0        ; offset, high
mov     dx,-80      ; offset, low: back up 80 bytes
int     21h
```

13. Yes, the file pointer may be moved anywhere in a text file. At the same time, it might be difficult to know where a particular record is located, because the records usually have different lengths.

14. The instructions to locate the file pointer 20 bytes beyond the end of the file are:

```
mov    ah,42h       ; move file pointer
mov    al,2         ; relative to end of file
mov    bx,filehandle
mov    cx,0         ; offset, high
mov    dx,20        ; offset, low
int    21h
```

15. The offset (950) may be found using the following formula:

    Offset = (20 − 1) * 50

16. Input records are buffered whenever possible in order to speed up file processing. The slowest operation a computer performs is input/output. If the records are buffered, fewer disk accesses are needed.

17. The bit values are:

11000101	store = 6	department = 5
00101001	store = 1	department = 9
01010101	store = 2	department = 21

18. DOS does not set the Carry flag when the disk is full. Instead, you must compare AX to CX after INT 21h is called in order to find out if all bytes were written.

19. DS and ES contain the PSP segment address when the program is loaded, but this program changes both registers before moving DS to BX. According to the procedure specifications, BX must contain the PSP segment address.

13

Macros and Advanced MASM

MACROS

A *macro* is a symbolic name given to one or more assembly language statements. Once created, it may be used as many times in a program as you wish. When creating a macro, you *define* it; when using a macro, you *call* it. An advantage of defining a macro is that its statements need only be coded once. Each time the macro is called, the assembler generates the statements in the macro for you. Suppose we plan to write the following instructions to display the contents of DL several times in a program:

```
mov  ah,2       ; write DL to the console
int  21h        ; call DOS
```

We could store these instructions in a procedure and call it each time it was needed. But this would create the added overhead of the CALL and RET instructions, which tend to slow a program down. A better way would be to create a macro called PUTCHAR.

Once PUTCHAR has been defined, it can be called from anywhere in the code segment. Calling a macro is not the same as calling a procedure. It means the macro's statements are inserted in the program from where it was called. Let's define the macro PUTCHAR:

```
putchar  macro    ; begin macro definition
    mov  ah,2
    int  21h
endm              ; end macro definition
```

In the code segment, one calls PUTCHAR just by coding its name. Each time the macro is called, MASM inserts the instructions from the original macro definition into the program (marked here with a + sign):

Source Code	Generated Statements
.code	.code
main proc	main proc
.	
.	
mov dl,'A'	mov dl,'A'
putchar	+ mov ah,2
.	+ int 21h
.	.
.	.
mov dl,'*'	mov dl,'*'
putchar	+ mov ah,2
.	+ int 21h
.	

This expansion is performed by MASM during its first pass through the source file, and the resulting statements are shown in the listing (.LST) file.

Macros execute more quickly than procedure calls. Macros require no CALL and RET instructions, whereas procedures do. Macros tend to make a program larger than do procedures, because each macro call inserts a new copy of its code in the program.

Passed Values. Macros can handle passed values. When calling PUTCHAR, for example, one loads DL with the character to be displayed before calling the macro. But if we add a parameter to the macro definition (**char**), we can pass the character on the same line when calling the macro:

```
putchar macro  char  ; begin macro definition

    mov  ah,2
    mov  dl,char     ; char takes on a new value
    int  21h

endm

.code
    .
    .
    putchar 'A'      ; call the macro here
```

Passing values to a macro makes it more flexible and convenient and should be done whenever possible.

Macros to Create Data. Macros may be called from the data segment. For instance, they may be used to allocate space variables. In the next example, each table entry created by the ALLOC macro consists of 4 spaces and 4 bytes of zeros:

```
alloc  macro varname,numbytes
    varname  db  numbytes dup('    ',0,0,0,0)
endm
    .
    .
.data
alloc value1,20     ; allocate 20 entries
alloc value2,50     ; allocate 50 entries
```

Generated statements:

```
value1  db  20  dup('    ',0,0,0,0)
value2  db  50  dup('    ',0,0,0,0)
```

Varname and **numbytes** are names that take on whatever values are passed when the macro is called. The first is assembled as the variable's name, and the second determines the number of bytes to be allocated by the DUP operator.

Defining and Calling Macros

A macro can be defined anywhere in a program, using the MACRO and ENDM directives. The syntax is:

```
macroname MACRO [parameter-1] [,parameter-2] ...
  statements
ENDM
```

There is no rule regarding indentation, but one can indent statements between *macroname* and ENDM to make them easier to identify.

The statements between the MACRO and ENDM directives are not assembled until the macro is called. *Macroname* may be any symbolic name. The *parameters* are optional. There may be any number of parameters in the macro definition, as long as they are separated by commas and they all fit on the same line. These parameters, often called *dummy parameters,* represent values that will be supplied when the macro is used.

All statements before the ENDM are considered part of the macro. If a macro is never called, its statements are not assembled.

Calling a Macro. A macro is called by coding its name, along with any values to be passed. Of course, calling a macro really means that statements generated by the macro are inserted directly in the program. It is not *called* as a procedure is, because no branching takes place. The syntax for a macro call is:

```
macroname [argument-1] [,argument-2] ...
```

Macroname must be the name of a macro defined earlier in the source file. An *argument* is a value passed to the macro, which will, in turn, replace a parameter in the original macro definition. The order of arguments must correspond to the original parameters, but the number of arguments does not have to match the number of parameters. If too many arguments are passed, the extra ones are ignored. If too few are passed, the remaining parameters default to null strings.

Example: The DISPLAY Macro. To see how this all works, let's create a macro called DISPLAY that displays a string pointed to by DX. No parameters are specified in the macro definition:

```
display macro       ; begin macro definition

    push ax
    mov  ah,9
    int  21h
    pop  ax

endm                ; end macro definition
```

As in procedures, one often pushs and pops registers within macros in order to preserve their values. To call the DISPLAY macro, we write:

```
        mov   dx,offset message
        display
        .
        .
message db 'This string is displayed.',0Dh,0Ah,'$'
```

Passing Parameters

By using parameters in a macro's definition, we make it more flexible. Let's rewrite the DISPLAY macro with a parameter called **string**, the name of the string to be displayed:

```
display macro string

    push ax
    push dx
    mov  ah,9
    mov  dx,offset string
    int  21h
    pop  dx
    pop  ax

endm
```

String is replaced each time the macro is called. To display three different strings, we call the macro three times, passing a different argument each time:

```
          display msg1
          display msg2
          display msg3
          .
          .
msg1    db   'This is message 1.',0Dh,0Ah,'$'
msg2    db   'This is message 2.',0Dh,0Ah,'$'
msg3    db   'This is message 3.',0Dh,0Ah,'$'
```

Parameter names do not appear in a program listing and may be duplicates of other names (labels, variables, etc.).

The passed argument makes the DISPLAY macro more useful now. We can avoid the usual complications involved in passing values to procedures. The following example shows the statements generated by MASM (the macro calls themselves are listed ahead of the statements they have generated). We do, however, pay a price in program code size by using macros:

```
display msg1
      push ax
      push dx
      mov  ah,9
      mov  dx,offset msg1
      int  21h
      pop  dx
      pop  ax
display msg2
      push ax
```

```
            push dx
            mov  ah,9
            mov  dx,offset msg2
            int  21h
            pop  dx
            pop  ax
      display msg3
            push ax
            push dx
            mov  ah,9
            mov  dx,offset msg3
            int  21h
            pop  dx
            pop  ax
```

The LOCATE Macro. The LOCATE macro listed here locates the cursor at a desired row and column on the screen:

```
locate macro  row, column

     push  ax
     push  bx
     push  dx
     mov   bx,0          ; choose page 0
     mov   ah,2          ; locate cursor
     mov   dh,row
     mov   dl,column
     int   10h           ; call the BIOS
     pop   dx
     pop   bx
     pop   ax

endm
```

LOCATE may be called and passed 8-bit immediate values, memory operands, and register values:

```
locate 10,20    ; immediate values
locate row,col  ; memory operands
locate ch,cl    ; pass registers
```

Be careful when passing values in registers, because they may conflict with register usage in the macro. If we called LOCATE using AH and AL, for instance, the macro would not work properly. To see why, let's look at the generated statements after the parameters have been substituted:

```
        locate  ah,al

     1:      push ax
     2:      push bx
     3:      push dx
     4:      mov  bx,0       ; choose page 0
     5:      mov  ah,2       ; locate cursor
     6:      mov  dh,ah      ; (too late: AH changed)
     7:      mov  dl,al
     8:      int  10h        ; call the BIOS
     9:      pop  dx
    10:      pop  bx
    11:      pop  ax
```

Assuming that AH is passed as the row value and AL is the column, line 5 replaces AH before we have a chance to move it to DH on line 6. Therefore, the macro will incorrectly locate the cursor on screen row 2.

The STARTUP Macro. The STARTUP macro initializes DS and ES to the location of the data segment and copies the DOS command tail to a memory buffer. STARTUP is designed to work with the MASM simplified segment directives. Call it once at the beginning of a program and pass it the name of a buffer, which will then receive a copy of the command tail:

```
startup macro buffer

    extrn get_command_tail:proc
    mov   bx,ds                ; get copy of PSP segment
    mov   ax,@data             ; initialize DS, ES
    mov   ds,ax
    mov   es,ax
    mov   dx,offset buffer     ; copy the command tail
    call  get_command_tail

endm
```

Sample call:

```
 startup filename    ; init DS,ES, put command tail
                     ; in filename
```

Nested Macros

One way to simplify a macro is to borrow from existing ones. A *nested* macro calls another macro. Let's create a macro called DISPLAY_AT that displays a string at a requested row and column. It calls the LOCATE and DISPLAY macros by taking its own parameters and passing them as arguments to the other two macros:

```
display_at macro row,col,string

   locate  row,col     ; call LOCATE macro
   display string      ; call DISPLAY macro

endm
```

Sample call:

```
    display_at  10,15,greeting
    .
    .
greeting  db  'Hello from row 10, column 15.$'
```

The statements generated by the macros appear in the following table. Notice that the nesting level is 2, because both macros are being called from within a macro. The source line that calls LOCATE does not appear in the listing file:

Nesting Level	Statements
	display_at 10,15,greeting
2	push ax (LOCATE macro)
2	push bx
2	push dx
2	mov bx,0
2	mov ah,2
2	mov dh,10
2	mov dl,15
2	int 10h
2	pop dx
2	pop bx
2	pop ax
2	push ax (DISPLAY macro)
2	push dx
2	mov ah,9
2	mov dx,offset greeting
2	int 21h
2	pop dx
2	pop ax

The LOCAL Directive

The LOCAL directive forces MASM to create a unique name for a label each time a macro is called. The syntax is:

```
LOCAL  labelname
```

A macro may need to use labels as reference points for jump and loop instructions. Let's create a macro named REPEAT that displays any character a requested number of times. The LOCAL directive tells MASM to change L1 to a *unique* name each time the macro is called:

```
repeat macro  char,count

    local L1         ; declare a local label
    mov  cx,count
L1: mov  ah,2
    mov  dl,char
    int  21h
    loop L1

endm
```

By calling REPEAT more than once, we can see how MASM creates a different label each time. It numbers the labels from 0000h to FFFFh and precedes them with two question marks:

```
         repeat  'A',10     ; call the macro

         mov  cx,10
??0000:  mov  ah,2
         mov  dl,'A'
         int  21h
         loop ??0000

         repeat  '*',20     ; call the macro

         mov  cx,20
??0001:  mov  ah,2
         mov  dl,'*'
         int  21h
         loop ??0001
```

Using a Macro to Call a Procedure

We have already hinted at a small disadvantage of using macros: They increase the amount of code generated by the assembler, because each macro call becomes a *separate copy* of the macro statements. In terms of program size, procedures are more economical. On the other hand, procedure calls can be awkward when passed parameters are involved.

The best compromise between the two is to use macros to streamline parameter passing for procedure calls. A macro can place each procedure argument in its required register before calling a procedure. We will use this technique to call the WRITEINT procedure, which displays an unsigned integer on the console.

Calling the WRITEINT Procedure. The CALL_WRITEINT macro listed here calls the WRITEINT procedure from CONSOLE.LIB. The two parameters, **value** and **radix**, are loaded into AX and BX. We save and restore the two registers before and after the procedure call in order to minimize the impact on the surrounding program:

```
call_writeint macro  value, radix

     push  ax          ; save AX, BX
     push  bx
     mov   ax,value    ; value to be displayed
     mov   bx,radix    ; radix to be used
     call  writeint    ; display AX on console
     pop   bx
     pop   ax

endm
```

One can call this macro using registers, variables, or constants. For example:

```
    call_writeint  2000h,10    ; immediate value in decimal
    call_writeint  dx,16       ; register value in hexadecimal
    call_writeint  wordval,2   ; memory value in binary
    .
    .
wordval  dw  1000h
```

Conditional-Assembly Directives

Twelve different conditional-assembly directives may be used in conjunction with macros to make them even more powerful. The general syntax for all conditional-assembly directives is:

```
IF condition

  statements

[ELSE

  statements]

ENDIF
```

Specific directives will now be discussed. When we say that a directive *permits assembly,* we mean that any following statements will be assembled until the ENDIF directive is encountered:

IF — Syntax: IF *expression*
Permits assembly if the value of *expression* is true (nonzero). The following example permits assembly if **count** < 20:

```
IF count LT 20
```

Possible relational operators are LT, GT, EQ, NE, LE, and GE.

IFE — Syntax: IFE *expression*
Permits assembly if the value of *expression* is 0, or false. In the following example, this happens if **count** = 10:

```
IFE (count - 10)
```

IF1 — Syntax: IF1
Permits assembly if this is currently the assembler's first pass through the source program.

IF2 — Syntax: IF2
Permits assembly if this is currently the assembler's second pass through the source program.

IFB — Syntax: IFB <*argument*>
Permits assembly if *argument* is blank, because it was not passed to the macro. The argument name must be enclosed in angle brackets (<>).

IFNB — Syntax: IFNB <*argument*>
Permits assembly if *argument* is not blank, because it was passed to the macro.

IFIDN — Syntax: IFIDN <*argument1*>,<*argument2*>
Permits assembly if the two arguments are equal. The comparison may be made case insensitive if the IFIDNI directive is used.

IFDIF — Syntax: IFDIF <*argument1*>,<*argument2*>
Permits assembly if the two arguments are unequal. The comparison is case insensitive if the IFDIFI directive is used.

IFDEF — Syntax: IFDEF *name*
Permits assembly if *name* has been defined.

IFNDEF — Syntax: IFNDEF *name*
Permits assembly if *name* has not been defined.

ENDIF Ends a block that was begun using one of the conditional-assembly directives.

ELSE Assembles all statements up to ENDIF if the condition specified by a previous IF directive is false.

Checking for Macro Arguments. A macro may have one or more optional parameters. It should check to see if each argument was actually passed. If not, MASM returns a blank value for the parameter. This could cause meaningless instructions to be assembled. Suppose we called the CALL_WRITEINT macro but did not pass a radix value. The macro would assemble with an invalid instruction on line 5:

Macro call:

```
call_writeint  1000h
```

Generated statements:

```
1:   call_writeint
2:        push  ax        ; save AX, BX
3:        push  bx
4:        mov   ax,1000h  ; value to be displayed
5:        mov   bx,       ; radix to be used (?)
6:        call  writeint  ; display AX on console
7:        pop   bx
8:        pop   ax
```

The IFB (if blank) directive returns *true* if a macro argument is blank, and IFNB (if not blank) returns *true* if a macro argument was supplied.

For example, the following macro, called MYMAC, checks to see if a value for **parm1** was passed when the macro was called. If MYMAC is called with no arguments, the EXITM directive prevents any statements from being generated:

```
mymac macro parm1
   ifb <parm1>          ; no argument supplied?
     exitm              ; then exit the macro
   endif                ; and generate no statements
   .
   .
endm

.code
   .
   .
   mymac                ; omit the argument
   mymac val1           ; pass an argument
```

The EXITM Directive

The EXITM directive tells MASM to exit from a macro and stop generating statements. This can reduce the length of the final program by eliminating unnecessary instructions. The following GOTOXY macro positions the cursor on the screen. We want to exit the macro if either argument is less than 0 (of course, this requires them to be constants). The IF condition compares **xval** to 0, using LT (*less than*), and exits if the result is true. The same is done for **yval**:

```
gotoXY macro  xval,yval

     if xval LT 0         ; xval < 0?
       exitm              ; if so, exit
     endif

     if yval LT 0         ; yval < 0?
       exitm              ; if so, exit
     endif

     mov  bx,0            ; choose video page 0
     mov  ah,2            ; locate cursor
     mov  dh,yval
     mov  dl,xval
     int  10h             ; call the BIOS

endm
```

A conditional directive such as IF must be followed by an expression that can be evaluated to either true or false at assembly time. This will not work for values in registers or memory variables, because they are known only at run-time. The ENDIF directive must be used to mark the end of each IF conditional block.

Displaying Messages During Assembly. The %OUT directive displays a string during assembly. This might be used with the GOTOXY macro to display a message whenever an invalid argument is passed. We have used the IF2 directive in the following example, to make sure the %OUT messages only display once during the assembler's second pass:

```
gotoXY macro  xval,yval

   if xval LT 0         ; xval < 0?
    if2
     %out GOTOXY: First argument (xval) is invalid.
     %out (value must be >= 0)
    endif
   endif
```

```
      if  yval LT 0          ; yval < 0?
       if2
        %out GOTOXY: Second argument (yval) is invalid.
        %out (value must be >= 0)
       endif
      endif

      mov   bx,0             ; choose video page 0
      mov   ah,2             ; locate cursor
      mov   dh,yval
      mov   dl,xval
      int   10h              ; call the BIOS

   endm
```

Imagine calling GOTOXY with two invalid arguments, −1 and −2. The following messages would display during assembly:

```
GOTOXY: First argument (-1) is invalid.
(value must be >= 0)

GOTOXY: Second argument (-2) is invalid.
(value must be >= 0)
```

Clearly, range checking of parameters is a good way to improve the reliability of macros, and diagnostic messages are a great help when learning to use a macro.

The WRITE Macro. Let's create a macro called WRITE that writes a literal to standard output. The literal is passed as an argument in single quotation marks. An optional parameter, **creturn**, indicates that a carriage return is to be displayed:

```
write macro  text, creturn
   local string,strlen      ; local labels

   push   ax
   push   dx
   mov    ah,40h            ; display the string
   mov    bx,1              ; handle = console
   mov    dx,offset string
   mov    cx,strlen
   int    21h
   pop    dx
   pop    ax

   .data                    ; define the string

   ifb <creturn>            ; CR/LF specified?
     string  db  text
   else
```

```
            string  db  text,0Dh,0Ah
        endif
        strlen  equ  $-string

        .code

    endm
```

This example shows how the .DATA directive may be included in a macro before variable definitions. The variable **string** will be assembled in the data segment. The LOCAL directive ensures that **string** and **strlen** will not conflict with any other names in the program.

The WRITE macro is especially good for displaying a literal on the console, as one avoids having to code a separate data definition (DB) for the string. In the first sample call shown here, the argument *N* could be any character, as long as the parameter is not blank:

```
write 'Hello there',N           ; include CR/LF
write 'No return on this line' ; no CR/LF
```

Macro Operators

There are five macro operators that serve to make macros more flexible when called. One, the macro comment (;;), is not an operator in the usual sense. It suppresses printing of comment lines when a macro is expanded:

&	Substitute operator
%	Expression operator
<>	Literal-text operator
!	Literal-character operator
;;	Macro comment

Substitute (&) Operator. The & operator replaces a parameter with an argument value. The syntax is:

```
&parameter
```

This operator is particularly useful when text passed as an argument must be inserted into a string or instruction within the macro. For example, the following DOSmsg macro lets you create storage for the string passed as an argument:

```
DOSmsg macro  num,string
    msg&num  db   'DOS error: &string',0
endm
```

The following table shows sample calls to DOSmsg, along with the statements generated by MASM:

Called As	Generated Statements
DOSmsg 1,<Invalid function>	msg1 db 'DOS error: Invalid function',0
DOSmsg 2,<File not found>	msg2 db 'DOS error: File not found',0
DOSmsg 3,<Path not found>	msg3 db 'DOS error: Path not found',0

Notice that I enclosed the strings passed to DOSmsg in angle brackets (<>). These tell MASM that the entire string is to be passed as a single argument.

Expression Operator (%). Sometimes the result of an expression must be passed as an argument. Use the % operator at the beginning of the expression to tell MASM that the result of the expression, not the expression itself, is to be passed to the macro.

Suppose the macro MEMDISPLAY writes a string directly to the video buffer. We want to pass the macro either a single numeric value or an expression:

```
memdisplay macro ofset,string
    mov   ax,videoseg       ; address of video buffer
    mov   es,ax
    mov   di,ofset          ; offset into video buffer
    .
    .
endm
```

When calling MEMDISPLAY, the first argument is the desired offset into the video buffer. The second argument is the name of the string. The offset can be a single value such as 320, or it can be the result of an expression involving constant symbols:

```
row = 10      ; constant symbols
col = 40
.
.
memdisplay %((row * 160) + (col * 2)),string1
memdisplay 320,string2
```

Literal-Text Operator (<>). The literal-text operator groups a list of characters into a single string. It prevents MASM from interpreting members of the list as individual arguments. (This operator is also required around the operands in conditional-assembly directives such as IFB and IFIDN.) This is particularly important when the string contains special characters (, %, &, and ;) that would otherwise be interpreted as macro operators. Let's use a macro named MESSAGE as an example:

```
message macro text
    db '&text',0      ; create a string
endm
```

The macro call

```
message <Efficiency is 50%, & falling;>
```

would be assembled as

```
db  'Efficiency is 50%, & falling;',0
```

Literal-Character Operator (!). The literal-character operator was invented for much the same purpose as the literal-text operator: It forces MASM to treat a special character as a character instead of an operator. Using the MESSAGE macro again as an example, we might want to pass a string containing the > character:

```
message  <Efficiency is !> 50%>
```

This would be assembled as

```
db  'Efficiency is > 50%', 0
```

Sample Macros

Following are a few general-purpose macros illustrating some of the special macro operators.

The CCALL Macro. One excellent use for macros is to enhance the Intel instruction set—this can make programs easier to write. The following CCALL (conditional call) macro makes it possible to call a procedure based on the flags, using a single instruction:

```
Ccall macro   cond,procname
      local   L1,L2

      j&cond  L1
      jmp     L2
  L1: call    procname
  L2: exitm

endm
```

The macro can be based on any flag condition. For example, we might wish to call the DOS_error procedure when the Carry flag is set. The macro allows us to write:

```
Ccall  c,DOS_error
```

Or we may wish to call LOWER if **value1** is less than or equal to AX:

Original		**Generated Statements**
cmp value1,ax		cmp value1,ax
Ccall le,lower		jle ??0002
		jmp ??0003
	??0002:	call lower
	??0003:	exitm

We can call NOT_EQUAL if AX is not equal to BX:

```
cmp    AX,BX
Ccall  ne,not_equal
```

After comparing two strings, we can call EXCHANGE:

```
call   compare    ; compare two strings
Ccall  a,exchange ; exchange if source > destination
```

The CMPJ Macro. CMPJ (compare and jump) compares two operands and jumps to a label based on the flags:

```
cmpj macro  dest,flag,source,label
    cmp   dest,source
    j&flag  label
endm
```

Sample calls:

```
cmpj  ax,le,bx,label1  ; if AX <= BX, jump to label1
cmpj  cx,e,count,exit  ; if CX = count, jump to exit
```

The MULT Macro. As you know, the MUL instruction imposes certain limitations. AL or AX is automatically the implied destination operand, and immediate source operands are not allowed. The MULT macro in the following example allows you to multiply any 16-bit operand by a register, memory operand, or immediate operand:

```
mult macro  dest,source

    push  ax            ; save registers
    push  bx
    mov   ax,dest       ; AX = destination
    mov   bx,source     ; BX = source
    mul   bx            ; DX:AX = product
    mov   dest,ax
    pop   bx
    pop   ax

endm
```

MULT multiplies **dest** by **source,** placing the result in **source**. If the result is larger than 16 bits, the Carry flag is set, and the high part of the result is in DX.

The following calls to MULT demonstrate its flexibility in multiplying operands of various types:

```
      mov   cx,value1         ; CX = 0100h
      mult  cx,5              ; CX = 0500h
      mult  value1,value2     ; value1 = 0200h
      mult  value2,5          ; value2 = 0Ah
      .
      .
value1  dw  100h
value2  dw  2
```

You may have noticed a small limitation of the MULT macro: AX cannot be used as the source operand, because its value is replaced by the **dest** parameter.

The MMOVE Macro. The Intel instruction set does not include a memory-to-memory move instruction other than MOVS. The MMOVE macro accomplishes this—the TYPE operator determines if the operands are 8 or 16 bits, and then **source** is moved to **dest** via AL or AX:

```
mmove macro  dest,source

    push ax
    if (type dest) EQ 1    ; 8-bit type?
      mov  al,source       ; yes: use AL
      mov  dest,al
    else
      if (type dest) EQ 2 ; 16-bit type?
        mov  ax,source     ; yes: use AX
```

```
                    mov  dest,ax
                  endif
                endif
                pop  ax

            endm
```

Sample calls:

```
mmove word2,word1     ; 16-bit move
mmove byte2,byte1     ; 8-bit move
```

Because the TYPE operator is used in this macro, MASM generates an error message unless the .DATA directive is located before the macro definition. This is because MASM needs to locate the variables during its first pass before it can evaluate their type. The following segment order works:

```
.stack 100h
.data
 (variables here)

 (macro definition here)

.code
 (instructions here)
```

Conditional Jumps and Loops. The Intel instruction set limits the span of conditional jump instructions—including LOOP—to 127 bytes forward or 128 bytes backward. Particularly when your program has a number of macro calls within the area spanned by a conditional jump or loop, the jump or loop may be out of range. Imagine that we have converted the WRITESTRING, READSTRING, and WRITEINT procedures to macros and used them in a program:

```
    mov   cx,10                  ; loop counter
L1: writestring  prompt          ; display a prompt
    readstring   buffer          ; input a string
    writeint     1000h,10        ; display 1000h in decimal
    loop  L1                     ; loop out of range
```

This example would cause a syntax error because the code produced by the macros inside the loop exceeds 127 bytes; the loop is out of range.

The LLOOP Macro. The LLOOP (long loop) macro allows you to loop to any label in the current segment. It does this by looping to a JMP instruction that, in turn, jumps to the destination. JMP, unlike LOOP, can reach any label in the segment:

```
LLoop macro dest

     local A1,A2
     loop  A1          ; loop to short label
     jmp   A2
A1:  jmp   dest        ; jump to destination

A2: endm
```

This macro uses the LOOP instruction in an unusual way: It loops *forward* to the label **A1**. At this location, the JMP instruction takes us back to **dest**. If CX is decremented to zero, the LOOP falls through and jumps to A2, which is the location of the next program instruction. A small amount of execution overhead is added, but then we would use the macro only for an important reason. The following example shows the new macro in place of the LOOP instruction in our original example:

```
     mov   cx,10                   ; loop counter
L1:  writestring  prompt           ; display a prompt
     readstring   buffer           ; input a string
     writeint     1000h,10         ; display 1000h in decimal
     LLoop L1                      ; use LLoop macro
```

Defining Repeat Blocks

One or more statements may be repeated using the REPT, IRP, and IRPC directives. This makes it possible for a single macro to create a large data structure.

REPT Directive. The REPT directive repeats a block of statements based on a counter. The syntax is:

```
REPT expression
  statements
ENDM
```

Expression determines the number of repetitions and must evaluate to a 16-bit unsigned number. You may recall that in Chapter 12 we used REPT to define space for an index in the Student Index program. The constant **max_index_entries** specified the number of repetitions:

```
index label byte         ; index stored here
rept max_index_entries   ; create space for the index
    db  7 dup(?)         ; student number
    dw  ?                ; status
    dw  ?                ; record pointer
endm
```

One could use the same technique to create a macro that shifts an operand left a specific number of times. In the following example, **count** determines the number of repetitions of the SHL instruction:

```
mshl macro dest,count
  rept count              ; repeat the following statement
    shl dest,1
  endm
endm
```

This is a nested macro definition. We can see the macro called two different ways here, followed by the statements generated by MASM:

```
mshl ax,1
mshl bx,4
```

Generated statements:

```
shl ax,1
shl bx,1
shl bx,1
shl bx,1
shl bx,1
```

IRP Directive. The IRP directive creates a repeat block in which each repetition contains a different value. The syntax is:

```
IRP parameter,<argument [,argument]...>
  statements
ENDM
```

The block is repeated once for each argument. Each time it repeats, the current argument value is substituted for the parameter. This directive is useful for initializing a table or block of data in which some of the values are varied. The arguments may be symbol names, strings, or numeric constants:

Original Repeat Block	Generated by the Assembler
irp parm,<10,20,30,40>	dw 10, 10*2, 10*3, 10*4
dw parm, parm*2, parm*3, parm*4	dw 20, 20*2, 20*3, 20*4
endm	dw 30, 30*2, 30*3, 30*4
	dw 40, 40*2, 40*3, 40*4

IRP can initialize a table of procedure offsets. This may prove useful if you want to code a multiway branch based on the value of an index. For example,

```
mov  bx,indexvalue   ; BX = indexvalue
call proctable[bx]   ; indirect call
```

Four procedure names are passed as arguments in the following IRP example. Each is inserted where **procname** appears, resulting in a table containing the procedures' offsets:

```
proctable label word
irp  procname,<movup,movdn,movlft,movrt>
  dw procname
endm
```

The following statements are generated:

```
proctable label word
dw movup
dw movdn
dw movlft
dw movrt
```

Earlier, we used the REPT directive to form a macro called MSHL that shifts an operand left a specified number of times. If we want the same macro for each of the other shift and rotate instructions, we have to create eight different macros. There is a much better way: The IRP directive may be combined with a macro definition to create variations on the macro. The following macro generates eight macros named MSHL, MSHR, MSAL, MSAR, MROL, MROR, MRCL, and MRCR:

```
irp styp,<shl,shr,sal,sar,rol,ror,rcl,rcr>
  m&styp macro dest,count
    rept count
      &styp  dest,1
    endm
  endm
endm
```

The substitute operator (&) used here allows substitution of an argument string in the macro definition. At the outermost level, IRP repeats the macro definition eight times, using a different value for **styp** each time. The macro M&STYP, in other words, is actually eight macros, because it changes its name each time the IRP loop repeats. The innermost loop (using REPT) is identical to that shown earlier in the MSHL macro. It codes the number of shift or rotate instructions determined by the value of **count**. Oddly enough, none of the eight macros actually appear in the program listing. We see their effects only when code is generated. Sample calls are as follows:

```
mshl ax,3      ; shift AX left
mrcl count,2   ; rotate count left through Carry
mshr bx,4      ; shift BX right
mror ax,5      ; rotate AX right
```

This is a triple-nested macro, which only begins to show the real power of macro definitions. In the hands of an expert, macros can create high-level language statements such as IF...THEN, FOR...NEXT, and so on.

The instructions generated by our sample calls are:

```
mshl ax,3
     shl  ax,1
     shl  ax,1
     shl  ax,1

mrcl count,2
     rcl  count,1
     rcl  count,1
```

IRPC Directive. The IRPC directive is essentially the same as IRP, except that the number of characters in the argument string determines the number of repetitions. The syntax is:

```
IRPC parameter,string

  statements

ENDM
```

String must be enclosed in angle brackets (<>) if it contains spaces, commas, or any other special characters. The following example generates five variables (value_A, value_B, etc.), using the characters in the string ABCDE as arguments:

```
irpc  parm,ABCDE
   value_&parm db '&parm'
endm
```

Generated statements:

```
value_A db 'A'
value_B db 'B'
value_C db 'C'
value_D db 'D'
value_E db 'E'
```

No doubt there are many other clever ways to use the REPT, IRP, and IRPC directives, particularly when combined with macro operators. Macros represent the ultimate extension of the assembler instruction set; you will find yourself limited only by your imagination.

Additional Tips

Store Macros in an Include File. Once you collect a wide assortment of macros, it becomes inconvenient to copy them into each new program. Instead, create a file containing only macros and let the INCLUDE directive copy them at assembly time. Only the macros actually used will become part of your final program. It is a good idea to surround the INCLUDE with the IF1 and ENDIF directives, telling MASM to include the macros only on its first pass:

```
if1                     ; if the first pass,
  include lib1.mac      ; include macro listings
endif
```

Listing Directives. The following assembler directives control the content of your listing files (.LST). Many of them relate to macros and conditional directives:

Directive	Action
.LIST	List all statements (default)
.XLIST	Suppress listing of statements
.LFCOND	List false-conditional blocks
.SFCOND	Suppress listing of false-conditional blocks (default)
.TFCOND	Toggle false-conditional listing
.LALL	List macro expansions (default)
.SALL	Suppress listing of macro expansions
.XALL	Exclude comments from macro listing

From the Macro Assembler 5.1 *Programmers Guide,* copyright 1987, by Microsoft Corporation.

The .SALL directive is useful for suppressing macro expansions so they do not clutter up your program listings. Place the .SALL directive anywhere in the file before the macros are called. To reenable macro expansions, use .LALL.

Debugging with CODEVIEW. When you debug a program with macros in source mode, CODEVIEW suppresses macro expansions. To view and trace through the expanded code, change the VIEW option to *mixed* or *assembly*.

ADVANCED MASM OPERATORS AND DIRECTIVES

Type Operators

All of the assembler operators discussed in this section return the *type,* or *attribute,* of a name or label. The operators are listed here in alphabetical order:

Syntax	Return Value
HIGH *expression*	High-order byte of an expression
LENGTH *variable*	Number of elements in a variable
LOW *expression*	Low-order byte of an expression
OFFSET *expression*	Offset address of an expression
type PTR *expression*	Forces expression to a desired type
SEG *expression*	Segment address of an expression
SHORT *label*	Sets a label type to SHORT
SIZE *variable*	LENGTH of a variable times the TYPE
THIS *type*	Creates an operand of the desired type
.TYPE *expression*	Mode and scope of an expression
TYPE *expression*	Number of bytes in a variable or structure

SEG Operator. The SEG operator returns the segment address of a label, variable, segment name, group name, or other memory operand. This operator is particularly valuable if you do not know the segment name for a variable that is located in another program module. The following example places the segment address of **array** in AX and then copies it to DS:

```
mov  ax,seg array
mov  ds,ax
```

SHORT Operator. The SHORT operator is often used with a JMP instruction when we know that a forward jump will be less than or equal to +127 bytes from the current location. This allows MASM to generate a short jump rather than a near jump, which is a longer instruction.

TYPE Operator. The TYPE operator returns the size, expressed as the number of bytes, of a single data element of a variable. For example, an 8-bit variable would return a TYPE value of 1, a 32-bit variable would return 4, an array of bytes would return 1, and an array of 16-bit integers would return 2. If the expression is a NEAR label, a value of 0FFFFh is returned, and a FAR label returns 0FFFEh. Examples of several variable types are shown here:

```
        mov   ax,type var1    ; AX = 0001
        mov   ax,type var2    ; AX = 0002
        mov   ax,type var3    ; AX = 0004
        mov   ax,type var4    ; AX = 0001
        mov   ax,type msg     ; AX = 0001
        .
        .
var1   db   20h
var2   dw   1000h
var3   dd   ?
var4   db   10,20,30,40,50
msg    db   'File not found',0
```

LENGTH Operator. The LENGTH operator counts the number of individual elements in a variable that have been defined using DUP. If the DUP operator is not used, LENGTH returns a value of 1. Examples:

```
         mov   ax,length val1      ; length = 1
         mov   ax,length val2      ; length = 1
         mov   ax,length array     ; length = 20h
         mov   ax,length message   ; length = 1
         .
         .
val1      dw   1000h
val2      db   10,20,30
array     dw   20h dup(0)
message db   'File not found'
```

A string variable returns a value of 1. If nested DUP operators are used, only the outer one is counted by LENGTH.

SIZE Operator. Using the SIZE operator is equivalent to multiplying the LENGTH of a variable by its TYPE value. For example, the following array of 16-bit values has a type of 2 and a length of 20h. Its size is 40h:

```
int_array   dw   20h dup(0)    ; SIZE = 0040h
```

The following string has a size of 1 because its length and type are both equal to 1:

```
message  db  'This is a message'
```

The STRUC Directive

The STRUC directive defines a *structure* (template, or pattern) that can be overlaid on an area of memory. A structure can also initialize an area within a program to default values. The individual parts of a structure are called *fields*.

We define a structure much the same as a macro—ahead of the point where it will be used. For example, we can define a structure describing fields from a student record. The following *structure definition* should be placed in the source file ahead of the data segment:

```
st_struc struc       ; begin structure definition

  stnumber  db '0000000'
  lastname  db '                    ' ; 20 spaces
  credits   dw 0
  status    db 0

st_struc ends        ; end of structure
```

The fields within the structure add up to a total of 30 bytes. Within the data segment, we can define a *structure variable* that allocates 30 bytes of memory:

```
.data
srec  st_struc <>
```

The required angle brackets (<>) tell MASM to keep the default field values provided in the structure definition.

Override Default Values. One can override the default values with new ones. The new values must be separated by commas, and each leading field may be skipped by writing a comma. The following statements override various fields in the **st_struc** structure:

```
srec st_struc <'1234567','Irvine',30,1> ; override all fields
myrecord     st_struc <,,50,0>          ; override last two fields
your_record  st_struc <,'Gonzalez'>     ; override second field
```

Note, however, that any fields using the DUP operator in the original structure declaration cannot be overriden. Suppose the **lastname** field in the **st_struc** declaration had been

```
lastname db 20 dup(' ')
```

The following attempt by a structure variable to override this field would generate a syntax error:

```
srec st_struc <,'Jones'>        ;(incorrect)
```

A structure may include the DUP operator, resulting in an array of structures:

```
students  st_struc  100 dup(<>)
```

Using Structure Fields. Once a structure variable has been created, references to individual fields are made by separating the variable name and the field name by a period:

```
mov  dl,srec.stnumber
mov  ax,srec.credits
```

MASM adds the offset of the structure variable to the offset of the field within the structure in order to generate an effective address. In the **st_struc** structure, for example, the offset of **stnumber** is 0, because it is the first field in the structure. The offset of **credits** is 27, the offset of **lastname** is 7, and so on.

If a base or index register points to a structure, a period separates the index from the field:

```
mov  bx,offset srec
.
.
mov  ax,[bx].credits
mov  dl,[bx].status
```

Various other addressing modes may be used, depending upon one's imagination:

```
mov  ax,srec[si].credits
mov  dl,[bx+si].status
mov  dl,srec[bx+di].stnumber
```

The RECORD Directive

The RECORD directive is not to be confused with a *record* in high-level languages. It is, rather, a description of bit groups within a byte or word operand. We use it primarily to make bit masking and bit shifting easier. First, a record must be defined with the record name and the name and width of each field. The syntax for a record definition is:

```
recordname RECORD field [,field] ...
```

The syntax for a *field* is:

```
fieldname:width[= expression]
```

Fieldname is the name of a particular field within the record, and the first field is stored in the most significant bits of the byte or word.

Let's use the RECORD directive to define the bit layout of a 16-bit date stored in the disk directory. You may recall from Chapter 11 that the date is bit-mapped, with 7 bits for the year, 4 bits for the month, and 5 bits for the day of the month:

```
1 1 1 1 1 1 1 1 1 1 1 1 1 1 1 1
└───year────┘ └month┘ └──day──┘
```

A suitable use of the RECORD directive for the date would be:

```
date_record record  year:7, month:4, day:5
```

Notice that each field name must be followed by its width, expressed as the number of bits. It is also possible to give default values to the fields. Let's initialize **date_record** to January 1, 1980 (a year value of 0 indicates 1980):

```
date_record record  year:7 = 0, month:4 = 1, day:5 = 1
```

If one defines a record containing 8 bits or less, the record automatically refers to a byte; otherwise, it refers to a word.

If some bit positions are unused, the bit fields are right justified. For example, the following record defines only 12 bits. MASM sets the bits to the low positions in the field and sets the unused high 4 bits to 0:

```
bitrec record field1:6 = 111111b, field2:6 = 111111b
```

The value of the entire 16 bits is:

```
0000111111111111
```

Creating a Record Variable. Once a record has been defined, it may be used to create a *record variable*. The syntax is:

```
[name] recordname < [initialvalue [,initialvalue]] ...>
```

You can assign a starting value to any of the bit fields. If the assigned value is too large, MASM will display an error message.

Let's create a record variable, using the **date_record** defined earlier. The following declaration retains the default values (0, 1, 1) for January 1, 1980:

```
date_record record  year:7 = 0, month:4 = 1, day:5 = 1
.
.
daterec  date_record <>
```

On the other hand, we might want to initialize **daterec** to May 30, 1990:

```
daterec date_record <10,5,30>
```

Shifting and Masking. Last of all, the field names in a record help you to mask and shift the bit fields more easily. In Chapter 11 we retrieved the date stamp of a file, using INT 21h. The 4 bits making up the month number were isolated, using the SHR and AND instructions. Here we have modified the approach by ANDing AX first and then shifting it to the right:

```
mov  ax,file_date          ; get the date
and  ax,0000000111100000b  ; clear unused bits
mov  cl,5
shr  ax,cl                 ; shift right 5 bits
```

MASK Operator. If we have used the RECORD directive to define **date_record**, we can improve the preceding statements. The MASK operator creates a bit mask. All bits corresponding to the field position are set, but all other bits are cleared:

```
mov   ax,file_date      ; get the date
and   ax,mask month     ; clear unused bits
mov   cl,month
shr   ax,cl             ; shift right 5 bits
```

When **date_record** is defined, MASM automatically assigns a numeric value to each field, depending on its *shift value*. This may be interpreted as the field's bit offset from bit position 0. In the foregoing example, **month** was moved to CL, affecting the shift count. The following table shows the shift value of each field (the same technique would work for the **day** and **year** fields):

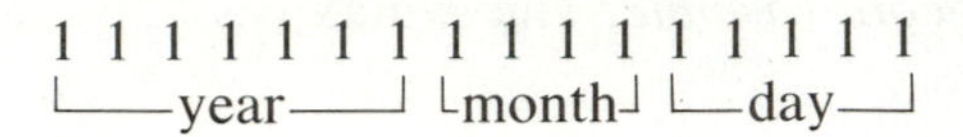

Field	Shift Value
year	9
month	5
day	0

WIDTH Operator. The WIDTH operator returns the number of bits in a record field. The following example shows the width value returned for each of the fields in **date_record**, as well as the width of the record itself:

```
date_record record  year:7 = 0, month:4 = 1, day:5 = 1
.
.
size_of_year   equ  width year      ; width = 7
size_of_month  equ  width month     ; width = 4

.code
mov  ax,width day                   ; width = 5

if (width date_record) gt 8         ; 16-bit record?
  mov  ax,daterec                   ; move to AX
else                                ; 8-bit record?
  mov  al,daterec                   ; move to AL
endif
.
.
.data
daterec date_record <>
```

POINTS TO REMEMBER

Macros. A macro is a symbolic name given to one or more assembly language statements. Macros may be used to generate instructions or data definitions. A macro must be defined before it may be called. A macro definition generates no code or data storage, but each macro call generates a copy of the statements in the macro. For this reason, macros tend to make programs larger when they are called more than once.

A macro definition may include dummy parameters, which are symbolic names used within the macro statements. When the macro is called, arguments are passed that replace the dummy parameters. In this way, the statements generated by a macro may vary each time it is called.

Some sample macros introduced in this chapter were:

PUTCHAR	Display a character
DISPLAY	Display a string
LOCATE	Locate the cursor
DISPLAY_AT	Combine the LOCATE and DISPLAY macros
STARTUP	Set up DS and ES, and get the DOS command tail
REPEAT	Display a character multiple times
CALL_WRITEINT	Call the WRITEINT procedure
GOTOXY	Locate the cursor at column, row
WRITE	Display a literal
CCALL	Conditional procedure call
CMPJ	Compare operands and jump to label
MMOVE	Memory to memory 8/16-bit move
LLOOP	Long loop to any near label
MSHL	Multiple shift left instructions
M&STYP	All eight multiple shifts and rotates

The purpose of using macros in your programs is not to make them more complicated or to emulate a high-level language. No doubt, you could completely rewrite assembly language as a collection of macros. The problem with this approach is that someone reading your code would still have to look at the code generated by the assembler to know exactly what was going on.

Use macros to make both coding and debugging of your programs as easy as possible. This allows you to concentrate on the application being written.

Operators. A number of advanced operators were introduced in this chapter. For instance, the SEG operator obtains the segment address of a label; the TYPE operator returns the number of bytes in each data object of a variable; the LENGTH operator returns the number of individual elements in a variable defined using DUP; and using the SIZE operator is the same as multiplying a variable's TYPE by its LENGTH.

STRUC. The STRUC directive defines a structured variable containing elements of different sizes (called a *record* in Pascal or COBOL). A structure definition is a lot like a pattern or template, which can be applied to any area of memory.

RECORD. The RECORD directive defines bit patterns within a byte or word variable. It can define a template that overlays an existing variable, or it can allocate memory for a new variable. Each field name in a record automatically implies a width, a bit mask, and a shift count.

REVIEW QUESTIONS

1. Write a macro called PUSH_DATAREGS that pushes AX, BX, CX, and DX on the stack, and another macro called POP_DATAREGS that pops the same registers off the stack.

2. Write a macro that creates a data definition for a buffer. Pass the length of the buffer as an argument.

3. Write a macro called READ that reads a sequential data file into a memory buffer. Pass the handle of a currently open file, the name of the input buffer, and the number of bytes to be read. A sample call is as follows:

```
read  infile, inbuf, 80
```

4. Write a macro called DEFINE_STR that creates a data definition for a literal. Pass the literal as an argument, and return a pointer to the ASCIIZ string containing the literal. Sample macro call:

```
define_str  'This is a literal.',SI
```

5. The following TJNZ macro tests a destination operand with a source operand and jumps to a label based on the Zero flag. For example, it may be called thus:

```
tjnz al,1,NZ,L2   ; (test AL,1 and jump if not zero to L2)
```

Find and correct any errors in the macro:

```
tjnz macro dest,source,result,label
   test source,dest
   j%result label
endm
```

6. For each of the following variables, supply its TYPE, LENGTH, and SIZE values:

	Variable	TYPE	LENGTH	SIZE
a.	var1 dd 5 dup(0)			
b.	var2 dw 10 dup(0FFFFh)			
c.	var3 db 20			
d.	msg db 'Hello there'			

7. Assume that the following structure has been defined:

```
rental_st struc
  invoice_num  db  5 dup(' ')
  daily_price  dw  ?
  days_rented  dw  ?
rental_st ends
```

State whether each of the following structure variable declarations are valid or invalid:
a. rentals rental_st <>
b. rental_st rentals <>
c. march rental_st <'12345',10,0>
d. rental_st <,10,0>
e. current rental_st <,15,0,0>

8. Assume that the following record has been defined:

```
myrec record  fld1:4,fld2:3,fld3:3,fld4:6
```

State whether each of the following record variable declarations are valid or invalid:
a. myrec rec1 <>
b. db myrec <5>
c. rec1 myrec <5,2>
d. rec1 myrec <16,2,8>
e. bit_pattern myrec <,,,3>

9. Assume that the following record has been defined:

```
myrec record  fld1:4,fld2:3,fld3:3,fld4:6
```

Give the mask, shift, and width values in hexadecimal for each of the fields (the first is done for you):

	Field	Mask	Shift	Width
	fld1	F000h	0Ch	4
a.	fld2			
b.	fld3			
c.	fld4			

10. Assume that the following macro has been defined:

```
repeat macro char,count
    local L1
    mov  cx,count
L1: mov  ah,2
    mov  dl,char
    int  21h
    loop L1
endm
```

Write the code that will be generated by MASM when the macro is called as follows:

```
repeat 'X',50
```

11. Assume that the following macro has been defined:

```
gotoXY macro xval,yval

        if xval LT 0          ; xval < 0?
          exitm               ; if so, exit
        endif

        if yval LT 0          ; yval < 0?
          exitm               ; if so, exit
        endif

        mov    bx,0           ; choose video page 0
        mov    ah,2           ; locate cursor
        mov    dh,yval
        mov    dl,xval
        int    10h            ; call the BIOS

endm
```

Write the code that will be generated by MASM if the macro is called as follows:

```
gotoXY  -2,20
```

12. Assume that the following macro has been defined:

```
mymsg macro num,string
  msg&num db  'Status: &string',0
endm
```

Write the statement that will be generated when the macro is called as follows:

```
mymsg  10,<Currently printing.>
```

13. Write the statements that will be generated by the following repeat macro:

```
irp  val,<100,20,30>
  db  0,0,0,val
endm
```

PROGRAMMING EXERCISES

Exercise 1 **MASM Operators**

Write a program that demonstrates each of the following operators:

SEG
SHORT
HIGH, LOW
LENGTH
TYPE
SIZE

In the listing file, circle the values generated by MASM each time one of the preceding operators was used.

Exercise 2 Student File Structure

Modify the Student File program from Chapter 12. Use the STRUC directive to define the record format for the student record. Use the structure to allocate space for **student_record**.

Exercise 3 Date Stamp Record

Modify the Date Stamp program from Chapter 11 (Figure 11-9). Use the RECORD directive to define the bit fields. Use the mask and shift values defined in the record fields to extract and display the date.

Exercise 4 Call WRITEINT with a Macro

Modify the WRITEINT procedure from Chapter 9 as follows. If DL = 1, WRITEINT writes an optional carriage return (0Dh,0Ah) after the number. The calling program passes a file/device handle in DH that is used when writing the number. This means, of course, that DOS function 40h (write to a file or device) should be used:

AX	Value to be written
BX	Radix to be used
DH	File/device handle to be used
DL	Carriage return flag

Once the procedure is tested by passing all parameters in registers, write a macro to make the procedure call smoother. Include the following parameters in the macro definition:

VALUE	The 16-bit value to be displayed
RADIX	Numeric radix to be used: 2, 8, 10, or 16
CRETURN	Write a carriage return? (1 = true, 0 = false)
DEVICE	Output device (1 = console, 4 = printer, *nn* = currently open file handle)

Write a program to test the macro. Call the macro at least 10 times, using every combination of valid arguments you can create. Then pass it a few invalid arguments to see if the macro handles the error as smoothly as possible. For example, you might pass a radix of 50 or pass a file handle that is not open.

The macro should still work properly if the caller passes arguments in registers. At the beginning of the macro, you may want to save a copy of the arguments in variables or on the stack in order to avoid inadvertently changing a register that contains an argument. (This problem was mentioned earlier in the chapter when discussing the LOCATE macro.)

Exercise 5 Enhanced MULT Macro

The MULT macro introduced in this chapter has one limitation: AX cannot be used as the source operand. Revise the macro and eliminate this restriction so any register may be used as the source operand.

Further, enhance the macro so it will allow an 8-bit source operand to be multiplied by a 16-bit destination operand.

Hint: Use the TYPE operator to determine the size of each parameter.

Exercise 6 The DOIF Macro

Write a macro called DOIF that executes a given instruction when a condition is true. Sample calls are as follows:

```
cmp  bx,20                        ; compare two values
doif E, <mov ax,bx>               ; execute if BX = 20
cmp  cx,count
doif B, <call subroutine_1>       ; execute if CX < count
```

The first argument is the condition to be tested, which may be any of the following:

E, NE, Z, NZ, B, A, BE, AE, C, NC, G, NG, GE, L, NL, LE

The second argument must be enclosed in angle brackets (<>) when it contains more than one word. Test the macro by calling it several times from the same program. Be sure to use the LOCAL directive to avoid duplicate labels.

Exercise 7 Keyboard Input Macro

Write a keyboard input macro with the following parameters:

INBUF	Offset of the input buffer created by the macro
MAX	Maximum number of characters to be input
NUMCHARS	Number of characters actually input (returned by the macro)

Let the macro allocate its own storage for the input buffer, the length of which is determined by the value of MAX. Write a program to test the macro, calling it at least five times.

Exercise 8 Enhanced Keyboard Input Macro

Enhance the keyboard input macro described in Exercise 7. Write a program that calls the macro at least five times, passing it a wide variety of arguments. Define the macro with the following parameters:

INBUF	Offset of the input buffer created by the macro
MAX	Maximum number of characters to be input
NUMCHARS	Number of characters actually input (returned by the macro)
RANGE_L	Lowest ASCII code to be allowed as input
RANGE_H	Highest ASCII code to be allowed as input

The RANGE_L and RANGE_H parameters are 8-bit values that limit the input to a specified range of ASCII codes. For example, values of 30h and 39h would limit keyboard input to the characters 0 through 9. Values of 41h and 5Ah would limit input to uppercase letters.

RANGE_L and RANGE_H should be optional parameters. If they are blank when the macro is called, assign default values (0 and 255).

Exercise 9 The SCROLL Macro

Write a SCROLL macro that will scroll a window on the screen. Include the following parameters in the macro definition:

ULROW	Upper-left window row
ULCOL	Upper-left window column
LRROW	Lower-right window row
LRCOL	Lower-right window column
NLINES	Number of lines to scroll (optional)
DIR	Direction to scroll (optional: up or down)
ATTRIB	Attribute or color of scrolled lines (optional)

If NLINES is blank, the entire window is to be scrolled (cleared). If DIR is blank, the window is to be scrolled up. If ATTRIB is blank, use an attribute of 7 (normal). Sample calls:

```
scroll                   ; scroll entire screen up, normal attribute
scroll 0,0,24,79         ; scroll entire screen up, normal attribute
scroll 5,10,20,70,1      ; scroll a window up 1 line
scroll ,,,,1,D           ; scroll entire screen down 1 line
scroll 5,10,20,70,,,70h  ; scroll entire window up in reverse video
```

Exercise 10 CREATE Macro

Write and test a macro that creates a new file. Include the following parameters:

FILENAME	The name of a variable containing an ASCIIZ file specification.
HANDLE	A 16-bit file handle returned by DOS after the file has been created.

STATUS A 16-bit value set to 0 if the file was created successfully; otherwise set to a DOS error code.

ATTRIB The desired file attribute. If the parameter is blank, use a normal attribute. Other valid argument values are:
- R Read-only
- H Hidden
- M Hidden and read-only
- S System

When decoding the ATTRIB values, use the IFIDNI directive, as it ignores differences between uppercase and lowercase letters.

Exercise 11 CONSOLE Library Macros

Choose four string manipulation procedures from the CONSOLE library introduced in Chapter 10, and write macros that call them in a more flexible manner. Write a program to test the macros. For example, the STRCHR procedure uses the character in AL to find a match in the string pointed to by DS:DI. A sample macro to call STRCHR follows. Notice that we must check to see if DI has been passed as the **position** parameter. Without checking, we might erase the value when DI is popped from the stack:

```
m_strchr macro char,string,position

        push   ax                    ; save AX, DI
        push   di
        mov    al,char               ; character to be found
        mov    di,offset string      ; string to be searched
        call   strchr                ; call CONSOLE routine

        ifidni  <position>,<di>      ; position = DI?
          pop    ax                  ; yes: don't change it
        else
          mov    position,di         ; no: move DI to position
          pop    di                  ; restore DI
        endif

        pop    ax                    ; restore AX

endm
```

(The POP AX instruction after the IFIDINI directive is just a dummy pop so that the stack will be restored correctly.)

Sample calls to the M_STRCHR macro:

```
m_strchr  'A',buf1,bx      ; find 'A' in buf1, store position in BX
m_strchr  'B',buf1,di      ; find 'B' in buf1, store position in DI
m_strchr  char,buf1,result ; find char in buf1, store position in result
.
.
char   db  'E'
buf1   db  'ABCDEFG',0
result dw  ?
```

ANSWERS TO REVIEW QUESTIONS

1.

```
push_dataregs macro          pop_dataregs macro
     push  ax                     pop  dx
     push  bx                     pop  cx
     push  cx                     pop  bx
     push  dx                     pop  ax
endm                         endm
```

2.

```
allocate macro len
   db  len dup(0)     ; allocate the buffer
endm
```

3.

```
read macro handle,buffer,count
   mov  ah,3Fh
   mov  bx,handle
   mov  cx,count
   mov  dx,offset buffer
   int  21h
endm
```

4.

```
define_str  macro literal, strptr
   local start
   .code
   mov strptr, offset start
   .data
   start label byte
   db &literal,0
   .code
endm
```

5. The corrected form follows (there were two errors):

```
tjnz macro dest,source,result,label
   test dest,source
   j&result label
endm
```

6. a. type = 4, length = 5, size = 20
   b. type = 2, length = 10, size = 20
   c. type = 1, length = 1, size = 1
   d. type = 1, length = 1, size = 1

7. a. valid
   b. invalid: the structure name must follow the variable name
   c. invalid: it may not override the DUP field
   d. valid
   e. invalid: too many arguments

8. a. invalid: the record name must follow the variable name
   b. valid
   c. valid
   d. invalid: the first argument is too large
   e. valid

9. a. mask = 0E00h, shift = 09, width = 3
   b. mask = 01C0h, shift = 06, width = 3
   c. mask = 003Fh, shift = 00, width = 6

10. The generated code is as follows:

```
         mov  cx,50
??0000:  mov  ah,2
         mov  dl,'X'
         int  21h
         loop ??0000
```

11. No code will be generated, because the following conditional directive checks to see if **xval** is less than zero:

```
if xval LT 0      ; xval < 0?
  exitm           ; if so, exit
endif
```

12. The generated statement will be:

```
msg10 db 'Status: Currently printing.',0
```

13. The statements will be:

```
db 0,0,0,100
db 0,0,0,20
db 0,0,0,30
```

14

Advanced Topics

IBM-PC SYSTEM HARDWARE

The system board components introduced in Chapter 2 were just a small part of the overall hardware on the IBM-PC. Other devices on the system board are listed here (all are produced by the Intel Corporation):

- The *8087 Math Coprocessor* is an optional coprocessor chip that handles floating-point and extended integer calculations (covered in Chapter 15).
- The *8284 Clock Generator,* known simply as the *clock,* oscillates at a speed ranging from 4.77 megahertz (MHz) on the original IBM-PC to 25 MHz on some machines using the 80386 processor. The clock generator synchronizes the CPU and the rest of the computer.
- The *8259A Interrupt Controller* handles external interrupts from hardware devices such as the keyboard, system clock, and disk drives. These devices literally "interrupt" the CPU and make it process their requests immediately.
- The *8255 Programmable Peripheral Interface* speeds up parallel input-output between the CPU and peripherals such as disk drives and the video display.

- The *8237 DMA Controller* handles transfers of data to and from memory, freeing the CPU to do other work.
- The *8253 Programmable Interval Timer/Counter* interrupts the system 18.2 times per second, updates the system date and clock, and controls the speaker. It is also responsible for constantly refreshing memory, since RAM memory chips can remember their data for only a few milliseconds.

On the expansion cards, three processors are used on the original IBM-PC:

- The *Motorola 6845 Video Controller,* used on both monochrome and color video adapter cards, is responsible for all details of the video display.
- The *Intel 8272 Floppy Disk Controller,* located on the disk controller card, handles the interface between the operating system and the physical details of different disk drives.
- The *Intel 8251 Programmable Serial Interface Controller* is the controller for the asynchronous communications port. This chip handles *handshaking,* that is, the way serial devices and computers communicate with each other.

The CPU

The various parts of the Intel 8088 processor are seen in Figure 14-1. Along the sides of the chip are 40 pins that plug into a socket in the system board, connecting it to the rest of the computer system. The registers are inside the CPU. The CPU transfers data and instructions through the system via the data and

Figure 14-1 Basic Intel 8088 architecture (conceptual drawing only).

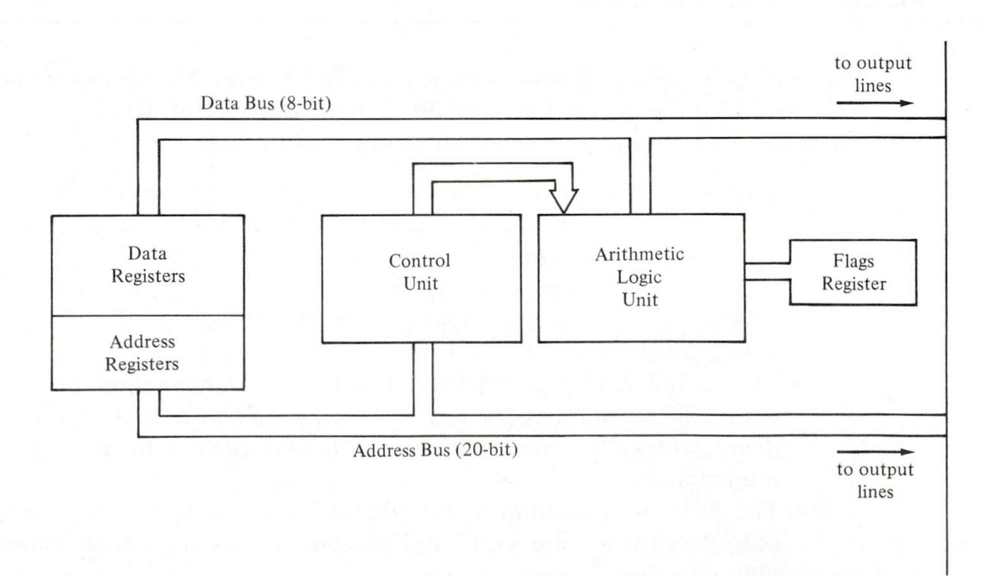

address buses. The *data bus* transfers data between the CPU registers and memory or between the CPU and the input-output chips. The *address bus* is used to transfer the addresses (locations) of instructions and data. The *clock* synchronizes the CPU with the data and instruction buses.

The CPU is logically divided into two parts: The *arithmetic logic unit* (*ALU*) carries out arithmetic, logical, and shifting operations. The *control unit* (*CU*) fetches data, increments the program counter, and decodes addresses for the ALU. The ALU is also known as the *execution unit* (*EU*), and the CU is also known as the *bus interface unit* (*BIU*).

Instruction Cycle. When the CPU executes an instruction, it goes through an instruction cycle containing three basic steps: *fetch, decode,* and *execute*:

1. The CU fetches the instruction, copying it from memory into the CPU.
2. The CU increments the program counter and decodes the instruction. If other operands are specified by the instruction, the CU decodes their addresses and fetches the operands. It passes the instruction and operands to the ALU via the *prefetch queue,* a 4-byte area that acts as a waiting area for the ALU.
3. The ALU executes the operation and passes the result operands to the CU, where they are returned to registers and memory.

Each step in the instruction cycle takes at least one tick of the system clock, called a *clock cycle*.

One of the most important developments in microprocessors is their division of labor between the ALU and the CU, allowing them to work in parallel. Instead of waiting for the ALU to finish each instruction, the CU fetches the next instruction from memory and loads it into the instruction queue.

Calculating Instruction Timings

There are applications in data communications, engineering, and realtime processing that require us to choose the most efficient way to code a group of instructions. By calculating the relative amount of time different instructions take to execute, we can write better programs. In order to calculate the time taken for a particular instruction, one must know the following:

The CPU type (8088, 8086, 80286, etc.)

The clock speed of the CPU

The instruction mnemonic

The addressing mode

Because of the great variety of CPUs available for the IBM-PC family, we won't deal with the possible variations on CPUs and clock speeds. Instead, we will select the original IBM-PC whose clock speed is 4.77 MHz, with the understanding that the same principles apply to other IBM-compatible computers. You can find a list of instruction times for each of the CPUs in Intel's reference manuals.

Clock Cycles. We measure the speed of an instruction by the number of clock cycles required to execute it. The speed of the clock itself is determined by the chip manufacturer and the computer designer. A CPU might be capable of running at 16 MHz, for example, but the memory chips might be able to respond at only 10 MHz. In general, a computer system is designed as a compromise between the abilities of each of its components.

Each instruction takes a specific number of clock cycles to execute, depending on the types of operands. For example, the INC instruction is one of the fastest, requiring as few as 2 clock cycles (called *clocks*):

INC INSTRUCTION TIMINGS

Operand Type	8-Bit	16-Bit	
Register	3	2	
Memory	15	23	(plus effective address)

A 16-bit INC is much faster when incrementing a register rather than a memory operand. This is true for nearly all instructions, so one tends to use registers when speed is the primary goal.

Effective Address. A memory operand requires extra work by the 8088 CPU: Its address must be decoded, and the operand must be fetched. The clock time depends on the addressing mode used; predictably, more advanced addressing modes require more time. The Intel 80286 and 80386 processors, on the other hand, are able to calculate effective addresses using hardware. Instruction timings are affected only by the *based indexed with displacement* addressing mode (e.g. [BX+SI+2].

The following table shows how many additional clocks each memory addressing mode adds to an instruction on the 8088 processor:

EFFECTIVE ADDRESS CALCULATION (FOR MEMORY OPERANDS)

Addressing Mode	Additional Clocks	Operand Types
Direct	6	disp
Register indirect	5	[bx], [bp], [si], [di]
Based	9	disp[si], disp[di]
		disp[bx], disp[bp]
Based indexed	7	[bp+di], [bx+si]
	8	[bp+si], [bx+di]
Based indexed with	11	[bp+di+2], [bx+si+3]
displacement	12	[bp+si+1], [bx+di+4]

(add 2 more clocks for a segment override)

Execution Time. Using this table, we know the required time for the following instruction would be 23 clocks, using a 16-bit memory operand, plus 9 clocks for the effective address:

```
INC word ptr table[bx]
```

The instruction would take 32 clocks, as opposed to the 2 clocks required for a register operand. That represents a 16:1 difference in execution speed.

To calculate the actual execution time of an instruction, we need to take the speed of the CPU into account. If a CPU operates at 4.77 MHz, 1 clock cycle takes 1/4,770,000 of a second (0.00000020964 seconds). Using the INC instruction that requires 32 clocks, multiply 32 by 0.00000020964, giving a total instruction time of 0.0000067086 seconds.

LOOP Example. We can easily calculate how long a loop takes to execute. The following routine clears the high bit from each character in a buffer. Let's calculate the time taken by the instructions beginning at the label L1:

```
    mov   di,offset buffer   ; point to buffer
    mov   cx,1000            ; loop count
L1: and   byte ptr [di],7Fh  ; clear high bit
    inc   di                 ; point to next
    loop  L1                 ; repeat until CX = 0
    .
    .
buffer    db 1000 dup(?)
```

The AND instruction here takes 22 clocks: 17 for the instruction itself and 5 more to calculate the effective address. The INC instruction takes 2 clocks. The LOOP instruction takes 17 clocks each time it repeats (the very last time, it takes only 5 clocks). Therefore, each iteration of the loop takes 41 clocks:

$$22 + 2 + 17 = 41 \text{ clocks}$$

The loop will be repeated 1,000 times, so we multiply 41 by 1,000:

$$(41 * 1{,}000) = 41{,}000 \text{ clocks}$$

Now we multiply this by the clock time (0.00000020964), and the result is a fairly accurate representation of the loop timing:

$$41{,}000 * 0.00000020964 \approx 0.0086 \text{ seconds}$$

This tends to put time into perspective, when you consider that it would take at least 1/4 second to open a file and fill a buffer of 1,000 bytes from a floppy disk. It would then take only 8.6 thousandths of a second more to clear all the high bits!

The Prefetch Queue. But wait a moment—our simple method of calculating instruction times is not perfect. You may recall that the CU fetches instructions and places them in a 4-byte *prefetch queue*. There they are held until the ALU can execute them. Whenever the ALU is busy executing an instruction, the BIU is busy refilling the queue. (The 8086 and 80286 processors have a 6-byte prefetch queue.)

It takes the 8088 4 clock cycles to fetch an instruction from memory and load it into the queue. As long as the ALU is executing an instruction that takes at least 4 clocks, the CU keeps up quite well. But the prefetch queue is depleted when instructions of less than 4 clocks are executed. The following instructions each take 2 clocks to execute and are 2 bytes long:

```
shl  al,1
shl  al,1
shl  al,1
```

Let's assume that the prefetch queue was full when we started. After 6 clocks have passed, the 4 bytes in the queue have been depleted, and the CU has not had enough time to fetch the fourth instruction. This means the ALU will have to wait for the queue to be filled before going on. Therefore, it is more efficient to write the following than to code five individual shift instructions:

```
mov  cl,5
shl  al,cl
```

Loop Example Compiled by a High-Level Language. Let us look at the same loop example written in Pascal. By comparing the number of clock cycles (41 for the assembly language version versus 134 for the Pascal version), we see that the former is over three times faster. The Pascal source code is listed here:

```
PROGRAM Buffertest;
VAR
  buffer :ARRAY[1..1000] OF BYTE;
  n :integer;
BEGIN
  FOR n := 1 TO 1000 DO
    buffer[n] := buffer[n] AND $7F;
END.
```

The disassembled code produced by the Pascal compiler follows. The original Pascal statements have been inserted to make the listing clearer. To the right of each instruction within the loop is the number of required clock cycles:

```
FOR n := 1 TO 1000 DO
     mov    N,offset buffer + 1
     jmp    L2
buffer[n] := buffer[n] AND $7F;   (clocks)
L1:  inc    word ptr N            ; 29
L2:  mov    di,N                  ; 12
     mov    al,[di-1]             ; 17
     and    al,7Fh                ; 4
     mov    di,N                  ; 18
     mov    [di-1],al             ; 18
     cmp    N,1000                ; 20
     jnz    L1                    ; 16  Total clocks: 134
```

You can see the assembly instructions by loading a compiled program into memory with a debugger. It is worthwhile to disassemble the code, because it gives you a glimpse of how high-level languages work. The code compiled by the Pascal program in our example is fairly efficient; there is no obvious duplication. But there is no question that if speed is your goal, you can write much faster code in assembly language.

Near Calls and Far Calls. Much has been written in IBM-PC programming literature about using near calls as much as possible, rather than far calls to procedures in other segments. The difference stems from the fact that a far call requires both CS and IP to be pushed on the stack and both registers to be set to the segment/offset address of the subroutine.

We can see just how much difference there is between the two by measuring the relative execution times. In the following example, the call to NEARPROC requires (23 + 20) = 43 clocks, while the call to FARPROC requires (36 + 32) = 68 clocks, or nearly twice as much time:

```
cseg segment

main proc
    call   nearproc     ; 23 clocks
    call   farproc      ; 36 clocks
main  endp

nearproc proc
    ret                 ; 20 clocks (near return)
nearproc endp

cseg ends

otherseg segment        ; new segment begins here
```

```
farproc proc far          ; far procedure
    ret                   ; 32 clocks (far return)
farproc endp

otherseg ends
```

The Intel Microprocessor Family

The recent history of the Intel microprocessor family begins with the Intel 8080 processor, an 8-bit CPU that accessed a maximum of 64K of memory and contained 8-bit registers. This was superseded by the Z80 processor, produced by Zilog, Inc. The Z80 was the foundation of the famous CP/M operating system, which was a major influence on the microcomputer world prior to the appearance of the IBM-PC. Both the Z80 and the 8080 operate primarily on 8-bit operands, limiting them in terms of speed and memory addressing.

The iAPX 8088. The Intel iAPX 8088 was next, providing a major advance over the 8-bit microprocessors. Used on the original IBM-PC and PC/XT, it manipulates both 8-bit and 16-bit values and uses 20 bits to address memory. Because of this, the 8088 is able to address up to 1 MB of memory.

The 8088's greater addressing ability makes it possible for programs on 8088-based machines to be much larger than was previously possible. Software developers have taken advantage of this capability. DOS has more than doubled in size since it was introduced, and many programs require a full 640K of memory.

The iAPX 8086. The 8086 is the more powerful cousin of the 8088, with exactly the same instruction set and memory addressing, but with greater speed. The 8086 has a 16-bit data bus, so it can input and output 16-bit values directly to ports and memory. The 8088, by contrast, uses an 8-bit data bus.

Downward Compatibility. One can tie the advancement of microcomputers in recent years directly to advances in microprocessor chip design. More advanced processor chips seem to appear each year, but there has been a conscious effort by manufacturers such as Intel to make the new chips downwardly compatible. This means programs written for the older processors (such as the 8088) will run on the newer processors, such as the iAPX 80286 and iAPX 80386.

Recent Advances. After the Intel 8086 processor, the Intel iAPX 80186 was a short-lived improvement, with an 8-MHz clock and ten new instructions intended to increase the processor's efficiency. At the same time, the 80186 could execute all instructions used on the 8088 and 8086.

The Intel iAPX 80286 quickly replaced the 80186, with greater speed and power. The 80286 allows up to 16 MB of addressable RAM. Its internal architecture is still 16-bit: The largest operands allowed in instructions are 16 bits long. The 80286 was chosen by IBM for the IBM-AT computer, widely used as an upgrade from the original IBM-PC, and at present, can exceed 12 MHz. One major advance over the earlier processors is the ability of the 80286 to run in either *real address mode* (the same as the 8088) or in *protected mode*. The latter mode allows separate programs to be run in memory at the same time without disturbing each other.

The next step in Intel's evolution was the introduction of the iAPX 80386 processor, first used on the *COMPAQ Deskpro 386* and *IBM RT* computers. The 80386 runs at 16–24 MHz, can address up to 4 billion bytes of real memory, and contains 32-bit instructions. Probably most outstanding is its ability to work with *virtual memory,* a feature previously available only on minicomputers and mainframes. MS-DOS and OS/2 do not yet take advantage of the 80386's features, but future versions probably will.

In the second quarter of 1987, IBM introduced its *IBM Personal System/2* line of microcomputers. The Model 30 uses the Intel 8086 processor, Models 50 and 60 use the Intel 80286, and the Model 80 uses the Intel 80386. Models 50 through 80 use IBM's proprietary *micro-channel bus architecture,* resulting in increased throughput along the system bus. Most importantly, the operating system (OS/2), developed jointly by IBM and Microsoft, is multitasking. *Multitasking,* or *concurrent processing,* is the running of two or more independent programs at the same time.

The OS/2 operating system still runs most DOS applications in its DOS Compatibility Environment, a part of the operating system set aside for this purpose. At the same time, these programs are not multitasking.

It should be noted also that a number of other multitasking operating environments exist for 80286 and 80386-based computers. Among them are UNIX, XENIX, PC-MOS/386, DESQview, Concurrent DOS 386, and Windows/386.†

DEFINING SEGMENTS

The great majority of assembly language programs can use the simplified segment directives provided with MASM. We have used them in this book for two reasons. First, they are compatible with Microsoft C, Pascal, QuickBASIC, and FORTRAN. Second, they are convenient to use and relatively bulletproof. At the same time, what we gain in convenience we sometimes lose in flexibility.

There are a few occasions when you may prefer to code explicit segment definitions. You may wish, for instance, to write a COM-format program in order to keep it as small as possible. A program in COM format must have its segment definition coded manually. Alternatively, you may be writing a routine to be called from a high-level language that does not use Microsoft's segment names.

The SEGMENT and ENDS directives define the beginning and end of a segment. A program may contain almost any number of segments, each with a unique name. Segments can also be grouped together. In short, we can do everything simplified directives do, and more.

Each segment can be up to 65,536 bytes long (0000-FFFFh). Each begins on a 16-byte boundary, so it can be addressed by one of the segment registers. You

†See Ed McNierney, "386 Operating Environments," *PC Tech Journal,* Vol. 6, No. 1, January 1988, for an excellent discussion of operating environments.

may recall that a segment address includes 4 additional implied zero bits. Thus a segment address of 1B65h really represents an absolute address of 1B650h, shown here in binary:

```
0001 1011 0110 0101 0000
   1    B    6    5  └──(4 implied bits)
```

This is why a segment can begin only on a 16-byte boundary: The 4 implied bits of its absolute address are always zeros.

A program with explicit segment definitions has two tasks to perform. First, a segment register (DS, ES, or SS) must be set to the location of each segment before it may be used. Second, MASM must be told how to calculate the offsets of variables in the segments.

The SEGMENT and ENDS Directives

An EXE program needs at least two segments—one for its code and another for its stack. A program containing variables also needs a segment for its data. The SEGMENT directive begins a segment and the ENDS directive ends it. Their syntax is:

```
name SEGMENT [align] [combine] ['class']
statements
name ENDS
```

Align types: BYTE, WORD, DWORD, PARA, PAGE

Combine types: PUBLIC, STACK, COMMON, MEMORY, AT *address*

The segment *name* may be a unique name or the name of another segment.

Align Type. When the segment being defined is to be combined with another segment, the align type tells the linker how many bytes to skip. Sometimes called *slack bytes,* these bytes are inserted between segments to make the CPU more efficient. Again, this only affects segments that are combined—the beginning of the first segment in a group must still begin on a paragraph boundary, because segment addresses always contain four implied low-order bits.

The BYTE align type causes a segment to begin immediately after the previous segment. The WORD align type causes the segment to start on the next 16-bit boundary, and DWORD starts at the next 32-bit boundary. The align type of PARA (the default) starts the segment at the next available 16-byte paragraph boundary. The PAGE align type starts at the next 256-byte boundary.

If a program will likely be run on an 8086 or 80286 processor, a WORD align type is best for data segments. This is because both CPUs have a 16-bit data bus. A variable on an even boundary requires only one memory fetch, while a variable on an odd boundary requires two. Virtually all programs written for the IBM-PC today must run on the PC/AT (which uses the 80286) so the WORD align type should be used. If a program will be run on an 80386 processor, the DWORD align type is most efficient for some operations.

The EVEN directive may also be used within a segment to force the next instruction or variable to an even boundary. In the following example, **var3** would have been located at an odd-numbered address if not for the EVEN directive. Instead, MASM inserts a byte containing 90h (a NOP, or *no operation* instruction) before **var3** to set it to an even address:

```
dseg segment word
  var1   dw  1000h
  var2   db  ?
  even
  var3   dw  2000h
dseg ends
```

The purpose of inserting a NOP is clearer when the EVEN directive is used within the code segment: A NOP instruction is ignored by the CPU.

Combine Type. The combine type tells the linker how to combine segments having the same name. The default type is *private,* meaning that such a segment will not be combined with any other segment.

The PUBLIC and MEMORY combine types cause a segment to be combined with all other public or memory segments by the same name; in effect, they become a single segment. The offsets of all labels are adjusted so they are relative to the start of the same segment.

The STACK combine type resembles the PUBLIC type in that all stack segments will be combined with it. DOS automatically initializes SS to the start of the first segment it finds with a combine type of STACK and sets SP to the segment's length when the program is loaded. In an EXE program, there should be at least one segment with a STACK combine type; otherwise, the linker displays a warning message.

The COMMON combine type makes a segment begin at the same address as any other COMMON segments with the same name. In effect, the segments overlay each other. All offsets are calculated from the same starting address, and variables can overlap.

The AT *address* combine type lets you create a segment at an absolute address. No variables or data may be initialized, but you can create variable names that refer to specific offsets. The keyboard status byte is a good example:

```
BIOS segment at 40h
     org 17h
keyboard_flag  db  ?
BIOS ends
```

Class Type. A segment's class type provides a way of controlling the ordering of segments in an executable program. The class type is simply a string (case insensitive) enclosed in single quotation marks. Segments with the same class type are loaded together, although they may be in a different order in the original program. One standard type, 'CODE', is recognized by the linker and should be used for segments containing instructions. You must include this type label if you plan to use CODEVIEW.

Code Segment. Let us start with the segment containing code, or instructions. If the code is less than 64K in size, we can include all procedures in the same segment:

```
mycode segment 'code'    ; all procedures go here
  main proc
    .
    .
  main endp

  subroutine_1 proc      ; NEAR procedure
    .
    .
  subroutine_1 endp
    .
    .
mycode ends
```

In fact, procedure calls within the same segment are more efficient, because only the offset of the return address is pushed on the stack. A call to a procedure in the same segment is a near call.

If a called procedure is in a different segment, reaching it requires a far call: The current values of CS and IP are pushed on the stack, and then both are set to the segment-offset of the called procedure. The following is an example:

```
mycode segment 'code'   ; starting code segment

  main proc
    call  near_routine  ; near call
    call  far_routine   ; far call
    .
    .
  main endp

  near_routine proc     ; accessed via a NEAR call
    .
    .
  near_routine endp

mycode ends             ; end of MYCODE segment

;---------------------------------------------------
```

```
otherseg segment 'code' ; this is a separate segment

  far_routine proc      ; accessed via a FAR call
    .
    .
  far_routine endp
    .
    .
otherseg ends
```

This would not be as common when all procedures are in the same program module, but it could likely happen if modules were compiled separately and later linked together. An example is shown here:

```
PROG1.ASM:

    mycode segment 'code'     ; main procedure here
      main proc
        call subroutine_x     ; far call
        .
      main endp
    mycode ends

SUB1.ASM:

    otherseg segment 'code'   ; this is a separate segment

      subroutine_x proc       ; calls to these procedures
        .                     ; are far calls
        .
      subroutine_x endp

      subroutine_y proc
        .
        .
      subroutine_y endp

    otherseg ends
```

The Data Segment. Normally, all variables are placed in a separate *data* segment. It can have any name, unless the assembly program is being called from a high-level language. In the latter case, certain segment-naming conventions may apply. With Microsoft high-level languages, for example, the data segment is called _DATA.

When an EXE program is loaded into memory, DS and ES point to the PSP. It is your responsibility to set them to the start of the segment containing data. For example:

```
        mov    ax,mydata
        mov    ds,ax
        mov    es,ax
        .
        .
mydata segment 'data'     (variables here)
   .
   .
mydata ends
```

The ASSUME Directive

The ASSUME directive makes it possible for MASM to calculate the offsets of labels and variables at assembly time. It is usually placed directly after the SEGMENT directive in the code segment, but you can have as many additional ASSUMEs as you like. Each time a new one is encountered, MASM modifies the way it calculates addresses.

In the following example, ASSUME tells MASM to use DS as the default register for the MYDATA segment. CS is identified as the default segment register for CSEG, and SS is associated with MYSTACK:

```
title  Segment Example

cseg  segment 'code'          ; class type is CODE
assume cs:cseg, ds:mydata, ss:mystack
main proc
    mov   ax,mydata           ; point DS to MYDATA
    mov   ds,ax
    mov   bx,value1 + 2       ; requires ASSUME DS:MYDATA
    jmp   L1                  ; requires ASSUME CS:CSEG
    push  ax
    pop   ax
L1: mov   ax,4C00h            ; return to DOS
    int   21h
main endp
cseg  ends

mydata segment 'data'         ; class type is DATA
  value1  dw  1000h,2000h
mydata ends

mystack segment stack         ; combine type is STACK
    db  100h dup('S')
mystack ends
end main
```

Notice that we must still set DS to the start of MYDATA, because DOS always initializes DS to the start of the PSP when the program is loaded. The ASSUME for CSEG makes it possible to refer to labels in the code area of the program:

```
jmp  L1
```

The ASSUME for MYDATA makes it possible to address variables in that segment:

```
mov   bx,value1 + 2        ; requires ASSUME DS:MYDATA
```

The ASSUME for MYSTACK is not required in this example and is included simply for completeness. There is only one segment in this program declared with a combine type of STACK, so MASM automatically sets SS to its starting location.

The most common mistake made by beginners in regard to ASSUME is their belief that the directive will change the values in DS and ES. Nothing could be further from the truth. One must change these registers at *runtime* by moving the segment addresses into DS and ES.

Segment Override Operator. The segment override operator (:) tells MASM to calculate an offset relative to a segment other than the instruction's default segment. For example, there may be a variable in the code segment that you want to access. The MOV instruction assumes DS is the default segment register, but you can override it:

```
mov   al,cs:localvariable
```

You may wish to access a variable in a segment currently pointed to by ES:

```
mov es:variable1,ax
```

The following instruction obtains the offset of a variable in a segment not currently pointed to by either DS or ES:

```
mov   bx,offset otherseg:var2
```

If more than a few instructions must be overridden, you can use an ASSUME to change the default segment references:

```
assume ds:otherseg
mov   ax,otherseg   ; set DS to otherseg
mov   ds,ax
mov   al,var1
.
.
```

```
mov   ax,mydata     ; set DS to mydata
mov   ds,ax
assume ds:mydata
```

Combining Segments. Multiple segments may be combined by giving them the same name and specifying a PUBLIC combine type. This happens even if the segments are in separate program modules. If you use a BYTE align type, each segment will immediately follow the previous one. If a WORD align type is used, the segments will follow at the next even word boundary. The align type defaults to PARA, in which each segment follows at the next paragraph boundary.

Figure 14-2 shows two program modules with two code segments, two data segments, and one stack segment that combine to form only three segments: CSEG, DSEG, and SSEG. The main module contains all three segments, and both CSEG and DSEG are given a PUBLIC combine type. A BYTE align type is used for CSEG to avoid creating a gap between the two CSEG segments when they are combined.

Figure 14-2 Multimodule program with combined segments.

```
title    Segment Example (main module,  SEG1.ASM)

extrn var2:word, subroutine_1:proc

cseg  segment byte public 'code'
assume cs:cseg,ds:dseg, ss:sseg

main proc
    mov   ax,dseg         ; initialize DS
    mov   ds,ax

    mov   ax,var1         ; local variable
    mov   bx,var2         ; external variable
    call  subroutine_1    ; external procedure

    mov   ax,4C00h
    int   21h
main endp
cseg  ends

dseg segment word public 'data'   ; local data segment
  var1  dw  1000h
dseg ends

sseg segment stack        ; stack segment
    db  100h dup('S')
sseg ends
end main
```

Figure 14-2 *(Cont.)*

```
title  Segment Example (submodule, SEG1A.ASM)

public subroutine_1, var2

cseg  segment byte public 'code'
assume cs:cseg, ds:dseg

subroutine_1 proc                    ; called from MAIN
    mov   ah,9
    mov   dx,offset msg
    int   21h
    ret
subroutine_1 endp

cseg ends

dseg segment word public 'data'
  var2  dw  2000h                    ; accessed by MAIN
  msg   db  'Now in Subroutine_1'
        db   0Dh,0Ah,'$'
dseg ends
end
```

```
The SEG1.MAP file, showing only three segments:

 Start  Stop   Length Name
 00000H 0001BH 0001CH CSEG  (combined code segments from both modules)
 0001CH 00035H 0001AH DSEG  (combined data segments from both modules)
 00040H 0013FH 00100H SSEG

Program entry point at 0000:0000
```

The GROUP Directive

Multiple segments can be grouped together under a single segment name, using the GROUP directive. GROUP is used most often in programs that are restricted to a size of 64K. Programs in COM format, for example, often use GROUP when linking separate program modules together. The MASM simplified segment directives also use GROUP to create programs in EXE format.

The individual segments may have different class or combine types, but they can be combined so all references are to near labels. The syntax is:

```
name GROUP segment [,segment] ...
```

The offsets of all labels and variables are calculated relative to the start of the group, rather than to the start of each of their individual segments.

The segments do not have to be contiguous, that is, they do not have to appear sequentially in the source program. The size of a group may not exceed 64K.

GROUP Example. The following example shows two segments grouped under a single name called DGROUP. In addition, each segment is assigned a class ('CODE', 'DATA', 'STACK') to make it compatible with Microsoft high-level languages, which use the same names:

```
title  Segment Group Example

dgroup group _data,stack
       assume cs:_text,ds:dgroup,ss:dgroup,es:dgroup

extrn  subroutine_1:proc, var2:word

_text segment 'CODE'
main  proc
    mov   ax,dgroup          ; initialize DS
    mov   ds,ax
    call  subroutine_1       ; call submodule
    mov   bx,offset var2     ; refer to external variable
    mov   ax,4C00h           ; end program
    int   21h
main  endp
_text ends

_data segment 'DATA'
var1  dw  1000h
_data ends

stack segment stack 'STACK'
db 100h dup(0)
stack ends

end main
```

By coincidence, we have used exactly the same segment names and group name used by Microsoft when simplified segment directives (.CODE, .DATA, .STACK) are used. We are not restricted to these names, of course, but this program would be compatible with other Microsoft languages.

Now we can link this program to other program modules containing the same GROUP directive. Although these modules may use *different* segment names, the final EXE program contains references to variables with all offsets relative to the start of the group. All procedure calls, even between modules, will still be near. We will add the following two submodules:

```
title  Sample Submodule Number 1
public subroutine_1
assume cs:seg_A

seg_A segment 'CODE'      ; segment containing code
subroutine_1 proc
    mov   ax,1000h
    ret
subroutine_1 endp
seg_A ends
end
```

```
title  Sample Submodule Number 2
dgroup group  data2     ; add DATA2 to DGROUP
public var2

data2 segment 'DATA'    ; segment containing data
   var2  dw 2000h
data2 ends
end
```

In the second of these modules, the GROUP directive mentions only DATA2. This submodule does not need to know the names of the other segments that are already part of the group. The MAP file for the combined program shows the grouping of segments. Both segments with a class of 'CODE' have been placed together, and the DATA, DATA2, and STACK segments are part of DGROUP:

```
Start   Stop    Length Name        Class
00000H 0000FH 00010H _TEXT        CODE
00010H 00013H 00004H SEG_A        CODE
00020H 00021H 00002H _DATA        DATA
00030H 00031H 00002H DATA2        DATA
00040H 0013FH 00100H STACK        STACK

Origin   Group
0002:0   DGROUP
```

The GROUP directive, therefore, has important implications for the assembly programmer who writes subroutines for other programs. By using a group name that is compatible with a main program, we can add new modules (with new segment names) to the group and still be assured that all code and data references will be near, that is, within a single segment.

Simplified Segment Directives

In the great majority of assembler programs, the Microsoft simplified segment directives may be used. These include the segment directives for .CODE, .DATA, and .STACK, as well as the .MODEL and DOSSEG directives. They ensure that your program will be compatible with high-level languages. Programs written under versions of MASM prior to 5.0 were required to contain explicit segment definitions; they will still compile under later MASM versions.

A complete list of simplified segment directives is given in the following table:

Directive	Comment
.STACK [*size*]	Stack segment
.CODE [*name*]	Code segment
.DATA	Initialized near-data segment
.DATA?	Uninitialized near-data segment
.FARDATA [*name*]	Initialized far-data segment
.FARDATA? [*name*]	Uninitialized far-data segment
.CONST	Constant-data segment

The optional *name* next to the CODE, FARDATA, and FARDATA? segments is used only if you wish two . . . segments to have different names. This feature may be used only with a memory model that allows multiple code segments (medium, large, or huge). You may recall from Chapter 3 that tiny and small model programs place all their code and data in a single segment.

If your program uses a directive such as .CODE more than once in a program, the linker concatenates all instructions under each of these directives into a single segment. This makes it possible to freely intermix instructions and data. It is debatable whether this is a good programming practice, but at least it shows how the directives work. In the following example, **var1** is placed in the data segment, and there is no break between the instructions:

```
.code                                   ; part of code segment
       mov    ax,var1
       mov    bx,10
.data                                   ; part of data segment
       var1   dw   1000h
.code
       call   writeint                  ; follows immediately after
                                        ; the MOV instruction
       .
       .
```

Segments defined with the .STACK, .CONST, .DATA, and .DATA? directives are placed in a group called DGROUP. This means they are essentially in a single segment, and all offsets are calculated relative to the starting address of the group.

Segments defined using .FARDATA and .FARDATA? are not included in DGROUP. They are restricted to medium model and larger programs.

The .CONST directive identifies constant data that will not change at runtime. It is used primarily when linking to high-level language programs and has no particular meaning when used in a stand-alone assembly language program.

Predefined Equates. When using simplified segment directives, you can obtain the address of either DGROUP or the code segment (called _TEXT):

```
mov   ax,@data   ; address of DGROUP
mov   bx,@code   ; address of code segment
```

There are a number of other equates described in the MASM manual: @CURSEG contains the name of the current segment, @FILENAME contains the name of the current source file, and @CODESIZE and @DATASIZE return 1 or 0, depending on the type of program model.

RUNNING PROGRAMS UNDER DOS

By now, you realize that an effective assembly language programmer needs to know a lot about DOS. This section describes COMMAND.COM, the Program Segment Prefix, and the structure of COM and EXE programs. It is my hope that this discussion will prompt you to study DOS more carefully, using the available reference books.

The COMMAND.COM program supplied with DOS is called the *command processor.* It interprets each command typed at the DOS prompt. DOS goes through the following sequence when you type a command:

1. It checks to see if the command is internal, such as DIR, REN, or ERASE. If it is, the command is immediately executed by a memory-resident DOS routine.
2. It looks for a matching file with an extension of COM. If the file is in the current directory, it is executed.
3. It looks for an executable program (extension EXE). If the file is in the current directory, it is executed.
4. It looks for a matching file with an extension of BAT. If the file is in the current directory, it is executed. A file with an extension of BAT is called a *batch file,* which is a text file containing DOS commands to be executed as if they had been typed at the console.
5. If DOS is unable to find a matching COM, EXE, or BAT file in the current directory, it searches the first directory in the current *path*. If it fails to find a match there, it proceeds to the next directory in the path and continues this process until either a matching file is found or the path search is exhausted.

Application programs with extensions of COM and EXE are called *transient programs*. They are loaded into memory long enough to be executed, and then the memory they occupied is released when they finish. DOS creates a PSP for a transient program as it is loaded into memory, containing the following information:

PROGRAM SEGMENT PREFIX MAP

PSP Offset	Comments
0h–15h	DOS pointers and vector addresses
16h–2Bh	Reserved by DOS
2Ch–2Dh	Segment address of the current environment string
2Eh–5Bh	Reserved by DOS
5Ch–7Fh	File control blocks 1 and 2, used mainly by pre-DOS 2.0 programs.
80h–FFh	Default disk transfer area and a copy of the current DOS command tail

COM Programs

There are two types of transient programs, depending on the extension used: COM and EXE. The differences go beyond the filename extension. DOS uses a program's extension to detect its format.

A *COM* (command) program is simply a binary image of a machine-language program. It is loaded into memory at the lowest available segment address, and a PSP is created at offset 0. The program code begins at offset 100h, the location immediately following the PSP. All segment registers are set to the base segment address of the program. For example, a typical memory map of a COM program is shown in Figure 14-3. We will assume that the program contains 200h bytes of code and data.

A COM program keeps its code, data, and stack within the same segment. Thus its total size (in memory) cannot exceed 65,536 bytes.

A COM program called SAMPLE is shown here. The program's only segment (CSEG) must be declared using explicit segment directives:

```
title Exchange Two Variables              (SAMPLE.ASM)

cseg segment
    assume cs:cseg, ds:cseg, ss:cseg
    org  100h                  ; required for COM programs

main proc
    mov   al,value1            ; exchange the two values
    xchg  al,value2
    mov   value1,al
    mov   ax,4C00h             ; return to DOS
    int   21h
main endp
```

```
value1  db   0Ah
value2  db   14h
cseg ends

end main
```

The ORG directive sets the location counter to offset 100h before generating any instructions. This leaves room for the PSP, which occupies locations 0 through 0FFh. A COM program takes up less space on disk compared to an EXE program. The foregoing program, for example, is only 17 bytes long.

Figure 14-3 Memory map of a typical COM program.

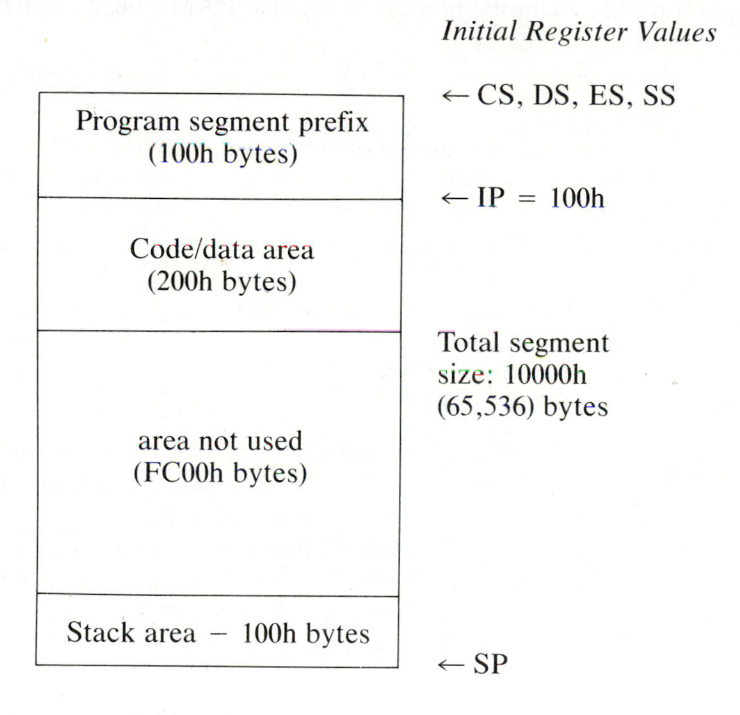

Sample Values	(Bytes)
PSP	100h
Code/data	200h
Stack	100h
Unused	FC00h
Total	10000h

Freeing Unused Memory. Although a COM program takes up little space on disk, it allocates all of available RAM when loaded. COM programs require at least one full segment, because they automatically place their stack at the end of the segment. You can get around this limitation if you move the stack up to the lowest available location and then release memory above the stack.

A COM program's memory use has not been a problem when it was the only transient program in memory. Now, however, multitasking software makes it possible to load several programs at once, each competing for available RAM. The term *well-behaved* refers to programs that take only the memory they need and release the rest for other programs. When writing a COM program that must run under multitasking software, you need to release all memory not used by the program right after it is loaded by DOS.

Freeing up unused memory is a two-step process. First, move the program stack up to the first available location in your program. Then call DOS function 4Ah (modify memory blocks) to release RAM you do not need. Here is an example of this procedure:

```
main proc
   mov  sp,offset mystack_end    ; point to local stack
   mov  ah,4Ah                   ; modify memory blocks
   mov  bx,256                   ; reserve 256 paragraphs
   int  21h                      ; shrink the program
   jc   cannot_shrink            ; exit if DOS failed
   .
   .
mystack  db  256 dup(0)
mystack_end label word           ; point SP to here
```

The value in BX refers to the number of 16-byte paragraphs, so we are really requesting 4,096 bytes (256 * 16). The PSP and stack take up 512 of these bytes, so that leaves 3,584 bytes for the code and data.

You may recall from Chapter 12 that function 4Ah requires ES to be set to the segment of the modified memory block. This has already been done for us by DOS, because COM programs set all segment registers to the same base segment. Here is a diagram showing their values:

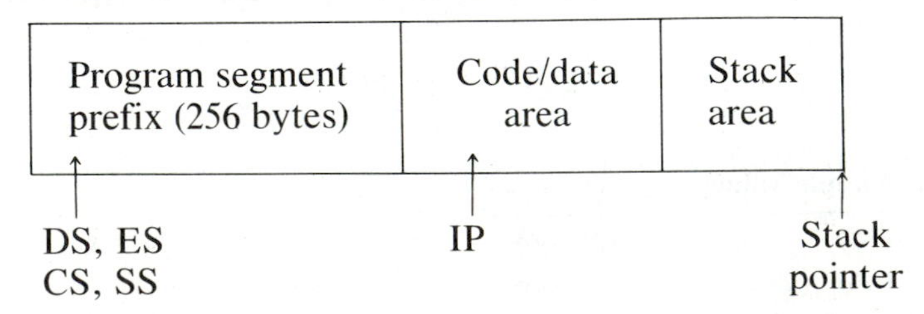

EXE Programs

An EXE program is stored on disk with an *EXE header* followed by a *load module* containing the program itself. The program header is not actually loaded into memory; instead, it contains information used by DOS to load and execute the program.

When DOS loads an EXE program, a PSP is created at the first available address, and the program is placed in memory just above it. As DOS decodes the program header, it sets DS and ES to the program's load address. CS and IP are set to the entry point of the program code, from where the program begins executing. SS is set to the beginning of the stack segment, and SP is set to the stack size.

The load module consists of separate *segments,* which may be thought of as reserved areas for instructions, variables, and the stack. Suppose we have a program containing three segments of the following lengths:

Segment Name	Length
CODE	20h
DATA	10h
STACK	100h

An EXE program may contain up to 65,535 segments, although there are only four segment registers. To switch to another segment, you need only set your segment register to point to the new segment. The memory layout of a typical EXE program is shown here, with code, data, and stack segments:

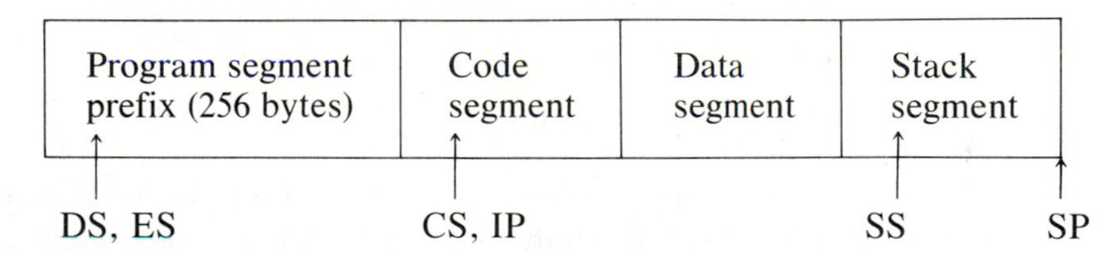

Of course, most EXE programs will not have segments that are exactly the same size. Only the PSP will remain at 256 bytes. The amount of memory an EXE program uses is determined by its program header—in particular, the values for the minimum and maximum number of paragraphs needed above the program. By default, the linker sets the maximum value to 65,535, which is more memory than could be available under DOS. When the program is loaded, therefore, DOS automatically allocates whatever memory is available.

The maximum allocation may be set when a program is linked, using the /CP option. This is shown here for a program named PROG1.OBJ:

```
link/cp:1024 prog1;
```

The number 1024 refers to the number of 16-byte paragraphs, expressed in decimal.

These values can also be modified after an EXE program is compiled, using the EXEMOD program supplied with MASM. For example, the command to set the maximum allocation to 400h paragraphs (16,384 bytes) for a program named PROG1.EXE is:

```
exemod prog1/max 400
```

The EXEMOD utility can also display important statistics about a program. Just type EXEMOD, followed by the name of the executable program. Sample output is shown here for PROG1 after it was linked with the maximum allocation set at 1,024 paragraphs:

PROG1	(Hex)	(Dec)
.EXE size (bytes)	876	2166
Minimum load size (bytes)	786	1926
Overlay number	0	0
Initial CS:IP	0000:0010	
Initial SS:SP	0068:0100	256
Minimum allocation (para)	11	17
Maximum allocation (para)	400	1024
Header size (para)	20	32
Relocation table offset	1E	30
Relocation entries	1	1

This program was linked with CONSOLE.LIB, so the program contains one relocation entry.

Most high-level compiled languages use the EXE format rather than COM for several reasons. Program modules can be compiled separately and then linked together, resulting in simplified program maintenance; programs can exceed 64K in size; and, last of all, only EXE programs are supported in OS/2's multitasking mode. For MASM programmers, there is an additional incentive—only EXE programs may be debugged in source mode by CODEVIEW.

EXE Header. The header area of an EXE program is used by DOS to correctly calculate the addresses of segments and other components. The header contains information such as the following:

- A *relocation table,* containing addresses to be calculated when the program is loaded
- The *file size* of the EXE program, measured in 512-byte units
- *Minimum allocation*: minimum number of paragraphs needed above the program
- *Maximum allocation*: maximum number of paragraphs needed above the program

- *Starting values* to be given to the IP and SP registers
- *Displacement* (measured in 16-byte paragraphs) of the stack and code segments from the beginning of the load module
- A *checksum* of all words in the file, used in catching data errors when loading the program into memory

Memory Models

Microsoft high-level languages are based on different *memory models* to distinguish between different program sizes. Some model types are recognized by other compilers, those by Borland, for example. Any assembler program using simplified segment directives must include the .MODEL directive. In general, one uses the smallest memory model that is adequate. The various memory models are as follows:

Tiny. All data and code must be within a single segment. Written in COM format, these programs cannot be generated by Microsoft high-level languages, and tiny model programs cannot be debugged in source mode using CODEVIEW.

Small. The data and stack segments fit within a single 64K segment, and the code fits within another segment. This model is used by the majority of stand-alone assembler programs because it is efficient. All procedures may be accessed via near calls.

Compact. The code fits within a single segment, but the data may be larger than 64K. All procedure calls are near, and no single array may be larger than 64K. Most Microsoft languages support this model.

Medium. The data and stack fit within a single segment, but the code may be larger than 64K. Thus, DS and ES remain set to a single segment, but procedure calls between segments are far calls.

Large. Both code and data may be larger than 64K, calls between segments are far calls, and data may be located in multiple segments. All Microsoft languages support this format.

Huge. Identical to the large model, except that arrays may be larger than 64K, and array indices are 32-bit segment/offset values. Most Microsoft languages support this model.

IBM Compatibility

Much has been said and written about the compatibility of various computers with the IBM-PC. As an assembly language programmer, you will have to consider how your programs will behave on various IBM-compatible computers. When programming in a high-level language, details of the computer's hardware tend to be hidden from the user. In assembly language no such restriction exists, and you can communicate directly with the computer's hardware and operating system.

Many early programs for the IBM-PC were tailored specifically to IBM hardware and did not work on IBM-compatible computers. With improved versions of DOS (and more compatible *compatibles*), standards have been set up to aid in writing well-behaved programs that run on a greater number of machines. The introduction of the IBM-PC/AT computer also made it necessary for the same programs to work on the IBM-PC, PC/XT, and PC/AT. Probably the most problematic programs at this time are those employing disk-based copy protection. They tend to have trouble running on all IBM-compatible computers.

Most IBM-compatible computers are identical at certain key points. When the same video memory addresses are used, high-performance application programs such as word processing and graphics programs can write directly to memory. Programs dealing with asynchronous communications need to access specific input-output port addresses, because the DOS and BIOS support for communications is inefficient. Last of all, thousands of available commercial expansion/option cards work on all IBM-compatible computers. IBM compatibility exists at three levels: hardware, BIOS, and DOS.

Hardware-Compatible. A computer that is hardware-compatible with an IBM will run virtually any program written for the IBM-PC without any modifications. The computer must have the same memory addresses for video memory and must use the same addresses for input-output ports to the various hardware devices. This level of compatibility has even led to legal wrangles between IBM and its competitors. One reason for the appearance of computers in this category stems from IBM's decision to use an open architecture on the IBM-PC. This policy meant that all details about the IBM-PC's hardware and BIOS were made available to the public. This open architecture spawned a massive industry of hardware and software add-ons for the IBM-PC.

BIOS-Compatible. At this level, a computer may have slightly different hardware, even with different locations for video memory and input-output ports. The differences, however, are compensated for by the programs in the ROM BIOS. The BIOS used by many non-IBM computers has been written to emulate all of the functions in IBM's own BIOS without actually duplicating IBM's code. An example is the popular Phoenix BIOS, used on many IBM-compatible computers.

DOS-Compatible. The lowest level of compatibility exists when the hardware and BIOS are both different, but both computers run DOS. Some machines in this category use the Intel 8086 processor instead of the 8088. Their BIOS is tailored to the computer's hardware and is functionally different from IBM's BIOS. Programs that use the accepted programming conventions suggested by the DOS and DOS reference manuals will still run on DOS-compatible computers. Programs making direct references to either hardware locations or specific ROM BIOS routines will usually not work correctly.

Configuring DOS

The final step in the startup sequence after DOS is loaded into memory is under your control. First, DOS checks to see if a *configuration file* called CON-

FIG.SYS is on the directory of the boot disk. The complete set of CONFIG.SYS commands is explained in IBM DOS manual, and the more common ones are listed here:

SELECTED CONFIG.SYS COMMANDS

Set extended checking of Ctrl-Break (BREAK)
Specify the number of disk buffers (BUFFERS)
Specify the country whose date and time format you want to use (COUNTRY)
Install device drivers (DEVICE)
Specify the number of files that can be opened by file control blocks (FCBS)
Specify the number of files that can be open at one time (FILES)
Set the maximum drive letter that you may access (LASTDRIVE)
Specify the name of a top-level command processor (SHELL)

The CONFIG.SYS file is a text file containing commands from the preceding list designed to override DOS's default values. If changes are made to the file, the effects will not be seen until the computer is rebooted. A few of the more commonly used commands will now be explained.

The BUFFERS command lets you override the default number (2) of disk buffers used by DOS when accessing files. When reading an input file, data is read one sector at a time. If a request is made for a record, DOS reads the entire sector and passes the record to the application program. When the next record is read, DOS checks to see if the sector is already in memory. If it is, DOS passes the record to the application program without rereading the disk. Many database programs require the number of buffers to be increased. An example of the command (in CONFIG.SYS) is:

```
buffers = 5
```

The FILES command, used to specify the number of file handles that may be open at one time, extends the default number of 8 up to as many as 20. DOS keeps 5 file handles (0–4) for itself, so the default of 8 files really means that your program can open only 3 files at once. If FILES is set to 20, you can open as many as 15 files. Many database programs and language compilers require the FILES command in CONFIG.SYS.

The DEVICE command specifies the name of a device driver program to be loaded into memory when the system is booted. A *device driver* is a machine language program that acts as an interface between a physical device and DOS. It must be written in a special format required by DOS, so that it can be "chained" together with other device drivers. One can write a new driver for an existing device (e.g., keyboard, console) or for a new device, such as a pen plotter. Two drivers supplied by DOS can be optionally specified in the CON-

FIG.SYS file: ANSI.SYS and VDISK.SYS. To be used, the programs themselves must be made available to the system when DOS is booted.

The ANSI.SYS device driver gives the PC extended screen and cursor control features through DOS. The command in the CONFIG.SYS file is:

```
device = ansi.sys
```

This driver replaces the standard DOS console input and output drivers. The ANSI.SYS driver is required when accessing some electronic bulletin boards, as it allows transmission of graphics characters and cursor positioning commands to remote terminals. In general, strings of characters beginning with the *escape* character (1Bh) are written to the standard output device, which interprets them as commands. The entire list of codes is described in the IBM DOS *Technical Reference Manual*.

The VDISK.SYS driver creates a *RAM disk,* which is a simulated disk drive kept in RAM memory. For example, the CONFIG.SYS command to create a 200K RAM disk is:

```
device = vdisk.sys 200
```

This virtual disk uses part of memory, so its size is limited by the available memory in your system. A RAM disk operates many times faster than a floppy disk. All data on the RAM disk are lost if the computer is rebooted, so the disk should be backed up frequently.

POINTS TO REMEMBER

System Hardware. The CPU consists of a data bus, address bus, registers, a clock, an arithmetic logic unit (ALU), and a control unit (CU). The CU fetches data and instructions and decodes addresses; the ALU carries out arithmetic, logical, and shifting instructions. The instruction cycle consists of three steps: fetch, decode, and execute. The speed of each step is controlled by the clock, and the execution time of an instruction is determined by its required number of clock cycles. The elapsed time for a clock cycle is determined by dividing 1 by the clock speed. When calculating the number of clock cycles required by an instruction, you must first look up the timings for the particular types of operands, and then add on any additional cycles required by the effective address calculation.

Segment Definitions. Explicit segment definitions are used when we need more flexibility than allowed by the MASM simplified segment directives. An EXE program can contain almost any number of segments, each of which may be as large as 64K. A segment definition may include an align type, a combine type and a class.

Use the align type when the segment will be combined with another segment. Use the combine type if you want to control the way the linker combines separate segments with the same name. Use the class if you want segments of the same type (e.g., code) to be located together in the executable program. In particular, the code segment should set its class to 'CODE' to remain compatible with CODEVIEW.

Whenever possible, try to keep procedures in the same segment in order to make procedure calls more efficient. Access to variables and other data is faster if they are all located in the same segment.

The ASSUME directive ties a segment register to a particular segment. This makes it possible for MASM to calculate offsets of labels and variables. ASSUME is required only when you want to use explicit segment definitions.

The GROUP directive allows segments with different names to be grouped into a single segment, even when the segments appear in different program modules. This is the approach used in the MASM simplified segment directives, where the .STACK, .CONST, .DATA, and .DATA? segments belong to DGROUP.

Running Programs Under DOS. When running programs under DOS, keep in mind the default precedence of program types: COM—EXE—BAT. For instance, a program with a file extension of COM will always be executed before a program by the same name with an extension of EXE or BAT. If no matching program is found in the current directory, DOS searches each directory in the current path.

Application (transient) programs are loaded and executed by DOS. Once finished, the memory they used is released. This makes it possible for other programs to reuse the same memory. DOS creates a program segment prefix (PSP) at the beginning of a program. A COM program is stored on disk as a binary image of the original code and data. An EXE program is stored on disk with a program header that contains information about the program. DOS uses this header to load the program into memory.

Techniques were shown to release memory not in use by an application program. This helps to make programs compatible with multitasking software.

The CONFIG.SYS file must be in the boot directory if you want to increase the number of disk buffers or the maximum number of open files. In addition, CONFIG.SYS may be used to load device drivers.

REVIEW QUESTIONS

1. Can you think of any programming applications in which the MASM simplified segment directives are not appropriate?

2. When using simplified segment directives, is there any reason why variables should not be placed in the .CODE segment?

3. In a small model program, what is the maximum size of the combined stack and data segments?

4. In a small model program, what is the maximum size of the entire program?

5. What does the ASSUME directive do, and what happens if it is left out of a program that uses explicit segment definitions?

6. Explain what happens when the GROUP directive is used with segments in different program modules.

7. What is the difference between the *combine type* and the *class* of a segment?

8. How does MASM know which segment to set SS to when loading an EXE program?

9. Where do DS and ES point to when an EXE program is loaded?

10. How does the starting value of CS differ between COM and EXE programs?

11. Where is the stack located in a COM program?

12. What determines the amount of memory allocated to an EXE program when it is loaded by DOS?

13. What absolute address is implied by the segment address 2CDAh?

14. Assume that **segment_A** ends at absolute location 0F102h and is immediately followed by **segment_B**. If the latter has an align type of PARA, what will be its starting address?

15. In the following example, assume that **segA** begins at address 1A060h. What will be the starting address of the *third* segment, also called **segA**?

```
segA segment common
  var1  dw  ?
  var2  db  ?
segA ends

stack segment stack
  db 100h dup(0)
stack ends

segA segment common
  var3  dw  3000h
  var4  db  40h
segA ends
```

16. Describe the difference between a near call and a far call. Explain why a far call takes longer to execute.

17. If a procedure is located in another program module, must it always be accessed via a far call? Explain.

18. The following program contains three erroneous statements relating to segments. Write any corrected statements on the right-hand side of the program:

```
title  Segment Example

cseg  segment
assume ds:dseg, ss:stack
main proc
    mov   ax,dseg
    mov   ds,ax
    mov   bx,value1 + 2
    jmp   L1
    push  ax
    pop   ax
L1: mov   ax,4C00h
    int   21h
main endp
cseg ends

dseg segment
  value1  dw   1000h,2000h
ends

sseg segment
    db  100h dup('S')
sseg ends
end main
```

19. What are the main differences between the early microprocessors such as the Intel 8080 and the processor used on the IBM-PC?

20. Which processor is the more powerful cousin of the Intel 8088, sharing the same instruction set? What makes it faster?

21. How fast is the clock on a standard IBM-PC?

22. Which processor interrupts the system 18.2 times per second? What are some of its practical uses?

23. The CPU contains two buses that transfer data and other information to memory, registers, and input-output ports: the data bus and the ________ bus.

24. Which part of the CPU fetches data from memory and decodes the addresses in instructions?

25. In the typical CPU *instruction cycle,* what happens after the instruction and its operands have been fetched from memory?

26. Which part of the CPU carries out arithmetic, logical, and shifting operations?

27. The three basic steps in the instruction cycle of a microcomputer CPU are fetch, __________ , and execute.

28. Which part of the CPU calculates the addresses of memory operands?

29. When the CU locates an instruction in memory, it passes the instruction to the ALU in the *prefetch queue*. What advantage is gained by doing this?

30. A major feature of the Intel iAPX 80286 processor makes it possible for programs to share memory without disturbing each other. This is called the __________ mode.

31. Why is a *transient program* given its name?

32. What is the name of the 256-byte area at the beginning of a transient program?

33. Where in a transient program is the *command tail* (characters typed on the command line) saved?

34. How many program segments can a COM program occupy?

35. In what way does a COM program make inefficient use of memory?

36. When stored on disk, the two main parts of an EXE program are the *header* and the __________ module.

37. Many early programs written for the IBM-PC would not run on IBM-compatible computers. Why?

38. (Y/N) Does a hardware-compatible computer require any software modifications to run IBM software?

39. What does the term *open architecture* mean? Does it offer any advantages to the average computer user?

40. Name at least one microcomputer system that employs *closed architecture*. Can you think of any disadvantages to this approach for the computer manufacturer?

41. T/F: *Well-behaved* programs generally will run on BIOS-compatible computers but not on DOS-compatible computers.

42. Explain each of the following CONFIG.SYS file commands:
    a. BREAK
    b. BUFFERS
    c. DEVICE
    d. FILES

43. Write a CONFIG.SYS command to make extended screen and keyboard control available through DOS.

44. Write a CONFIG.SYS command to create a 300K RAM disk.

PROGRAMMING EXERCISES

Exercise 1 Segment Combine Types

Write a short program that contains the following segments:

CSEG (code)
DSEG (data)
SSEG (stack)
DSEG (another data segment)

Choose a *combine type* for SSEG so that MASM and the linker will set SS to the segment's starting address. Choose a combine type for DSEG that will cause both segments with the same name to be conbined. Code an ASSUME directive to identify the segment register tied to each segment. Place several variables in the two data segments, and code instructions to access the data. Run the program using a debugger to make sure the segments were constructed correctly.

Exercise 2 Executing Far Calls

Write a short main program made up of the following three segments:

CODE1, DATA, and STACK

Write another program module containing a single segment: CODE2. Write a statement in the main procedure that calls a procedure in the CODE2 segment. Assemble each module separately, link the two modules, and trace the final program with a debugger to make sure a far call was executed.

Exercise 3 Text File Listing Program

Modify the Text File Listing program introduced in Chapter 12 (LISTFIL.ASM, Figure 12-2) so that some of its procedures are placed in a separate program module under a different segment name. Use the GROUP directive to group the code, data, and stack segments. Link the program modules together. Use explicit segment definitions.

Exercise 4 Loading File Buffers

Write a program that loads a text file into two 64K buffers, each in its own data segment. As the first buffer fills up, switch to the second. Make sure DS points to the correct segment as the file is loading. To maximize efficiency, use a single read for each buffer. Use explicit segment definitions.

Exercise 5 Execute an Overlay Program

Write a short .COM-format program that displays a message, such as:

```
'Overlay Program Currently Running'
```

The last instruction in this program should be RET. Assemble, link, and convert this program to a .COM file. Do not attempt to run it from DOS. We will call this the *overlay program*.

Next, write a main program (.EXE format) that contains a buffer large enough to hold the overlay program. For example:

```
overlay_prog db 100h dup(0)
```

In the main program, do the following:

1. Open the .COM file holding the overlay program and read it into the buffer.
2. CALL the label that identifies the first instruction in the buffer (the overlay program will execute).
3. The RET at the end of the overlay program will return to your main program. Display a message, and return to DOS.

Exercise 6 Multiple Overlay Programs

Modify Exercise 5 by creating four separate overlay programs. In the main program, set up a loop so that each overlay program is loaded and executed in turn, using the same buffer area.

ANSWERS TO REVIEW QUESTIONS

1. One application would be when linking an assembler routine to Turbo Pascal, Turbo C, or Turbo BASIC, where the segment-naming conventions are different from those of Microsoft. Another would be when positioning a segment at a specific location in memory, such as the DOS data area that begins at 0040:0000h.

2. When simplified directives are used, MASM assumes that variables will be an offset from one of the segments in DGROUP. If you place a variable in the .CODE segment, you need to set DS to the location of @CODE before referencing the variable and then reset it to @DATA afterwards.

3. The combined data and stack must fit within 64K.

4. 128K: 64K for the code, and 64K for the data.

5. The ASSUME directive tells MASM the names of the segments that will hold code, data, and the stack. Syntax errors would result when references to labels and variables were made.

6. The GROUP directive identifies any segments that are to be grouped together. The segments may have different names, but MASM will adjust all offsets so they are from the beginning of the group.

7. The combine type combines segments with the same name. The class places all like segments together in the executable program.

8. MASM looks for the first segment that has a combine type of STACK and sets SS to its starting location. It also sets SP to the length of the segment.

9. DS and ES point to the PSP area.

10. In a COM program, CS points to the PSP; in an EXE program, CS points to the start of the code segment.

11. In a COM program, the stack is located at the end of the program segment.

12. The maximum allocation field in the EXE program header determines the amount of memory allocated to the program.

13. The segment address 2CDAh is really the absolute address 2CDA0h.

14. The second segment, **segment_B**, will begin at the next paragraph boundary, which is location 0F110h.

15. The third segment (**segA**) will begin at the same address as 1A060h, because their combine types are COMMON.

16. A near call means the CPU pushes IP on the stack and loads the destination offset into IP. A far call requires both CS and IP to be pushed on the stack, CS to be set to the destination segment address, and IP to be set to the destination offset.

17. No. If simplified segment directives are used with a small or compact memory model program, all code is automatically combined into a single segment. If the GROUP directive is used, segments with different names may be combined. Last of all, code segments with the same name using the same combine type will be joined into a single segment.

18. The three corrected lines are:

```
assume cs:cseg,ds:dseg,ss:sseg
dseg ends
sseg segment stack
```

19. The IBM-PC processor is a 16-bit processor. It uses 20 bits to address memory and contains instructions to manipulate 16-bit operands. The Intel 8080 is an 8-bit processor.

20. The Intel iAPX 8086. It uses the same instruction set as the 8088, but it has a 16-bit data bus.

21. The clock runs at 4.77 MHz on a standard IBM-PC. It is controlled by the Intel 8284 Clock Generator chip.

22. The Intel 8253 Programmable Interval Timer/Counter. It updates the system time and clock, controls the speaker, and refreshes memory.

23. Address.

24. The control unit.

25. The control unit passes instructions and operands to the ALU via the prefetch queue.

26. The arithmetic logic unit.

27. Decode.

28. CU.

29. Speed. This allows overlapping execution of the control unit and the arithmetic logic unit.

30. Protected.

31. It is loaded into memory only temporarily; when the program ends, all memory used by the program is released.

32. The program segment prefix, or PSP.

33. Offset 80h in the PSP.

34. Only one segment.

35. There is a large gap between the code and stack areas of the program.

36. Load.

37. The programs were written specifically for IBM-PC hardware.

38. No.

39. Details about the hardware and BIOS are made available to the public. Yes, hardware expansions may be purchased more cheaply on the open market.

40. Apple MacIntosh and Commodore Amiga are two. Fewer software and peripheral developers are available, since one cannot easily obtain details about the system.

41. False. MS-DOS computers depend on programs to be well behaved.

42. a. Check for CTRL-BREAK and halt a program in progress.
    b. Specify the number of disk buffers.
    c. Install a device driver.
    d. Specify the maximum number of files that may be open at the same time.

43. DEVICE = ANSI.SYS.

44. DEVICE = VDISK.SYS 300.

15

Numeric Processing

This chapter is loosely called "Numeric Processing," although it combines topics related to input-output, advanced addressing, and floating-point arithmetic. We will cover the remainder of the Intel instruction set by looking at specialized instructions for controlling interrupts, pointers, the CPU, flags, and I/O ports. We will survey the MASM directives used in defining real (floating-point) numbers. Finally, we will examine the Intel 8087 math coprocessor, used primarily for performing arithmetic on real numbers.

COMPLETING THE INSTRUCTION SET

Somehow we have reached this advanced stage of IBM-PC assembly language programming without having discussed a few remaining instructions. In this section we will look at the following:

Address manipulation instructions	(LEA, LDS, LES)
Interrupt control instructions	(STI, CLI)
Processor control instructions	(ESC, HLT, LOCK, WAIT)

I/O port instructions	(IN, OUT)
Flag manipulation instructions	(LAHF, SAHF, PUSHF, POPF)

Address manipulation instructions load 16-bit and 32-bit pointers. Interrupt control and processor control instructions are the domain of systems-level programming. We use them to start and stop the CPU, to process hardware interrupts, and to pass instructions to the 8087 math coprocessor. The I/O port instructions allow us to access the system hardware directly, in order to control the speaker, the serial communications port, or other devices. The flag manipulation instructions are used to store and retrieve the contents of the Flags register.

Loading Pointers

A *pointer* is a variable that contains the address of some other data. There are two types of pointer variables. A *near* pointer is a 16-bit offset that points to data within the current segment. A *far* pointer is a 32-bit segment–offset address that points to data outside the current segment. In assembly language, we extend the concept of pointers to include base and index registers (BX, BP, SI, and DI). Examples of near pointers pointing to a variable called **array1** are:

```
        mov   bx,offset array1      ; base register
        mov   si,pntr1              ; index register
        .
        .
    pntr1  dw array1                ; pointer variable
    array1 db 200 dup(?)            ; array
```

Suppose **array2** is located in a segment called **otherseg**. Examples of initializing pointers to the array are presented here. Example 1 initializes DS:BX as a far pointer to **array2** at runtime; Example 2 shows how a pointer may be initialized at assembly time:

Example 1: Initializing a pointer at runtime

```
    mov   ax,seg array2        ; get segment value
    mov   ds,ax                ; move to DS
    mov   bx,offset array2     ; place offset in BX
```

Example 2: Initializing a pointer at assembly time

```
dseg segment
  farptr  dd  array2   ; far pointer initialized by MASM
dseg ends
```

(The data being pointed to)

```
farseg segment
   array2  dw  100 dup(0)
farseg ends
```

LEA Instruction. The LEA (load effective address) instruction loads a register with the offset address of a variable. In particular, use LEA when the effective address of an operand must be calculated at runtime. Examples of direct and indirect operands are shown here with LEA:

```
lea  si,array      ; direct operand
lea  string1+2     ; direct operand
lea  si,array[bx]  ; indirect operand
lea  bx,[si]       ; indirect operand
```

Indirect Jumps and Calls

Indirect jumps and calls are particularly powerful in assembly language, because they can use an address stored in a variable. Therefore, the destination of a jump or call can be *dynamic*—it can change at runtime. A base or index register may be set to the offset of a pointer variable. MASM then jumps or calls to the location the variable points to. The following examples help to illustrate:

```
 1:        mov   bx,offset ptr_16
 2:        jmp   [bx]                   ; jump to location CS:0150h
 3:        jmp   bx                     ; jump to location CS:0000h
 4:
 5:        mov   bx,2
 6:        jmp   ptrlist[bx]            ; jump to location CS:0020h
 7:
 8:        mov   si,offset ptr_32
 9:        call  far ptr [si]           ; call location 6BA7:000Ah
10:
11: ;(offset)
12:    0000    ptr_16     dw   0150h             ; 16-bit pointer
13:    0002    ptr_32     dd   6BA7000Ah         ; 32-bit pointer
14:    0006    ptrlist    dw   0010h, 0020h, 0030h
```

(The offset values at the beginnings of lines 12–14 are provided only for reference and would not appear in a source program.) Line 2 jumps to the location stored inside **ptr_16**. Line 3 jumps to the offset of **ptr_16**. Line 6 jumps to the address stored in the second element of **ptrlist**. Line 9 calls a far procedure whose 32-bit address is stored in **ptr_32**.

Using Direct Memory Operands. Addressing when using JMP or CALL to an address stored in a direct operand can be quite subtle. There are two ways to make MASM generate the right code. A segment override (CS or DS) may be supplied, or DWORD PTR may be used. Each of the following works correctly:

```
        call cs:ptr_16
        call ds:ptr_16
        call cs:ptr_32
        call dword ptr ptr_32
        .
        .
ptr_16  dw   near_procedure
ptr_32  dd   far_procedure
```

Although the two pointers in this example are declared in the data segment, the CS and DS segment overrides appear to work equally well.

The following calls will assemble with no errors, but they cause the program to call the *operand's* address, rather than the location it points to. Brackets around a direct memory operand, incidentally, have no effect:

```
call ptr_16
call ptr_32
call [ptr_32]
call far ptr ptr_32
```

Array of Pointers. Let's say that **pointer_array** is actually an array of pointers; that is, each word in the array contains a 16-bit address that points to other data. We can place an index value in SI and load the address of an individual array element:

```
mov  si,index              ; start with index value
lea  bx,pointer_array[si]  ; get offset of operand pointed to by SI
mov  si,[bx]               ; SI contains pointer from pointer_array
```

Each array entry contains an address that points to data elsewhere in memory. If SI contained 0002h, for example, the effective address in BX would be **pointer_array + 2**:

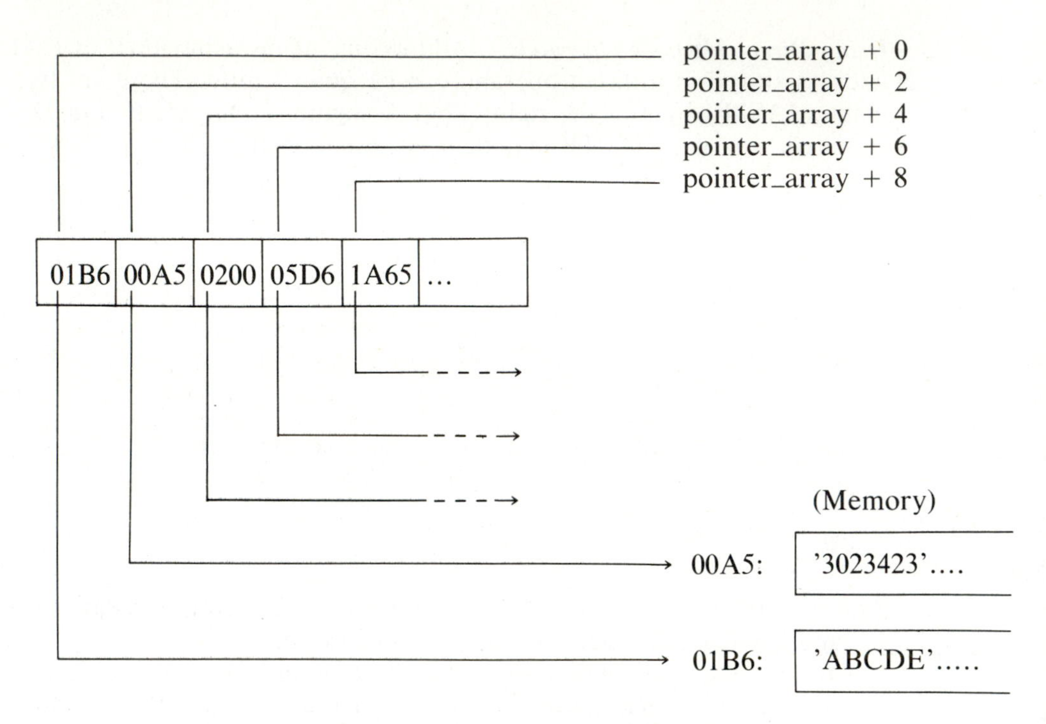

The contents of **pointer_array + 2** are 00A5h, which is the address of a string of numbers: 3023423. This is an example of two *levels of indirection,* used here to get the address of an operand that is known only at runtime.

Loading Far Pointers

LDS Instruction. The LDS (load register and DS) instruction loads a 32-bit variable into DS plus another register. The high word is placed in DS and the low word is placed in the destination register. The syntax is:

```
LDS register,memory
```

LDS does not obtain the *offset* of an operand, as you might suspect. It merely loads the *contents* of the operand into two registers. The memory operand must either be defined with DD or given a DWORD label. Examples are:

```
lds  ax,double_word      ; move DOUBLE_WORD to DS:AX
lds  si,farptr           ; move FARPTR to DS:SI
.
.
```

```
double_word  dd  10002000h

farptr label dword
   offset_part   dw   ?
   segment_part  dw   ?
```

If you caught the error in the foregoing example, you are indeed a sharp reader. The first LDS instruction sets DS:AX to 1000:2000h. The second LDS instruction uses the offset of the variable **farptr** (0004h) correctly, but unfortunately, DS has changed. Thus, it loads the contents of memory location 1000:0004h. This is further proof of what we already know: The offset of a variable may be calculated correctly by MASM, but a segment register can change at runtime. Be extremely careful when modifying segment registers. The corrected instructions for the previous example are:

```
push  ds                  ; save current DS
lds   ax,double_word      ; move DOUBLE_WORD to DS:AX
pop   ds                  ; restore DS
lds   si,farptr           ; move FARPTR to DS:SI
```

The LES (load register and ES) instruction is identical to LDS, except that the high word of the 32-bit memory operand is moved to ES. The syntax is:

```
LES register,memory
```

32-Bit Pointer Table. The following example shows how to initialize a table of 32-bit pointers at assembly time. **Ptrtable** contains far pointers to four different buffers located in FARSEG. The LES instruction combines the offset of **ptrtable** with an index value in BX to produce an effective address. We use this address to copy an entry from the table into ES:DI:

```
     mov   bx,index             ; index into the table
     les   di,ptrtable[bx]      ; get pointer from the table
     mov   al,byte ptr es:[di]  ; get a byte from the buffer
     .
     .
dseg  segment
  ptrtable  dd  buffer1     ; far pointer to BUFFER1
            dd  buffer2     ; far pointer to BUFFER2
            dd  buffer3     ; far pointer to BUFFER3
            dd  buffer4     ; far pointer to BUFFER4
dseg  ends

farseg  segment             ; separate segment
  buffer1  db  1024 dup(0)
  buffer2  db  1024 dup(0)
  buffer3  db  1024 dup(0)
  buffer4  db  1024 dup(0)
farseg  ends
```

Suppose that **index** was equal to 8. This would cause LES to move the segment-offset address of **buffer3** to ES:BX. The subsequent MOV statement would move the first character of the buffer into AL.

Interrupt Control Instructions

The CPU has a flag called the *Interrupt flag* (IF) that controls the way the CPU responds to external interrupts. If the Interrupt flag is set (IF = 1), we say that interrupts are *enabled*; if the flag is clear (IF = 0), interrupts are *disabled*. An external interrupt might be triggered by any of the following devices:

Interrupt Level	Interrupting Device
0	System timer (18.2/second)
1	Keyboard
2	(Not used)
3	Asynchronous communications 1
4	Asynchronous communications 2
5	Hard disk
6	Diskette
7	Printer

Each device has a priority, based on its *interrupt level,* or *IRQ*. Level 0 has the highest priority, and level 7 has the lowest. A lower-level interrupt cannot interrupt a higher-level one still in progress. For instance, if communications port 1 (COM1) tried to interrupt the keyboard interrupt handler, it would have to wait until the latter was finished. Also, two or more simultaneous interrupt requests are processed according to their priority levels.

STI Instruction. The STI instruction enables external interrupts. For example, the system responds to keyboard input by suspending a program in process and doing the following: It calls INT 9, which stores the keystroke in a buffer and then returns to the current program.

Normally, the interrrupt flag is enabled. Otherwise, the system timer would not calculate the time and date properly, and input keystrokes would be lost.

CLI Instruction. The CLI instruction disables external interrupts. It should be used sparingly—only when a critical operation is about to be performed, one that cannot be interrupted. When an interrupt occurs, the current values of the flags, CS, and IP are pushed on the stack. The interrupt processing program executes, and then the old values of the flags, CS, and IP are restored.

When changing the value of SS and SP, for example, most programmers clear the Interrupt flag. Otherwise, the correct values of SS and SP might be lost if a hardware interrupt occurred between transfers. The following statements, for example, set SS:SP to **mystack**:100h.

```
cli                    ; disable interrupts
mov   ax,seg mystack   ; reset SS
mov   ss,ax
mov   sp,100h          ; reset SP
sti                    ; reenable interrupts
```

Interrupts should never be disabled for more than a few milliseconds at a time, or you may lose keystrokes or slow down the system timer. When the CPU acknowledges either a software or a hardware interrupt, other interrupts are disabled. One of the first things the DOS and BIOS interrupt service routines do is to reenable interrupts.

Processor Control Instructions

The ESC, HLT, LOCK, and WAIT instructions all control the CPU. They are primarily used in systems programming and in programs that use the 8087 math coprocessor.

ESC Instruction. The ESC instruction passes an instruction and/or operand to the math coprocessor. Also called the *access memory location* instruction, it places the contents of a memory operand on the data bus. This makes it possible for the 8087 coprocessor to take advantage of the 8088 addressing modes. The ESC instruction is automatically inserted by MASM before each 8087 instruction.

HLT Instruction. The HLT instruction halts the program until a hardware interrupt occurs. Be sure hardware interrupts have been enabled before executing the HLT instruction, or the system will simply lock up.

LOCK Instruction. The LOCK instruction locks out other processors from the system bus until the immediately following instruction finishes. LOCK is an instruction prefix that prevents the math coprocessor from carrying out any operation prematurely. In the following example, LOCK affects only the MOV (not the MUL) instruction:

```
lock              ; lock bus for next instruction
mov   ax,var1
mul   bx          ; bus is no longer locked
```

WAIT Instruction. The WAIT instruction tells the CPU to stop processing until it receives a signal from a coprocessor that has finished its task. For example, the CPU may ask the 8087 math coprocessor to do a calculation. It then waits for the result before going on.

WAIT can be temporarily suspended if interrupts are enabled (IF = 0) and an external interrupt occurs. After the interrupt is serviced, the CPU returns to the WAIT instruction.

Accessing Input/Output Ports

Ports are connections, or gateways, between the CPU and other devices connected to the computer. Each port has a specific address; the CPU is capable of addressing up to 65,536 of them. Ports may be used to control the speaker, for example, by turning the sound on and off. We can communicate directly with the asynchronous adapter through a serial port by setting the port parameters (baud rate, parity, etc.) and we can send data through the port.

The keyboard port is a good example of an input/output port. When a key is pressed, the keyboard controller chip sends an 8-bit scan code to port 60h. The keystroke triggers a hardware interrupt, which prompts the CPU to call INT 9 in the ROM BIOS. INT 9 inputs the scan code from the port, looks up the key's ASCII code, and stores both values in the DOS keyboard buffer. If we wanted to, we could bypass the operating system completely and read characters from the input port ourselves. But that would be inefficient, as we would have to check the port constantly to see if a character was available.

Most devices have one or more *status* ports. In the case of the keyboard, you might use this port to see if a character is ready. There is also usually a *data* port, through which input–output data is transferred.

IN Instruction. The IN instruction inputs a byte or word from a port. The syntax is

```
IN accumulator,port
```

Port may be a constant in the range 0–FFh, or it may be a value in DX between 0 and FFFFh. *Accumulator* must be AL for 8-bit transfers and AX for 16-bit transfers. Examples are:

```
in   al,3Ch     ; input byte from port 3Ch
in   al,dx      ; DX contains a port address
in   ax,60h     ; input word from port 60h
in   ax,dx      ; input word from port named in DX
```

OUT Instruction. The OUT instruction outputs a byte or word to a port. The syntax is:

```
OUT port,accumulator
```

The same rules apply to the port and accumulator operands as to the IN instruction.

Controlling the Speaker. We can write a program that uses the IN and OUT instructions to generate sound. The speaker control port (number 61h) turns the speaker on and off by manipulating the Intel 8255 *Programmable Peripheral In-*

terface chip. To turn the speaker on, input the current value in port 61h, set the lowest 2 bits, and output the byte back through the port. To turn the speaker off, clear bits 0 and 1 and output the status again.

The Intel 8253 *Timer* chip controls the frequency (pitch) of the sound being generated. To use it, we send a value between 0 and 255 to port 42h. The following Speaker Demo program shows how to generate sound by playing a series of ascending notes:

```
 1:    title Speaker Demo Program                       (SPKR.ASM)
 2:
 3:    ;
 4:    ;  This program plays a series of ascending notes on
 5:    ;  an IBM-PC or compatible computer.
 6:    ;
 7:    dosseg
 8:    .model small
 9:    .stack 100h
10:        speaker  equ  61h
11:        timer    equ  42h
12:        delay    equ  0D000h ; delay between notes
13:
14:    .code
15:    main  proc
16:        in     al,speaker      ; get speaker status
17:        push   ax              ; save status
18:        or     al,00000011b    ; set lowest 2 bits
19:        out    speaker,al      ; turn speaker on
20:        mov    al,60           ; starting pitch
21:
22:    L2: out    timer,al        ; timer port: pulses speaker
23:        mov    cx,delay        ; hold the note
24:    L3: loop   L3
25:        sub    al,1            ; raise pitch
26:        jnz    L2              ; play another note
27:
28:        pop   ax               ; get original status
29:        and   al,11111100b     ; clear lowest 2 bits
30:        out   speaker,al
31:
32:        mov    ax,4C00h        ; return to DOS
33:        int    21h
34:    main  endp
35:    end main
```

Lines 18–19 turn the speaker on, using port 61h, by setting the lowest 2 bits in the speaker status byte. Line 20 sets the pitch by sending 60 to the timer chip. A delay loop makes the program pause before changing the pitch again (lines 23–24).

After the delay, lines 25–26 subtract 1 from the frequency value, which raises the pitch. The new frequency is output to the timer at line 22. This continues until the frequency counter in AL equals 0. Lines 28–30 pop the original status byte from the speaker port and turn the speaker off.

Flag Manipulation Instructions

In this section, we will discuss instructions that save and restore the entire Flags register. In previous chapters, we discussed instructions that manipulate specific flags:

STC	Set Carry flag
CLC	Clear Carry flag
CMC	Complement Carry flag
STD	Set Direction flag
CLD	Clear Direction flag

LAHF Instruction. The LAHF (load AH from flags) instruction copies the lower half of the Flags register into AH. The following flags are copied:

Flag	Bit Position
Sign flag	7
Zero flag	6
Auxiliary carry flag	4
Parity flag	2
Carry flag	0

Using this instruction, one can save a copy of the flags in a memory variable or test several flags at once:

```
lahf                   ; load flags into AH
mov    saveflags,ah    ; save them in a variable
test   ah,10000001b    ; check for Sign or Carry flag
jnz    flags_set       ; jump if either is set
```

SAHF Instruction. The SAHF (store AH to flags) instruction copies AH into the Flags register. This instruction is often used to transfer flag settings from the math coprocessor to the 8088 Flags register.

PUSHF Instruction. The PUSHF (push flags) instruction pushes the entire 16-bit flags register on the stack. This is the best way to save the current flags, in case they are about to be changed. They can later be restored, using the POPF instruction.

POPF Instruction. The POPF (pop flags) instruction pops the top of the stack into the flags register. If the flags were previously pushed, they can be restored to their original value. For example, we might want to call SUBROUTINE, but we don't want it to modify the current flags. We can push and pop the flags within the subroutine, along with selected data registers:

```
call   subroutine
.
.
subroutine proc
    pushf              ; save the flags
    push   ax
    push   bx
    .
    .
    pop    bx
    pop    ax
    popf               ; restore the flags
    ret
subroutine endp
```

DEFINING REAL NUMBERS

In this section, we will use assembler directives to define real numbers. MASM is able to translate a number in decimal representation in a source program into an encoded real format recognized by the math coprocessor.

A *decimal real* number consists of a mantissa and an optional exponent. The *mantissa* contains the sign, integer portion, and fractional portion. In the number 234.56E+02, for example, the mantissa is 234.56 and the exponent is +02. Other examples of reals are:

```
2.5
+0.4646
1.024E+04       ; (1.024 × 10⁴)
-80000.21
```

We need not go into the details of bit mapping all the various real number formats. Instead, let's look at an example of a 4- byte real number in IEEE format. The sign occupies 1 bit, the exponent is 8 bits, and the mantissa is 23 bits long:

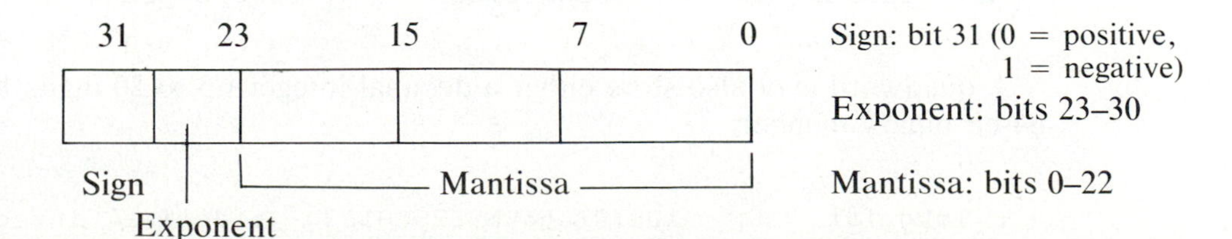

A similar format is used for the various types of real numbers. By encoding individual bits for the exponent, sign, and mantissa, MASM stores very large or small real numbers efficiently.

Define Doubleword (DD)

The DD directive tells MASM to create storage for a 4-byte number. A real number stored as a doubleword is called a *short real*. The number may be declared using either hexadecimal or decimal digits. The latter is called a *decimal real* and can have up to 8 digits of precision. Examples of *short reals* are shown here:

```
dd  12345.678      ; digits, decimal point
dd  +1.5E+02       ; value is 1,500
dd  2.56E+38       ; largest positive exponent
dd  3.3455E-39     ; largest negative exponent
```

An *encoded real* is a real number that is expressed as a string of hexadecimal digits. The hexadecimal digits reflect the number's exact binary contents, with the mantissa, exponent, and sign already included. MASM requires the letter *R* to be used as a radix indicator. For example, the number +1.0 would be represented by the following encoded real:

```
dd  3F800000r     ; encoded real, equal to +1.0
```

Encoded reals have limited usefulness, because you have to encode the bit patterns for the mantissa, sign, and exponent, which is no easy matter.

Define Quadword (DQ)

The DQ directive creates storage for an 8-byte (quadword) variable. The initial value may be an 8-byte encoded real, a decimal real, a decimal integer, or a binary integer.

DQ can be used to create a *long real* number, either as a decimal real or an encoded real:

```
float1  dq  +1.5E+10            ; decimal real
float2  dq  2.56E+307           ; largest exponent
float3  dq  3F00000000000000r   ; encoded real
```

A quadword may also store either a decimal integer up to 20 digits long or a 64-bit binary number:

```
long_int   dq   10030768458923589123   ; decimal integer
big_binary dq   0FFFFFFFFFFFFFFFh      ; binary integer
```

Define Tenbyte (DT)

The DT directive creates storage for a 10-byte variable. The contents may be an encoded real, a decimal real, a packed-decimal number, or a binary integer. The bytes are stored in reverse order.

Decimal digits are assumed to be stored in packed BCD format (2 digits per byte). The most significant byte is reserved for the sign. The number itself may be up to 18 digits long, positive or negative, as the following examples show:

```
packed_1    dt   123456789012345678
packed_2    dt  -004600238646485678
```

The sign byte contains 0 for positive numbers and 80h for negative numbers.

MASM assumes the radix of a number declared with DT is hexadecimal; therefore, the decimal radix indicator (d) must be used if you wish to declare a decimal value:

```
bin_integer  dt  1234567890123456789012345d
```

(Decimal value: 1,234,567,890,123,456,789,012,345)

Temporary Real. The DT directive creates a 10-byte real number conforming to the IEEE *temporary real* format (this format is also used by the 8087 coprocessor). A real number may be specified in either decimal or hexadecimal format. A hexadecimal encoded real must be 20 digits long:

```
float1  dt 1.5                       ; decimal real
float2  dt 3F000000000000000000r     ; encoded real
```

THE INTEL 8087 FAMILY MATH COPROCESSORS

The 8087 math coprocessor is an optional feature added to the IBM-PC. It is also known as the *Numeric Data Processor* (*NDP*). The IBM-PC was designed so the 8087 can be plugged into an empty socket on the system board. The 80287 and 80387 math coprocessors work with their cousins, the 80286 and 80386. The 80287 and 80387 recognize all 8087 instructions and add a number of their own enhancements. From this point on, when we refer to the 8087, it should be assumed that we are referring to the 80287 and 80387 as well.

In general, a *coprocessor* is a second CPU that works in parallel with the primary CPU. This boosts a computer's power tremendously, as certain tasks can be offloaded onto specialized processors. Coprocessors are used in many computer systems for video graphics, data communications, sound synthesis, floating-point math, and direct memory access.

The 8087 performs integer and floating-point calculations automatically, because the logic is designed into the chip. This makes doing calculations with the 8087 at least 7–10 times faster than with the 8088, because the latter must emulate the 8087's math functions through software. Many computer languages today offer you the option of using the 8087 to generate more efficient programs.

The 8087 has eight registers, each 80 bits long. They are arranged in the form of a stack and given the names ST(0), ST(1), ST(2), ST(3), ST(4), ST(5), ST(6), and ST(7). Register ST(0), usually called ST, is located at the top of the stack. Numbers are held in registers while being used for calculations, and their format is identical to the IEEE 10-byte temporary real format. When the 8087 stores the result of an arithmetic operation in memory, it automatically translates the number from temporary real format to one of the following formats: integer, long integer, short real, or long real.

Numbers are transferred to and from the main CPU via memory, so one always stores an operand in memory before invoking the 8087. The 8087 loads the number from memory into a register, performs an arithmetic operation, stores the result in memory, and signals the CPU that it has finished.

Control Registers. The 8087 has five control registers, which are of interest mainly to systems programmers. They are the *control word,* the *status word,* the *tag word,* the *instruction pointer* (32-bit), and the *operand pointer* (32-bit).

Instruction Format. The 8087 instructions always begin with the letter *F,* to distinguish them from 8088 instructions. The second letter of an instruction (often *B* or *I*) indicates how a memory operand is to be interpreted: *B* indicates a binary-coded decimal (BCD) operand, and *I* indicates a binary integer operand. If neither is specified, the memory operand is assumed to be in real-number format. For example, FBLD operates on BCD numbers, FILD operates on integers, and FMUL operates on real numbers.

Operands. An 8087 instruction can have up to two operands, as long as one of them is a coprocessor register. Immediate operands are not allowed, except for the FSTSW (store status word) instruction. CPU registers, such as AX and BX, are not allowed as operands. Memory-to-memory operations are not allowed.

Arithmetic Formats. There are four arithmetic instruction formats: *Classical–stack, memory, register,* and *register pop*. In the following table, *n* refers to a register number (0–7), *memory* refers to an integer or real memory operand, and *op* refers to an arithmetic operation:

Instruction Form	Syntax	Implied Operands	Example
Classical–stack	F*op*	ST(1),ST	FADD
Memory	F*op* *memory*	ST	FADD memloc
Register	F*op* ST(*n*),ST		FADD ST(5),ST
	F*op* ST,ST(*n*)		FADD ST,ST(3)
Register pop	F*op*P ST(*n*),ST		FADDP ST(4),ST

Implied operands are not coded, but are understood to be part of the operation. *Op* (operation) may be one of the following:

ADD	Add source to destination
SUB	Subtract source from destination
SUBR	Subtract destination from source
MUL	Multiply source by destination
DIV	Divide destination by source
DIVR	Divide source by destination

A *memory* operand may be one of the following: a 4-byte short real, an 8-byte long real, a 10-byte packed BCD, a 10-byte temporary real, a 2-byte word integer, a 4-byte short integer, or an 8-byte long integer.

The *classical–stack* instruction form refers to the top operand or operands on the register stack. No operands are needed, because ST and ST(1) are implied. When performing arithmetic, for example, ST is always the source operand and ST(1) is the destination. The result is temporarily stored in ST(1). ST is then popped from the stack, leaving the result on the top of the stack. The FADD instruction, for example, adds ST to ST(1) and leaves the result at the top of the stack:

Instruction: **fadd**

	Before		After
ST	100.0	ST	120.0
ST(1)	20.0	ST(1)	

The *memory* instruction form also treats the registers like a stack. Memory operands are either pushed on or popped from the stack. Only the top of the stack (ST) may be accessed. There are two basic types of memory instructions. A *load* instruction loads ST from a memory operand and pushes all other registers down; a *store* instruction copies ST to a memory operand.

For instance, FADD is an arithmetic memory instruction. In the following example, it adds the contents of **var1** to ST:

Instruction:

```
fadd var1
.
.
var1 dd 2.0
```

	Before		After
ST	26.0	ST	28.0
ST(1)		ST(1)	

The *register* instruction form uses coprocessor registers as ordinary operands. Each register, other than ST, must be given a subscript. One of the operands must always be ST. The general format is:

```
instruction  dest-register,source-register
```

For example, the following FADD instruction adds ST(1) to ST:

Instruction: **fadd st,st(1)**

	Before		After
ST	26.0	ST	28.0
ST(1)	2.0	ST(1)	2.0

The *register–pop* instruction form treats the registers as a stack and requires the source operand to be ST. Such instructions always pop the source operand off the stack when they finish. For example, the following FADDP instruction adds ST to ST(1) and places the result in ST(1). Then when ST is popped from the stack, the contents of ST(1) slide up into ST. The result is that neither register keeps its old value:

Instruction: **faddp st(1),st**

	Before		After
ST	200.0	ST	232.0
ST(1)	32.0	ST(1)	

Evaluating an Expression. Register–pop instructions are a beautiful example of the process used by an assembler or compiler when evaluating arithmetic expressions. Consider a routine that evaluates the following postfix (*reverse Polish*) expression:

$$6\ 2 * 5\ - \qquad \text{(same as: } 6 * 2 - 5)$$

Many calculators use this format, in which the two operands are keyed in before the operator. The rule is simple: When reading an operand, we push it on the stack. Upon reaching an operator, the top two numbers in the stack are operated on. The result is placed back on the top of the stack:

Step	Input Values	Instruction		Register Stack	
1	6 2 * 5 – ▲	FILD	Push mem into ST	ST	6
2	6 2 * 5 – ▲	FILD	Push mem into ST	ST ST(1)	2 6
3	6 2 * 5 – ▲	FMUL	Multiply ST by ST(1), pop result into ST	ST	12
4	6 2 * 5 – ▲	FILD	Push mem into ST	ST ST(1)	5 12
5	6 2 * 5 – ▲	FSUBR	Subtract ST from ST(1), pop result into ST	ST	7

Let's go through each step carefully. In step 1, FILD pushes 6 onto the stack. In step 2, FILD pushes 2 onto the stack, which moves the 6 down one position. In step 3, FMUL multiplies the two stack operands together, places the result in ST(1), and pops ST off the stack. Step 4 pushes 5 on the stack. In step 5, ST is subtracted from ST(1) and ST is popped from the stack. The result (7) is left on the top of the stack.

Application: Payroll Calculation Program

The program listed in Figure 15-1 shows how the 8087 may be used to perform a simple payroll calculation. Input to the program is the number of hours worked by an employee. The program calculates the following values:

Regular hours worked

Overtime hours worked

The pay rate for each category

Total gross pay for the employee

Figure 15-1 *The Payroll Calculation program. (Used by permission of Bob Galivan.)*

```
title   Payroll Calculation Program  (8087 demo)

dosseg
.model small
.8087                          ; enable 8087 instructions
.stack 100h
.code
```

Figure 15-1 *(Cont.)*

```
main proc
     mov     ax,@data           ; initialize DS
     mov     ds,ax
     finit                      ; initalize the 8087 coprocessor
     fld     regRate            ; push regRate into ST
     fld     regConst           ; push regConst into ST
     fld     totalHours         ; push totalHours into ST
     fsub    st,st(1)           ; subtract ST(1) from ST:
                                ;  overtime hours = regConst - regRate
     ftst                       ; compare ST to zero
     fstsw   status             ; store coprocessor status word in
                                ;   the memory variable STATUS
     fwait                      ; tell the system processor to wait until
                                ;   8087 has completed the FSTSW
     mov     ax,status          ; load STATUS into AX
     sahf                       ; store AH into the 8088 flags
     jle     calcRegular        ; no overtime if hours ≦ zero

calcOvertime:                   ; overtime hours > zero
     fst     otHours            ; store ST to otHours
     fld     otRate             ; push otRate into ST
     fmul    st,st(3)           ; ST = ST * ST(3)      (otRate * regRate)
     fmul                       ; multiply ST by ST(1), pop result into ST
     fst     grossPay           ; store ST in grossPay
     fstp    otpay              ; pop ST into otPay
     fldz                       ; push zero into ST

calcRegular:                    ; If this is reached following an overtime
                                ;   pay calculation, then ST = 0.
     fadd                       ; ST = ST + ST(1)
     fst     regHours           ; store ST in regHours
     fmul                       ; ST =  ST * ST(1)
     fadd    grossPay           ; add grossPay to ST
     fstp    grossPay           ; pop ST into grossPay, the final result
     mov     ax,4C00h           ; return to DOS
     int     21h
main endp

.data
status          dw  ?           ; holds the 8087 status word
otRate          dd  1.5         ; The four variables are data that could be
regRate         dd  5.0         ;   input from a data file. They hold the data
regConst        dd  40.0        ;   to be processed by the coprocessor.
totalHours      dd  46.0
regHours        dd  0.0         ; The next five variables hold the results
otHours         dd  0.0         ;   of the calculations.
otPay           dd  0.0
grossPay        dd  0.0
netPay          dd  0.0
end main
```

Each program step is described in the following commented listing:

Instruction	Notes
finit	Initalize the 8087 coprocessor.
fld regRate	Push the regular pay rate into the ST register.

ST	5.0	(regRate)

Instruction	Notes
fld regConst	Push **regConst** into ST. This represents the standard 40 hours worked by an employee in one week.

ST	40.0	(regConst)
ST(1)	5.0	(regRate)

Instruction	Notes
fld totalHours	Push the total hours actually worked by the employee into ST.

ST	46.0	(totalHours)
ST(1)	40.0	(regConst)
ST(2)	5.0	(regRate)

Instruction	Notes
fsub st,st(1)	Subtract ST(1) from ST, and place the result in ST. (We subtract 40 from **totalHours** to see if there were any overtime hours.)

ST	6.0	(overtime hours)
ST(1)	40.0	(regConst)
ST(2)	5.0	(regRate)

Instruction	Notes
ftst	Compare the overtime hours in ST to 0.
fstsw status	Store the coprocessor status word in a memory variable named **status**.

Instruction	Notes
fwait	Tell the main processor to wait until the coprocessor has completed the last instruction. This prevents the 8088 from accessing **status** too soon.
mov ax, status	Load **status** into AX (coprocessor flags).
sahf	Store AH into the CPU flags.
jle calcRegular	If ZF = 1 or CF = 1, the overtime hours were <= 0, and overtime pay should not be calculated.
calcOvertime:	If this label is reached, the overtime hours were > 0.
fst otHours	Store ST in overtime hours.
fld otRate	Push the overtime pay rate into ST. All other values are pushed down:

ST(1)	1.5	(otRate)
ST(1)	6.0	(otHours)
ST(2)	40.0	(regConst)
ST(3)	5.0	(regRate)

Instruction	Notes
fmul st,st(3)	Multiply ST by ST(3), and store the result in ST (**otRate** * **regRate**). The 7.5 now represents the actual overtime pay rate:

ST	7.5	(otRate)
ST(1)	6.0	(otHours)
ST(2)	40.0	(regConst)
ST(3)	5.0	(regRate)

Instruction	Notes
fmul	Multiply ST by ST(1), and pop the result into ST. (The overtime rate is multiplied by the overtime hours.) Both operands are changed after the operation:

Instruction	Notes

ST	45.0	(overtime pay)
ST(1)	40.0	(regConst)
ST(2)	5.0	(regRate)

Instruction	Notes
fst grossPay	Store ST in **grossPay**.
fstp otPay	Pop ST in **otPay**:

ST	40.0	(regConst)
ST(1)	5.0	(regRate)

Instruction	Notes
fldz	Push zero into ST to initialize it for the regular pay rate calculation:

ST	0.0	
ST(1)	40.0	(regConst)
ST(2)	5.0	(regRate)

Instruction	Notes
calcRegular:	If this label is reached following an overtime pay calculation, then ST = 0. If there was no overtime, the value in ST will be zero. If fewer than 40 hours were worked, ST will be negative.
fadd	Add ST(1) to ST. The result is popped into ST, destroying both operands. Whatever value remains will be the actual time worked:

ST	40.0	(regular hours)
ST(1)	5.0	(regRate)

Instruction	Notes
fst regHours	Store ST in **regHours**.

Instruction	Notes
fmul	Multiply ST by ST(1), and pop the result into ST (both operands are destroyed): ST 200.0 (regular pay)
fadd grossPay	Add **grossPay** to ST. (**GrossPay** contains 45.0 from the earlier calculation.) ST 245.0 (grossPay)
fstp grossPay	Pop ST into **grossPay**, which holds the final value of the calculations. ST is now empty.

In the **calcOvertime** section, the last instruction (FLDZ) pushes zero into ST. This gives the coprocessor something to add to the regular rate constant stored in ST(1) at the beginning of the **calcRegular** section. If there is any overtime, there *must* be at least 40 hours of regular time. If there is no overtime, the employee must have worked 40 hours or less.

POINTS TO REMEMBER

A near pointer is a 16-bit offset calculated from the beginning of the current segment or group. A far pointer is a 32-bit segment-offset value that points to data outside the current segment.

The LEA instruction is particularly well suited to loading a variable's offset when the offset is known only at runtime. The LDS instruction loads a 32-bit value into DS plus another register. The LES instruction does the same, using ES. Both LDS and LES are typically used to load far (32-bit) pointers.

The STI and CLI instructions enable and disable hardware interrupts, respectively. We disable interrupts when performing critical operations involving segment registers and the stack. Interrupts should not be disabled for more than a few milliseconds. Keystrokes may be lost, and your system timer may begin to lose accuracy.

Ports are connections, or gateways, to the hardware devices connected to a computer. Each port on the IBM-PC has a unique address, and the ports are accessed using the IN and OUT instructions. There are two basic types of ports.

Status ports tell you about the status of a device or controller chip; data ports send and receive data.

The LAHF instruction loads the lower half of the Flags register into AH. The SAHF instruction does just the opposite— it stores AH back into the flags. Instructions such as these are often used when we need to retrieve results from the math coprocessor, because it saves flag status results in memory.

The PUSHF and POPF instructions are an effective way of preserving the entire Flags register. We often use these instructions at the beginning and end of procedures.

Real Numbers. In this chapter we showed how real numbers may be defined, using the DD, DQ, and DT directives. The DD directive defines a 4-byte short real, the DQ defines an 8-byte long real, and the DT directive defines a 10-byte temporary real. The last is compatible with the 8087 coprocessor's internal registers.

8087 Coprocessor. The 8087 math coprocessor is a second, specialized CPU. It performs floating-point calculations about 7–10 times faster than the 8088. Without an 8087, programs must perform all floating-point operations through software.

At least one of the 8087's eight registers is used in almost all operations. The registers are designed as a stack. A value may be pushed on the top of the stack, causing other registers to move down. A register may be popped from the stack, so the other registers move up.

REVIEW QUESTIONS

1. Name two common sizes of pointer variables.
2. How is a pointer variable usually used?
3. Are there any reasons why you would want to locate all variables in the same segment?
4. Describe the difference between the following two instructions from the points of program efficiency and the resulting value(s) in SI:

```
mov  si,offset count
lea  si,count
```

5. Describe the difference between the following two instructions:

```
mov  si,offset [bx+2]
lea  si,[bx+2]
```

6. Describe the contents of SI and DS after the following instruction is executed. Assume that the variable **long_ptr** is located at offset 0 from the beginning of the data segment:

```
lds si,long_ptr
.
.
long_ptr  dd 0123ABCDh
```

7. What is the difference between the following two instructions?

```
les  si,bigval
lds  si,bigval
```

8. When is it important to clear the Interrupt flag?

9. Why is it important to set the Interrupt flag soon after clearing it?

10. Explain the difference between the HLT and WAIT instructions.

11. Which register must hold 8-bit data that is being output to a port?

12. What is wrong with each of the following instructions?
    a. `out 3BD   Fh,0`
    b. `out 26,   DL`
    c. `in DX,    BL`
    d. `in 3BD    Fh,AX`

13. Explain the difference between LAHF and SAHF instructions.

14. Which flags are not affected by LAHF and SAHF?

15. Using the DD, DQ, and DT directives, give examples of each of the following declarations:
    a. decimal short real
    b. encoded short real
    c. decimal long real
    d. encoded long real
    e. 10-byte real in BCD format
    f. 8-byte decimal integer

PROGRAMMING EXERCISES

Exercise 1 Offset Address Table

Create a table containing ten 16-bit subroutine offsets. Write a program that displays a menu with the subroutine names, and inputs a number between 1 and 10 from the console. Use the number to locate the address of the corresponding procedure in the table. Call the procedure, using indirect addressing. Return to the menu and continue the cycle until ESC is pressed.

Exercise 2 Linked Name List

Write a program that creates a linked list containing names of people. Each node in the list consists of a 20-byte string, followed by a 16-bit pointer to the next entry. As the user inputs each name from the keyboard, insert it in the list.

Create space for 20 nodes at assembly time by using the REPT directive. The expression: $+2 tells MASM to add 2 to the location counter and initialize the memory operand to this value:

```
name_list label byte
rept 20
   db  20 dup(' ')      ; store a person's name
   dw  offset $+2       ; pointer to next entry
endm
```

Be sure to inspect the listing file generated by this REPT macro in order to verify that the pointers have been initialized correctly. Once all the names have been input, display them on the screen and write them to an output file as fixed-length records.

Exercise 3 Linked Name List, Enhanced

Enhance the Linked Name List program from Exercise 2 in the following ways:

- Make the list doubly linked so each node has pointers to the previous and next nodes.
- Read the names from a text file rather than the keyboard.
- Display the list in reverse order on the screen.
- Prompt the user for a name; then search the list (from the beginning) for the name. Print out a number, showing its relative position in the list. For example:

```
Name to find: JONES

JONES found in position 5.

Find another (Y/n)? y
```

Exercise 4 Printer Control Program

Write a program that sends escape sequences to control your printer. Use a table containing menu letter choices, followed by printer commands you want to send.

Display a menu with single-letter choices, such as *B* (boldface), *C* (compressed), and so on. Input a single keystroke, convert it to uppercase, and use it to search through the table of printer commands. A sample table for Epson-compatible printers is shown here:

```
escp    equ 1Bh                       ; define the escape character
table   db   '6',escp,32h,0           ; 66 lines/page
        db   '8',escp,30h,0           ; 88 lines/page
        db   'B',escp,45h,0           ; boldfaced type
        db   'C',0Fh,escp,30h         ; compressed type
        db   'D',escp,57h,31h         ; double width
        db   'E',escp,4Dh,0           ; elite type
        db   'I',escp,34h,0           ; italics mode
        db   'Q',escp,78h,0           ; near letter quality
        db   'P',escp,50h,0           ; pica
        db   'R',escp,40h,0           ; reset printer
        db   'S',escp,4Eh,0           ; skip over perforation
        db   'X',0,0,0                ; exit to DOS
```

Each entry is exactly 4 bytes long, making a sequential search easy to perform. When you find a matching table entry, output each following character to the printer until a zero terminator byte is reached.

As each selection is made, highlight the menu choice when you redisplay the menu. Continue doing this until the user presses X to exit to DOS.

If you have another type of printer, consult its manual for the correct escape sequences.

Extra: Most printers do not allow some options to be in effect at the same time. The Epson, for example, does not allow the compressed and boldface options to be used together. When you highlight the menu choices that have already been selected, check for any conflicting cross references and remove the highlighting. If compressed were chosen after boldfaced, for example, you would automatically toggle the boldfaced option off. If boldfaced were chosen after compressed, you would toggle the compressed option off.

Exercise 5 Quadratic Equation Calculation (math coprocessor required)

Create a table containing the following doubleword real numbers, representing the values of a, b, c, and x:

```
dd  1.0, 2.0, 3.0, 4.0  ; a, b, c, x
dd  4.0, 3.0, 2.0, 1.5  ; a, b, c, x
```

Plug these values into the following quadratic equation and calculate the result:

$$ax^2 + bx + c$$

Exercise 6 Synthetic Division (math coprocessor required)

Write a program that carries out a single step of synthetic division of a polynomial. Use CODEVIEW to trace the program, and print a dump of the coefficients of the quotient at the end of the program. The program should be able to handle up to a sixth-degree polynomial.

Synthetic division provides an easy way to factor a polynomial by successively dividing it by the quantity $(x - a)$, where a is a constant. Let's perform the following division using 2 as a possible value for a:

$$\frac{3x^4 + 2x^3 - 16x^2 + 10x - 20}{(x - 2)}$$

(divisor)

2	3 + 2 − 16 + 10 − 20	(coefficients of the dividend)
	+ 6 + 16 + 0 + 20	(product of divisor and previous coefficient)
	3 + 8 + 0 + 10 + 0	(coefficients of the quotient)

Since the remainder is 0, we know that $(x - 2)$ is a factor, and the polynomial may now be expressed as follows:

$$(x - 2)(3x^3 + 8x^2 + 10)$$

Exercise 7 **Synthetic Division (math coprocessor required)**

Enhance the Synthetic Division program written for Exercise 6 by carrying out the synthetic division until the polynomial is expressed as the product of linear factors, such as

$$(x - 2)^2 (x + 1)(3x - 5)$$

Exercise 8 **Quadratic Equation (math coprocessor required)**

Write a program that will solve a quadratic equation, using the binomial theorem:

$$\frac{-b \pm \sqrt{b^2 - 4ac}}{2a}$$

Thus, zeros of $x^2 - 2x - 8$ may be calculated as:

$$\frac{2 \pm \sqrt{(-2)^2 - (4)(1)(-8)}}{(2)(1)} = x = (2 + 6) / 2 = 4$$

or

$$= (2 - 6) / 2 = -2$$

Therefore, the zeros of the equation are 4 and -2.

Extra: Check the value inside the radical to be sure it is positive before calculating the square root. If it is negative, display an error message and quit.

ANSWERS TO REVIEW QUESTIONS

1. Near pointers and far pointers.
2. It usually contains the address of another variable or data structure.
3. If all variables are located in the same segment, they may be accessed via near references (offset only). It is not necessary to modify DS.
4. Both instructions move the offset address of **count** into SI. The MOV...OFFSET, however, calculates the offset of **count** at assembly time, while LEA does it at runtime. The former is more efficient.
5. The MOV...OFFSET instruction is illegal, because the value of BX cannot be known at assembly time.
6. DS will contain ABCDh, and SI will contain 0123h.
7. LDS loads DS and SI with the contents of **bigval**, and LES loads ES and SI with the contents of **bigval**.
8. Whenever you are changing the value of SS and SP. An interrupt at such a time would be disastrous, because the return address of your program would be lost.
9. To reenable hardware devices, including the system timer.
10. The HLT instruction remains in effect until a hardware interrupt occurs; the WAIT instruction waits for the 8087 numeric coprocessor to finish a task.
11. AL must hold 8-bit data.
12. a. A constant value for the port number must be in the range 0–255.
    b. Only AL or AX may be the source operand.
    c. Only AL or AX may be the destination operand.
    d. DX must be used to hold a port address greater than 255.
13. LAHF loads the lower byte of the Flags into AH; SAHF stores AH in the lower byte of the Flags register.

14. Overflow, Direction, Interrupt, and Trap flags.

15. a. DD +1.23
    b. DD 0FB002300r
    c. DQ 2.45E+96
    d. DQ 12A55BC896842300r
    e. DQ 268493820370983436
    f. DQ 1234567891223947d

16

High-Level Linking and Interrupts

LINKING TO HIGH-LEVEL LANGUAGES

If you were to poll a group of programmers who know assembly language, you would find that many use it for specialized tasks, but few use it to develop complete applications. The reasoning is clear: Where convenience and development time are more important that speed or code size, applications can be effectively written in a high-level language. Then such programs can be fine-tuned in assembly language for the routines that must be optimized.

Assembly language is also used when controlling high-speed hardware devices, for DOS memory management routines, for memory-resident code, and so on. Our focus in this chapter is on the *interface,* the connection, between high-level languages and assembly language. We will select a few languages to be used as examples: Turbo Pascal, Turbo C, and Microsoft QuickBASIC. After learning how to interface to these languages, you should be able to use other high-level languages with no problem.

A Few Words About Terminology. There appears to be some variation in the way programmers discuss the passing of data to subroutines. As in earlier discussions regarding macros, we will refer to *arguments* as values passed from a main program to a subroutine. *Parameters,* on the other hand, are values used inside a subroutine that have been passed from the calling program. We also use *formal parameters* in a procedure or function declaration. The following examples help to show the difference, using Pascal as an example:

```
procedure  Sub1 (var1, var2 :integer);     (formal parameters)

  var
    total : integer;
  begin
    total := var1 + var2;       (var1 and var2 are parameters)
    .
    .
  end;

begin {---------- main program ----------}
  .
  .
  Sub1 (10,20)      (10 and 20 are arguments)
  .
  .
end.
```

Each high-level language has a different syntax for describing procedures and functions. In this chapter, we will use the term *subroutine* to describe either a function or a procedure. Subroutines may be divided into two types, depending on whether or not they return a value:

Language	Return Value	No Return Value
BASIC	function procedure	subprogram
C	function	(void) function
FORTRAN	function	procedure
Pascal	function	procedure
Assembler	procedure	procedure

The following general considerations need to be addressed when calling an assembly language subroutine from a high-level language:

The *naming convention* used by a language refers to the way segments and modules are named, as well as rules or characteristics regarding the naming of variables and procedures.

The *memory model* used by a program (tiny, small, compact, medium, large, and huge) determines the way external procedures and data will be handled—specifically, whether calls and references will be near (within the same segment) or far (between different segments).

The *calling conventions* used by a program refer to the low-level details about how procedures and functions are called. We need to know the following:

- Which registers must be restored
- The parameter passing order
- Whether arguments are passed by value or by reference (address)
- How the stack pointer is restored
- How function results are returned

Names of Variables and Procedures. When calling an assembly language subroutine from another language, you need to choose names that are compatible with both languages. The linker can resolve external references only if the names used are compatible.

BASIC, assembly language, and Pascal translate all names into uppercase. The C language, on the other hand, recognizes differences between uppercase and lowercase letters. Compilers recognize different lengths of identifiers, as shown by the following sample list:

Compiler	**Significant Characters in Identifiers**
Microsoft QuickBASIC	40
MASM	31
Turbo Pascal	63
Microsoft Pascal	8
Microsoft C	31
Turbo C	32
Turbo Prolog	250
Microsoft FORTRAN	6

When two program modules are written in different languages, any identifiers shared by them must use the shorter name limit. For example, if an assembly language subroutine contains two names that are identical in the first 8 characters, a Microsoft Pascal program will mistake them for the same name:

```
read_next_record
read_next_byte        ; appears to be the same name
```

Segment Names. When linking an assembly routine to a high-level language, you must use segment names that are compatible with the calling program.

Memory Models. Borland and Microsoft languages support standard memory models. The choice of memory model affects the way arguments are passed to a subroutine. *Large* and *medium* memory model programs require far calls to external subroutines; the current CS and IP are both pushed on the stack. *Tiny, small,* and *compact* memory model programs require near calls to external subroutines, so only IP is pushed on the stack. Whenever possible, use a .MODEL directive in your assembly subroutine that matches the default model for the calling program.

Calling Conventions. A language's calling convention refers to the way it implements a subroutine call. This is often referred to as a *low-level protocol.* One problem we face is that the same subroutine cannot be automatically called by different languages. A subroutine called by Pascal, for example, cannot be automatically called by C, because each language has a different way of passing arguments and restoring the stack to its original state.

One principle seems to be universal: When a high-level language calls a subroutine, it pushes its arguments on the stack before executing a CALL instruction. But beyond this, languages vary in their calling conventions.

A calling program needs to know how arguments are to be passed to the subroutine. It must also know whether or not it is responsible for restoring the original value of the stack pointer after the call.

A called subroutine uses a calling convention to decide how to receive parameters. If a function subroutine is called, both the calling program and the subroutine need to know how the function result will be returned.

The approach we will use in this chapter is to introduce several popular computer languages and compilers. By seeing specific ways in which various languages implement calling conventions, you should gain a general understanding of how the whole process works.

LINKING TO TURBO PASCAL

An assembly language subroutine called by Turbo Pascal must be assembled into an .OBJ file and then linked to the main program by the Pascal compiler. The subroutine declares its name and any public variables, using the PUBLIC directive. In the main Pascal program, we use the EXTERNAL directive to declare the name of the subroutine. Examples of both procedure and function declarations are shown:

```
procedure Locate (row,col :integer);  external;

function  StrtoUpper (st :string) :string; external;
```

$L Directive. The $L directive identifies an .OBJ file containing the external subroutine to be linked to the main program. The Turbo Pascal compiler automatically converts the object file from the Intel object format into Borland's own format.

If, for example, we wish to link our Pascal program to the assembled program ASMRTN.OBJ, the $L directive must be placed somewhere in the Pascal program before the BEGIN for the main body of the program. Or if it is being linked to a Pascal unit, it must appear before the BEGIN in the unit's initialization section. The following directive would link ASMRTN.OBJ to a Pascal program:

```
{$L ASMRTN}
```

Near and Far Calls. Turbo Pascal automatically selects the correct type of call (near or far) based on the way a procedure is declared. A far procedure or function is declared in the interface section of a unit and may be called from other programs or units. A near procedure is declared either within a program or in the implementation section of a unit and may only be called from within the same program or unit.

You must declare your assembly language procedure as either near or far, to match Pascal's interpretation. This lets MASM generate the correct type of RET instruction (RET or RETF):

Assembly Language Procedure Declaration	**Type of RET Instruction Generated by MASM**
subroutine_1 proc near	RET (near)
subroutine_2 proc far	RETF (far)

Segment Names. Turbo Pascal expects certain segment names to be used in an assembly language subroutine: Code and instructions should be placed in a segment named **code** (or **cseg**), and variables local to the module should be placed in a segment named **data** (or **dseg**). Variables in the data segment cannot be initialized to starting values, as we are used to doing in assembly language. The Turbo linker will just ignore initialized values.

Other segment names and GROUP directives are ignored. Segments should not have class names. Either a BYTE or a WORD align type is allowed, but Turbo will ignore this and automatically make each segment word aligned.

Arguments. Pascal arguments are pushed on the stack before a procedure or function is called. The number of arguments is determined by the number of parameters in the procedure or function declaration.

Registers. You must preserve the BP, SP, SS, and DS registers in your MASM subroutines. Other registers may be modified.

Sample Procedure

Let's write a subroutine called LOCATE, to be called by Turbo Pascal. It locates the cursor at a chosen row and column on the screen, regardless of any limits set by Turbo's WINDOW procedure. Two integer parameters are specified in the procedure declaration:

```
procedure Locate (trow, tcol :byte); external;
```

Listings of LOCATE.PAS and LOCATE.ASM are shown in Figure 16-1. Any modifications made to the parameters within LOCATE will not affect the actual

Figure 16-1 The LOCATE.PAS and LOCATE.ASM programs.

```
Program Calling_Locate;                { LOCATE.PAS }

uses Crt;

Procedure Locate (trow,tcol :byte); external;
{$L LOCATE}      { link to LOCATE.OBJ }

const
   row = 10;
   col = 20;

begin  { main }

   ClrScr;
   Locate (row, col);
   write ('*');

end.
```

```
 1:    title  LOCATE Procedure, Called from Turbo Pascal
 2:    ;      (LOCATE.ASM)
 3:
 4:    ; The locate procedure is called from Turbo Pascal.  It
 5:    ; locates the cursor based on the passed row and column.
 6:    ; It operates independently of the current Pascal
 7:    ; WindMin and WindMax values.
 8:
 9:
10:    code segment
11:         assume cs:code
12:         public locate      ; make this procedure public
13:
14:    locate proc near
15:
16:        push   bp
```

Figure 16-1 *(Cont.)*

```
17:          mov    bp,sp
18:          mov    dx,[bp+6]      ; get the row
19:          mov    dh,dl          ; place in DH
20:          or     dx,[bp+4]      ; get the column
21:          dec    dh             ; adjust for Pascal ranges:
22:          dec    dl             ;      (1-80, 1-24)
23:
24:          mov    ah,2           ; locate cursor function
25:          mov    bh,0           ; video page 0
26:          int    10h            ; call the BIOS
27:
28:      ;   Create two local variables:
29:      ;          row_val, at  [bp-2]
30:      ;          col_val, at  [bp-4]
31:
32:          sub    sp,4
33:          mov    ax,[bp+6]      ; copy row to row_val
34:          mov    [bp-2],ax
35:          mov    ax,[bp+4]      ; copy column to col_val
36:          mov    [bp-4],ax
37:
38:          mov    sp,bp          ; restore SP and BP
39:          pop    bp
40:          ret    4              ; return and clear the stack
41:
42:      locate endp
43:      code ends
44:      end
```

passed variables because LOCATE does not have access to their locations. We would call the procedure thus:

```
Locate (row, col);
```

Let's assume **row** and **col** are equal to 10 and 20, respectively. Pascal pushes their values on the stack, followed by a 16-bit return address. Pascal pushes arguments from left to right, so **row** is pushed first. In the following illustration, we see the instructions executed by the calling program and the stack after the CALL is executed:

Instructions		**Stack**	
push row		10	(row)
push col		20	(col)
call Locate	SP →	ret addr	

When LOCATE takes control, SP points to the return address, as we would expect when any subroutine is called. We push a copy of BP on the stack to preserve it, and then set BP to SP:

Instructions		Stack	
		10	(row)
push bp		20	(col)
mov bp,sp		ret addr	
	BP = SP →	BP	

Local Variables. A subroutine creates local variables by reserving space for them on the stack below the stack pointer. It does this by subtracting a value from SP equal to the size of all local variables. Suppose our LOCATE subroutine has two local variables, **row_val** and **col_val**. Each variable is 2 bytes long, so we subtract 4 from SP. From this point on, the subroutine refers to **row_val** as [BP−2], and to **col_val** as [BP−4]:

Instructions			Stack	
		[BP+6]	10	(row)
sub sp,4		[BP+4]	20	(col)
		[BP+2]	ret addr	
		BP →	BP	
		[BP−2]	xx	row_val
	SP →	[BP−4]	xx	col_val

xx = indeterminate value.

This example helps to show why the contents of local variables are indeterminate until they are initialized; they simply overlay an unused portion of the stack.

This combination of return address, passed parameters, and local variables is called the *stack frame*. Now the LOCATE subroutine can access local variables by subtracting offsets from BP, or it can access passed parameters by adding offsets to BP. To show the difference, lines 33–36 in Figure 16-1 copy the passed parameters into the local variables.

When a subroutine is ready to return to the calling program, it sets SP back to its original value and restores BP. Thus, it "throws away" the two local variables, making them no longer accessible:

Instructions		Stack	
mov sp,bp		10	(row)
pop bp		20	(col)
ret 4	SP →	ret addr	

Finally, the RET 4 instruction tells the CPU to set SP back 4 bytes after popping the return address into IP. This clears the stack of the two integer arguments passed to the subroutine.

Passing Arguments by Value

When Turbo Pascal passes an argument by value, the size and type of the variable determine how it will be passed. If a parameter is 1, 2, or 4 bytes long, its value will be pushed on the stack. If the parameter is larger than 4 bytes, its address will be pushed on the stack. The subroutine may copy the parameter to a local storage variable to avoid modifying the original.

A *byte* parameter is passed as a word on the stack, with the ASCII code of the character in the low byte. The high byte is undefined.

A *character* parameter is always passed as a byte. A *boolean* parameter is passed as a byte containing a value of 1 or 0. An *enumerated type* parameter is passed as an unsigned byte if it has 256 or fewer values; otherwise, it is passed as an unsigned word. For example:

Procedure Sub1 (ch :char; flag:boolean);

Stack frame inside Sub1:

	Stack	
	ch	[BP+6]
	flag	[BP+4]
	ret addr	[BP+2]
BP = SP →	BP	

Inside the subroutine we would be wise to clear the high byte of each parameter, because its value is undefined:

```
and    [bp+4],0FFh       ; clear high byte of flag
and    [bp+6],0FFh       ; clear high byte of ch
```

A *real number* argument is passed directly on the stack. Turbo Pascal's default format for real numbers is its own 6-byte real. If the 8087 coprocessor is installed, you have the option of passing an 8087-type argument (single, double, extended, or comp). The number is then pushed directly on the top of the 8087 stack.

A *pointer* parameter is passed as 2 words on the stack. The segment portion is pushed first, followed by the offset. The following illustration shows how the stack looks inside a subroutine after a pointer has been pushed:

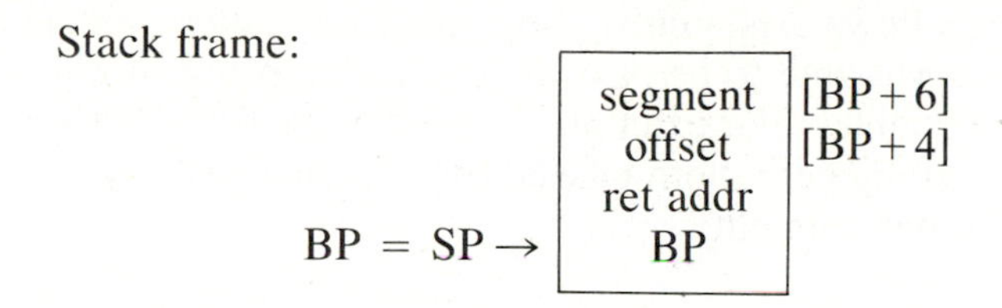

Thus, [BP+6] contains the segment value of the pointer, and [BP+4] contains the offset value. This makes it easy for the subroutine to load the pointer using (LDS or LES) into a segment and index register:

```
push   ds            ; remember to save DS
lds    si,[bp+4]     ; load pointer into DS:SI
```

A *string* or *array* parameter is passed as a 32-bit pointer. A Pascal subroutine would automatically copy the string or array to a local variable on the stack. For example:

Procedure WriteUpCase (st :string80);

```
            DS
            (st)      [BP+4]
            ret addr
BP = SP→    BP
```

```
lds    si,[bp+4]     ; get address of st
sub    sp,81         ; create space for local string
mov    ax,ds         ; make ES = DS
mov    es,ax
lea    di,[bp-2]     ; ES:DI points to local string
cld                  ; set Direction flag to up
mov    cx,81
rep    movsb         ; copy the string
```

(The compiled Turbo Pascal code is actually less efficient than this.)

Clearly, there is considerable execution time overhead involved when a string must be copied to a local variable. Passing a pointer to the string would be more efficient, and that is why many Pascal programmers prefer to pass strings as VAR parameters. Of course, this gives the subroutine the power to modify the string. Your own assembly language subroutines are not obligated to copy passed strings even when they are passed by value. Just realize that any change made to such a string will be global.

Passing Arguments by Reference

Pascal also allows arguments to be passed by *reference*. This causes the 32-bit address of a variable to be passed. The called procedure has the option of modifying the variables. For example, the following SWAPINT procedure exchanges two unsigned integers, both passed by reference. We will assume both variables are in the same segment:

```
 1:      public SwapInt
 2:
 3:  SwapInt proc near
 4:      push  bp            ; save BP
 5:      mov   bp,sp
 6:      push  ds            ; save DS
 7:      lds   bx,[bp+8]     ; get 32-bit address of int1
 8:      mov   ax,[bx]       ; move contents to AX
 9:      lds   bx,[bp+4]     ; get 32-bit address of int2
10:      xchg  ax,[bx]       ; exchange with AX
11:      mov   [bx+8],ax     ; store AX in int1
12       pop   ds            ; restore DS
13:      pop   bp            ; restore BP
14:      ret   8
15:  SwapInt endp
```

As you can see, there is considerable execution time overhead in this small example. In everyday practice, we would probably not bother writing a separate subroutine to carry out the exchange. Lines 7 and 9 use LDS to load each 32-bit address from the stack into registers. Once the offset is placed in BX, we use indirect addressing to get the actual value of each variable (line 8). This two-step process is only necessary when variables are passed by reference.

Calling a Function. Turbo Pascal returns ordinal-type results in registers: 8-bit values are returned in AL, 16-bit values are returned in AX, 32-bit values are returned in DX:AX, and 6-byte reals are returned in DX:BX:AX. Pointers are returned in DX:AX. If a string is returned by a function, the calling program pushes a 32-bit pointer to a temporary storage location before pushing any other parameters, and the function places the result string in that same location.

Example: The COUNT_CHAR Function

The COUNT_CHAR subroutine (Figure 16-2) counts the number of times a particular character is found in a string. The calling program passes a single character and the address of a string. The assembly language subroutine returns the count as an integer. The calling Pascal program and the assembly subroutine are both listed in the figure.

```
 1:   Program Pascal_Example_1;                          { PASEX1.PAS }
 2:
 3:   uses Crt;
 4:
 5:   {$L PASEX1A}        { link to PASEX1A.OBJ }
 6:
 7:   VAR
 8:     st :string;
 9:     ch :char;
10:     count :integer;
11:
12:   Function Count_Char (st :string; c :char) :integer; external;
13:
14:   BEGIN
15:
16:     Write ('Input a string: ');
17:     Readln (st);
18:
19:     Write ('Character to be counted? ');
20:     ch := ReadKey;
21:     Writeln (ch);
22:
23:     count := Count_Char (st,ch);
24:
25:     Writeln ('The character ',ch,' was found ',count,' times.');
26:
27:   END.
```

```
 1:   title   Count_Char Procedure                      (PASEX1A.ASM)
 2:
 3:   ;  This routine is called by a Turbo Pascal program.  It
 4:   ;  counts the  number of occurrences of a single character
 5:   ;  in a string.  It is called as a near procedure.
 6:
 7:   char    equ    [bp+4]      ; passed as a 16-bit value
 8:   string  equ    [bp+6]      ; passed as a 32-bit pointer
 9:
10:   public count_char
11:
12:   code  segment
13:       assume cs:code
14:
15:   count_char proc near
16:       push  bp                ; set BP to the top of stack
17:       mov   bp,sp
18:       push  ds                ; save DS
19:       mov   bx,0              ; character count
20:       mov   ax,0              ; loop counter
21:
22:   ;   Char is located in the lower half of the word at stack
23:   ;   position [bp+4].  String was passed as a 32-bit pointer,
```

Figure 16-2 Pascal program and assembly language subroutine.

Figure 16-2 *(Cont.)*

```
24:    ;   with the offset portion at position [bp+6].
25:
26:        mov   dl,char           ; character to count
27:        lds   si,string         ; DS:SI = address of string
28:        lodsb                   ; get length
29:        mov   cx,ax             ; use as loop counter
30:
31:    ;   Scan each byte of the string, using the count in CX
32:    ;   and the search character in DL.  Increment BX whenever
33:    ;   a matching character is found.
34:
35:    L1: lodsb                   ; load string byte into AL
36:        cmp   al,dl             ; character found?
37:        jne   L2                ; no: look for next
38:        inc   bx                ; yes: increment counter
39:    L2: loop  L1                ; repeat for loop count
40:
41:    ;   Turbo expects the function result to be in AX.  Both
42:    ;   DS and BP must be restored to their original values.
43:    ;   SP must be restored to its original value before the
44:    ;   parameters were pushed.
45:
46:        mov   ax,bx             ; function result in AX
47:        pop   ds
48:        pop   bp
49:        ret   6                 ; clear parameters from stack
50:    count_char endp
51:
52:    code ends
53:    end
```

The Pascal program uses the $L directive to identify the name of the assembled object program:

```
{$L PASEX1A}
```

(Be sure not to leave a space between the left brace and the $.) The Pascal function declaration for COUNT_CHAR includes the EXTERNAL directive:

```
Function Count_Char (st :string; c :char) :integer; external;
```

When COUNT_CHAR is called, it returns a count showing how many times the character was found in the string:

```
count := Count_Char (st,ch);
```

In the assembly language module containing COUNT_CHAR, we name the segment CODE so the subroutine will be compatible with Pascal's default segment names. The name COUNT_CHAR is declared PUBLIC so the linker will pass this information to the Pascal program.

Notice that equates are set up in lines 7 and 8 to make references to passed parameters simpler. **Char** and **string** are used in lines 26–27.

Lines 26–29 set up SI and CX before the search begins: The search character is placed in DL. The string address is placed in DS:SI. The LODSB instruction copies the string descriptor byte into AL, and AL is copied into the loop counter (CX).

The core of the procedure consists of scanning each character to see if it matches the character we are searching for (lines 35–39). Line 38 increments a counter of the number of matches found.

After the end of the loop, line 46 moves the character count in BX to AX, which is the standard register for function return values.

LINKING TO QUICKBASIC

Microsoft QuickBASIC is a basic compiler that represents a new trend in BASIC compilers: It offers both an integrated programming environment with an editor, and a command-line compiler. In this chapter, we will use only the command-line version.

Declaring a Subroutine. The DECLARE statement is used in a QuickBASIC program to declare the name of an external subroutine. The syntax is:

```
         { FUNCTION }
DECLARE  {          }  name [CDECL] [ALIAS "aliasname" [([parameterlist])]
         { SUB      }
```

The CDECL option is used only if a C function is being called. The ALIAS option is used if the subroutine name contains characters that are illegal in QuickBASIC, such as the underscore (_). The name enclosed in quotation marks represents the actual name of the external subroutine. Examples of subroutine declarations follow:

```
DECLARE  SUB Subrtn1
DECLARE  FUNCTION Upcase
DECLARE  SUB ScrollWin ALIAS "Scroll_Window"
```

Parameterlist is optional, but if parameters are supplied, they must be enclosed in parentheses. The syntax for the list of parameters is:

```
[{BYVAL | SEG}] variable [AS type]
[,{BYVAL | SEG}] variable [AS type]] ...
```

The ellipses (...) at the end indicate that you can repeat everything in the square brackets as many times as you wish. For example:

```
DECLARE SUB Subrtn1 (value1 AS INTEGER)
DECLARE SUB Count (BYVAL a1, BYVAL a2)
DECLARE FUNCTION Doit (val1, val2, val3)
DECLARE SUB Total (SEG a3, SEG a4, SEG a5)
```

By default, QuickBASIC passes an argument's 16-bit offset on the stack. The BYVAL keyword forces the argument to be passed by value. The SEG keyword causes the 32-bit segment–offset of the argument to be passed. The AS *type* option overrides the default type declaration of the variable. A list of available types is shown in the QuickBASIC reference manual.

Segment Names. The MASM simplified segment directives make interfacing to QuickBASIC and other Microsoft languages fairly easy. Assembly language subroutines should use the .MODEL MEDIUM directive. This causes procedure calls to be far and data references to be near. The subroutine should contain the DOSSEG, .CODE, and .DATA directives. The .STACK directive is not necessary, because QuickBASIC maintains its own stack.

Preserving Registers. You must preserve the BP, SI, DI, SS, and DS registers inside a subroutine called from QuickBASIC.

Passing Arguments. QuickBASIC passes arguments by *reference,* so the addresses of variables are pushed on the stack. If you want the arguments to be passed by value, use the CDECL or BYVAL option.

Function Results. 16-bit function results are returned in AX, and 32-bit function results are returned in DX:AX. For numeric return values other than 16-bit or 32-bit integers, a calling QuickBASIC program pushes a 16-bit pointer on the stack as the last argument. This points to a memory location where the function result is to be stored.

Example: The DISPBINARY Procedure

The QuickBASIC program in Figure 16-3 calls an assembly language subroutine named DISPBINARY. The subroutine displays each of the bits in a 16-bit number (we wrote such a program in Chapter 8). The main program declares DISPBINARY as a subroutine, with a single integer parameter, **value%**. The INPUT statement reads an integer from the console. This value is passed to the assembly subroutine.

Assembly Subroutine. The DISPBINARY subroutine (Figure 16-3) is written in assembly language. The procedure name must be declared with the PUBLIC directive. Assuming that the filename of the main QuickBASIC program is BASEX1.BAS and the assembly subroutine is BASEX1A.ASM, the commands to compile and link the two programs are:

```
bc basex1;              (compile BASEX1.BAS, create BASEX1.OBJ)
masm basex1a;           (assemble BASEX1A.ASM, create BASEX1A.OBJ)
link basex1+basex1a;    (link BASEX1 and BASEX1A, create BASEX1.EXE)
```

The subroutine contains the DOSSEG, .MODEL, and .CODE directives in order to make it compatible with QuickBASIC. QuickBASIC programs default to a medium model size, so procedure calls to external modules are far, and all data references default to near.

The DISPBINARY program calls a local procedure, DISPLAY_BITS (lines 21–33), which takes the number in AX and displays each bit on the console. This procedure is not declared PUBLIC, so the main QuickBASIC program has no way to access it.

Let's look at the way DISPBINARY retrieves the argument passed by the main program. QuickBASIC pushes both a segment and an offset return address on the stack following the passed argument, so the latter is found at location [bp+6]:

At the beginning of DISPBINARY, the stack contains the 32-bit return address and the passed value:

	offset of **value%**	[BP+6]
	ret seg	[BP+4]
	ret ofs	[BP+2]
BP = SP →	BP	

Thus, the main program placed the offset of **value%** on the stack at location [BP+6]. To make the program easier to read, we have defined [BP+6] as **address_parm1** on line 7.

Line 12 loads the address of the passed parameter into BX, so now BX points to **value%**. Lines 13 and 14 copy its value into AX and call the DISPLAY_BITS procedure.

When we return to the calling program, the RET instruction is coded as

```
ret 2
```

so SP will return to its original value before the address of **value%** was pushed on the stack.

```
 1:    declare SUB DispBinary (value%)
 2:
 3:    Cls
 4:    input "Value to be displayed in binary: ",value%
 5:
 6:    locate 3,1
 7:    call  DispBinary (value%)
 8:
 9:    locate 5,1
10:    print "Returning to BASIC"
11:    end
```

```
 1:    title  Subroutine Called by QuickBASIC
 2:
 3:    public DispBinary
 4:    dosseg
 5:    .model medium
 6:    .code
 7:    address_parm1  equ  [bp+6]
 8:
 9:    DispBinary proc
10:        push   bp
11:        mov    bp,sp
12:        mov    bx,address_parm1  ; pointer to parameter
13:        mov    ax,[bx]           ; get its value
14:        call   display_bits      ; display the bits
15:        pop    bp
16:        ret    2          ; clear parameter from stack
17:    DispBinary endp
18:
19:    ;   Display each binary bit in the integer.
20:
21:    display_bits proc  near
22:        mov   cx,16           ; number of bits in AX
23:    L1: shl   ax,1            ; shift AL left into Carry flag
24:        mov   dl,'0'          ; choose '0' as default digit
25:        jnc   L2              ; if no carry, then display
26:        mov   dl,'1'          ; else move a '1' to DL
27:    L2: push  ax              ; save AX
28:        mov   ah,2            ; display DL
29:        int   21h
30:        pop   ax              ; restore AX
31:        loop  L1              ; shift another bit to left
32:        ret
33:    display_bits endp
34:
35:    end
```

Figure 16-3 Calling assembly language from QuickBASIC.

Debugging with CODEVIEW. You can use CODEVIEW to debug the executable program, and you will be able to view the source code of both the main program and the assembly language subroutine. CODEVIEW automatically loads the current source program. Use the /ZI option when compiling and assembling, and use the /CO option when linking. Note that QuickBASIC requires the /ZI option to be placed after the source file name:

```
bc basex1/zi;
masm/zi basex1a;
link/co basex1 basex1a;
```

If you plan to use DEBUG to debug the program instead, you can skip over the QuickBASIC code by inserting a breakpoint instruction (INT 3) at the beginning of the assembly subroutine. This inserts a single-byte machine instruction (CCh) in the program:

```
DispBinary proc  far
   int  3                  ; set a breakpoint
   push bp
   mov  bp,sp
   .
   .
```

When you type G (Go) in DEBUG, the program executes at full speed until it reaches the breakpoint. In order to trace or execute the rest of the program, you must increment IP so the CPU can skip over the breakpoint.

LINKING TO TURBO C

Compiling and Linking

Turbo C has an integrated environment that includes a text editor, and it comes with a command-line compiler (TCC.EXE). For the examples shown here, we will use the latter. It has an unusual feature: It automatically executes both TLINK.EXE, the Borland linker, and the assembler.

Let's assume the following files are either in the current directory or DOS path:

TCC.EXE	Turbo C compiler
TLINK.EXE	Turbo C linker
MASM.EXE	Microsoft macro assembler

All library and header files required by Turbo C

We want to compile a C program called CEX1.C, assemble CEX1A.ASM, and link the two together. This may all be accomplished using a single command line, shown here for Turbo C version 2.0:

```
tcc -Emasm.exe cex1 cex1a.asm
```

Each part of the command line is explained here:

tcc	Name of the Turbo C compiler
-Emasm.exe	Name of the assembler, defaults to TASM.EXE
cex1	Name of the main C program
cex1a.asm	Name of the assembly subroutine

Segment Names

Turbo C programs use a small memory model by default, but any of the other standard models may be selected. The segment names used by Turbo C depend on which memory model is being used. For example, a small model program uses the following declaration for the code segment:

```
_TEXT segment byte public 'CODE'
```

For the data segment containing initialized data, the declaration is:

```
_DATA segment word public 'DATA'
```

For uninitialized data, the segment declaration is:

```
_BSS segment word public 'BSS'
```

It is possible to override these segment names, using options with the command-line compiler. This might be useful if you want the same assembly subroutine to link to programs compiled by different C compilers. In our examples, however, we will use the standard names.

Saving Registers. You must save BP, CS, DS, SS, and ES at the beginning of a subroutine and restore them when returning to C. You must also save SI and DI unless you have used the -r- compiler option that disallows register variables.

Identifiers. C automatically appends an underscore (_) to the beginning of any identifier before saving it in an object file. Therefore, any names in your assembly subroutine that will be referenced by a C program should begin with an underscore. For example:

_TEXT segment	Segment name (must be capitalized)
_addem proc	Procedure name
public _addem	Public declaration
_count dw 0	Public variable

Likewise, if your assembly subroutine references any variables in the main C program, those names must also begin with an underscore.

Defining the Function. In C, all subroutines are functions. A function normally returns a value, but C has a special function type called *void* that returns no value; it is just like a Pascal procedure. You must use the EXTERN label before a function declaration, as in the declaration for SUB1 shown here:

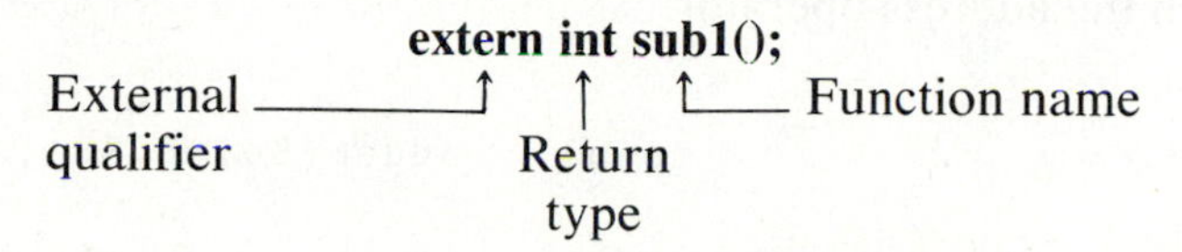

If the function has no return value, the return type is void:

```
extern void sub1();
```

If the function has parameters, they may be coded within the parentheses. Here, **parm1** and **parm2** are integer parameters:

```
extern int sub1(int parm1, int parm2);
```

Function Results. Turbo C functions return 16-bit values in AX and 32-bit values in DX:AX. Larger data structures (structure values, arrays, etc.) are stored in a static data location, and a pointer to the data is returned in AX. (In medium, large, and huge memory model programs, a 32-bit pointer is returned in DX:AX.)

Example: Calling the ADDEM Function

Let's write a C program that calls an assembly language subroutine called ADDEM. This subroutine adds up the values of three integers and returns their sum. In the C program, we assign values to the variables **a**, **b**, and **c** and pass their values to ADDEM. The result is returned in the variable **total**. The C program is as follows:

```
/*   C Example Number 1     (CEX1.C) */

#include <stdio.h>

extern int addem(int p1, int p2, int p3);
int  a,b,c,total;
```

```
main()
{
  a = 1;
  b = 2;
  c = 3;
  printf("\nAdding 1 + 2 + 3:   ");
  total = addem(a,b,c);
  printf("Total = %d\n",total);
}
```

A C program passes arguments by value, so the subroutine has no way to change them. If we wanted to pass the addresses of **a**, **b**, and **c**, we could preface each with the address operator:

```
total = addem(&a,&b,&c);
```

Then the subroutine would have access to the original variables if it wanted to modify their contents.

The output from the CEX1.EXE program is:

```
Adding 1 + 2 + 3:   Total = 6
```

The ADDEM Subroutine. We will not pretend that using ADDEM is faster than simply coding the add statements in C. In fact, there is considerable overhead (seven or eight instructions) involved in just calling a subroutine. But right now, we're more interested in seeing how it all works.

C functions always return a 16-bit function result in AX, so ADDEM does the same. Note that all public symbols are coded with leading underscore characters. The segment names are compatible with Turbo C's small memory model:

```
 1:  title  Subroutine called by  CEX1.C    (CEX1A.ASM)
 2:
 3:      public _addem
 4:
 5:  _TEXT segment byte public 'CODE'
 6:      assume cs:_text
 7:  _addem proc near
 8:      push  bp
 9:      mov   bp,sp
10:      mov   ax,[bp+8]    ; third argument
11:      add   ax,[bp+6]    ; second argument
12:      add   ax,[bp+4]    ; first argument
13:      pop   bp
14:      ret
15:  _addem endp
16:  _TEXT ends
17:  end
```

Stack Frame. As in previous examples, we push BP and set BP to the stack pointer at the beginning of the routine (lines 8 and 9). Notice that the RET instruction contains no constant, as did the Pascal and QuickBASIC examples. This is because a calling C program automatically resets the stack pointer to its starting value after the subroutine returns.

The calling C program pushed the third argument on the stack first, then the second argument, and finally the first argument. (This is opposite the order used in Pascal programs.) A picture of the stack after pushing BP is shown here:

Address	Stack		
[BP+8]	0003	c	parameters
[BP+6]	0002	b	parameters
[BP+4]	0001	a	parameters
[BP+2]	ret addr		
BP →	BP	← SP	

The following is a sample disassembly of the instructions used by the C program to call the subroutine. The value of each argument is pushed on the stack before the call. After the call, 6 is added to SP to return it to its original value, and the function result in AX is moved to **total**:

Offset	Instruction		
018E	push	[0352]	; c
0192	push	[034C]	; b
0196	push	[0350]	; a
019A	call	01B1	; addem
019D	add	SP, +06	
01A0	mov	[034E],AX	; total

Case Sensitivity. C programs are case sensitive, meaning that the name **addem** is considered different from **Addem**, **ADDEM**, **addEM**, and so forth. This has the potential to create compatibility problems, because the macro assembler automatically converts all identifiers to uppercase. When the Turbo C compiler (TCC.EXE) assembles an assembly language subroutine, it uses the /mx option by default; this tells MASM not to convert public names to uppercase.

INTERRUPT HANDLING

In this section, we discuss ways to customize the BIOS and DOS by installing *interrupt handlers* (or *interrupt service routines*). Interrupt handlers are generally in the domain of assembly language, because they require straightforward control over registers and DOS function calls. One of the greatest features of DOS is its flexibility. The BIOS and DOS contain interrupt service routines designed to make programming easier. DOS also allows you to replace any of these service routines with one of your own.

An interrupt handler might be written for a variety of reasons. You might want a special program to activate when a "hot" key is pressed, even while you are running another program. For example, Borland's *SideKick* was one of the first programs that was able to pop up a notepad or calculator whenever a special combination of hot keys was pressed.

You can also replace one of DOS's default interrupt handlers in order to provide more complete services. For example, the *divide by zero* interrupt is activated when the CPU tries to divide a number by zero, but there is no standard way for a program to recover.

You can replace the DOS *critical error handler* or the CTRL-BREAK handler with one of your own. DOS's critical error handler causes a program to abort and return to DOS when a disk drive door is left open, for example. Your own routine can recover from the error and return the current application program.

A user-written interrupt service routine can handle hardware interrupts more effectively than DOS. For example, the IBM-PC's standard asynchronous communication routine (INT 14h) performs no input or output buffering. This means that an input character is lost if it is not read from the port before another character arrives. A memory-resident program can wait for an incoming character to generate a hardware interrupt, input the character from the port, and store it in a buffer. This frees an application program from the need to take valuable time away from other tasks to check the serial port repeatedly.

Interrupt Vector Table. The key to DOS's flexibility lies in the interrupt vector table located in the IBM-PC's first 1,024 bytes of RAM (locations 0–3FFh). Each entry in the table (called an *interrupt vector*) is a 32-bit segment-offset address that points to one of the BIOS or DOS service routines. Let's look at a sample of the first ten entries. You can display a similar table on your own computer by using the DD (dump doubleword) command in CODEVIEW:

Interrupt Number	Offset	Interrupt Vectors			
00-03	0000	02C1:5186	0070:0C67	0DAD:2C1B	0070:0C67
04-07	0010	0070:0C67	F000:FF54	F000:837B	F000:837B
08-0B	0020	0D70:022C	0DAD:2BAD	0070:0325	0070:039F
0C-0F	0030	0070:0419	0070:0493	0070:050D	0070:0C67
10-13	0040	C000:0CD7	F000:F84D	F000:F841	0070:237D

Your interrupt vectors will probably be different from these, because they depend on the version of the ROM BIOS in the machine, as well as on the DOS version.

Each interrupt vector corresponds to an interrupt number. In the preceding example, the address of the standard routine for INT 0 (divide by zero) is 02C1:5186h. The offset of a particular interrupt vector may be found by multiplying its number by 4. Thus, the offset of the vector for INT 9h is (9h * 4h), or 0024h.

Triggering Interrupts. An interrupt service routine may be executed in one of two ways: An application program containing an INT instruction could cause a call to the routine. This is called a *software interrupt*. Another way for an interrupt routine to be executed is via a *hardware interrupt,* when a hardware device (asynchronous port, keyboard, timer, etc.) sends a signal to the Intel 8259A Programmable Interrupt Controller chip.

Let's use the keyboard as an example. When a key is pressed, the 8259A locates the vector for INT 9 in the interrupt vector table. The segment-offset values in the vector are loaded into CS and IP, and the BIOS routine for INT 9 executes. One of the first things it does is to reenable hardware interrupts, which were temporarily disabled by the 8259A chip. This is done using the STI instruction.

Next, the INT 9 routine inputs a character from the keyboard port and stores it in a 32-byte circular keyboard buffer located in low memory. It then returns to whatever program was executing when the interrupt was triggered, using the IRET (interrupt return) instruction. IRET pops the stack into IP, CS, and the Flags register, in that order. The following illustration shows the stack before the IRET instruction is executed:

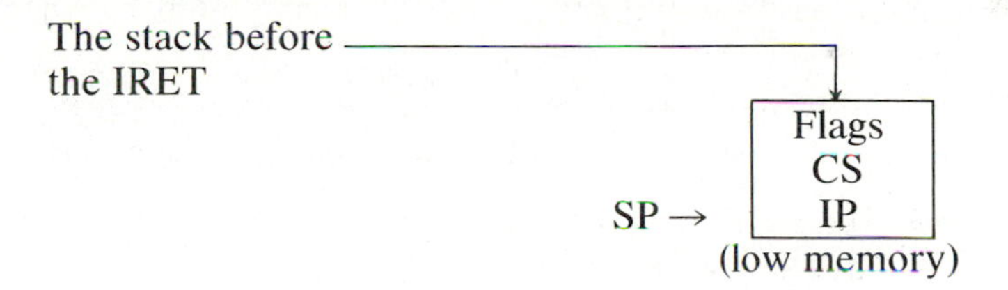

Sample BIOS Routine. Let's look at a sample disassembly of INT 16h in the ROM BIOS. This routine examines the keyboard buffer in low memory, checking to see if a character is waiting. On entry to the routine, interrupts are disabled, so they will soon have to be reenabled with the STI instruction. Otherwise, the system clock and system performance would be affected:

```
    push  ds
    push  si
    xor   si,si
    mov   ds,si
    mov   si,041Ah      ; locate keyboard buffer head pointer
    dec   ah
    jnz   L1
    mov   ax,[si]       ; get buffer head
    mov   si,0400h      ; point to DOS data area
    add   si,ax
    cmp   ax,[041C]     ; buffer tail = buffer head?
    mov   ax,[si]       ; move char and scan code into AX
L1: sti                 ; reenable interrupts
    pop   si
    pop   ds
    iret                ; return, pop flags from the stack
```

Replacing Interrupt Vectors

One might ask why the interrupt vector table exists at all. We could, of course, call specific subroutines in ROM to process interrrupts. The designers of the IBM-PC wanted to be able to make modifications and corrections to the BIOS routines without having to replace the ROM chips. One can replace addresses in the interrupt vector table with those of new subroutines in RAM.

You can also replace interrupt vectors, making them point to memory-resident assembly language routines. One could even go to the trouble of writing a brand-new keyboard interrupt routine, replacing the existing one. There would have to be a compelling reason to do this, of course. A more likely alternative would be to inspect characters coming from the keyboard first and then forward them to the existing INT 9 routine.

DOS has two INT 21h functions that help you install an interrupt handler: DOS function 35h (get interrupt vector) returns the segment-offset address of an interrupt vector. Call the function with the desired interrupt number in AL. The 32-bit vector is returned by DOS in ES:BX. For example:

```
          mov   ah,35h      ; get interrupt vector
          mov   al,9        ; for INT 9
          int   21h         ; call DOS
          mov   int9,BX     ; store the offset
          mov   int9+2,ES   ; store the segment
          .
          .
     int9  label word
           dd   ?           ; store old INT 9 address here
```

DOS function 25h (set interrupt vector) lets you replace one of the interrupt vectors with a routine of your own. Call it with the interrupt number in AL and the segment-offset address of your own interrupt routine in DS:DX. For example:

```
          mov    ax,seg kybd_rtn
          mov    ds,ax
          mov    ah,25h      ; set interrupt vector
          mov    al,9        ; for INT 9
          mov    dx,offset kybd_rtn
          int    21h         ; call DOS
          .
          .
     kybd_rtn proc   ; (new INT 9 interrupt handler here)
```

CTRL-BREAK Handler Example. The best way to show how an interrupt service routine gains control is to write a short program that replaces the DOS CTRL-BREAK handler. When CTRL- BREAK is pressed, the CPU immediately jumps to the subroutine pointed to by INT 23h in the interrupt vector table. As written, the DOS routine immediately terminates the program. Most application programs substitute their own routine for this vector to prevent DOS from terminating the program when CTRL-BREAK is pressed. Files might be left open, records might be only partially updated, and so on.

The CTRLBK.ASM program (Figure 16-4) is a simple example of a CTRL-BREAK handler. The main program initializes the vector for INT 23h. Notice that we must set DS to the offset of the code segment (lines 16–18) before calling DOS, because DS:DX has to point to the segment address of the BREAK_HANDLER routine (lines 36–45). Lines 18–21 call DOS function 25 (set interrupt vector).

The main program loop (lines 24–27) simply inputs and echoes keystrokes until ESC is pressed. The BREAK_HANDLER routine beeps whenever CTRL-BREAK is pressed and immediately returns to the calling program. The IRET instruction on line 43 returns from the interrupt back to the main program.

Sample output when the program was run is shown here:

```
Ctrl-Break demonstration.       (CTRLBK.EXE).
This program disables Ctrl-Break. Press any
keys on the keyboard, and press ESC to return to DOS.
ABCDEFGHIJKLM^C    (beep sounds)
^C                 (beep sounds)
^C                 (beep sounds)
```

Incidentally, when your program is terminated by INT 21h function 4Ch, DOS cleverly restores its original CTRL-BREAK vector, which it stored at offset 0Eh in your program's PSP.

Figure 16-4 Control-Break Handler program.

```
 1:    title  Control-Break Handler                  (CTRLBK.ASM)
 2:
 3:    dosseg
 4:    .model small
 5:    .stack 100h
 6:    .code
 7:    main  proc
 8:        mov   ax,@data     ; initialize DS
 9:        mov   ds,ax
10:        mov   dx,offset msg  ; display greeting message
11:        mov   ah,9
12:        int   21h
13:
14:    install_handler:
15:        push  ds             ; save DS
16:        mov   ax,@code      ; initialize DS
17:        mov   ds,ax
```

Figure 16-4 *(Cont.)*

```
18:         mov    ah,25h         ; function: set interrupt vector
19:         mov    al,23h         ; for interrupt 23h
20:         mov    dx,offset break_handler
21:         int    21h
22:         pop    ds             ; restore DS
23:
24:     L1: mov    ah,1           ; wait for a keystroke
25:         int    21h
26:         cmp    al,1Bh         ; ESC pressed?
27:         jnz    L1             ; no: continue
28:         mov    ax,4C00h       ; yes: return to DOS
29:         int    21h
30:     main  endp
31:
32:     ;   The following routine executes when Ctrl-Break
33:     ;   is pressed.
34:
35:     break_handler proc
36:         push   ax
37:         push   dx
38:         mov    ah,2           ; sound a beep
39:         mov    dl,7
40:         int    21h
41:         pop    dx
42:         pop    ax
43:         iret
44:     break_handler endp
45:
46:     crlf    equ   <0Dh,0Ah>
47:
48:     .data
49:     msg label byte
50:      db 'Ctrl-Break demonstration.       (CTRLBK.EXE).',crlf
51:      db 'This program disables Ctrl-Break.  Press any',crlf
52:      db 'keys on the keyboard, and press ESC to return to DOS.'
53:      db  crlf,'$'
54:
55:     end main
```

Memory-Resident Programs

A memory-resident program, also known as a *terminate and stay resident (TSR)* program, is one that is installed in memory and stays there either until it is removed by the user or the computer is rebooted. Such a program might remain hidden and then be activated only when a particular combination of keys is pressed. It is quite common for such programs to replace the keyboard interrupt vectors (INT 9h and INT 16h) with their own routines. For example, Borland's popular SideKick is a pop-up notepad, calendar, calculator, and phone dialer.

SideKick replaces a number of interrupts. The following illustration shows part of an interrupt vector table after SideKick has been loaded. Selected vectors that have been replaced are shown in boldface:

Interrupt Number	Interrupt Vectors			
00-03	02C1:5186	0070:0C67	0DAD:2C1B	0070:0C67
04-07	0070:0C67	F000:FF54	F000:837B	F000:837B
08-0B	**11C5:08E5**	**11C5:0A7E**	0070:0325	0070:039F
0C-0F	0070:0419	0070:0493	0070:050D	0070:0C67
10-13	**11C5:1106**	F000:F84D	F000:F841	**11C5:0A01**

SideKick also replaces several other interrupt vectors. In the early days of TSRs, compatibility problems occasionally arose when two or more programs replaced the same interrupt vectors with their own addresses. Older programs simply replaced the interrupt vector and provided no forward chaining method to other programs that needed it.

Keyboard Example. Suppose we have a program in memory at location 10B2:0020h that needs to inspect each character from the keyboard. We can fetch the current INT 9 vector from the table, save it, and then replace the table entry with the address of our own program. Whenever a key is pressed, the character is ready to be input from the keyboard port, and a hardware interrupt is triggered. This causes the 8259A Interrupt Controller to take control. It locates the address of INT 9 in the vector table, which in turn points to our program. When our program has finished looking at the keyboard, we jump to the original INT 9 routine and let it process the keyboard character as it always does. This chaining process is shown in the following illustration:

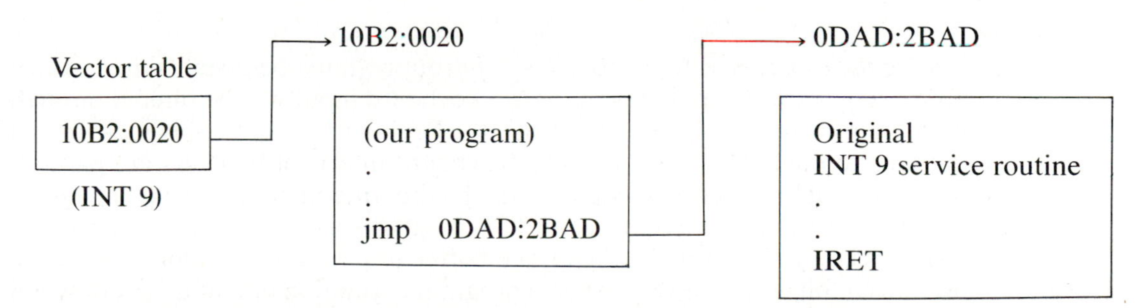

Our program would contain a JMP instruction to jump to the old INT 9 routine. When this routine finishes, the IRET instruction pops the flags off the stack and returns to whatever program was executing when the character was pressed.

Application: The NO_RESET Program

Let us write a memory-resident program that will prevent the system from being reset when Ctrl-Alt-Del is pressed. The program will be assembled as a COM program to keep it as small and simple as possible. Once our program is installed in memory, the system may be reset only by pressing a special combination of keys: Ctrl-Alt-Right shift-Del. The only other way to deactivate the program is to turn the computer off and do a cold start.

The DOS Keyboard Status Flag. One bit of information we need before we start is the location of the keyboard status flag kept by DOS in low memory. Our program will inspect this flag to see if the Ctrl, Alt, Del, and Right-Shift keys are held down. On IBM-compatible computers, the flag is stored at location 0040:0017h. The labels on the right side of the diagram show what each bit means when it is equal to 1:

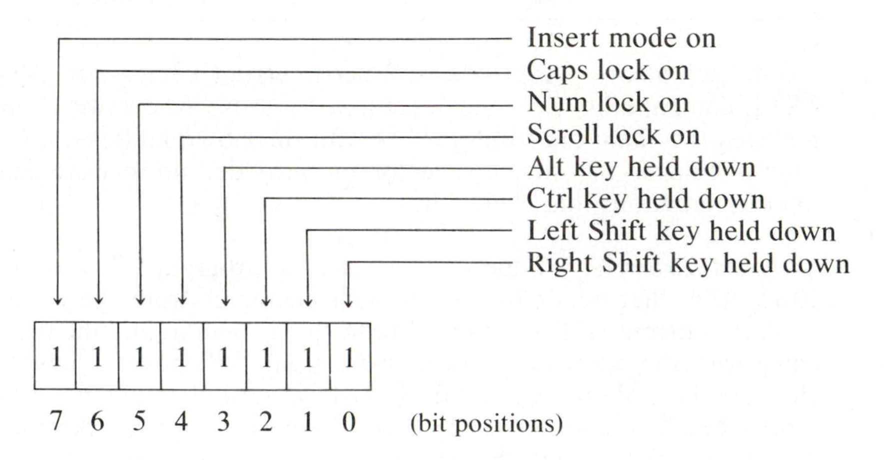

There is one additional keyboard status byte located at 0040:0018h that duplicates these flags, except that bit 3 shows when Ctrl-NumLock is currently active.

Installing the Program. A memory-resident routine must be installed in memory before it will work; from that point on, all keyboard input will be filtered through the program. If the routine has any bugs, the keyboard will probably lock up and require us to cold start the computer. Keyboard interrupt handlers are particularly hard to debug, because one uses the keyboard constantly when debugging programs. Those who regularly write TSR programs usually invest in hardware-assisted debuggers that maintain a trace buffer in protected memory. Often the most elusive bugs appear only when a program is running in real time, not when one is single-stepping through it.

Program Listing. In the NO_RESET program (Figure 16-5), the installation code is located at the end because it does not remain resident in memory. The resident portion, beginning with the label **int9_handler**, is left in memory and pointed to by the INT 9 vector.

First, let's look at the instructions that install the program. Lines 83–84 use DOS function 35h to get the current INT 9 vector, which is then stored in **old_**

```
 1:    title  Reset-Disabling Program               (NO_RESET.ASM)
 2:
 3:    ;
 4:    ;  This program disables the usual DOS reset command
 5:    ;  (Ctrl-Alt-Del) by intercepting the INT 9 keyboard
 6:    ;  hardware interrupt.  It checks the shift status
 7:    ;  bits in the DOS keyboard flag, and changes any
 8:    ;  Ctrl-Alt-Del to Alt-Del.  The computer can be
 9:    ;  rebooted only by typing Ctrl-Alt-Right shift-Del.
10:    ;  Assemble, link, and convert it to a COM program:
11:    ;          masm no_reset;
12:    ;          link no_reset;
13:    ;          exe2bin no_reset no_reset.com
14:
15:
16:    rt_shift        equ    01h        ; Right shift key: bit 0
17:    ctrl_key        equ    04h        ; Ctrl key: bit 2
18:    alt_key         equ    08h        ; Alt key: bit 3
19:    del_key         equ    53h        ; scan code for Del key
20:    kybd_port       equ    60h        ; keyboard input port
21:
22:    code    segment
23:            assume cs:code,ds:code
24:            org   100h                 ; this is a COM program
25:    start:
26:        jmp   setup         ; jump to installation routine
27:
28:    ;   Memory-resident code begins here.
29:
30:    int9_handler proc far
31:        sti                    ; reenable hardware interrupts
32:        pushf                  ; save registers and flags
33:        push  es
34:        push  ax
35:        push  cx
36:        push  di
37:
38:    ;   Point ES:DI to the DOS keyboard flag byte.
39:
40:    L1: mov   ax,40h         ; DOS data segment is at 40h
41:        mov   es,ax
42:        mov   di,17h         ; location of keyboard flag
43:        mov   ah,es:[di]     ; copy keyboard flag into AH
44:
45:    ;   Test for the Ctrl and Alt keys.
46:
47:    L2:
48:        test  ah,ctrl_key          ; Ctrl key held down?
49:        jz    L5                   ; no: exit
50:        test  ah,alt_key           ; Alt key held down?
51:        jz    L5                   ; no: exit
```

Figure 16-5 Example of a memory-resident program.

Figure 16-5 *(Cont.)*

```
52:
53:     ;   Test for the Del and Right-shift keys.
54:
55:     L3: in    al,kybd_port          ; read keyboard port
56:         cmp   al,del_key            ; Del key pressed?
57:         jne   L5                    ; no: exit
58:         test  ah,rt_shift           ; Right shift key pressed?
59:         jnz   L5                    ; yes: allow system reset
60:
61:     L4: and   ah,not ctrl_key       ; no: turn off CTRL
62:         mov   es:[di],ah            ; store keyboard_flag
63:
64:     L5: pop   di                    ; restore registers and flags
65:         pop   cx
66:         pop   ax
67:         pop   es
68:         popf
69:         jmp   cs:[old_interrupt9]   ; jump to INT 9 routine
70:
71:     old_interrupt9   dd ?
72:
73:     int9_handler endp
74:     end_ISR label byte
75:
76:     ; -------- (end of TSR program) --------
77:
78:     ; Save a copy of the original INT 9 vector, and set
79:     ; up the address of our program as the new vector.
80:     ; Terminate this program, and leave INT9_HANDLER in memory.
81:
82:     setup:
83:         mov   ax,3509h                      ; get INT 9 vector
84:         int   21h
85:         mov   word ptr old_interrupt9,bx  ; save INT 9 vector
86:         mov   word ptr old_interrupt9+2,es
87:
88:         mov   ax,2509h              ; set interrupt vector, INT 9
89:         mov   dx,offset int9_handler
90:         int   21h
91:
92:         mov   dx,offset end_ISR   ; end of resident code
93:         int   27h                   ; terminate and stay resident
94:     code    ends
95:     end     start
```

interrupt9 (line 71). We do this so that we will be able to locate the ROM BIOS keyboard handler routine once we have finished checking the keyboard.

Next, lines 88–90 use DOS function 25h to set interrupt vector 9 to the address of the resident portion of our program. The address must be in DS:DX when calling the function.

This method, incidentally, is preferable to moving a new address directly into the vector table. In future versions of DOS, the vectors may be at new locations or the interrupt vector table may be in protected memory.

Lines 92–93 exit to DOS using INT 27h, which leaves the resident program in memory. DOS automatically saves everything from the beginning of the PSP to the offset placed in DX.

The Resident Program. The resident interrupt handler (lines 30–73) has now been installed in memory and will be executed every time a key is pressed. Line 31 reenables interrupts as soon as the program begins, because the 8259A Interrupt Handler automatically disables interrupts.

Lines 32–36 push the flags and registers that will be changed, so they can be restored to their original values when we return. We must keep in mind that a keyboard interrupt will often occur while another program is executing. If we modified the registers or flags here, this would cause unpredictable results in an application program.

Lines 40–43 locate the keyboard flag byte stored in low memory at address 0040:0017h and copy it into AH. The byte needs to be tested to see which keys are currently being pressed. Lines 48–51 check for both the Ctrl and Alt keys. If both are not currently held down, we exit.

If the Ctrl and Alt keys are both held down, the operator may be trying to reboot. We know there is an input character waiting at the keyboard port, because that's how INT 9 was triggered in the first place.

To find out what the character is, lines 55–56 input the character and compare it to the scan code of the Del key. If it's not DEL, we simply exit and let INT 9 process the keystroke. If DEL was pressed, line 58 looks for the Right shift key. If the latter was pressed, we exit and allow the computer to be booted. Otherwise, line 61 turns off the Ctrl key bit in the keyboard flag byte and disables the system reset.

Notice that line 69 executes a far jump to the original ROM BIOS INT 9 routine, so that all keystrokes can be processed normally. This forward chaining is vital to the program's success.

Other Actions. This program opens up a whole world of possibilities for your programs. By being able to examine keyboard input before it reaches the BIOS or DOS, you can remove keys from the keyboard buffer, add new keystrokes, or force certain keys to be ignored, as we have done. You can rearrange all the keyboard scan codes by using a translate table: As each key is read from the input port, change its scan code, and DOS will never suspect a thing.

It should be said in passing that there is another side to this picture: The more hardware-specific your programs are, the more they will be prevented from running on non–IBM-compatible computers. And such programming runs counter to the intent of multitasking operating systems, which depend on the ability of programs to coexist in memory as peacefully as possible. When possible, use the existing DOS resources to accomplish your goal. If there are none available, write your own interrupt handler in a way that will make it as universal as possible.

POINTS TO REMEMBER

Linking to High-Level Languages. Arguments are values passed from a calling program to a subroutine, and parameters are the values used by the subroutine. There are a number of issues that must be addressed when calling an assembly routine from a high-level language.

The calling convention refers to the way parameters are passed: their order, how they are removed from the stack after the call, how function results are returned, and so on.

The naming convention refers to the allowable characters and lengths of identifiers in each language. Each language compiler also expects certain names to be used for segments and groups.

The memory model is also determined by the calling language, because it must know whether to pass near or far references to data on the stack, and it must also push either a near or far return address on the stack.

Another major point regarding variables has to do with passing by value or by reference. Pascal and C programs usually pass variables by value, so the variables themselves cannot be modified by a subroutine. This provides an important level of data security, as the calling program needs to know exactly what has changed. Usually this is accomplished by having the subroutine return a function result. A QuickBASIC program normally passes each argument by reference, which means its address is passed to a subroutine. QuickBASIC contains an option, however, that allows a variable to be passed by value.

Interrupt Handling. Interrupt handlers, also called interrupt service routines, can either take over or modify exising DOS functions. An interrupt may be activated either by software, using the INT instruction, or by a hardware device. In the latter case, a device sends a signal to the 8259A Interrupt Controller. The system timer, keyboard, and asynchronous adapter are all examples of devices that generate hardware interrupts.

To install your own interrupt handler, call a DOS function to replace the interrupt's vector. This is located in the interrupt vector table in low memory (locations 0:0 through 0:03FF). DOS function 35h (get interrupt vector) may be used to retrieve an existing interrupt vector so you can save it in a variable. DOS function 25h (set interrupt vector) may be used to make an interrupt vector point to your own program. As soon as your program no longer needs to process the interrupt, you should reset the vector back to normal. In this chapter, we wrote a simple CTRL-BREAK interrupt handler that was activated whenever CTRL-BREAK was pressed.

A memory-resident program, also called a terminate and stay resident (TSR) program, is one that stays in memory after being executed. Many memory-resident programs are also interrupt handlers, although they do not have to be. We looked at the NO_RESET program, which traps INT 9, the keyboard hardware interrupt. Once installed in memory, this program prevents a user from resetting (booting) the computer with the Ctrl-Alt-Del keys.

REVIEW QUESTIONS

1. Explain the difference between arguments and parameters in the context of a subroutine call.

2. How does the memory model of a calling program affect the way a subroutine accesses its parameters? Be specific in regard to the small and large memory models.

3. What special naming convention is used by a C program when it refers to an identifier from another program module?

4. How does an assembly language program deal with the fact that C programs recognize differences between uppercase and lowercase letters in identifiers?

5. If a Pascal procedure declaration is

```
Procedure Subrtn1 (var  int1, int2 :integer);
```

   what will be passed on the stack, the values of the arguments or the addresses?

6. How is C different from both QuickBASIC and Pascal in regard to the way arguments are pushed on the stack?

7. What advantage is there to the way C pushes arguments on the stack?

8. How is the $L compiler directive used in Turbo Pascal? (Include an example.)

9. Assume the following Pascal function declaration refers to an assembly language subroutine and **table** is an array:

```
Function  FindIt (table :bigarray; value:integer):
                position; external;
```

   Draw a picture of the stack frame right after the subroutine has pushed BP.

10. How does QuickBASIC return a 32-bit function result?

11. How does Turbo Pascal determine whether a subroutine call will be near or far?

12. What type of call (near or far) is the default for QuickBASIC?

13. How is a 6-byte real function result returned by Turbo Pascal?

14. In a QuickBASIC, Pascal, or C subroutine, what is implied by the the following addressing?

```
[bp-4]
```

15. What is wrong with the following instruction in a subroutine called by a C program?

```
ret  6
```

16. Explain the difference between an interrupt handler and a memory-resident program.

17. When a key is pressed on the keyboard, which hardware interrupt is executed?

18. When an interrupt handler finishes, how does the CPU resume execution at the address that was current before the interrupt was triggered?

19. If your program is in the process of creating a disk file and you press a key on the keyboard, when will the key be placed in the keyboard buffer—before or after the file has been created?

20. What do you think would happen if a system timer interrupt occurred between the second and third instructions shown here?

```
mov   ax,mystack
mov   ss,ax
mov   sp,100h
```

21. At which address is the interrupt vector for INT 10h stored?

22. The following statements are designed to modify the interrupt vector for INT 23h, the DOS CTRL-BREAK handler. Write any corrections that are needed:

```
push  ds
mov   ax,@code
mov   ds,ax
mov   ah,25h
mov   ax,offset break_handler
int   21h
pop   ds
```

23. In the following example, a QuickBASIC program calls an assembly language subroutine. Explain what is wrong with the way the assembly subroutine retrieves parameters from the stack:

```
'-------------- QuickBASIC program ----------------

declare SUB Subroutine1 (value1%,value2%,sum%)
```

```
N1% = 20
N2% = 30

call  Subroutine1 (N1%,N2%,sum%)

end

;---------------- Assembly subroutine ----------------

title  Subroutine called by QuickBASIC

public Subroutine1
dosseg
.model medium
.code

Subroutine1 proc
    push  bp
    mov   bp,sp
    mov   ax,[bp+10]     ; get 1st parameter
    add   ax,[bp+8]      ; add 2nd parameter
    mov   [bp+6],ax      ; store the sum
    pop   bp
    ret   6
Subroutine1 endp
end
```

PROGRAMMING EXERCISES

Exercise 1 Interrupt Vectors

Print a dump of interrupt vectors 0–15h on your computer. Then run a memory-resident program such as Borland's Sidekick. Now print another dump of the vector table, and note where the vectors have changed. Choose one of the interrupts, say INT 9, and unassemble the code in memory at the address pointed to by the vector. If the program looks for a hot key, see if you can tell if it inputs a key from port number 60h or if it checks the keyboard flag at address 0040:0017h.

Note: In the next several programming exercises, we are assuming that you have access to Turbo Pascal, Microsoft QuickBASIC, and Turbo C. If this is not the case, you may substitute another language compiler.

Exercise 2 Block Comparison

Turbo Pascal has no built-in function for comparing two memory blocks. Write one in assembly language, and call it from Pascal. You will need to pass the following arguments:

Offset of the first block
Offset of the second block
Number of bytes to compare

The function returns a boolean result (true or false). A sample function declaration is:

```
Function Block_Compare (block1,block2 :word;
      count :integer) : boolean; external;
```

Call the function, using the offsets of two arrays. For example:

```
if Block_Compare (ofs(array1), ofs(array2), 1000) then
 writeln ('The arrays are equal');
```

Extra: Have the function return an enumerated type indicating whether the first block was less than, equal to, or greater than the second block. The type declaration might be:

```
comparetype = (less,equal,greater);
```

Exercise 3 **Search for a String**

Write a subroutine in assembly language that searches for a string inside a large buffer. The routine should then be called from Pascal, QuickBASIC, or C. Write a main program that calls your subroutine. Pass it the name of an array of characters and a short string to be found. Return a value of 0 if the string was not found; otherwise, return the position in the buffer where the string was found. Use the following sample Pascal program to call the routine, if you wish:

```
Program Test;
TYPE
  string80 = string[80];
  chararray = array[1..4096] of char;
VAR
  buffer :chararray;
  n :word;

{$L SRCHSTR}

Function Search_String (var buff :chararray; var st :string80 )
                       : word; external;

BEGIN
  n:= Search_String (buffer,'ABC');
  if n > 0 then
     writeln ('ABC was found at position ',n)
  else
     writeln ('ABC was not found');
END.
```

Exercise 4 Read a Sector

Write a subroutine in assembly language that reads a requested logical sector from the default drive. Call the subroutine from Pascal, QuickBASIC, or C. The calling program must pass the name of a buffer where the sector data will be stored. In Pascal, for example, the procedure call would be:

```
TYPE  buffarray = array[1..512] of byte;
VAR   buffer :buffarray;
      secnum :word;
      .
      .
Read_Sector (secnum, buffer);
```

Exercise 5 CTRL-BREAK Handler

Write your own CTRL-BREAK handler program, modeled after the one presented in this chapter. Add the handler to one of your existing file programs from Chapter 12. When the user presses CTRL-BREAK, display a small window on the screen asking if he or she wishes to return to DOS. If the answer is yes, close any open files and exit to DOS, using INT 21h function 4Ch.

Exercise 6 Library of String Manipulation Routines

Modify three string manipulation routines presented in Chapter 10 so they may be called from Pascal, BASIC, or C. Assemble them into a single .OBJ file, and call each from the chosen high-level language. If the same routines exist in the high-level language, compare their speeds to yours.

Exercise 7 Extended String Manipulation Routines

Find three string manipulation routines that are not available in BASIC or Pascal. Write them in assembly language and call them from a high-level language program. Here are some suggested operations that may be performed on strings:

1. Remove all redundant spaces.
2. Remove all leading spaces.
3. Remove all trailing spaces.
4. Convert the entire string to uppercase or lowercase.
5. Right justify all nonblank characters in the string.
6. Compare two strings without case sensitivity.
7. Copy all characters from one string to another until a selected terminator character is found.
8. Scan a string backwards for a selected character.

Exercise 8 **Keyboard Redefinition**

Write a TSR program that will redefine the IBM-PC keyboard. The NO_RESET program presented in this chapter showed how you can intercept keystrokes before they are passed to the ROM BIOS INT 9 keyboard interrupt. Using this program as a model, write a program that will look up each keyboard scan code in a translate table and change it to another value. Find a way to pass the revised scan code to the original INT 9 handler.

ANSWERS TO REVIEW QUESTIONS

1. Arguments are passed by a calling program to a subroutine. Parameters hold the values inside a subroutine that were passed.

2. A large memory model program pushes a 32-bit return address on the stack, so the first parameter is located at [bp + 6]. A small memory model program pushes a 16-bit return address, and the first parameter is located at [bp + 4].

3. A C program always inserts a leading underscore character before external identifiers.

4. Use the /mx option when assembling the subroutine, which preserves differences between uppercase and lowercase.

5. Since INT1 and INT2 are VAR parameters, their addresses will be passed.

6. QuickBASIC and Pascal push their arguments in order from left to right, whereas C does the opposite.

7. The method used by C makes it possible for a subroutine to have a variable number of parameters.

8. The $L directive is used to name an .OBJ file containing an external subroutine—for example, {$L SUBRTN}.

9. Stack frame in the subroutine after BP has been pushed:

```
          (top of stack)
          +----------+
          |  table   |
          |  value   |
          | ret addr |
   SP →   |    BP    |
          +----------+
```

10. QuickBASIC returns a 32-bit function result in DX:AX.

11. A far procedure or function is declared in the interface section of a unit and may be called from other programs or units. A near procedure is declared either within a program or in the implementation section of a unit and may only be called from within the same program or unit.

12. QuickBASIC defaults to a far call.

13. In DX:BX:AX.

14. [bp – 4] refers to a local variable that is using stack space below the calling program's return address.

15. A subroutine called by a C program should not adjust the stack pointer to compensate for passed parameters. The calling program will do it instead.

16. An interrupt handler is a program or routine that takes over one of the interrupt vectors; it does not have to be memory resident. A memory-resident program is any program that remains in memory after it has finished executing; it need not have anything to do with interrupt vectors.

17. Interrupt 9h.

18. When the interrupt occurs, the Flags, CS, and IP values are pushed on the stack. When the interrupt handler finishes, it uses an IRET instruction to pop the stack into IP, CS, and the Flags.

19. The keyboard interrupt will process the interrupt immediately, unless the program accessing the disk has specifically disabled interrupts (using CLI).

20. The SS register would point to a new stack, while the offset in SP was intended to point to the old stack.

21. The vector for INT 10h is stored at 0000:0040h.

22. The corrected code is as follows:

```
push  ds            ; save DS
mov   ax,@code      ; initialize DS to code segment
mov   ds,ax
mov   ah,25h        ; function: set interrupt vector
mov   al,23h        ; for interrupt 23h
mov   dx,offset break_handler
int   21h
pop   ds            ; restore DS
```

23. The subroutine seems to assume that the arguments were passed by value, as one does in C or Pascal. In this example, however, the QuickBASIC program is passing the offsets of the arguments. This means the subroutine must take an extra step to use the passed address of each variable to obtain the variable's value. For example:

```
mov    bx,[bp+10]        ; get 1st parameter
mov    ax,[bx]
mov    bx,[bp+8]         ; add 2nd parameter
add    ax,[bx]
mov    bx,[bp+6]         ; store the result
mov    [bx],ax
```

Binary and Hexadecimal Tutorial

BINARY NUMBERS

Binary numbers are called *base 2* numbers because each digit is either 0 or 1. Computers store instructions and data as a series of binary digits, called *bits*. The binary digits are organized into groups of 8 called *bytes*. Two bytes together make a *word*, although this number will vary, depending on the size of the computer.

Counting and Addition. If a carry results when two binary digits are added together, the carried digit is moved to the next highest position:

$$1 + 1 = 10$$

The following shows what happens if we add 1 to 10b and continue the process:

$$\begin{aligned} 10 + 1 &= 11 \\ 11 + 1 &= 100 \\ 100 + 1 &= 101 \\ 101 + 1 &= 110 \end{aligned}$$

Addition Examples. When several digits are involved, the arithmetic always begins with the rightmost digits, carrying into the next highest position when necessary:

Add Binary 0011 and 0101

```
        1        ← Step 1: 1 + 1 = 0, carry generated
   0 0 1 1
 + 0 1 0 1
 ---------
         0
```

```
      1 1        ← Step 2: 1 + 1 + 0 = 0, carry generated
   0 0 1 1
 + 0 1 0 1
 ---------
       0 0
```

```
    1 1 1        ← Step 3: 1 + 0 + 1 = 0, carry generated
   0 0 1 1
 + 0 1 0 1
 ---------
     0 0 0
```

```
    1 1 1        ← Step 4: 1 + 0 + 0 = 1, no carry generated
   0 0 1 1
 + 0 1 0 1
 ---------
   1 0 0 0       (result)
```

Add Binary 0011 and 0011

```
        1        ← Step 1: 1 + 1 = 0, carry generated
   0 0 1 1
 + 0 0 1 1
 ---------
         0
```

```
      1 1        ← Step 2: 1 + 1 + 1 = 1, carry generated
   0 0 1 1
 + 0 0 1 1
 ---------
       1 0
```

```
    ' '           ← Step 3: 1 + 0 + 0 = 1, no carry
  0 0 1 1
+ 0 0 1 1
---------
    1 0 0


    ' '           ← Step 4: 0 + 0 = 0, no carry
  0 0 1 1
+ 0 0 1 1
---------
  0 1 1 0         (result)
```

Binary to Decimal Conversion

To convert a binary number to its decimal equivalent, we evaluate each digit position as a power of 2. Thus, $2^0 = 1$, $2^1 = 2$, $2^2 = 4$, and so on. Let's use the binary number 1111 as an example—its decimal value is 15:

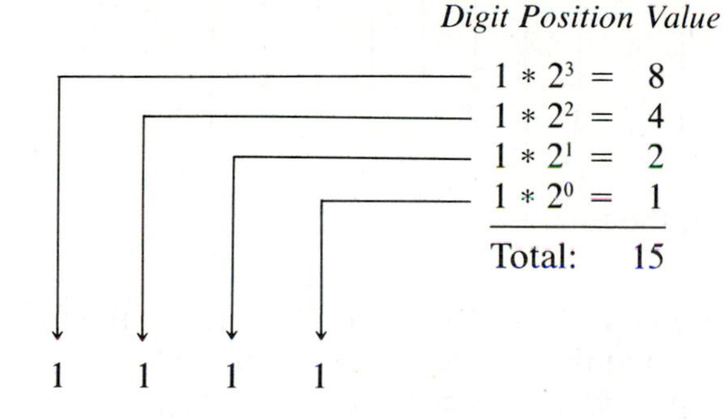

Find the Value of Binary 1010. Bits 1 and 3 are set, so we add 8 and 2 to get decimal 10:

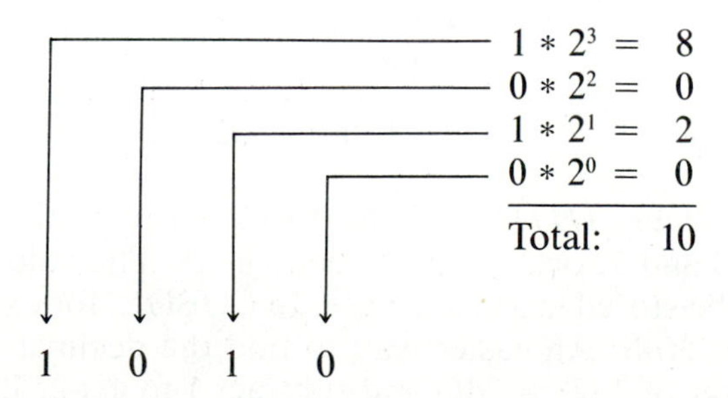

At first glance, it would seem that only small numbers could be represented in binary. When you include 16 bits in a number, the values increase quickly. To see this, you might want to add up the values for each bit position in the following table:

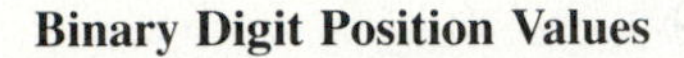

Binary Digit Position Values

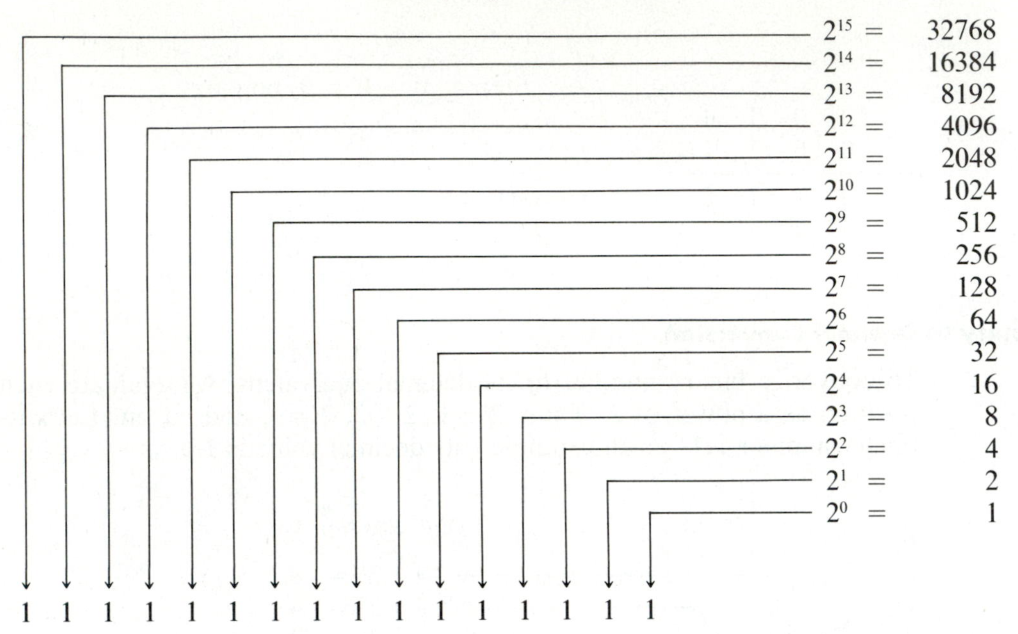

To save you the trouble, the total for 16 bits is 65,535.

Decimal Value of Binary 11001010. We can refer to the foregoing table of digit position values to find the decimal value of an 8-bit binary number. The following bit positions are added together (the lowest digit in a binary number is *bit 0*):

$$
\begin{array}{rr}
\text{bit } 7 = & 128 \\
+ \text{ bit } 6 = & 64 \\
+ \text{ bit } 3 = & 8 \\
+ \text{ bit } 1 = & 2 \\
\hline
\text{Total} = & 202
\end{array}
$$

Decimal Value of Binary 11111111. This turns out to be the sum of all digit positions between 0 and 7, or $2^7 + 2^6 + 2^5 \ldots + 2^0$. The value is 255, the largest number that can be stored in a single byte. In COBOL, for example, this is called HIGH-VALUES. *Hint*: An easier way to find the decimal value is to take the next highest power of 2 ($2^8 = 256$) and subtract 1 to get 255.

Decimal Value of Binary 1000000010000000. Since this is a *16-bit* number, bit 15 is set (2^{15}), and bit 7 is set (2^7). The sum of 32,768 and 128 is 32,896.

Decimal Value of Binary 1111111111111111. This is the largest possible unsigned 16-bit number. One way to find its decimal value is to add up all the bit positions using the Powers of 2 table:

$$\begin{array}{ccccccccc} 2^{15} & + & 2^{14} & + & 2^{13} & + & 2^{12} \ldots & + & 2^{0} \\ (32{,}767 & + & 16{,}384 & + & 8{,}192 & + & 4{,}092 \ldots & + & 1) = 65{,}535 \end{array}$$

An easier way is to find the value of 2^{16} and subtract 1:

$$\begin{array}{l} 2^{16} - 1 \quad = 65{,}535 \\ (65{,}536 - 1) \end{array}$$

Decimal to Binary Conversion

When debugging or testing assembly language programs, you often need to know in advance how big a decimal value will be. You must be able to convert the decimal value into binary and compare it with the actual contents of memory and registers.

Convert by Inspection. If the number to be converted is a power of 2, we can usually perform the conversion to binary intuitively. Suppose we want to find the binary representation of the number 66. We know the binary equivalent of 64 is 01000000. We can verify this by noting the entry for 2^6 in the Powers of 2 table. We also know that 2 is really 2^1 and the sum of 64 and 2 is 66, so we set bits 1 and 6. The result is 66, or 01000010b.

Method 1: Divide by Powers of 2. The intuitive method becomes hard to follow for larger decimal numbers. Instead we can divide a decimal number by powers of 2. Suppose we would like to find the binary equivalent of 76. The largest power of 2 that fits into 76 is 64 (2^6); therefore, bit 6 in the binary value is set:

0 1 0 0 0 0 0 0 = 64

If we subtract 64 from 76, the result is 12. The largest power of 2 that fits into 12 is 8 (2^3); therefore, bit 3 is also set:

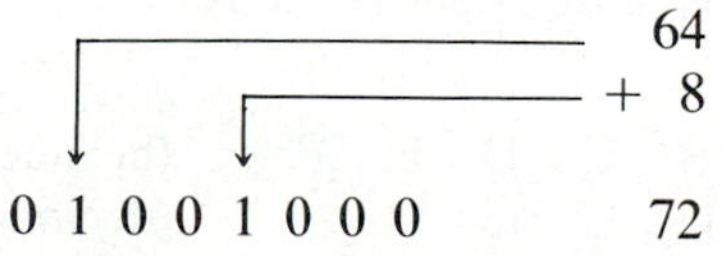

```
 ┌────────────────────── 64
 │        ┌───────────── + 8
 ↓        ↓
0 1 0 0 1 0 0 0          72
```

If we subtract 72 from 76, the result is 4, which is 2^2. Therefore, bit 2 is also set. The final result is 76, or 01001100b.

Therefore, we were able to convert 76 to binary by dividing successively smaller powers of 2 into the decimal number. The steps may be listed as follows:

72 / 64	=	1,	remainder 12
12 / 8	=	1,	remainder 4
4 / 4	=	1,	remainder 0

As soon as the remainder equals 0, we stop. This method involves some trial and error, yet it works well when conversions are done by hand.

Method 2: Divide by 2. Another way to convert a decimal number to binary is to first divide the number by 2; take the quotient and divide it by 2; take the next quotient and divide it by 2; and so on. The remainder from each division becomes one of the binary digits. Let's use this method to find the binary equivalent of 76:

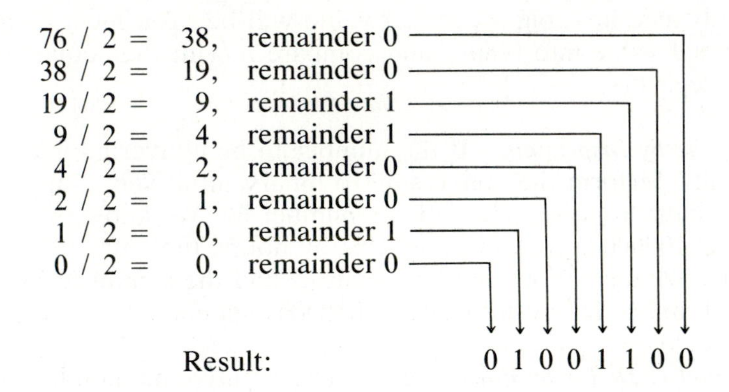

As we see, the division was carried out eight times. The first remainder is placed in bit position 0. This method is ideally suited to a looping algorithm in a computer program but is time-consuming when performed by hand.

HEXADECIMAL NUMBERS

Hexadecimal numbers are *base 16* numbers, containing digits from 0 to 9 and letters from *A* to *F*. Each digit value is shown here:

0	1	2	3	4	5	6	7	8	9	A	B	C	D	E	F	(hexadecimal digit)
0	1	2	3	4	5	6	7	8	9	10	11	12	13	14	15	(decimal value)

Computer storage and addresses are almost always expressed in hexadecimal on the IBM-PC. Large values may be stored in just a few digits, and the digits correspond closely to binary numbers. In this book, I follow the notation used by the Macro Assembler: Hexadecimal numbers are followed by a lowercase *h*. For example, 45h is a hexadecimal number, while 45 is a decimal number.

Binary to Hexadecimal Conversion

The following table shows how each sequence of 4 binary bits may be translated into a single hexadecimal digit:

Binary	Hex	Binary	Hex	
0000	0	1000	8	
0001	1	1001	9	
0010	2	1010	A	(10)
0011	3	1011	B	(11)
0100	4	1100	C	(12)
0101	5	1101	D	(13)
0110	6	1110	E	(14)
0111	7	1111	F	(15)

Large binary numbers may be converted to hexadecimal. Each group of 4 bits is converted as if it were an independent number. With practice, this may be done quickly:

```
 A     B       9     7       8     6       E     5
1010  1011    1001  0111    1000  0110    1110  0101   =   AB9786E5
```

Converting a large hexadecimal number to binary is easy also, because each hexadecimal digit converts to 4 bits:

8A 26 40 = 1000 1010 0010 0110 0100 0000

More examples are listed here:

Hex	Binary
0AF6	0000 1010 1111 0110
D58C	1101 0101 1000 1100

Hexadecimal to Decimal Conversion

Each digit position in a hexadecimal number may be thought of as a power of 16, as shown by the following table:

HEXADECIMAL TO DECIMAL CONVERSION TABLE

	Digit Position			
Digit	**3**	**2**	**1**	**0**
1	4,096	256	16	1
2	8,192	512	32	2
3	12,288	768	48	3
4	16,384	1,024	64	4
5	20,480	1,280	80	5
6	24,576	1,536	96	6
7	28,672	1,792	112	7
8	32,768	2,048	128	8
9	36,864	2,304	144	9
A	40,960	2,560	160	10
B	45,056	2,816	176	11
C	49,152	3,072	192	12
D	53,348	3,328	208	13
E	57,344	3,584	224	14
F	61,440	3,840	240	15

Example. Using this table, we can calculate the value of 2412h:

1. The highest digit in the number 2,412 is 2, located in digit position 3. Add the value 8,192 in row 2 to the total.
2. The next digit is 4, in digit position 2. Add the value 1,024 to the total.
3. The next digit is 1, in digit position 1. Add the value 16 to the total.
4. The next digit is 2, in digit position 0. Add the value 2 to the total.

The total (8,192 + 1,024 + 16 + 2) is 9,234.

Hexadecimal Digit Position Values. Converting numbers from hexadecimal to decimal is similar to converting from binary to decimal. One method involves using the values of each hexadecimal digit position. To do this, we multiply each digit by its digit position value. If we use the hexadecimal to decimal conversion table as a guide, we can imagine 42h as the sum of 64 and 2:

```
     64      (4 * 16)
 +    2      (2 * 1)
 ----------------------
     66 decimal
```

Example: Convert 0146h to Decimal. We multiply 0 by 4,096, 1 by 256, 4 by 16, and 6 by 1. The sum of these operations is 326:

	0	(0 * 4096)
	256	(1 * 256)
	64	(4 * 16)
+	6	(6 * 1)
	326	(total)

Example: Convert 3BA4h to Decimal. Before multiplying each digit by its position value, we need to remember that the hexadecimal digit "B" is equal to 11 and the digit "A" is equal to 10:

	12,288	(3 * 4,096)
	2,816	(11 * 256)
	160	(10 * 16)
+	4	(4 * 1)
	15,268	decimal

Decimal to Hexadecimal Conversion

Successive Division by 16. A good way to convert from decimal to hexadecimal is to divide the number by 16; take the quotient of this and divide it by 16; take the next quotient and divide by 16, and so on. The remainder from each division becomes a hexadecimal digit. Let's use this method to find the hexadecimal equivalent of 48:

```
48 / 16 =  3,  remainder 0 ──────────────────┐
 3 / 16 =  0,  remainder 3 ───────────────┐  │
                                          ↓  ↓
                  Hexadecimal result:     3  0
```

Example: Convert 326 to Hexadecimal. Divide 326 by 16; then divide each quotient by 16. Each remainder becomes a digit in the result:

```
326 / 16 = 20,  remainder 6 ──────────────────┐
 20 / 16 =  1,  remainder 4 ───────────────┐  │
  1 / 16 =  0,  remainder 1 ────────────┐  │  │
                                        ↓  ↓  ↓
           Hexadecimal result:          1  4  6
```

Example: Convert 15,268 to Hexadecimal. This is the reverse of an example shown earlier, when 3BA4h was converted to 15,268 decimal:

```
15,268 / 16 = 954,   remainder  4
   954 / 16 = 59,    remainder 10
    59 / 16 = 3,     remainder 11
     3 / 16 = 0,     remainder  3

     Hexadecimal result:         3 B A 4
```

ARITHMETIC

The 8088/8086 performs all arithmetic in binary, so it is particularly important for you to be able to check calculations manually when debugging programs.

Signed and Unsigned Numbers

Binary numbers may be either *signed* or *unsigned*. The CPU performs arithmetic and comparison operations for both types. Let's use an 8-bit number as an example. If *unsigned*, all 8 bits contribute to the number's value, as with binary 11111111:

```
1 1 1 1 1 1 1 1   =   255
```

Therefore, 255 (hexadecimal FF, binary 11111111) is the largest value that may be stored in a single byte. The largest 16-bit value that may be stored in a word (2 bytes) is 65,535:

```
1111111111111111   =   65,535
```

A *signed* number is used when an arithmetic operation might involve a negative number. A signed number may be either negative or positive, as indicated by the number's highest bit. If the bit is set, the number is negative:

```
(sign bit)
   ↓
   1 0 0 0 1 0 1 0   (negative)
   0 0 0 0 1 0 1 0   (positive),   +10
```

The positive number above is +10 (decimal). What about the negative number: Is it −10? Negative values are not as easy to recognize. Instead, they are stored in a special format called *twos complement notation* for machine efficiency reasons.

Twos Complement Notation

When a signed number has its highest bit set, the number must be converted back into normal notation before we can tell what its value is. To find the twos complement of a number, do two things: Reverse all bits, and then add 1 to the result. Using the negative binary number 11111010 as an example, we can see that its value is −6:

```
     1 1 1 1 1 0 1 0
     0 0 0 0 0 1 0 1    ← reverse all bits
+                  1    ← add 1
 -------------------
     0 0 0 0 0 1 1 0    ← result:  6
```

After adding 1, the number 6 is generated. We add the negative sign to the result, which becomes −6.

Maximum and Minimum Signed Values. The highest bit of a signed number is called the *sign bit,* because it is reserved for the sign. A signed byte value has only 7 bits to use for the number's value, making the highest value possible equal to +127, or 7Fh. A 16-bit signed number has a maximum value of +32,767, or 7FFFh:

```
           (sign bit)

Byte:          0 1 1 1 1 1 1 1                   =  +127
Word:          0 1 1 1 1 1 1 1 1 1 1 1 1 1 1 1   =  +32,767
```

The smallest negative value a byte may have is −128, and the smallest negative value a 16-bit word may have is −32,768:

```
Byte:          1 0 0 0 0 0 0 0                   =  −128
Word:          1 0 0 0 0 0 0 0 0 0 0 0 0 0 0 0   =  −32,768
```

Example: Convert Signed Binary 11111111 to Decimal. First, find the twos complement, and then convert it to decimal. Binary 11111111 is actually the same as decimal −1:

```
   11111111
   00000000    ← reverse all bits
+         1    ← add 1
 ----------
   00000001    ← result:   −1
```

Example: Convert Signed Binary 11101100 to Decimal.

```
  11101100

  00010011     ← reverse all bits
+        1     ← add 1
----------
  00010100     ← result:   −20
```

Example: Convert Signed 9Bh to Decimal. We know that 9Bh is negative because its highest bit is set:

```
10011011
```

To convert it to decimal, we find its twos complement:

```
  10011011  =  9Bh
  01100100  =  64h
+        1
----------
  01100101  =  65h   (result: −101)
```

Hexadecimal Twos Complement. The ones complement of a hexadecimal number may be found by subtracting each digit from 15. Try this using 9Bh:

$15 - 9 = 6$

$15 - B = 4$

This yields 64h. To get the twos complement of the original number, add 1 to 64h, giving 65h. Thus, the twos complement of 9Bh is 65h.

What's the twos complement of 6A295CD4h? The ones complement is 95D6A32Bh, found by subtracting each original digit from 15. Adding 1 to this, we get 95D6A32Ch. This shows that larger numbers present no special difficulty.

Binary Subtraction

Before subtracting one binary number from another, it must be converted to its twos complement. Then the two operands may be added together. Suppose you want to subtract 00010000b from 00011100b. Intuitively, we understand that this is the same as $28 - 16 = 12$. The twos complement of the first number is 11110000b, or −16. We add this to the second number:

```
    00011100       (+28)
+   11110000   +   (-16)
   ----------
    00001100  <-   result =  (+12)
```

Hexadecimal Addition and Subtraction

When we add two hexadecimal numbers, each digit of the first number is added to the corresponding digit of the second. As long as no carry is generated, the addition is simple. Each value in the following example is shown in hexadecimal:

```
    0 4 A 0
+   3 6 7 5
  ---------
    3 B 1 5
```

When two digits generate a value larger than 15, a carry is generated. For example, 0Ah + 7 = 17: We divide 17 by the hexadecimal number base (16), carrying the quotient (1) to the next highest digit position. The remainder is placed in the lowest digit position of the result, which is 11h:

```
   1
     A
+    7
  ----
   1 1
```

Example: Add 3BA8h and 02B5h. First, 8 + 5 = 13 (Dh); then Ah + Bh = 21, which requires a carry; then 21 / 16 = 1, remainder 5. Carry the 1, and place the 5 in the current digit position. Next, 1 + Bh + 2 = Eh. Finally, 3 + 0 = 3:

```
      1
    3 B A 8
+   0 2 B 5
  ---------
    3 E 5 D
```

Example: Subtract 0009h from 3E62h. Fortunately, unsigned hexadecimal numbers may be subtracted directly, without having to use twos complement notation. In the following example, a *borrow* was generated in the first digit position, since 9 is greater than 2. In a base-16 numbering system, a borrow returns a value of 16. We can interpret the subtraction in the first digit position as 18 − 9 = 9:

```
        -1         <- borrow
    3 E 6 2
-   0 0 0 9
  ---------
    3 E 5 9
```

REVIEW QUESTIONS

1. What is the largest unsigned hexadecimal value that may be stored in (a) a single byte? (b) a single word?

2. Convert the following decimal numbers to hexadecimal:
   a. 26
   b. 435

3. Convert the following decimal numbers to 16-bit binary:
   a. 4,096
   b. −128
   c. 256
   d. 514
   e. −1
   f. −32,768

4. Convert the following hexadecimal numbers to binary:
   a. 6AFCh
   b. 204Eh
   c. BDCAh

5. Convert the following unsigned hexadecimal numbers to decimal:
   a. 100h
   b. 6BCh

6. What is the hexadecimal representation of the following sequence of binary bits?

   1011 1000 1010 1111

7. Convert the following unsigned binary numbers to decimal:
   a. 00010110
   b. 11010101
   c. 10001000
   d. 01111100

8. Convert each signed 16-bit binary number to decimal:
   a. 1111111111111110
   b. 1111111111111000

9. Convert each signed binary number to its twos complement, and write the decimal value of the latter:
   a. 11110101
   b. 00011010
   c. 10000000
   d. 11111111

10. Convert the following signed hexadecimal values to decimal:
    a. EFFFh
    b. 200h
    c. B6DCh
    d. FFFFh

11. Assemble and execute the following instructions, using a debugger. Assuming both numbers are signed, write down the contents of AL after the second instruction and explain what has happened. Use decimal values in your explanation:

```
mov  al,51h
add  al,FEh
```

ANSWERS TO REVIEW QUESTIONS

1 a. 255
  b. 65,535

2. a. 1Ah
   b. 1B3h

3. a. 00001000 00000000b
   b. 11111111 10000000b
   c. 00000001 00000000b
   d. 00000010 00000010b
   e. 11111111 11111111b
   f. 10000000 00000000b

4. a. 01101010 11111100b
   b. 00100000 01001110b
   c. 10111101 11001010b

5. a. 256
   b. 1724

6. B8AFh

7. a. 22
   b. 213
   c. 136
   d. 124

8. a. FFFEh = −2
   b. FFF8h = −8

9. a. 00001011 = 11
   b. 11100110 = −26
   c. 10000000 = 128
   d. 00000001 = 1

10. a. The twos complement of EFFFh is 1001h, which, when converted to decimal, is 4,097. The sign bit was set, so the value is −4,097.
    b. The number 200h is positive, so we don't need to find its twos complement. Its decimal value is 512.
    c. The twos complement of B6DCh is 4924h, which, when converted to decimal, is 18,724. The sign bit was set, so the value is −18,724.
    d. The twos complement of FFFFh is 0001h, which translates to a decimal value of −1.

11. First, 51h = decimal 81, and 0FEh = decimal −2. Therefore, the sum of these should be 79, or 4Fh. When you run the program, the answer in AL is 4Fh, and the Carry flag is set because the sum of 51h and FEh is greater than 8 bits. The carry is irrelevant, because the numbers are signed.

Using DEBUG

As you learn assembly language programming on the IBM-PC, the importance of using a debugger program cannot be stressed too much. A debugger displays the contents of memory quickly and easily, showing registers and variables as they change. You can step through a program one statement at a time, making it easier to find logic errors.

Beginning assembly language programmers often underestimate the value of a debugger and do not spend enough time mastering it. I use a debugger almost daily to test assembler instructions, to try out new programming ideas, or to step through new programs. It takes supreme self-confidence to write an assembly language program and run it directly from DOS the first time! If one should forget to match pushes and pops, for example, a return from a subroutine will branch to an unexpected location. Any call or jump to a location outside your program will almost surely cause DOS to crash. For this reason, you would be wise to run newly written programs in DEBUG first. Watch the stack pointer (SP) very closely as you step through the program, and note any unusual changes to the CS and IP registers.

This appendix covers the DEBUG.COM utility supplied with DOS that helps you test and debug assembly language programs. DEBUG is small enough to be included on the same floppy disk with the Macro Assembler or your favorite text editor.

Debugging Functions. Some of the most rudimentary functions that a debugger can perform are the following:

- Assemble short programs
- View a program's source code, along with its machine code
- View the CPU registers and flags
- Trace or execute a program, watching variables for changes
- Enter new values into memory
- Search for binary or ASCII values in memory
- Move a block of memory from one location to another
- Fill a block of memory
- Load and write disk files

Many commercial debuggers are available, ranging widely in sophistication and cost: CodeView, Periscope, Atron, SYMDEB, Codesmith-86, and Turbo Debugger, to mention just a few. When you first start out, DEBUG is the simplest and is provided with DOS.

DEBUG is called an *assembly level* debugger because it displays only assembly mnemonics and machine instructions. Even if you use it to debug a compiled Pascal program, for instance, you will simply see a disassembly of the program's machine instructions. It is ideally suited to assembling and debugging short, simple programs. You may load and run it by typing the command DEBUG from the DOS prompt.

In order to trace or execute a machine language program, you must type the name of the program being debugged on the same command line. To debug the program SAMPLE.EXE, for example, we would type:

```
debug sample.exe
```

If we could picture RAM memory after typing this command, we would see DOS loaded in the lowest area, DEBUG loaded above DOS, and the program SAMPLE.EXE loaded above DEBUG. In this way, several programs are resident in memory at the same time. DOS retains control over the execution of DEBUG, and DEBUG controls the execution of SAMPLE.EXE.

Printing a DEBUG Session. If you want a printed copy of everything you've done during a DEBUG session, type CTRL-PRTSC right after loading DEBUG. This command is a toggle, so it may be typed a second time to turn the printer output off.

DEBUG COMMAND SUMMARY

DEBUG commands may be divided into four categories: program creation/debugging, memory manipulation, miscellaneous, and input-output.

Program Creation and Debugging

A Assemble a program using instruction mnemonics
G Execute the program currently in memory
R Display the contents of registers and flags
P Trace past an instruction, procedure, or loop
T Trace a single instruction
U Disassemble memory into assembler mnemonics

Memory Manipulation

C Compare one memory range with another
D Dump (display) the contents of memory
E Enter bytes into memory
F Fill a memory range with a single value
M Move bytes from one memory range to another
S Search a memory range for specific value(s)

Miscellaneous

H Perform hexadecimal addition and subtraction
Q Quit DEBUG and return to DOS

Input-Output

I Input a byte from a port
L Load data from disk
O Output a byte to a port
N Create a filename for use by the L and W commands
W Write data from memory to disk

When DEBUG is first loaded, the following defaults are in effect:

1. All segment registers are set to the bottom of free memory, just above the DEBUG program.
2. IP is set to 0100h.
3. DEBUG reserves 256 bytes of stack space at the end of the current segment.
4. All of available memory is allocated (reserved).
5. BX:CX are set to the length of the current program or file.
6. The flags are set to the following values: NV (Overflow flag clear), UP (Direction flag = up), EI (interrupts enabled), PL (Sign flag = positive), NZ (Zero flag clear), NA (Auxiliary Carry flag clear), PO (odd parity), NC (Carry flag clear).

Command Parameters

DEBUG's command prompt is a hyphen (-). Commands may be typed in either uppercase or lowercase letters, in any column. A command may be followed by one or more parameters. A comma or space may be used to separate two parameters. The standard command parameters are explained here.

Address. A complete segment-offset address may be given, or just an offset. The segment portion may be a hexadecimal number or segment register name:

F000:100	Segment, offset
DS:200	Segment register, offset
0AF5	Offset

Filespec. A file specification, made up of a drive designation, filename, and extension. At a minimum, a filename must be supplied. Examples are:

```
b:prog1.com
c:\asm\progs\test.com
file1
```

List. One or more byte or string values, separated by commas:

```
10,20,30,40
'A','B',50
```

Range. A range refers to a span of memory, identified by addresses in one of two formats. In Format 1, if the second address is omitted, it defaults to a standard value. In Format 2, the value following the letter *L* is the number of bytes to be processed by the command. A range cannot be greater than 10000h (65,536):

Syntax		Examples
Format 1:	address [,address]	100,500 CS:200,300 200
Format 2:	address L [value]	100 L 20 (refers to the 20h bytes starting at location 100)

Sector. A sector consists of a starting sector number and the number of sectors to be loaded or written. You can access logical disk sectors using the L (load) and W (write) commands.

String. A string is a sequence of characters enclosed in single or double quotes. For example:

```
'COMMAND'
"File cannot be opened."
```

Value. A value consists of a 1- to 4-character hexadecimal number. For example:

```
3A
3A6F
```

INDIVIDUAL COMMANDS

This section describes the most common DEBUG commands. A good way to learn them is to sit at the computer while reading this material and experiment with each command.

A (Assemble)

Assemble a program into machine language. The syntax is

```
A [address]
```

Address is assumed to be an offset from the address in CS, unless another segment value is given.

Example	Comment
A 100	Assemble at CS:100h.
A	Assemble from the current location.
A DS:2000	Assemble at DS:2000h.

Each time you press ENTER at the end of a line, DEBUG prompts you for the next line of input. Each input line starts with a segment-offset address. To terminate your input, press ENTER on a blank line. For example:

```
-a 100
5514:0100 mov ah,2
5514:0102 mov dl,41
5514:0104 int 21
5514:0106
```

(boldface text typed by the programmer)

D (Dump)

The D command displays memory on the screen as single bytes in both hexadecimal and ASCII. There are two syntax formats:

```
Format 1: D[address]
Format 2: D[range]
```

If no address is specified, the location begins where the last D command left off, or at location DS:0 if the command is being typed for the first time. An address may consist of a segment-offset address or just an offset:

```
D  F000:0     (segment-offset)
D  ES:100     (segment register-offset)
D  100        (offset)
```

The default segment is DS, so leave it out unless you want to dump an offset from another segment location.

A range may be given, telling DEBUG to dump all bytes within the range:

```
D  150 15A   ; Dump DS:0150 through 015A
```

Other segment registers or absolute addresses may be used, as the following examples show:

Example	Comment
D	Dump 128 bytes from the last referenced location.
D SS:0 5	Dump the bytes at offsets 0–5 from SS.
D 915:0	Dump 128 bytes at offset zero from segment 0915h.
D 0 200	Dump offsets 0–200 from DS.
D 100 L 20	Dump 20h bytes, starting at offset 100h from DS.

Memory Dump Example. The following figure shows an example of a memory dump. The numbers at the left are the segment and offset address of the first byte in each line. The next 16 pairs of digits are the hexadecimal contents of each byte. The characters to the right are the ASCII representation of each byte. The dump appears to be of machine language instructions, rather than displayable characters (from COMMAND.COM):

```
DEBUG COMMAND.COM
-D 100

1CC0:0100  83 7E A4 01 72 64 C7 46-F8 01 00 8B 76 F8 80 7A   .~$.rdGFx...vx.z
1CC0:0110  A5 20 73 49 80 7A A5 0E-75 06 C6 42 A5 0A EB 3D   %sI.z%.u.FB%.k=
1CC0:0120  8B 76 F8 80 7A A5 08 74-0C 80 7A A5 07 74 06 80   .vx.z%.t..z%.t..
1CC0:0130  7A A5 0F 75 28 FF 46 FA-8B 76 FA 8B 84 06 F6 8B   z%.u(.Fz.vz...v.
1CC0:0140  7E F8 3A 43 A5 75 0C 03-36 A8 F4 8B 44 FF 88 43   ~x:C%u..6(t.D..C
1CC0:0150  A5 EB 0A A1 06 F6 32 E4-3B 46 FA 77 D8 8B 46 F8   %k.!.v2d;FzwX.Fx
1CC0:0160  40 89 46 F8 48 3B 46 A4-75 A1 A1 06 F6 32 E4 3B   @.FxH;F$u!!.v2d;
1CC0:0170  46 FC B9 00 00 75 01 41-A1 A8 F4 03 46 FC 8B 16   F:9..u.A!(t.F:..
```

This is a different part of COMMAND.COM. Since memory at this point contains a list of the command names, the ASCII dump is more interesting:

```
1CD6:3AC0  05 45 58 49 53 54 EA 15-00 04 44 49 52 01 FA 09   .EXISTj...DIR.z.
1CD6:3AD0  07 52 45 4E 41 4D 45 01-B2 0C 04 52 45 4E 01 B2   .RENAME.2..REN.2
1CD6:3AE0  0C 06 45 52 41 53 45 01-3D 0C 04 44 45 4C 01 3D   ..ERASE.=..DEL.=
1CD6:3AF0  0C 05 54 59 50 45 01 EF-0C 04 52 45 4D 00 04 01   ..TYPE.o..REM...
1CD6:3B00  05 43 4F 50 59 01 CC 1A-06 50 41 55 53 45 00 1F   .COPY.L..PAUSE..
1CD6:3B10  13 05 44 41 54 45 00 38-18 05 54 49 4D 45 00 CE   ..DATE.8..TIME.N
1CD6:3B20  18 04 56 45 52 00 57 0E-04 56 4F 4C 01 C8 0D 03   ..VER.W..VOL.H..
1CD6:3B30  43 44 01 A6 12 06 43 48-44 49 52 01 A6 12 03 4D   CD.&..CHDIR.&..M
1CD6:3B40  44 01 D9 12 06 4D 4B 44-49 52 01 D9 12 03 52 44   D.Y..MKDIR.Y..RD
1CD6:3B50  01 0E 13 06 52 4D 44 49-52 01 0E 13 06 42 52 45   ....RMDIR....BRE
1CD6:3B60  41 4B 00 92 17 07 56 45-52 49 46 59 00 C7 17 04   AK....VERIFY.G..
1CD6:3B70  53 45 54 00 0F 10 07 50-52 4F 4D 50 54 00 FA 0F   SET....PROMPT.z.
1CD6:3B80  05 50 41 54 48 00 A0 0F-05 45 58 49 54 00 C9 11   .PATH. ..EXIT.I.
1CD6:3B90  05 43 54 54 59 01 F7 11-05 45 43 48 4F 00 59 17   .CTTY.w..ECHO.Y.
1CD6:3BA0  05 47 4F 54 4F 00 96 16-06 53 48 49 46 54 00 56   .GOTO....SHIFT.V
1CD6:3BB0  16 03 49 46 00 50 15 04-46 4F 52 00 68 14 04 43   ..IF.P..FOR.h..C
1CD6:3BC0  4C 53 00 53 12 00 00 00-00 00 00 00 00 00 00 00   LS.S...........
```

E (Enter)

The E command places individual bytes in memory. You must supply a starting memory location where the values will be stored. If only an offset value is entered, the offset is assumed to be from DS. Otherwise, a 32-bit address may be entered, or another segment register may be used. The syntax is:

`E` *address*	Enter new byte value at *address*
`E` *address* `[`*list*`]`	Replace the contents of memory starting at the specified address with the values contained in the list.

To begin entering hexadecimal or character data at DS:100, type

```
E 100
```

Press the space bar to advance to the next byte, and press ENTER to stop. To enter a string into memory starting at location CS:100, type

```
E CS:100 "This is a string."
```

F (Fill)

The F command fills a range of memory with a single value or a list of values. The range must be specified as two offset addresses or segment-offset addresses. The syntax is:

F *range list*

Examples are given in the following table:

Example	Comment
F 100 500,' '	Fill with spaces.
F CS:300 CS:1000,FF	Fill with hex 0FF.
F 100 L 20 'A'	Fill 20 hex bytes with the letter 'A', starting at location 100.

G (Go)

Execute the program in memory. You can specify a starting address and a breakpoint, causing the program to stop at a given address. The syntax is:

G [=*startaddress*] *brkptaddress* [*brkptaddress...*]

If no breakpoint is specified, the program runs until it stops by itself and returns to DEBUG. Up to 10 breakpoints may be specified. Examples are given in the following table:

Example	Comment
G	Execute from IP to the end of the program.
G 50	Execute from the IP to CS:50h and stop.
G=10 50	Begin execution at offset 10h and stop before the instruction at offset 50h.

H (Hexarithmetic)

The H command performs addition and subtraction on two hexadecimal numbers, entered in the following format:

```
H value1 value2
```

For example, the hexadecimal values 1A and 10 are added and subtracted here:

```
H 1A 10

002A 000A        ← displayed by DEBUG
```

L (Load)

The L command loads a file (or disk sectors) into memory. To read a file, you must first initialize its name with the N (Name) command. If no address is specified, the file is loaded at CS:100. DEBUG sets BX and CX to the number of bytes read. Syntax:

```
L [address]
```

Example:

```
N B:PROG1.COM        (Initialize the file name)
L                    (Load at CS:100)
```

M (Move)

The M command copies a block of data from one memory location to another. The syntax is:

```
M range address
```

Range consists of the starting and ending locations of the bytes to be copied. *Address* is the target location, to which the data will be copied. All offsets are assumed to be from DS, unless specified otherwise.

Example	Comment
M 100 105 110	Move bytes in the range DS:100–105 to location DS:110.
M CS:100 105 CS:110	Same as above, except that all offsets are relative to the segment value in CS.

Sample String Move. The following example uses the M command to copy the string 'ABCDEF' from offset 100h to 106h. First we enter the string at location 100h; then we dump memory, showing the string. Next we move (copy) the string to offset 106h and dump offsets 100h–10Bh:

```
-E 100 "ABCDEF"
-D 100 105
19EB:0100 41 42 43 44 45 46                                 ABCDEF
-M 100 105 106
-D 100 10B
19EB:0100 41 42 43 44 45 46 41 42 43 44 45 46   ABCDEFABCDEF
```

N (Name)

The N command initializes a filename (and file control block) in memory before using the *Load* or *Write* commands. The syntax is:

```
N [d:][filename][.ext]
```

Example:

```
N b:myfile.dta
```

P (Ptrace)

Execute the next instruction and stop; if the instruction calls a procedure, execute the procedure and then stop. The LOOP instruction and string primitive instructions (SCAS, LODS, etc.) are executed completely up to the next instruction.

LOOP Example. Let's look at an example where the P command steps through MOV and ADD instructions one at a time. When the P command reaches the LOOP instruction, however, the complete loop is executed five times.

Assemble the following program:

```
-A 100
4A66:0100 mov  cx,5      ; loop counter = 5
4A66:0103 mov  ax,0
4A66:0106 add  ax,cx
4A66:0108 loop 106       ; loop to location 0106h

AX=000F  BX=0000  CX=0000  DX=0000  SP=FFEE  BP=0000  SI=0000  DI=0000
DS=4A66  ES=4A66  SS=4A66  CS=4A66  IP=0100   NV UP EI PL NZ NA PE NC
4A66:0100 B90500          MOV     CX,0005
-P
```

```
AX=000F  BX=0000  CX=0005  DX=0000  SP=FFEE  BP=0000  SI=0000  DI=0000
DS=4A66  ES=4A66  SS=4A66  CS=4A66  IP=0103   NV UP EI PL NZ NA PE NC
4A66:0103 B80000         MOV     AX,0000
-P

AX=0000  BX=0000  CX=0005  DX=0000  SP=FFEE  BP=0000  SI=0000  DI=0000
DS=4A66  ES=4A66  SS=4A66  CS=4A66  IP=0106   NV UP EI PL NZ NA PE NC
4A66:0106 01C8           ADD     AX,CX
-P

AX=0005  BX=0000  CX=0005  DX=0000  SP=FFEE  BP=0000  SI=0000  DI=0000
DS=4A66  ES=4A66  SS=4A66  CS=4A66  IP=0108   NV UP EI PL NZ NA PE NC
4A66:0108 E2FC           LOOP    0106
-P

AX=000F  BX=0000  CX=0000  DX=0000  SP=FFEE  BP=0000  SI=0000  DI=0000
DS=4A66  ES=4A66  SS=4A66  CS=4A66  IP=010A   NV UP EI PL NZ NA PE NC
```

R (Register)

The R command may be used in one of three ways:

- Display the contents of one register, allowing it to be changed.
- Display registers, flags, and the next instruction about to be executed.
- Display the eight flag settings, allowing any or all of them to be changed.

Syntax:

```
R [registername]
```

Example	Comment
R	Display the contents of all registers.
R IP	Display the contents of IP and allow it to be modified.
R CX	Same (for the CX register).
R F	Display all flags and change them if desired.

Once the R F command has displayed the flags, you can change an individual flag by typing its new state. For example, we could set the Zero flag by typing the following two commands:

```
R F
ZR
```

The following is a sample register display (all values are in hexadecimal):

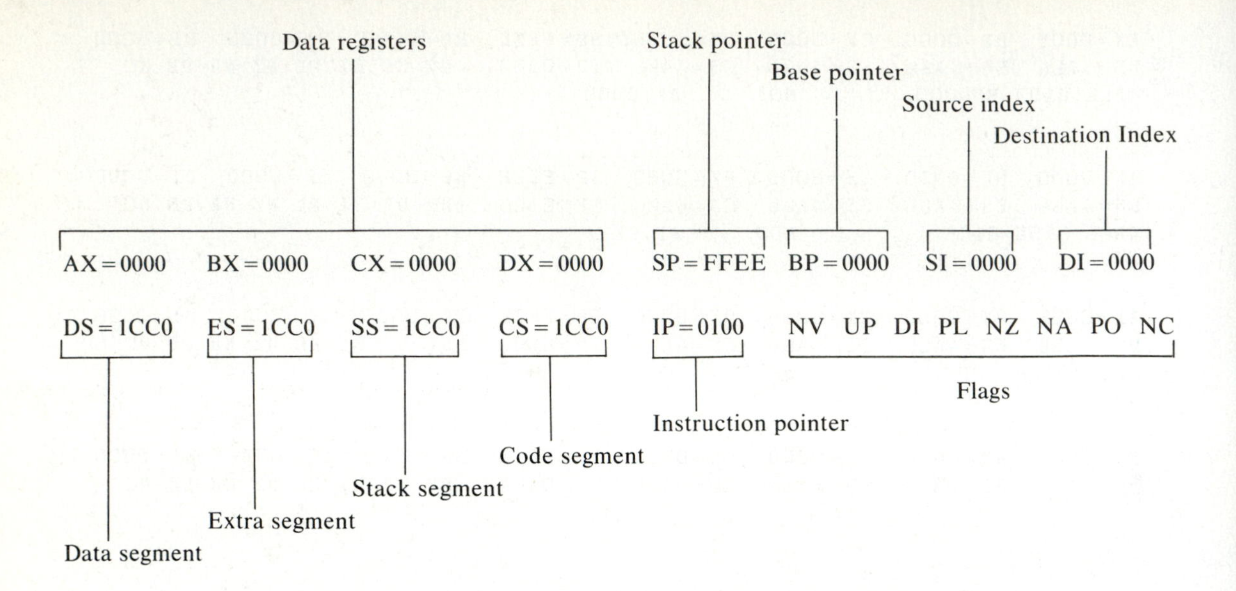

The R command also displays the next instruction about to be executed:

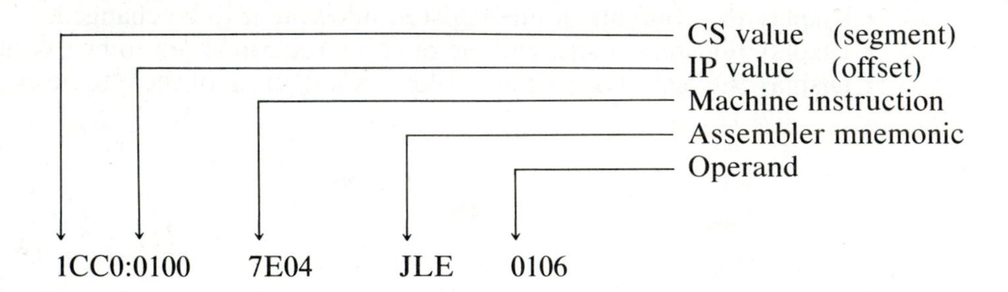

S (Search)

Search a range of addresses for a list of bytes or a string. Syntax:

```
S range list
```

Example	Comment
S 100 1000 0D	Search DS:100 to DS:1000 for the value 0Dh.
S 100 1000 CD,20	Search for the sequence CD 20.
S 100 9FFF COPY	Search for the word COPY.

T (Trace)

Execute one or more instructions from the current CS:IP location or an optional address, if specified. The contents of the registers are shown after each instruction is executed. Syntax:

```
T [=address] [,value]
```

Example	Comment
T	Trace one instruction from the current location.
T 5	Trace five instructions.
T=5,10	Start tracing at CS:5, and trace the next 16 steps.

This command traces individual loop iterations, so you may want to use it to debug statements within a loop. Also, the T command traces into procedure calls, whereas the P command executes a procedure call in its entirety without tracing.

U (Unassemble)

The U command translates memory into assembly language mnemonics. This is called *unassembling* or *disassembling* memory. If you don't supply an address, DEBUG disassembles from the location where the last U command left off. If the command is used for the first time after loading DEBUG, memory is disassembled from location CS:100. Syntax:

```
Format 1:    U [address]
Format 2:    U [range]
```

Example	Comment
U	Unassemble the next 32 bytes from the current location.
U 0	Unassemble 32 bytes from location 0.
U 100,108	Unassemble all bytes from offset 100h-108h.

W (Write)

Write a block of memory to a file or to individual disk sectors. If you want to write to a file, it must first be initialized with the N command. (If the file was just loaded either on the DOS command line or with the Load command, you do not need to repeat the Name command.)

Place the number of bytes to be written in BX and CX (BX contains the high 16 bits, and CX contains the low 16 bits). If a file is 256 bytes long, for example, the BX and CX registers will contain the following:

BX = 0000   CX = 0100

Example	Comment
N EXAMPLE.COM	Initialize the filename EXAMPLE.COM on the default drive.
R CX 20	Set the CX register to 20h, the length of the file.
W	Write 20h bytes to the file, starting at CS:100.
W 0	Write from location CS:0 to the file.

SEGMENT DEFAULTS

DEBUG recognizes the CS and DS registers as default segment registers when processing commands. Therefore, the value in CS or DS acts as a *base location* to which an offset value is added. The Assemble command, for example, assumes that CS is the default segment. If CS contained 1B00h, DEBUG would begin assembling instructions at location 1B00:0100h when the following command was issued:

```
-A 100
```

The Dump command, on the other hand, assumes that DS is the default segment. If DS contains 1C20h, the following command dumps memory starting at 1C20:0300h:

```
-D 300
```

The following table lists the default segment register for selected DEBUG commands:

Default	Description	Default Segment
A	Assemble	CS
D	Dump	DS
E	Enter	DS
F	Fill	DS
G	Go (execute)	CS
L	Load	CS
M	Move	DS
P	Procedure trace	CS
S	Search	DS
T	Trace	CS
U	Unassemble	CS
W	Write	CS

USING SCRIPT FILES WITH DEBUG

A major disadvantage of using DEBUG to assemble and run programs shows up when the programs must be edited. Inserting a new instruction often means retyping all subsequent instructions and recalculating the addresses of memory variables.

There is an easier way: All of the commands and instructions may first be placed inside a text file, which we will call a *script file*. When DEBUG is run from DOS, you can use a redirection symbol (<) to tell it to read input from the script file instead of the console. For example, let us create a script file named INPUT.TXT containing the following text:

```
a 100
mov ax,5
mov bx,10
add ax,bx
int 20

p 4
q
```

Once the script file has been created, DEBUG can be run using the script file as input:

```
debug < input.txt
```

I often create a script file with a pop-up editor like Borland's SideKick, so I can quickly modify the file and rerun it in DEBUG. Thus a program may be modified, saved, assembled, and traced within a few seconds. While DEBUG is displaying the program trace, type CTRL-NUMLOCK (or CTRL-S) to pause the screen scrolling; then press any other key to resume.

If you would like the output to be sent to a disk file or the printer, just redirect the output:

```
debug < input.txt > prn          (printer)
debug < input.txt > output.txt   (disk file)
```

C

BIOS and DOS Interrupts

Interrupt Number	Description
0	*Divide by Zero*. Internal: activated when attempting to divide by zero.
1	*Single Step*. Internal: active when the CPU Trap flag is set.
2	*Nonmaskable*. Internal: activated when a memory error occurs.
3	*Breakpoint*. Internal: activated when the 0CCh (INT 3) instruction is executed.
4	*Overflow*. Activated when the INTO instruction is executed and the Overflow flag is set.
5	*Print Screen*. Activated either by the INT 5 instruction or by typing SHIFT-PRTSC.
6	*(Reserved)*
7	*(Reserved)*
8	*Timer Interrupt*. Updates the BIOS clock 18.2 times per second. For your own programming, see INT 1Ch.
9	*Keyboard Hardware Interrupt*. Activated when a key is

	pressed. Reads the key from the keyboard port and stores it in the keyboard typeahead buffer.
0A–0D	*(Reserved)*
0E	*Diskette Interrupt*. Activated when a disk seek is in progress.
0F	*(Reserved)*
10	*Video Services*. Routines for manipulating the video display (see the complete list in a subsequent table).
11	*Equipment Check*. Returns a word showing all the peripherals attached to the system.
12	*Memory Size*. Returns the amount of memory (in 1,024-byte blocks) in AX.
13	*Disk Services*. Reset the disk controller, get the status of the most recent disk access, read and write physical sectors, and format a disk.
14	*Asynchronous (Serial) Port Services*. Initialize and read or write the asynchronous communications port, and return the port's status.
16	*Keyboard Services*. Read and inspect keyboard input (see the complete list in a subsequent table).
17	*Printer Services*. Initialize, print, and get the status of the printer.
18	*ROM BASIC*. Execute cassette BASIC in ROM.
19	*Boot Strap*. Reboot DOS.
1A	*Time of Day*. Get the number of timer ticks since the machine was turned on, or set the counter to a new value. Ticks occur 18.2 times per second.
1B	*Keyboard Break*. This interrupt handler is executed by INT 9h when CTRL-BREAK is pressed.
1C	*User Timer Interrupt*. Executed 18.2 times per second. May be used by your own program.
1D	*Video Parameters*. Point to a table containing initialization information for the Video Controller chip.
1E	*Diskette Parameters*. Point to a table containing initialization information for the diskette controller.
1F	*Graphics Table*. Table kept in memory of all extended graphics characters with ASCII codes greater than 127.
20	*Terminate Program*. Terminate the current program (INT 21h, function 4Ch should be used instead).
21	*DOS Services* (see the complete list in the next table).
22	*DOS Terminate Address*. Point to the address of the parent program or process. When the current program ends, this will be the return address.
23	*DOS Break Address*. DOS jumps here when CTRL-BREAK is pressed.

24	*DOS Error Address*. DOS jumps to this address when there is a critical error in the current program, such as a disk media error.
25	*DOS Disk Read*. Used for reading logical sectors from the disk.
26	*DOS Disk Write*. Used for writing logical sectors on the disk.
27	*Terminate and Stay Resident*. Exit to DOS or the calling program, but leave the current program in memory.
28–3F	(Reserved)
40,41	*Fixed Disk Services*. Fixed disk controller.
4B–7F	(Most are available for application programs)
80–F0	(*Reserved*: used by BASIC)
F1–FF	(Available for application programs)

INTERRUPT 21h FUNCTIONS (DOS SERVICES)

Function Number (hex)	Description
0	*Program Terminate*. Terminate the current program (use function 4Ch instead).
1	*Keyboard Input*. Wait for a character from the standard input device; echo it on the console. Output: AL = character.
2	*Display Output*. Display the character in DL on the standard output device (console).
3	*Auxiliary Input*. Wait for a character from the standard auxiliary device (serial). Output: AL = character.
4	*Auxiliary Output*. Send the character in DL to the standard auxiliary device (serial).
5	*Printer Output*. Send the character in DL to the standard printer device.
6	*Direct Console Input/Output*. If DL = FFh, read a waiting character from the console. Output: AL = character. If DL = 00h-FEh, output a character instead.
7	*Direct Console Input Without Echo*. Wait for a character from the standard input device. The character is returned in AL but is not echoed.
8	*Console Input Without Echo*. Wait for a character from the standard input device. The character is returned in AL but is not echoed. May be terminated by CTRL-BREAK.
9	*Print String*. Output a string of characters to the

	standard output device. Input: DS:DX = address of the string.
0A	*Buffered Keyboard Input*. Read a string of characters from the standard input device. Input: DS:DX = address of the buffer.
0B	*Check Standard Input Status*. Check to see if an input character is waiting. Output: AL = FFh if the character is ready; otherwise, AL = 0.
0C	*Clear Keyboard Buffer, Invoke Input Function*. Clear the console input buffer, and then execute an input function. Input: AL = desired function (1, 6, 7, 8, or 0Ah).
0D	*Disk Reset*. Flush all file buffers.
0E	*Select Disk*. Set the default drive. Input: DL = drive number (0 = A, 1 = B, etc.)
0F	*Open File*. Open a file described by an FCB (file control block). Input: DS:DX = address of the unopened FCB.
10	*Close File*. Close the file whose FCB is pointed to by DS:DX.
11	*Search for First Entry*. Search for the first matching filename in the current directory. Input: DS:DX = address of an unopened FCB.
12	*Search for Next Entry*. Search for the next matching filename in the current directory. Input: DS:DX = address of an unopened FCB. Output: AL = 0 if filename found, FFh if not found.
13	*Delete File*. Delete all matching directory entries that match the filename. Input: DS:DX = address of an unopened FCB with the filename. Output: AL = 0 if the file was deleted, AL = FFh if the file was not found.
14	*Sequential Read*. Read the next record of the file pointed to by an opened FCB into memory, and increment the record number. Input: DS:DX points to the FCB. Output: AL = 0 if successful.
15	*Sequential Write*. Write the record identified by the FCB from the current disk transfer address (DTA). Input: DS:DX points to the FCB. Output: AL = 0 if successful.
16	*Create File*. Create a new file, or open one if it already exists. Input: DS:DX points to an unopened FCB. Output: AL = 0 if successful.
17	*Rename File*. Rename a file. Both the old and new names are in a modified, unopened FCB. Input: DS:DX points to the FCB. Output: AL = 0 if

	successful; AL = FFh if the file was not found or the new name currently exists.
18	*(Reserved)*
19	*Current Disk.* Return the current default drive. Output: AL = drive number (0 = A, 1 = B, etc.).
1A	*Set Disk Transfer Address.* Set the DTA to the location pointed to by DS:DX.
1B	*Allocation Table Information.* Get information about the allocation table for the default drive. Output: DS:BX points to the media descriptor byte, DX = number of clusters, AL = number of sectors per cluster, and CX = sector size.
1C	*Allocation Table Information for Specific Device.* Same as function 1Bh, except that you can specify the drive number in DL when the function is called (0 = default, 1 = drive A, etc.).
1D, 1E, 1F, 20	*(Reserved)*
21	*Random Read.* Read the record addressed by the current FCB into memory at the disk transfer address. Input: DS:DX points to the FCB. Output: AL = 0 if successful.
22	*Random Write.* Write the record addressed by the current FCB from the disk transfer address to disk. Input: DS:DX points to the FCB. Output: AL = 0 if successful.
23	*File Size.* Return the number of records in a file based on the record size in the file's FCB. Input: DS:DX points to the unopened FCB. Output: If successful, AL = 0 and the random record field in the FCB contains the number of records in the file.
24	*Set Relative (Random) Record Field.* Set the random record field to the offset as the current block and record fields in the file's FCB. Input: DS:DX points to the FCB.
25	*Set Interrupt Vector.* Set an entry in the Interrupt Vector Table to a new address. Input: DS:DX points to the interrupt-handling routine that will be inserted in the table; AL = the interrupt number.
26	*Create New Program Segment.* Create a new program segment by copying the current program segment prefix (PSP) to a new segment address. Modify the PSP so it can be used by a new program. This function has been superseded by function 4Bh (EXEC).

27	*Random Block Read.* Read a specified number of records from the file based on the random record field in its FCB. Input: DS:DX points to the opened FCB, and CX = number of records to read. Output: AL = 0 if successful, and CX = number of records read.
28	*Random Block Write.* Write a specified number of records to the file based on the random record field in its FCB. Input: DS:DX points to the opened FCB, and CX = number of records to be written. Output: AL = 0 if successful, and CX = number of records written.
29	*Parse Filename.* The command line is parsed for a filename in the form *d:filename.ext,* and an unopened FCB is created.
2A	*Get Date.* Return the system date. Output: AL = day of the week (0–6, where Sunday = 0), CX = year, DH = month, and DL = day.
2B	*Set Date.* Set the system date. Input: CX = year, DH = month, and DL = day. Output: AL = 0 if the date was valid.
2C	*Get Time.* Return the system time. Output: CH = hour, CL = minutes, DH = seconds, and DL = hundredths of seconds.
2D	*Set Time.* Set the system time. Input: CH = hour, DH = seconds, CL = minutes, and DL = hundredths of seconds. Output: AL = 0 if the time was valid.
2E	*Set/Reset Verify Switch.* Either set or turn off the switch that DOS uses to perform an extra verify during each disk read/write operation. Input: AL = 0 to turn verify switch off, or AL = 1 to turn the switch on.
2F	*Get Disk Transfer Address (DTA).* Return the current DTA in ES:BX.
30	*Get DOS Version Number.* Return the current DOS version number. Output: AL = major version number, and AH = minor version number.
31	*Terminate Process and Remain Resident.* Terminate the current program or process, and attempt to set the current memory allocation to the number of paragraphs specified in DX. Input: AL = return code, and DX = requested number of paragraphs.
32	*(Reserved)*
33	*CTRL-BREAK Check.* Set or get the state of CTRL-BREAK checking. Input: AL = 0 to get the current state, AL = 1 to set the current

	state, DL = 0 to turn CTRL-BREAK checking off, and DL = 1 to turn it on. Output: DL = current state (0 = off, 1 = on).
34	*(Reserved)*
35	*Get Interrupt Vector.* Get the segment-offset value of an interrupt vector. Input: AL = interrupt number. Output: ES:BX = address of the interrupt handler.
36	*Get Disk Free Space.* Return the amount of disk free space. Input: DL = drive number (0 = default, 1 = A, etc.). Output: AX = sectors per cluster, or FFFFh if the drive number is invalid; BX = number of available clusters, CX = bytes per sector, and DX = clusters per drive.
37	*(Reserved)*
38	*Return Country Dependent Information.* Return a pointer to a list of country-specific data, such as the currency symbol, thousands separator, and decimal separator. See the DOS Technical Reference manual for details.
39	*Create Subdirectory.* Create a new subdirectory based on a given path name. Input: DS:DX points to an ASCIIZ string with the path and directory name. Output: AX = error code if the Carry flag is set.
3A	*Remove Subdirectory.* Remove a subdirectory. Input: DS:DX points to an ASCIIZ string with the path and directory name. Output: AX = error code if the Carry flag is set.
3B	*Change the Current Directory.* Change to a different directory. Input: DS:DX points to an ASCIIZ string with the new directory path. Output: AX = error code if the Carry flag is set.
3C	*Create a File.* Create a new file or truncate an old file to 0 bytes. Open the file for output. Input: DS:DX points to an ASCIIZ string with the filename, and CX = file attribute. Output: AX = error code if the Carry flag is set; otherwise AX = the new file handle.
3D	*Open a File.* Open a file for input, output, or input–output. Input: DS:DX points to an ASCIIZ string with the filename, and AL = the access code (0 = read, 1 = write, 2 = read/write). Output: AX = error code if the Carry flag is set; otherwise AX = the new file handle.
3E	*Close a File Handle.* Close the file or device specified by a file handle. Input: BX = file

handle from a previous open or create. Output: AX = error code if the Carry flag is set.

3F *Read from a File or Device*. Read a specified number of bytes from a file or device. Input: BX = file handle, DS:DX points to an input buffer, and CX = number of bytes to read. Output: AX = error code if the Carry flag is set.

40 *Write to a File or Device*. Write a specified number of bytes to a file or device. Input: BX = file handle, DS:DX points to the output buffer, and CX = number of bytes to write. Output: AX = error code if the Carry flag is set.

41 *Delete a File*. Remove a file from a specified directory. Input: DS:DX points to an ASCIIZ string with the filename. Output: AX = error code if the Carry flag is set.

42 *Move File Pointer*. Move the file read/write pointer according to a specified method. Input: CX:DX = distance (bytes) to move the file pointer, AL = method code, and BX = file handle. The method codes are as follows: 0 = move from beginning of the file, 1 = move to the current location plus an offset, and 2 = move to the end of file plus an offset. Output: AX = error code if the Carry flag is set.

43 *Get/Set File Attribute*. Get or set the attribute of a file. Input: DS:DX = pointer to an ASCIIZ path and filename, CX = attribute, and AL = function code (1 = set attribute, 0 = get attribute). Output: AX = error code if the Carry flag is set.

44 *I/O Control for Devices*. Get or set device information associated with an open device handle, or send a control string to the device handle, or receive a control string from the device handle.

45 *Duplicate a File Handle*. Return a new file handle for a file that is currently open. Input: BX = file handle. Output: AX = error code if the Carry flag is set.

46 *Force a Duplicate of a Handle*. Force the handle in CX to refer to the same file at the same position as the handle in BX. Input: BX = existing file handle, and CX = second file handle. Output: AX = error code if the Carry flag is set.

47 *Get Current Directory*. Get the full path name of the current directory. Input: DS:SI points to a

	64-byte area to hold the directory path, and DL = drive number. Output: A buffer at DS:SI is filled with the path, and AX = error code if the Carry flag is set.
48	*Allocate Memory*. Allocate a requested number of paragraphs of memory, measured in 16-byte blocks. Input: BX = number of paragraphs requested. Output: AX = segment of the allocated block, BX = size of the largest block available (in paragraphs), and AX = error code if the Carry flag is set.
49	*Free Allocated Memory*. Free memory that was previously allocated by function call 48h. Input: ES = segment of the block to be freed. Output: AX = error code if the Carry flag is set.
4A	*Modify Memory Blocks*. Modify allocated memory blocks to contain a new block size. The block will shrink or grow. Input: ES = segment of the block, and BX = requested number of paragraphs. Output: AX = error code if the Carry flag is set, and BX = maximum number of available blocks.
4B	*Load or Execute a Program*. Create a PSP for another program, load it into memory, and execute it. Input: DS:DX points to an ASCIIZ string with the drive, path, and filename of the program; ES:BX points to a parameter block, and AL = function value. Function values in AL: 0 = load and execute the program; 3 = load but do not execute (overlay program). Output: AX = error code if the Carry flag is set.
4C	*Terminate a Process*. Usual way to terminate a program and return to either DOS or a calling program. Input: AL = 8-bit return code, which can be queried by DOS function 4Dh or by the ERRORLEVEL command in a batch file.
4D	*Get Return Code of a Process*. Get the return code of a process or program, generated by either function call 31h or function call 4Ch. Output: AL = 8-bit code returned by the program, AH = type of exit generated: 0 = normal termination, 1 = terminated by CTRL-BREAK, 2 = terminated by a critical device error, and 3 = terminated by a call to function call 31h.
4E	*Find First Matching File*. Find the first filename that matches a given file specification. Input: DS:DX points to an ASCIIZ drive, path, and file specification; CX = file attribute to be used

	when searching. Output: AX = error code if the Carry flag is set; otherwise, the current DTA is filled with the filename, attribute, time, date, and size. DOS function call 1Ah (Set DTA) is usually called before this function.
4F	*Find Next Matching File*. Find the next filename that matches a given file specification. This is always called after DOS function 4Eh. Output: AX = error code if the Carry flag is set; otherwise, the current DTA is filled with the file's information.
50–53	(*Reserved*)
54	*Get Verify Setting*. Get the current value of the DOS verify flag (see DOS function 2Eh). Output: AL = current verify flag (1 = on, 0 = off).
55	(*Reserved*)
56	*Rename a File*. Rename a file or move a file to another directory. Input: DS:DX points to an ASCIIZ string that specifies the current drive, path, and filename; ES:DI points to the new path and filename. Output: AX = error code if the Carry flag is set.
57	*Get/Set a File's Date and Time*. Get or set the date and time stamp for a file. Input: AL = 0 to get the date/time, or AL = 1 to set the date/time; BX = file handle, CX = new file time, and DX = new file date. Output: AX = error code if the Carry flag is set; otherwise, CX = current file time, and DX = current file date.
58	*Get/Set Memory Allocation Strategy*
59	*Get Extended Error Information*. Return additional information about a DOS error, including the error class, locus, and recommended action. Input: BX = DOS version number (0 for version 3.xx). Output: AX = extended error code, BH = error class, BL = suggested action, and CH = locus.
5A	*Create Unique File*. Generate a unique filename in a specified directory. Input: DS:DX points to an ASCIIZ pathname, ending with a backslash (\); CX = desired file attribute. Output: AX = error code if the Carry flag is set; otherwise, DS:DX points to the path with the new filename appended.
5B	*Create New File*. Try to create a new file, but fail if the filename already exists. This prevents you from overwriting an existing file. Input: DS:DX points to an ASCIIZ string with the path and

	filename. Output: AX = error code if the Carry flag is set.
5C	*Lock/Unlock File Access.* Lock or unlock a range of bytes in an opened file (networking).
5D	*(Reserved)*
5E00, 5E02, 5E03, 5F02, 5F03, 5F04h.	Functions designed for Networks.
62	*Get Program Segment Prefix (PSP) Address.* Returns the PSP address of the current program in BX.

INTERRUPT 10h (VIDEO) FUNCTIONS

Function	Description
0	*Set Video Mode.* Set the video display to monochrome, text, graphics, or color mode. Input: AL = display mode.
1	*Set Cursor Lines.* Identify the starting and ending scan lines for the cursor. Input: CH = cursor starting line, and CL = cursor ending line.
2	*Set Cursor Position.* Position the cursor on the screen. Input: BH = video page, DH = row, and DL = column.
3	*Get Cursor Position.* Get the cursor's screen position and its size. Input: BH = video page. Output: CH = cursor starting line, CL = cursor ending line, DH = cursor row, DL = cursor column, AH = status.
4	*Read Light Pen.* Read the position and status of the light pen. Output: CH = pixel row, BX = pixel column, DH = character row, DL = character column, AH = status.
5	*Set Display Page.* Select the video page to be displayed. Input: AL = desired page number.
6	*Scroll Window Up.* Scroll a window on the current video page upward, replacing scrolled lines with blanks. Input: AL = number of lines to scroll, BH = attribute for scrolled lines, CX = upper left corner row and column, and DX = lower right row and column.
7	*Scroll Window Down.* Scroll a window on the current video page downward, replacing scrolled lines with blanks. Input: AL = number of lines to scroll, BH = attribute for scrolled lines, CX = upper left corner row and column, and DX = lower right row and column.
8	*Read Character and Attribute.* Read the character and its attribute at the current cursor position. Input: BH = display page. Output: AH = attribute byte, and AL = ASCII character code.

9	*Write Character and Attribute.* Write a character and its attribute at the current cursor position. Input: AL = ASCII character, BH = video page, BL = attribute or color, and CX = repetition factor.
0A	*Write Character.* Write a character only (no attribute) at the current cursor position. Input: AL = ASCII character, BH = video page, and CX = replication factor.
0B	*Set Color Palette.* Select a group of available colors for the color or EGA adapter. Input: BL = color value, and BH = color palette ID.
0C	*Write Graphics Pixel.* Write a graphics pixel when in color graphics mode. Input: AL = pixel color, CX = *x* coordinate, and DX = *y* coordinate.
0D	*Read Graphics Pixel.* Read the color of a single graphics pixel at a given location. Input: CX = *x* coordinate, and DX = *y* coordinate. Output: AL = pixel color.
0E	*Write Character.* Write a character to the screen and advance the cursor. Input: AL = ASCII character code, BH = video page, BL = attribute or color.
0F	*Get Current Video Mode.* Get the current video mode. Output: AL = video mode, and BH = active video page.
10	*Set Video Palette.* (EGA and PCjr only) Set the video palette register, border color, or blink/intensity bit. Input: AL = function code (00 = set palette register, 01 = set border color, 02 = set palette and border color, 03 = set/reset blink/intensity bit), BH = color, BL = palette register to set. If AL = 02, ES:DX points to a color list.
11	*Character Generator.* Select the character size for the EGA display. For example, an 8 by 8 font is used for the 43-line display, and an 8 by 14 font is used for the 25-line display.
12	*Alternate Select Function.* Return technical information about the EGA display.
13	*Write String.* (PC/AT only) Write a string of text to the video display. Input: AL = mode, BH = page, BL = attribute, CX = length of string, DH = row, DL = column, and ES:BP points to the string (will not work on the IBM-PC or PC/XT).

INTERRUPT 16h FUNCTIONS (KEYBOARD)

Function	Description
00	*Read Character.* Wait for an input character and keyboard scan code. Output: AH = scan code, and AL = ASCII character.

01	*Get Keyboard Status.* Find out if a character is waiting in the keyboard typeahead buffer. If one is, return the scan code in AH and the ASCII code in AL, and clear the Zero flag. If no key is waiting, set the Zero flag. (*Note*: the same character will remain in the keyboard buffer.)
02	*Get Keyboard Flags.* Return the keyboard flag byte stored in low RAM in AL. The meaning of each bit is:

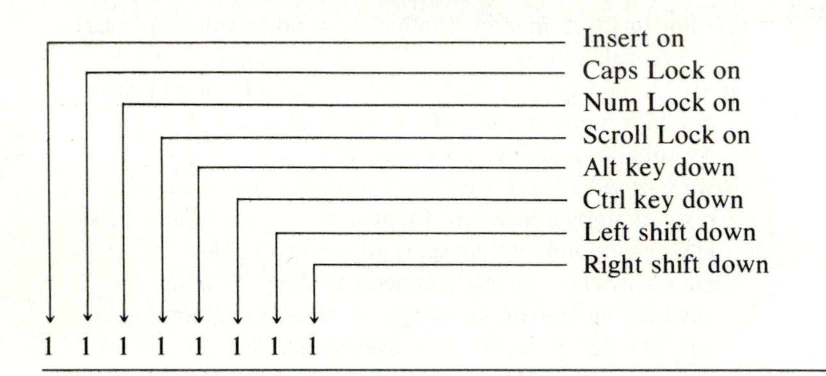

Intel 8086/8088 Instruction Set

The following notation is used:

Flags

Each of the eight flags is identified by a single letter:

O	Overflow	S	Sign	P	Parity
D	Direction	Z	Zero	C	Carry
I	Interrupt	A	Auxiliary Carry		

Inside the boxes, the following notation shows how each instruction will affect the flags:

1	Sets the flag
0	Clears the flag
?	May change the flag to an undetermined value
(blank)	The flag is not changed
*	Changes the flag according to specific rules associated with the flag

Instruction Formats

There may be several formats available for a single instruction. The following symbols are used:

reg	An 8-bit or 16-bit general purpose register (AX, BX, CX, DX, AH, AL, BH, BL, CH, CL, SI, DI, BP, SP)
segreg	A 16-bit segment register (CS, DS, ES, SS)
accum	AX or AL
mem	A memory operand, using any of the standard memory addressing modes
shortlabel	A label within −128 to +127 bytes from the next instruction
nearlabel	A label in the current code segment.
farlabel	A label in another code segment.
source	The source operand
dest	The destination operand, that is, the one that will be changed by the instruction
immed	An immediate operand
instruction	An 8086/8088 assembly language instruction

AAA

O	D	I	S	Z	A	P	C
?			?	?	*	?	*

ASCII adjust after addition: Adjusts the result in AL after two ASCII digits have been added together. If AL > 9, the high digit of the result is placed in AH, and the Carry and Auxiliary Carry flags are set.

Format: AAA

AAD

O	D	I	S	Z	A	P	C
?			*	*	?	*	?

ASCII adjust before division: Converts unpacked BCD digits in AH and AL to a single binary value in preparation for the DIV instruction.

Format: AAD

AAM

ASCII adjust after multiply: Adjusts the result in AX after two unpacked BCD digits have been multiplied together.

O	D	I	S	Z	A	P	C
?			*	*	?	*	?

Format: AAM

AAS

ASCII adjust after subtraction: Adjusts the result in AX after a subtraction operation. If AL > 9, AAS decrements AH and sets the Carry and Auxiliary Carry flags.

O	D	I	S	Z	A	P	C
?			?	?	*	?	*

Format: AAS

ADC

Add carry: Adds the source and destination operands and adds the contents of the Carry flag to the sum, which is stored in the destination.

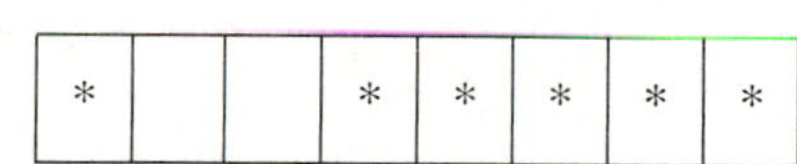

O	D	I	S	Z	A	P	C
*			*	*	*	*	*

Formats:

ADC *reg,reg*
ADC *mem,reg*
ADC *reg,mem*
ADC *reg,immed*
ADC *mem,immed*
ADC *accum,immed*

ADD

Add: Adds a source operand to a destination operand and stores the sum in the destination.

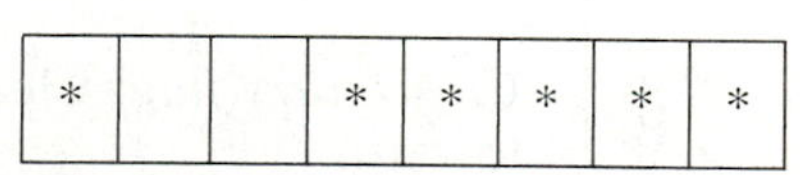

O	D	I	S	Z	A	P	C
*			*	*	*	*	*

Formats:

ADD *reg,reg*
ADD *mem,reg*
ADD *reg,mem*
ADD *reg,immed*
ADD *mem,immed*
ADD *accum,immed*

AND

Logical AND: ANDs the bits in the destination operand with the source operand.

O	D	I	S	Z	A	P	C
*			*	*	?	*	0

Formats:

AND *reg,reg*
AND *mem,reg*
AND *reg,mem*
AND *reg,immed*
AND *mem,immed*
AND *accum,immed*

CALL

Call a procedure: Pushes the location of the next instruction on the stack and transfers to the destination location. If the procedure is near (in the same segment), only the offset of the next instruction is pushed; otherwise, both the segment and the offset are pushed.

O	D	I	S	Z	A	P	C

Formats:

CALL *nearlabel*
CALL *farlabel*
CALL *reg*
CALL *mem16*
CALL *mem32*

CBW

Convert byte to word: Extends* the sign bit in AL throughout the AH register.

O	D	I	S	Z	A	P	C

Format: CBW

CLC

Clear carry flag: Clears the Carry flag to zero.

O	D	I	S	Z	A	P	C
							0

Format: CLC

*Often referred to as *propogating* the sign, where all bits in AH are affected.

CLD

O	D	I	S	Z	A	P	C
	0						

Clear direction flag: Clears the Direction flag to zero. String primitive instructions will automatically increment SI and DI.

Format: CLD

CLI

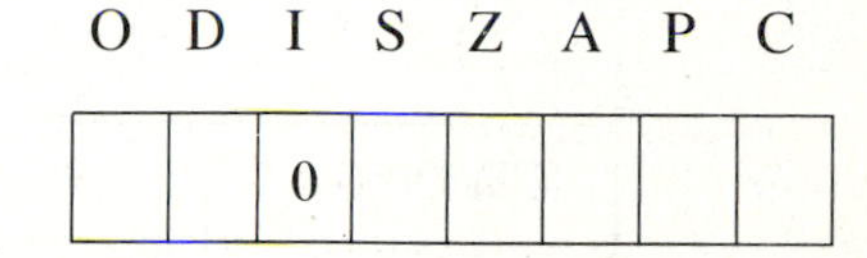

Clear interrupt flag: Clears the Interrupt flag to zero. This disables maskable hardware interrupts until an STI instruction is executed.

Format: CLI

CMC

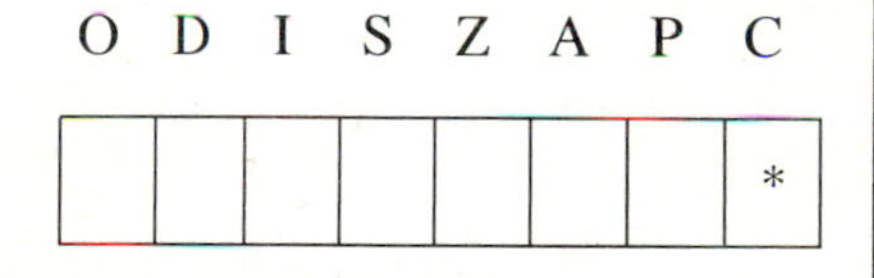

Complement carry flag: Toggles the current value of the Carry flag. A 0 is changed to a 1, and vice versa.

Format: CMC

CMP

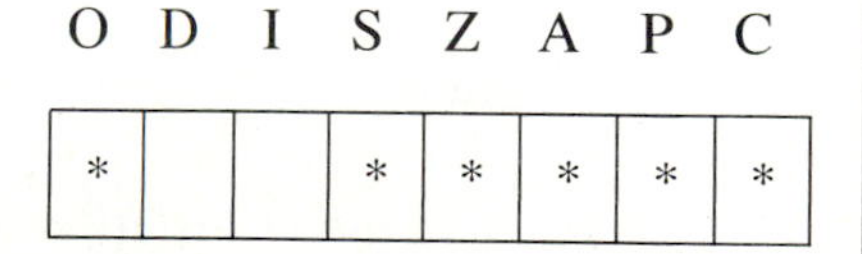

Compare: Compares the destination to the source by performing an implied subtraction of the source from the destination.

Formats:

CMP *reg,reg*	CMP *reg,immed*
CMP *mem,reg*	CMP *mem,immed*
CMP *reg,mem*	CMP *accum,immed*

CMPS, CMPSB, CMPSW

O	D	I	S	Z	A	P	C
*			*	*	*	*	*

Compare strings, addressed by DS:SI and ES:DI. Carries out an implied subtraction of the destination from the source. SI and DI are incremented if the Direction flag is clear, or they are decremented if the flag is set. CMPSB compares byte operands, and CMPSW compares word operands.

Formats:

CMPS	*source,dest*	CMPSB
CMPS	*segreg:source*,ES:*dest*	CMPSW

CWD

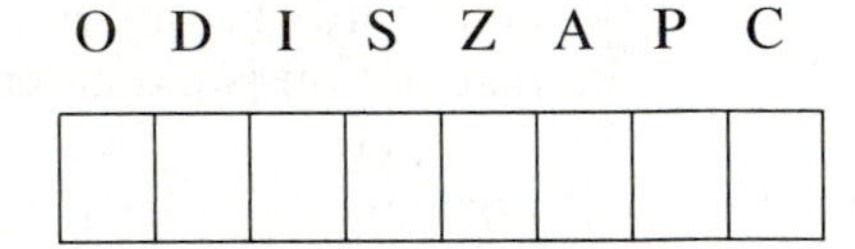

Convert word to doubleword: Extends the sign bit in AX into the DX register. This is usually done in preparation for a signed division (IDIV) operation.

Format: CWD

DAA

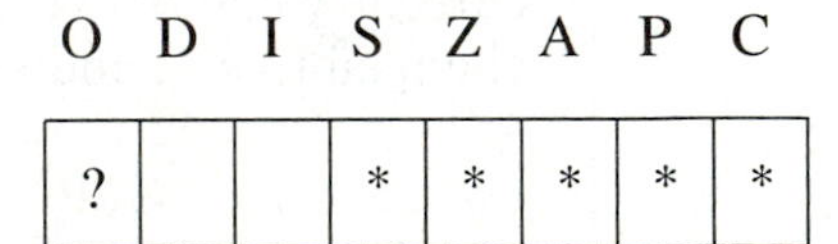

Decimal adjust after addition: Adjusts the binary sum in AL after 2 packed BCD values have been added. Converts the sum to two BCD digits in AL.

Format: DAA

DAS

O	D	I	S	Z	A	P	C
?			*	*	*	*	*

Decimal adjust after subtraction: Converts the binary result of a subtraction operation to 2 packed BCD digits in AL.

Format: DAS

DEC

O	D	I	S	Z	A	P	C
*			*	*	*	*	

Decrement: Subtracts 1 from a byte or word operand. Does not affect the Carry flag.

Formats:

DEC *reg*
DEC *mem*

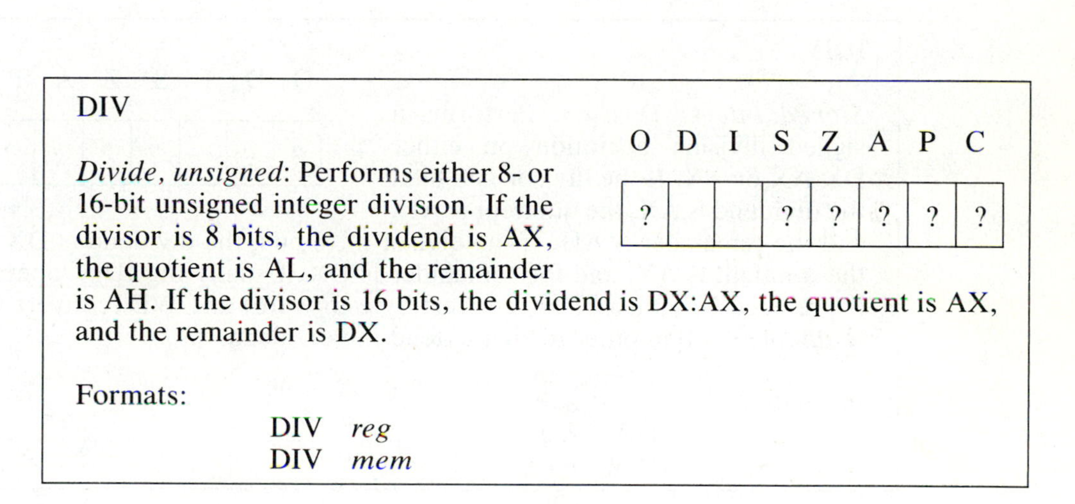

DIV

O	D	I	S	Z	A	P	C
?			?	?	?	?	?

Divide, unsigned: Performs either 8- or 16-bit unsigned integer division. If the divisor is 8 bits, the dividend is AX, the quotient is AL, and the remainder is AH. If the divisor is 16 bits, the dividend is DX:AX, the quotient is AX, and the remainder is DX.

Formats:

DIV *reg*
DIV *mem*

ESC

O	D	I	S	Z	A	P	C

Escape: Provides an instruction and an optional operand to a coprocessor. The first operand specifies the bits of the coprocessor instruction, and the second operand is a register or memory operand that will be used by the coprocessor.

Formats:

ESC *immed,reg*
ESC *immed,mem*

HLT

O	D	I	S	Z	A	P	C

Halt: Stops the CPU until a hardware interrupt occurs. Note that the Interrupt flag must be set by STI, in order for a hardware interrupt to occur.

Format: HLT

IDIV

O	D	I	S	Z	A	P	C
?			?	?	?	?	?

Signed Integer Division: Performs a signed division operation on either DX:AX or AX. If the divisor is 8 bits, the dividend is AX, the quotient is AL, and the remainder is AH. If the divisor is 16 bits, the dividend is DX:AX, the quotient is AX, and the remainder is DX. Usually the IDIV operation is prefaced by either CBW (convert byte to word) or CWD (convert word to doubleword) in order to sign-extend the dividend.

Formats:

IDIV *reg*
IDIV *mem*

IMUL

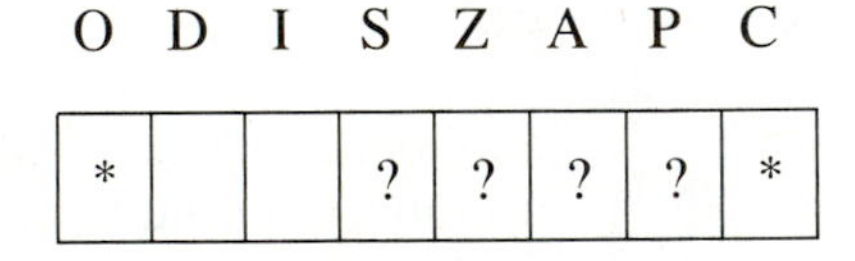

Signed integer multiply: Performs a signed integer multiplication on either AL or AX. If the multiplier is 8 bits, the multiplicand is AL and the product is AX; otherwise, the multiplicand is AX and the product is DX:AX. The Carry and Overflow flags are set if a 16-bit product extends into AH or a 32-bit product extends into DX.

Formats:

IMUL *reg*
IMUL *mem*

IN

O	D	I	S	Z	A	P	C

Input from port: Inputs a byte or word from a port into AL or AX. The source operand is a port address, expressed as either an 8-bit constant or a 16-bit address in DX.

Formats:

IN *accum,immed*
IN *accum*,DX

INC

O	D	I	S	Z	A	P	C
*			*	*	*	*	

Increment: Adds 1 to a register or memory operand, but does not affect the Carry flag.

Formats:

INC *reg*
INC *mem*

INT

O	D	I	S	Z	A	P	C
		0					

Interrupt: Generates a software interrupt, which in turn calls a routine in the ROM BIOS or RAM. Clears the Interrupt flag and trap flag; pushes the flags, CS, and IP on the stack before branching to the interrupt routine. A special form, the INT 3 instruction, generates a breakpoint.

Formats:

INT *immed*
INT 3

INTO

O	D	I	S	Z	A	P	C
		*	*				

Interrupt on overflow: Generates internal CPU Interrupt 4 if the Overflow flag is set. No action is taken by DOS if INT 4 is called, but a user-written routine may be substituted instead.

Format: INTO

IRET

O	D	I	S	Z	A	P	C
*	*	*	*	*	*	*	*

Interrupt return: Returns from an interrupt handling routine. Pops the stack into IP, CS, and the flags.

Format: IRET

Jcondition

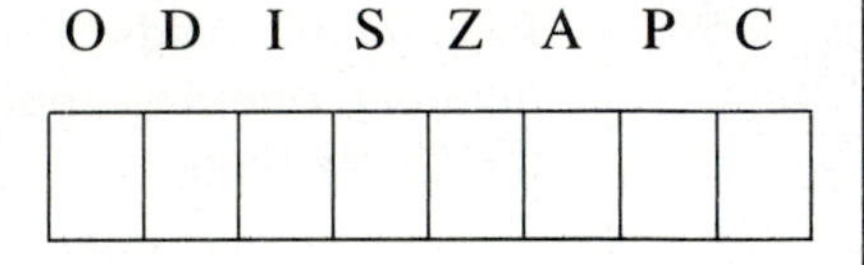

Conditional jump: Jumps to a label if a specified flag condition is true. The label must be in the range of −128 to +127 bytes from the next instruction.

Format: J*condition* *shortlabel*

Available mnemonics:

JA	jump if above	JE	jump if equal
JNA	jump if not above	JNE	jump if not equal
JAE	jump if above or equal	JZ	jump if zero
JNAE	jump if not above or equal	JNZ	jump if not zero
JB	jump if below	JS	jump if sign
JNB	jump if not below	JNS	jump if not sign
JBE	jump if below or equal	JC	jump if carry
JNBE	jump if not below or equal	JNC	jump if no carry
JG	jump if greater	JO	jump if overflow
JNG	jump if not greater	JNO	jump if no overflow
JGE	jump if greater or equal	JP	jump if parity
JNGE	jump if not greater or equal	JPE	jump if parity equal
JL	jump if less	JNP	jump if no parity
JNL	jump if not less	JPO	jump if parity odd
JLE	jump if less or equal		
JNLE	jump if not less or equal		

JCXZ

O	D	I	S	Z	A	P	C

Jump if CX is zero: Jump to a short label if the CX register is equal to zero. The short label must be in the range −128 to +127 bytes from the next instruction.

Format: JCXZ *shortlabel*

JMP

O	D	I	S	Z	A	P	C

Jump unconditionally to a label: The label may be short (−128 to +128 bytes), near (current segment), or far (different segment).

Formats:

JMP *shortlabel*
JMP *nearlabel*
JMP *farlabel*
JMP *reg16*
JMP *mem16*
JMP *mem32*

LAHF

O	D	I	S	Z	A	P	C

Load flags into AH: The lowest 8 bits of the flags are transferred, but not the Trap, Interrupt, Overflow, and Direction flags.

Format: LAHF

LDS

O	D	I	S	Z	A	P	C

Load register and DS: Loads the contents of a doubleword memory operand into DS and the specified register.

Formats: LDS *reg,mem32*

LEA

O	D	I	S	Z	A	P	C

Load effective address: Calculates and loads the 16-bit effective address of a memory operand.

Format: LEA *reg,mem*

LES

O	D	I	S	Z	A	P	C

Load register and ES: Loads the contents of a doubleword memory operand into ES and the specified register.

Format: LES *reg,mem32*

LOCK

O	D	I	S	Z	A	P	C

Lock the system bus: Prevents other processors from executing during the next instruction. This instruction is used when another processor might modify a memory operand that is currently being accessed by the CPU.

Format: LOCK *instruction*

LODS, LODSB, LODSW

O	D	I	S	Z	A	P	C

Load string: Loads a memory byte or word addressed by DS:SI into the accumulator. If LODS is used, the memory operand must be specified. LODSB loads a byte into AL, and LODSW loads a word into AX. If the Direction flag is clear, SI is automatically incremented; otherwise, SI is decremented.

Formats:

LODS *mem* LODSB
LODS *segreg:mem* LODSW

LOOP

O D I S Z A P C

Loop: Decrements CX and jumps to a short label if CX is greater than zero. The short label must be in the range −128 to +127 bytes from the next instruction.

Format: LOOP *shortlabel*

LOOPE, LOOPZ

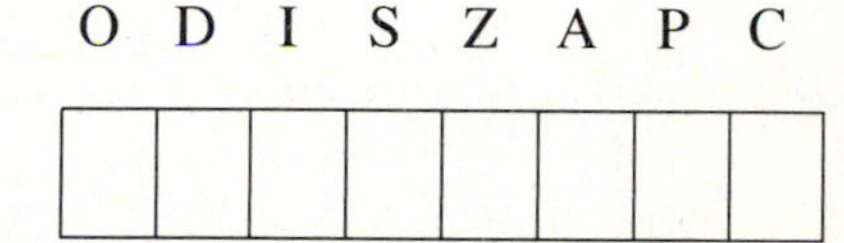

Loop if equal (zero): Decrements CX and jumps to a short label if CX > 0 and the Zero flag is set.

Formats:

LOOPE *shortlabel*
LOOPZ *shortlabel*

LOOPNE, LOOPNZ

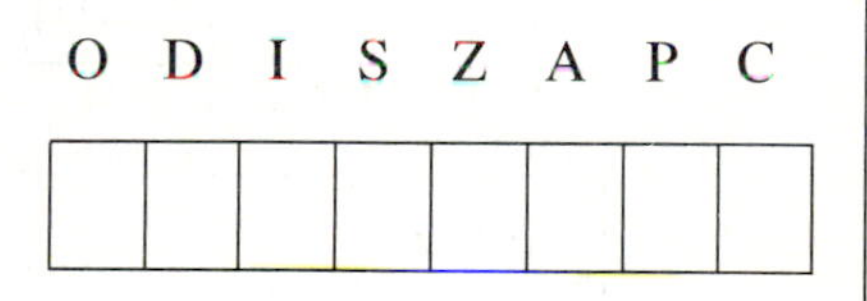

Loop if not equal (not zero): Decrements CX and jumps to a short label if CX > 0 and the Zero flag is clear.

Formats: LOOPNE *shortlabel*
LOOPNZ *shortlabel*

MOV

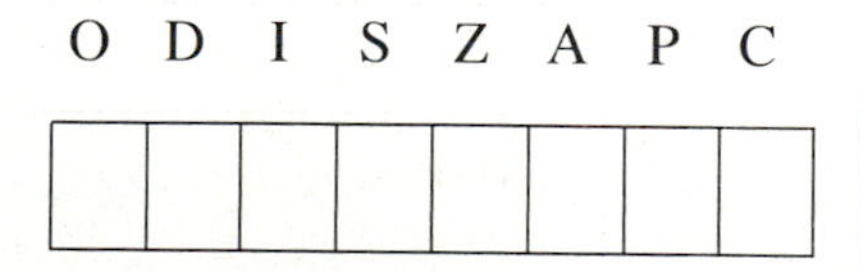

Move: Copies a byte or word from a source operand to a destination operand.

Formats:

MOV *reg,reg*
MOV *mem,reg*
MOV *reg,mem*
MOV *reg16,segreg*
MOV *segreg,reg16*
MOV *reg,immed*
MOV *mem,immed*
MOV *mem16,segreg*
MOV *segreg,mem16*

MOVS, MOVSB, MOVSW

O	D	I	S	Z	A	P	C

Move string: Copies a byte or word from memory addressed by DS:SI to memory addressed by ES:DI. MOVS requires both operands to be specified. MOVSB copies a byte, and MOVSW copies a word. If the Direction flag is clear, SI and DI are incremented; otherwise, SI and DI are decremented.

Formats:

MOVS *dest,source*
MOVS ES:*dest,segreg*:*source*
MOVSB
MOVSW

MUL

O	D	I	S	Z	A	P	C
*			?	?	?	?	*

Unsigned integer multiply: Multiplies AL or AX by a source operand. If the source is 8 bits, it is multiplied by AL and the product is stored in AX. If the source is 16 bits, it is multiplied by AX and the product is stored in DX:AX.

Formats:

MUL *reg*
MUL *mem*

NEG

O	D	I	S	Z	A	P	C
*			*	*	*	*	*

Negate: Calculates the twos complement of the destination operand and stores the result in the destination.

Formats:

NEG *reg*
NEG *mem*

NOP

O	D	I	S	Z	A	P	C

No operation: This instruction does nothing, but may be used inside a timing loop or to align a subsequent instruction on a word boundary.

Format: NOP

NOT

Not: Performs a logical NOT on an operand by reversing each of its bits.

O	D	I	S	Z	A	P	C

Formats:

NOT *reg*
NOT *mem*

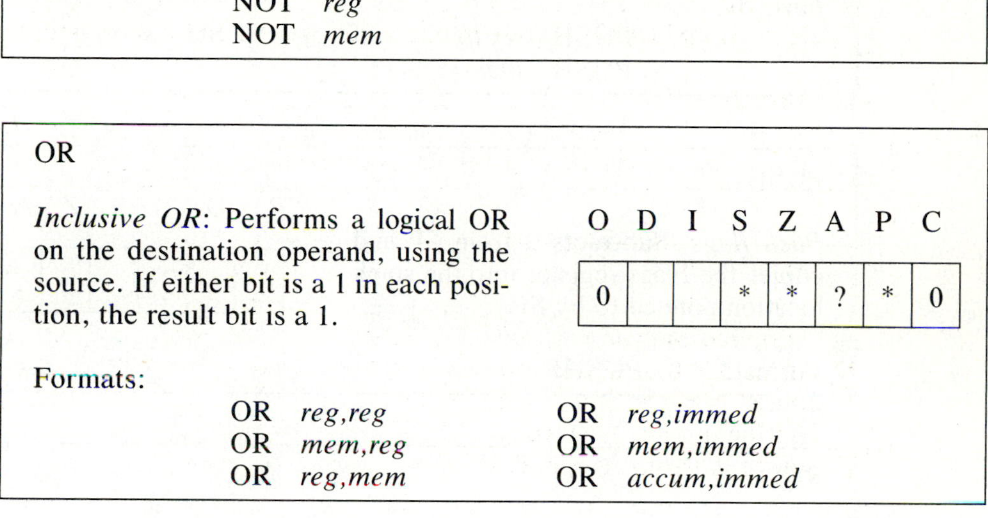

OR

Inclusive OR: Performs a logical OR on the destination operand, using the source. If either bit is a 1 in each position, the result bit is a 1.

O	D	I	S	Z	A	P	C
0			*	*	?	*	0

Formats:

OR *reg,reg*
OR *mem,reg*
OR *reg,mem*
OR *reg,immed*
OR *mem,immed*
OR *accum,immed*

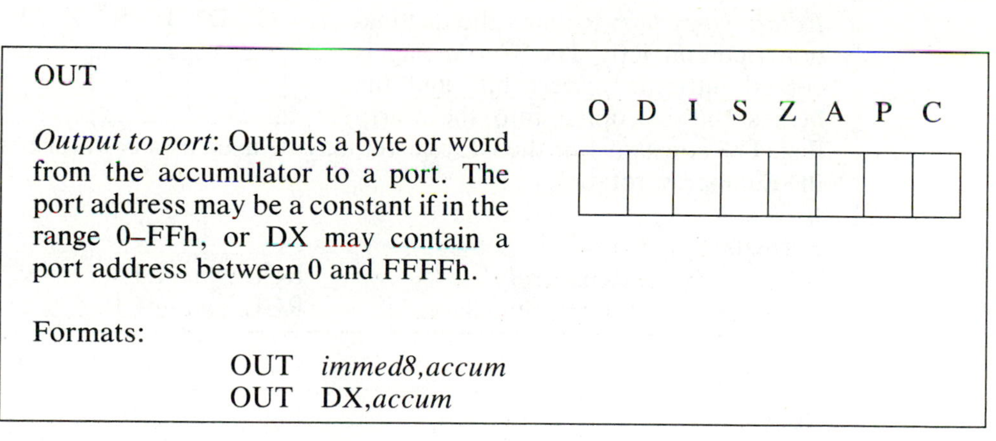

OUT

Output to port: Outputs a byte or word from the accumulator to a port. The port address may be a constant if in the range 0–FFh, or DX may contain a port address between 0 and FFFFh.

O	D	I	S	Z	A	P	C

Formats:

OUT *immed8,accum*
OUT DX,*accum*

POP

Pop from stack: Copies a word at the current stack pointer location into the destination operand and adds 2 to SP.

O	D	I	S	Z	A	P	C

Formats:

POP *reg16*
POP *mem16*
POP *segreg*

PUSH

Push on stack: Subtracts 2 from SP and copies the source operand into the stack location pointed to by SP.

O	D	I	S	Z	A	P	C

Formats:

PUSH *reg16*
PUSH *mem16*
PUSH *segreg*

PUSHF

Push flags: Subtracts 2 from SP and copies the Flags register into the stack location pointed to by SP.

O	D	I	S	Z	A	P	C

Format: PUSHF

RCL

Rotate carry left: Rotates the destination operand left. The Carry flag is copied into the lowest bit, and the highest bit is copied into the Carry flag. The constant 1 or the CL register may be used as a counter controlling the number of rotations.

O	D	I	S	Z	A	P	C
*							*

Formats:

RCL *reg*,1
RCL *reg*,CL
RCL *mem*,1
RCL *mem*,CL

RCR

Rotate carry right: Rotates the destination operand right. The Carry flag is copied into the highest bit, and the lowest bit is copied into the Carry flag. Either the constant 1 or the CL register may be used as a counter controlling the number of rotations.

O	D	I	S	Z	A	P	C
*							*

Formats:

RCR *reg*,1
RCR *reg*,CL
RCR *mem*,1
RCR *mem*,CL

REP

O	D	I	S	Z	A	P	C

Repeat string: Repeats a string primitive instruction, using CX as a counter. CX is decremented each time the instruction is repeated, until CX = 0.

Format (shown here with MOVS):

REP MOVS *dest,source*

REPcondition

O	D	I	S	Z	A	P	C
				*			

Conditional repeat string: Repeats a string primitive instruction until CX = 0 and while a flag condition is true. REPZ (REPE) repeats while the Zero flag is set, and REPNZ (REPNE) repeats while the Zero flag is clear. Only the SCAS and CMPS instructions modify the Zero flag.

Sample formats used here with SCAS:

REPZ SCAS *dest*	REPNZ SCAS *dest*
REPZ SCASB	REPNE SCASB
REPE SCASW	REPNZ SCASW

RET, RETN, RETF

O	D	I	S	Z	A	P	C

Return from procedure: Pops a return address from the stack. RETN (return near) pops only the top of the stack into IP. RETF (return far) first pops the stack into IP, and then into CS. RET may be either near or far, depending on the attribute specified or implied by the PROC directive. An optional 8-bit immediate operand tells the CPU to add a value to SP after popping the return address.

Formats:

RET	RET *immed8*
RETN	RETN *immed8*
RETF	RETF *immed8*

ROL

Rotate left: Rotates the destination operand left. The highest bit is copied into the Carry flag and moved into the lowest bit position. Either the constant 1 or the CL register may be used as a counter controlling the number of rotations.

O	D	I	S	Z	A	P	C
*							*

Formats:

ROL *reg*,1	ROL *mem*,1
ROL *reg*,CL	ROL *mem*,CL

ROR

Rotate right: Rotates the destination operand right. The lowest bit is copied into both the Carry flag and the highest bit position. Either the constant 1 or the CL register may be used as a counter controlling the number of rotations.

O	D	I	S	Z	A	P	C
*							*

Formats:

ROR *reg*,1	ROR *mem*,1
ROR *reg*,CL	ROR *mem*,CL

SAHF

Store AH into flags: Copies AH into bits 0 through 7 of the Flags register. The Trap, Interrupt, Direction, and Overflow flags are not affected.

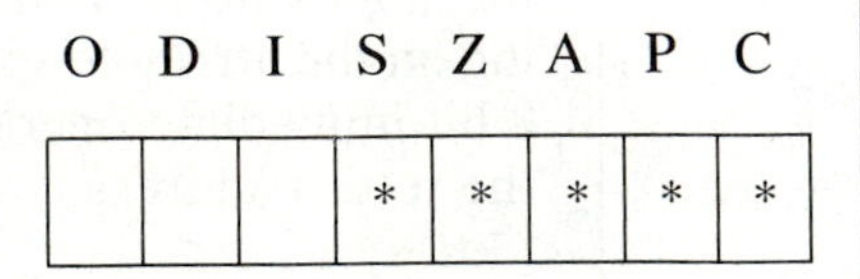

Format: SAHF

SAL

Shift arithmetic left: Shifts each bit in the destination operand to the left. The highest bit is copied into the Carry flag, and the lowest bit is filled with a zero. Identical to SHL.

O	D	I	S	Z	A	P	C
*			*	*	?	*	*

Formats:

SAL *reg*,1 SAL *mem*,1
SAL *reg*,CL SAL *mem*,CL

SAR

Shift arithmetic right: Shifts each bit in the destination operand to the right. The lowest bit is copied into the Carry flag, and the highest bit retains its previous value. This shift is often used with signed operands, because it preserves the number's sign.

Formats:

SAR *reg*,1 SAR *mem*,1
SAR *reg*,CL SAR *mem*,CL

SBB

Subtract with borrow: Subtracts the source operand from the destination operand and then subtracts the Carry flag from the destination.

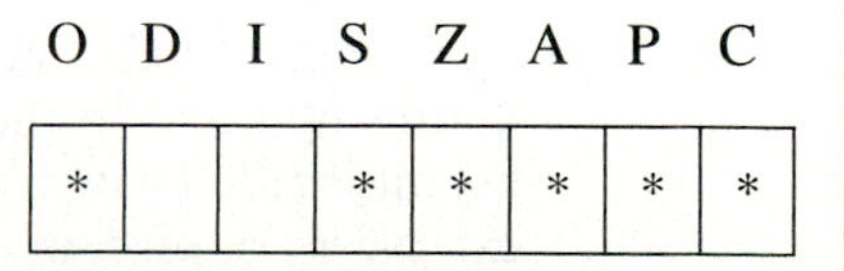

Formats:

SBB *reg,reg* SBB *reg,immed*
SBB *mem,reg* SBB *mem,immed*
SBB *reg,mem* SBB *accum,immed*

SCAS, SCASB, SCASW

O	D	I	S	Z	A	P	C
*			*	*	*	*	*

Scan string: Scans a string in memory pointed to by ES:DI for a value that matches the accumulator. SCAS requires the operands to be specified. SCASB scans for a value matching AL, and SCASW scans for a value matching AX.

Formats:

SCAS	*dest*	SCASB
SCAS	ES:*dest*	SCASW

SHL

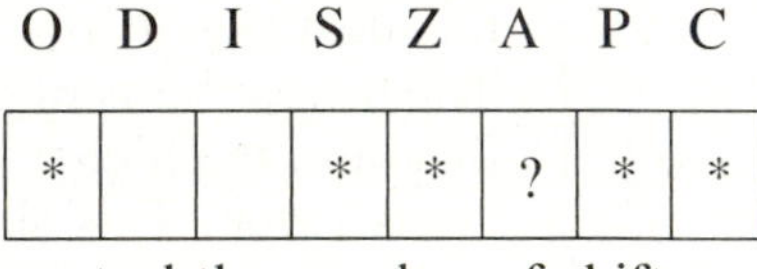

Shift left: Shifts each bit in the destination operand to the left. The highest bit is copied into the Carry flag, and the lowest bit is filled with a zero (identical to SAL). Either a constant or CL may control the number of shifts.

Formats:

SHL	*reg*,1	SHL	*mem*,1
SHL	*reg*,CL	SHL	*mem*,CL

SHR

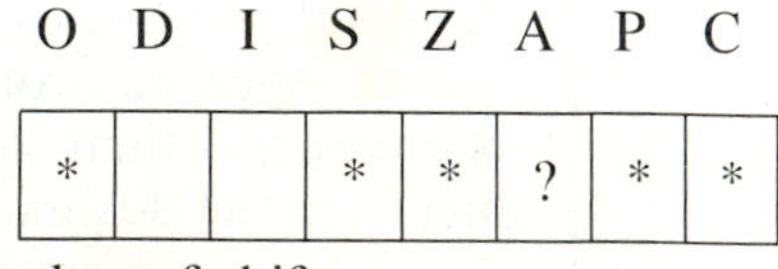

Shift right: Shifts each bit in the destination operand to the right. The highest bit is filled with a zero, and the lowest bit is copied into the Carry flag. Either a constant or CL may control the number of shifts.

Formats:

SHR	*reg*,1	SHR	*mem*,1
SHR	*reg*,CL	SHR	*mem*,CL

STC

O	D	I	S	Z	A	P	C
							1

Set Carry flag: Sets the Carry flag. This may be done by a procedure that wants to signal an error condition to a calling program.

Format: STC

STD

O	D	I	S	Z	A	P	C
	1						

Set Direction flag: Sets the Direction flag, causing SI and/or DI to be decremented by string primitive instructions. Thus, string processing will be from high addresses to low addresses.

Format: STD

STI

O	D	I	S	Z	A	P	C
		1					

Set Interrupt flag: Sets the Interrupt flag, which enables maskable interrupts. Interrupts are automatically disabled when an interrupt occurs, so an interrupt handler procedure immediately reenables them, using STI.

Format: STI

STOS, STOSB, STOSW

O	D	I	S	Z	A	P	C

Store string: Stores the accumulator in the memory location addressed by ES:DI. If the Direction flag is clear, DI is incremented; otherwise, DI is decremented. If STOS is used, a destination operand must be specified. STOSB stores the byte in AL into memory, and STOSW stores the word in AX into memory.

Formats:

STOS *mem*	STOSB
STOS ES:*mem*	STOSW

SUB

Subtract: Subtracts the source operand from the destination operand.

O D I S Z A P C

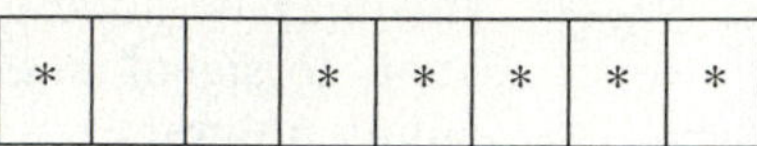

Formats:

SUB *reg,reg*
SUB *mem,reg*
SUB *reg,mem*
SUB *reg,immed*
SUB *mem,immed*
SUB *accum,immed*

TEST

Test: Tests individual bits in the destination operand against those in the source operand. Performs a logical AND operation that affects the flags but not the destination operand.

O D I S Z A P C

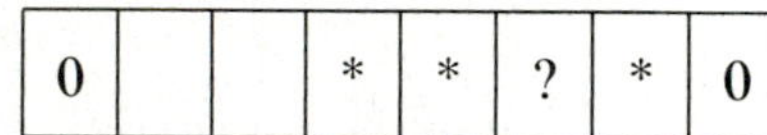

Formats:

TEST *reg,reg*
TEST *mem,reg*
TEST *reg,mem*
TEST *reg,immed*
TEST *mem,immed*
TEST *accum,immed*

WAIT

Wait for coprocessor: Suspends CPU execution until the coprocessor finishes its current instruction.

O	D	I	S	Z	A	P	C

Format: WAIT

XCHG

Exchange: Exchanges the source operand with the destination operand.

O	D	I	S	Z	A	P	C

Formats:

XCHG *reg,reg*
XCHG *mem,reg*
XCHG *reg,mem*
XCHG *reg,immed*
XCHG *mem,immed*
XCHG *accum,immed*

XLAT

Translate byte: Uses the value in AL to index into a table pointed to by DS:BX. The byte pointed to by the index is moved to AL. An operand may be specified in order to provide a segment override. Beginning with MASM 5.0, XLATB may be substituted for XLAT.

O	D	I	S	Z	A	P	C

Formats:

XLAT
XLAT *mem*
XLAT *segreg*:*mem*

XOR

Exclusive OR: Each bit in the source operand is exclusive ORed with its corresponding bit in the destination. The destination bit is a 1 only when the original source and destination bits are different.

O	D	I	S	Z	A	P	C
0			*	*	?	*	0

Formats:

XOR *reg,reg*
XOR *mem,reg*
XOR *reg,mem*
XOR *reg,immed*
XOR *mem,immed*
XOR *accum,immed*

Index

ASCII CONTROL CHARACTERS

The following list shows the ASCII codes generated when a control key combination is pressed. The mnemonics and descriptions refer to ASCII functions used for screen and printer formatting and data communications.

ASCII Code*	Ctrl-	Mnemonic	Description	ASCII Code*	Ctrl-	Mnemonic	Description
00		NUL	Null character	10	Ctrl-P	DLE	Data link escape
01	Ctrl-A	SOH	Start of header	11	Ctrl-Q	DC1	Device control 1
02	Ctrl-B	STX	Start of text	12	Ctrl-R	DC2	Device control 2
03	Ctrl-C	ETX	End of text	13	Ctrl-S	DC3	Device control 3
04	Ctrl-D	EOT	End of transmission	14	Ctrl-T	DC4	Device control 4
05	Ctrl-E	ENQ	Enquiry	15	Ctrl-U	NAK	Negative acknowledge
06	Ctrl-F	ACK	Acknowledge	16	Ctrl-V	SYN	Synchronous idle
07	Ctrl-G	BEL	Bell	17	Ctrl-W	ETB	End transmission block
08	Ctrl-H	BS	Backspace	18	Ctrl-X	CAN	Cancel
09	Ctrl-I	HT	Horizontal tab	19	Ctrl-Y	EM	End of medium
0A	Ctrl-J	LF	Line feed	1A	Ctrl-Z	SUB	Substitute
0B	Ctrl-K	VT	Vertical tab	1B	Ctrl-[	ESC	Escape
0C	Ctrl-L	FF	Form feed	1C	Ctrl-\	FS	File separator
0D	Ctrl-M	CR	Carriage return	1D	Ctrl-]	GS	Group separator
0E	Ctrl-N	SO	Shift out	1E	Ctrl-^	RS	Record separator
0F	Ctrl-O	SI	Shift in	1F	Ctrl--†	US	Unit separator

*ASCII codes are in hexadecimal.
†ASCII code 1Fh is Ctrl-Hyphen (-).

ALT-KEY COMBINATIONS

The following hexadecimal scan codes are produced by holding down the ALT key and pressing each character:

Key	Scan Code	Key	Scan Code	Key	Scan Code
1	78	A	1E	N	31
2	79	B	30	O	18
3	7A	C	2E	P	19
4	7B	D	20	Q	10
5	7C	E	12	R	13
6	7D	F	21	S	1F
7	7E	G	22	T	14
8	7F	H	23	U	16
9	80	I	17	V	2F
0	81	J	24	W	11
–	82	K	25	X	2D
=	83	L	26	Y	15
		M	32	Z	2C